MINNESOTA STUDIES IN THE PHILOSOPHY OF SCIENCE

Minnesota Studies in the
PHILOSOPHY OF SCIENCE

HERBERT FEIGL AND GROVER MAXWELL, GENERAL EDITORS

VOLUME IX

Perception and Cognition
Issues in the Foundations of Psychology

EDITED BY

C. WADE SAVAGE

FOR THE MINNESOTA CENTER FOR PHILOSOPHY OF SCIENCE

UNIVERSITY OF MINNESOTA PRESS, MINNEAPOLIS

The University of Minneosta
is an equal opportunity
educator and employer.

Library of Congress Cataloging in Publication Data

Main entry under title:

Perception and cognition.

(Minnesota studies in the philosophy of science;
v. 9)
"Co-sponsored by the Minnesota Center for Research
in Human Learning and the Minnesota Center for
Philosophy of Science."
Includes indexes.
1. Cognition—Addresses, essays, lectures.
2. Human information processing—Addresses, essays,
lectures. 3. Psychology—Philosophy—Addresses,
essays, lectures. I. Savage, C. Wade.
II. Minnesota. University. Center for Research in
Human Learning. III. Minnesota. University. Center
for Philosophy of Science. IV. Series.
Q175.M64   vol. 9   [BF311]   501s   [153]   78-12743
ISBN 0-8166-0841-5

Preface

The philosophy of mind has acquired new life from recent work in cognitive psychology, linguistics, and the information sciences. Scientists in these fields are addressing questions about thinking, perceiving, and imagining that were once thought to be the exclusive concern of (mentalist) philosophers. An extensive and often technical interchange between philosophers of psychology and cognitive psychologists is under way.

This volume is part of that interchange. Most of the papers were read or previewed at a conference on perception and cognition held at the University of Minnesota in June of 1975, co-sponsored by the Minnesota Center for Research in Human Learning and the Minnesota Center for Philosophy of Science. The rest appear by invitation of the editor.

The papers are grouped roughly according to subject matter. Papers in the first group (chs. 1-7) deal with imagery, mental representation, and perception; the second group (chs. 8-9) with difficulties in psycholinguistic models; the third group (chs. 10-12) with so-called functionalist models of thinking and consciousness. Papers in the fourth group (chs. 13-15) either discuss or present comprehensive theories of the relationship of mind to the rest of the world. The final paper (ch. 16) is both an introduction and a contribution to the theory of psychophysical measurement.

The nonspecialist may find it useful to read the papers in the order presented. The specialist will no doubt impose his or her own order.

Many of the papers deal, in one way or another, with computational, information-processing models of cognitive processes. A cognizing organism is viewed as a "computer," that is, as the embodiment of a group of computational devices in a physical or biological system. To take a specific example, the multiplication table is a computational device embodied in my brain. More generally, rules (mechanisms) by means of which humans understand language, make deductive and inductive inferences, solve problems, perceive, and fantasize are computational devices embodied in human brains. The major function of the brain-computer is to process and utilize information about the organism and about its physical and social environment. Some of this information may have been genetically stored; but most of it is obtained through the organism's sensory systems, encoded, stored, and reorganized into hypotheses, or plans, that direct the behavior of the organism.

This computational, information-processing approach now dominates cognitive psychology, and has had a profound effect on philosophy of mind. Many philosophers now answer such questions as, "What are images?", "What is a belief?", and "What is consciousness?" as do the psychologists—by locating the cognitive object or process in the latest computer model of cognition. Thus, an image of a geometrical figure may be said to be a special system for storing geometrical information in and retrieving it from a brain. Some philosophers believe that the approach can be expanded to explain motivational, emotional, aesthetic, moral, and all other human and animal mental processes; and that with this expansion the last great metaphysical problem—that of the nature of the relation between mind and body—will have been solved, or dissolved. For a mind will have been shown to be a vastly complicated system of computational devices embodied in a brain; and there is no greater difficulty understanding the relation of the mind thus conceived to brain, than there is in understanding the relation of a computer program driving a computer to the electronic hardware of the computer being driven. Other philosophers, including some of the contributors to this volume, believe that there are insurmountable philosophical and scientific difficulties in the above approach, and that the "solution" it envisages is specious.

It is my hope that, in addition to offering useful papers on some fundamental topics concerning cognition and perception, this volume will assist in assessing the current status of the problem of mind and body.

I wish to thank Grover Maxwell, J. J. Jenkins, Keith Gunderson, and D. C. Dennett, who provided encouragement and editorial assistance; Caroline Cohen, who helped in assembling and preparing the manuscript; Marilyn Bennett, who prepared the index; and, of course, the contributors.

C. W. Savage

Contents

MINNESOTA STUDIES IN THE PHILOSOPHY OF SCIENCE

──────── HERBERT A. SIMON ────────

On the Forms of Mental Representation

The human brain encodes, modifies, and stores information that is received through its various sense organs, transforms that information by the processes that are called "thinking," and produces motor and verbal outputs of various kinds based on the stored information. So much is noncontroversial—only the most radical of radical behaviorists question it. What *is* highly controversial is *how* information is stored in the brain—in the usual terminolgy, how it is "represented" —or even how we can describe representations, and what we mean when we say that information is represented in one way rather than another.

There is not a single problem of representation; there are several, each referring to a different level of analysis. There is, of course, the basic physiological question of the nature of the "engram"; but I shall not be concerned with that question here. In talking about a computer memory, we do not need to concern ourselves with magnetic cores and integrated circuits; we can talk about memory structures at the information-processing level, in terms of symbol structures and the operators that act upon them. In different computers, these symbol structures and operators may be realized by quite different physical devices. In the same way, our interest here will lie in the symbol structures in the human mind and in the operators that act on them to transform them. A theory of mental representation at this symbolic level may be compatible with a variety of different biological realizations. That is fortunate, for very little indeed is known about the biological foundations of human memory.

Note: This research was supported by Research Grant MH-07722 from the National Institute of Mental Health.

Since we are concerned with representation at the symbolic or information-processing level, it will matter little whether the memory we are talking about resides in a human head or in a computer. Hence we may use what we know about computer memories to clarify our notions about human memory. This should be helpful since it is very much easier to find out in detail what is going on inside a computer than to find out what is going on inside a human brain. I shall base the discussion on evidence drawn from both artificial intelligence and experimental psychology.

Equivalence of Representations

It is impossible to find an entirely neutral language in which to describe representations of information, for a language is itself a form of representation. We can avoid this difficulty, at least in part, by not attempting to describe representations directly, but by talking instead in terms of the equivalence of representations. It is essential that we define carefully what we mean by "equivalence," and that we distinguish among the various kinds of equivalences that can hold between representations. Specifically, I shall talk about *informational* equivalence and *computational* equivalence.

Informational Equivalence. Two representations are informationally equivalent if the transformation from one to the other entails no loss of information, i.e., if each can be constructed from the other.

Thus, in an appropriate information-processing system, the statements "Distance equals average velocity times time" and "$S = w*T$" are informationally equivalent. There is informational equivalence, also, between appropriately axiomatized formulations of Euclidean geometry and analytic geometry, respectively.

On the other hand, consider a system that receives information via a two-dimensional spatially extended "retina" but stores a particular three-dimensional interpretation of this information. What is presented to the system is, say, the familiar Necker Cube of Figure 1, and what is stored is the information about the vertices, edges, and faces of this cube, with the face ABCD labeled "front" and the face EFGH labeled "back."

Now the important feature of the Necker Cube is that this is not the only possible three-dimensional interpretation of the presented

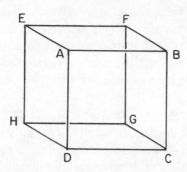

Figure 1. The Necker Cube

figure. It is equally consistent with that figure to label the face ABCD the "back" and the face EFGH the "front." It is precisely because of this ambiguity that the Necker Cube is reversible—i.e., that a normal subject can alternate at a rate of several times per second between the two internal three-dimensional representations. Hence we must conclude that the two-dimensional stimulus and the internal representation are not informationally equivalent: the former can always be obtained univocally from the latter, but not vice versa.[1] These examples should suffice to illustrate the meaning of informational equivalence. We turn now to computational equivalence.

Computational Equivalence. Two representations are computationally equivalent if the same information can be extracted from each (the same inferences drawn) with about the same amount of computation.

For certain purposes, we may wish to weaken this definition slightly, replacing it by: Two representations are computationally equivalent *in the extended sense* if the same information can be extracted from each by the same amounts of computation, up to a factor of proportionality.

Thus, if we had two computers (like the IBM 709 and IBM 7090) that were essentially isomorphic at the information processing level, but one of which, for hardware reasons, had a much faster operation cycle than the other, all operations would take on the slower machine a fixed multiple of the time that they would take on the faster machine. If the processing of some particular representations on the two machines differed only by this fixed factor, we would say that the representations were computationally equivalent in the extended sense. This weaker definition of equivalence is crucial in comparing computer simulations with human performance, since the representations in this case, having different hardware realizations, will have different processing times associated with the corresponding primitive operations.

Consider the following information: $ABCD$ is a rectangle with AB twice as long as BC. It is bisected into two squares by the line EF, where E is the midpoint of AB, and F the midpoint of CD. $ABCD$ is also bisected into two triangles by the line AC. Now we ask the following question of a system that has been given this information: Do EF and AC have a point of intersection inside the rectangle?

The information about the rectangle and the processes for answering questions about it might be represented in a variety of ways. (1) They might be represented as a set of propositions (more or less isomorphic with the verbal statement), together with an appropriate axiomatization of plane geometry. Then the question could be answered by proving the theorem that EF must intersect AC. (2) Or they could be represented as a set of coordinate pairs for the points A through F, together with an appropriate set of rules for constructing the equations of the lines joining these points and for finding points of intersection of these lines. Then the question could be answered by solving a pair of simultaneous linear equations. (3) Or they could be represented by a drawing on paper (see Figure 2), together with some visual scanning processes capable of noticing the intersection at G.

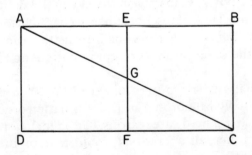

Figure 2. "Computation" with a visual image (by drawing the lines EF and AC, infer the existence of G).

Although these three representations are informationally equivalent, they are not at all computationally equivalent. For human beings, at least, answering the question with the use of the first representation would generally be the most difficult, and answering it with the third representation, the least difficult. Most human beings, upon being given this problem verbally, would promptly translate it into an internal ("visual" or "pictorial") representation that is more or less computationally equivalent with the third representation. But I am getting ahead of my story.

Representation in Discrete Associative Memories

There is no close relation between a system's "hardware" and the representations it may employ. The observation has already been made that computers that are quite different physically may use representations that are informationally, and even computationally, equivalent. As a matter of fact, virtually all computers of the so-called von Neumann type, that is to say, almost all general-purpose computers that have been built in the past 25 years, are very close to being computationally equivalent in the extended sense, so far as their basic machine-language representations are concerned.

The converse proposition holds also. Not only may the same representation be realized with different physical systems, but different representations may be realized with a single physical system—by superimposing the higher level representations upon the underlying physical scheme. There is, for example, a widespread belief today, based on a fair amount of evidence, that the left and right hemispheres of the human brain use different representations. In some versions of this theory, the left hemisphere employs "verbal" and "symbolic" representations, the right hemisphere, "pictorial" or "holistic" representations. Yet there is no known basic difference in the tissues of the two hemispheres, and indeed, if the left hemisphere of a child is damaged, the right hemisphere is often capable of taking over the usual functions of the other with little or no evidence of deficit.

Returning again from the obscurities of the human brain to computers, let us consider how specific representations are defined for a system, and how higher level representations are superimposed upon a hardware representation. Defining a representation means

(1) specifying one or more data types, and (2) specifying the primitive (i.e., "fast") operations that can be performed on information in those data types.

A *data type* is some particular way of organizing information in memory. For example, among the data types that are commonly used in computing are lists and arrays. A list is an ordered set of symbols or symbol structures; an array is a set of symbols or structures to each of which has been assigned *n* coordinates, so that (in the case of a two-dimensional array) we can refer, say, to the symbol with coordinates (i, *j*).

The declaration that information will be represented in lists or in arrays does not say anything about the physical location of the information in memory. Two adjacent items on a list need not occupy adjacent memory locations. Rather, the declaration of a data type means that certain *primitive operations* are available for accessing, storing, and modifying data. A list representation requires a primitive operation of *find.next*, which, given a particular symbol as its argument, will access the succeeding symbol in the list to which the first belongs. In a list representation, other primitive operations are available for inserting a symbol in a list (i.e., after symbol *X* has been inserted between *Y* and *Z*, execution of *find.next* (*Y*) will yield *X*); for deleting a symbol from a list; and so on.

We may indicate, for illustration, one way in which a list representation could be realized with standard computer hardware. At a hardware level, information is held, say, in the form of *words*, which are individually *addressable*. That is, with each word is associated a number, its address; so that a primitive operation, *find* (*X*), will access the symbol whose address is the number *X*. To superimpose a list representation upon this hardware addressing scheme, a new level of primitive operations is defined (higher-level language), each element of which is a small algorithm of the original hardware-level primitive operations (machine language). The convention could be adopted, for example, that symbols are to be stored in the odd-numbered addresses of the machine-level locations, and in each succeeding even-numbered address is to be stored the address of the *next* symbol in the list. Thus, if *X* were stored in hardware location 17, the number "25" in location 18, and the symbol *Y* in location 25, then the list operation *find.next* (*17*) would access location 25, i.e., the symbol *Y*. For further discussion of representations, the reader may consult Newell and Simon (1972, pp. 21-38), or for a more technical account, Galler and Perlis (1970) or Knuth (1968).

It is commonly thought that human memory is *associative*. In an associative memory, the basic *find* operation takes the form *find* (X, Y); e.g., "find (the name of) the father of John." With each symbol stored in such a memory is associated a set of labeled links. Given a symbol and one of the labels, we can find a second symbol that is associated with the first by that particular link.[2] It is a matter of considerable disagreement, however, whether the mental visual imagery of which humans appear capable can be accounted for in terms of such an associative structure. That question will provide a major theme for the next section of this paper.

What Is Visual Imagery?

Modern computers have freed our thinking about representations. First, they have taught us how representations can be defined operationally by specifying data types together with their associated primitive operations. Second, they have taught us that representations can be superimposed on one another, in the manner that was described in the last section, so that hardware organization need not consititue a severe constraint on the representations that are available. Third, they have taught us that a multiplicity of representations may exist side by side, realized in the same hardware.

In the enjoyment of this freedom, we can now discuss representation in human memory without undue concern for our ignorance of hardware realization. We can ask, as an empirical question, how many representations are employed by the human mind, what kinds of data types they are built upon, and what kinds of primitive operations. Empirical evidence can be gathered by presenting human subjects with various kinds of information and instructing them to perform a variety of tasks that draw upon that information. The possibility or impossibility, ease or difficulty, of performing the tasks will inform us about the characteristics of the memory representation the subjects are using, and about the informational and computational equivalence of different representations.

In this section I would like to sketch out the evidence for the proposition that most of the phenomena associated with human visual imagery can be realized in a representation that is superimposed on a basic associative system (see also Simon, 1972). Subsequently I shall expand the argument to claim that all of the known human memory representations—"pictorial," "propositional," or whatever—are subspecies of associative representation; but that inside the human head everything is lists and node-like structures of symbols.[3] This does not mean, of course, that all of these representations are computationally equivalent. It is precisely because they are not computationally equivalent that it is convenient for the system to have more than one of them.

In making my case, I shall refer only occasionally to formal experiments published in the psychological literature. Instead I shall rely mainly on informal experiments that you can perform, using yourself as subject, as you read about them. In fact, I have already asked you to perform two such experiments: one having to do with the Necker Cube (Figure 1), the other with a rectangle that was several times bisected by lines (Figure 2). Let me revert briefly to those examples, and then introduce some additional ones.

The Necker Cube. The Necker Cube can illustrate for us how a system with associational capabilities could picture a three-dimensional structure. The full scheme is fairly elaborate, so I can only sketch it here.[4] Vertices, edges, and faces will be represented in memory by nodes. These nodes will be connected by labeled links. For example, the labels "left.edge," "down.edge," and "back.edge" will associate the edges BA, BC, and BF, respectively, with the node B; the face ABCD will have the attribute "front," and EFGH, the attribute "back"; and so on.

The ambiguity of the Necker Cube (i.e., the fact that face ABCD could have the attribute "back," and the face EFGH the attribute "front," instead of vice versa) can arise in constructing the internal representation from the two-dimensional stimulus of Figure 1 as follows. Suppose a scanner were to begin by fixing on point B. The horizontal line segment BA would be interpreted as the right.edge of B. Similarly, the vertical segment BC would be interpreted as the down.edge of B. Since the system is programmed to interpret all angles as right angles unless a contradiction arises, BF must be labeled the forward.edge or the back.edge of B. Convention determines which label is chosen. Suppose it is the latter. Then, for consistency, the edge DH will later have to be interpreted as the back.edge of D and the forward.edge of H, thus placing H behind B. If, on the other hand, the processing had begun at point H, the same convention would have placed H and F on the front face, and D and B on the back. If this hypothetical account has any relation to the ways in which people process and store the Necker Cube, then it should be possible to induce a figure reversal by shifting attention from point B to point H of the figure. The reader can verify for himself that he can indeed do this.

The Dissected Rectangle. The dissected rectangle of Figure 2 provides an argument against simple node-link processes as the *sole* means for processing and storing information about geometric figures. How is the point of interesection G created in the mental representation of the verbally described rectangle when AC is added to the description of the figure? If the annexing process had some implicit knowledge of plane topology, it would know that A could not be joined to C without penetrating the boundaries AEFD and EBCF. However, that information alone is not enough to infer an intersection of EF with AC; metrical information about the lengths of the segments and the angles, and guaranteeing the straightness of the lines, is also needed. If only topological information were processed, segments like DF and FE could be replaced by curved lines, and the intersection of AC with EF could not be inferred.

Considerations of this kind argue for the availability of a "mind's eye" that has some of the capabilities of an analytic geometry representation, or a representation by means of a fine grid, to encode verbally presented descriptions into visual images that can be stored in memory.[5] On the other hand, if it seems difficult to account for the creation of such images in terms of an associational representation alone, such a representation may be fully adequate for storing the visual image once it has been generated (e.g., once the existence of the point G has been inferred).

The amount and kinds of information that can be stored in a visual image can be assessed by elaborations on the rectangle-generating task. Remembering that the rectangle of Figure 2 is twice as wide as high—that AB is twice AD—we now draw a diagonal in the right-hand square connecting B with F. BF will intersect AC at a point we will call H. Finally, we mark the midpoint of BF, calling it J.

Now we ask a subject who has been synthesizing this mental image from the verbal description (without Figure 2 before him) to tell us whether JH is longer or shorter than HF. If the answer is "shorter," we then ask how much longer HF is than JH.

In informal experiments with this task, I have found that most, but not all, subjects can answer the first question correctly. (JH is shorter than HF.) Fewer than half of the subjects can answer the second question correctly. (HF is twice as long as JH.) This task seems to strain to the capacity point, or just beyond, the ability of most persons to assemble a mental picture of a geometric figure. Hence the task demonstrates that the total amount of information that can be held in such a picture is quite modest, so that it could readily be accommodated in an associational representation.[6]

A Block Test. Baylor has constructed a computer simulation, using an associational representation, of tasks involving mental visualization of blocks. A typical task is the following: Imagine a cube that is three inches on a side. Paint one face of the cube red, and two other faces, adjacent to the red face and opposite to each other, blue. Now slice the cube into one-inch cubes. How many of the one-inch cubes have exactly one red and one blue side?

Most people can answer this particular question correctly. (There are six such cubes.) It is also interesting that they can tell you *which* face of the cube they colored red, and which faces blue, although the instructions did not require them to determine that. Hence we can conclude that the representation-building process synthesizes the figure in a particular orientation.

Baylor's simulation of the processes used by subjects in this task is also able to answer the question. The symbol manipulation required, however, to create and modify the representation (e.g., to "slice" the cube) is quite extensive. With problems that are somewhat more difficult than this one, the simulation makes errors that are similar to typical human errors—it is unable to process the information in such a way as to draw all the inferences correctly. Hence Baylor's experiments and simulation add a little more credence to the idea that associational representations may be computationally equivalent, or approximately so, to the representations that people use to store visual images.[7]

Summary of Evidence on Visual Representation. The kinds of experiments we have been reporting illustrate how much information, and what kinds of information, people can store in visual images. It is clear from such experiments that visual images permit certain types of inferences to be drawn that would be difficult or impossible to draw by verbal or even mathematical reasoning without those images. On the other hand, these same experiments show that the amount of information that can be held in a visual image is modest. For a scene of any complexity, the image falls far short of a photograph in information content.

Finally, with one important exception (a phenomenon like the generation of the point G in Figure 2), the evidence seems to be compatible with the idea that the underlying representation is wholly composed of list structures in an associational memory. The exception, however, is not an isolated phenomenon, and cannot be ignored. It suggests the availability of somewhat more elaborate processes for operating on images, even if these processes are not needed for storing them, once generated. Baylor's evidence on this point is inconclusive. His simulation shows that accomplishing the block-slicing tasks requires fairly elaborate, but not inconceivably complex, information processing capabilities if an associational representation is used.[8]

How Many Representations in the Head?

Much of the information that a person receives comes to him in the form of natural language discourse, oral or written. As we saw in the last section, if the natural language sentences describe concrete objects, it is possible that they may be encoded as visual images, not computationally equivalent to linguistic strings. But much information derived from natural language is abstract and not readily encoded in pictures. How is such information stored, and in particular, how closely does the stored information resemble the linguistic strings that are input?

At least two experimental techniques are available for investigating the processing of memory contents that were derived originally from natural language inputs. Time measurements can be made of the speed of response (response latency) for different kinds of tasks using the stored information; or subjects may be tested on their ability to remember which of a set of stimuli they have seen previously.

A Chronometric Study. An example of the first paradigm is the well-known experiment of Chase and Clark (1972) seeking to test how subjects determine whether a given sentence, such as, "The star is above the cross," is or is not true of a simple picture shown to them simultaneously with the sentence. To answer such questions, the subject must (1) have some way of translating the language of the sentence into the representation used for pictures, (2) perform the inverse translation from picture to language, or (3) translate both stimuli into some common representational form in which they can be compared. While the experiments do not choose unequivocally among these three alternatives, they tend to support the third.[9]

A Recognition Study. The second paradigm, first applied by Bransford and Franks (1971), has been used to show that the internal representation of information obtained through natural language inputs is not informationally equivalent to those inputs, having lost a substantial amount of syntactic information during the encoding and storage processes. Using this paradigm, Rosenberg and Simon (1977) gave subjects a sequence of stimulus sentences, one at a time. Subsequently they presented a second set of sentences, asking the subject each time whether he had seen precisely that sentence in the original set. When half the original sentences were in English and half in French (but on the same general subject matter in both languages), bilingual subjects frequently stated that they had previously seen sentences that they had in fact seen only in translation in the other language. The same experiment was performed in another variant in which half of the original stimuli were English sentences and half were simple drawings pertaining to the same subject matter. Again, subjects were frequently unable to distinguish between having seen a particular sentence and having seen a picture whose content was approximately equivalent to that sentence.

These experiments might be taken as evidence for the view that there is a *single* internal representation—a semantic or conceptual representation—into which all inputs, whatever their sensory modality or external coding, are translated. However, we must avoid overinterpreting the evidence. First, subjects did not make these errors in every case; sometimes they remembered syntactic details that enabled them to distinguish sentence inputs from pictures or from sentences in another language. Moreover, these experiments used very simple sentences, and correspondingly, very simple pictures whose content was easily describable in language.

If the experiments do not demonstrate conclusively that there is a single form of internal representation, they at least argue for relatively simple and straightforward translatability from one internal representation to another. In this way, they lend some support to our hypothesis that underlying the modality-specific representations employed by the human processor there is a common associational memory in terms of whose primitives all the higher-level and more specific representations are coded.

Dual Representations in Simulations. Several problem-solving systems show us how two representations may be better than one in carrying out heuristic search. Although these systems must be classified primarily as experiments in artificial intelligence, the methods they employ are probably not far from the methods used by people in these same task environments.

An early example of an automatic theorem-proving system was Gelernter's geometry theorem-proving machine (1963). As its name indicates, this system was capable of discovering proofs for theorems in Euclidean geometry. It employed a dual representation of each problem, one symbolic and syntactical, the other in the form of a diagram of the geometric figure. Before the system attempted to prove syntactically that corresponding angles, say, or corresponding sides of a pair of triangles were equal, it first tested for approximate equality on the diagram. The space of the diagram therefore served as a planning space that prescreened proof attempts and saved effort in fruitless proof attempts. People probably use diagrams in geometry for the same purpose.

Recently Novak (1976) built a computer program (ISAAC) for solving physics (statics) problems presented in natural language. This program, after some initial syntactic parsing of the input sentences, generates a diagram-like representation of the problem situation, then uses the diagram in constructing the algebraic equations that translate the problem statements. The diagram contains sufficient information so that it can be used to generate pictures of the situation on a cathode-ray tube. Thus Novak's program uses a variety of representations: the input language strings, the tree-like parsed sentences, the diagrams, the equations, and the output drawings on the CRT.

Both the Geometry Theorem Prover and ISAAC superimpose all of their representations on an associational, list-processing memory, although both have some capability for performing analytic geometry calculations on their pictorial images. Both demonstrate that "pictorial" representations can be realized on the basis of an underlying associational representation.

Conclusion

In this paper I have tried to show that the question, "How are ideas represented in the mind?", can be given a perfectly operational meaning and can be investigated experimentally. In order to study representations, we must first define what we mean by two representations being equivalent. We have seen that there are at least two distinct notions of equivalence, informational equivalence and computational equivalence, and that both are important for an understanding of representation.

The empirical evidence available today leads me, cautiously and tentatively, to believe that the brain operates basically as a system of labeled associations. This system may require supplementation from a specifically visual system ("the mind's eye) to account for some of the mind's capabilities for drawing inferences about the intersections and metrical properties of lines in geometrical figures.

Other specialized forms of representation in the brain may well be achieved by encoding higher level primitives at a level above the basic system of labeled associations. If one had to conjecture how many such specialized representations there might typically be, a plausible guess would be three: a verbal representation, perhaps not unlike the "deep structures" postulated by the transformational linguists; a visual representation, capable of holding, if not always generating, the information about spatial figures; and a conceptual representation, more "abstract" than the other two and particularly essential for handling abstract meanings.

But whether this is a correct description of the human representational system is not important. What is important is that we now have a variety of means for exploring representational issues empirically, so that these questions can no longer be settled from the comfort of an armchair. Identifying the representations used by the brain is an operational, researchable task.

Notes

1. Caution: in speaking here of the internal representation as "three-dimensional," I do not, or course, mean to imply that it occupies a three-dimensional region of the brain. I simply mean that it is described in terms of the attributes of a cube.

2. The need for a labeled or "colored" link to model human associative memory, rather than a simple "next" association, was first noted by the Würzburg psychologists early in this century. This requirement follows from a simple experimental datum. If, in an association experiment, a subject is given the stimulus "white," he is likely to respond "color" or "black," respectively, depending on whether he has previously been given the set to respond with superordinates or with opposites.

3. Presently I shall qualify my "everything" to "almost everything." Certain operations on visual images seem to call for processes that go beyond the usual basic primitives of the node-link scheme.

4. For a discussion of how a system like the one described here can account for the reversibility of the Necker Cube and for "impossible figures" like the drawings of Escher, see Simon (1967). Computer systems for "scene analysis," i.e., for three-dimensional interpretation of two-dimensional drawings, have been studied extensively by Guzman and Waltz, among others. See Waltz (1975).

5. Nothing mysterious is meant by the "mind's eye" metaphor; the same apparatus that is used to process the retinal image of an external stimulus might, for example, be used to process an image that had previously been stored in memory. All that is required is a set of processes to perform the inverse operations to those performed in encoding the retinal image in node-link form. See Novak (1976) for an artificial intelligence program that has precisely this capability of displaying the information from a node-link representation of a physics problem as a picture on a cathode ray tube. A similar view of imagery will be found in Chase and Clark (1972), pp. 224-230.

6. The reader may want to try a second task of the same nature. Imagine a square with sides labeled clockwise from the upper left corner, ABCD. Draw a circle with radius equal to AD and with D as center. Draw a second circle, with radius equal to one-half AB and with B as center. Do the two circles intersect?

7. See Baylor (1971). Additional evidence supportive of this hypothesis is provided by the works of Moran (1973) and Farley (1974).

8. Some well-known experiments by Shepard on the "mental rotation" of objects have been widely interpreted as denying the possibility of a discrete representation of mental images. (See Shepard & Metzler, 1971.) However, this interpretation has been challenged by the research of Just and Carpenter (1976), who provide a specific discrete processing system to account for the phenomena described by Shepard.

9. This experiment is just one of many directed at this issue, most of which support the conclusion reached here. Another good example is that of Potter and Faulconer (1975).

References

Baylor, G. W. Program and protocol analysis on a mental imagery task. *Proceedings of the Second International Joint Conference on Artificial Intelligence*, 1971.

Bransford, J. D. & Franks, J. J. The abstraction of linguistic ideas. *Cognitive Psychology*, 1971, 2, 331-350.

Chase, W. G. & Clark, H. H. Mental operations in the comparison of sentences and pictures. In L. Gregg (Ed.), *Cognition in learning and memory*. New York: John Wiley & Sons, 1972.

Farley, A. M. *A visual imagery and perception system: The results of a protocol analysis*, Vol. 1 & 2. Pittsburgh, Pa.: Department of Computer Science, Carnegie-Mellon University, 1974. (NTIS No. A-004 090 for Vol. 1 and NTIS No. A-004 091 for Vol. 2)

Galler, B. A., & Perlis, A. J. *A view of programming languages*. Reading, Mass.: Addison-Wesley, 1970.

Gelernter, H. Realization of a geometry-theorem proving machine. In E. Feigenbaum & J. Feldman (Eds.), *Computers and thought*. New York: McGraw-Hill, 1963.

Just, M. A. & Carpenter, P. A. Eye fixation and cognitive processes. *Cognitive Psychology*, 1976, 8, 441-480.

Knuth, D. E. *The art of computer programming*, Vol. I, Chap. 2. Reading, Mass.: Addison-Wesley, 1968.

Moran, T. P. The symbolic nature of visual imagery. *Proceedings of The Third International Joint Conference on Artificial Intelligence*, 1973.

Newell, A., & Simon, H. A. *Human problem solving*. Englewood Cliffs: Prentice-Hall, 1972.

Novak, G. S., Jr. Computer understanding of physics problems stated in natural language. Technical Report NL-30, Department of Computer Sciences, the University of Texas, Austin, Texas, 1976.

Rosenberg, S. & Simon, H. A. Modeling semantic memory: Effects of presenting semantic information in different modalities. *Cognitive Psychology*, 1977, 9, 292-325.

Shepard, R. N. & Metzler, J. Mental rotation of three-dimensional objects. *Science*, 1971, 171, 701-703.

Simon, H. A. An information processing explanation of some perceptual phenomena. *British Journal of Psychology*, 1967, 58, 1-12.

Simon, H. A. What is visual imagery? In L. W. Gregg (Ed.), *Cognition in learning and memory*. New York: John Wiley & Sons, 1972.

Waltz, D. Machine vision, understanding line drawings of scenes with shadows. In P. Winston (Ed.), *The psychology of computer vision*. New York: McGraw-Hill, 1975.

Imagery and Artifical Intelligence

1. Introduction

In this paper I shall attempt to summarize and extend some of the arguments I have advanced against the use of the notion of mental image as an explanatory construct in cognitive psychology (e.g., in Pylyshyn, 1973). In the first part (sections 2-4) I shall review some of my reasons for preferring to speak of cognitive representations — such as those involved in memory and thinking — as structured descriptions (albeit rather different from the usual linguistic descriptions) instead of images. I shall try to show that the facts of human perception, storage, and retrieval argue against the view that what is involved in such cognitive activity is some iconic and uninterpreted sensory pattern, as is implied when we speak of images. The point is not that there is no such object as an image, only that an adequate theory of the mental representation involved in imaging will depict it as having a distinctly nonpictorial character. Although the main arguments in the first part of the paper will be directed at the question of how knowledge is represented in long-term memory, most of the points apply equally to those transient structures constructed during imaging and thinking.

In the second part of this paper (sections 5-8) I shall examine the growing trend (at least in psychology) of referring to something

Note: I wish to thank Jerry Fodor for his careful and critical reading of an earlier draft of this paper. Part of the work of writing this paper was done while I was a visiting faculty member at the Artificial Intelligence Laboratory of M.I.T. Discussions with various members of the laboratory were invaluable in clarifying many problems in my earlier thinking (which is not to say that no errors of confusions remain in the present version). Research reported herein was supported by the National Reasearch Council of Canada, Operating Grant A4092.

called an analogical representation as a way of representing nonlinguistic information. I shall argue that much of the attraction of this notion stems from a failure to recognize some fundamental differences between the objects of perception (i.e., the physical environment) and the objects of cognition (i.e., mental representations). In this connection I shall examine some evidence frequently cited as supporting an analogical view of mental representation—in particular, experiments on such mental manipulations as "mental rotation" of figures.

2. What Is a Mental Representation Like?

It is schemata, not images of objects, which underlie our pure sensible concepts. No image could ever be adequate to the concept of a triangle in general. . . . Still less is an object of experience or its image ever adequate to the empirical concept; . . . The concept "dog" signifies a rule according to which my imagination can delineate the figure of a four-footed animal in a general manner, without limitation to any single determinate figure such as experience, or any possible image that I can represent *in concreto*, actually presents.

Emmanuel Kant
(*Critique of pure reason*, 1781)

To begin, I shall give you an informal and somewhat discursive review of why I believe mental representations are appropriately thought of as a type of description. Consider what happens when a scene is perceived and becomes assimilated into our store of knowledge, and what happens when we later access this knowledge from memory in recalling the scene.

It is useful to distinguish two phases of the process that intervenes between the arrival of a proximal stimulus and its interpretation and assimiliation as knowledge. There is some reason to believe there is an early phase in this process that has considerable autonomy—i.e., it does not depend upon higher cognitive processes except in a very general way, such as by adjusting peripheral receptors. Various phenomena that appear early in life and seem to be resistent to learning—such as figure-ground separation, certain illusions, gestalt laws of pragnanz, and perhaps some stereoscopic and temporal integration—may be identified with this phase. Roughly speaking, processes such as that which Julesz (1971) refers to as "cyclopean vision" or which Hochberg (1968) has characterized as the "mind's eye" in perception may occur immediately after this stage.

David Marr (1975) has investigated the computational requisites of this lowest level of vision and has proposed a model of this process up to figure-ground isolation. The process first computes a rich description of the optical intensity level differences present in the image; this description is called the "primal sketch." Marr then posits certain "non-attentive" groupings and first-order discriminations acting on the primal sketch. Higher-level knowledge and purpose are brought to bear on only very few of the decisions taken during this processing.

I would argue that from a computational point of view it is appropriate to treat this early semi-autonomous phase of vision as a special purpose transducer, which takes physical magnitudes as inputs and produces symbol structures as outputs. Regardless of the precise details of this phase (it is not clear, for example, whether Julesz, Hochberg, and Marr are describing precisely the same level), there is reason to believe that: (a) there is a semi-autonomous, pre-attentive phase in visual perception, (b) this phase is initiated by energy arriving at the sense organs, (c) only the output of this phase, and not intermediate steps, are available for further perceptual analysis, and (d) such cognitive processes as "noticing" and the assimilation of sensory patterns into cognitive structures take place after this phase. These characteristics are ones that one would expect a "wired-in" transducer to possess.

Because of the nature of this transducer itself, it may be excluded from the process of imaging, since there are literally no adequate physical stimuli—no light patterns—to which it can apply. It is not so obvious, however, that the output of the transducer—say the aggregated primal sketch—cannot be stored in memory or even generated in the process of imaging. I shall argue, however, that it is extremely unlikely that any preconceptual, preassimilated, or knowledge-independent data are stored or otherwise used in thinking or imaging.

Consider what happens to the transducer output as it is assimilated into some cognitive structure and stored in memory for later retrieval. First of all, we are clearly highly selective in what (and how) we notice. We have to be, since not only the scene itself but the transducer output is literally unlimited in its potential for interpretation.

So much is not controversial. But now let us look more closely at the *nature* of this selection or "noticing function." What follows is a sketch of some of the characteristics of the transformation that relates the output of a transducer and a memory representation of some event. Taken together, it seems to me, they provide a strong case against viewing cognitive (or memory) representations of perceptually acquired knowledge as consisting of unprocessed (unabstracted) records of transducer outputs. Note that this argument is being made not only against the view that memory consists of pictures, a view that may well be a straw man. It applies equally well if memory is thought to consist of collages of pictoral segments, sketches, dynamic motion pictures, holograms, encoded multidimensional intensity matricies, or any other form of record of a particular concrete event (the one-time output of the transducer). Properties of the transformation and of the memory representation that lead us to this view include the following.

(1) The transformation between transducer and memory does not simply produce a degradation of resolution (a blurring or a mapping of a coarser grid), since we clearly do not perceive (in any sense of that word) or remember something that is complete in all aspects but low in detail or in precision. As Bobrow (1975, p. 8) puts it, "Human visual memory does not seem to have (the) property of uniform extraction of detail, or of exhaustiveness."

(2) The transformation is not a continuous topological deformation of the pattern of stimulation. No continuous transformation results in such commonplace phenomena as, for example, failure to notice objects or relations in a scene, perceptual addition of features that were not there (e.g., "cognitive contours"), or noticing the "what" but not the "where" or "when" of scene contents. Furthermore, the radical manner in which perception is influenced by such things as motivation, expectation (e.g., see the review by Bruner, 1957), prior knowledge, or even stage of cognitive development, attests not only to the general malleability of perception, but to the high degree of stimulus-independent knowledge-based *construction* that goes into the mental representation. Although this simple point is frequently forgotten, it has been made repeatedly and eloquently in the psychological literature by people like Hochberg (1968),

Gombrich (1961), and Gregory (1974), and in the philosophical literature by people like Hanson (1953) and Goodman (1968).

(3) The representation of a scene contains many non-pictorial (and non-sensory) aspects—aspects that cannot realistically be said to be in the sense data at all. Examples of the latter are the perceived relation of causality (Michotte, 1963) or the relations of attack and defence on a chess board (Simon and Barenfeld, 1969). In fact I would argue that all relations are of this type: that there is no fundamental difference between the relations "is to the left of," "is under attack by," or "causes," inasmuch as none of them is any more "directly in the scene" than any other. These are all abstract conceptual relations far removed from the output vocabulary of the transducer.

(4) Although we often appear to go through a process of recalling an image of a scene and then of noticing or perceiving aspects of that image, this recall-reperceive sequence is extremely problematic. The fact that we can recall a scene, or part of a scene, by addressing aspects of the perceptually interpreted content of the scene argues that what we have stored is *already interpreted* and not in need of reperception as we supposed. Retrieval of images is clearly hierarchical to an unlimited degree of detail and in the widest range of aspects. Thus, for example, I might image a certain sequence of events as I recall what happened at a conference session. Such images may be quite global and could involve a whole scene in a room over a period of time. But I might also image someone's facial expression, or the substance of his remarks, or my reactions to the papers, or the approximate location of a questioner in the audience, without first calling up the entire scene. Such perceptual attributes must therefore be available as interpreted integral units in my representation of the whole scene. Not only can such recollections be of fine detail, but they can also be of rather abstract qualities, such as the mood of the assembly. Furthermore, when there are parts missing from one's recollections, these are never arbitrary pieces of a visual scene. We do not, for example, recall a scene with some arbitrary segment missing, such as a torn photograph. What is missing is invariably some integral perceptual attribute or relation; for example, colors, patterns, events, or spatial relations (I might, for example, recall the

people who were in the front row without recalling exactly where they were sitting or what they were wearing). When our recollections are vague, it is always in the sense that certain perceptual qualities or attributes are absent or vague, not that there are geometrically definable pieces of a picture missing. All of the above suggest that one's representation of a scene must contain already differentiated and interpreted perceptual aspects. In other words, the representation is far from being raw and, so to speak, in need of "perceptual" interpretation. Because retrieval must be able to address perceptually interpreted content, the network of cross-classified relations must have interpreted objects (i.e., concepts) at its nodes.[1] This does not mean, of course, that what we retrieve cannot be further processed. The argument is simply that they are not subject to *perceptual* interpretation the way pictures are interpreted; by "perceptual" I refer to the processes of transduction and of interpretation or assimilation into cognitive conceptual structures.

Because the representation is so obviously selective and conceptual in nature, referring to it as an image—a term that has pictorial or projective connotations—is very misleading. Although there are some who have no objections to speaking of "conceptual images," I prefer the term "description" or "structural description" because this carries certain desirable connotations. For example, it implies that the representation is something that (a) must be constructed out of a vocabulary of available concepts (Kant's "Categories of understanding"), (b) bears a referential relation to the object it represents rather than a relation of "resembling," and (c) has its semantics defined by an accessing function that is not assumed to be the entire visual apparatus (I shall have more to say about (b) and (c) in section 6 below). The structured description approach also gives one a psychologically appropriate way of talking about the complexity of a representation. Such complexity is not a property defined over a material layout (e.g., extent, dimensionality, number of topologically defineable segments, etc.) but rather a property defined over a symbol structure (e.g., number of symbols, relations, etc. or, better still, number of nodes at different levels of a tree structure—some details for the latter measure have been proposed and successfully tested in a limited context by Palmer, 1974). Complexity, in others words, is a measure over a description in symbolic or conceptual terms, not over a description in geometric or physical terms.

3. Some Illustrative Examples

To give an idea of what I believe can be gained by this approach to imagery, signalled as it were by the new terminology, I shall describe several phenomena—mostly ones observed in children (who incidentally have been shown to have particularly good "visual imagery" ability)—and then give an account of the phenomena in terms of the notion of "description."

Figure 1a schematically depicts some findings reported in Piaget and Inhelder (1956). When young children below the ages of four or five years are shown a colored fluid in an inclined transparent container and are later asked to draw (or to indicate by describing and pointing) what they saw, they typically indicate the fluid as being parallel to either the bottom or the side of the container. Two other related figural "errors" of reproduction or recognition that occur with young children are shown in Figures 1c and 1d. The first part of Figure 1c illustrates the well-known mirror image confusion common in children. Figure 1d (reported by Eve Clark, 1973) illustrates the following phenomenon. When young children are shown a small object being placed next to a container and are asked to imitate exactly the action they have just observed, they most frequently place the object *inside* the container. There are a number of other similar transformations that children systematically produce in imitating actions.

Such "errors" can be simply accounted for if we assume that children's internal vocabulary of descriptive concepts is limited or that the priorities they place on the use of such concepts differ from those of adults. For example, without a concept for the relation "is left of" or "is right of," no description of an asymmetrical figure is possible that distinguishes that figure from its mirror image (Figure 1c). Similarly, if a child lacks the concept of "geocentric level," his percept of the fluid in the inclined container may not be the same as an adult's. In such a case the nearest appropriate concepts (e.g., perpendicular, parallel) may be used, producing the observed errors. Of course such differences in the availability of figural concepts do not always produce a failure to make a distinction. In some cases

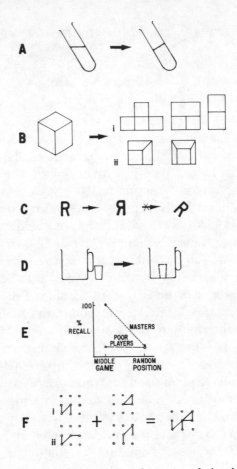

Figure 1. Examples of the conceptual nature of visual mental images. A: Typical recall error made by children who have not mastered the concept of "level" (Piaget & Inhelder, 1956). B: Common errors in children's drawings of a cube (adapted from Weinstein, 1974). C: Children are more likely to confuse a figure and its mirror image than a figure and a misoriented copy (e.g., Rock, 1973). D: When imitating the action of placing an object beside a container, a child is more likely to place the object inside the container (Clark, 1973). E: Chess masters' superior "visual recall" of chess positions holds only when the the positions are taken from real middle games (reported in Chase and Simon, 1973). F: When subjects are asked to synthesize a figure by mentally superimposing two given figures, their performance depends on the way the figure is decomposed (adapted from Palmer, 1974).

they result in a failure to perceive similarities. Thus, as illustrated in the second part of Figure 1c, children tend to treat a figure in a different orientation as a different figure. For example (see Rock, 1973), young children make fewer orientation generalization errors, confusing figures in different orientations in a discrimination learning experiment, than their older counterparts. (The apparent indifference of young children to the orientation of pictures and print may simply be due to their failure to recognize the importance of orientation to recognition—see Rock, 1973.) In our terms, for the same form in different orientations to be perceived as similar it would have to be represented in terms of appropriate orientation-independent concepts (e.g., relations like centripetal-centrifugal).[2]

The case of imitation is very similar. For what is considered to be mere mechanical imitation must be mediated by a memory representation, which, we have been arguing, depends on the availability of descriptive concepts. Of course imitation also depends on other factors such as preferred response strategies. Eve Clark (1973) found that if she asked a child to imitate the experimenter's action of moving a small object and placing it beside a container, the child most frequently performed a similar movement but left the object *inside* the container (as depicted in Figure 1d). One might be inclined to say that the child saw an object being placed in some appropriate proximate relation to a container and constructed an internal representation that recorded this observation. In imitating, the child selects an action in his repertoire, according to some preferences such as discussed by Clark (1973), which is compatible with this representation. For the child, then, the observed and produced actions fall in the same equivalence class—as captured by its internal representation—just as a figure and its mirror image are in the same class because the child's representation is conceptually less differentiated than that of the adult.

Figure 1b depicts a related situation in which children's drawings of a cube deviate from those made by adults. Notice that relative to the more familiar perspective drawing, the children's renderings are *more* faithful to a description of the cube (e.g., the angles are mostly 90°, faces are square and perpendicular to other faces, etc.). Weinstein (1974) found that older children produce hybrid drawings (such as the two on the second line) as they attempt to incorporate

If kids have perfect imagery, but their own set of percept-action mappings, & if they applied these mappings to their images, you'd happily predict all of these results.

the perspective conventions that the Western adult community did not adopt uniformly until the Renaissance (and that, conceivably, are considered the veridical rendering because they represent the way cameras operate). The point is that "optical projection onto a single stationary point of view" is only one of a large number of ways of transforming a mental representation of a three-dimensional object into a two-dimensional drawing. Since the mental representation is necessarily not identical with any of the drawings, it does not independently determine one of them as the unique "correct" rendering. The process of selecting from among the set of drawings compatible with the mental representation of the object must depend on other, probably learned and culturally specific principles — often collectively called "drawing skill."

Because children do not have so refined a vocabulary of descriptive figure-concepts as adults do, their mental representations may tend to be less differentiated than those of adults. In addition, children have not mastered adult conventions and various physical principles, so their reproductions and imitations are a source of more dramatic illustrations of the abstract conceptual or descriptive nature of mental representation. The principle is not by any means, however, confined to children. Consider the following two published results from adult subjects.

Chase and Simon (1973) describe a series of ingenious experiments on the visual memory of chess players. Chess masters are known to have a vastly superior memory for board positions than mediocre chess players. The question arises whether chess ability rests in part on exceptionally good visual imagery ability. Chase and Simon conclude, in effect, that such ability is very important but that it does not consist simply of a general visual imagery talent. The superior performance of chess masters in reproducing a board position after only a few seconds' exposure is manifest *only* when it is a true board position taken from an actual chess game. The difference between masters and duffers disappears when a random arrangement of the same pieces is used as the stimulus (see Figure 1e). Thus what appears to be strictly visual memory is extremely sensitive to chess-specific patterns. Chase and Simon conclude that the exceptional visual memory of chess experts derives from their very large repertoire of familiar chess configurations. Such "configurations"

are not defined simply by geometrical patterns, since they are independent of the shape, size, or color of chess pieces but are sensitive to nongeometrical relations such as attack, defence, control,
etc., which may even be spatially nonlocal. In our terms chess masters may be said to have a rich internal vocabulary with which to
construct a representation of the board. Their representation can
thus be constructed rapidly and is also conceptually simple—i.e., it
consists of a compact description constructed from a rich vocabulary
appropriate to the game of chess. Even though the memory is of
an apparently visual pattern, the particular internal representation
constructed depends on nonvisual factors. As a further corroborating
example Eisenstadt and Kareev (1975) have shown that the pattern
of errors in the recall of a particular Go board configuration depends
on whether a subject perceives it as a position in the game of Go
or in the game of Gomoku. In this case geometrically identical patterns are shown to be represented differently depending on highly
cognitive factors.

Another study illustrating the large conceptual component involved in visual imagery was reported by Palmer (1974). He presented subjects with two patterns (each with the same number of
line segments), which they were to superimpose to yield a third
synthesized pattern. The difficulty subjects experienced (measured
in terms of both latency and accuracy) in synthesizing a particular
pattern depended on the way it had been presented as subpatterns
to be superimposed. Thus the subpatterns designated as "good" configurations (e.g., Figure 1e(i)), which shared a larger number of major
integrated substructures with the required figure (defined by Palmer
in terms of a hierarchical description), were easier to synthesize.

Again, as in the other evidence cited above, Palmer found that
in what appears to be fundamentally a visual imagery task it is the
conceptual rather than some sort of graphic complexity that is the
essential determiner of task difficulty. Apparently even when visual
imagery seems clearly implicated, the underlying representation is
best characterized as something more abstract and conceptual—i.e.,
what we have been calling a structured description. The point is not
simply that there are tasks in which something beyond an iconic
image is involved, but that even in cases in which visual images would
appear to be the chief mode of representation, task complexity

OK. So it's not iconic. Now where?

measures lead one to recognize that what serves as the mental representation is highly cognitive. Furthermore, the most perspicuous way of talking about such representations is in terms of such notions as a vocabulary of internal concepts, compactness of descriptions couched in this vocabulary, and other locutions much more appropriate to descriptions than to pictures. I should emphasize, however, that in using the term "description" I am not referring to linguistic objects in the conventional sense. Such internal descriptions (e.g., those discussed in the next section) cannot be directly externalized as sentences. The reasons for this are, first, that the symbols involved may not have corresponding lexical labels in any natural language and, second, that the descriptive structures are not discursive in the sense that they must be scanned in a fixed sequence (as in the case with sentences). The primary reason for persisting in calling them "descriptions" lies in the way these representations are related to what they represent, as discussed in (a)-(c) in section 2 above.

4. Symbol Structures for Imagery

Those who are familiar with work in artificial intelligence will recognize that most computational data structures (e.g., semantic networks) have properties that make them suitable candidates for internal descriptions. Although they are all articulated symbol structures, most have very different formal properties from those of natural language or even of predicate calculus. For example, they contain flexible access paths among symbols that can be tailored to specific goals, they may designate procedures that can be evoked at appropriate times, and they may contain propositional forms that are asserted only in appropriate contexts, when bindings for free variables are provided. Although the formal properties of such descriptive systems as a class are not yet well understood (see Woods, 1975), it seems clear that they are at least a promising candidate as a formalism for internal representations, not only because of their descriptive power but also because of their structural flexibility. The latter quality is most important in the present context because we are presumably interested in finding a psychologically adequate form of representation as well as a logically adequate one. In particular we are interested in accounting for certain properties of natural intelligence. We would like to be able to give an account of why certain tasks are easier than others (i.e., why some take less time, result in fewer errors), why certain types of systematic errors occur, how representations are transformed in memory and thought, etc. From this perspective there are good reasons for believing that different representational structures are used at different times and for different purposes. For example, representations that are temporarily constructed in the course of activity we call imaging have some properties not shared by those constructed during episodes we would describe as inner speech. Evidence for this need not rely solely on reports that these activities are accompanied by different subjective experiences. Various measures of access and manipulatory complexity (as assessed, for example, by reaction times) also supports this view. My contention is, however, that there is at present no good reason to reject the view that a common articulated descriptive system underlies all of these representations and that the apparent differences arise from such things as the particular vocabulary of symbols (i.e., designations of concepts and relations) that are used, accessibility paths that are set up among parts of the representation, and the particular operations that are evoked to process these symbol structures. For example, some characteristics of temporary symbol structures that have been developed to model aspects of imaging (as in the work of Baylor, 1972; Moran, 1973; Farley, 1974) include the following:

(1) Representations of physical objects and their attributes are *individuated*—i.e., individual objects are distinguished by distinct internal symbols, and attributes are often attached to them (i.e., attributes are accessible through these symbols). Thus individuals in such representations can be *counted*. For example, there would be no atomic symbol corresponding to "*n* windows." Rather *n* distinct symbols would be generated one for each imagined window. These might even have to be related to one another by relations such as "above," "to the right of," etc.

(2) Spatial and temporal relations in such imaginal data structures are often found to provide particularly good access paths. For example, given an object in such an imaginal structure, it is easier to retrieve an object that is in the relation "next to" or "above" to it than in the relation "larger than" or "same color as" to it (e.g., see Collins and Quillan, 1969).

(3) When a temporary data structure corresponding to an image is constructed, many "default values" are included so that ready access is provided to some details not obviously relevant to the task at hand.

(4) In such workspace data structures we would not have quantifiers or logical connectives (i.e., we would not have an "image symbol structure" for the proposition of "all red blocks"), although sometimes prototypical patterns might be made to serve some of these functions.

(5) Common symbol systems, particularly those designating spatial relations, might be shared by various modalities and by the motor functions as well as the perceptual and image functions. This may explain why coordination is possible and why phenomena such as stimulus-response compatability (Fitts and Seeger, 1953) and intramodality interference (Brooks, 1968) are observed.

(6) We might even postulate that certain operations performed on objects in the "imaginal workspace" are computational primitives. Suggestion (2) above can be thought of in this way—i.e., given a reference to an element, retrieving the element that designates some spatially adjacent object may be computationally cheap. In fact this could be the theoretical interpretation of the claim that images are "spatially organized"—the reason is not that image data structures are distributed in space (whatever that could mean), but rather that spatial relations such as adjacency can be used as access paths. One must be careful, however, in positing computational primitives for the image workspace. As I shall argue it later, it is very tempting to posit as primitive operations, processes that conceal a major part of what one is trying to explain (as occurs if we take metaphors such as the "mind's eye" or "mental rotation" too literally).

But attempts to develop formal models of imagery are just beginning, and most of the story is yet to be told. Should it be possible to model all forms of cognition (in a manner that takes into account not only logical requisites but also psychological complexity evidence) in a single formalism, not only would be have achieved considerable theoretical parsimony, but we would also have made a significant contribution to bringing some integration to many classical philosophical puzzles of cognition.

I might remark that I have occassionally heard objections to such data structures on the grounds that the symbols are arbitrary atomic elements. As in mathematics, the symbol that designates some quality or some object is chosen for the theorist's convenience; hence in computer science the symbol is usually a string of letters forming a mnemonic word or phrase. What troubles some people is the fact that one must at some point bridge the gap between the symbol and the world outside. Thus, even admitting that much of the representation is symbolic, they would prefer to have some nonarbitrary symbolic content in the representation. For example, one proposal is that a fragment of a representation of a checkered tablecloth might be expressed as something like: "(TEXTURE TABLECLOTH ▨)," where the third term is a piece of template that can both designate checkeredness and be used to identify this texture in some transducer (the same might be done for TABLECLOTH but perhaps not for the more abstract concept TEXTURE). But although this hybrid expression may *look* different from a standard data structure, this is a property only of the way we have chosen to display it. It is no different from (TEXTURE TABLECLOTH Q137) provided the atom Q137 is used consistently (a) when a reference to a checkered pattern is intended; (b) when a checkered pattern is detected by the transducer hardware; (c) when a verbal reference to checkered patterns is received or generated, etc. (The last condition is contingent on the system having "learned" the relation between Q137 and a verbal label such as "checkered.") The nonarbitrariness of a symbol arises entirely from the system of symbols within which it occurs as well as the way in which input-output transducers are wired to translate between energy patterns and symbols.

5. Are Images Analogue?

Although enthusiam for pictorial representations, which resemble what they represent, or for some kind of "sensory storage" may be waning (at least in the case of representations stored in long-term memory), many people do not subscribe to the view that articulated symbol systems are sufficient to account for many of the phenomena that have been studied by psychologists interested in imagery. These people feel we are forced into the position of admitting at least two radically different types of representations—one to encompass articulated, verbal, or factual information, and the other to capture continuous, analogical, sensory, or wholistic types of phenomena implicated in imagery and perhaps other areas of cognition and thought. Within artificial intelligence the study of different types of representational systems is very much an active frontier, and it is impossible to rule out such a hypothesis—however vague the current notions of what constitutes an "analogical" representation. Whatever the outcome of this research, however, it nevertheless appears to me that the arguments and evidence that people have typically presented as favoring such nonarticulated representations have been far short of persuasive.

A wide variety of experimental phenomena has been cited in support of the claim that such nonarticulated imagery representations must be entertained. For example, there are experiments demonstrating differences in recall between concrete imaginable situations and abstract ones, and between performance under instructions to image vs. instructions to rehearse; experiments demonstrating confusion errors based on appearances as opposed to category membership; experiments showing intramodality interference during imaging; and more recently, experiments using reaction time measures, which show that relative difficulty of some tasks performed imaginally mirrors the relative difficulty of such tasks performed perceptually, i.e., while examining actual displays (see Kosslyn & Pomerantz, 1977). In addition there are a number of ingenious experiments (mostly by Roger Shepard and his students; e.g., Shepard, 1975; Cooper & Shepard, 1973; Metzler & Shepard, 1974) also using reaction time measures, which suggest that mental manipulation of images involves carrying out a sequence (or possibly a continuum) of transformations paralleling those that would be carried out in manipulating real objects. For example, the time taken to determine that two figures are identical except for their relative orientation has been found to be a linear function of the angle between them. This effect has been demonstrated in a variety of ways, including asking a subject to prepare mentally for the second of the two figures at some prescribed angle. The preparation time appears to be the same linear function of angular deviation (Cooper & Shepard, 1973).

This is explained by saying that subjects rotate an image of the presented form at some constant rate.

Taken as a whole these studies have persuaded many psychologists that mental representations of objects, particularly in the visual modality, must be structurally isomophic to the objects they represent. This is often phrased by saying that representations are *analogical* rather than descriptive or articulated and that they are transformed by wholistic analogue processes. The argument is often made that although it *might* be possible to fabricate an account of how such results could arise from articulated descriptive representations, such accounts are always post hoc and unnatural. Accounts based on positing the manipulation of internal analogues are invariably more natural and are independently motivated by the observation that the same laws of perception and transformation can be applied to the internal representation as are known to apply to external stimuli. My response to this is threefold.

(1) If one takes the position I outlined earlier—viz., that perception involves the construction of an internal description—then it should not be surprising that cognitive operations (e.g., judgments) occurring during perception bear some strong relation to cognitive operations occurring during imaging. On this account both involve the further processing of these internal descriptions.

Furthermore, it should not be surprising if operations upon internal representations show some systematic relationship to operations that would be carried out upon the corresponding objects in the world. We surely have some representation of physical operations as well as of objects. Our knowledge of what it means to manipulate objects derives at least in part from our experience in carrying out actions on real objects. Thus if someone asked me whether a piece of paper of a certain shape could be folded up to form a certain polyhedral form, I would not attempt to solve the problem by applying any arbitrary transformation to my representation of the paper. Instead I would go through a process of solving a series of subproblems, each of which involved answering the question, "What will happen to the shape if I make the following fold?" But this is far from being an argument for internal analogues, as many writers have claimed (e.g., Shepard, 1975). In any problem the solution method I use depends on both the demands of the task (e.g., in this case only physically possible transformations are legitimate) and on the way my knowledge about such transformations is structured. Presumably my knowledge of folding consists of such facts as what happens to the shape of an object when a single fold is made in it, just as my knowledge of addition consists of such atomic facts as $2 + 3 = 5$, which I use in the solution of more complex problems. But notice that all this implies only that I solve the problem in stages by applying operations to representations. There need literally be nothing in common between my mental representation of folding and actual folding, other than that one can be used in certain situations to compute the effect produced by the other—i.e., to compute what could result from actually completing a fold. In fact I shall argue in the next section that theoretical adequacy will force the mental operation to be unlike the physical operation in certain critical respects, giving the theory that "unnaturalness" that bothers many people.

If there were a high degree of correspondence between operations in the world and mental operations (including comparable complexities and constraints on what could be performed), one might perhaps be justified in speaking of the mental activities as in some sense "analogue." But the correspondence is highly partial: only certain aspects of some physical operations have correspondences. Although mental operations have few of the constraints that affect physical operations (i.e., it is easy to imagine physically impossible phenomena), they are also subject to many constraints for which there are no physical counterparts. There are countless simple operations that are impossible to imagine accurately. Sometimes we cannot keep track of all the relations. For example, imagine a familiar scene; now try to image it upside down, out of focus, viewed through a green filter, etc. Or sometimes we lack the tacit knowledge of the physical laws governing the phenomena. Examples of this are a child asked to imagine what will happen when a block is pushed over the edge of a table, or an adult asked to imagine the trajectory of a weight being dropped behind a screen. Ian Howard (1974) has discussed an interesting series of experiments in which he shows that adults' "perceptual schemata" are often not consonant with the laws of physics. In fact in a recent ingenious experiment, using trick

3-D photography and motion pictures, he showed that (a) about half the college students he tested could not articulate the principle that fluid levels in a container remain horizontal as the container is tilted, and (b) those who could not articulate this principle could not recognize gross anomalies (up to 30° from horizontal) in fluid levels, whereas those who did articulate the principles were very accurate in their detection of anomalies (Howard, in press). The failure of "perceptual schemata" to be veridical has also been demonstrated for fluid levels by Thomas, Jamison, and Hummel (1973). The point is that even in perception, the detection of deviations from physical laws is far from automatic. Obviously in the case of imaging physical transformations, the ability to image the correct effect is highly dependent on what the subject knows and does not merely follow from the behavior of internal analogues. It is especially not a consequence of any intrinsic property of some analogue "medium," as I shall argue presently. I shall return to the differences between physical and mental operations in sections 7 and 8 when I discuss mental rotation experiments.

(2) Although there are similarities between cognitive operations in perception and in imaging, there are also some outstanding differences that may be more revealing of the underlying processes. For example, the order of scanning and the sorts of things that can be "noticed" in imaging are much more constrained than in perception. The reason for this is partly that a scene has a stable independent existence and can be reexamined at will to produce new interpretations. In contrast, the construction of an internal description from stored knowledge can hardly be divorced from its interpretation. While some reinterpretation is certainly possible, it surely is more like the derivation of new entailments from the stored knowledge than like the discovery of new aspects of an environment by the usual visual means. Discovering even moderately novel readings from a mental image such as those required to find simple embedded figures in a pattern, have been shown to be exceedingly difficult (Reed, 1974). Another important property of an image that distinguishes it from perception is that it is quite limited in its content. This limitation, however, does not appear to depend on any simple measure of geometrical complexity so much as on conceptual, or what I would call descriptive, complexity. The latter in turn varies depending on

the availability of appropriate concepts for describing the display, as I have already argued.

(3) My third reaction to the arguments for analogical representations based on the parallels between imaging and perception is the following. I maintain that the reason why structured descriptions and the computational processes that go with them appear unnatural is precisely that they are an earnest attempt to make explicit the detailed structure of the entire cognitive system involved in imagery, down to the level of mechanically realizable processes. It seems that naturalness of theoretical accounts of imagery can be gained by sweeping a large part of the puzzle under one of two rugs: we can attribute some of the phenomena to unexplained properties of the "mind's eye" or some other interpreting process, or we can attribute some of them to instrinsic properties of the analogical representational *medium*. I shall suggest that both of these moves involve us in the game of *obscurum per obscurus*, an unreasonable price to pay for naturalness.

6. Properties of the Mind's Eye

I shall begin this sketch by giving the following caricature of a class of arguments for "analogical" or "direct" or "presentational" representations. Consider the parallel between the pairs "organism-environment" and "mental process-representation" (Figure 2a, b).

The system depicted in Figure 2a must surely have many properties in common with the system depicted in Figure 2b; otherwise thought would be irrelevant to action, and our chances of survival would be negligible. From this one is tempted to say that representations and the objects they represent must have much in common. Beginning with this innocent remark we are irresistably and imperceptibly drawn towards the fatal error of attributing more and more of the properties of the environment, as described by the physical sciences, to the representation itself. If I were permitted to misappropriate other people's terms slightly, I might call this the tendency to commit the "stimulus error" after Titchner or to succumb to the "objective pull" after Quine. It is in the failure to emphasize the fundamental differences between the mental object, which we call the representation, and the physical object (i.e., the two right-hand elements in Figure 2) that we run ourselves into various traps. The physical object has a stable existence, its transformations are governed by natural laws, and it is open to as many readings or interpretations as are compatible with the cognitive powers of its perceiver. The representation, on the other hand, is already an interpretation or reading given to the object by an act of conceptualization, and any transformations of the representation are determined by cognitive operations that may or may not bear any relation to the laws

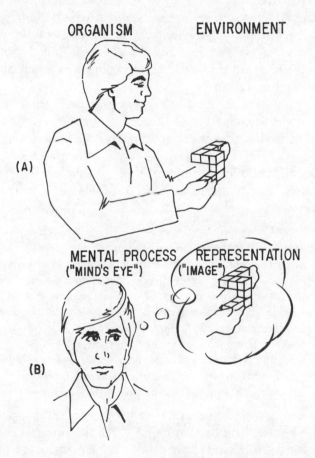

Figure 2. Because the object-organism relation depicted in A must share some functional properties with the "mental image"-"mind's eye" relation depicted in B, we can be seduced into attributing many object properties to the image and many perception properties to the mind's eye.

of physics. These may seem like rather obvious differences, but I shall argue that the failure to keep them in focus has been behind some of the arguments for analogical representations.

The temptation to draw the external world inside the head leads to a classical dilemma of imaginal representation: if the representation is too similar to the world it represents, it is of no help in apprehending the world, since it merely moves the problem in one layer; but if it is too dissimilar, then how can it represent the world at all? This apparent dilemma turns on the use of the word "similar," which surely is appropriate only when two things are examined by the same process (e.g., when they are both viewed). This, however, is a gratuitous assumption that underlies and confuses much of the discussion of representation.

For example, one frequently hears that a "nonverbal" representation preserves the structure of the environment it represents. Such preservation of structure is taken by many to be a defining characteristic of analogical representations. Aaron Sloman (1971, pp. 216-217) makes the following comparison in contrasting analogical representations with a pedicate calculus formulation, or what he calls Fregean systems:

> In an *analogical* system properties of and relations between parts of the representing configuration represent properties and relations of parts in a complex configuration, so that the structure of the representation gives information about the structure of what is represented. . . . By contrast, in a Fregean system there is basically only *one* type of 'expressive' relation between parts of a configuration, namely the relation between 'function-signs' and 'argument-signs'. . . . For example, the denoting phrase 'the brother of the wife of Tom' would be analyzed by Frege as containing two function-signs 'the brother of ( )' and 'the wife of ( )' and two argument-signs 'Tom' and 'the wife of Tom' as indicated in 'the brother of (the wife of (Tom))'. Clearly the structure of such a configuration need not correspond to the structure of what it represents or denotes.

Now this may sound like a reasonable claim until one tries to interpret the phrase "the structure of X." All the phrase can mean is that some function (which I have called the "semantic interpretation function") can give X an interpretation as a structure. There is literally nothing intrinsic in any object that can be called its "structure." Sloman's distinction is empty unless we are told which of an unlimited number of potential structures it refers to. For example,

Sloman notes that in the above example the sign "Tom" is *part of* the sign "the wife of Tom," whereas in the situation represented, the thing designated by the sign "Tom" is certainly not part of the thing designated by the sign "the wife of Tom." Thus, he argues, the structure of the representation does not reflect the structure of what is represented. But the point is that so long as the function that interprets the phrase shows no inclination to attend to what you and I might call the relation "is a part of," or, if it does attend to such a relation, does not identify it with a similarly named (but in fact quite different) relation in the world, the problem does not arise. In this case "is a part of" is simply not a *signifying* relation. In fact it would be correct to say that from the point of view of the "semantic interpretation function" such a relation does not exist. Thus it is true that a potential relation in the representation does not signify a relation in the world. But neither does the relation "is heavier than" in a picture represent a relation in the scene depicted—e.g., the part of a picture corresponding to a cloud may weigh more than the part of the picture representing a building, but so long as the interpretation function does not attend to relative weights, this remains irrelevant. Or to take a less farfetched example, the relation among areas in a Mercator map projection is not signifying, although a compass direction is.[3]

Thus discussions about the nature of mental representations should really be discussions about representational *systems* consisting of the pair "representation" and 'semantic interpretation function." Furthermore, my earlier claim that representations are descriptions should more properly be put as a claim that representations *function* as descriptions—i.e., they are related to the objects they represent in the way sentences are related to the objects they describe (i.e., via an interpretation or something like Wittgenstein's "laws of projection) rather than the way photographs are related to the objects they picture (i.e., via laws of optics and principles of projective geometry).

Occasionally writers have recognized the importance of the semantic interpretation function. In one recent case it has been used to resolve a long-standing philosophical puzzle relating to the indeterminateness of images. This is a problem that Dennett (1969) considers a serious difficulty with the imagery view. Recently, however,

[handwritten margin note: It's a good point that there's some confusion over whether the imagery claim is about the representation or about the interpretive device.]

Fodor (1975, p. 191) has argued that such indeterminateness is not problematic for a pictoral view of images. Fodor's argument rests on a recognition that the content of a mental representation is always relative to some interpretation. This is precisely the point we have been discussing above (as well as in Pylyshyn, in press). Let us look briefly at Fodor's argument that what we call images can reasonably be understood as indeterminate.

> What makes my stick figure an image of a tiger is not that it looks much like one (my drawings of tigers don't look much like tigers either) but rather that it's *my* image, so I'm the one who gets to say what it's an image of. My images (and my drawings) connect with my intentions in a certain way; I *take* them as tiger-pictures for purposes of whatever task I happen to have in hand. Since my mental image *is* an image, there will be some visual descriptions under which it is determinate; hence there will be some question whose answers I can 'read off' the display, and the more pictorial the display is the more such questions there will be. But, in the case of any given image, there might be arbitrarily many visual properties which would not be pictured but, as it were, carried by the description under which the image is intended.

This is an important and relevant observation. But notice what it has done to the notion of an image. The image has lost its essential quality. It has become an object that must be *read* via an intention and that can be read in many different ways. In other words, it contains forms or symbol tokens exactly as does a structured description.[4] What makes it pictorial, according to Fodor, is that there are many properties that can be "read off," presumable with low computational cost. But this is precisely what happens when we enrich a structured description by making it more elaborate and detailed. The advantages of thinking of this as the elaboration of a description, rather than of the image being more pictorial (apart from the vagueness of the notion of "degree of pictorialness"), are that (a) this interpretation gives recognition to the fact that the elaboration is done within the constraints of available concepts rather than by the addition of arbitrary pictorial fragments; (b) "reading off" becomes a well-defined symbol-matching operation rather than involving all of the perceptual apparatus driven by intentions; (c) no matter how much elaboration of detail is carried out, there will always be an arbitrarily large amount of indeterminateness in the resulting representation (it will always fail to be determinate with respect to some aspects which are not only determinate in the scene but which no picture would leave uncommitted), and furthermore, as noted in section 2 (1), the representation is not homogeneous in the amount of determinateness of various aspects; (d) this interpretation discourages the view, invariably associated with the term "image," that there exists an object that is interpreted the way a scene is interpreted (i.e., visually), that has a stable simultaneous existence so that it can be scanned perceptually for new readings, and that inherits certain intrinsic properties from the material medium in which it is embedded (e.g., rigidity under various transformations—see the discussion below).

Replacing "images" with "images under descriptions," as Fodor does, frees the term from many of the philosophical problems that plagued it in the past. The trouble with this move is precisely the problem of making clear the sense in which images under descriptions are to be distinguished from descriptions. Fodor (p. 190) puts it this way: "Images under description share their nondiscursiveness with images *tout court*. What they share with descriptions is that they needn't look much like what they represent." Thus discursiveness seems to be the crucial property. But, as we have seen, symbol structures are not discursive in the sense that sentences are — i.e, they need not be read in a prescribed order. The order of "scanning" is determined by the accessing algorithm and makes use of the relations that are the access paths of the structured description, just as a visual scan of an image would presumably be determined by the intentions of the perceiver together with something like peripheral vision. This amounts to saying that we have yet to see a viable distinction among images, images under descriptions, and structured descriptions when any of these is embedded within a representational system—i.e., when paired with the appropriate semantic interpretation function. Given the advantages of the nonpictorial description option mentioned above, I see no reason to abandon this approach, which at least has some theoretical exemplars in current computational models.

It is important to keep in mind the central role the semantic interpretation function plays in the whole issue of representation. One of the reasons why imagistic representations appear so natural is that they can literally *resemble* the objects they depict, just as we might think of the contents of our recollections as resembling the recalled situation. But this can be paraphrased as saying that the relation between images (or pictures) and their designata is clear when the semantic interpretation function in both cases is nothing less than the whole of intelligent human perception. That this way of characterizing representations is plagued with difficulties has been amply discussed by Wittgenstein (1953), Goodman (1968), Dennett (1969), Fodor (1975), and others, so I shall pass up the opportunity to add my comments. However, there are also more subtle errors based on tacit assumptions regarding the nature of the interpretation function. For example, there are frequent claims that certain kinds of information are "directly available" in an analogue representation and need merely to be "read off," as opposed to being computed from a descriptive representation. But as we have seen above, such claims are not about the merits of one *form* of representation as opposed to another, but about which aspects of a situation are explicitly built into the representation in advance and which types of operations are primitive in the semantic interpretation function.

It has long been recognized in computer science that there is a trade-off between the complexity of data structures and the complexity of algorithms for processing them. For example, at one extreme one of the simplest forms of representation is a list of propositions in the predicate calculus. However, extracting answers from such a representation requires a combinatorially explosive theorem-proving system. At the other extreme are some exhaustively cross-referenced data networks from which most of the more frequent questions can be answered by pattern-matching and graph-processing techniques. The difference is that in one case the work is done when new information is entered, whereas in the other case it is done at the time information is retrieved. For the psychologist, choosing some intermediate ground between these is at least partly an empirical issue, since he wishes to model the accessing complexity exhibited by human cognition. The trap here is that representations appear "natural" in proportion to the intelligence attributed to the accessing function. The most natural representation (the picture in the head) requires a full-fledged homunculus for its interpretation. Few psychologists would opt for this alternative. Next in attractiveness comes the wholistic analogue. What type of interpreting function this requires is not clear, but one that is sometimes hinted at would simply compute some similarity metric, such as implied by Quine's "quality space," or a function that recognizes something like Wittgenstein's "family resemblances." Such a function could thus indicate how similar some whole configuration was to, say, a prototypical one. Unfortunately we know nothing about how such similarity metrics can be "wholistically" computed. Even if we dropped the "wholistic" requirement, no one has been able to show general dimensional characteristics of similarity. In fact what evidence there is, such as the failure to find dimensions of generalization or dimensions of similarity in multidimensional scaling of structured stimuli (Shepard, 1964), suggests that a dimensional approach to similarity is probably doomed to failure.

As we depart from these direct or analogue representations and build more complex articulated descriptions, we find we can get away with somewhat better understood symbol-processing algorithms. What we lose in naturalness of representation we gain in approaching realizeable systems. Since we are still far from an adequate overall model of imagery, it is not a closed issue as to whether we will eventually run into fundamental difficulties. But at least the problems are out in the open—in all their unnatural nakedness— where they can be examined, rather than hidden in metaphors, such as that imagery involves perception.

7. Properties of the Medium

In the first place, I declare to you, sir, that when one has only confused ideas of *thought* and of *matter*, as one ordinarily has, it is not to be wondered at if one does not see the means of solving such questions.

Leibniz
New essays on the understanding, 1704

The second rug under which people have attempted to hide some of the puzzle of representation has been the representational medium itself. This approach is often taken in attempting to account for certain mental operations performed on representations. Before describing this approach I should like to describe a problem known as the "frame problem," which researchers in artificial intelligence have studied in the context of robot-planning, since it illuminates a relevant point.

Suppose we have a robot that has perceptual and motor capabilities and can be directed to move about, grasp objects, and generally follow a simple sequence of commands while observing what is going on around it. Such a robot has no difficulty with inconsistencies in its world model, since it merely observes what happens and updates its knowledge base. Sooner or later we would want to be able to give the robot more general goals that would require it to plan out an effective series of actions in advance. This, it turns out, is a qualitatively very different task from the one it has been performing. For now there is a problem of consistency. After each planned action the robot must, in effect, recompute its representation of the entire state of the world, since it must take into account all the possible effects of the action on every aspect of the environment. Such a recomputation may in fact involve referring to the laws of physics. The problem of reasoning about actions, in contrast with merely acting, gets us into a very difficult set of problems stemming from the interdependence of actions. A number of approaches to this so-called frame problem have been proposed (see Simon, 1972; McCarthy & Hayes, 1969; Raphael, 1971). All of them appear somehow to be unduly complex and unnatural. It is clear, however, that part of their unnaturalness rests on the fact that a great deal of knowledge must explicitly be brought to bear in reasoning about actions that we are not aware of using and that indeed we may not have to use when we operate directly on the world. In the latter case relevant interactions are given to us for free by the environment. In the case of reasoning, however, the relations are not free. We must in some way explicitly build in the knowledge regarding what effects do and do not follow from any action.[5]

It seems to me that the notion of an analogue representation medium is in part an attempt to get this information for free again. Consider the claim that data on the time-course of mental rotation (e.g., Shepard, 1975) argues that the process is analogue (since, as some people have been known to ask innocently, "How can you rotate a data structure through its intermediate positions?"). This carries the implication that once we start a rotation the medium will take care of maintaining the rigidity of the total pattern and carry along all the parts for us—just as the laws of physics take care of this for us in the real environment. But, as in the frame problem, we are overlooking the fact that the person must know what will and will not happen to the bottom part when the top part starts to rotate. In a descriptive structure this is precisely what makes "mental rotation" appear awkward and computationally unduly costly. But this is unavoidable unless we have an analogical modeling medium which intrinsically follows the laws of physics.[6] Unless we are willing to ascribe such laws to brain tissue (which, to some extent, is what Gestalt psychologists attempted to do), we are stuck with locating knowledge of such laws explicitly in some part of the total representation or in what I have called the semantic interpretation function (which does not, incidentally, preclude such knowledge from being a distributed computation attached to the data structure itself). If we admit this, however, we lose one of the main attractions of the "analogical medium" gambit. For now actions such as rotations must be accounted for by cognitive operations that are themselves not prima facie analogue, since they must in turn refer to knowledge about what happens to forms under certain transformations (we shall return to the notion of image rotation in the next section). Observations of children by Piaget as well as the experiments by Howard cited in section 5 (1) show that when such "operational knowledge" is not available, imagining actions does not lead to veridical conclusions, the supposedly analogical nature of the representation notwithstanding.

The phenomenon of attributing to the intrinsic nature of a representation some of the crucial aspects that need to be taken into account (because these are so intuitively obvious to the theorist) is not confined to analogical representations. Woods (1975) has recently shown that we frequently commit the same oversight in the case of semantic networks. For this reason it is important to attempt to simulate a significant portion of cognition by machine (although even here the existence of such built-in functions as an arithmetic processor may create the illusion that we get magnitudes for free— i.e., we need not account for how they are mentally represented).

8. What Is Rotated in Mental Rotation?

The mental rotation example raises a number of other related problems worth exploring. Let us suppose that an empirically adequate computational model of some cognitive process—say, for comparison of rotated forms, as in the Shepard (1975) experiments—is developed. What then would be the status of a description of the comparison process which used phrases such as "the image is mentally rotated"? There are several ways of approaching this question. One is to say that no rotation in fact takes place, since all behavorial data are accounted for by a model which contains no rotating entities. The only thing conceivably left to explain is why the subject reports "rotating an image."[7] This question might then be approached by an analysis such as that provided by Dan Dennett in his paper in this volume, in which he explores the source of introspective reports about cognitive processes.

A second approach is to say that "rotation" is the name we give to the result of a certain subprocess within the model that at a more microscopic level may or may not be carried out by a discrete symbolic computation. In other words, the "mental rotation" account is simply a description in a higher level language of a certain computation that takes place in the cognitive system. Furthermore, it could be argued that this is not just any arbitrary higher-level description but one that is particularly appropriate because (a) it is consonant with subjects' reports of what they do and (b) it alone accounts for the empirical constraints on the transformations applied to the representation—i.e., of all the logically possible ways of solving the comparison problem by transforming the symbol structure that is the mental representation of the stimulus, only the one describable as "rotation" (or, in other contexts, as "enlargement" or some such equally plausible pictorial manipulation) offers a natural account of the empirical regularities. Thus "rotation" is more than a convenient global description of the computation involved; the term has additional explanatory power because it captures the significant generalization, as the linguist would say, which underlies the empirically observed, as opposed to the logically possible, transformations.

In fact one might even cast the computational model or simulation in a higher-level language that had ROTATE as one of its primitive operations. This would make the computational model, in a sense, isomorphic to the imagery account (although presumably more complete in its detail and not necessarily analogue in any strong sense).

Such a defence of the "image rotation" account, if correct, would reduce the distinction between the imagery approach and the artificial intelligence approach. It would not entirely eliminate the distinction, since the latter group, not satisfied with an *explanation* that rests on the statement that comparisons require a subject first to "rotate an image," demands a more complete explication of the entire process. It would, however, eliminate some of the arguments over what is meant by words like "rotation" used in a technical theoretical sense.

Unfortunately such a translation from the language of images and rotations leaves some residual difficulties. In particular there are reasons for resisting the use of global operations like ROTATE as computational primitives. Presumably any operation that is a computational primitive need not be decomposed (i.e., no new understanding of the underlying *psychological* process is gained by expressing the primitive operation in terms of still smaller steps, even though such an analysis may be required in order to get it to execute on some particular device or perhaps to relate it to neurophysiology). But if the operation is to be treated as a single computational step, then surely the amount of computational resources (time and memory capacity) the operation uses must be independent of the context in which it is used. In particular the amount of computational resources used by a primitive operation should be independent of the representation to which it is applied.

Thus it should take t seconds to "rotate" a representation by Θ degrees regardless of what it is a representation of. If this were not the case, then we should further want to know what made one stimulus faster and another slower to rotate, which would be tantamount to asking what process takes place within the primitive operation ROTATE.

This approach reflects a general phenomenon in cognitive psychology. In constructing theories we often have the option of either postulating a large number of independent processes or else postulating a smaller number of more primitive interacting processes. In the former case variety of computations is accomplished by a variety of elementary processes, whereas in the latter case the variety comes from the way a few primitive processes interact. Given the option, the latter approach is usually preferred as providing the more powerful explanation—i.e., as being able to capture more significant generalizations with fewer theoretical entities.

Although such discussion rapidly gets into some deeper issues concerning the appropriate level of description of psychological processes, which cannot be discussed in general terms in this paper, the particular example of rotation should be clear enough. If the empirical evidence were compatible with the existence of a primitive cognitive operation for rotating a percept or an imaginal representation (which proceeded at some fixed rate of so many degrees per second), then it would be useful to speak of image-rotation as a description of part of the cognitive process. If, on the other hand, we have to qualify this description by saying that the cognitive process appears to be like a rotation of 360° per second for this kind of figure but of 60° per second for that kind of figure, or that some parts of a figure behave as if they were rotated but others do not, or that only certain kinds of figures can be subjected to rotation or only certain kinds of properties are contained in the rotated figure, then we have lost the most important currency this term had.[8] It then no longer acts like a primitive cognitive operation, since we are forced to expose the underlying computations covered by the term in order to account for the qualifying conditions. In addition it no longer has the virtue of distinguishing between permissible and impermissible transformations on representations, since clearly more is going on than simple rotation. So the usefulness of the image rotation account turns on a set of empirical questions.

Although there is not a great deal of evidence bearing on the kinds of possibilities raised above, there is some reason to believe that the hypothetical examples cited may very well be the case. In the first place, the ability to "mentally rotate" a presented figure clearly depends on the nature and complexity of that figure. For example, people find it almost impossible to recognize faces from inverted photographs (Rock, 1973) by performing a "mental rotation." The difficulty here does not seem to be associated with such geometrical attributes of the figure as its extent or the number of its components or attributes, as one might expect if the percept were thought of as some sort of iconic display. Numerous experiments have shown that the ability to recall a display (Chase and Simon, 1973), to construct an image mentally from a description (Moran, 1973), or to synthesize a composite figure mentally from component subfigures (Palmer, 1974) depends on the conceptual or descriptive complexity of the figures. Although I know of no published studies showing that the ability to manipulate images (e.g., by rotation) depends on conceptual complexity, this would certainly be a reasonable expectation, given, for example, the instability of complex images and the variable difficulty in retrieving different kinds of information from apparently clear initial images that are subjected to different transformations (e.g., in such tasks as the Guilford Spatial Visualization test—see Baylor, 1972).

In the second place, there is reason to believe that apparent rates of mental rotation depend on conceptual complexity. Metzler and Shepard (1974) found that line drawings of simple three-dimensional figures were rotated at only $60°$ per second, whereas Cooper and Shepard (1974) obtained a rate of $360°$ per second with letters of the alphabet. Hochberg and Gellman (1977) also report evidence that the apparent rate of rotation does depend on figural complexity, and in particular on the presence of "landmark features" in the figures. In fact, where salient landmark features are absent (as with certain patterns of filled and empty dots), *no* evidence of rotation is found (Hochber & Gellman, 1976). I have also obtained data (Pylyshyn, 1977) showing that apparent rates of rotation of line drawings are sensitive to such factors as practice and the type of discriminations that are to be performed on the rotated figures, suggesting that what passes for rotation in such experiments is not simply a rigid angular transformation of a gross iconic image.

There are, of course, many other proposals that could be made to account for data such as those cited here. These include proposals for various hybrid models involving iterating over features of the figure using some kind of relaxation method. Such iterations could involve small local rotations, rotations of a skeletal frame followed by partial reconstruction of the figure, or even iterations over descriptions with no obvious analogue (in the sense of continuous spatial function) processes involved. In the absence of a model worked out in detail, as well as of additional experimental analyses of factors affecting rotation, it is not clear how such proposals would fare. In any event it would seem that a major part of the evidence cited in support of "mental rotation" will be accounted for by computational processes of various kinds and not by properties of some analogue medium.

In conclusion let me reiterate that I do not claim to have made an argument against analogical modes of representation, and still less am I satisfied that semantic networks, procedures, etc. are adequate to handle all forms of knowledge. I have simply tried to argue that many of the reasons people have for jumping on the "analogical" (whatever that may be) bandwagon are insufficient. Furthermore, we are so far from understanding the semantics of discrete data structures (as Woods has cogently argued) that any mass movement to abandon them, or even augment them with something radically different is at the very least premature.

Notes

1. One might respond to Kant's objection that "concepts without percepts are blind" by pointing out that (a) 'concepts' in our sense can refer to an equivalence class of transducer outputs—i.e., they may correspond to perceptual patterns; and (b) nodes need not be iconic or sense-resembling in order to represent percepts (see the last paragraph of section 4 for more on this point).

2. It is also worth pointing out another advantage of thinking of such figures as being represented by structured descriptions. This approach resolves an old psychological puzzle of why figures' shapes remain perceptually invariant, for both adults and children, when we view them lying down or with our heads at an angle: if the figures are described in relation to their background the description remains the same.

3. This is not to suggest that no useful distinction can be made between analogical and Fregean or between pictorial and discursive representations. The point here is that one cannot make the distinction by simply examining the representation itself. One must, in addition, know something about how it is being used or interpreted. In fact the notion of isomorphism between representations is not a useful one. A more useful notion of isomorphism is the one that appears in algebra—i.e., isomorphism between systems.

4. When it is sometimes claimed that a painting or sketch can be abstract, this surely means that it can be interpreted to bear an abstract relation to the object depicted. The picture itself is never abstract or vague. But this simply means that two-dimensional displays can sometimes, in certain respects, do the work of descriptions.

5. This is not to suggest that people solve the frame problem as it is described. In fact there is good reason to believe that our ability to plan, anticipate, etc. is rather limited precisely because we cannot bring all relevant facts to bear. The point is merely to argue that when we do anticipate successfully we bring to bear multifarious knowledge, including tacit knowledge of physical laws. In some cases we can design representational structures in such a way that certain consequences appear to follow without explicit appeal to stored principles. For example, by choosing a list representation for objects related by a total ordering and by examining the list serially we seem to obtain the transitivity property of such relations as a by-product. Finding such representations is an important goal in building efficient computational models. From a psychological point of view, however, it should be noted that (at least in this example) a commitment to transitivity is made along with

the decision to place particular objects on a particular list, and this decision (and hence the representation of transitivity) may then simply fall outside the domain of what is being modeled. But in general we shall want to model the implicit knowledge of such principles. The need to model intellectual structures explicitly arises because of the kind of independence of properties of thought and properties of the world that we see in cognitive development in children as well as in the nonveridical nature of perceptual schemata discussed in section 5 (2).

6. The more general problem, one that vexed Leibniz in the above quotation is that the most tempting way to represent property P is to attribute P to the representation. However, when P is a *physical* predicate and we are dealing with *mental* representations, we must guard against reifying the physical world in the mind. The seductiveness of applying physical predicates (e.g. those pertaining to physical magnitudes) to images appears to be almost irresistible. For example, in a recent response to my critique of imagery, Kosslyn and Pomerants (1977, p. 13) begin by carefully noting that images themselves are neither large nor small but that they only "register size in the same way that the corresponding representations evoked during perception register size." Now this unexceptionable position does not itself say anything about the form of the representation. However, in each case in which they find that "imaginal" accounts are more "natural" than "propositional" accounts, this is the case precisely because a *literal* interpretation of terms like "large-small" or "near-far" is being applied to images projected onto a hypothetical screen. The Kosslyn and Pomerantz paper is one of most carefully argued expositions of the imagery position, one that emerged after considerable communication with the author of the present paper. The reader is invited to consult the Kosslyn and Pomerantz paper for a revealing sample of how precipitous the "analgoical" slope can get and how arguments in psychology can slip past one another in recycling classical philosophical puzzles.

7. Whether or not even at a pretheoretical level, the relevant phenomena are best described as "rotation" or something else, such as serial piece-by-piece analysis of where relevant portions of a figure would be were a rotation of the object actually carried out, is an empirical question. Although adequate fine-grain data bearing on this question are not available at present, such tentative evidence as introspective reports (e.g., gathered in our laboratory) and preliminary eye-movement evidence mentioned by Metzler and Shepard (1974) suggest that serial scanning and recomputation may in fact be a better description of the processes occurring in the comparison experiment than wholesale rotation. Recently detailed monitoring of eye-movements by Just and Carpenter (1976) has confirmed that there are several distinct phases to the rotation task, many of which clearly involve piecemeal search and comparison operations. In certain cases, however, such as closing one's eyes and imagining a rotating object, rotation may be the appropriate phenomenological description, so we shall stick with this for the time being.

8. There remains of course the serious methodological problem of empirically estimating the computational complexity of an operation. Presumably response latency arises from several sources that may interact in various ways. This, however, is a problem for everybody's theory, and we are here simply taking the current first-order view that variation in reaction time directly reflects changes in computational complexity of the primary operation. The next step would involve a theory of how such factors as attention and memory load interact with latency—i.e., a theory of computing under limited resources.

References

Baylor, G. W. A treatise on the mind's eye: An empirical investigation of visual mental imagery. (Unpublished doctoral dissertation, Carnegie-Mellon University.) Ann Arbor, Mich.. University Microfilms, no. 72-13, 699, 1972.

Bobrow, D. G. Dimensions of representation. In D. G. Bobrow & A. Collins (Eds.), *Representation and understanding: Studies in cognitive science*. New York: Academic Press, 1975.

Brooks, L. R. Spatial and verbal components in the act of recall. *Canadian Journal of Psychology*, 1968, 22, 349-368.

Bruner, J. S. On perceptual readiness. *Psychological Review*, 1957, 64, 123-152.

Chase, W. G. & Simon, H. A. Perception in Chess. *Cognitive Psychology*, 1973, 4, 55-81.

Clark, E. V. Non-linguistic strategies and the acquisition of word meanings. *Cognition*, 1973, 2, 161-182.

Collins, A. M., & Quillian, M. R. Retrieval time from semantic memory. *Journal of Verbal Learning and Verbal Behavior*, 1969, 8, 240-247.

Cooper, L. A., & Shepard, R. N. Chronometric studies of the rotation of mental images. In W. G. Chase (Ed.), *Visual information processing*. New York: Academic Press, 1973.

Dennett, D. C. *Content and consciousness*. New York: Humanities Press, 1969.

Eisenstadt, M., & Kareev, Y. Aspects of human problem solving: The use of internal representations. In D. A. Norman & D. E. Rumelhart (Eds.), *Explorations in cognition*. San Francisco: W. H. Freeman, 1975.

Farley, A. VIPS: A visual imagery and perception system. Unpublished doctoral dissertation, Computer Science Department, Carnegie-Mellon University, Pittsburgh, 1974.

Fitts, P. F., & Seeger, C. M. SR compatibility: Spatial characteristics of stimulus and response codes. *Journal of Experimental Psychology*, 1953, 46, 199-210.

Fodor, J. *The language of thought*. New York: Crowell, 1975.

Gibson, J. J. The information available in pictures. *Leonardo*, 1971, 4, 27-35.

Gombrich, E. H. *Art and illusion: A study in the psychology of pictorial representation*. Princeton: Princeton University Press, 1961.

Goodman, N. *Languages of art: an approach to a theory of symbols*. New York: Bobbs-Merrill, 1968.

Gregory, R. L. Choosing a paradigm for perception. In E. C. Carterette & M. P. Friedman (Eds.), *Handbook of perception* (Vol. 1). New York: Academic Press, 1974.

Hanson, V. R. *Patterns of discovery*. Cambridge: Cambridge University Press, 1953.

Hochberg, J. In the mind's eye. In R. N. Haber (Ed.), *Contemporary theory and research in visual perception*. New York: Holt, Rinehart and Winston, 1968.

Hochberg, J., & Gellman, L. Feature saliency, "mental rotation" times, and the integration of successive views. Mimeo, 1976.

Hochberg, J., & Gellman, L. The effect of landmark features on mental rotation times. *Memory and Cognition*, 1977, 5, 23-26.

Howard, I. P. Proposals for the study of anomalous perceptual schemata. *Perception*, 1974, 3, 497-513.

Howard, I. P. Recognition and knowledge of the water-level principle. *Perception*, 1978, 7.

Julesz, B. *Foundations of Cyclopean Perception*. Chicago: The University of Chicago Press, 1971.

Just, M. A., & Carpenter, P. A. Eye fixations and cognitive processes. *Cognitive Psychology*, 1976, 8, 441-480.

Kosslyn, S. M. & Pomerantz, J. R. Imagery, propositions and the form of internal representation. *Cognitive Psychology*, in press.

Marr, D. Analysing natural images: A computational theory of texture vision. M.I.T. A.I. Laboratory memo 334, 1975.

McCarthy, J. & Hayes, P. Some philosophical problems from the standpoint of artificial intelligence. In B. Meltzer & D. Minchie (Eds.), *Machine Intelligence 4*. Edinburgh University Press, 1969.

Metzler, J. & Shepard, R. N. Transformational studies of the internal representation of three-dimensional objects. In R. L. Solso (Ed.), *Theories of cognitive psychology, The Loyola Symposium*. Hillsdale, N.J.: Lawrence Erlbaum, 1974.

Michotte, A. *Perception of Causality*, London: Metheun, 1963.

Moran, T. The symbolic imagery hypothesis: A production system model. Unpublished doctoral dissertation, Carnegie-Mellon University, 1973.

Neisser, U. Changing conceptions of imagery. In P. W. Sheehan (Ed.), *The function of nature of imagery*. New York: Academic Press, 1972.

Palmer, S. E. Structural aspects of perceptual organization. Unpublished doctoral dissertation, University of California, San Diego, 1974.

Piaget, J. & Inhelder, B. *The child's conception of space*. New York: The Humanities Press, 1956.

Pylyshyn, Z. W. What the mind's eye tells the mind's brain: A critique of mental imagery. *Psychological Bulletin*, 1973, 80, 1-24.

Pylyshyn, Z. Factors influencing the apparent rate of "mental rotation." Research Bulletin no. 412, Department of Psychology, University of Western Ontario, 1977.

Pylyshyn, Z. W. The symbolic nature of mental representations. In S. Kaneff and J. R. O'Callaghan (Eds.), *Objectives and methodologies in artificial intelligence*, New York: Academic Press, in press.

Raphael, B. The frame problem in problem-solving systems. In N. V. Findler & B. Meltzer (Eds.), *Artificial intelligence and heuristic programming*. Edinburgh. Edinburgh University Press, 1971.

Reed, S. K. Structural descriptions and the limitations of visual images. *Memory and Cognition*, 1974, 2, 329-336.

Rock, I. *Orientation and Form*. New York: Academic Press, 1973

Shepard, R. N. Attention and the metric structure of the stimulus space. *Journal of Mathematical Psychology*, 1964, 1, 54-87.

Shepard, R. N. Form, formation, and transformation of internal representations. In R. Solso (Ed.), *Information processing and cognition: The Loyola Symposium*. Hillsdale, N.J.: Lawrence Erlbaum Assoc., 1975.

Shepard, R. N. & Metzler, J. Mental rotation of three-dimensional objects. *Science*, 1971, 171, 701-703.

Simon, H. A. On reasoning about actions. In H. A. Simon and L. Siklossy (Eds.), *Representation and meaning*. Englewood Cliffs, N.J.: Prentice-Hall, 1972.

Simon, H. A. & Barenfeld, M. Information-processing analysis of perceptual processes in problem solving. *Psychological Review*, 1969, 76, 473-483.

Sloman, A. Interactions between philosophy and artificial intelligence: The role of intuition and non-logical reasoning in intelligence. *Artificial Intelligence*, 1971, 2, 209-225.

Thomas, H., Jamison, W., & Hummell, D. D. Observation is insufficient for discovering that the surface of still water is invariantly horizontal. *Science*, 1973, 181, 173-174.

Weinstein, E. L. The influence of symbolic systems on perspective drawings: A developmental approach. Unpublished M.Sc. thesis, Department of Psychology, University of Toronto, Canada, 1974.

Wittgenstein, L. *Philosophical investigations*. Oxford: Blackwell, 1953.

Woods, W. What's in a link: Foundations for semantic networks. In D. Bobrow & A. Collins (Eds.), *Representation and understanding: Studies in cognitive science*. New York: Academic Press, 1975.

Is There Mental Representation?

We tend to take it for granted that there is such a thing as mental representation. People obviously have beliefs, desires, hopes, and fears, and it seems obvious that such mental states involve mental representation. Consider the following mental states: the belief that Paul is in Pittsburgh, the desire that Paul should be in Pittsburgh, the hope that he is in Pittsburgh, and the fear that he is. These are different attitudes *toward* Paul's being in Pittsburgh: belief, hope, desire, fear. They are attitudes *about* Paul—a belief about him, a desire about him, a hope about him, a fear about him. Presumably these attitudes therefore must involve mental representation. For, it seems, to speak of mental representation is simply to make the obvious point that mental states are often attitudes *toward* one or another state of affairs, that they are attitudes *about* one thing or another.

In the same way we assume there are mental representations. For the belief that Paul is in Pittsburgh is itself a mental representation of Paul's being in Pittsburgh; the desire that Paul should be in Pittsburgh is a different representation of the same thing. Similarly for other mental states that are attitudes toward some state of affairs or other, attitudes about one thing or another. All such mental states are, or seem to be, themselves mental representations.

It seems almost as obvious that there is some sort of system to mental representation. We cannot accept as a brute unanalyzable fact about a mental state that it represents Paul's being in Pittsburgh. Such a mental state must surely have something nontrivial in common with other mental states that represent Paul's being in various other places and must also have something nontrivial in common with other mental states that represent other persons' being in Pittsburgh. There must be some identifiable aspect of the mental state, an aspect it can share with other mental states, an aspect by virture of which it is a representation of *Paul*. It must also have a different aspect by virtue of which it and other states with that aspect are representations of someone's being in *Pittsburgh*. What a mental state represents must surely be determined by the way in which certain elements are combined in that state, just as what a sentence represents is determined by the way in which certain words are combined in that sentence. Just as a finite stock of words can be combined in an infinite number of possible ways to form an infinite number of sentences, so too, it seems, a finite stock of mental elements must be combinable in a indefinite number of ways to form an indefinite number of mental representations. Mental states must have elements and structure in a way that is analogous to the way in which sentences have elements and structure. There must be, as it were, mental words, mental structure, mental names, mental predicates, mental connectives, and mental quantifiers.

This should not be surprising. We presuppose as much whenever we offer reasons to explain why someone has done something or has a given desire or belief. Suppose someone explains why Ned wants to hold a conference on mechonetics in Pittsburgh, by citing Ned's desire that Paul should be in Pittsburgh and Ned's belief that Paul will be in Pittsburgh if he, Ned, holds a conference on mechonetics there. This explanation invokes the commonsense principle that a desire that *P* and a belief that *P, if Q* can lead to a desire that *Q*. As Israel Scheffler has observed, such commonsense principles clearly presuppose that mental states can have logical structures, in this case that a belief can have a conditional structure. The idea that there is some sort of system of mental representation seems therefore required by common sense.

Now, given that there is such a system of mental representation, it can be argued that a natural language like English or German will be part of the system of mental representation possessed by someone who speaks that language. For one thing, there is the experience familiar to second language learners of no longer having to translate between their first language and the language they are learning, when they come, as we sometimes say, to be able to "think in" the new language. Second, when we learn a new theory of some sort, a new branch of physics or mathematics, learning the language of the theory and learning to think in the new way required by the theory seem impossible to separate. Third, giving arbitrary labels to aspects of the natural environment seems to have an immediate effect on the way we perceive that environment. Fourth, in most conversations we do not plan our remarks ahead of time but, as it were, simply "think out loud."

I would suggest that these four points are best explained by supposing that language learning involves modifying our system of mental representation so as to incorporate the language being learned. This is not of course to say that all mental representation is in language. Much, perhaps most, is not. This other nonlinguistic representation may be very much like linguistic representation, or alternatively may involve something like the sort of representation that is involved in pictures, maps, or diagrams. I am not sure what to say about this. The main claim I wish to make is that some mental representation is in language.

Now, however, I must confess that I have some doubts about what I have just said. What worries me is not, as you might suppose, the last suggestion that some mental representation is in language. I am instead worried by the more basic claim that there is such a thing as mental representation in the first place. This strikes me as much less obvious than I have been pretending. On the other hand, I am strongly inclined to think that, if the basic claim is correct, then almost certainly some mental representation is in language. But, as I say, I am worried about the basic claim.

Notice, first of all, that not all beliefs, desires, hopes, or fears consist in *explicit* mental representations of what is believed, desired, hoped, or feared. Almost everyone believes that $104 + 3 = 107$, but few people believe this in any explicit way. Few people have in their minds, either consciously or unconsciously, an explicit mental representation of this particular sum. Rather, we might be inclined to say, they believe it implicitly. It is, we suppose, clearly implied by things they believe more explicitly.

The example reveals something very important. The fact that someone believes, desires, hopes, or fears that something is the case does not by itself entail that he or she has an explicit mental representation of that being the case. So the claim that there is mental representation does not follow trivially from the existence of beliefs, desires, hopes, and fears. How then is that claim to be supported? That is my worry.

What does it mean to say that a given person only implicitly believes that 104 + 3 = 107? Presumably, to say that he does not explicitly believe this is to deny that his belief that 104 + 3 = 107 is a real state of him, a state that is part of the causal order, a state that might play a role in getting him to believe other things or act in various ways. To say that he believes implicitly that 104 + 3 = 107 is to say rather that this belief is merely implicit, perhaps implicit in things he believes explicitly so that it is obviously implied by his explicit beliefs and easily "reachable" by him from his explicit beliefs without any real thought.

But then we must at least consider the possibility that all alleged mental representation might be somehow merely implicit. Do mental representations ever play a real causal role? Are beliefs, desires, hopes, and fears ever part of the real causal order or are they always to some degree implicit in something else in approximately the way in which an average person's belief that 104 + 3 = 107 is thought to be a merely implicit belief?

One reason we take an average person to believe that 104 + 3 = 107 is that, if we ask him what the sum of 104 + 3 he will say that it is 107, and he will say this immediately without laborious calculation. He can give this answer immediately even though he has no prior explicit mental representation of this sum. But then maybe all beliefs are like this—involving no explicit mental representation but only the ability to respond appropriately if one is aked certain questions or if one is put in certain other situations.

The question whether a belief is explicit, in this sense, is of course not the same as the question whether it is an "occurrent belief," i.e., a belief of which one is now consciously aware. A defender of mental representation might well maintain that one has a large number of explicit beliefs that are part of the causal order but that for the most part never become conscious or "occurrent." On the other hand, I am worried whether any beliefs, including "occurrent" conscious beliefs, are ever explicit in this sense, being themselves part of the causal order and not merely implicit in other things that are part of the causal order.

The issue here is that raised by behaviorism. Do mental states ever play an explanatory role? Are they part of the causal order? Or are they merely part of an interpretation we make, something that is only implicit in the causal order in the way that the average person's belief that $104 + 3 = 107$ is merely implicit? What is at issue here is not the existence of mental states. Of course mental states exist; the issue is whether they ever exist explicitly rather than merely implicitly. Nor is there a serious issue here of verbal analysis. The issue is not whether mental terminolgy can be translated into some combination of behavioral and neurophysiological terminology. Whether or not such translation is possible, the challenge of behaviorism remains: What reason is there to suppose that mental states are real parts of the causal order? In other words, what reason is there to suppose that mental representation is ever anything more than implicit representation?

Now it might be argued that implicit representation somehow depends on explicit mental representation. I am inclined to think it does, but I am not sure how the argument is to be put. One possibility would be to argue like this:

There is implicit mental representation only if there is a disposition to form a corresponding explicit mental representation under certain conditions. We can ascribe an implicit belief that $104 + 3 = 107$ to the average person because the average person is disposed to believe this explicitly if asked, "What is $104 + 3$?"

This argument is hardly compelling, however. Why must we suppose that the relevant disposition is a disposition to form an explicit *mental* representation? Consider the following analogy. Someone might suppose that linguistic representation is sometimes implicit in mental representation, without having to suppose that mental representation is ever explicit representation in language. This person might agree that there is implicit linguistic representation only if there is some sort of disposition to produce an explicit linguistic representation. But this does not have to be a disposition to produce an explicit *mental* representation in language. It could be (this person might suppose) a disposition to produce an explicit linguistic representation out loud or in writing.

Objection: sometimes one simply says something silently to one-self. Won't that have to count as an explicit mental representation in language? Not necessarily. It might be argued that this is a case in which one produces an explicit mental but nonliguistic represen-tation *of* a nonmental linguistic representation.

I am not endorsing this position, since I am inclined to believe there is mental representation in language. But I think this other position is a possible position to take, one that is in no way inco-herent. If so, the claim that there is implicit mental representation of a certain sort does not logically entail the claim that there is a disposition to form an explicit mental representation of that sort. But then, the argument as I have stated it must be rejected since it assumed that there is such an entailment.

Perhaps we could make do with a weaker assumption. Consider this argument.

There is implicit mental representation only if there is a disposition to form a corresponding explicit representation. Sometimes this will be a disposition to form an outer nonmental representation, such as an utterance in a language, but not always. There are thoughts that cannot be expressed in language. Fur-thermore, animals and human infants have beliefs, desires, hopes, and fears without possessing any language. They must therefore be disposed to form corresponding explicit representations that are not in language. Such repre-sentations can only be explicit mental representations. So there are after all some explicit mental representations.

I am not sure this is conclusive. Precisely because animals and hu-man infants do not have language, some philosophers and psycholo-gists deny that they have beliefs, desires, fears, and so forth, in the full sense of these terms and hold that implicit mental representa-tions can be ascribed to such creatures only to the extent that they are disposed to act in ways that can be interpreted as behavioral representations of one or another state of affairs.

A somewhat different and possibly more compelling argument might go like this:

There is implicit representation only where there is something that is implicit in—implied by—the content something has explicitly. So there is implicit men-tal representation only if there is explicit mental representation.

As an a priori argument, this will not do, since behaviorists are not committing a logical error in rejecting the argument. But the argument seems plausible to me if interpreted as saying that:

The best account we have at present of implicit mental representation assumes that there is explicit mental representation and takes something to be implicitly mentally represented only if it is fairly obviously implied by what is explicitly mentally represented.

This seems plausible to me even though I am not altogether sure what the alleged "best account" is supposed to be. I do not know of any very specific plausible account of mental representation. There is, of course, the ordinary commonsensical idea that people act as they do because of their beliefs, desires, hopes, fears, and so forth. According to common sense, such mental states do sometimes play a part in the causal order, which is sufficient if true for them to count as explicit mental representations. And common sense is sometimes willing to speak of belief in a case in which the belief is merely implicit in what someone explicitly believes. So I suppose there is some sort of commonsensical account of implicit and explicit mental representation. That is, I guess, our "best account." I do not know of any clearly better account.

True, there are a number of interesting proposals by psychologists that postulate mental representations of various sorts. But where these proposals clearly go beyond common sense, they seem to me so speculative that I hesitate to include any of them as part of our "best current account." Maybe I am being overly cautious here. If so, I hope someone will tell me why.

Of course, if I am right about common sense being the best account, the situation is unstable. Common sense does not seem to yield much in the way of an explicit theory and, if psychologists do develop a fairly specific theory to account for various aspects of mental life, it is not obvious to me that their theory will have to be in any way an extension of common sense, nor is it obvious that such a theory will have to include an important role for mental representations. But, at least for the time being, our best account does assume that explicit mental representations are part of the causal order, which gives us some reason to *believe* that explicit mental representations are part of the causal order.

There is the same weak sort of reason to think that mental representations have logical structure. For, as I have already mentioned, commonsensical explanations that appeal to a person's reasons presuppose that beliefs and other mental representations sometimes have, for example, the structure of a conditional.

And there is, I think, almost the same weak sort of reason to think that "one's system of mental representation," (if I may call it that), incorporates one's natural language. True, common sense does not seem to be committed to this assumption. But the four points mentioned earlier are best explained, I think, by supposing that language learning modifies one's system of mental representation by incorporating the language being learned. To repeat those points, they are (1) that language learners come to be able to "think in" the new language, (2) that learning a new theoretical terminology seems to involving learning new methods of thinking, (3) that giving arbitrary labels to things helps to structure one's perceptions, and (4) that conversation is often unplanned and involves a certain amount of something it is natural to call "thinking out loud." The explanation here is quite unspecific, so these points provide at best very weak evidence for the claim that some thought is in language. But our evidence that there is any such thing as mental representation at all seems to be also of this extremely weak sort.

—— WALTER REITMAN, ROBERT NADO, AND BRUCE WILCOX ——

Machine Perception: What Makes It So Hard for Computers to See?

Introduction

Go is a board game with an intellectual role in the Orient comparable to that of chess in the West. Several years ago we began work on a program we hoped would be capable of playing interesting Go. Though not intended as a strict simulation, insofar as possible the program was to be modeled after what we could learn of how a highly skilled human player plays the game.

Go is played with black and white tokens (called stones) on the 361 points of a 19 x 19 grid. Black and white take turns, each placing one stone at a time upon the board. Once played, the stones generally remain on the board until the end of the game. Figure 1 illustrates what a Go board looks like somewhere in mid-game, in this case after about 100 moves. As is evident, play typically results in highly intricate patterns of stones. Figure 2 (p. 76) shows an earlier stage of the same game, after approximately 25 moves. There are only a few locally complex patterns, but even at this stage there are quite complex global interrelations among friendly and hostile stones all around the board.

As these figures may suggest, the perception of local patterns and global interrelations among stones is a major factor in skilled play. Since our program was to function as an intelligent human player does, it became obvious that we would have to design perceptual

Note: We would like to thank I. Cantrall for his vivid account of web processing in nature, and M. Alpern, D. Krantz, R. Pachella, J. Reitman, L. Springer, S. Stich, and W. Utall for their helpful comments on an earlier draft.

Support from NSF Grants Nos. DCR71-02038 and MCS77-00880 is gratefully acknowledged.

65

components for the program. Furthermore, since the system was to be not only a game-playing program, but an instantiation of a more general model of human intelligence, we wanted to develop these perceptual components in ways that would be consistent with a reasonable conception of human perceptual activity.

The first part of this chapter is a brief summary and critique of one approach to machine vision that is now attracting a great deal of attention among those interested in endowing machines with something analogous to human perceptual capabilities. We present it here to suggest some of the main current issues and to motivate what we believe to be a more appropriate set of propositions. The second

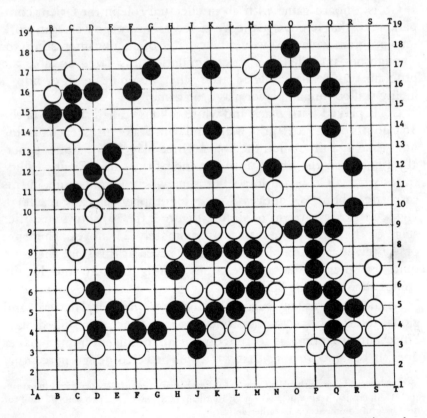

Figure 1. Five-stone handicap game after move 96. From Kerwin and Reitman (1973).

part of the paper describes in some detail one of the major components of the Go program's perception system. This component is certainly not a general theory, either of machine perception or of human perception. The specifics make sense only in the context of Go. But the basic ideas underlying the component and its relations with the rest of the program are, we believe, a reasonable view of the perceptual process, and thus the program illustrates how one can begin to incorporate such ideas in a machine implementation.

Minsky's Frame System Theory of Vision

Artificial intelligence approaches to perception have passed through at least two major phases over the course of their 20-year history. Until quite recently, most work aimed at trying to build perception from the bottom up. One built systems that tried first, for example, to organize points into lines, then to organize lines into regions and simple objects, and finally to describe the interrelations of the simple objects in the scene. Even though almost all of this work has been restricted to static complexes of relatively simple polyhedral objects (pyramids, cubes, etc.), a great deal of work turned out to be needed to get computers to carry out such scene description successfully.

More recently, Minsky (1975) has proposed an approach to vision that emphasizes the perceptual role of what we already know about objects and their interrelations. According to Minsky, the essence of frame system theory is this. When one encounters a new situation, one selects from memory a structure called a frame. This is a remembered data structure that can be adapted to fit the present reality by changing details as necessary. A frame consists of a network of nodes and relations. The top levels of the frame are fixed. They represent things that are always true about the supposed situation. The lower levels have many terminals or slots that must be filled by specific instances or data. Each terminal can specify conditions its assignments must meet. Attached to a frame are several kinds of information—for example, about what one can expect to happen next.

The effects of important actions are mirrored by transformations from one frame to another. As applied to visual scene analysis, a system of interrelated frames might be thought of as describing the scene from different viewpoints. The transformations from one frame of such a system to another represent the effects of moving from place to place.

According to Minsky (p. 213), the power of the theory hinges on the way in which frames account for expectations and other kinds of presumptions. A frame's terminals normally are already filled with "default" assignments. Thus, when used to organize a visual scene, a frame may contain many details not actually warranted by the situation. These default assignments "are attached loosely to their terminals, so that they can be easily displaced by new items that better fit the current situation."

Frame systems are linked in memory by an information retrieval network. When a proposed frame cannot be made to fit reality in the sense that we cannot find terminal assignments that suitably match the terminal conditions, the network provides a replacement frame. Once a frame is proposed to represent a situation, a matching process tries to assign each frame's terminals values consistent with the constraints associated with the terminals.

When we try to take frame theory as an explanatory account of visual perception, a number of objections arise. How is it possible to account for the perception of three-dimensional structure and for the apparent continuity of visual experience in terms of a model whose elements are a list-structured system of nodes and relations? Minsky acknowledges both of these questions, but his attempts to deal with them hardly seem satisfying.

With respect to the problem of the experience of three-dimensional space, for example, Minsky asserts (p. 220), "surely everyone would agree that at some level vision is essentially symbolic," and then argues that at the symbolic level the issue of dimensionality evaporates and the very concept of dimension becomes inappropriate. But the fact that vision is at some level symbolic does not mean that it must be so at every level, particularly if "symbolic" refers to whatever we can represent in structures of nodes and relations. How, for example, do we use such a structure to account for our perceptual experience when we look at the walls of our offices? We might be able to represent our ideas of rooms and blue walls with such structures, but how can they represent our experience as we observe that spatially extended expanse of blue on the other side of the room?

As for the experience of visual continuity, Minsky suggests (p. 221) this is an illusion due to the persistence of assignments to terminals common to the different viewpoints. "Continuity depends on the confirmation of expectations which in turn depends on rapid access to remembered knowledge about the visual world." For example, "just before you enter a new room, you usually know enough to 'expect' a room rather than, say, a landscape . . . and you can often select in advance a frame for the new room. Very often, one expects a certain particular room. Then many assignments are already filled in."

Such an approach may be useful as far as it goes, but it does not seem to go very far. Suppose we toss a pack of matches in the air and watch it carefully as it rises and falls, twisting and turning as it goes. We may not know exactly what it means to say that our perception of the object's path is temporally continuous, but still less is it clear how we account for our visual experience in terms of a sequence of static frames imposed from within.

Much of the inadequacy of Minsky's account arises from his unwillingness to distinguish sharply between experiences with eyes opened and eyes closed. Thus, discussing whether vision is symbolic, Minsky observes (p. 220) that "people have great difficulty keeping track of the faces of the six colored cube if one makes them roll it around in their mind." So they may, but what has that to do with the symbolic or nonsymbolic character of *vision*, as opposed to *imagination*? Perhaps a frame system may be useful for thinking about what happens when we imagine objects in space, or objects changing over time. But it hardly seems to account for the perceptual experience we have when we actually watch and see things going on in our environment.

Minsky's account also fails to distinguish adequately between what we can perceive and what we can recall. Minsky notes our inability to remember large amounts of perceptual detail after a perceptual experience. But that does not really speak to the role of that detail at the time of the experience. I may very well chuck out my intermediate calculations once I have arrived at my income tax. But my inability to retrieve those intermediate calculations *now* is no evidence at all for the view that I never made them, or that they were not absolutely necessary for arriving at the final result in the first place.

As we noted above, Minsky recognizes and attempts to deal with the two objections to his theory we have just discussed. There are other problems he does not deal with that should also be pointed out. The first is the problem of perceptual autonomy. Engrossed in a conversation or a chain of thought, you can walk for blocks or drive for miles with apparently only minimal awareness of your surroundings. But although you may have walked or driven in the wrong direction in such circumstances more times than you would care to count, rarely did you bump up against a wall or another car. Such observations suggest that whatever you were thinking about, your perceptual-motor system was doing a nice job all on its own of maintaining object separation and keeping you posted at least on the significant physical masses you were encountering in the course of your excursions. It is easy to think of such experiences, at a general sort of level, in terms of a semi-autonomous perceptual system operating largely independently of frame structures and processes. It seems difficult to account for such experiences in terms of a fundamentally serial frame-based system of the sort Minsky describes.

Even the basic paradigm for recognition that Minsky uses is suspect. Sitting in a dark room, you can see and identify an unanticipated object under a single flash of stroboscopic illumination even though the light falling on your retina lasts less than a thousandth of a second. It is difficult to see how such an experimental fact is to be accounted for in terms of a model that talks of pulling frames from memory on the basis of cues, checking out the various candidate frames against incoming data, etc.

To be sure, as any experimental psychologist will tell you, the information conveyed to the retina by a flash of light does not disappear instantaneously. A detailed record of the experience at something close to the level of the original sense data (Neisser's [1967] term is *icon*) endures for at least a tenth of a second, and some trace may be present for as much as half a second or even longer. Furthermore, the lowest levels of the perceptual system feed upward, and we do not know how long the "intermediate calculations" made at higher levels remain available. Note, however, that we now are talking about information and perceptual components that are neither part of the environment (the room is dark again) nor part of frame system theory (long-term memory has not yet even been accessed).

In our view, these lower and intermediate level perceptual components are fundamentally important in perception. They are, we suggest, the physiological bases of the perceptual manifold, the rich, detailed experience we have of the environment around us. No doubt we have symbolic representations of faces, which lead us to expect to see two eyes, a nose, and a mouth together, with the nose positioned roughly between the eyes and the mouth. We also may have frames embodying previous experience with the different kinds of scratches one can have on a face. But when your daughter comes running in to you after the cat has been at her cheek, you *see* where the scratch is, its color, how it runs, what its orientation is, and so on. Minsky never suggests how such visual experience (everything we actually see of the scratch and its relations to the face) is to be represented in terms of interconnections among the terminals of frames, and frame systems appear to us an inherently unsatisfactory way to account for the perceptual manifold.

Minsky no doubt would agree that the lower-level sensory systems are important. He might also grant that they are not well represented by symbolic structures of nodes and relations. Our disagreement with Minsky concerns the intermediate levels. For Minsky the organization imposed by the frame systems is primary, and the low-level sensory information is used only to suggest and confirm frames and to furnish values to be assigned to frame terminals. For us the lower and intermediate level perceptual-motor components are semi-autonomous. As the driving and walking examples suggest, they lead a life of their own. They are essential to the experience of spatial extent, exact spatial locations and relations, spatial and temporal continuity, and the perceptual manifold in general. What we know affects that perceptual experience, not by providing a structure of symbolic slots, but by sculpting and interpreting the shapes, masses, and colors directly represented within the intermediate perceptual components.

We hope the foregoing discussion has indicated what we see as some of the main problems of machine perception, and suggest why we see frame theory in its present form as inadequate in the light of these problems. In what follows, we list some general propositions we would want to include in a more adequate theory of perception, and then show how one may begin to incorporate such ideas in a machine implementation for the game of Go.

Some Propositions for a Theory of Perception

The propositions we wish to consider all have to do with how humans perceive a collection of objects. We are not concerned here with specific sensory mechanisms involved; we wish to assert certain general functional propositions about the overall perceptual process itself.

(1) Perception of the external world is inherently spatial. The human perceiver does not use numerical coodinates to compute the spatial interrelations among objects. He has a unitary overall sense of the general positions of objects in relation to one another and to himself. He can tell directly which are close together (locally connected) and which are far apart. He has a sense of angle and direction. If one object is between two others in his visual field, he sees it directly. The inherent spatial quality of perception is most readily apparent when we consider such phenomena as the perception of symmetries. Complex symmetric relations requiring detailed computation on a point-by-point basis the human perceives immediately.

(2) The example of symmetry perception also suggests, at least as far as the distal senses, vision and audition, are concerned, that perception handles space in volume, not point by point. A slow processor, required to keep up to date on a more or less continuous basis, and often at a very fine level of detail, could hardly afford to process point by point, like a blind man with a cane, or like Shrdlu the simulated robot (Winograd, 1972) trying to find space for a block on a table. When we look up and see clouds, we are simultaneously seeing the absence of any sizeable opaque objects in the volume of space between us and the clouds. The "points" of the intervening space are handled simultaneously, in parallel.

(3) Those concerned with the analysis of static scenes tend to view perception as a matter of describing, symbolizing, and recording. Once these operations have been carried out, no further use is usually made of the information in the scene itself. But if we consider everyday perception over time, attempts at detailed, once-and-for-all recording for its own sake are very infrequent. The primary function of perception is to keep our internal framework in good registration with that vast external memory, the external environment itself. With the exception of eidetic imagery, an odd phenomenon seen mostly in children, and even then not very often (Neisser, 1967),

there is no evidence to suggest that man constantly takes in and stores in long-term memory great quantities of information from the environment. Why should he? When he wants the information he can look. Thus much of the describing, symbolizing, and recording that goes on is instrumental, sustaining the one critical condition the perceptual system must satisfy: that it maintain good alignment between the real world and the internal spatial model so that when we do want to use the external memory to find something out, we know both what we are looking for and what we are looking at. On this point, incidentally, our view and Minsky's appear to coincide.

(4) As was suggested earlier, however, the fact that we do not regularly store quantities of environmental detail permanently should not be taken to mean that we cannot see it, or that the perceptual system somehow operates without taking that detailed information into account. We can and often do ignore such information, and we generally cannot remember or reproduce much of it. But seeing at a glance is a fact, not an illusion, and can hardly be accounted for without reference to the rich detail the senses provide.

(5) One great advantage of the environment as an external memory is that it updates itself automatically. Viewed as a representation of itself, the information in the environment is never incorrect, never obsolete. For example, when the position of an object changes, its spatial relations to all other objects in the visual field change simultaneously, with absolutely no rescanning and recalculation necessary on the part of the perceiver. Whenever the perceiver wants to know the current state of some aspect of his immediate world, he can always be sure the information at his sensorium is up to date.

(6) At its most fundamental level, the human perceptual system is built sensitive to change, and in particular to movement. In the visual system, for example, change detection is built in right at the retinal level. The perceptual system thus need not waste time and effort in constantly scanning the environment. When significant change occurs, it is detected directly.

(7) When the person we are talking with frowns, we are aware of the global change of expression, the face frowning. Only with deliberate effort do we move from the overall expression to focus upon particular details. At one end, the perceptual system is tied into the current state of the sensorium. But at the other, as Minsky

emphasizes, it has access to a vast complex body of knowledge that enters, by means we are only beginning to examine in detail, into the definition of the current internal model of the environment. At some level we are of course simultaneously seeing at least some of the low-level sensory detail. What the perceptual component puts out to the rest of the system, however, are not aggregates of sense data but percepts, meaningful collections of objects meaningfully organized in space.

(8) Observe, finally, that most of us have no trouble conversing while driving, and we can solve complex problems walking across campus from classroom to office. It is hard to say anything about the intrinsic economy and efficiency of human perception in and of itself. But with respect to the control overhead it requires of the rest of the system, it is economical and efficient indeed. The perceptual component alerts us to significant environmental changes, and it provides the percepts we need, all with a minimum of deliberate interference and control from the problem-solving component.

To summarize, we suggest that the human perceptual system includes an intrinsically spatial component. This component processes space in bulk, focusing upon things that are there rather than things that are not. It keeps our internal perceptual representation well aligned with a self-updating environment, alerts us to significant changes, and provides meaningfully organized percepts to the other components of human intelligence with a minimum of extrinsic direction and control. We do not regard these assertions as necessarily self-evident; they certainly are not provable in any sense at the present time. But they seem at least plausible, and thus may serve as useful in thinking about the design of perceptual components for an artificial intelligence system. In this light, what follows may be viewed as an exploration of these principles as applied to the problem of designing an intelligent Go playing program.

Go hardly seems a very rich or dynamic perceptual situation. The processing that goes on involves only a few of the many capabilities involved in perception generally. There are no textures, no shading, and no third spatial dimension to worry about. The perception of spatial continuity reduces to a matter of recognizing local connectivity among neighboring discrete points separated by unit distances in the grid. With the exception of captures (relatively infrequent events involving removal of one or more stones from the board), stones once played remain where they are until the game ends. Thus the changes that occur generally come slowly, in discrete increments, as black and white each in turn place one stone at a time upon the board. But although the perceptual component for a Go program will be far simpler than a general perception system, the design problem is not trivial, especially if the design is constrained to satisfy propositions about human perceptual processes in general; and the overall design of the component may be useful as we assess the prospects for future work on more general machine perception systems.

The Elements of Go

Go is a contest for control of *territory* (the vacant intersections of the 19 x 19 grid). For detailed rules, see any good introduction to the game, for example Iwamoto (1972). In addition to the individual white and black stones, the Go program recognizes a variety of higher order units. A *string* consists of a single isolated stone, or of two or more stones of the same color located on immediately adjacent grid points. In Figure 2, for example, the two white stones at Q7 and Q8 form a string. Two strings of the same color, in close proximity, with no intervening enemy stones, are considered by the program to be *linked*. In Figure 2, for example, the white stones at J5 and M4 are considered to be joined by a "large knight's move" link. Strings in close proximity to the edge of the board, with no intervening enemy stones, are considered to be linked to the edge.

The single black stone at J3 is *enclosed* by an uninterrupted set of links running from the edge point F1 through the white stones F3, F5, J5, M4 and back to the edge at M1. Links and enclosures may under some conditions be broken by the interposition of enemy stones, but if conditions are unfavorable, this can lead to fighting that will be disadvantageous to the player attempting to break through.

A *group* consists of a single isolated string, or of two or more strings of the same color in close proximity, with no intervening enemy stones or links. The seven white stones on the lower right side in the figure form a group. So do the four white stones at the bottom of the figure, since there are uninterrupted links connecting each stone in the group to at least one other and therefore, by transitivity, to all of the others. The group is the primary unit of interest for our purposes in this paper, since what we are after is a fast, effective procedure for perceiving the strategic implications of moves, and this entails noticing and taking account of the significant spatial relations between a given new move and the existing groups on the board.

The extent and degree of prospective territorial control exercised by each side at any time during the game is a function of the relative security of each side's groups and the interacting dispositions of the two sets of groups over the board. For example, in Figure 2, black has some measure of control over the upper right side, and white is strong around the middle of the bottom.

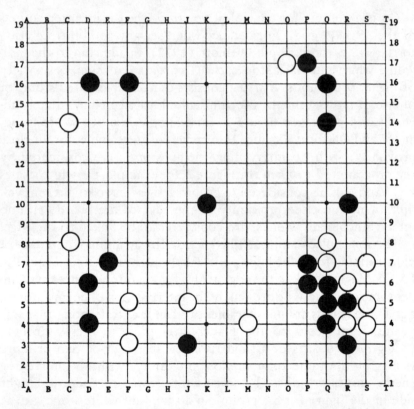

Figure 2. Early stage in a five-stone handicap game, i.e., a game beginning with black stones at D4, D16, Q16, Q4, and K10. From Kerwin and Reitman (1973).

The Go program associates with each group a set of *options* (see Reitman, Kerwin, Nado, Reitman & Wilcox, 1974). These are general ways in which that particular group may be developed, protected, and used. The white group at C8 in Figure 2, for example, may develop in subsequent moves along the left side, or out towards the center. Similarly the white group at O17 may develop along the upper side, or escape out into the center, or serve as a sacrifice stone to minimize black's territorial profits along the upper side or in the upper right corner.

Plays at one point on the board may augment, modify, or reduce the options of groups elsewhere on the board. Just as a car emerging from a side street may significantly affect the options of several other cars at some distance from it on the main road, so the play of a white stone at one point may affect the development of a remote black group—for example, by obstructing a potential escape route of that group. In particular, a group that earlier had several options for development and protection may, as a result of several remote plays by the opponent, be left with only one. Consequently, protection of that group becomes urgent. Otherwise, with a single additional move, the opponent may be able to disrupt the group entirely. In this sense, changes in option sets significantly affect the *focus* of the game.

Note that Go is a resource-limited problem. Not only do the two players compete with one another, but each side's groups compete for resources among themselves. Each player wants to develop each of his groups, to make them more secure. He also wants to establish new groups, to exert influence over a greater prospective territorial area. But he may only put down one token per turn. If he focuses too singlemindedly upon securing a small number of existing groups, his opponent will achieve broader influence than he does. If he spreads himself too thinly, setting up many insecure groups around the board, he risks undergoing attacks that may wipe out a large part of the influence and control he is trying to achieve. As we have seen, however, a single move by a player can have more than a single local effect. It also may broaden his options elsewhere, or restrict those of his opponent. This interactive resource-bound character of Go places a premium on multipurpose moves.

With resources limited and many things to be done, it is important that the perception component of the Go program include a means for determining, quickly and effectively, the multiple strategic implications of a single move. Our goal was to design such a system in accordance with the perceptual principles outlined earlier in this paper. For reasons that will become apparent in what follows, we call our result the web perception process.

The Web Perception System

The general operation of this system is most easily understood in terms of a pair of metaphors. First, to define the maximum scope of the system, imagine each group on the Go board as having its own two-dimensional radar, which operates in the plane of the board. Radar waves from the group pass through vacant points, but are reflected back by stones, links, and the edges of the board. Thus in Figure 2, for example, the white group at C8 can "see" from left to right: the left edge of the board; white C14 and its link to the left edge; black D16, F16, and the link between them; the upper edge of the board from about G19 to O19; white O17; and so on. Since the radar waves do not penetrate past stones or links, C8 cannot see such other stones on the board as white F3 or F5.

Now imagine that each group on the board also has its own spider. Each group's spider spins a web in all directions, over exactly those points of the board passed through or reached by that group's radar. The web terminates wherever it runs into a stone, a link, an edge of the board, or a radar shadow cast by some other stone (once we are clear about the scope of the web, we can forget about the radar). Thus the scope of the web is the entire area contained within the bounds defined by the set of stones, links, and edges visible from that particular group.

The overall process responsible for producing a web is SPINWEB. To understand how the web for a group is constructed, consider first the creation of a web for a one stone group, black B2, on an otherwise empty board (the truncated 7 x 7 grid shown in Figure 3a). The first circumferential strand of the web is spun around the *hub*, B2. It consists of nodes for the four points (A2, B3, C2, B1) directly connected to B2 by the horizontal and vertical grid lines passing through the stone. This strand forms a complete ring. To

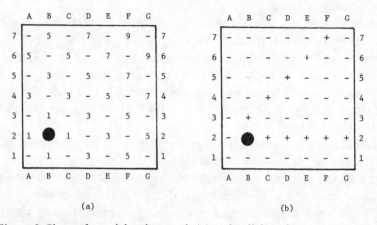

Figure 3. Circumferential web strands (a) and radial predecessor-successor strands (b) generated for a one-stone group on an otherwise empty board (for easier reading, only odd-numbered circumferential strands and two of the radial strands are shown).

generate the second level circumferential strand from the first, or more generally, the $n + 1$th level strand from the nth level *basis* strand, SPINWEB calls SPINSTRAND. SPINSTRAND determines each node in the $n + 1$th strand from three contiguous nth strand nodes. Of these, the two side nodes may correspond to vacant, occupied, link, or shadow points on the board. The center node, however, must correspond to a vacant point. If the center node corresponds to an occupied point, or an edge, link, or shadow point, it forms part or all of a segment boundary. and this segment of the web ends there.

The three contiguous level n nodes define a local directional sense, which may be thought of as a segment of a straight line from the hub out through the center node. Whatever the specific pattern of the corresponding board points, NEXT uses the X, Y displacement from the first point to the second, and from the second to the third, to generate by table lookup 0, 1, or 2 nodes on the $n + 1$th level circumferential strand. Each of these new nodes is connected into this strand. At the same time, it also is connected into a radial strand emerging from the hub by means of a bidirectional connection back to the point of generation in the predecessor strand, the basis strand. SPINSTRAND now moves one node clockwise around the nth strand, and generation of the nodes of the $n + 1$th strand continues. To illustrate with respect to Figure 3, using the level 1 nodes corresponding to the configuration formed by A2, B3, and C2, SPINSTRAND generates level 2 nodes corresponding to B4 and C3. It now moves one node clockwise, and since B3, C2, and B1 form an identical configuration, SPINSTRAND adds nodes for D2 and C1 to the second level strand.

Generation of nodes on the $n + 1$th strand halts when SPINSTRAND either reaches its starting node in the basis strand or else come across a basis node corresponding to a nonvacant board point. If all of the nodes of a basis strand are vacant, all of the nodes of the next level strand are generated in one uninterrupted sequence by the process just described. In this case, the nodes just generated form a complete $n + 1$th level ring. If SPINSTRAND encounters in the basis strand a node corresponding to a stone, an edge point, or a link or shadow point, however, it treats that node as a boundary node and generation of further $n + 1$th level nodes ceases for the time being. In this case, the nodes just generated form not a complete ring but a ring arc. In either case, the ring or arc just created is now taken as the new basis, and generation of nodes on the next strand out begins.

This means that the web is spun segment by segment. Only when the outermost strand of the present web segment has been finished —that is, when no further strands can be generated because the current strand consists entirely of one or more boundary nodes—does SPINWEB move back in one strand, to the right-hand boundary node of the immediately preceding strand. If that right-hand boundary node has an unprocessed vacant node anywhere after it in the strand, then the spinning of another segment begins there. Otherwise SPINWEB again moves inward one level and proceeds in the manner just described. At some point SPINWEB either finds some portion of an inner circumferential strand that can be spun out further, in which case the process continues as before, or it reaches its starting point on the innermost level strand, and the web for the group is finished.

For every board point visible from the hub, there is now a corresponding web node. Every nonboundary web node is connected in its circumferential strand to its immediate left and right neighbors, and it also is tied into a radial strand formed by the chain of bidirectional connections running out through it from the hub. Figure 3, a visualization of the resulting web for the example just discussed, shows separately (3a) the odd-numbered circumferential strands and (3b) two of the radial strands formed by the bidirectional connections between adjacent circumferential strands.

WEB ALTERATION

The web for a group will be updated whenever a friendly or enemy stone is played within its scope. Consider first what happens when a friendly stone is added to the hub. To be specific, assume black adds a stone at B3 to the group shown in Figure 3a, with the result shown in Figure 4. Note that the new stone must always be played at a point corresponding to a node in the level 1 strand of the old web. This node already is tied to a level 1 node immediately to its left, in this case the node corresponding to the board point A2. Now, beginning from that node, REWALK adds to the strand new nodes for A3, B4, and C3. When it reaches C2, it recognizes the node for C2 in the existing strand and reconnects the two ends of the strand at that point. Each successive $n + 1$th strand of the web is then augmented in its turn, using the newly added level n nodes as the basis.

A similar web modification process is initiated when a friendly stone is played within linking distance of an existing group. The details of this process are more complex because a number of pos-

	A	B	C	D	E	F	G	
7	5	–	5	–	7	–	9	7
6	–	3	–	5	–	7	–	6
5	3	–	3	–	5	–	7	5
4	–	1	–	3	–	5	–	4
3	1	●	1	–	3	–	5	3
2	1	●	1	–	3	–	5	2
1	–	1	–	3	–	5	–	1
	A	B	C	D	E	F	G	

Figure 4. Web modification following the addition of a friendly stone to the hub.

sibilities are involved. Consider, for example, a white play at D11 in Figure 2. That stone forms links to both white C8 and white C14. Thus two webs have to be modified and, in effect, merged in order to come up with an appropriate web structure for the new three-string group. Conceptually, however, the end result is identical to that just discussed. The scope of the new web structure includes all those board points in direct line of sight from any string in the group.

When a friendly stone is played beyond linking distance to a group, or when an enemy stone is played anywhere within the scope of a web, a new process, DEWEB, becomes involved. DEWEB rips out from the existing web for the group all points lying in the shadow created by the play of the new stone (this includes points falling in the shadow of any links the play of that stone may have created). In the modified web, the new stone and the points at the border of the shadow now are boundary points, as are any new link points not already removed from the web. Consider, for example, Figure 5. This is the same as Figure 4 except that white has now played a stone at E3. This creates a link from E3 through E2 to the edge at E1. The nodes for these three points now form a new boundary for the redefined black group web, and they occlude the three bottom points on lines F and G. Since the six former web points can no longer be seen from B2 and B3, they are no longer in the scope of the black group's web.

	A	B	C	D	E	F	G	
7	5	–	5	–	7	–	9	7
6	–	3	–	5	–	7	–	6
5	3	–	3	–	5	–	7	5
4	–	1	–	3	–	5	–	4
3	1	●	1	–	○	–	–	3
2	1	●	1	–	3	–	–	2
1	–	1	–	3	–	–	–	1
	A	B	C	D	E	F	G	

Figure 5. Web modification after a white play at E3.

WEB PERCEPTION IN OPERATION

Two brief examples will help to show how the web perception system works in a game context. Figure 6 shows the web for the white stone at C8 in the game situation originally introduced in Figure 2. As in Figure 3, only odd-numbered circumferential strands and a few of the radial strands are shown. Circumferential strands are represesented by unit digits throughout (e.g., 13th-level nodes are represented by 3s, and so on).

Suppose for the first example that the next black play is at D9. This stone links to black E7, black D6, and the edge at A9. Associated with D9 and the link points are lists of web nodes, one node in each list for each group having an unobstructed view of that point. The web for each such group now "vibrates" at those nodes, and

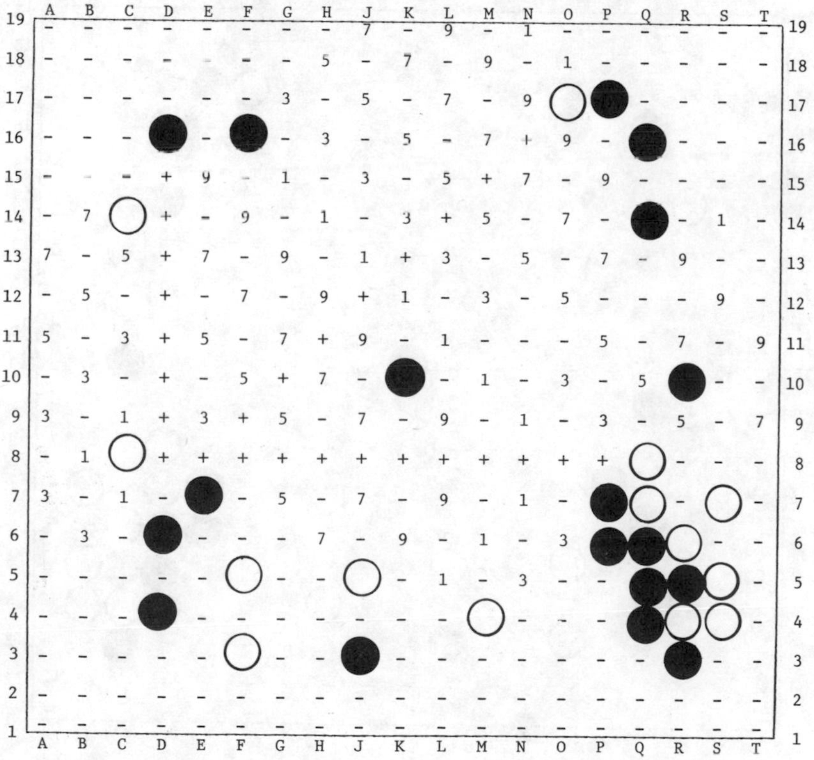

Figure 6. Actual game situation, with web for white C8 shown.

each group for which the play may have strategic significance is immediately alerted. Every such group knows not only that the play has occurred, but also the relative spatial position of the points involved, as given by their radial distances and directions from the hub and their circumferential relations to other nearby groups. In addition, once the web modification process is complete for all affected webs, each group also can see exactly what the immediate strategic effects upon its options are. To appreciate this, consider Figure 7, which shows the web for white C8 after black D9 is played. As a comparison of the two webs in Figure 6 and 7 will show, black's one move effectively encloses the white C8 stone, wiping out its previous developmental options along the left side and out to the center.

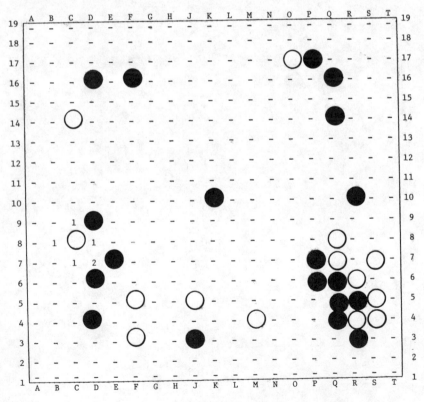

Figure 7. Web for white C8 after black play at D9.

Consider now as a second example a white play at R17. Though premature at this stage of the game because it lacks strategic significance, later on such a move would give white a chance to steal black's corner. The interesting point to notice is that since R17 is enclosed by black stones and links, only one web vibrates, the web for the black group in the upper right corner. In other words, the *absence* everywhere else on the board of any immediate strategic effect is "noticed" directly, with a minimum of computation. It simply falls out of the structure of the webs and the way the web processor works. In the early stages of the game, web processing requires considerable computational and storage overhead. But as this second example suggests, once there are a substantial number of stones on the board and the webs of most groups are, accordingly, quite closely restricted, web processing is not only a conceptually attractive means of handling the resulting complex spatial interrelations, but computationally a rather efficient means as well.

WEB PERCEPTION IN A GO PROGRAM

The system just described is part of a general Go playing program being written in LISP/MTS (Hafner & Wilcox, 1974). An interim version of the system is running on the University of Michigan's Amdahl/470 system. For details of the system and an assessment of its performance, see Reitman and Wilcox (in press). The web processor is only one of several interrelated components responsible for all aspects of spatial perception and representation in the program. Among the others completed or under development are a sectors processor and a patterns processor. The sectors processor complements the web system in maintaining global information about the arrangement of all groups on the board, but with none of the detail provided by the webs. It thus corresponds to what the program *knows* in general about the overall spatial situation, while the webs correspond to exactly what the program can (and cannot) *see* from the vantage point of each group. The patterns processor recognizes configurations of stones the program is acquainted with, and organizes the analysis of all other patterns that fail to match some stored representation.

The web processor serves a number of other functions in addition to determining the immediate strategic implications of plays. In conjunction with the program's lookahead system, and with web scope restricted to link distance, it contributes to tactical lookahead. In this case, the webs correspond to the spatial perception of a player focusing upon the delimited board area involved in a given tactical problem. The web processor also is used in working out the remote strategic consequences of a move, i.e., those consequences that follow not so much from the move itself as from the tactical sequence of plays the move initiates.

The Web Perception System in Perspective

Now that we have considered the details of the web perception system, it may be useful to look at it on a more general level. Interpretation is risky; it is easy to get carried away. But if we do not take the enterprise too seriously, thinking about the system in more general contexts may be suggestive.

(1) Any information-processing system must make choices between storage costs and computing costs. In the case of the web perception system, and perception generally, however, the trade-offs involve real time. Just as the orb spider invests considerable time and energy in creating its tactile amplifier beforehand, thus ensuring a fast and appropriate response when its prey appears, so the web perception system invests in its webs, to respond quickly and effectively when a new stone is played.

(2) One of the basic bottlenecks for machine perception and problem-solving is the cost and difficulty of effective search. But as the web perception system suggests, if we are willing to invest in building up the appropriate information structures, we can cut down radically on the amount of search required for effective performance. The webs function as a dynamic indexing scheme. They guarantee the Go program that it will be able to relate environmental events (the play of new stones) to exactly those existing structures (the groups) strategically affected by them, and under conditions in which extended search might entail prohibitive time and computational costs.

(3) The webs may also be thought of as a solution in the context of Go to the problem of interfacing general purpose knowledge with ongoing events. Note that although the web-weaving and detection algorithms are fixed and autonomous, the particular webs resulting

from the weaving process are dependent upon and exquisitely sensitive to subtle differences in the configurations on the board.

(4) The web perception system's work results in a significant reduction in the data that have to be considered by higher-level components of the program. Thus web perception may be thought of as a procedure for answering general strategic questions ("which groups are affected by that move?") for higher-order units in the system. In this sense, the role of the web component within the Go program as a whole is consistent with the general "question-answering" organizational scheme for complex artificial intelligence proposed by Bobrow and Brown (1975).

(5) Finally, as we indicated above, the web perception system may be thought of as a first exploration of a set of general principles for dealing with problems of natural and artificial perception. We do not want to argue this point too strongly; what seems to us a reasonable instantiation of a principle may appear strained and farfetched to someone else. But we do feel the general principles outlined earlier have had substantial heuristic significance for us, and we believe they also may prove useful to others.

References

Bobrow, R. J., & Brown, J. S. Systematic understanding: Synthesis, analysis, and contingent knowledge in specialized understanding systems. In D. G. Bobrow & A. Collins (Eds.), *Representation and understanding. Studies in cognitive science*. New York: Academic Press, 1975.

Hafner, C., & Wilcox, B. *LISP/MTS programmer's manual*. The University of Michigan, Computing Center Memo M251, 1974.

Iwamoto, K. *Go for beginners*. Tokyo: Ishi, 1972.

Kerwin, J., & Reitman, W. *Video game #3: A Go protocol with comments*. Unpublished paper, The University of Michigan, Mental Health Research Institute, 1973.

Minsky, M. A framework for representing knowledge. In P. H. Winston (Ed.), *The Psychology of computer vision*. Princeton, N.J.: McGraw-Hill, 1975.

Nado, R., & Reitman, W. *Natural and artificial intelligence*. Hillsdale, N.J.: Lawrence Earlbaum Assoc., in preparation.

Neisser, U. *Cognitive psychology*. New York: Appleton-Century-Crofts, 1967.

Reitman, W., Kerwin, J., Nado, R., Reitman, J., & Wilcox, B. Goals and plans in a program for playing Go. *Proceedings of the 29th National Conference of the Association for Computing Machinery*, 1974, 123-127.

Reitman, W., & Wilcox, B. Pattern recognition and pattern-directed inference in a program for playing Go. In D. Waterman & F. A. Hayes-Roth (Eds.), *Pattern-directed inference systems*. New York: Academic Press, in press.

Winograd, T. *Understanding natural language*. New York: Academic Press, 1972.

Perceiving, Anticipating, and Imagining

What is the relation between perception and mental imagery? It has often been suggested, by myself (Neisser, 1967) among others, that the same processes underlie both. More specifically, it has been assumed that while the early processing stages of a percept may be missing from the development of the corresponding image, their later stages (resulting in awareness) are more or less the same. Yet this cannot be right; it would leave us in continual doubt about whether we were seeing something or merely imagining it. Common experience suggests, however, that such doubts rarely arise in the waking lives of ordinary people. (The apparently contrary evidence of Perky's (1910) experiment can probably be ignored. Although her subjects did seem to confuse pictures with images, the demand characteristics of the experiment actually gave them little choice. Segal's (1971, 1972) extended efforts to replicate Perky's work produced some cases of "incorporation" but few documented instances of confusion.) I shall argue here that imaging and perceiving are not confusable, because they differ fundamentally—as sharply as a phenotype differs from a genotype, or a plan from an action. Indeed, I shall suggest that images are precisely plans for the act of perceiving.

How are we to think of perception itself? The most popular current view treats it as a case of information-processing (e.g., Lindsay & Norman, 1972; Posner, 1973; Massaro, 1975). Perceiving is assumed to begin with the stimulation of a sensory surface, and to

Note: A preliminary version of this paper was presented as an invited address to the Division of Philosophical Psychology, American Psychological Association, Chicago, 1975. An extended version of the same argument appears in the author's book *Cognition and Reality*, W. H. Freeman and Company. Copyright © 1976.

end with the formation of a "percept," given in consciousness. Visual perception, for example, begins when neural mechanisms in the retina, called "detectors," respond to features of the retinal image. Information about these features is passed on to the higher states, where it is combined with stored information. This series of processes eventually results in a perceptual experience. Theories of this genre are inevitably illustrated with flow charts, like the one caricatured in Figure 1. Information arrives at the left, is processed through various stages, and eventually reaches its mysterious destination at the right. The whole train of events is inflicted on a passive perceiver, who takes what he is given and must be grateful for it.

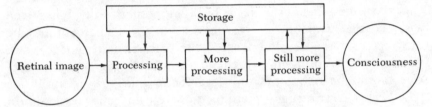

Figure 1. The internal flow chart model of perception. Reprinted with permission from *Cognition and Reality* (Figure 1) by Ulric Neisser, W. H. Freeman and Company. Copyright © 1976.

There is some supporting evidence for this view. Certain neural mechanisms do respond selectively to features of the retinal image; their existence has been demonstrated both neurophysiologically and psychologically (e.g., Hubel & Wiesel, 1959; Lindsay & Norman, 1972). Nevertheless, such a model leaves many questions unanswered. How does it happen that different people notice different things? How are units formed, so that some portions of the input are treated as belonging to one object, some to another? How are successive glances at the same scene integrated with one another? And what about mental images?

In an information-processing model, an image is treated as a train of processes that arises in the middle of the apparatus instead of at the left-hand end and then proceeds along the sequence normally. To *see* a unicorn is to have one's retina stimulated by unicorn-shaped rays of light and to process the resulting detector activity through (say) eight stages. To *imagine* a unicorn is to skip the first two stages or so and begin the processing a little further along. How, then, do we know whether we are seeing or imagining one? Moreover, how would we go about *looking for* unicorns if we wanted to see them? The model makes no provision for perceptual search.

Another difficulty for the passive information-processing model concerns the use of information from several sensory modalities. In real life we constantly listen to things we are also looking at, and often touch them as well. How are all these inflows coordinated? How do we know which ones to filter out and which to admit to the inner sanctum?

A particularly serious problem is posed by the fact that perception is generally accurate and veridical. It must be, if it is to play a useful role in our lives. As psychologists, we sometimes overlook the accuracy of perception in our fascination with *illusions*, which have made claims on our theoretical interest far out of proportion to their ecological significance. In real life, perceptual illusion is as rare as political illusion is common; people usually see the sizes, shapes, colors, positions, and potential manipulability of objects quite accurately. The most fundamental problem for theories of perception is to account for this success, achieved despite the inadequacy of every momentary retinal image. It is far from clear whether the presently fashionable mixed bag of sophisticated detectors and corrections based on past experience can do so satisfactorily. At one time I thought it would help to insist (1967) that perceiving is a "constructive" process rather than a passive one. I still think so, but this claim does not really come to grips with the basic question: how do we know just what to construct?

The accuracy of perception under ordinary conditions suggests that the optically-available information is highly *specific*: so specific that we can make only one construction, the right one. If this is true, however, the notions of "construction" and "processing" seem almost superfluous. One is tempted to abandon them altogether, as J. J. Gibson has done (1966). He insists that invariant features of the optical array specify the real environment quite precisely, and need not be "processed" at all. For Gibson, a theory of perception need only describe the information that is being picked up. But although there can be no doubt that such a description is necessary, it does not seem sufficient. Another part of the psychologists's job is surely to describe the perceiver's contribution: the internal structure that accepts and uses information. There must be processes in the perceiver that are attuned to the relevent information in the environment. What do they do? Did they evolve merely to fashion "percepts" out of "stimuli"?

There is another and more natural alternative, which becomes plausible as soon as one examines ordinary perceptual acts more closely. Such as examination soon reveals (and undermines) several assumptions that have been accepted uncritically for many years. It has traditionally been assumed that visual perception is something discrete (i.e., beginning at one point in time and ending at another) and intrapsychic (occurring entirely inside the head). In fact, however, visual perception is a continuous activity. We look at things over extended periods of time, through many fixations. For this reason, looking must involve the *anticipation* of information as well as its pickup. I suggest that it depends on certain crucial internal structures, or "schemata," that function as anticipations and as plans. It is these schemata, together with the information actually available in the environment, that determine what is seen. Perception is indeed a constructive process, but what is constructed is not an inner image to be admired by an inner man; it is a plan for obtaining more information. At any moment the perceiver anticipates that a certain sort of information will become available, and he gets ready to accept it. Often he actively explores with his eyes or his hands in order to obtain more of it. The outcome of these explorations modifies the original schema, permitting it to direct further explorations and to prepare for still more information. This cycle is diagrammed in Figure 2.

Perceptual activity is not restricted to a single sensory system. Even newborn babies look in the direction from which a sudden sound has come: initial information in one modality leads to exploration in another. Adults have sophisticated schemata that accept information from many sources simultaneously and direct explorations of many kinds. When we look at someone who is speaking, the visual information about his lip movements supports the auditory information about the movements of his tongue and his articulators. We call this "hearing him speak," but it is really a multimodal enter-

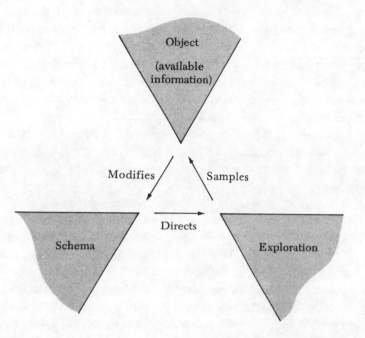

Figure 2. The perceptual cycle. Reprinted with permission from *Cognition and Reality* (Figure 2) by Ulric Neisser, W. H. Freeman and Company. Copyright © 1976.

prise because it is based on multimodal anticipations. When these anticipations are not fulfilled, as in a dubbed movie, the result can be very disturbing.

The anticipatory schema plays a critical role in every perceptual act. Nevertheless it is not a "percept," nor does it produce one anywhere in the perceiver's head. I submit that perceiving does not involve any such things as "percepts." We perceive, attend to, and are conscious of objects and events, not ghostly mental representations. The schema is just one phase of an ongoing interaction with the environment. Perception is the entire cycle illustrated in Figure 2, not any single part of it. It never occurs instantaneously, and it does not just happen in the head.

The idea that visual perception is continuous over time represents a radical break with most perceptual theory. Despite their disagreements, for example, the Gestalt psychologists and their classical opponents shared the assumption that visual perception begins with a pattern on the retina and ends with a percept in the mind. It is time, I think, to give up this assumption. It is already clear that the analogues of the assumption in other perceptual fields are unacceptable. In speech perception, we have finally rid ourselves of the notion that phonemes (or any units) are perceived one by one, independent of context. Where haptic perception is concerned (the active exploration of objects with our hands), no one would ever have been tempted by such a notion in the first place. It hangs on only in vision.

This assumption has had, and is still having, serious consequences. For example, it has created a virtual addiction to the tachistoscope as an experimental tool. By limiting the subject to a single brief flash of light, falling willy-nilly onto a receptor system he does not have time to adjust, this tempting device allows one to specify just when perception "begins." A great many clever experiments have been conducted with tachistoscopic techniques, but I think they have misled us. In the normal course of events perception does not "begin" at a sharply specified moment at all, and it ends only when the perceiver is tired of looking at something.

Consider a few natural examples of perception. In one very frequent case, a perceiver at rest watches a moving object: a running animal, perhaps, or a thrown ball. Usually he follows the object with his eyes. Even an infant only a few days old can track an optical motion under the right conditions, and adults are highly skilled at doing so. Successful tracking of this sort implies both anticipation and information pickup. Information about how the object is moving determines how the eyes and the head must move in order to follow it. When these movements have been made, still more information about the object and its motion can be acquired, leading to still further tracking. It is obvious, then, that this kind of perception is cyclical and extended in time.

If the moving object turns, or tumbles, or has limbs that shift their positions, more information becomes available. Parts of the object occlude and reveal other parts as it goes. The projected shapes and sizes of its surfaces at the eye of the observer keep changing. These changes do not result in confusion or blur, as they would if the static retinal image were the basis of perception. On the contrary, they represent information that can be used. The perceiver who pays attention to such a moving object continually develops general anticipations of its coming movements, which are continually being confirmed and made specific by the movements that actually occur. Indeed, that is what "paying attention" means. In recent experiments at Cornell, Becklen and I (1975) have superimposed the optical images of two natural events, both involving motion, and asked subjects to attend to one while ignoring the other. They find this very easy to do. They need no special "filtering mechanism" to block out the unwanted event; they simply do not follow it. It is as easy to follow one movement and ignore others as it is to follow one conversation and ignore another in a crowded room; the same principles apply in both cases. Nor are eye movements necessary for this kind of attention, although they naturally occur unless they are deliberately prevented (Littman & Becklen, 1976). What people see depends on the anticipations they develop, the perceptual explorations they carry out, and the information they find available; in other words, on the perceptual cycle in which they are engaged.

This principle applies not only to continuous and familiar motions; it is equally applicable when a new object enters the field of view. In laboratory studies, new visual objects are often presented artificially. They appear as soon as the experimenter closes a switch to turn on some display device. This procedure is poorly adapted to the study of normal perception. Perceivers usually have a good deal of advance information about new objects before the first visual fixation, which they have acquired from various sources. As a result, their first looks are well prepared.

Suppose, for example, that an unexpected visitor arrives at my office, where I am hard at work on this manuscript. It is surprisingly difficult to define the specific instant at which I first perceive him. In most cases I will be engaged in some particular activity when he arrives, and then look up and toward the door. Why do I look? Probably either because I *hear* him or because I see him in *peripheral vision*, "out of the corner of my eye." (These two possibilities are functionally similar, since both provide information that is used to direct further perceptual exploration.) Having picked up this information, I swivel my head and eyes around for a better look. In that look, the visitor's face (say) will be properly imaged on the central fovea of my eye. But this first foveal glance is not the beginning of perception; I already have the information about his position and movement that I acquired a moment before. Nor is this all: during the next few seconds the direction of my gaze will shift repeatedly as I look at him. Each of these eye movements will be made as a consequence of information already picked up, in anticipation of obtaining more. At what moment in all this activity can perception be said to occur? There is no such moment. Indeed, I am not even aware of the fixations, or of their sequence; only of the visitor himself. What I see is not in my head but in the world, and I see it over time.

Even without the contribution of peripheral vision, my visitor would not find me perceptually unprepared. After all, he must appear in the doorway. If I am working in my office, I already know where the doorway is, and what lies beyond it, just as I know the location of other familiar objects. This means that I can anticipate the distances and possible motions of *any* arriving guest. Information about his location and movements fits into a preexisting spatial schema, or cognitive map, and thereby modifies that schema. A visitor who entered through the wall, or materialized in the middle of the room, would be more like a ghost than a person. His ghostliness would be the first thing I noticed about him, and would color everything I saw afterward. Psychologists do not believe in ghosts, of course, but they often experiment with stimuli that appear just as mysteriously.

Of course, one can see stationary objects as well as moving ones. Sitting quietly at my desk, I may decide to look at the clock on the wall, for example. I already know where the wall is, and roughly where the clock is. I continue with a series of successive glances, each of which provides more detail. An anticipatory schema directs my looking from the first, and is modified by additional information as it becomes available so that further looks can be successfully executed. The perceptual cycle diagrammed in Figure 2 applies to such stationary cases just as it does to situations involving movement.

The claim that perception involves "anticipation" is easily misunderstood. It does *not* mean that one can see only what one expects to see. If the clock has been moved or even removed since the day before, I will surely realize it. The first direct glance will provide information that changes the schema, which will direct further and more appropriate exploration of the new object. When a perceptual cycle is carried out normally, schemata soon tune themselves to the information actually available. They must do so, since people are not always in familiar environments, and they often look at unfamiliar objects. The function of perception is to acquire new information, not merely to confirm preexisting assumptions! Nevertheless, it seems equally obvious that without some appropriate preexisting structure, no information could be acquired at all.

There is a dialectical contradiction between these two requirements. We cannot perceive *unless* we anticipate, but we must not see *only* what we anticipate. If we were restricted to isolated and unconfirmed glances at the world, this contradiction would prove fatal. Under such conditions we could not consistently disentangle what we see from what we expect to see, nor distinguish objects from hallucinations. This dilemma cannot be resolved in the internal processing model of perception. Its resolution is achieved only through the perceptual cycle. Although a perceiver always has at least some (more or less specific) anticipations before he begins to pick up information about a given object, these are corrected as may be necessary while he continues to look.

Anticipation is the function of the structures that I am calling "schemata," a term borrowed from Piaget and Bartlett. My own usage of this term is somewhat different from theirs. A schema is here defined as that portion of the perceptual cycle that is inside the observer, modifiable by experience, and somehow specific to what is being observed. The schema accepts information as it becomes available, and is changed by that information. Thus it undergoes what Piaget would call *accommodation*. But there is no need to postulate any process analogous to his *assimilation*: the sensory information is not changed by the perceiver, it is merely selected. Moreover, schemata are not passive; they direct movements and exploratory activities of many kinds that make more information available, by which they are further modified.

In some respects, a schema resembles a *format* in a computer programming language. Formats specify that information must be of a certain sort if it is to be interpreted coherently. Anything else will be ignored, or will lead to meaningless results. From another side, however, a schema is like a *plan*, of the sort described some years ago by Miller, Galanter, and Pribram (1960). Perceptual schemata are plans for finding out about objects and events, plans for obtaining more information to fill in the format. They often direct exploratory movements of the eye, head, and hands. It is important to stress, however, that schemata are equally functional in cases where no overt orienting movements occur. In such cases (listening is a typical example), the acquisition of information is still determined by the perceiver's developing format. Information that does not fit the schema either alters it substantially or goes entirely unused. Perception is inherently selective.

The analogy between schemata and formats or plans is not complete. In real formats and plans, one can make a sharp distinction between form and content; this is not true of schemata. The information that fills in the format at one point in the cycle becomes a part of the format in the next, determining how further information is accepted. The schema is not only the plan but also the executor of the plan. It is a pattern *of* action as well as a pattern *for* action.

The schema at any given moment resembles a "genotype" rather than a "phenotype" as these concepts are defined in genetics. It offers a possibility for development along certain lines, but the precise nature of that development is determined only by interaction with a real environment. It would be a mistake to identify the schema with the "percept," just as it is a mistake to identify any gene with a definite characteristic of an adult organism. Perception is determined by schemata in the same sense that the observable properties of organisms are determined by their genes. It results from the interaction of schema and available information; indeed, it *is* that interaction itself.

The cyclic and anticipatory nature of perception is especially obvious in one case that has not yet been considered: motion of the observer himself. Motion always changes the available information, and in ways that can be at least roughly anticipated. A sideways shift of the head is enough to reveal new aspects of most nearby objects. More extensive movements—going around a corner or looking into a new room—present whole new layouts of objects that were previously hidden. Every occluding edge defines a region that could be brought into view by some movement, and thus marks the potential location of things presently unseen. Perceptual schemata incorporate this fact. What the perceiver will see when he has moved stands in an already defined relation to what is presently visible, so that the relative positions of objects are "known" before they are imaged on the retina. Information picked up as a result of motion is systematically related to existing schemata, and in particular to a *cognitive map* of the nearby environment.

A cognitive map is essentially a larger kind of schema. That is, it accepts information and directs action. Just as an object schema accepted information about the clock on my office wall and directed further visual exploration, so my cognitive map of the entire building and its geographical setting accepts information about the larger environment and directs my actual explorations. The schema of the clock is a part of the cognitive map, just as the clock itself is a part of the real environment. The perceptual cycle itself is embedded in a more inclusive cycle that covers more ground and more time. Figure 3 illustrates this relationship. The schema directs looking, the cognitive map directs traveling. Both are simultaneously active and offer each other mutual support.

Although perceiving and traveling are similar activities, there is a crucial difference between them. In perception, successive phases follow one another very rapidly, and we are often unaware of them. In traveling, however, there are often prolonged periods during which we anticipate objects or events that have not yet appeared. During the time it takes me to get home from my office, for example, my cognitive map is preparing to pick up the information that will become available when I get there, as well as for the territory in between. Throughout the trip I have active but still "unfulfilled" expectations. This is not an unusual circumstance: all mobile organisms must often be in such a state. The proper term for this state, I suggest, is "mental imagery."

This definition of imagery differs from more familar ones in two ways. First, it is not introspective. Any organism that anticipates the layout of objects in the environment and directs appropriate movements as a result may be said to have spatial imagery. Second, while the image represents "stored information" in a certain sense of that word, it is not ordinarily used as stimulus information would be.

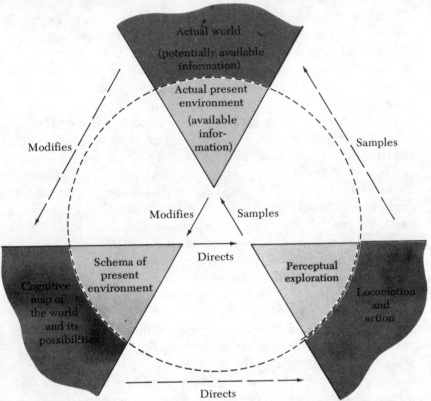

Figure 3. Perceiving as embedded in traveling. Reprinted with permission from *Cognition and Reality* (Figure 4) by Ulric Neisser, W. H. Freeman and Company. Copyright © 1976.

The traveler need not *examine* his cognitive map, as he might study a real map to determine his route. A mental image is not a picture of the world, but a plan for obtaining information from parts of it that have not yet been reached. It is the inner aspect of a spatial anticipation. When a subject reports verbally about an image, he is really reporting quite literally what he—or at least his visual system —is prepared to see. The referents of language about images are possible perceivable objects in the environment, not phantasms in the head.

It is evident that if cognitive maps are essentially perceptual anticipations, they must be flexible and easily altered. After all, the world itself changes: we find a visitor in the living room, or a package on the desk, and we replan our information-gathering activity as a result. Schemata and cognitive maps can change even while they are actively controlling behavior. All of us know how to alter them, on the basis not only of what we see but also of what we are told. If we learn that there is a body or a treasure chest or a traffic jam at a certain point on the way home, for example, it is easy to modify our perceptual anticipations and our travel plans. Many people have learned to take advantage of this flexibility in a way that gives images a secondary function. Besides being plans for traveling and looking, they can serve as mnemonic devices.

Consider first the "method of loci," a curious and ancient trick for remembering things that has intrigued contemporary psychologists to no small degree. This device, invented by the Greeks in classical times, is suitable for remembering any arbitrary list of items. To use it, you must first familiarize yourself with some series of locations along a particular route or path. (For the ancients this was often walking through a large temple with many niches and statues; nowadays a university campus is more convenient.) Once learned, such a cognitive map can be used over and over again for mnemonic purposes. To remember any particular list, simply visualize the successive items as if they were situated at consecutive spots, or "loci," along your path. When you wish to recall them, take a mental stroll along the path; you will find the items all still comfortably in place (Ross & Lawrence, 1968). Of course there is some "suspension of disbelief" involved: you need not really believe that the objects are there. But you are prepared to see them, and an appropriate test might well show that you *could* perceive them easily and quickly. That is why everyone can use this method: in many classroom demonstrations, I have never found a student unable to do so. Everyone who gets around in the world must be able to form and modify cognitive maps, and the method of loci is nothing but the use of a cognitive map for an unusual purpose.

The cognitive map is the most basic form of imagery, but not the only form. Perception is a cyclic process even when a stationary observer views a single object; anticipatory schemata play a crucial role. Normally perceptual plans and their executions succeed one another so rapidly that we are aware only of the object itself, not of the individual glances or the states of preparation that precede them. Nevertheless, these states are present, and when they are prolonged for any reason we may notice them. We call them, too, "images."

This kind of imagery underlies other imaginal mnemonic devices. When subjects remember a pair of nouns by visualizing the corresponding objects in interaction, they are preparing to see these two objects themselves, to move their eyes and their heads as would be necessary if the objects were present, and to pick up the kind of information that such movements would bring. A subject who memorizes the pair "shark-crib" by imagining a shark in a crib is making just such a plan. In this case his plan has no perceptual function — neither the shark nor the crib will actually come into view — but he can report on what he would expect to see if they did.

This interpretation explains why imagery instructions work well only with so-called concrete words (Paivio, 1971). In fact, it provides a specific definition of "concrete." Words are concrete to the extent that they denote objects that offer *anticipatable* sensory information. Nothing else can be visualized, because to visualize is to anticipate. This interpretation also explains why the objects must be imagined in some kind of *interaction*. Two objects interact, in this sense, if the perceiver must take their relationship into account in order to see them properly. That is why the shark had best be imagined inside the crib, or eating it, but not merely next to it, if they are to be remembered together.

Because schemata and cognitive maps are anticipations, they can and do represent objects that are temporarily concealed or obscured as well as those in plain sight. This suggests that one can imagine a concealing, nonpicturable relationship between two objects as easily as any other kind, and use it as a mnemonic device. It should be just as effective to imagine the crib completely inside the shark as the shark inside the crib, for example. This turns out to be true, as Nancy Kerr and I reported recently (Neisser and Kerr, 1973). Although our subjects reported that images of concealed objects were less "vivid" or "good" than other images, they were no less effective as mediators for memory. Images are not like pictures; indeed, they are not even exclusively visual. An anticipatory schema can direct reaching and touching and listening as well as looking. If a schema can be said to represent anything—and I have some doubts that it can—it represents the spatial arrangement of objects rather than just the way they look.

From this point of view, the fact that images facilitate rapid perception of an imagined object is not a minor byproduct of the act of visualizing; it is the essence of that act. To have a perceptual set for something is to have an anticipatory image. The more precisely the image anticipates the actual information to come, the more effective it will be. Posner and his colleagues have demonstrated many times that a subject who has just seen a particular letter, say a capital *A*, will respond to it more quickly if it appears again in the same form and less quickly if it now appears in a different form, say as a lower-case *a* (e.g., Posner, Boies, Eichelman, & Taylor, 1969; Beller, 1971). Indeed, facilitation occurs even if the subject is merely told what the coming letter will be, so that he can imagine it. I believe the facilitation occurs because the subjects actually *perceive* the relevant information more quickly when they are appropriately prepared. If images are essentially perceptual anticipations, this result is easily understood.

Anticipations may be formed at various levels of detail. One can look at something casually or carefully, from close up or far away, with an interest in one part of it or another. All these kinds of looking require different plans, and hence they correspond to differences in imagery. Kosslyn (1975) has recently shown that one's ability to report small details of the appearance of an imagined animal, for example, depends on how large and how close he imagines the animal to be. This need not mean that an image of a large animal is a big, detailed picture and that of a small animal a small picture: our plans for looking at a large animal are simply different from our plans for looking at a small one. Similarly, our plans for looking at a rotating or a rotated object are different from our plans for looking at an upright and stationary object, and it takes time to convert from one plan to the other.

If images are anticipatory schemata, they should serve to direct anticipatory behavior. This suggests that one should make the same kinds of eye movements in imagining something as in actually looking at it. Such a proposition cannot be tested with ordinary images, because there are too many different ways to look at things. The eye movements made in examining a chair, say, will vary with the intent, skill, and momentary inclination of the observer, and thus cannot easily be predicted. For the reason an equally wide range of eye movement patterns, including no movement at all, may occur as one *imagines* a chair, i.e., develops a particular plan for looking at it. A test becomes possible, however, if one imagines an event involving systematic motion, like a tennis match. Under these conditions, the eye movements of imagers do follow the expected pattern (Antrobus, Antrobus, & Singer, 1964). The same principle applies even to dreamers. When the content of a dream includes regular movements, as indicated by the dreamer's subsequent report, appropriate eye movements often occur (Koulack, 1972). The reason for this is not that the dreamer first has a mental picture and then moves his eyes to examine it. Rather, he just anticipates seeing something, plans to look at it, and executes as much of his plan as he can.

In summary, the reason that we do not regularly confuse imagining with perceiving—or images with objects—is that these are activities of fundamentally different kinds. Perception is a cyclic interaction with the world; an image is a single phase of that interaction. Treating them as equivalent would be like identifying fulfillment with promise, or a plant with its seed. Such a mistake is impossible under normal conditions. To be sure, we may make perceptual errors, mistaking a stranger for a friend or a tree for a looming monster. Such errors confuse objects with one another, but not images with objects. Errors occur because not enough information has been picked up; perhaps too little exploratory activity was conducted, or an anticipatory image misdirected the perceptual process. Usually enough information is picked up to correct such mistakes quickly. When they go uncorrected in the hallucinator or the dreamer, it is in some sense because he is "not really trying"; his problem is fundamentally one of motivation, not of perception.

Perceiving is like science—subject to many errors, but self-correcting in the long run. Eventually we obtain better information about the world than we had before. Let us hope this proves true of the scientific study of perception and imagery as well as of the directed activity of perceivers and imaginers.

References

Antrobus, John S., Antrobus, Judith S., & Singer, J. L. Eye movements accompanying daydreaming, visual imagery, and thought suppression. *Journal of Abnormal Psychology*, 1964, 69, 244-252.

Beller, H. K. Priming: Effects of advance information on matching. *Journal of Experimental Psychology*, 1971, 87, 176-182.

Gibson, J. J. *The senses considered as perceptual systems*. Boston: Houghton-Mifflin, 1966.

Hubel, D. H., & Wiesel, T. N. Receptive fields of single neurones in the cat's striate cortex. *Journal of Physiology*, 1959, 148, 574-591.

Kosslyn, S. M. Information representation in visual images. *Cognitive Psychology*, 1975, 7, 341-370.

Koulack, D. Rapid eye movements and visual imagery during sleep. *Psychological Bulletin*, 1972, 78, 155-158.

Lindsay, P. N., & Norman, D. A. *Human information processing*. New York: Academic Press, 1972.

Littman, D., & Becklen, R. Selective looking with minimal eye movements. *Perception and Psychophysics*, 1976, 20, 77-79.

Massaro, D. W. *Experimental psychology and information processing*. Chicago: Rand McNally, 1975.

Miller, G. A., Galanter, E., & Pribram, K. H. *Plans and the structure of behavior*. New York: Holt, 1960.

Neisser, U. *Cognitive psychology*. New York: Appleton-Century-Crofts, 1967.

Neisser, U., & Becklen, R. Selective looking: Attending to visually-specified events. *Cognitive Psychology*, 1975, 7, 480-494.

Neisser, U., & Kerr, N. Spatial and mnemonic properties of visual images. *Cognitive Psychology*, 1973, 5, 138-150.

Paivio, A. *Imagery and verbal processes*. New York: Holt, Rinehart, & Winston, 1971.

Perky, C. W. An experimental study of imagination. *American Journal of Psychology*, 1910, 21, 422-452.

Posner, M. I. *Cognition: An introduction*. Glenview, Illinois: Scott Foresman, 1973.

Posner, M. I., Boies, S. J., Eichelman, W. H., & Taylor, R. L. Retention of visual and name codes of single letters. *Journal of Experimental Psychology Monographs*, 1969, 79, 1, part 2.

Ross, J., & Lawrence, K. A. Some observations on memory artifice. *Psychonomic Science*, 1968, 13, 107-108.

Segal, S. J. Processing of the stimulus in imagery and in perception. In S. J. Segal (Ed.), *Imagery: Current cognitive approaches*. New York: Academic Press, 1971.

Segal, S. J. Assimilation of a stimulus in the construction of an image: The Perky effect revisited. In P. W. Sheehan (Ed.), *The function and nature of imagery*. New York: Academic Press, 1972.

The Role of the Percept in Visual Cognition

In his recent book (1975, p. 24) Irvin Rock remarks on the way specialists in the study of perception have staked out certain problem areas that are more or less distinguishable from those of neighboring disciplines. The field of perception can be said to lie between the field of sensory processes on the one side and of cognitive processes on the other. Investigators of sensory processes are typically concerned with the psychophysical relationship between stimulation and sensation and with the physiological mechanisms that mediate sensation. On the other hand, investigators of cognitive processes are concerned with problems that begin where preception ends. They begin with the perceived object as given and tend to concentrate on such processes as recognition, recall, association, attention, understanding, problem-solving, and thinking.

Another way to put this same point is to say that there are both an etiological and a functional story to tell about perception. The etiological story is concerned with the causal antecedents of our perceptual experience, the sorts of mechanisms, processes, and factors that go into determining the character of that experience. The functional story, on the other hand, looks to the results, the effects, of such experience on the organism's continuing adjustment to its environment. Here we are concerned with the role, the upshot, of perception in the satisfaction of the organism's needs, desires, and purposes.

Note: I wish to thank the participants of the Information-Cognition-Perception Symposium for their helpful comments on an earlier version of this paper. I would also like to thank Professor Len Uhr for his probing questions while I was writing the paper and Professor William Epstein of the Psychology Department, University of Wisconsin, for his advice and suggestions. No one seems to agree fully, but as a philosopher, accustomed to blank stares of incomprehension, I find the fact of disagreement itself an encouraging sign of communication.

It is hard to fault either approach to the study of perception—unless, of course, it purports to be the *whole* story. It seems reasonable enough to suppose that perception falls somewhere between the S-R poles and even more narrowly, as Rock suggests, somewhere between the sensory and cognitive process with which it is so intimately connected. It is the purpose of this paper to explore just where (if anywhere) on this flow chart, this bluprint of the organism reacting to and interacting with his environment, we may best locate perceptual phenomena. I shall suggest that there is, in some quarters, a tendency to overfunctionalize perception, a tendency to assimilate it to the genuine cognitive processes to which it gives rise. I hope to nudge it, ever so slightly, away from the response and back toward the stimulus end of this spectrum.

If I understand them, many psychologists and philosophers mean to speak of a certain internal, conscious state when they speak about a subject's *perception* of an object or event. In other words, in speaking of S's perception of depth or S's perception of motion, they mean to refer to S's perceptual state—something we might also refer to as the *way things look* to S or the *way he perceives* things quite apart from the way things actually are. I shall not use this terminology. I shall, instead, speak about S's percepts. This terminology, although it horrifies some and is avoided by others, has a decided advantage. It clearly suggests that what we are talking about is some internal state of S and *not* some relationship between S and the objects in his environment. Although this is merely a terminological point, the terminology is important; it has been responsible for some confusion. Let me take a moment, therefore, to explain what I see as the difference between S's percept of something and S's perception of something, and why I prefer the former terminology.

If S owns a house, we can speak of S's owning the house or of the house S owns. These are different things and not likely to be confused. We can paint the house S owns, but we cannot paint S's ownership of the house. If S sells the house, his ownership ceases, but the house he owned may persist unaltered. S's owning the house is a *relationship* that exists between S and the house; the house S owns is the object to which he is related.

The distinction is obvious enough in terms of this example. Yet it tends to get blurry when we move to other cases. For example, we can distinguish between my being frightened by you, and my fright. My being frightened by you is a complex relational state of affairs that involves you as an essential ingredient; you are a *part* of this relational state. I cannot be frightened by you unless you exist. On the other hand, my fright is some internal state of me. It is something of which you are not a part although it is something of which you are the cause.

Similar remarks can be made about S's perception of O and S's percept of O. S's perception of O is a relationship that exists between S and O; it is a state of affairs that cannot exist unless both S and O exist and stand in the appropriate relation to each other. S's percept of O, however, is a state of S *alone*. It does not have O as a part even though it is brought about or produced by O (thereby allowing us to refer to it as a percept *of* O). The point can be put this way: just as my being frightened by you involves (very roughly) your producing in me a certain internal state, a state to which we may refer with the phrase "my fright," so, also, my perception of you involves (again, very roughly) your producing in me a certain internal state, a state to which we may refer with the phrase "my percept."

The confusion between S's perception of O and S's percept of O appears in the dispute about whether perception of something (a table, say) is possible when there is no table (no *real* table) present. If one uses the phrase "S's perception of a table" to refer to S's percept of a table, then it is easy enough to suppose that since *such* percepts can occur without a real table being present, one's perception of a table does not *require* a real table. This, it seems to me, is a confusion that could easily be avoided by making a clear distinction between S's perception of a table (which, being a relationship between S and a table, requires the existence of some table) and S's percept of a table. The latter is the sort of thing that *can* exist without a real table being present (although, of course, if there were no real table present, we would not refer to S's percept as a percept *of* a table). We can have "table percepts" just as we can have "ghost fears" without real tables or real ghosts, but we cannot *perceive* a table or be *frightened by* a ghost without encountering the genuine articles.

This distinction, once mentioned, is rather obvious, and I assume that my readers will find it so. I remark on it, not with the intention of saying anything novel, but only for the purpose of marking a difference and noting the somewhat confusing way this difference is sometimes expressed. In this paper I want to talk about our percepts (roughly: our perceptual experience or the way we perceive things)—a type of internal state that is typically produced in us as a result of our interactions with our surroundings. Some people, perhaps skittish about the mentalistic or imagistic connotations of the word "percept," prefer to talk about the same thing by speaking of our perception of things. For the reasons just given, I shall not talk this way. I hope it will be clear, however, that this is *just* a difference in the way we choose to talk; we *are* talking about the same thing.

I have already suggested a preliminary characterization of a percept: it is some type of internal state that is (under normal circumstances) causally dependent on the objects and events that we are said to perceive. There is, unquestionably, this type of causal dependence.[1] Nevertheless, it also seems clear from a variety of experimental studies that our percepts, though dependent to a greater or less degree on the distal and proximal stimuli, are not wholly *determined* by these stimuli. There is an obvious dependence on the state of the receptors, the neural pathways, and the brain. But even holding these variables fixed, or as fixed as we can hold them, we have efferent effects on our percepts of motion and position, the shifting perception of ambiguous figures (where there is a change in the percept without a corresponding change in the proximal stimulus), and the influence of such factors as set, attention, and past experience on the resultant percept. Gibson's advocacy of an updated psychophysical correspondence (1950, 1966) has made it more common to hear about the availablility *in* the stimulus of information formerly taken to be an enrichment *of* the stimulus (or stimulus dependent sensations) by habit, memory and inference. But this constancy hypothesis is acknowledged to have only limited validity; experiments establishing the influence of set and attention on our perception of ambiguous figures (e.g., Steinfield, 1967), our variable perception of moving forms (Johansson, 1975), and the older experiments of the transactionalists (Kilpatrick, 1952)[2] serve well enough, it seems to me, to belie any full correspondence between stimulus and percept.

Equally obvious is the underspecification of the percept by the subject's behavioral responses. Although a subject's behavior, verbal and otherwise, is (often enough) conditioned by his concurrent perceptual state, his perceptual state is only one of the many variables that go to determine his behavior and his disposition to behave (Garner, Hake, & Eriksen, 1956). This means that the percept is left underspecified by the kind of information available in the subject's overt responses. Methodologically, of course, one is forced to rely on the subject's reports and other discriminatory behavior (using, whenever possible, converging operations) in framing hypotheses about his percepts, but this is clearly the relationship between indicator and indicated. There are a variety of factors that can influence the reliability of this index. The subject's overt behavior is presumably a function, not only of his percepts, of how things look and sound to him, but also of his beliefs, attentiveness, habits, expectations, interests, purposes, and values. The notion of a response bias seems to presuppose the distinction between the percept itself and the array of behavioral responses we exploit to specify it. These other variables help to determine, not only the character of the response, but whether there is a response at all; from signal detection theory (Engen, 1972, and Swets, Tanner, & Birdsall, 1961) we learn that whether or not a response is forthcoming depends, not only on the effect of the stimulus relative to the noise, but also on what the observer *expects* in the situation and the potential consequences of his decision.

We can, of course, *call* the percept itself a kind of response—e.g., a central response—but this verbal maneuver accomplishes nothing. The fact remains that these "central responses" are as loosely associated with the overt responses in terms of which one identifies and characterizes these central states as they were when called by another name. Referring to these central states as dispositions to behave, or (Pitcher, 1971) suppressed dispositions to behave, is equally futile; we are still left with something whose character is underspecified by the available input and output data.

I shall have more to say in a moment about the relationship between a subject's responses and his percepts. For the moment I shall simply assume, without further discussion, that the idea of a percept, or a perceptual state, is the idea of an internal state which, though conditioned by the stimulus and in turn a possible factor in the response, is not wholly determinable by either. It is this under-determination of the percept that I mean to signal by my use of the adjective "internal" in referring to a percept as an internal state of the subject. It is internal in the sense in which the totality of stimu-lation and the totality of behavioral responses are external.

If this is all that could be said about the notion of a percept, there would (or should) be little debate about the existence or role of such elements in visual cognition. For there clearly are stages in the processing of sensory information that fit the characterization of a percept just given. For instance, there are neurophysiological states or processes (perhaps the neural activity in the superior colliculus) that depend on, but are not wholly determined by, the character of the incoming stimulation and that, in turn, affect (but do not wholly determine) the subject's motor responses. What is missing in my description of a percept is that feature that distinguishes this particular internal state from a variety of other intermediate stages in the processing of sensory information. The feature usually men-tioned in this regard is our conscious awareness of the percept, its introspective accessibility, its phenomenal character. The idea of a percept, after all, is supposed to be the idea of an internal state that somehow constitutes our visual experience; and it is this experiential quality that is usually invoked to distinguish a percept from the variety of other internal states that can be given similar functional and etiological characterizations.

I think there is some merit in talking about our perceptual states in the language of "conscious experience" and "phenomenal appear-ances," but, unfortunately, the merit does not lie in the precision or illumination that such language provides. The merit in using this kind of language is that it indicates, in a rough and familiar way, what it is that we want to talk about. The trouble is that it does not supply us with the means for talking about these things in a precise enough way to allow us to determine whether what we say, or want to say, about them is true or not. Such language has the further demerit of stirring up a swarm of philosophical and terminological problems that I am anxious to avoid. Therefore I propose to retreat slightly and approach the question of what it is, specifically, that we mean to talk about when we refer to a subject's percepts in a slightly different way.

Suppose objects of type O have a peculiar effect on humans; they induce a kind of neurological activity (call it N) that quickly, in a matter of minutes, manifests itself in a periodic twitching of the cheek muscles. There is no pain or other discomfort associated with this effect, and with most subjects the twitching goes unnoticed. If we suppose that the neurological state N is specific to objects of type O, we can describe the subject's reaction to O in informational processing terms. The state N embodies information about the subject's surroundings, information to the effect that there is (or was, a few minutes earlier) an object of type O nearby. The involuntary twitching, being a distinctive symptom of state N, also contains the information that there is or was an object of type O nearby. There are, in a sense, coding, storage, and retrieval of information.

The fact that such a regular sequence of events can be described in informational terms should not suggest that the subjects *in whom* such information is being processed know anything related to the information passing through them. One could say, I suppose, that the subject's *body* knows that an O is present, but it is fairly clear that *the subject* does not (or need not) know that an O is present. The information passes through without becoming available to the subject himself. Although he embodies an O-detecting mechanism, although his nervous system is acting as a channel for the transmission, and temporary storage, of this information, the subject himself does not *have* the information about the presence of an O. He may not suspect that an O is present; he may even disbelieve in the *existence* of Os and act in accord with this conviction. The fact that our subject is in a certain internal state, a state that can for certain informational purposes be described as an O-positive state, is quite irrelevant to determining *his* cognitive capabilities. One needs more than a built in O-detector to be a detector of Os. One needs some kind of mediating process (Hebb, 1966) to convert these reflexes into perceptual responses.[3]

Our hypothetical subject might, by glancing in a mirror, realize that an O was nearby by noticing the abnormal twitching in his cheek. This, however, is a new and different story. He is now using his body as he might a piece of litmus paper, and his body does not know, any more than does a piece of litmus paper, what *he* can come to know by observing it. The information about the presence of an

O is now being *reprocessed* through a different system, the visual system, capable of giving the subject information that formerly, when he served merely as a conduit, was denied him.

When we speak, as we naturally do, of certain neural networks or cells as edge-detectors or movement-detectors, we should similarly bear in mind the fact that the subject himself (the *total* system, if you will) in which these detectors are found as parts, need not be able to detect either edges or movement (although from an evolutionary standpoint, it would be surprising indeed if this were so). Whether the system as a whole can detect edges depends on how its component edge-detectors are integrated into the system. That subassembly that we choose to call an edge-detector must not only detect edges, thus having *its* output conditioned by the presence of an edge, it must make this information available to the system of which it is a part for purposes of shaping *its* responses. A system cannot live on the reputation or performance record of its parts. *You* earn no cognitive credits for the detective capabilities of your parts—not unless the results are made available to you for modulation of *your* responses.

If we keep this point in mind, I think it is easier to see what kind of internal state we mean to describe when we talk about a subject's perceptual state. We do not want just any stage in the processing of sensory information, nor do we want a composite of *all* stages. We want that point in the process at which the information from the assorted detection mechanisms *is made available to the system as a whole*. We want that point in the flow of information at which further activity, if any, may be counted as responses of *the system* and not just as outputs or responses of its components. Before we reach the point at which the information is made available to the system as a whole we have detector mechanisms responding in their appointed way, but the system containing these mechanisms has not yet detected anything. After this point we have a response, the onset of behavior, by the system itself—an output that is to be accounted for, partially at least, by the information made available to the system by the foregoing processes. We have, in short, a genuine *perceptual* response.

What is to be counted as a response of the system as a whole, as genuine behavior of the system itself, and not merely as a reflex or a response of some component of the system? This is a sticky question, and I am not really going to attempt a full answer. Dennett (1969; see also Rundle, 1972, pp. 85-86) takes an approach that I consider promising. In discussing the distinction between what he calls intelligent and nonintelligent storage of information (p. 46) Dennett describes intelligent storage as the storage of information that is *for the system*. Information *for* the system is information the system can *use*, and useful information is ultimately to be understood in terms of the system's needs and purposes. I am interested not so much in the details of this view as I am in the general program it represents and the implications of this general approach for understanding perception. For what we are now embarking upon, if we follow through this line of thought, is a shift to a functional characterization of the percept. The general outline of this approach goes something like this: perception is the pickup of information. But, as we have just seen, not all the information a system absorbs is perceptual in character. Only that is to be counted as perceptual that is made available to the system as a whole and can therefore figure, more or less directly, in the system's pattern of responses. And the *system's responses*, in contrast to the responses of its gall bladder, sweat glands, basilar membrane, or cheek muscles, are those responses that are determined, not only by the incoming stimulus information, but also by the needs, purposes, and desires of the system as a whole. Hence perception is to be understood as the pickup of information available to the organism and serviceable to it in the satisfaction of its needs and purposes.[4]

A simple analogy is available. The ordinary home thermostat monitors the room temperature and responds by sending a signal to the furnace. The signal sent to the furnace is a function of two things: the information received about the temperature of the room, and the desired temperature of the room as given by the preadjusted setting of the thermostat itself. The thermostat's response is therefore determined by *both* the information received about the temperature of the room *and* the desired state of the room as reflected in its preadjusted setting. If we trace the flow of incoming information, we can treat the bimetal strip, whose curvature depends on the ambient temperature, as a temperature detector. Its responses depend, simply, on the temperature of the room. The responses of this crucial component, however, are not to be counted as responses of the thermostat itself. The thermostat itself has a different function than merely registering the temperature; its function or purpose is to send a signal to the furnace about the *difference* between the actual temperature and the desired temperature. In light of this function we can identify responses of the thermostat itself, in contrast with responses of its various components (e.g., the bimetal strip), as responses that are determined not simply by the incoming information, but by this information *together with* the adjusted setting indicative of the desired temperature.

At what stage is the information about the room temperature made available to the thermostat for use in determining its responses? Clearly enough, the information about the room temperature is available *in* the configuration of the bimetal strip. *That* is where the information is, but what makes this information *available* to the thermostat itself is the positioning of the bimetal strip relative to the electrical contacts completing the circuit to the furnace. Move these contacts far enough and the information, though still there *in* the thermostat, as it were, is no longer available to the thermostat. We shall have a temperature detector (the bimetal strip), but *the thermostat* cannot detect the temperature. *It* cannot detect the temperature because the information is not available to it for modulating its responses to the furnace—and *that* is its function.

The configuration of the bimetal strip in a properly manufactured thermostat is, therefore, the analogue of a percept or a perceptual state. It is that internal state of the system in which stimulus information is made available to the system as a whole for the purposes of determining its responses.[5] The system's responses, in turn, are to be measured in terms of its function, purpose, or (should it have such) needs and desires.

We now have a dual specification of a percept; the description is partly etiological, partly functional. We are talking about something that has a certain origin, something with causal antecedents in the stimulus, something that (normally, at least) embodies information about these causal antecedents. But we mean to speak of only some of these etiologically described elements, only those that also have a certain functional role to play in the behavior of the organism itself, only those that have, or can have, *certain sorts of effects* on the output of the system as a whole.

If something like this dual characterization of a percept is even roughly correct, and it seems to me that it is, we should expect to be able to investigate perceptual phenomena from the point of view of both input and output, cause and effect, etiology and function. And this, it would appear, is our actual practice. To put it somewhat crudely, our inferences about what people see, about the character of their perceptual experience, is sometimes based on what goes in and sometimes based on what comes out. When the sleeping cat opens its eyes, looks about the room for a moment, yawns, and goes back to sleep, we may suppose that it saw us despite the absence of any overt responses to indicate that it did. And when, despite our efforts at concealment, the rabbit raises its head, tenses, and then darts into the underbrush, we suppose it somehow sensed our presence, although we might not be sure just how. There are, however, methodological reasons for placing greater, almost exclusive, reliance on the output or response end of this inferential base. For the matter under investigation is often what the relationship is between stimulus input and the percept itself, and when *this* is the empirical question under investigation one cannot, on pain of circularity, rely on the stimulus itself to determine what features will be assigned to the percept. This would trivialize the entire project. One needs an independent determination of the percept for an investigation of this sort, and the only independent basis available for defining the character of the perceptual experience is the response of the subject. In a study of this sort one is, of necessity, restricted to a response-based specification of the percept.

This methodologically induced restriction is innocent enough as long as it is properly understood as a constraint on empirical investigations of a certain sort. There is, however, a tendency to interpret it as something more fundamental, as somehow a manifestation of the underlying *functional* nature of perception itself. Restriction to a subject's responses in determining the way he perceives what he perceives fosters the idea that if something goes in and does not come out, and cannot be made to come out under properly controlled conditions, then it did not really get in—not, at least, in the way that deserves to be called *perceptual*. To concede it a perceptual status, in the minds of some, would be to remove perception from the realm of empirical science since there is no way (given the methodological limitation) to determine that such perceptual events are occurring.

This, I suggest, is an overfunctionalization of the concept of a perceptual state. It is to take something that is functional and transform it into something that is *only* functional. But functional states also have an etiology, and it would be surprising indeed if nature were so streamlined in its operation that it could produce functional elements without, in the process, creating a few superfluous, functionally superfluous, adjuncts. Valve-lifters (Fodor's example, 1969) are certainly functional devices, and when we refer to them as valve-lifters we refer to them in explicitly functional language. But these facts should not prevent one from appreciating that what we are referring to is something that also has an origin and a nature quite independent (logically) of the purpose it serves in the larger system of which it is a part. If I were eccentric and wealthy enough, I could have my car's valve-lifters inlaid with pearls. This would not make any difference to the valve-lifter as a valve-lifter, since its performance in lifting valves would be unimpaired. But it would be a gross overfunctionalization of the notion of a valve-lifter, a confusion between *what* we were talking about with *how* we were talking about it, to argue that from a functional standpoint my valve-lifters could not be studded with pearls because such decoration would have no discernible effect on their performance in lifting valves. True enough, but the question of whether my valve lifters are so adorned is still a legitimate question; one must simply look to something other than their output or performance in answering it.

I believe a similar point can be made about our percepts or perceptual experience. Consider, first, the well-known experiments by Sperling (1960) and Averbach and Coriell (1961), in which subjects were exposed to an array of nine or more letters for a brief period (50 milliseconds). It was found that after removal of the stimulus there was a persistence of the "visual image"; subjects reported that the letters appeared to be visually present and legible at the time of a tone occurring 150 milliseconds after the stimulus had been removed. Niesser (1967) has dubbed this iconic memory—a temporary storage of sensory information in perceptual form. It is unimportant (for our purposes) whether we think of this as the persistence of *an image* or not. What is important to notice is that although subjects could identify only three or four letters under these brief exposure conditions, *which* three or four letters they succeeded in identifying depended on the character of a later stimulus—a stimulus that only appeared 150 milliseconds *after* removal of the original array of letters. This later stimulus (a marker appearing in different locations) had the effect of shifting the subject's attention to different parts of the *persisting icon*. This was not a case of shifting the subject's attention to different parts of the *stimulus*; for, of course, the time at which the shift occurred was 150 milliseconds *after* the stimulus had been removed.

These experiments suggest that although there may be an information-extracting limitation on the subjects, the same limitations do not apply to our visual system. Although the subjects could succeed in identifying only three or four letters, information about *all* the letters was contained in the persisting icon. The visual system had information about the character of all nine letters in the array, whereas the subject had information about at most four. The availability of this information is demonstrated by the fact that after removal of the stimulus the subject could (depending on later stimulation) extract information about *any* letter in the array; hence, information about *all* the letters in the array was available *in* the persisting icon. The visual system was processing and making available a quantity of information in excess of what the subject (or the higher cognitive centers) could absorb.

The sense in which this perceptual information is available to the subject is the sense in which we might say that all the information in the public library is available to you even though you are allowed to check out only three books. The percept is like a well-stocked library; it constitutes a pool of information from which you, given your limited check-out privileges, can extract only a fraction. The remaining information is available to you in the sense that although you can leave with only a part of the whole, you can leave with *any* part of the whole. After leaving the library with your three books there is a sense in which the only information *now* available to you is the information contained in those three books you selected. You exercised your option, you made your selection, and the information *now* available to you is but a part of what *was* available to you when you were in the library before making your selection.

There is a similar difference between perception and such higher-level cognitive processes as recognition, identification, discrimination, and learning. The subjects in the above experiment could "check out" only four letters; these are the letters they recognized or identified. But while they were *in* the library, during that fraction of a second in which the stimulus was present and the icon persisted, *all* of the letters were available to them. Once the stimulus had been removed, once the subject closed his eyes, looked elsewhere, or moved on to other things (thus leaving the library), the amount of available information was reduced; the subject was left (in short-term or long-term memory) with what he had succeeded in extracting from that larger pool of information (the percept) available to him during stimulation. These subjects perceived all nine letters in the array; this was the information available to them during (and shortly after) stimulation—available to them, not only *in the stimulus*, but *in the percept* generated by that stimulus. Though perceiving all nine letters, these subjects recognized or identified only three of four letters; this is a measure of the information they extracted from the percept, information that was available for shaping their responses (including their verbal responses to questions about *what* they had perceived). To confuse the information that was available in the percept with the information that is actually extracted, stored, and effective (or potentially effective) in determining behavior is to confuse perception with cognition. In terms of our analogy, it is to confuse the total informational resources of the library with the more limited quantity of information one extracts from it.

I am afraid this talk of libraries and the information available in the books one may or may not choose to read will make it sound as though I view the percept, the sensory information available to the subject, as a stack of mental "bulletins" that the busy homunculus has scarcely time to read. I hope not one will take my illustration that literally. I do not think the percept is something that the subject scans, perceives, decodes, interprets, or is even aware of if by "aware of" we mean something like that perceptual relation between subject and object in which we speak of ourselves as aware of flowers and people. Quite the contrary. If the subject perceives anything, he perceives (I would argue) causal antecedents of his percept, those objects and events in his environment that the information in his percept is information *about*. My library example was only meant to illustrate the distinction between the information available to the subject and the information the subject actually extracts—the distinction I take to be fundamental between perception and cognition. If the percept is to be understood in informational terms, as I have suggested it can be, we must remember that it is the visual system, *not* (or not *necessarily*) the subject, that has the information. Whether the subject himself knows anything, whether he stands in any cognitive relation to the events and objects responsible for his percept, is a question of what sensory information he succeeds in extracting from the information embodied in this percept. The information in the percept is information available to the subject, not in the sense that *he has the information*, but in the sense that (during stimulation) *he could have had it*—perhaps not *all* of it, but certainly any part of it.

My lengthy discussion of tachistoscopic experiments may suggest that the distinctions I am urging are a special feature of such situations. Let me try, therefore, to make the same point with homelier examples. Think of occasions on which you have looked at a fairly complex scene: a crowd of youngsters playing in a schoolyard, a shelf full of books and knick-knacks, or a display of the American flag with all the stars and stripes fully visible. I think a reaction typical of such encounters is that we have seen a great deal more than we noticed or consciously attended to. There were 43 children in the playground, and although we may have seen them all, we do not know *how many* we saw. We perceived 43, but this numerical information is not information that we generally extract from such experiences. Some children wore blue shirts, some red shirts, some white shirts, but we noticed only the cute little girl in red who was jumping rope. Some children were tall, others were short, some were moving, others were still. Much of this, I submit, is information available to us in the perceptual experience, but it is not information that *we* (the subject) succeed in extracting (either consciously or unconsciously, in long-term or short-term memory) under routine perceptual conditions. Notice, I am not denying that this information *is* extracted and processed, is made available to us by our visual systems. What I am denying is that in typical cases the *subject* extracts all this information.

It will certainly be said that I am assuming something for which I have given no argument: viz., that the visual system does make available in our percepts the kind, and variety, of information just described. Before trying to answer this charge, let me hasten to emphasize that I am not asserting or assuming any simple psychophysical correspondence between information available in the percept and information available (in the stimulus) at the retina. There is obviously a *loss* of information between that which arrives at the receptor and that which is available in the percept (and, conversely, there may be a *restoration* of information not available in the stimulus—see, e.g., Warren, 1970). If one saw all 43 children but saw some of them only peripherally, it seems unlikely that information pertaining to the color of their clothing would be available in the percept. If such color information, contained in the light reaching the retina, does not reach the color-sensitive cones in the fovea, it will obviously not be available in the resultant percept. But even with these peripherally seen children, information about their relative location, size, and spacing will be transmitted. Even if, following Neisser (1967), we suppose that the preliminary operations associated with the preattentive processes (prior to the more elaborate processing associated with focal attention) yield only segregated figural units, units that lack the richness of information available in those portions of the field to which attention is given, there is (I suggest) more information embodied in these figural units than we, as subjects, normally extract: information about the spacing, number, and relative size and position of the objects represented. Typically the output of our sensory systems overloads the information-handling capacity of our cognitive centers so that not all that is given to us in perception can be digested. The rule of seven (Miller, 1956) applies to cognition, not to perception: to the information *we* can absorb, not to the information our sensory system can absorb and transmit. If it applied to perception one would expect a sky with 10 visible stars to look the same (to generate the same precept) as one with 10,000 visible stars, and it clearly does not.[6]

Taking a cue from the tachistoscopic experiments described above, consider the following thought experiment (I do not know whether anything resembling it has been performed). Imagine yourself viewing a field containing 45 discrete objects. Recently, for example, I found myself observing an American flag manufactured around the turn of the century. It contained (as I later determined) 45 stars. Was this numerical information available to me in my percept during my first, casual, inspection of the flag? Clearly, *I* did not have this information; quite the contrary, I thought there were 48 (or perhaps 50) stars on the flag. Was this information nonetheless contained in my percept? If so, in what sense? Suppose I viewed the flag in such a way that a faint after-image was created when I turned away. Suppose, furthermore, that this after-image was projected into a carefully contrived background consisting of 45 dots spaced in such a way that each dot fell within the area of a projected star. Suppose, finally, that I could tell immediately that no star's after-image was without an enclosed dot, and no dot lacked an enclosing image (by "immediately" I mean "before the after-image faded"). We can now (knowing how many dots were on the background) say with some confidence that the after-image contained exactly 45 discrete elements. What does this tell us about the original percept? It tells us, I suggest, that our original percept of the flag contained this numerical information about the number of stars on the flag, information that I failed to extract and would, in normal circumstances, find almost impossible to extract without counting. Still, there is a clear sense in which the visual system made this information available to me, the same sense in which the tachistoscopic experiments showed that information about the unidentified letters was nonetheless available to the subjects.

Consider finally (and very briefly) an example from developmental studies. Eleanor Gibson (1969), in reporting Klüver's studies with monkeys, describes a case in which the animals were trained to the larger of the two rectangles. When the rectangles were altered in size the monkeys continued to respond to the larger of the two rectangles—whatever their absolute size happened to be. In the words of Klüver (Gibson, p. 284): "If a monkey reacts to stimuli which can be characterized as belonging to a large number of different 'dimensions', and if in doing so he reacts consistently in terms of one relation, let us say, in terms of the 'larger-than' relation, he may be said to 'abstract'." Klüver's monkeys succeeded in "abstracting" the larger-than relation. But how shall we describe the perceptual situation *before* they learned to abstract this relation? Did the rectangles *look* different? If not, how could the monkeys ever learn to distinguish between them? It seems natural enough to say in a situation of this sort that prior to learning, prior to success in abstracting the appropriate relation, the monkey's percepts embodied the information that they only later succeeded in extracting. In such a case there is certainly learning taking place, but I see no reason to suppose that there is any change in perception, any change in the percept, any change in the information *available to* the monkeys. And if one thinks of *perceptual* learning, as it is common to think of it (Epstein, 1967), as the modification of the percept as the result of repeated experience, I see no reason to think of this as a case of *perceptual* learning at all. Indeed, a great many instances of so-called perceptual learning seem to me to be obviously cases of learning, but just as obviously *not* cases of perceptual change.

The situation becomes even clearer if we present our monkeys with three rectangles and try to get them to abstract the "intermediate-size" relation. This more difficult problem proved capable of solution by chimpanzees (Gibson, p. 292), but let us suppose our monkeys are incapable of solving the problem. Once again, what shall we say about the perceptual situation? Since the monkeys have abstracted the "larger-than" relation, the three rectangles must look different to them; the intermediate rectangle looks smaller than the larger one and it looks larger than the smaller one. But the information about which rectangle is intermediate, though obviously available in the percept itself, is not, and apparently *cannot* be, extracted by the monkey.[7] Here is an instance in which the difference between *perception*, the kind of sensory information *available* to the organism, and *cognition*, the kind of information *actually extracted* from that which is made available, is most obvious and compelling.

In conclusion, let me simply say that the idea of a percept is a functional notion, but only in an indirect way. It is functional in the same way a library with too many books for anyone ever to read is functional. It is functional in that it defines the informational upper limit of what can be functional. But if, in our efforts to understand perception, we restrict ourselves to what *is* functional, we shall be missing most of what is fundamental and characteristic of perception itself.[8] We shall, I suggest, be neglecting what it is about perception that makes it, in contrast to its discursive and cognitive consequences, so rich, concrete, and informationally profuse. Just as most libraries contain more than we can ever take from them, we perceive more than we will, or can, ever know.

Notes

1. The causal theory of perception, understood as a philosophical theory about the meaning or truth conditions for the statement that S percieves O, makes the existence of such a causal dependence between O and S a *necessary consequence* of the fact that S perceives O. See Grice (1961), pp. 121 ff.

2. The experiments I have in mind are those demonstrating the "Honi" phenomenon and those with a trapezoidal window and intersecting bar, in which perceptual differences emerged as a result of different assumptions about the rigidity of the bar.

3. I have heard it said that vaccination produced memory. Apparently this was to be called memory because the subject's response to some later, similar event (exposure to smallpox) was modified as a result of his previous exposure. The subject "learned" something. The subject may, of course, remember the inoculation, but his immunity to smallpox is not itself a case of memory. Or, if it is to be called memory, then tempered metals, watered lawns, and sun-tanned skin have very good memories indeed. I have no objection to speaking of this as a kind of memory, but I think it should be carefully distinguished from the kind of memory we mean to describe when we say that the subject (not just his body) remembers being inoculated.

4. It should be noted that the usefulness of the response to the organism as a whole (the appropriateness of the response) does not itself confer on the internal informational state that generates that response a *perceptual* status. Even if Os were dangerous predators and cheek-twitching tended to frighten them away, this would not mean that our subjects thereby perceived Os. What is required is that the response (whether useful or not) *be* a response of the system as a whole, that it be generated, in part at least, *by* the needs or desires of the system whose perceptual capacities are in question.

5. If we take time into account there is also information embodied in the bimetal strip about the rate of change of temperature, information that thermostats are not designed to extract. Unlike human subjects, they are not properly wired to allow them to "shift attention" to this additional piece of information; hence this piece of information is not available to them in the way analogous information is available to human subjects.

6. J. R. Pierce (1961, pp. 248-49) makes a similar point in discussing the information processing capacity of subjects:

Now, Miller's law and the reading rate experiments have embarrassing implications. If a man gets only 27 bits of information from a picture, can we transmit by means of 27 bits of information a picture which, when flashed on a screen, will satisfactorily imitate any picture? If a man can transmit only about 40 bits of information per second as the reading rate experiments indicate, can we transmit TV or voice of satisfactory quality using only 40 bits per second? In each case I believe the answer to be no. What is wrong? What is wrong is that we have measured what gets *out* of the human being, not what goes *in*. Perhaps a human being can in some sense only notice 40 bits/sec. worth of information, but he has a choice as to what he notices. He might, for instance, notice the girl or he might notice the dress. Perhaps he notices more, but it gets away from him before he can describe it.

7. If the monkey *cannot* extract the information, in what sense is it *available* to the monkey? The same sense in which information about *all* the letters in the array was available to the subjects in the experiments of Sperling, Averbach, and Coriell (although the subjects *could* not extract *all* this information), and in the same sense in which the information about the number of stars was available to me in my thought experiment (although I could not extract this information during brief inspection). Our conviction that this information was available to the monkeys, in their percepts, is based on our knowledge that the information that was available (relating to the "larger than" relationship) required (logically) the availability of the information about which rectangle was of intermediate size. That is, if we grant that the information that A is larger than B, and that B is larger than C, is available to the monkey in his perception of the rectangles, we are committed to treating the information that B is intermediate in size as also available. This is simply to say that the context "Information——is available to S" is transparent to substitution of logically equivalent expressions, whereas the context "S knows that——" is not.

8. Dennett (1969, p. 78) denies *content* to all those elements in (what I am calling) the percept for which there is no "demonstrably appropriate chain between the afferent and the efferent." As I understand this, Dennett is denying any content to the perceptual experience other than that which is somehow extracted by the organism for use in determining its motor responses. I think this is an unfortunate restriction in the idea of "content" and represents a mistaken conflation of perception with recognition (or cognition).

References

Averbach, E., & Coriell, A. S. Short-term memory in vision. *Bell System Technical Journal*, 1961, 40, 309-328.

Dennett, D. C. *Content and consciousness*. London: Routledge & Kegan Paul, 1969.

Engen, T. Psychophysics. In J. W. Kling & Lorin A. Riggs (Eds.), Woodworth and Schlosberg's *Experimental psychology* (3rd ed.). New York: Holt, Rinehart and Winston, 1972.

Epstein, W. *Varieties of perceptual learning*. New York: McGraw-Hill, 1967.

Fodor, J. *Psychological explanation*. New York: Random House, 1968.

Garner, W. Hake, H. & Eriksen, C. Operationism and the concept of perception. In Peter A. Fried (Ed.), *Readings in perception: Principle and practice*. Lexington, Mass.: D. C. Heath and Co., 1974. (Reprinted from *Psychological Review*, 1956, 63.)

Gibson, E. *Principles of perceptual learning and development*. New York: Appleton Century Crofts, 1969.

Gibson, J. *The perception of the visual world*. Boston: Houghton Mifflin Company, 1950.

Gibson, J. *The senses considered as perceptual systems*. New York: Houghton Mifflin, 1966.

Grice, P. The causal theory of perception. *Proceedings of the Aristotelian Society, Supplementary Volume XXXV*, 1961.

Hebb, D. O. *A textbook of psychology* (2nd ed.) Philadelphia: Saunders, 1966.

Johansson, G. Visual motion perception. *Scientific American*, 6 June 1975, 232, 76-88.

Kilpatrick, F. P. *Human behavior from the transactional point of view*. Washington, D.C.: Department of the Navy, 1952.

Miller, G. A. The Magic Number seven, plus or minus two: Some limits on our capacity for processing information. *Psychological Review*, 1956, 63, 81-97.

Neisser, Ulric. *Cognitive Psychology*. New York: Appleton Century Crofts, 1967.

Pierce, J. R. *Symbols, signals and noise*. New York: Harper & Row, 1961.

Pitcher, George. *A theory of perception*. Princeton, N.J.: Princeton University Press, 1971.

Rock, I. *An introduction to perception*. New York: Macmillan, 1975.

Rundle, B. *Perception, sensation and verification*. Oxford: Clarendon Press, 1972.

Sperling, G. The information available in brief visual presentations. *Psychological Monographs*, 1960, 74 (11).

Steinfeld, G. J. Concepts of set and availability and their relation to the reorganization of ambiguous pictorial stimuli. *Psychological Review*, 1967, 75 (6), 505-522.

Swets, J. Tanner, W., & Birdsall, T. Decision processes in perception. *Psychological Review*, 1961, 68, 301-340.

Warren, R. M. Perceptual restoration of missing speech sounds. *Science*, 1970, 167, 392-393.

—— JAMES J. JENKINS, JERRY WALD, AND JOHN B. PITTENGER ——

Apprehending Pictorial Events:
An Instance of Psychological Cohesion

Much of contemporary experimental psychology concerns the modeling of how people process information, whether it be information contained in a text or on a Go board. For modeling to be successful, a complementary task must be accomplished: the specification of the units of analysis. Specification of the units of analysis and the processes that operate on them are interdependent endeavors, and both depend in turn on the problem area under study.

In some psychological research, the specification of appropriate units does not seem to be a problem. For example, if one models the earlier stages of reading, distinctive features of letters, individual letters, and words suggest themselves as units (or data) to be processed (e.g., Gough, 1972). When one models a particular reading task or the acquisition of reading as a skill, one may begin to determine which units are functionally important, and when and how they are used (e.g., LaBerge & Samuels, 1974. For other examples, see several of the papers in Kavanagh & Mattingly, 1972).

Note: The research reported in this paper was supported by grants to the Center for Research in Human Learning, University of Minnesota from the National Science Foundation (GB 17590), The National Insititue for Child Health and Human Development (HD 01136), and the Graduate School, University of Minnesota. The second author is a predoctoral trainee of the National Institute for Child Health and Human Development under Training Grant, HD 00098. The third author expresses thanks to the University of Arkansas for a travel grant that made collaboration possible. The authors are happy to express their appreciation to Martin Wurthman and Vincent Berg, who helped with the photographic work involved in these studies. The debt the authors owe to Robert Shaw for intellectual stimulation and inspiration is evident throughout the paper; it is gratefully acknowledged. We are also grateful to the following colleagues for criticism and comments: C. Bremer, L. Brownston, D. LaBerge, L. Larkey, K. McGovern, S. Soli, W. Strange, and G. Widin.

In other research domains, however, the units of analysis are more obscure. For example, Jenkins (1974a, 1974b) suggests that both the kinds of units and the kinds of processes involved in verbal recall and recognition change with variations in the nature of the material to be remembered and the orienting task being performed by the subject. The result of this state of affairs is that processing models are harder to specify. Visual perception, with which we shall be concerned in this paper, is another such domain of uncertainty. In the past, several kinds of units have been proposed, ranging from punctate stimuli to the holistic visual Gestalt. Associated with these units are pattern recognition devices and processing models that rely on analysis-by-synthesis routines, template matches, or the like (see Neisser, 1967). However, neither these units nor the processing models based on them seem adequate. As Neisser (1967) points out, they encounter difficult problems (such as orienting or normalizing the input stimuli) and are not always compelling as psychological models of visual processing or visual perception.

It is our aim to suggest another way to proceed. Rather than relying on neutral stimuli or forms as our basic units, we propose to adopt an ecological approach to the problem. In what follows we shall regard the *event* as primary. At the outset, we shall use the term only in its intuitive sense. We cannot at this time give a satisfactory definition of what an event is. We believe that with sufficient experimental and theoretical work, however, the concept will find an increasingly adequate definition. (Shaw and Pittenger, in press, have made first steps in this direction.)

We have taken the intuitive approach for two reasons. First, we acknowledge that events exist at several levels. One might point to microscopic events (such as chemical changes), to ecological events (such as the sun's rising), or to astronomical events (such as the expansion of the universe). Furthermore, events are usually embedded in other events. Consider one's taking one's seat to listen to the first movement of a Brahms symphony during a Brahms-Beethoven-Bach Festival. Because events are nested within events (as one's sitting down is a subevent within the overall event of the festival) and because of the related problems posed by multiple levels of analysis (e.g., the detailed analysis of the first movement of a Brahms symphony versus the more general analysis of the symphonic structure itself), finding one set of defining properties that cuts across all manner of events presents formidable difficulties.

Second, we believe that the intuitive notion of an event can be specified more closely only when we know what supports (or specifies) an event to a perceiving organism. In this paper we are concerned with visual events, so we shall focus on those characteristics that support the perception of events in the visual world. We shall report some beginning studies of the apprehension of visual events. As we go along, certain psychological consequences of having perceived an event will become apparent and certain characteristics of the stimuli that make event perception possible will begin to be seen.

This paper, then, is a first attempt to lift ourselves by our empirical bootstraps to a position from which we may see the nature of various ecological units more clearly. With such information in hand, the complementary task of modeling the apprehension of visual events should also be clarified.

Events: Some Initial Considerations

For our present purposes we may regard events as pertaining to both objects and the changes (or transformations) defined over objects. We must note, however, that although objects and transformations are conceptually distinct, they are not independent of one another. Objects, for example, may be in part defined as those "things" or properties left invariant under certain transformations, such as translation. It is best, perhaps, to regard objects and transformations as two aspects of an event.

To help clarify this view we may recall some properties of objects that are said to be conserved under certain transformations, properties that contribute to our meaning of *object*. Consider, for example, the Piagetian experiments on "conservation." The point of the experiments for our purposes is not that properties are invariant (or conserved) under all possible changes that may occur; indeed, the point is just the opposite. Some properties are conserved under some types of changes or alterations, and those properties left invariant contribute to our meaning of the object within the situation. For example, *number* of marbles is conserved over various spatial arrangements of the marbles, but it is not conserved over the operation of running the marbles through a grinder or smashing them with a sledgehammer. *Volume* of a liquid is conserved over various transformations of shapes of containers, but it is not conserved over evaporation, loss through spilling, addition of more liquid, drinking some of the liquid, etc. *Amount* of matter is conserved over translation, reshaping, amalgamation, and subdivision, but not over burning, addition, subtraction, eating, dissolving, etc. It is precisely the relation between the type of change and the relevant property of concern that is being investigated in such experiments. For the sophisticated organism the crucial perception is that the operations performed on the material in question do or do not constitute a type of change that affects the property, and hence the object, whose invariance is at test. It makes no sense at all to talk about the conservation of number, volume, or matter without talking about the nature of the changes involved.

In the above examples it is easy to lose sight of the importance of the transformational aspect of an event; the object and its properties seem to predominate. But the importance of change cannot be overlooked. In many domains we know that the rate of change itself is a critical determiner of perception. Michotte's classic experiments demonstrate that the relative rates of movement of two objects striking one another determine whether the event is seen as "entraining," "launching," or "triggering" (Michotte, 1963). And in other domains it is the "style" of change that not only specifies the nature of the event but also the nature of the object under change. Johansson (1975) has made elegant motion pictures of "point-light people" that show the power of change in the configuration of lights over time. These films were made in the dark and show only the patterns of movement and the disappearance and appearance of point-light sources mounted at the joints of the human subjects being pictured (shoulders, elbows, wrists, hips, knees, and ankles, with a single light at the crown of the head). In a static frame of the film, an observer sees nothing but an unorganized jangle of lights. In the running film the moving patterns of lights are sufficient not only to specify the actions of walking, running, dancing, approaching, receding, and transversing, but they enable the observer to specify that the moving "object" is a human of a particular sex.[1]

What is crucial, then, is the nature of the change as well as the object and its properties left invariant under the change, for these jointly influence (if not determine) the quality of the event that is perceived. Only the two aspects taken together can make the event cohere.

Some Experiments on Pictorial Events

Many years ago, Esper (1925) published an experiment that demonstrated that people may learn more than they have experienced. He presented subjects with pictures of four forms, each of which appeared in four different colors, and required the subjects to learn the names that he had systematically paired with the colored forms. The labeling system was such that the shape of the form determined the first syllable of the name and the color of the form determined the second syllable. Instead of presenting all 16 instances of the colored forms, however, Esper withheld two particular instances. Following training on the 14 items, he tested all 16 items in a naming test. He found that the subjects correctly named the two new items when they were presented. Surprisingly, the subjects could not even say which items were old and which items were new. Thus Esper demonstrated that when there is a systematic relation between stimulus variation and response variation, subjects may learn the complete system of relations even though they do not see all the members, and that once they learn the *system*, they may not even know which instances they have seen and which they have not.

Esper's study is not just a selected curiosity; many studies of the Esper sort have been conducted (see Esper, 1975, for an extensive account), and this result is frequently found. In attempting to explain the Esper results, one is forced to conclude that subjects go beyond the learning of the finite set of stimuli with which they have been presented. That is, the stimuli that are presented to the subjects appear to specify a system of relations within which the individual stimuli cohere. Furthermore, these relations apparently specify additional stimuli that were not in fact shown. In some experiments (e.g., Foss, 1968) the additional stimuli were recognized as belonging to the system of relations and were correctly named, but the additional stimuli were also usually recognized as being new. In other cases (e.g., Segal, 1962) the new stimuli were recognized as belonging and correctly named but were not distinguished from the training stimuli; i.e., the subjects did not know that the stimuli were new. The first case (the Foss experiment) may be called *co-herence*, and the second case (the Segal experiment) may be called *fusion*. It will be seen that coherence is the general case and fusion is the special case observed when specific memory for exemplars is lost or overwhelmed by the constraints of the system.

Although Foss's and Segal's data appear inconsistent, the inconsistency is more apparent than real. The difference in their findings points instead to a critical distinction, a distinction to which we shall repeatedly return. The distinction is this: when presented with any set of related stimuli (i.e., coherent stimuli), subjects may acquire two forms of knowledge—knowledge of the particular stimuli experienced and knowledge of the underlying coherent system of relations. The first may be said to be concerned with the experimental setting itself as an event (e.g., with the particular materials and tasks at hand) and the second with the system as an event. Consequently any experimental outcome will be some product of both of these bases of knowledge, the contribution of each to any particular situation being determined by a host of factors.

We should also note that the characteristic findings of Esper, Foss, and Segal are not limited to their particular experimental paradigm; analogous findings obtain with other procedures and materials. Several experimental examples might be cited (Franks & Bransford, 1971; Posner & Keele, 1968, 1970; Strange, Keeney, Kessel, & Jenkins, 1970), but for our present purposes the conclusions from one such study may suffice. Wilson, Wellman, and Shaw (reported in Shaw & Wilson, 1975) used a system in which four simple geometric forms were orbited around the four corners of a square. From the total set of 16 stimuli two subsets were selected: one subset constituted a generator set; when presented to subjects these stimuli and their transformational relations were sufficient to specify the total set of 16 stimuli. The second subset was not a generator—i.e., it could not specify the complete system. One group of subjects saw the generator subset; another group saw the nongenerator subset. The subsets were presented only once. Following this presentation, each group was given a recognition test consisting of all 16 stimuli plus 9 control items. Only the group seeing the generator set falsely recognized the appropriate new items, items that belonged to the coherent system specified by the original generator set. Shaw and Wilson (1975) concluded that what one remembers depends upon the generative power of the set of instances to which the subject has been exposed. In short, as Garner (1974) has noted, experimental subjects do not deal in some simple fashion with only the stimuli that the experimenter presents. Clearly they respond on the basis of a set of possibilities that the presented stimuli may be said to define or generate.

These findings seem at odds with much recent work that implies that visual memory is precise and virtually unlimited. Shepard (1967) and Standing and his colleagues (Standing, 1973; Standing, Conezio, & Haber, 1970; also see Haber, 1970) have demonstrated that if subjects are shown large numbers of slides (up to 2,000), they can identify them with high accuracy on a forced-choice recognition test. (Subjects are asked to choose the slide they have seen before when an old slide is paired with a new slide). Standing (1973) has carried this demonstration to the extreme of 10,000 slides presented over a period of five days. He found high accuracy of recognition for sample sets of these slides and estimated total retention as 6,600 items. Postman (1975) was so impressed by this demonstration that he offers it as evidence to "anyone who doubts that pictures are easy to remember" (p. 322).

Obviously these results are in striking contrast to the findings of Esper and the data obtained by Shaw and Wilson for their visual materials. With unrelated visual materials, memory for pictures seems virtually unlimited and precise. With just a few systematically related slides, on the other hand, memory for particular instances of visual displays is poor. One may, of course, attribute the conflicting results to differences in experimental paradigms (forced-choice recognition versus a variety of other operations); indeed, some of the difference may reside in the sensitivity of the forced-choice technique, but we believe that a major difference in outcomes is attributable to a radical difference in stimulus materials. In the experiments with arrays of forms, colors, patterns, etc., the stimuli form a system, some kind of coherent whole that the subject apprehends. In the experiments with massive numbers of slides, every effort is made to keep the pictures unrelated; i.e., each slide is a slice of a separate event, unassimilated and unassimilable except as a discrete event in itself. Such a slide, then, constitutes an event with a frequency of one exposure that is later to be compared with some other slide, another unique event, that has a frequency of zero in the subject's experience. Put in this way, the recognition of large numbers of slides may not seem to be such a dramatic feat as we had first supposed. Perhaps we should have suspected some such performances, given the older literature on frequency effects. In many identification and recognition tasks there is a sharp discontinuity in familiarity between a stimulus that has been experienced once and a stimulus that has never been experienced. As long as the events stay separate and unique and have frequencies of zero or one, there is little remarkable about knowing which is which.

Shepard's work, in fact, suggests that frequency of exposure was important in achieving the results mentioned earlier. In another experiment, he discovered that the high accuracy of recognition of selected pictures was lost if *pairs* of slides were originally presented to subjects who were asked to remember only one of the two slides. In this case both of the slides now had an exposure frequency of one, and the subjects no longer performed with high accuracy on a forced-choice recognition test that asked them to pick from the two slides the one they were supposed to learn. One possible interpretation is that picture memory itself is not being tested in these experiments; the experiments may be testing for the recognition of events one has formerly experienced (even though in impoverished form) as opposed to events one has not previously experienced. (But, as we shall see, this cannot be the whole story.)

Striking evidence that effects are different when the pictures to be remembered bear some relation to each other is found in a study by Goldstein and Chance (1970). These investigators discovered that memory for pictures was seriously impaired when the pictures were all of the same genre: all ink blots, all faces, or all snowflakes. In sharp contrast to the high accuracy of recognition usually observed for unrelated pictures, and in spite of the very modest number presented to a subject (only 14 exemplars of one of the three classes), the results in a "yes-no" recognition test showed 28% errors on faces, 49% errors on ink blots, and (despite their legendary differences in form) a whopping 64% errors on snowflakes. Thus, when the "experimental event" becomes one of viewing related, though highly differentiated and discriminable, members of a class of objects, a decrement of absolute recognition is observed.

Perhaps a *gedanken* experiment is appropriate at this point. Suppose we take a motion picture film as our visual display. If we show a portion of the film consisting of some simple event, we can assume that observers will report having witnessed that event. Now suppose we take all the odd-numbered frames of the film and splice them together, and all the even-numbered frames and splice them together. If we show the odd-numbered sequence to an observer and then show him the even-numbered sequence, he will almost certainly report that he is seeing the same thing, namely, a somewhat "jumpy" movie of a single event. We would be surprised if he reported that he had never seen the second film before, although in the technical, physical sense, he has not.

The *gedanken* experiment suggests a continuum of relatedness running from the intact movie on one end, through a series of frames with an increasing number of intervening frames removed, to the presentation of a series of scenes of isolated events of the Shepard, Haber, and Standing variety on the other end. Reflecting on this potential continuum enticed us to approach the event perception problem through a series of still pictures which were in themselves separate and distinct enough that the question of their confusability would not arise but that, taken together, presented a dynamic event: something like a picture story or a slide show that tells a story.

The question we posed was the following: If a subject saw an appropriately ordered sequence of pictures that was sufficient to give him all the necessary information for an event, would he give us evidence that he had experienced that event in its entirety? Would he, for example, falsely recognize pictures of the event that he had not seen before? Would he be able to reject pictures that were highly similar to the pictures he had seen but that violated some invariant of the event or some detail of the observation?[2]

We decided to begin with some natural but simple, everyday events: a woman making a cup of tea, a teenage girl answering the telephone, and, as one kind of control event, some pictures of people at a party. The first two cases clearly told a story. In the first, the woman standing beside a table in a dining room unwrapped a tea bag and put it in a cup on the table. She left the room and returned with a sugar bowl, which she put on the table. She left again and returned with a tea kettle from which she poured water into the cup. She then returned the kettle to the kitchen, came back into the room, sat down at the table, removed the tea bag from the cup, added sugar, and took a cautious sip of tea. Pictures were taken from a fixed station point, with the camera oriented so that the woman was always near the center of the picture.

In the second event, pictures were again taken from a fixed station point. A girl appeared in the doorway, crossed the room, and picked up the phone. She talked for a few moments while standing, then sat at the desk on which the phone rested, put her feet up on the desk, smiled and laughed, put her feet down, and hung up the phone.

The third sequence of slides *could* have been construed to make a loose story, but the pictures were taken from two different station points and no particular story was apparent. A graduate student was seen arriving at a party, walking across a room, sitting on a couch with other students, talking to a visitor (who was also shown alone). Several new people came and went from subsequent pictures, which were mainly of a single corner of the room.

In each situation, "control" pictures were taken. For the Tea Sequence, additional pictures were taken with a new brightly-colored object on the table with the tea things, with the woman wearing glasses, with the woman pouring water with her left hand instead of her right, with the camera very close to the table, and with the camera at a new station point across the table. Control pictures for the Telephone Sequence involved changes in distance of the camera from the girl, a station point diagonally across the room so that the direction of the girl's walk was from right to left instead of from left to right, and different postures at the desk with the phone. Controls for the Party Sequence were other pictures of the party from the same station points. The pictures involved the same people but they were in different postures and different combinations.

These pictures were presented to subjects in the following fashion: For each sequence the original series of pictures was shown except that every third picture in the sequence was removed. For example, in the Tea Sequence, 26 pictures had been taken. In the initial presentation the subjects were shown pictures 1, 2, 4, 5, 7, 8, 10, 11, etc. up to 26. Each slide was shown for about five seconds. This presentation was then repeated to ensure that subjects were familiar with the pictures. At this point subjects were told they would see a test series of pictures. They were asked to indicate which pictures they had seen before. Subjects were then shown a random series of slides consisting of 8 of the original pictures (Originals), the 8 pictures that belonged in the series but that had not been shown (Belonging slides), and 8 slides that did not fit the sequence (Controls). For the Telephone Sequence, 10 slides were presented initially. The test series consisted of 4 Originals, 4 Belonging slides, and 4 Controls. For the Party Series, 10 slides were presented for learning. The test series consisted of 4 Originals, 5 slides that could have been used to make a loose story (Belonging slides?), and 3 Controls.

It should be noted that this experiment is a very strong test of our hypothesis. Our fundamental assumption is that if the pictures show an event taking place over time, the subjects will apprehend the event. For our first test to work successfully a further assertion is necessary, namely, that having apprehended the event, the subject will be unable to reject a picture that fits the specifications of the event he has experienced. This is in spite of the fact that the two presentations in original learning ought to ensure specific memory of the slides. Thus we must argue that specific memory for individual pictures will be outweighed by the abstract or general memory for the event experienced. At the same time we shall argue that some aspects of memory will be enhanced; specifically, that any picture that violates the constraints or invariants of the experienced event will be detected as new, no matter how much it resembles the original pictures in terms of its elements.

The results of the experiments were very gratifying. For the Tea Sequence 80% of the Originals were recognized as originals, 50% of the Belonging slides were falsely called originals, and only 10% of the Controls were falsely called originals. This clearly demonstrates that false positive recognitions can be obtained for new slides when they fit the overall constraints of the experienced event. The fact that the subjects detected the Controls as being new is evidence both that they were attending to the event and that they were sensitive to the particular details of the event they had experienced.

Results for the Telephone Sequence convincingly corroborated the findings of the Tea Sequence. Ninety-four percent of the Originals were recognized as being originals and 42% of the Belonging slides were falsely called originals, but only 3% of the Controls were called originals.

As we had expected, the Party scenes yielded results different from those of the Tea Sequence and Telephone Sequence events. The Party results were much more in agreement with the traditional picture memory studies discussed above; Originals were correctly recognized as originals 83% of the time and Belonging and Control slides were falsely called originals less than 10% of the time. There were very few false positive recognitions.

A reasonable interpretation of these data seems to be that events can be (and are) apprehended when they are available in pictorial stimuli and that apprehension of the event has a marked effect on subsequent recognition behavior. Further, it seems appropriate to talk about "experiencing the event." The Control slides showed us that subjects were quite sensitive to the invariant details of an event. As one example, consider the station point of the camera. Subjects correctly identified as *new* any slide portraying the event from a station point or distance other than the one shown during the original presentation of the event, even though the slide was accurate with respect to all other details. A second example occurred in the Telephone Sequence, in which the only picture of the girl smiling happened to fall into the Belonging group of slides. Almost all subjects rejected this slide even though it was like the original sequence in all other respects. That is, they were extremely sensitive to the display of emotion on the face and correctly knew that they had not seen any such display during the course of the event they had witnessed.

As we went on to further studies, we were impressed with the sharp contrast between the effects seen in these experiments as compared to the studies of isolated pictures. First, recall that the traditional studies that used hundreds or thousands of isolated, unrelated pictures obtained their high levels of picture recognition with only one presentation of the stimulus set. In our studies of coherent events, in spite of the fact that the 10 to 20 slides were shown twice, we consistently obtained high levels of *false* recognition for the Belonging slides. Second, as mentioned above, the studies of isolated pictures are sensitive to frequency effects; once a subject has seen the pictures used as "lures" in the recognition test, his ability to discriminate original pictures from such lures is greatly reduced. This appears not to be the case with pictorial events, as our next experiments showed.

In one classroom experiment we presented the Tea Sequence twice at the beginning of class and then tested for recognition at the end of class. On the next class day we explained that we were going to do exactly the same experiment again, and we performed the experiment in the identical manner. Again on the third class day we performed another exact repetition. The results on all three days were virtually identical with the results we obtained on the single administration. Subjects got neither better nor worse. Apparently the information from the event was virtually complete with the original two showings; repeated exposures of the Originals, Belonging, and Control slides made little or no difference. The Belonging pictures that were originally judged to belong to the class of original pictures continued to be so assigned, and those that were not so judged at the start were not later on. Whatever kept these latter slides from being perceived as belonging to the event continued to prevent their false positive recognition. Similarly, reexposure of the Controls did not contribute to their false recognition; they were still clearly seen as *not* belonging to the event, and their repeated exposure did not change that categorization.

Anticipating the criticism that perhaps the waiting period (the 45-minute class period) disadvantaged the subjects in this experiment and prevented them from using "fresh" visual images even after they truly understood the task, we performed a replication of the repeated trials experiment in another class. In this case the procedure was the same except that the test series immediately followed the original learning series on each of the three days. The results were the same as in the earlier experiment; Belonging slides that were initially falsely recognized continued to be so, but Controls were consistently rejected. When we analyzed the responses to each slide over the three days, however, we did see an interesting trend in the Belonging slides. The eight slides in this category were divided evenly into four slides that the majority of the subjects thought had been in the original series, and four slides that the majority thought had not been in the original series. On successive trials these slides tended to polarize; i.e., the accepted slides became even more widely accepted and the unaccepted slides became even less well accepted.[3] This suggests that even though the event is well defined on the first occasion, it may become even better specified with repeated exposures.

Further Explorations

The major conclusion we draw from the studies we have just described is that events can be primary units of analysis. We can specify events with a sequence of slides and influence subjects' recognition responses when they perceive the coherence of the events. In this way our results resemble those of Esper (1925), and Shaw and Wilson (1976). When the experimenter specifies the structure of a system with a set of systematically related stimuli, subjects learn (or "pick up") that system. However, in the case of pictorial events, what is the nature of the relations that specify the event? An obvious, but overly simple, suggestion is that it is the raw physical similarity of the slides in the original set that makes them cohere. We have already seen that this cannot be the whole story, given the way we constructed our Control slides and the data we obtained from them. The next studies shed additional light on this suggestion.

In the next set of studies, we randomized the original order of presentation for each of the three picture sequences we discussed above. We predicted, of course, that the randomization would do nothing whatsoever to the recognition performance of our subjects in the Party Sequence. Since no event was picked up when the pictures were shown in their original sequence, there was no reason to suppose that an event would be created by their randomization. We predicted specific picture recognition as before, and that is exactly what we observed. The results for the Party pictures duplicated those of the first experiment.

We did not know what to predict for the organized events. One might suppose that some events are so intrinsically ordered that any presentation of details can be correctly ordered by the observer. If this is the case, the event will be apprehended in spite of random ordering (especially because the slides are presented twice prior to the recognition test.) Further, Garner (1974) argues that any subset of slides will specify a set of alternatives. Thus, while original order is lost, rather considerable constraints will remain as to the set of possible slides that the subject might have seen. If the information is coherent enough to specify the nature of the event, that may be sufficient to determine the same pattern of false positives for the Belonging slides that we had seen on the ordered presentation. On the other hand, if the event is intrinsically only weakly ordered or if it is time-dependent, perhaps the specific memory for individual pictures will be manifest.

Fortunately for the stimulation of future research, both of these outcomes were observed. The Tea Sequence pictures, even though randomly presented, yielded the same results observed above; about half the responses to Belonging slides were false positives, but Control slides were rejected. When the Telephone Sequence was presented randomly, however, the test series yielded high recognition responses only to the Original slides, with almost no false positives for the Belonging slides or the Control slides. Although we cannot at this time specify the source of the coherence of the Tea Sequence as opposed to the Telephone Sequence, we see such specification as an attractive research possibility.

The fact that the Telephone series breaks down when it is presented in random order is useful in that it furnishes valuable information about the role of picture similarity. Obviously similarity between individual pictures could not be the source of the false positives that were originally observed for the Belonging slides in this sequence. If the false positives had been due simply to picture similarity, there is no reason for the order of presentation to make any difference at all. It is tempting to think that the Telephone Sequence is close to some critical point on the continuum between the split movie and the array of isolated events discussed above. The set of pictures is apprehended as a coherent event when the appropriate order of presentation is followed, but the individual pictures are so dissimilar that they are perceived as a set of unrelated pictures when the order is scrambled. Thus order in time is an important source of information in specifying possible alternatives, at least for some events.[4]

These early experiments were crudely done with a hand-held household camera and with very little precision as to timing of the photographs, lighting, specification of the station point, etc. Given their promising outcomes, we decided to simplify our events and improve the technical quality of the materials. From these new experiments a few examples will show that the phenomena can be enhanced impressively.

One of the best series we have done to date is called Orbiting. This series shows an octagonal tray sitting on a black background. In the center of the tray is a large jam jar. The various pictures show the tray and jar immobile while a small saltcellar moves from one position to another around the rim of the tray through each vertex and each midpoint between vertices. Sixteen pictures make up the series and complete the orbit. The learning series was prepared by drawing randomly two slides from every subset of three ordered slides (so that the missing slides would not be periodic). As before, the sequence was shown twice. The subjects were then tested on five slides from the Original series, five Belonging slides, and five Control slides that violated some aspect of the experience of the event (distance, perspective, relation of the saltcellar to the rim, reversal of jar and saltcellar, missing objects). The effect was very striking. Subjects correctly recognized Original slides as originals 89% of the time. They incorrectly identified Belonging slides as originals 73% of the time (false positives) and *never* identified Control slides as originals (zero false positives). It is interesting to note that four of the Belonging slides are as well accepted as the actual originals. Most of the detection of a Belonging slide as a new slide occurred on one slide that showed the saltcellar emerging from behind the jam jar. This was the only picture in the series that showed partial occlusion of one object by another; this was apparently sufficiently important as a "subevent" that its distinctiveness was noted by most of the subjects.

This series illustrates how compelling the fusion process can be. The details that supported the apprehension of the event are almost completely lost or merged in the quality of overall event. One simply cannot believe that the Belonging slides are new because they are so much a part of the completely apprehended event. At the same time we can see that the test of event apprehension employed in these studies is too strong. All of the subjects knew that the slide showing occlusion belonged in the series, but they also knew they had not seen that particular instance *just because* it was a particularly distinctive portion of the event. It is in such cases that the difference between subjects' knowledge of the event and specific knowledge of what they have seen becomes apparent.

Fusion and the loss of memory for particular pictures is a phenomenon that serves to call our attention to the dominance of the event, but it is not a necessary phenomenon in that some specific knowledge of the specifying stimuli also occurs. Obviously we should be able to develop a variety of effective ways to explore the coherence of perceptual events. For example, if we were not interested in the subjects' knowledge of what was seen but were interested only in the coherence of the event and the subjects' knowledge of the quality of the event, a sufficient test would be to ask, "Does this picture belong in the event which you have just witnessed?" (rather than asking which slides had been seen before). (See Baggett, 1975 for some related research.)

Questions regarding both kinds of knowledge, particularly when asked of carefully constructed sequences and ingeniously selected Controls, should greatly enhance our understanding of the perception of events, the kinds of information that specify events, and the kinds of information that support the various qualities of the events we are interested in. The following incident is instructive. In examining the Control slides of the Orbiting series, we learned another aspect of what-is-perceived. Our camera man made one slide that fitted the series perfectly well but used a different position for the light sources. This slide is impressive because an observer knows immediately that it is not one of the series, but the source of the difference is not apparent for some time. Then one suddenly becomes aware that the shadows are wrong, something that almost no one would specify if asked to describe the picture. This points out again to us that any invariant in the situation can become an important cue to divergence. The invariants are accepted as the defining properties of the event or constraints on "what counts" in the pictures. One becomes aware of these invariants when they are violated, although they may not be given in the description of the event or even be available in consciousness (see Garner, 1974, for more on this point). It seems to us that the converse of this may also hold. If some aspect of the event varies freely in the learning series (e.g., the quality of lighting in the original Tea series), it is ruled out as a defining property of the event, and unless this variable reaches extreme values in the test series, it will be ignored. What is important here is that what is taken to be invariant or deviant for any event will be defined over the course of the event itself. In this sense events are self-defining, and they may be studied as such.

Studies bearing on the power of events to specify their own important characteristics have been carried out by Robert Kraft, who was interested in a special aspect of picture memory. Kraft pointed out to us that picture memory could hardly be images because left-right orientation was often not preserved. When Standing, Conezio, and Haber (1970) tested subjects for their knowledge of whether a slide was reversed or not, they found a marked drop in the accuracy of orientation information over 24 hours even though subjects were still highly accurate in identifying pictures they had seen against new pictures. In Kraft's own work on memory for orientation of human profiles he found virtually chance identification of the original left-right orientation, even when subjects were warned that they were going to be tested on orientation.

The point of view espoused in this paper suggests that it should be easy to enhance memory for orientation. If the event portrayed in a series of photographs had a natural movement through space that was an intrinsic part of the event, subjects should be able to remember orientation far above chance because orientation would be defined over (and hence a defining property of) the event. Kraft and Jenkins (1977) developed three picture sequences that portrayed events flowing to the left and to the right. Each event had both left-going and right-going actions, but these were part of the overall event in a natural way that made the orientation of objects and movements an integral part of the story. One story involved a boy and a girl. The girl dumped snow on the boy, the boy chased her and was about to hit her with a snowball. A second story showed a woman going out of the house to a shed, getting a box from the shed, and loading it in her car. The third story followed a girl to a skating rink and watched her put on her skates and then skate off across the pond into the distance.

One group of subjects saw these slides in their correct order and correct left-right orientation. They were then tested on a randomized set, half of which had been reversed in left-right orientation. The subjects were 94% correct in assigning the proper orientation to the slides. One group of subjects saw the slides in random order but with the proper orientation. These subjects apprehended the stories, despite the random order, and were 91% correct in assigning the correct orientation to the slides. A third group of subjects saw the slides in random order and with random orientation. (This group serves as a control for the memory for orientation of individual slides.) These subjects performed poorly when asked to designate original orientations; they were correct in only 67% of the cases. Thus, when orientation is an integral property of the event being portrayed, left-right orientation of test slides can be correctly designated. But when orientation is simply an arbitrary property of an individual slide, subjects are not very successful in remembering it.

As a further interesting variation, Kraft presented a group of subjects with the ordered set of slides in the correct orientations and then tested them on the orientation of Belonging slides (slides that fitted the stories but had not actually been presented). The subjects assigned the correct orientation to these new pictures 90% of the time. Kraft's work is both interesting in itself and suggestive of new directions for research and new methods of determining what subjects have learned about events.

Finally, one other direction of research must be mentioned. All the materials above have been developed from the perspective of the static observer, yet this is only one kind of visual experience giving rise to events. Information is also available over time to an observer who is moving through an environment (Gibson, 1966). Accordingly, we undertook an inverse experiment: the observer moving over the still landscape. The event in this case is a walk across a campus from the student union to the psychology building and back again. The pictures were taken early one Sunday morning and show the campus empty of people. Every 20 paces or so the walker (J.P.) took a photograph looking straight ahead on his walk. Control pictures were other scenes of the same campus, other pictures of some of the same buildings taken from positions off the walk, scenes taken along other walks at the university, etc.

The experiment presented a set of slides that "took the subjects for a walk," as described above, and a set of test slides that evaluated the subjects' ability to discriminate old from new slides among the Original, Belonging, and Control slides. In all but one respect, the procedure was similar to the procedures used above: the learning set was shown twice in the appropriate order, and uniformly distributed slides of the original series were held out as Belonging slides. In addition, however, we withheld a sequence of six consecutive slides from the return walk, thus leaving a considerable gap in the temporal-spatial sampling of the walk.

On the test sequence the subjects performed very much like subjects previously studied with the events from static points of observation: 82% of the Originals were correctly identified as having been presented before, 70% of the Belonging slides (including two from the "gap") were incorrectly identified as having been in the original set (false positives), and only 11% of the Control slides were falsely recognized as having been seen before. When separated from the other Belonging slides, the slides in the "gap" were identified only 27% of the time as having been seen before. With these slides removed, the overall results are even more impressive. The Belonging slides that were simply interspersed along the walk were falsely recognized 83% of the time as having been seen before. This means they were indistinguishable from the slides that were actually presented.

In this context one may ask why the Belonging slides in the gap were so poorly recognized. Because so many slides had been excluded, either the content of the gap was not specified for these subjects or the subjects became aware of the gap in the presentation and specifically noted that such views were excluded from the original series. In an effort to shed more light on this question, we repeated the experiment under different conditions.

In the repetition of the experiment, the learning set was presented in random order. We felt that the scrambling of space-time order would provide some evidence as to the coherence of the event and would help us decide between the alternative accounts of the slides in the gap. According to one alternative, subjects might still identify the nature of the walk in the random series but never notice the existence of the gap. If this were the case, it could be argued that the Belonging slides in the gap would not be different in recognition from the other Belonging slides from the random series. On the other hand, it could be argued that the Belonging slides in the gap would be treated just like Controls because no matter what the order of their presentation, there was not enough information in the learning series to specify them as possible alternatives.

The results of the random presentation were similar to those of the ordered presentation: 76% of the Originals were correctly recognized, 58% of the Belonging slides were falsely recognized, and only 8% of the Controls were falsely recognized. When the slides from the gap were considered alone, they showed 20% false recognition, just about the same percentage as that observed in the ordered presentation.

When we exclude the slides in the gap, the Belonging slides in the correctly ordered series received 15% more false positive responses than the same slides in the unordered condition (83% versus 68%). It appears, then, that the appropriate temporal-spatial order was important in inducing the high level of responding to the Belonging slides in the original experiment.

With respect to the slides in the gap, however, there seems to be little difference between the correctly ordered series and the random series; both show very low rates of recognition. Thus we can conclude that the slides from the gap are not well specified in either presentation. There simply is not sufficient information in the original set of slides to determine or support these alternatives.

These experiments with the moving observer, unlike our earlier experiments, offer the further possibility of determining how much of the false recognition effect was attributable to the general knowledge subjects had of the physical campus and how much was attributable to the visual information present in the slide series alone. To exploit this circumstance, we performed the same random and ordered experiments on a similar population of students at another university. These students, of course, could be expected neither to identify any of the buildings nor to have any knowledge of the general campus layout. If the false positives in the original experiments are attributable to extensive knowledge of the constraints of the campus and to the subjects' awareness of the nature of the walk, then the naïve subjects should show little or no false recognition of Belonging slides. If, on the other hand, the walk is specified as a coherent visual event in itself, then subjects from another campus may be expected to show the same phenomenon of false recognition.

The repetitions of the experiments with the second population of subjects yielded several interesting comparisons. The subjects who saw the ordered series responded in the usual fashion of subjects viewing some coherent event. They recognized Original slides 85% of the time, Belonging slides (excluding the gap slides) 54% of the time, and Control slides 4% of the time. The subjects who saw the randomized series responded somewhat more profusely to all cases: Originals 89%, Belonging slides (again without the gap) 66%, and Controls 9%.

When the data for these groups are compared with those for the students who knew the campus, the parallel is remarkable. The data for the randomized presentations are almost exactly the same (except that students who did not know the campus were somewhat more likely to recognize correctly the Original slides than students who did know the campus). The data for the *ordered* presentation, however, show a striking difference in the recognition rate for the Belonging slides. The subjects who knew the campus believed 83% of the time that they had seen the Belonging slides, whereas those who did not know the campus believed only 54% of the time that they had seen the same slides, a difference of 29%.

It appears that this series of pictures is fortuitously chosen to reveal both the nature of coherence of a new visual event and the contribution of personal knowledge to that event. The series is sufficient to specify the event in enough detail to make the interpolated slides "familiar" even to an outsider or even when presented in random order; but at the same time personal knowledge and correct temporal-spatial order specify the total event even more fully and result in almost complete fusion.

Frankly, we had not expected so strong an outcome. Even with two viewings, the slides leave the naïve observer with the impression that he knows very little about the walk. Yet one of the things he does know is that a walk is specified. Almost always one sees the path itself in a relatively constant position on the screen. This invariant alone is sufficient to reject some of the Control slides, but it will not, of course, reject any Belonging slide. That such a single cue is not sufficient to account for all the data is shown by the fact that some Belonging slides with this detail are rejected and the fact that some Control slides that show this invariant are likewise rejected. These results have sensitized us to the fact that real events may have many more sources of coherence than those of which we are typically aware. They challenge us to specify such sources sufficiently well that we can design (or synthesize) new slides that will behave like Control or Belonging slides as we manipulate the variables which specify the event.

A final study may be mentioned. Although it is a study of number recognition, it is included here because it is an extreme case in which a "hidden" invariant can be apprehended by the subject. When the invariant is apprehended, it makes a difference in his construal of the experimental event and results in false positive recognitions like those in the experiments described above.

In this study 30 numbers between 0 and 200 were presented to the subjects. They were told to study the numbers as they were presented one at a time and to attempt to remember them so that they could recognize them later. The numbers were shown for five seconds each; there was only one presentation. One group of subjects saw the numbers in ordinal sequence (e.g., 2, 12, 18, 22, 30, 34, . . . , 190); the other group was given the numbers in random order. The numbers were all multiples of two. Subjects were given a recognition test of 20 items; 6 Original, 6 Belonging (e.g., 8, 16, 24, . . .) and 8 Controls (e.g., 15, 23, 31, . . .).

The group receiving the ordered presentation responded correctly to 77% of the Originals, 46% of the Belonging numbers, and 8% of the Controls. The group receiving the unordered set responded correctly to 74% of the Originals, 49% of the Belonging, and 20% of the Controls. Except for the high rate of responding to the Controls in the unordered group, this result looks very much like the results obtained with the perception of simple events reported earlier. It appears that the invariant in this event (all numbers being even numbers) is a strong determiner of the recognition response and influences responses to about half of the possible numbers that fit this category even though they have not been exposed.

Limiting Factors

Lest we leave the reader with the feeling that everything we choose to display turns out to be an event, we would like to present some experimental "failures" that have taught us something more about the nature of events. Three experiments in particular are relevant: one an attempt to simplify the experiment, one an attempt to capture a "formless invariant" (Gibson, 1966), and one an adventure in the undergraduate's understanding of arithmetic.

The first experiment arose when we attempted to simplify our experiment and increase its analytic power by going to cartoons of movements. Four-panel cartoon sequences depicting particular events of motion were borrowed from Robert Verbrugge's (1974) studies of metaphors of movement. These sequences showed simple events such as an object falling from a support and smashing on the floor, an object being enclosed or entrapped by a structure with a door or gate, an object running into another object, etc. Figure 1 illustrates two variants of each of two sequences.

Our first attempt was to see whether subjects would apprehend an event if they were merely shown several overlapping portions of it. This experiment was designed as a visual analogue to the experiments of Bransford and Franks (1971), who showed that subjects presented with portions of a complex sentence will falsely recognize the complete sentence. For example, subjects who hear "The rock rolled down the mountain," "The rock crushed the hut at the edge of the forest," "The hut was tiny," "The rock that rolled down the mountain crushed the tiny hut," "The tiny hut was at the edge of the forest," etc., will falsely recognize a sentence that they have never heard: "The rock that rolled down the mountain crushed the tiny hut at the edge of the forest."

In this experiment, slide sequences instead of single pictures were presented to the subjects. Four events were chosen. Subjects saw pairs of slides or triples of slides from the separate events but did not see the critical events in their entirety. Thus of the four slides in one event, a subject might see slides 1 and 2, then later slides 1, 3, and 4, then later slides 2 and 4, and still later slides 2, 3, and 4. Proper sequence order of the slides was always preserved. Subjects were tested for recogntition of doubles and triples and full sequences. Almost no subjects showed the predicted false recognition of the 1, 2, 3, 4 sequences.

Reflecting on this study, we could see a number of possible shortcomings. Some were merely experimental: each sequence was very short and the subjects might have been aware of sequence length.

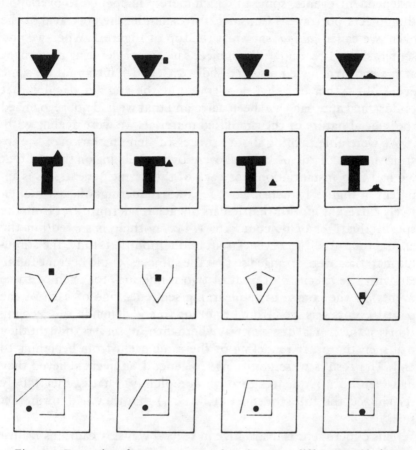

Figure 1. Examples of cartoon events of motion. Two different renderings of each of two events. From Verbrugge, 1974.

For the most part the events had very clear end points, and subjects seemed sensitive to the fact that they had not seen the full sequence from end point to end point. A major flaw, however, was conceptual; we ourselves had neglected the rate of change portrayed. Nonconsecutive samplings of the sequences of these slides automatically accelerated or decelerated the speed of the event being portrayed! Instead of providing samplings of the *same* event, we were presenting the subjects with sequences that differed in important properties.

Rather than presenting four events, we had been presenting many independent events, some of which merely happened to overlap in the objects portrayed. Consider, for example, the portrayal of the event we called *falling*, shown at the top of Figure 1. When we presented slides 1, 2, and 4, the subject saw an accelerating movement at the end. When we presented slides 1, 3, and 4, it was not the same event but rather one that decelerated at the end. We decided that our original approach had been naïve and that we had not recognized the special nature of the simplified materials we were dealing with.

We were able to bring about a successful demonstration of the abstract nature of the perceptual event by capitalizing on the fact that we had two instantiations for each of the "same" events. As is apparent in Figure 1, there are two separate renderings of each qualitatively different motion. Particulars of each rendering differ from the specific features of its counterpart; i.e., nothing is shared but the abstract nature of the event itself. In our modified study, the stimulus materials were arranged so that the subjects would become familiar with the specifics of each of two renderings for each of three events. In the course of the learning sequence one of each of the paired events was seen from beginning to end. Then in the recognition test the crucial question was whether the observers thought they had seen the other rendering of the same event from beginning to end. The results were gratifying. In general, subjects believed they had seen both sequences through completely. That is, they falsely recognized the full sequences (1, 2, 3, 4) that they had not in fact seen.

This experiment is instructive in several ways. It cautions against our identifying events with the objects or forms involved in the events or with a simplistic view of what constitutes a transformation. It argues that if the depicted transformations are different, the presence of "the same" objects may not be sufficient to define a common event. Furthermore, it argues that if the elements are familiar and the transformations are the same, the lack of common objects need not prevent two sequences as being seen as the same event. If only one illustration of a moving event is given, the knowledge of the event and the knowledge of the particulars are perfectly confounded. If there is more than one exemplar of the event, the abstract nature of the event itself can be separated from the particulars used to specify it, and the event may dominate its particular instantiations.

The second lesson we learned through experimental failure is almost the inverse of the conclusions just stated. We tried to construct an event that would be object-independent—i.e., defined solely in terms of its transformation. This experiment was arranged like the Orbiting experiment presented earlier. It differed only in one respect: the object that appeared at each position about the jam jar was different in every slide. Thus the subject saw a saltcellar in the first position, a pen in the second position, a screwdriver in the third position, an inkwell in the fourth, etc. Quite clearly, orbiting was taking place, but no specific object was doing the orbiting. Test slides used Original pictures, new objects at unseen positions of the orbit (Belonging slides), and various Control slides as before. Subjects were virtually perfect at identifying the slides they had seen before and in rejecting the new slides, whether Belonging or Control. In other words, our unnatural conditions had simply reduced the series to a set of independent events, not one overall event with object changes embedded in it. The data are entirely consistent with what one would expect from a study using unrelated slides.

The moral of this experimental failure is that abstraction may require a reasonable or coherent base. When the orbiting transformation is accompanied by object constancy, as in our earlier experiment, it is one of our strongest demonstrations of fusion. When the transformation is imposed on different, random objects, the effect disappears.

In this regard, our first two failures are perfectly consistent with one another. As we remarked earlier, transformations and objects are best viewed as two aspects of one event. When the stimulus materials are unrelated—whether by their depiction of different transformations (as in our cartoon study) or of different objects (as in the current Orbiting study)—the knowledge of the event is not separable from the knowledge of the materials per se. Only when the subject is able to perceive the invariants across instances—whether by being presented with different instantiations of the same event or by an invariant object's participation in the event—will the subject's knowledge of the event be different from his knowledge of the particulars. Only in such cases might we expect to find evidence supportive of fusion.

The final failure draws our attention to the subjects' knowledge as it contributes to the coherence phenomena we are discussing. We attempted to repeat the numerical experiment discussed above with multiples of three in place of the multiples of two used earlier. The experiment was designed in the same way and given to a comparable group of subjects. Subjects were presented with either an ordered series (3, 9, 12, 18, 27, . . . , 198) or a random arrangement of the same items (54, 174, 3, 183, etc.). As before, the test list contained Original, Belonging, and Control items. Subjects in both groups correctly recognized the Original items (74% and 71% respectively). They responded moderately well to the Belonging items (46% and 37%), but they responded almost as often to the Control items that should have been rejected (35% and 35%). In the Control items subjects seemed to be responding on the basis of numerical proximity. That is, a subject who had seen 378 on the learning list may have responded more to 376 (which is not divisible by 3) than he did to 375 (which *is* divisible by 3).

Inquiries by the experimenter revealed that over half of the subjects were not aware (did not perceive?) that the acquisition set consisted of multiples of three. What is more remarkable is that even those subjects who were aware of this responded at a high rate to the Control items that were not multiples of three. This apparently baffling finding has a simple explanation. The subjects do not know how to decide quickly and accurately whether a new number is divisible by three!

The implication of this experiment supports those of our other two failures and seems to return us to the beginning of our discussion; subjects can and do apprehend an event when there is a discernible invariant (e.g., even numbers), but they fail to do so when the invariant is not available to them or not detected by them. The invariant property in the case of multiples of three is not detected by the typical subject, and, even if he apprehends the property, he is unable to use it effectively because he cannot determine new instances readily. We assume this is the case with respect to many learned skills: i.e., the perception of special materials is vastly different for persons who have different backgrounds with respect to the materials. It is well known that the chess board is not the same to the master as it is to the novice, nor is the symphony the same to the amateur as it is to the virtuoso musician. Thus the example provided by the numerical case may be a simple illustration of the general case of the role of one's experience in the perception of coherent events.

Concluding Remarks

In this final section of the paper we shall briefly summarize the findings of our studies and comment on the wider implications we see in the research. Then we shall briefly mention issues we consider important for those who wish to model processes; and finally we shall engage in a little optimistic "handwaving" concerning the promise of our line of research.

Findings of our studies. The studies to date provide a set of demonstrations that are quite convincing at the phenomenal level. We have clearly shown that subjects can and do apprehend natural events portrayed over a series of slides. When subjects apprehend such events, they describe what they have perceived as an event (rather than as a collection of slides), and their behavior on subsequent recognition tasks is influenced in powerful ways by that perception: subjects often believe they have seen Belonging slides that, in fact, they have not seen. Subjects do not believe they have seen highly similar Control slides that violate either the static or dynamic invariants defined over the original set. That is, they detect discrepancies in station point, lighting, direction of action, event-specific transformations and relations, presence or absence of objects, etc.

We have also shown that analogous phenomena can be obtained under highly varied conditions. Most important, perhaps, is the demonstration that the observer moving over the still environment is just as much a natural event as the dynamic event presented to the stationary observer. Equally interesting are the demonstrations that artificial events (such as Orbiting) can be constructed and that such events may show greatly enhanced experimental effects. The promise here is of greater control and careful evaluation of specific aspects of the visual presentation and their contribution to the coherence of the event. We have also learned, however, that such artificial events may fail. To date they have failed in interesting ways that have directed our attention to constraints and considerations we neglected at first. Examples are the experiments with Verbrugge's cartoons, in which, by neglecting the effect of rate transformations, we created multiple separate events instead of several views of a single event; the Orbiting of Different Objects experiment, in which, by neglecting to specify object constancy, we failed to provide sufficient support for the apprehension of a unified event; and the experiment on "threeness," in which it appeared that subjects' lack of knowledge prevented them from apprehending the event we believed we were presenting.

Wider implications. At the general level these studies can be interpreted as adding to the evidence already available that shows that any set of slides implies some set of possible alternatives. In particular, we view these experiments as strong support for the position that coherent sets of slides, i.e., slides that relate to each other in some systematic fashion, specify other stimuli that may or may not be presented. Stimuli that are thoroughly specified are likely to be falsely recognized just because they fit all of the constraints or invariants of the system that has been apprehended. They may not be falsely recognized if they are only weakly specified or if there is some aspect of the particular stimulus that makes its very absence a salient feature of the presentation.

We see events as natural wholes that are, so to speak, perceived *through* the slides, rather than built up from the slides. The slides are windows through which the specifications of the event are glimpsed; they are not Tinker Toys that are used to construct some kind of event-like edifice. We believe events define their own invariants over time, and we now believe there are many more sources of coherence in real events than we had previously imagined. Perhaps any characteristic or change that can be specified in the visual array could become an invariant for some kind of event. Conversely, random variation in any aspect of an event may signify allowable variation and result in that aspect's being "ruled out" as a property relevant to that event.

We see a wealth of evidence that suggests that these experiments give rise to two kinds of knowledge: specific knowledge of what was seen in the experiment, and extensive knowledge of the event itself. In the extreme case of unrelated materials the two levels are the same; the independent slides presented are single representatives of the individual events experienced. As the event level comes to differ from the particular slide level through systematic relations (as in Esper's or Garner's experiments), through conceptual class relations (as in Goldstein and Chance's experiments), or through coherence in action patterns (as in our experiments), the two kinds of knowledge may coexist. At the extreme of relatedness, knowledge of the event itself may totally dominate knowledge of the specific inputs.

Several findings reflect the presence of these two levels of knowledge. Our subjects describe the event rather than the slides when we ask them what they have seen. When they apprehend the events, they show the false recognition of Belonging slides; when they do not apprehend events, they do not. Frequency effects play little or no role in the recognition data when coherent events are perceived, but they are predominant when one deals with unrelated events.

We believe we have shown that information is specified over time and that we have developed a technique for assessing the importance of the time course of the display in studying the event. The difference in natural- versus random-order displays offers us an opportunity to evaluate the contribution of time and rate information to the quality of an event. Some of the events we have studied so far (e.g., the Tea Sequence) seem to be so well specified or so constrained that random presentation does not prevent their veridical perception. Others are much less constrained (the Telephone Sequence) or are much more time-dependent (the Verbrugge cartoons) and lose their single-event quality under randomization.

Finally, we have reaffirmed the contribution of the subject's knowledge to the nature of the perceptual event. Our subjects' ability to pick up "twoness" but not "threeness" is a "poor man's demonstration" of the elegant work that has been done by others on the perceptual abilities of chess experts (e.g., Chase & Simon, 1973) and other specialists.

Implications for modeling processes. We attempt to study the perception of events and the characteristics of stimulus presentations that give rise to event perception. We are not trying to explain how the subjects apprehend these events; we are simply trying to say what supports the apprehension. We see the perception of the event as primary, for only after the event is apprehended can we appropriately analyze the "units" that contribute to its apprehension.

We regard the selection of materials to be studied as crucial and feel that the dramatic differences between the phenomena associated with unrelated pictures and the phenomena associated with related pictures are an important warning to investigators about permissible generalizations from impoverished materials and artificial laboratory settings. Furthermore, the choice of ecologically inappropriate materials will only result in the development of equally inappropriate models, since the two are complementary.

With respect to our experiments we see several thorny problems for any modeling approach that restricts itself to static displays. First, what is it that is taken from each individual slide and coded and stored? We think the evidence is fairly strong that whatever an image might be, it is not some sort of picture in the head; it is not another photographic representation. Second, what kind of device scans the stored representations? It seems to us that it must be some kind of dynamic "change detector." If there are such change detectors, perhaps they should work directly on the world, rather than on less-rich, static representations of the world. Third, given that our subjects seem to respond to event-specific invariants, how could the device get along with anything less than universal storage of all possible aspects of every visual representation? How would such a device discard the random changes from slide to slide but detect and represent as crucial the dynamic invariants? In brief, even in our simple experiments we see a set of challenges that will tax the ingenuity of model builders for some time to come.

We, along with the model builders, believe that the human being is a marvelous device, shaped by millions of years of evolution and millions of experiences to pick up the qualities of events. But we do not need to wait for a solution of the analytic processing dilemmas before we start to work on understanding event perception. We can simply move in the complementary direction, away from the machinery of the organism and toward the structure of the world that is to be processed. That is, we can try to understand what is perceived and what will provide sufficient ground for a coherent perception before we try to specify how it is done.

Directions of research. Starting with the assumption that events are primary, we see a rich set of questions within reach. We believe the line of investigation that we are pursuing can be readily exploited to explore the phenomena we have already tapped. We can ask what kinds of variables serve to increase coherence in events of a given kind without expecting to obtain transituational answers. We can begin to separate and study a subject's knowledge of the stimuli presented versus his knowledge of the event specified. We can ask under what circumstances we obtain coherence (what possible slides could belong to some event) and under what circumstances we obtain fusion (the inability to reject instances that belong to an event although they were not presented as part of the event). We can evaluate the role of past experience and knowledge of the observer in contributing to the coherence of an event. And we can explore the fashion in which a dynamic event creates its own "features" through the invariants it manifests over time.

These are exciting questions that we think will furnish new stimulation for both psychologists and philosophers of all orientations. They are questions pertaining to the perception of events that can be investigated at this very moment. We hope their answers will suggest new processing metaphors and new solutions to old problems.

Notes

1. Although all the experiments described here are in the visual domain, parallel arguments can be made for natural events in other modalities. A particularly good example is the perception of vowels as treated by Shankweiler, Strange, and Verbrugge (1977). These authors argue that the information that specifies a vowel cannot be found in any temporal cross section of the acoustic signal but can only be specified over time.

2. These studies are closely related to those of Bransford and Franks (1971), Franks and Bransford (1971) and Bransford, Barclay, and Franks (1972), as well as later studies in that tradition cited by Bransford and McCarrell (1974). The Franks and Bransford (1971) studies are especially significant because they demonstrate that subjects who were shown a small series of visual patterns, all of which were derived from a single prototype, falsely recognized the prototype figure and varied their recognition ratings of other figures in terms of transformational distance from the prototype.

3. Of the four slides that were not accepted, three showed the woman returning from the kitchen. This interesting accident in the selection of Belonging slides demonstrates two levels of knowledge of the event. The subjects knew that the slides belonged in the Tea Sequence but they also knew that they had not seen them because they had *never* seen the woman return to the room. This "sub-event", nested in the overall event, had a distinctiveness of its own. Because *all* "returning" pictures had been omitted from the learning series, this was an invariant of the presentation and could characterize the learning series itself.

4. Obviously, the similarity problem is a critical one and cannot be dismissed by the results of one experiment. We have currently developed several more tests of the effect

of slide similarity as opposed to "event-defined" similarity by designing intersecting events. For example, in contrast to the *orbiting* event discussed below, a *transversing* event can be created with the saltcellar moving across the tray and over the jam jar. The orbiting and transversing events intersect in two identical pictures at the edges of the tray. If a subject sees an orbiting sequence, we expect him to reject the adjacent, highly similar, slides that belong to the transversing sequence. If the subject sees the transversing sequence, we expect him to reject the highly similar slides that are adjacent in the orbiting sequence. Pilot studies show these effects are actually observed.

References

Bransford, J. D., Barclay, J. R., & Franks, J. J. Sentence memory: A constructive versus interpretive approach. *Cognitive Psychology*, 1972, *3*, 193-209.

Bransford, J. D., & Franks, J. J. The abstraction of linguistic ideas. *Cognitive Psychology*, 1971, *2*, 331-350.

Bransford, J. D., & McCarrell, N. S. A sketch of a cognitive approach to comprehension: Some thoughts about understanding what it means to comprehend. In W. B. Weimer & D. S. Palermo (Eds.), *Cognition and the symbolic processes*. Hillsdale, N.J.: Erlbaum: 1974.

Chase, W. G., & Simon, H. A. Perception in chess. *Cognitive Psychology*, 1973, *4*, 55-81.

Esper, E. A. *Analogy and association in linguistics and psychology*. Athens, Ga.: University of Georgia Press, 1973.

Esper, E. A. A technique for the experimental investigation of associative interference in artificial linguistic material. *Language Monographs of the Linguistic Society of America*, 1925, *1*.

Foss, D. J. An analysis of learning in a miniature linguistic system. *Journal of Experimental Psychology*, 1968, *76*, 450-459.

Franks, J. J., & Bransford, J. D. Abstraction of visual patterns. *Journal of Experimental Psychology*, 1971, *90*, 165-174.

Garner, W. R. *The processing of information and structure*. Potomac, Md.: Erlbaum, 1974.

Gibson, J. J. *The senses considered as perceptual systems*. Boston: Houghton-Mifflin, 1966.

Goldstein, A. G., & Chance, J. E. Visual recognition memory for complex configurations. *Perception and Psychophysics*, 1970, *9*, 237-240.

Gough, P. B. One second of reading. In J. F. Kavanagh & I. G. Mattingly (Eds.), *Language by ear and by eye*. Cambridge, Ma.: The M.I.T. Press, 1972.

Haber, N. R. How we remember what we see. *Scientific American*, 1970, *222*(5), 104-112.

Jenkins, J. J. Can we have a theory of meaningful memory? In R. E. Solso (Ed.), *Memory and cognition: The second Loyola symposium*. Potomac, Md.: Erlbaum, 1974, 1-20. (a)

Jenkins, J. J. Remember that old theory of memory? Well, forget it! *American Psychologist*, 1974, *29*, 785-795. (b)

Johansson, G. Visual motion perception. *Scientific American*, 1975, *232*(6), 76-88.

Kavanagh, J. F., & Mattingly, I. B. *Language by ear and by eye*. Cambridge, Ma.: The M.I.T. Press, 1972.

Kraft, R. N., & Jenkins, J. J. Memory for lateral orientation of slides in picture stories. *Memory and Cognition*, 1977, *5*, 397-403.

LaBerge, D., & Samuels, S. J. Toward a theory of automatic information processing in reading. *Cognitive Psychology*, 1974, *6*, 293-323.

Michotte, A. *The perception of causality*. London: Methuen & Co., Ltd., 1963.

Neisser, U. *Cognitive psychology*. New York: Appleton-Century-Crofts, 1967.

Posner, M. I., & Keele, S. W. On the genesis of abstract ideas. *Journal of Experimental Psychology*, 1968, *77*, 353-363.

Posner, M. I., & Keele, S. W. Retention of abstract ideas. *Journal of Experimental Psychology*, 1970, *83*, 304-308.

Postman, L. Verbal learning and memory. *The Annual Review of Psychology*, 1975, *26*, 291-335.

Segal, E. M. *Stimulus perception as a function of response set*. Unpublished doctoral dissertation, University of Minnesota, 1962.

Shankweiler, D. P., Strange, W., & Verbrugge, R. R. Speech and the problem of perceptual constancy. In R. E. Shaw & J. D. Bransford, (Eds.), *Perceiving, acting, and knowing: Toward an ecological psychology*, Hillsdale, N.J.: Erlbaum, 1977.

Shaw, R. E., & Wilson, B. E. Conceptual knowledge: How we know what we know. In D. Klahr (Ed.), *Cognition and instruction*. Hillsdale, N.J.: Erlbaum, 1976.

Shaw, R. E., & Pittenger, J. B. On perceiving change. In H. L. Pick & E. Saltzman (Eds.), *Modes of perceiving and processing information*. Hillsdale, N.J.: Erlbaum, in press.

Shepard, R. N. Recognition memory for words, sentences and pictures. *Journal of Verbal Learning and Verbal Behavior*, 1967, *6*, 156-163.

Standing, L. Learning 10,000 pictures. *Quarterly Journal of Experimental Psychology*, 1973, *25*, 207-222.

Standing, L., Conezio, J., & Haber, R. N. Perception and memory for pictures: Single-trial learning of 2500 visual stimuli. *Psychonomic Science*, 1970, *19*, 73-74.

Strange, W., Keeney, T., Kessel, F. S., & Jenkins, J. J. Abstraction over time of prototypes from distortions of random dot patterns. *Journal of Experimental Psychology*, 1970, *83*, 508-510.

Verbrugge, R. R. *The comprehension of analogy*. Unpublished doctoral dissertation, University of Minnesota, 1974.

———————— EDWIN MARTIN, JR. ————————

The Psychological Unreality of Quantificational Semantics

> . . . an endearing trait of canonical notations is that they do not bind.
>
> W. V. Quine

1. Introduction

A theory of the structure of a human language, as Chomsky has emphasized, is a theory of the mental processes and representations underlying human use of the language. Thus an adequate syntax of English will identify the syntactic structures and operations underlying recognition and production of English by fluent speakers. Adequacy consequently requires that the structural descriptions and transformations posited by a syntax be psychologically real. That is, the structures posited must be those that are actually internalized by the fluent speaker and that, in part, control his linguistic behavior. There is now good evidence that this requirement is met by at least some of the posits of transformational grammars (cf. Fodor, Bever, & Garrett, 1974, ch. 5). Similarly a semantic theory of a human language must identify the representations of the language's sentences, production of which is necessary and sufficient for *understanding* those sentences. Thus the posits of an adequate semantic theory — like those of an adequate syntax — will be psychologically real: they will be structures actually accessed during sentence comprehension.

Most models of sentence comprehension for achieving production or accessing of semantic representations posit a two-component process (e.g., Anderson & Bower, 1973, ch. 8; Winograd, 1972, pp. 16-34, 126-169; Schank, 1972). The first component of the process takes the sentence as input and yields a surface syntactical parsing of it. This parsed structure becomes input for the second component, which produces the canonical semantic representation of the sentence.

165

It is true of these models that in general, the more *complex* a sentence's semantic representation, the greater the amount of second-component processing required to produce that representation. Consequently any semantic theory with such a processing view will predict the relative amounts of processing required for comprehension of a pair of English sentences with identical or similar surface forms: comprehension of the sentence with the more complex semantic representation will require more processing and thus will take longer. Since difficulty of comprehension is correlative with amount of processing required for comprehension, a semantic theory of English will predict the relative comprehensional difficulty of pairs of English sentences: the sentence with the more complex semantic representation will be harder to understand.

It is also true of these models that the amount of second-component processing required for comprehension is a function of the representational *distance* between the surface form of the sentence and its semantic representation. For the greater the disparity in surface and semantic representations, the more second-component processing required to get from the one to the other. "Not all men didn't come," for example, might mean the same thing as "Some men came." Even though the two sentences would have the same semantic representation, however, the first could still be more difficult than the second. Plausibly the semantic representation underlying these sentences is more like the surface form of the second, so less second-component processing is required to understand it than to understand the first. On this hypothesis too a semantic theory will make predictions of relative comprehensional difficulty; of two sentences having the same semantic representation, the one whose surface representation is more dissimilar to that semantic representation is the harder to understand.

The hypothesis that the amount of processing required for comprehension is correlative with the complexity of the underlying semantic representation will be referred to as the *complexity hypothesis*. The hypothesis that the amount of processing required for comprehension is correlative with the dissimilarity of the surface and semantic representations will be called the *distance hypothesis*.[1] The two hypotheses are not mutually exclusive; comprehensional difficulty, that is, might be a function of both complexity and distance.

There is also wide agreement among semantic theorists that a number of semantic properties and relations should be formally characterizable in terms of semantic representations. These properties and relations include anomaly, ambiguity, and most important, entailment (implication, deductive validity). Thus an adequate semantic theory of English will provide a *formal characterization of entailment* in terms of the semantic representations it assigns to sentences.

There are a number of semantic theories of natural languages that derive from the classical quanitification theory of Frege. These use quantificational structures as semantic representations. They proceed by representing syntactically or morphologically simple expressions of natural languages by syntactically or morphologically complex constructions in the quantificational semantic metalanguage. In terms of these rather few quantificational constructions, such theories attempt formal characterizations of entailment for a wide variety of sentences. But if the theories are to be adequate theories of English, their representations must also underlie comprehension and thus be psychologically real. In what follows I urge that if either the complexity hypothesis or the distance hypothesis is true, then the known theories of semantic representation inspired by Frege's work make very implausible predictions of the relative comprehensional difficulty of certain pairs of English sentences. If this claim is true, then it follows that those representations do not underlie the comprehension of English: they are psychologically unreal. Thus quantificational semantic theories are inadequate as general theories of English competence and cannot contribute to a psychological model of a speaker of English in any straightforward way.[2]

2. Logical Form

The fundamental structures of quantification theory are: proper names, predicates (of any finite number of argument positions), sentential connectives (conjunction, disjunction, negation, conditional, biconditional), and two quantifiers (universal and existential). Some of these structures can be defined in terms of others, but for present purposes we can just as well think of them all as primitive. In terms of these structures quantificational semantic theories attempt to build semantic representations of English sentences. For example, the categorical statements of syllogistic theory are represented as follows:

All ducks are hurt	$\forall x \, (Dx \rightarrow Hx)$
Some ducks are hurt	$\exists x \, (Dx \, \& \, Hx)$
No ducks are hurt	$- \, \exists x \, (Dx \, \& \, Hx)$
Some ducks are not hurt	$\exists x \, (Dx \, \& \, -Hx).$

The power of quantification theory comes from its ability to represent a wide variety of quantificational constructions in a meager and uniform notation, and to characterize entailment in terms of that notation. Among these constructions are definite descriptions and number sentences. Russell (1905) showed that 'The duck is hurt' can be represented in quantificational notation as '$\exists x \, (Dx \, \& \, Hx \, \& \, \forall y \, (Dy \rightarrow x=y))$' (or alternately as '$\exists x \forall y \, [(Dy \leftrightarrow y=x) \, \& \, Hx]$'). And sentences like 'Exactly two ducks are hurt' can be represented as '$\exists x \, \exists y \, [Dx \, \& \, Hx \, \& \, Dy \, \& \, Hy \, \& \, -x=y \, \& \, \forall z \, (Dz \, \& \, Hz \rightarrow z=x \, v \, z=y)]$'.

It seems reasonable that the complexity of such a representation is in part a function of its length. That is, generally speaking, the more occurrences of predicates, connectives, and quantifiers in such a representation, the greater the amount of processing involved and the greater the comprehensional difficulty. Of course, some predicates or quantifiers may be more difficult than others. In the case of connectives such inequality seems clear, since negation is so difficult (Wason, 1961) and since different connectives affect the difficulty of rule-learning tasks to different degrees (Bourne, 1967). And, of course, structure—such as degree of embeddedness—will also be relevant to difficulty. But the complexity variations I shall consider will not require any knowledge of such differences. We shall be able to gauge roughly the complexity of a sentence by a triple $[p, c, q]$, where p is the number of occurrences of predicates in the sentence's semantic representation, c is the number of occurrences of connectives, and q is the number of occurrences of quantifiers. The representational triples of some familiar sentences representable in quantificational notation are as follows.

Every duck is hurt	[2, 1, 1]
A duck is hurt	[2, 1, 1]

No duck is hurt	$[2, 2, 1]$
The duck is hurt	$[3, 2, 2]$ or $[4, 3, 2]$
Exactly one duck is hurt	$[5, 4, 2]$
Exactly two ducks are hurt	$[9, 9, 3]$
Exactly n ducks are hurt	$[\frac{n^2}{2} + \frac{5}{2}n + 2, (n + 1)^2, n + 1]$.

As can be seen, the number of predicates, connectives, and quantifiers occurring in representations of simple number sentences goes up as a function of n^2. As n goes from 2 to 10 the total number of predicates, connectives, and quantifiers goes from 21 to 209. Thus, given the complexity hypothesis, 'Exactly ten ducks are hurt' is predicated to be roughly ten times as difficult as 'Exactly two ducks are hurt'. Of course that prediction is false, for the two sentences are approximately equally difficult to understand. The predictions become even more absurd, naturally, as n gets even bigger: thus 'Exactly one million ducks are hurt', though easy enough to understand, has on the order of 10^{11} times as many predicates, connectives, and quantifiers as does 'Exactly two ducks are hurt'.

Of course no quantificational theory is committed to this treatment of number sentences. However, there are what appear to be formally valid inferences containing such sentences. For example,
(1) Only one man was invited to dinner
  Two men came to dinner
  ∴ Some uninvited men came to dinner
is valid, and thus should be characterized as valid by a semantic theory. The only known way of doing this in a quantificational context is by representing number sentences in the Russellian way. So if quantification theory is to avoid making false relative difficulty predictions, new techniques of representation are required. It might be thought that such techniques are available in a semantic metalanguage that contains a set theory; here (1) could be represented as

The cardinal number of $\{x \mid x$ is a man & x was invited to dinner$\} = 1$
The cardinal number of $\{x \mid x$ is a man & x came to dinner$\} = 2$
∴ $\exists x$ (x is a man & $-x$ was invited to dinner & x came to dinner).

It seems extremely unlikely, however, that the unabbreviated forms of such representations will accurately reflect sentence difficulty: 'Two men came to dinner', for instance, seems much less difficult than 'There is a one-one function whose domain is $\{x \mid x$ is a man & x came to dinner$\}$ and whose range is $\{\emptyset, \{\emptyset\}\}$'. (And this second sentence still does not correspond to the unabbreviated form of the set theoretic representation.) Thus the apparatus of set theory seems not to help here; if anything, it puts us out of the frying pan and into the fire.

Further difficulties of this kind exist for any related attempt to represent sentences like 'Most ducks are hurt', 'Few ducks are hurt', or 'Half of the ducks are hurt'. The only known way of representing these sentences within quantificational structures is, again, to adopt a set theory as underlying logic of the metalanguage. 'Most ducks are hurt' then becomes representable as something like: the set of ducks that are not hurt can be mapped one-one into the set of ducks that are hurt, but not vice versa. Even in abbreviated form this is obviously a much more intricate representation than that posited for 'Some ducks are hurt.' But it seems very likely that 'Some ducks are hurt' and 'Most ducks are hurt' are approximately equally easy to understand; surely nothing like the differences predicted by the present account exist. And, of course, to waive these sentences would be to give up seemingly valid inferences like

(2) Most ducks are hurt

   Most ducks are hybrids

   ∴ Some hybrids are hurt.

There is evidence that negative quantifiers like 'no', 'few', and 'a minority' make sentences more difficult than do positive quantifiers like 'all', 'most', and 'a majority'. And there is also evidence that the 'all'-'some'-'no' group is easier than the 'most'-'many'-'few' group, which in turn is easier than the 'a majority'-'a minority' group. But there is no known evidence for the predictions of quantificational semantics. Just and Carpenter (1971), for example, found picture verification of 'most' and 'many' sentences no harder than 'no' and 'none' sentences. But if either the complexity or the distance hypothesis is true, quantificational semantics should predict 'most' much harder than 'no' for its quantificational representation is more complex and more distant from its surface form than is that for 'no'. Similarly Glass, Holyoak, and O'Dell (1974, experiment

II) found verification times for 'few' sentences on the average only 6% slower than for 'no' sentences, whereas 'no' sentences were 14% slower than 'some' sentences. Quantificational semantics, though, must predict that 'no' sentences are only slightly harder than 'some' sentences and that 'few' sentences are much harder than 'no' sentences. Thus the available evidence runs counter to the predictions of quantificational semantics.

Sentences involving number words or quantifiers such as 'most' are not the only ones about which quantification theory appears to make false predictions. For example, although parsing 'Only John came' should be but slightly harder than parsing 'John came,' quantificational semantics predicts the first to be much harder comprehensionally than the second. For while quantificational representation of the second is just 'Cj', the representation for the first is 'Cj & $\forall x \ (Cx \rightarrow x = j)$'; the quantificational triples are [1, 0, 0] and [3, 2, 1], thus marking a substantial difference in complexity between the two representations. Other cases similar to this abound.

What all of this seems to show is that if the complexity hypothesis is true, comprehension of an English sentence cannot involve production of the sentence's logical form if that form is given by traditional quantification theory. Relative ease of comprehension is simply not accurately predicted by such logical forms.

Most of the foregoing examples can be made to apply equally if the distance hypothesis is true. For example, 'Some ducks are hurt' and 'Most ducks are hurt' have very similar surface forms, so initial parsing of them should be equally difficult. But the surface form of the first sentence is much more like its presumed semantic representation than is the surface form of the second like its presumed semantic representation. That is, not only is quantificational representation of the second sentence more complex than that for the first sentence, but it is also more distant from the relevant surface form. Consequently, if the distance hypothesis is true, then many of the previous predictions will again be made. And so, if the distance hypothesis is true, comprehension cannot involve production of quantificational structure.

3. Senses

Frege thought sentence comprehension requires production of

sentence "sense," the "thought" expressed by the sentence. Every predicate, connective, and quantifier, Frege thought, has a function as sense, whereas proper names have objects as senses (cf. Frege, 1892a, b). The thought expressed by a sentence is then the value of the function that is the sense of the sentence's primary component when it takes as arguments the senses of the other relevant sentential parts. Consider for example a sentence of the form:

$$\forall x\ Fx \to Fa.$$

Here the arrow is the primary sentential component. It has as a sense a two-placed function that takes as arguments the senses of the sentences that are the antecedent and consequent of the conditional. The predicate 'F,' in turn, has a function as a sense. On the consequent side this function takes as argument the object that is the sense of the proper name 'a' and yields as value the thought expressed by the sentence 'Fa.' On the antecedent side, the sense of 'F' is the argument for the function that is the sense of the universal quantifier; the value is the thought expressed by the conditional's antecedent. These two thoughts, then, are the arguments for the sense of the arrow, which has as value the sense of the whole conditional. This account in terms of functions and arguments is generalized to all quanitficational structures (but cf. Martin, 1974). The thought expressed by a sentence can thus be computed by computing the functions that are the senses of sentential parts for arguments that are senses of other sentential parts.

On this view the logical form of a sentence is something like its deep syntax, and it is perhaps associated with the sentence's surface form by a series of presently unknown transformations. This syntactic representation directs semantic operations by pointing functions at arguments and by controlling the order in which computations are made. It is a view that is no more tenable than the view of comprehension by production of logical form, however. For on this view comprehension still requires production of logical form as a syntactic control for subsequent semantic processing; so the enormous differences predicted by a logical form semantics would still be expected on a theory of comprehension by computation of sense. Further, the number of semantic computations required for understanding a sentence will, on this view, increase with the total number of predicates, connectives, and quantifiers appearing in its logical form. Thus semantic processing—and with it comprehensional difficulty—would increase with length of logical form. Consequently the Fregean theory embraces the complexity hypothesis as an explicit consequence. And so Frege's theory of sense entails the resulting untenable predictions of comprehension by production of logical form.

All of the difficulties with logical form, then, are difficulties with any view that makes computation of senses necessary for comprehension as long as computational complexity is reflected in quantificational form. Frege's theory of sense thus is undone by the difficulties with logical form, so senses as he envisioned them cannot be psychologically real. Consequently computation of Fregean senses cannot be required by comprehension.

4. HAM

A canonical encoding notation much like that of quantification theory is proposed in Anderson and Bower's (1973) theory of semantic memory, HAM. HAM's encoding formalism is that of a binary labeled graph whose main branches are for subject, relation, and object. Complexity of a representation in this notation is plausibly a function of the size of the graph, the number of links or arcs it contains. For the more links there are in a graph, the greater the work needed to construct it, and the more processing steps required to check its structure during accessing.

Now HAM's graphs reflect quanitficational structure with the restriction to use of only unary and binary predicates. Indeed, Anderson and Bower (1973, pp. 167ff) claim that their notation is "equivalent" to a version of quantification theory. Consequently the size of a graph will directly correlate with the length of an "equivalent" quantificational representation. And so complexity of quantificational representation and complexity of graph will go hand in hand. Thus if HAM were to be considered a theory of language comprehension, the implausible predictions of quantificational form semantics would be made by it also. For example, HAM contains only three quantificational devices, reflecting universal and existential quantification and a kind of particular though indefinite instance quantification. Consequently number words and other quantifiers such as 'the', 'few', 'many', and 'most' must be dealt with by paraphrase in some way mirroring the options available to a quantification theoretic semantics. In terms of predicate and connective structure too, HAM will have to paraphrase in ways similar to quantificational semantics. Since HAM's paraphrases are similar to those of quantificational semantics, the distance between surface and canonical graph representations will generally vary with the distance between surface and quantificational representations.

Thus if either the complexity or distance hypotheses is true, HAM will make implausible predictions about the relative comprehensional difficulty of pairs of English sentences. Therefore HAM's structures cannot underlie language comprehension. In a curious passage Anderson and Bower (p. 169) admit that "it seems reasonable to suppose that neither human language nor human memory evolved in a way that enables them to deal easily with the expressive powers of the formal languages that have been developed only in the past century of man's history." One might well wonder, then, about the appropriateness of those formal languages as models for semantics or memory.[3]

5. Truth Conditions

Tarski (1936) showed how to construct truth conditions systematically for a set-theoretic language in a metalanguage that contains translations of the object language constructions, names of the object language constructions, and some auxiliary logical devices. Davidson (1967a, pp. 305, 310) has claimed that such a systematic construction of truth conditions for the sentences of a language is an adequate semantics for the language. The truth definition shows "how the meanings of sentences depend upon the meanings of words," and explains "the fact that, on mastering a finite vocabulary and a finitely stated set of rules, we are prepared to produce and to understand any of a potential infinitude of sentences."

The definition of truth proceeds in Tarski's work by defining the auxiliary notion of satisfaction. Intuitively a sequence of objects satisfies a predicate such as Dx_i just in case the ith object in the sequence is a duck. In fact Tarski's scheme requires a clause like this for every primitive predicate in the object language.[4] Next there is a series of clauses for the connectives. For example, the clause for conjunction says that a sequence satisfies an open sentence $t \mathbin{\&} w$ just in case the sequence satisfies t and also satisfies w. Finally come clauses treating quantifiers. For the universal quantifier the clause says that a sequence s satisfies an open sentence $\forall x_i t$ just in case s satisfies t and every sequence that differs from s in just the ith position satisifies t. A sentence is then true if and only if it is satisfied by every sequence. Using the clauses in the definitions of satisfaction and truth, a truth condition can be generated for every sentence of the object language. For example, the truth condition for a universal affirmative sentence will have something like the following form: for every sequence s, if the ith member of s is a duck then the ith member of s is hurt.

Davidson's claim that Tarski's construction provides an adequate semantics for English entails that truth conditions are psychologically real structures accessed during comprehension, and thus complexity of truth conditions or dissimilarity of surface form and statement of truth conditions predict comprehensional difficulty. Since Tarski's definition is wedded to quantificational structure as the underlying logical form, statements of truth conditions directly reflect quantificational form. If either the complexity hypothesis or the distance hypothesis is true, Davidson's claim will founder on the difficulties that demonstrate the psychological unreality of quantificational structures.

Another difficulty for Davidson is the apparent impossibility of extending Tarski's definition to handle opaque contexts—those in which coreferential substitutions are not always reference- or truth-preserving. If, for example, our object language contained an opaque operator that the metalanguage translated as 'it is widely believed that,' then the definition of satisfaction would need to contain an additional clause for belief. But no satisfactory clause seems to be available. We might say that s satisfies Bt just in case it is widely believed that s satisfies t; but this is wrong, since in most cases—if not all—there will be no widely shared beliefs about satisfaction even if there are widely shared beliefs about matters the object language discusses. The only way out of this difficulty within the framework of Tarski's definition seems to be to produce extensional, truth conditional-revealing translations of opaque contexts. Such translations are typically immensely more complex than the opaque constructions they translate (cf., for example Carnap, 1947).[5] Thus, for example, since 'John knew where the man was' contains an opaque construction whereas 'John looked where the man was' does not, these two sentences will be predicted to be miles apart in difficulty if either of the complexity or distance hypotheses is true, although in fact they are reasonably close. Another example of this phenomenon is Davidson's (1967b) analysis of action sentences. On this analysis 'Al is taller than Bob' might be represented by 'aTb'; but Al is kicking Bob' comes out as something like '$\exists x$ (Kx & xBa & xOb).' The quantificational triple for the first, then, is [1, 0, 0], while the triple for the second representation is [3, 2, 1]. Thus, given either the complexity hypothesis or the distance hypothesis, the two sentences are predicted to be quite different in comprehensional difficulty. Surely, though, that is not so. It might be countered that 'Al is taller than Bob' should be represented as '$\exists x \exists y$ (xHa & yHb & xGy)' ("there are things x and y such that x is a height of Al, y is a height of Bob, and x is greater than y"). Still the general point remains: there are simple relation sentences (perhaps 'Al is five feet tall' ($5'Ha$) is one) that do not appear to be very much easier than 'Al is kicking Bob.'[6]

Truth conditions so developed consequently do not seem an accurate indicator of comprehensional difficulty on either the complexity hypothesis or the distance hypothesis, and thus truth conditions cannot be the semantic representations that are accessed during sentence comprehension. They are, as semantic representations, psychologically unreal. It is worth emphasizing that the problems for truth conditions as a semantic theory are additional to those for quantificational form. We could, for example, easily add opaque constructions as primitive logical forms of the semantic metalanguage and add also rules of inference for them. The metalanguage would then have a more reasonable representation of the sentences as far as difficulty is concerned, and the additional inference rules would facilitate characterization of entailment. This route is blocked on Davidson's theory of truth conditions because extensionality is demanded (compare Martin, 1972).

6. Possible World Semantics

Possible world semantics attempts to circumvent Davidson's problems with opaque constructions by letting satisfaction be a relation between sequences of *possible* objects and open sentences. In practice this comes about by talking of possible worlds, each inhabited by possible objects and bearing some sort of accessibility relation to other possible worlds (cf. Kripke, 1963). Necessary truth is then truth in all possible worlds accessible from the actual world. Possible truth is truth in some possible worlds accessible from the actual world. And similar representations are supplied for other opaque constructions. The metalinguistic semantic representation for an object language sentence is then a quantificational structure, but one that talks about states of affairs in various possible worlds, not confining itself to talk of the actual world.

Since the representations that underlie possible world semantics are quantificational in form, they inherit all the implausibility of quantificational structures as semantic representations. But they produce implausible predictions of their own. For example, the two sentences 'If Plunkett played well, then we won' and 'If Plunkett had played well, then we would have won' must be in the same neighborhood in terms of comprehensional difficulty. Yet possible world semantics must say that the second is far more complex than the first.[7] The first is represented by a quantificational structure concerned only with the actual world, while the representation of the second must appeal to a complicated set of possible worlds and events in them. Thus if the complexity hypothesis is true the second sentence must be predicted by possible world semantics to be much harder than the first. Lewis (1973), for example, begins his book on counterfactuals by saying (p. 1) " 'If kangaroos had no tails, they would topple over' seems to me to mean something like this: in any possible state of affairs in which kangaroos have no tails, and which resembles our actual state of affairs as much as kangaroos having no tails permits it to, the kangaroos topple over." He later (p. 16) expands on this formula by saying that a counterfactual conditional with ϕ as antecedent and ψ as consequent is true in world i just in case either of the following two conditions is met:

(1) no ϕ-world belongs to any sphere S in $\$_i$, or
(2) some sphere S in $\$_i$ does contain at least one ϕ-world and $\phi \supset \psi$ holds in every world in S.

Of course full expansion requires saying what ϕ-worlds, spheres, and $\$_i$ are; but the difference in comprehensional difficulty is already quite clear. And if the distance hypothesis is true, possible world semantics will again predict great differences in comprehensional difficulty between indicative conditionals and counterfactual conditionals, since there are great differences of distance between their respective surface forms and their posited semantic representations.

There are other applications of the techniques of possible world semantics that produce equally implausible predictions (e.g., representations of epistemic or deontic constructions). Consequently possible world representations cannot be psychologically real, so possible world semantics cannot provide an adequate semantics of English.

7. Conclusion

In general, comprehensional difficulty of a sentence seems to be correlative with the complexity of its surface form. The more a semantic theory "analyzes" sentences in producing their semantic representations, then, the greater the disparity between difficulty predicted and difficulty acutally found. Logically loaded sentences must be represented in a logically loaded way rather than in a way that makes the logical form explicit. Only in this way will a semantic theory be able to predict that 'A man hit a ball' is as difficult as 'The man hit the ball', 'Exactly two ducks are hurt' is as difficult as 'Exactly one million ducks are hurt', 'John looked where the man was' is as difficult as 'John knew where the man was', 'John hit the man' is almost as difficult as 'John should have hit the man', 'No man is mortal' is easier than 'It is not the case that there is something which both is a man and is mortal', and 'Al is kicking Bob' is easier than 'There is an event which is a kicking event, is a by Al event, and is an of Bob event'. In order to be faithful to the facts about relative comprehensional difficulty, that is, sentences must *not* wear their entailments on the sleeves of their semantic representations.

In order to characterize entailments between sentences in terms of semantic representations, then, something like Carnap's (1952) meaning postulates is needed. In the case of number sentences these postulates should incorporate arithmetical laws in some way that makes inference (1) valid. There would have to be separate postulates for 'most' and other quantifiers, from which the validity of inferences like (2) would follow. And there would have to be postulates for special modal and epistemic constructions, and no doubt many others. Only by thus separating comprehension processes from inferential processes will it be possible to remain faithful to the differences in processing time required by them. As Fodor, Fodor, and Garrett (1975) point out, the distinction is between mandatory on-line processes and optional off-line processes. It is intuitively quite plausible that comprehension is an on-line process and that consequently the representations accessed during comprehension are very similar to the surface forms that are the prompting input. Inference, however, is typically more labored and time-consuming. Of course we cannot draw all the valid conclusions of some piece of information, and what inferences we do make are often context-dependent. This suggests that context has much to do with which meaning postulates are utilized, just as context generally has much to do with what is retrieved from long-term memory. Thus if entailment is characterized in terms of the semantic representations underlying comprehension processes it is not done in the neat formal way quantification theory proposes. Rather, a host of special postulates must be invoked. Consequently quantificational structures do not underlie comprehension or inference, and so are psychologically unreal.

It might be claimed that the theories discussed above were never meant to contribute to a psychological model of language comprehension, so that the criticisms lodged against them are fairly irrelevant. Thomason (1974, p. 2), for example, says that "according to Montague the syntax, semantics, and pragmatics of natural languages are branches of mathematics, not of psychology." What this outlook denies is much clearer than what it asserts. What, after all, is a mathematical theory of language? What constraints is it sensitive to? How do we know when such a theory is true? What are the phenomena it theorizes about? The answers to such questions are relatively clear in the case of a psychological theory of language; and it is difficult, I think, to envision a viable alternative here. The proponents of the theories discussed above may not describe their theories as mathematical. But if those theories are not intended to contribute to a psychological model of sentence comprehension then, at the very least, we are due an account of what they are theories of. To date, accounts of such alternatives have not been given.

Notes

1. The distance hypothesis is somewhat motivated by the demonstration that memory of linguistically presented material is independent of surface form (Bransford and Franks, 1971; Kintsch, 1974). Presumably the mnemonic representation is at least sometimes linguistically neutral. Sentence comprehension, possibly, involves producing a similar such abstract representation from the sentence's surface form. Anderson and Bower (1973, pp. 224ff) appeal to the distance hypothesis in discussing reaction time differences for active and passive sentences.

2. This paper derives its general direction from Fodor, Fodor, and Garrett (1975), who discuss in more detail the two conditions on the adequacy of a semantic theory as well as the general strategy of representing syntactically or morphologically simple expressions by complex constructions. Fodor et. al. contend that the lexical decompositions of generative and interpretive semantic representations are psychologically unreal. This paper and I have benefited from the advice of Michael R. Lipton and Jerry A. Fodor.

Davidson (1964) and Martin (1974) give two arguments — different from the ones that follow — that versions of quantificational semantics are inadequate.

3. It seems quite possible that the structures produced during sentence comprehension are subsequently stored for accessing in memory. If so, then the unsuitability of HAM's structures for underlying comprehension must imply that they are not the structures used in memory either. Other theories of semantic memory (e.g., those of Kintsch, 1974 and Rumelhart, Lindsay, and Norman, 1972) avoid these difficulties by allowing many quantifiers to be represented primitively.

4. Similarly, if the object language contains logically simple names, they must each be dealt with. The appropriate clauses are of the form: a sequence s satisfies Da just in case Al is a duck. Every combination of simple predicates and simple names must be similarly handled by a separate clause.

5. Davidson's own solution to this (Davidson, 1969) is to say that 'It is widely believed that the earth is round' has the joint structures of the two sentences.

The content of my next utterance is widely believed.

The earth is round.

In effect, the original sentence is banished from the object language.

6. These difficulties do not extend to adding quantifiers like 'most' or 'few'. Clauses for such quantifiers can be fairly straightforwardly added to the definition of satisfaction; cf. Wallace (1965).

7. On the basis of verification times, Carpenter (1973) theorizes that comprehension of counterfactual conditionals involves explicit negatives in the immediate representation of counterfactual clauses. She envisions nothing approaching the complexity of possible world semantics, however.

References

Anderson, J. R., and Bower, G. H. *Human associative memory*. Washington, D.C.: V. H. Winston, 1973.

Bourne, L. E., Jr. Learning and utilization of conceptual rules. In B. Kleinmuntz (Ed.), *Concepts and the structure of meaning*. New York: Wiley, 1967.

Bransford, J. D., and Franks, J. J. The abstraction of linguistic ideas. *Cognitive Psychology*, 1971, 2, 331-350.

Carnap, R. *Meaning and necessity*. Chicago: University of Chicago Press, 1947.

Carnap, R. Meaning postulates. *Philosophical Studies*, 1952, 3, 65-73.

Carpenter, P. A. Extracting information from counterfactual clauses. *Journal of Verbal Learning and Verbal Behavior*, 1973, 12, 512-521.

Davidson, D. Theories of meaning and learnable languages. In Y. Bar-Hillel (Ed.), *Logic, methodology, philosophy of science*. Amsterdam: North-Holland, 1965.

Davidson, D. Truth and meaning. *Synthèse*, 1967, 17, 304-323. (a)

Davidson, D. The logical form of action sentences. In N. Rescher (Ed.), *The logic of Decision and action*. Pittsburgh: University of Pittsburgh Press, 1967. (b)

Davidson, D. On saying that. In D. Davidson & J. Hintikka (Eds.), *Words and objections*. Dordrecht: Reidel, 1969.

Fodor, J. A., Bever, T.G., & Garrett, M. F. *The psychology of language*. New York: McGraw-Hill, 1974.

Fodor, J. D., Fodor, J. A., & Garrett, M. F. The psychological unreality of semantic representations. *Linguistic Inquiry*, 1975, 6, 515-531.

Frege, G. Über Begriff und Gegenstand. *Vierteljahrsschrift für wissenschaftliche*, 1892, 16, 192-205. (a)

Frege, G. Über Sinn und Bedeutung. *Zeitschrift für Philosophie und philosophische Kritik*, 1892 C, 25-50. (b)

Glass, A. L. Holyoak, K. J., & O'Dell, C. Production frequency and the verification of quantified statements. *Journal of Verbal Learning and Verbal Behavior*, 1973, 13, 237-254.

Just, M., & Carpenter, P. Comprehension of negation with quantification. *Journal of Verbal Learning and Verbal Behavior*, 1971, 10, 244-253.

Kintsch, W. *The representation of meaning in memory*. Hillsdale, N. J.: Lawrence Erlbaum Associates, 1974.

Kripke, S. A. Semantical considerations on modal logic. *Acta Philosophica Fennica*, 1963, 16, 83-94.

Lewis, D. K. *Counterfactuals*. Cambridge, Mass.: Harvard University Press, 1973.

Martin, Edwin, Jr. Truth and translation. *Philosophical Studies*, 1972, 23, 125-130.

Martin, Edwin, Jr. A note on Frege's semantics. *Philosophical Studies*, 1974, 25, 441-443.

Rumelhart, D. E., Lindsay, P. H., & Norman, D. A. A process model for long-term memory. In E. Tulving and W. Donaldson (Eds.), *Organization of memory*. New York: Academic Press, 1972.

Russell, B. On denoting. *Mind*, 1905, 14, 479-493.

Schank, R. C. Conceptual dependency. *Cognitive Psychology*, 1972, 3, 552-631.

Tarski, A. Der Wahreitsbegriff in den formalisierten Sprachen. *Studia Philosophica*, 1936, 1, 262-405.

Thomason, R. H. Introduction. In R. H. Thomason (Ed.), *Formal Philosophy: Selected Papers of Richard Montague*. New Haven: Yale University Press, 1974.

Wallace, J. Sortal predicates and quantifications. *Journal of Philosophy*, 1965, 62, 8-13.

Wason, P. C. Response to affirmative and negative binary statements. *British Journal of Psychology*, 1961, 52, 133-142.

Winograd, T. Understanding natural language. *Cognitive Psychology*, 1972, 3, 1-191.

Infinite Sets, Unbound Competences, and Models of Mind

Underlying a large number of proposals in cognitive theory is the conviction that mental activity should be seen as a series of discrete computational processes on sets of elements. It is felt, in turn, that formal programs or systems describing such computations provide us with the best (and perhaps the only possible) psychological theories of human cognition. Of course, once one settles on such a model of cognition, other things follow. In particular, there is the strong push to go from truths about the limits and capacities of certain formal systems and how they function to claims about the limit of the mind and how the mind itself must function. By focussing on some arguments about the significance of infinite sets and unbounded competences, I hope to show some of the problems involved in making this move from formal theory to psychological reality.

Although it has seemed obvious that human capacities are physically limited and finite, it is often observed that people can acquire certain competences that are unbounded or unlimited. This discrepancy between limited capacities and unbound competences is thought to have important psychological implications, particularly with regard to learning. In most cases, however, the resulting claims made about the mind are not themselves supported by empirical evidence; rather they are usually thought of as self-evident truths to be freely used as premises in support of some further position or theoretical point. In this chapter I intend to examine several arguments about language that depend on claims concerning infinity.

Note: I wish to thank M. Atherton, S. Morgenbesser, and D. Rosenthal for discussing some of these matters with me, and C. W. Savage for much helpful editorial advice. This work was supported by a Faculty research Award from the City University of New York.

I shall first present a sketch of an argument (A) and then examine (E) the psychological significance of the conclusions reached. I shall make no effort to attribute these arguments to individual theorists, nor shall I attempt to criticize specifically any theorist's pet versions of these arguments. For what I mainly wish to show is that infinitary arguments of this sort go through only if we make some additional assumptions about the nature and limits of mind or mental processes. And further, I wish to show that the assumptions needed are not at all obvious truths about cognitive capacity in general, but require supplementary evidence or argument to justify their use in individual cases. In particular, I think the additional assumptions necessary to make the infinitary arguments sound in the case of natural language are not readily extendible when we consider the full range of human symbolic competences, and even less so when we try to encompass cognitive skills in general.

Again, what interests me in each of the following examples is not the formal claim about the infiniteness of a set of items, but the psychological claim that is supposed to follow from it. For it is in shifting from formal fact to psychological conclusion that I believe unwarranted assumptions about the nature of mental processes are too readily accepted. Finally, it should be noted that I shall be using the terms 'infinite,' 'unlimited,' and 'unbounded' somewhat interchangeably throughout, not in their precise technical senses, but rather to describe sets of items for which there is no principled limit or cut-off point on the number of members they contain. I do this both for stylistic reasons and because, as I hope to show, the sense of infinity needed for arguments of this sort to proceed is itself part of the problem.

A Uniqueness Claim

(A) Natural languages are infinite. Linguistic competence is unbounded in the sense that the set of sentences a speaker of a natural language can produce and recognize as part of the language is theoretically infinite. This infinite nature of language makes linguistic competence qualitatively different from most other competences and thus shows the need for special learning capacities or processes not like those that might account for other skills.

(E) Whatever a correct account of language acquisition may turn out to be, there is nothing in the unboundedness of linguistic competence that serves to distinguish it from almost any other skill or competence we have. Our abilities to play chess, to identify baroque music, to add and subtract, to recognize and produce tables, chairs, triangles, doorknobs, the letter A, or, for that matter, almost anything else, are likewise unbounded skills. There is no fixed limit, for example, to the number of chairs we can recognize, and given some design skills, no fixed limit on the number of different kinds of chairs we can produce. This competence cannot reasonably be seen to involve the mastery of some list of chairs whose membership roll is consulted in each act of recognition or production. Not all chairs (or even kinds of chairs) to be dealt with will have been actually encountered in learning the concept 'chair,' and the creative designer can produce chairs vastly unlike those ever previously experienced. There is no reason to suppose that each new chair recognized or produced will be a mere copy or physically "similar" to earlier ones. Chairs may vary in color and size, in shape, style, and material, in beauty and comfort, and in whether or not they can function as seats. Chairs cannot be ordered or differentiated along some one or few linear stimulus dimensions. And to claim that identifying chairs is a case of mere pattern recognition, whereas determining which strings of words are grammatical is not, will remain a vacuous retreat, unless some cogent arguments can be given as to why the latter too is not a case of pattern recognition. Chairs are similar to one another in their chairness, and grammatical sentences are similar to one another in their grammaticality. Moreover, normal use of this chair competence would appear to be innovative and free from the control of detectable stimuli in ways not easily distinguishable from those assumed for language. The notions 'innovative' and 'stimulus-free' are not very clear, and a detailed analysis of them would sidetrack my main concern (but see Atherton, 1970). Loosely, my point is that we can design chairs to fit or to be appropriate to new situations and conditions, and that our designing activity does not in any simple way seem to be under the control of stimuli. All of these points could be made equally well about almost any other interesting competence we have mastered.

Now I am not here arguing that there are no important distinctions to be drawn between our various nonlinguistic skills and linguistic competence; nor am I maintaining that any creature capable of learning one must be capable of learning some or all of the others. My point is that if we are looking for characteristic differences among competences that will have psychological import, emphasis on the fact that the set of grammatical strings is infinite is misguided. If linguistic competence is to be distinguished from all these other skills, some feature other than unbounded recognition and productivity will be required. One obvious feature that would seem to separate linguistic competence from such skills as chair designing, chess playing, bicycle-riding, etc. is that our linguistic skill is essentially a symbolic skill—its products can stand for, denote, refer, or describe. To the extent that we focus our attention solely on our ability to pick out syntactically grammatical strings, there would seem to be little reason to distinguish this skill from other pattern recognition competences, for, by itself, this skill is hardly a symbolic competence. But, of course, to have learned a natural language, we must know how sentences relate to the world. It is in our having acquired an associated skill of interpretation that our manipulation of marks and utterances becomes a symbolic skill. So, if it is the symbolic nature of linguistic skill that is psychologically distinctive and important, then it is semantic competence that looms large.

Clearly any adequate theory of verbal learning must be able to account not only for our ability to recognize grammaticality, but for the way we learn the referential or descriptive force of sentences. And it might be thought that here considerations of infinity would lend uniqueness to language competence. For not only can we recognize the grammaticality of a theoretically infinite set of sentences, we also know how to interpret them, we know what conditions would make them true. We can produce and understand sentences never heard before, describing situations never before encountered. So it may be thought that the need to account for an unbounded semantics is what particularizes theories of natural language acquisition.

But again little argument is needed to show that if we are to establish the uniqueness of natural language competence, something other than appeal to the infinite is required. For even if we limit our consideration to symbolic skills, to skills that have an essential semantic or referential component, the unboundedness of natural language competence will not be distinctive. Most other symbol systems that we use every day (e.g., maps, models, pictures, diagrams, music notation) are likewise unbounded. Mastering any one of these systems enables us to recognize and understand the descriptive force of an unlimited set of new symbols and to use these symbols creatively to represent or describe an unlimited set of novel situations. Furthermore, unlike mastering some systems of animal communication, mastering these symbol systems requires more than being able to correlate a single stimulus dimension with some single property of the symbol scheme. And in general there will be no regular relationship between producing or understanding a given symbol in these systems and any immediately ensuing behavior pattern or emotional state. Nor do I think it can be argued, as it is sometimes said of artificial languages, that these systems all presuppose natural language or are merely notational variants of or parasitical on natural language.

So although the need to master the theoretically infinite semantic force of natural language may be of importance in distinguishing linguistic competence from various other skills, it will not separate out this competence from most of our symbolic skills. From the standpoint of learning theory, further differentiation would depend upon exposing distinctions between natural language competence and our other symbolic skills, and then providing empirical evidence that these distinctions have a critical effect on learning. Thus, for example, Katz (1972, pp. 22 ff), arguing along somewhat narrower lines than I, claims that the infinity of sentences will not set natural language apart from various other languages. Rather, he thinks natural languages are distinguished from other languages by their superior expressive power. I have qualms with aspects of this latter claim, which I am not going to pursue here. If Katz were correct, however, one might then want to show how the supposedly superior expressive power of natural language requires special learning capacities or processes.

From Infinity to Rules

(A) The infiniteness of natural language entails that anyone possessing the competence to understand or speak such a language must employ a set of rules.

(E) Here the difficulty lies with the term "employ." If the claim that rules must be employed is merely a way of saying that linguistic competence is an open-ended skill and that performance is not based on consulting an exhaustive list, then the claim is undoubtedly true. As we have suggested, hardly any interesting competence can be seen to involve the learning or memorization of a list that is consulted in each case. If, however, the argument is that the infiniteness of language entails the *use* of rules, that the speaker *employs* rules in recognition, understanding, and producing language, then it seems that without some additional empirical premises the inference is unsound.

From a logical standpoint the argument from infinity to rules breaks down; it leads to a regress. If rules are construed as internalized instructions, formulas, or principles that specify membership conditions or describe the members of a given infinite set, use of such rules would require the ability to apply the concepts or criteria employed in the rule specification. But the skills needed to apply the rule to a theoretically unlimited number of cases would themselves be unbounded and thus require the use of additional rules, and so on ad infinitum. For example, suppose the skill under consideration is that of recognizing Ps, and suppose x is a P if and only if x has properties $Q_1, \ldots, Q_n$. Determining the presence of $Q_1, \ldots, Q_n$ provides a rule for picking out Ps. However, if the set of Ps is unlimited, the ability to apply $Q_1, \ldots, Q_n$ must also be unlimited, and this skill would require the use of yet another set of rules, those that permit us to pick out cases of $Q_1, \ldots, Q_n$. So if we are to avoid a regress, we must allow that there are at least some unbounded competences which themselves are not to be accounted for in terms of employing rules. Thus in our example it might be claimed that the abilities to recognize $Q_1, \ldots, Q_n$, although unbounded skills, cannot be further reduced. But then it must be allowed that some other type or types of psychological processes can also account for unbounded competences. And in any particular case, determining which model will account for which competence remains an empirical matter. (Morgenbesser, 1969, Nagel, 1969, and Malcolm, 1971 have interesting things to say about the problems under consideration here and in what follows.)

Now, for many of our skills, I would argue that the rule-following model is unlikely to prove useful as a psychological explanation.

What, for example, is the significance of the claim that we master rules when we learn to recognize and produce chairs, or the letter "*A*"? Clearly most of us could not state a definition or rule that would enable us to pick out all chairs, or all "*A*"s. And even if we were to do so, there would be no good reason to assume that we had been unconsciously consulting the rule all along, or that it had played a role in bringing about our performance. That such definitions might pick out the class of objects that we call "chairs," or "*A*"s, does not by itself show that these definitions play any role in our processes of recognition or production. Indeed, the odds are that a satisfactory definition of "chair" or "letter *A*" will involve concepts more complex and difficult to apply than the predicates "chair" and "letter *A*" themselves. And, as our previous argument was meant to show, we cannot, on pain of regress, assume that each of our unbounded recognition and production skills requires the literal use of rules. Some of our skills must be irreducible, i.e., not explainable on a rule-following model.

But our chair and letter *A* competences seem to me to be as good candidates for unreduced status as any other. The mere fact that they are learned skills does not entail a rule mastery account of our present competence. The push to view all our learned cognitive competences as literally composed of or definable in combinatorial terms from some fixed set of elementary concepts results from assuming a priori that a reductionist computational model must be correct. On the other hand, I think it more reasonable to assume that many of our skills function as our unreduced skills must be thought to do. Hence these developed skills will not be adequately modeled by the sorts of reductive programs the computational approach usually promotes. Arguing for this latter position, though, would be a lengthy matter. What I have attempted to establish here is that for any given competence, empirical evidence is required to show that its use is mediated by the sort of processing a literal construal of the rule model would seem to demand.

It is true, perhaps, that linguistic competence may on the face of it appear to be a more promising realm for employing a rule model of processing. However, I do not believe we have at present adequate evidence or grounds for assuming it to be the only or most appropriate model for understanding these matters. This, of course, is not to imply that we cannot talk about the underlying neurological and/or psychological processes that accompany our linguistic accomplishments. My question is whether the set of formal rules that a grammarian or logician may propose provides such an account, and if so, what sort of account it provides. Are these rules merely descriptions of certain regularities in the speaker's competence, in the way that one or another axiomatization of logic may be seen as a representation of the ideal logician's reasoning competence; or is there some stronger sense in which the speaker can be said actually to employ or follow the rules? If the connection between rules and competence is thought of as similar to the logic case, then any direct application of the rule-model as a psychological account would seem an unpromising approach to learning theory. If a more central explanatory role is to be assigned to the rules of grammar, it would seem that some process, state, or internal phenomena must be seen as embodying, representing, or reflecting the particular rules. Just what such an embodiment of rules would reasonably be like and how it would play a role in verbal behavior I find unclear. I would claim, however, that recent attempts to explicate rule-mastery in terms of tacit or implicit knowledge do not help matters much. For the issue here at least is not whether linguistic competence is best described as having knowledge, tacit or otherwise. Rather, the main question is whether anything like a formal grammar plays a role in our processes of production and understanding, whether some mechanism involved in verbal performance actually goes about assigning sentences the full analysis a grammar does.

But it is not possible, nor would it be to the point, to rehash here the many problems involved in the idea of tacit knowledge and linguistic competence. More on this matter can be found in Harman (1967), Hook (1969), and elsewhere. For our primary task has been to show that claims about the routes of language-learning and performance do not follow by themselves, once it is noted that natural languages are formally infinite. If a rule-model of competence can be made clear and plausible, still justification for applying such a model to linguistic competence would require more than an appeal to the infinite. It would be necessary to demonstrate some particular features of linguistic skill that recommend a rule-model. And I should think that whatever these features turn out to be, they would continue to suggest such a rule-based psychological account whether the sentences of some natural language were finite or infinite in number.

The Assumption of a Finite Base

(A) The number of semantically primitive expressions of a language must be finite; otherwise the language would be unlearnable.

(E) The rationale for this claim seems obvious. The words "cow," "ink," and "shoe" each denote kinds of objects, and what each denotes is a matter of convention. There is no a priori reason why the word "cow" is used to denote cows rather than shoes and why "shoe" is used to denote shoes rather than ink. So it would seem that if the inventory of terms were infinite, we could not possibly learn the denotation of them all. Thus it is assumed that, for a language to be learnable, it must contain only a finite number of primitives.

Now the major problem in evaluating this claim is that the notion of a "semantic primitive" in a natural language is not a very clear one. A natural language, as opposed to an artificial language, is not given to us with a list prescribing its primitive vocabulary and a set of official definitions sanctioned in the system. Terms are usually characterized as primitive only relative to a particular formalization of a language, since expressions primitive in one formalization may be defined in another and vice versa. But even if a particular set of terms is not to be singled out as representing the primitives, when the system we are dealing with is not an artificially constructed one, perhaps the force of the learnability claim can still be made with a more relative notion of primitives. Suppose, as a first approximation, we allow that a term is primitive relative to the other terms in a set if it cannot be defined or its semantics specified using only these other terms. We can then interpret the psychological assumption as saying that, if the terms or semantic units of a system are infinite, the system will be unlearnable, unless it is possible to specify the semantics of the set using only some finite subset of itself.

But on this formulation of the learnability claim, is there any reason to believe it is a true psychological principle? After all, we do master certain unbounded symbol systems in which it seems unlikely that we can finitely specify the semantic significance of all members in terms of the content of some of the others. Consider such symbol systems as gestures (e.g., mime), models, or pictures. In these systems, each different gesture, model, or picture has its semantic function, and each seems to be primitive with respect to the other symbols in the system. In such symbol systems, I do not see the grounds for claiming that the semantic units of the system are reducible to a finite set. But surely these systems are learnable, and there is no reason to suppose that learning them must proceed via reduction to or specification of their semantics in some other system like natural language. What I am arguing, then, is that given practice in reading or interpreting gestures, models, and pictures, we can project from the finite teaching instances in a way that allows us to comprehend the semantic significance of a potentially infinite set of distinct symbols.

Now one major difference between natural languages and gestures, models, and pictures is that natural languages are syntactically notational whereas these other schemes are syntactically dense—they are nonnotational or analogue schemes. In the case of natural language we can isolate an alphabet and vocabulary of repeatable characters, and these characters are separable into disjoint, differentiated classes. (Goodman, 1968, develops these distinctions more precisely and in detail.) In the analogue cases division of the schemes into component characters of this kind is not possible. Perhaps it will be maintained that only in systems of this latter analogue sort can semantic learning proceed unbounded. Although this distinction among symbolic schemes marks a significant difference, I do not think it is one that can rescue this version of the learnability claim. Take, for example, a subsystem of standard Western music notation—a system having a vocabulary of only whole notes, each denoting a class of sounds, and containing no sharps or flats. Such a system is disjoint, notational, and not analogue. Within such a system there will be no way to define or specify the semantical force of a note in terms of other notes in the vocabulary, and if the system provides for higher and lower notes without limit, the vocabulary of notes will be theoretically infinite. And yet his system seems clearly learnable by inductive means. By providing someone with a finite set of teaching instances (a written note accompanied by a sound it denotes) the person will eventually be able to project to new cases. Shown a written note not among the teaching instances, the learner will understand what it says, and there will be no fixed limit on the number of new notes capable of being so handled.

I am not talking here about new combinations of previously learned notes, but of understanding new, hitherto unseen individual notes. There will, of course, be limits to how many new notes can actually be distinguished and applied, but such limitations would seem to be more a matter of bounds on discriminatory power rather than a limit on our ability to master semantic systems. According to our present interpretation of primitiveness, then, each of these notes will be construed as a semantic primitive, and their number is theoretically infinite. The obvious objection, that each is not really a primitive, will be taken up shortly.

But are there any sets of expressions in natural language that are like gestures, models, pictures, and music notation in that they are unlimited and learnable on the basis of selected instances? Right off it would seem that there are. Consider the indicator or token reflexive words "I," "here," "that," "you," etc. Tokens of each of these words have different denotations, and there is no fixed number of such tokens we can comprehend. Given some instances of these words, we seem to learn how to handle new cases. Mother, father, and sister use "I," and we are able to project from these instances the correct denotation of our aunt's "I." Of course there is the difference with indicator terms that each token, although possibly differing in denotation, is of the same type or is an instance of the same character in the language. However, there are examples of infinite sets of terms differing in type in which it seems possible that inductive learning could occur. Consider a vocabulary in which the numeral "1" is used to denote one-inch long objects, "2" to denote two-inch long objects, etc. Take someone with no mathematical vocabulary and teach this measurement system by inductive means, i.e., pair numerals with objects of the appropriate length. After suitable practice in associating numerals with objects, it is likely that the person will learn how to go on, how to apply new numerals correctly, and there would seem to be no fixed upper limit on the learner's ability to continue. There may be cases, then, in natural language similar to gestures, models, pictures, and music, in which we are able to work out how to handle an unlimited vocabulary from a finite number of teaching instances.

Of course the objection will be raised that in the case of "I" and this measurement system (as well as the music system and perhaps even the analogue systems mentioned), although the vocabulary is infinite, we really are not dealing with sets of infinite primitives. After all, it might prove possible to define or reduce the semantic import of the various occurrences of "I" to only one expression, such as "the present speaker," and we can finitely specify the semantics for the size numerals using only a few mathematical terms like "plus," "times," "power of," etc. So in these cases we are really dealing with finite sets of primitives.

The problem with this reply is that it involves a slight but psychologically important shift in the notion of a primitive. For notice that, although others may have resources in their vocabulary enabling them to specify finitely the semantics for these infinite sets, there is no reason to suppose that anyone who masters these sets also has the additional resources. Surely a child could learn to understand tokens of "I" before acquiring the expression "the present speaker." Similarly, although the set of numeral terms may not be primitive with respect to the mathematician's resources, there is no reason to assume such richness in every learner's vocabulary. And even if the learner does have this additional vocabulary, it is not at all likely that he or she will be able to specify the semantics for their infinite vocabulary with this finite base. If we or the child as language user cannot perform such definitional reduction or specification, however why isn't it the case that we have mastered an infinite set of primitives? From a psychological point of view, from considerations about how and what we can learn, the fact that someone else happens to be able to specify the semantics for our infinite vocabulary by finite means should not make any difference.

The reason such an external specification or reduction has been thought relevant to the issue of learning, I think, depends on the further assumption that something like this definitional reduction must psychologically underlie our semantic skill, or else we could not master an infinite vocabulary. It is assumed that in order for us to be able to extend our vocabulary in an unbounded way, we must have mastered a semantic rule. Somehow the reducing definition scheme marks more than a formalization of our semantics; it also plays a role in the underlying psychological processes, it serves as a rule we "follow." Although we cannot consciously perform the definitional reduction, this is what our mind or nervous system "has done." But what evidence or proof do we have that semantic learning can be accomplished only by means of our minds defining or specifying the semantic force of new expressions in terms of some more basic or previously available vocabulary? As was suggested in the previous section of this paper, I am not at all maintaining that nothing can be said in the way of explaining our unbounded competences. The problem here is to determine whether or in what way any particular definition or formal specification by something that can reasonably be called a "semantic rule" supplies such an account.

In any case, it should be clear that, unless we put some restrictions on what is to count as a semantic rule or as mastering a semantic rule, it is hard to see how to begin to establish the claim that only finitely based languages are learnable, or, on the other hand, to know what it would even mean to acquire an infinite set of primitives. For example, if merely mastering an infinite vocabulary is taken as synonymous with having a semantic rule, then the limitations claim would be vacuous. We could not learn an infinite set of semantic primitives, for learning the set would mean the same as mastering a semantic rule, and this would ensure that the number of primitives is finite. Similarly, consider again the case with the indicator terms. We could perhaps finitely specify the denotations of each of these, if we were to allow certain semantic or pragmatic terms to occur in our rules. We might specify that tokens of "here" are true of just the areas the speaker is indicating, or that tokens of "you" denote the person or persons addressed by the speaker. But if we are willing to allow semantic and pragmatic notions like "indicate" or "address" into our rules, it may not even be possible for there to be a vocabulary containing an infinity of primitives. We might be able to specify the semantics for all predicates or singular terms of the lexicon with some sort of single rule, saying that for arbitrary P, P refers to what the speaker indicates or denotes by using P in the sentence. But surely this would not prove anything about the number of primitives in the speakers language. (In a paper that just came to my attention, Cummins, 1975, addresses himself to aspects of these issues.)

And more importantly, returning to some of the nonlinguistic symbol systems we mentioned earlier, e.g., mime, models, and pictures, what sort of rules are we to allow in analyzing the semantic function of these symbols? Here it is at least doubtful that a componential semantic analysis of the sort usually offered for natural languages — analyses that start with an initial stock of words or morphemes and build up to sentences — can get off the ground, yet we can master these systems. But if we are to maintain the learning limitations claim in full generality, i.e., as a limit on the human ability to master symbolic systems, it would be necessary to show how these competences too are reducible to a finite number of semantic rules or primitives of the *specified* kind.

Obviously, if someone wishes to formalize finitely the semantics of a natural language or other symbol system, reducing the needed primitives to a finite stock will be in order. But such reduction will then be forced on semantic analysis by formal features of the type of analysis proposed and not by psychological demands. No claim about the impossibility of learning a language follows by itself from the fact that the language contains an infinite number of primitives on some particular analysis. Without additional assumptions, questions of formal analysis and questions of psychology remain separate issues. In order to support the claim that a language is unlearnable unless it turns out to be finitely based on a particular kind of analysis, it would be necessary to establish a connection between the analysis proposed and learning processes. It would be necessary to show how the proposed specification of the semantics of a given vocabulary is relevant to issues of acquisition. Only then might it be possible to begin to argue that unless the vocabulary can be finitely specified in that way, it could not be learned. As it is, I know of no argument yet proposed that goes to establish and give psychological content to these sorts of claims.

Nevertheless, at least in the case of some symbol systems like natural language, I think there is a point lying behind the assumed limit on primitives. It is just that the usual reasoning from infinity has matters backwards. The important difference between the set of words "shoe," "ink," "cow," etc., and the other systems considered is that the items in this set are abitrary relative to one another. They are arbitrary in the sense that learning one gives no substantial purchase or bias toward learning the denotation of other members of the set. Learning the use of "shoe" and "ink" does not enable one to understand "cow," and vice versa. On the other hand, the members of the music vocabulary, measurement systems, indicator terms, and various of the analogue systems cited are not arbitrary in this way. Learning some members of the system does significantly guide and shape our understanding of other members. (I have discussed this issue in more detail in Schwartz, 1975.)

Arbitrariness of this sort, though, is essentially a question of learnability and not definability. Whether a set of items is to be considered arbitrary depends on whether or not the items provide a basis for learning one another. As I have argued, the connection between learning and any particular type of semantic specification will, from a psychological standpoint, always be derivative. We shall not be able to determine that a set of symbolic items is inductively unlearnable by appeal to the impossibility of a particular type of formal reduction unless it is *first* established that such a definitional specification marks the route by which learning proceeds (or that other routes exist only when such specification is possible). As well as I can interpret it, the original claim that we can learn only a finite number of primitives, especially if it is to be construed as a claim about limits on human symbolic capacity in general, borders on the tautological. For the only sense I have been able to make of primitiveness has been in terms of learnability. But given any set of items, finite or infinite, semantic or other, if it turns out that learning the use of some does not provide sufficient experience for learning the rest, we shall not be able to learn the rest. The claim that we can learn only systems containing a finite number of primitives would then amount to the claim that what we find out we cannot learn under a given set of conditions, we cannot learn under those conditions.

If all this is correct then it also follows that we shall not be able to force any particular kind of semantic analysis on a language merely by citing the formal infiniteness of a linguistic class. Only be requiring that a semantic theory represent some additional specific psychological facts can we derive psychological support for assigning semantic structure. From this point of view, the significant point underlying the assumed limit on primitives may, I think, be brought to light. The claim cannot be interestingly construed as an established constraint on human symbolic capacities. Rather it might best be seen as suggesting a psychological criterion of adequacy for semantic theory. The criterion it suggests is that formal semantics should in some way indicate certain learning relationships among semantic items. Briefly, a semantic analysis should reflect such facts as that learning items of sort *A* enables us to understand items of sort *B*. Justification then for assigning structure will depend on judgments about whether specific learning relationships hold among items and not on whether or how the items can be defined or reduced to one another.

Tokens of a given indicator term will, for example, be construed as instances of one lexical item because learning the reference of some tokens enables us to understand new tokens of that type. Whether the semantics for the indicator can or cannot be specified in one finite fell swoop without appeal to other semantic or pragmatic notions is not to the point. Similarly, on this account, semantic structure will be assigned to the phrases "decoy duck," "centaur picture," and possibly "ran quickly," not because the semantics of the composite phrase can readily be defined in terms of the denotations of its components, but because there is an interplay between the learning habits associated with other tokens of these components, occuring in other contexts and different composites, which serve to guide our construal of the composite expression, and vice versa. The vice versa is significant here. For notice I am not claiming any necessary inferential relationship between composites and their parts, nor that in understanding the composite we actually project its meaning from that assigned its parts in isolation, nor that learning the parts must come first. We may come to learn the parts by being taught the compounds, e.g., when we teach a child the meaning of "tiger" by teaching the child to pick out which things are correctly called "tiger-pictures." Likewise, by appealing to learning relationships, we would justify treating a term and a metaphorical use of the term as one lexical item, rather than as an ambiguous term with two lexical entries, etc. To claim, though, that such learning relationships exist between tokens is not to claim that they have the same meaning or denotation or identical role in their home sentences. To assume that some fixed common property must run through or lie behind all cases of semantic learning is to accept a priori a reductionist view of learning that I have been cautioning against.

Obviously these last suggestions are only a sketch of an approach; much more needs to be said before its implications can be drawn out. Also, as should be clear by now, extending the notions of semantic unit and semantic primitive to other kinds of symbol systems will involve serious complications. I mention this proposal here only because I think something like it, rather than any informative thesis about human symbolic capacities, lies at the heart of the original claim that we can learn only finitely based languages.

Concluding Remarks

The purpose of this paper has been to explore several psychological claims concerning the infinite. These infinitary arguments are initially very appealing, since they appear to offer us insight into the learning process merely by looking at the logic of the situation. The theses are seen as a priori or transcendental principles of human behavior and mental activity that can be established by formal analysis alone, without the need for empirical support or argument. But this is surely a mistake. What can be established by any such formal analysis is that, if humans are systems of a specific sort, if they accept and process data in a certain way, then a particular limitation will exist. To show that a limitation actually exists, though, we must first show that humans are systems of that specific type, and that in a given case the material presented is processed in the specific way. In order to make the formal argument applicable or psychologically relevant, further assumptions must be added about the system at hand, which can only be justified by studying our actual competences and the ways we go about acquiring them. In the case of claims based on infinity, this is particularly striking. For the relevant notion of infinity will always be relative to some system of classifying, parsing, or individuating. The world comes to us neither as one nor as many. So we can establish infinity arguments intelligibly only after we have established something about how the given set is actually organized and processed, and only after we have understood what means are available to the organism for handling the material. Once this psychological study of the actual perceptual and learning processes is completed, moreover, it would seem that an appeal to the infinite will add relatively little. The important psychological insights will have been gained in determining what kind of a system the organism really is.

I have attempted to focus on this methodological issue concerning the relationship between formal theory and models of mind by examining several claims about learning natural language. I have argued that in each case a simple appeal to the infiniteness of some specified set is not sufficient to establish significant and interesting psychological principles. I have not sought to reject outright or to refute these various claims; for although it should be clear that I find these assumptions—as sometimes propounded—suspect, I think there are psychologically interesting points lurking behind them. In support of this feeling, in some areas, I have even offered tentative suggestions as to what I think would be a fruitful approach to the problems. My hope is that by being more prudent in our reliance on the infinite, we can progress toward a better account of the underlying psychological issues.

References

Atherton, M. *Nativism*. Unpublished doctoral dissertation, Brandeis University, 1970.

Cummins, R. Truth and logical form. *Journal of Philosophical Logic*, 1975, 4, (1), 29-44.

Goodman, N. *Languages of art*. Indianapolis: Bobbs-Merrill, 1968.

Harman, G. Psychological aspects of the theory of syntax. *Journal of Philosophy*, 1967, 64 (2), 75-87.

Hook, S. (Ed.) *Language and philosophy*. New York: New York University Press, 1969.

Katz, J. J. *Semantic theory*. New York: Harper and Row, 1972.

Malcolm, N. The myth of cognitive processes and structures. In T. Mischel (Ed.), *Cognitive development and epistemology*. New York and London: Academic Press, 1971.

Morgenbesser, S. Fodor on Ryle and rules. *Journal of Philosophy*, 1969, 66 (14), 458-472.

Nagel, T. Bounds of inner sense. *Journal of Philosophy*, 1969, 66, (14), 452-458.

Schwartz, R. Representation and resemblance. *Philosophical Forum*, 1975, 7, 499-512.

Toward a Cognitive Theory of Consciousness

I

Philosophers of mind and epistemologists have much to learn from recent work in cognitive psychology, but one of philosophy's favorite facets of mentality has received scant attention from cognitive psychologists, and that is consciousness itself: full-blown, introspective, inner-world, phenomenological consciousness. In fact if one looks in the obvious places (the more ambitious attempts at whole theories, overviews of recent research, and more specialized work in such areas as attention and "mental imagery") one finds not so much a lack of interest as a deliberate and adroit avoidance of the issue. I think I know why. Consciousness appears to be the last bastion of occult properties, epiphenomena, immeasurable subjective states—in short, the one area of mind best left to the philosophers, who are welcome to it. Let them make fools of themselves trying to corral the quicksilver of "phenomenology" into a respectable theory.

This would permit an acceptable division of labor were it not for the fact that cognitive psychologists have skirted the domain of consciousness by so wide a margin that they offer almost no suggestions about what the "interface" between the models of cognitive psychology and a theory of consciousness should be. I propose to fill this gap and sketch a theory of consciousness that can be continuous with, and help unify, current cognitivist theories of perception, problem-solving, and language use. I fear that to the extent that the view I put forward is seen to meet these desiderata it will *seem* not to do justice to the phenomena, so it would help if first I said just what I am trying to do justice to. Nagel (1974) has epitomized the problem of consciousness with the question: "What is it like to be something?" It is certainly not like anything to be a brick or a hamburger; it certainly is like something to be you or me; and it seems to be like something to be a bat or a dog or a dolphin, if only we could figure out what. The question, "is it like something to be an *X*?" may in the end be the wrong question to ask, but it excellently captures the intuitions that constitute the challenge to a theory of consciousness. Until one's psychological or physiological or cybernetic theory explains how it can be like something to be something (or explains *in detail* what is wrong with this demand), one's theory will be *seriously* incomplete. It is open to the theorist, of course, to reject the challenge out of hand. One can emulate those behaviorists who (it has been charged) "feign anesthesia" and categorically deny that anyone *has* an inner life. This course has little or nothing to recommend it. Some behaviorists may find this comfortable ground to defend, but it would be awkward at the very least for the cognitivist, who has to explain what is going on when, for example, one asks one's experimental subjects to form a mental image, or to give an introspective account of problem-solving, or to attend to the sentences in the left earphone rather than the sentences in the right earphone. The cognitivist must take consciousness seriously, but there are relatively noncommittal ways of doing this. One can somewhat paradoxically treat consciousness itself as something of a "black box" from which introspective and retrospective statements issue (with their associated reaction times, and so forth), but how is this black box fastened to the other boxes in one's model? I shall propose an answer to this question, one that will also be a partial account of what is going on inside the black box.

II

There is much that happens to me and in me of which I am *not* conscious, which I do not experience, and there is much that happens in and to me of which I *am* conscious. That of which I am conscious is that to which I have *access*, or (to put the emphasis where it belongs), that to which *I* have access. Let us call this sort of access the access of personal consciousness, thereby stressing that the *subject* of that access (whatever it is) which exhausts consciousness is the *person*, and not any of the person's parts. The first step in characterizing this access is to distinguish it from two other sorts of access that play important roles in cognitive theories. The first of these can be called *computational access*. When a computer program is composed of subroutines (typically governed by an "executive" routine) one can speak of one routine having access to the output of another. This means simply that there is an information link between them: the results of computation of one subroutine are available for further computation by another subroutine. A variety of interesting issues can be couched in terms of computational access. For instance, Marvin Minsky (1974) faults the design of current chess-playing programs by pointing out that the executive programs typically do not have enough *access* (of the right sort) to the routines that evaluate the various lines of play considered. Typically, the evaluator "has to summarize the results of all the search . . . and compress them into a single numerical quantity to represent the value of being at node A . . . [but] we want S [the output of the evaluator] to tell the Move Generator which kinds of moves to consider. But if S is a mere number, this is unsuitable for much reasoning or analysis." It would be better if the higher executive had more access to the details of the line of play evaluated, and not just a summary judgment.

In a very different context, Julesz's (1971) perception experiments using randomly generated dot displays show that at least some perceptual information about depth, for instance, is computed by a process that has *access* to highly uninterpreted information about the pattern of light stimulating the retinas. Lines of computational access are currently being studied in cognitive psychology and related fields, and there are useful characterizations of direct and indirect access, variable access, gated access, and so forth. Computational access has nothing *directly* to do with the access of personal consciousness, for *we* do not have access to many things that various parts of our nervous systems are shown to have access to. For instance, some levels of the visual processing system must have computational access to information about inner ear state changes and saccadic eye movements, but *we* do not, and *we* have virtually no access to the information our autonomic nervous systems must have access to in order to maintain the complex homeostases of health.

The second sort of access to distinguish from both computational access and the access of personal consciousness might be called *public access*. Often it is useful to a programmer to have access to what the computer is doing, so that the computer's progress on the program can be monitored; and to this end a "trace" is provided for in the program so the computer can print out information about the intermediate steps in its own operations. One provides for public access of this sort by designing a print-out subroutine and giving it *computational* access to whatever one wants public access to. This is a nontrivial additional provision in a program, for there is a difference between, say, the access the executive routine has to its subroutines, and the access the print-out routine has to the access the executive routine has. The domain of computational access for a system and the domain of public access for the system user are as distinct as the functions and offices of Secretary of State Henry Kissinger and Press Secretary Ron Nessen. Kissinger has computational access to much information that we the public have no access to because Nessen, our avenue of access, has no computational access to the information. What is used for control is one thing and what is available to the public is another, and there is at best a contingently large overlap between these domains, both in computer systems and in the White House.

The notion of public access seems to bring us closer to the personal access of consciousness, for we are speaking creatures (we have a sort of print-out faculty), and—at least to a first approximation —that of which we are conscious is that of which we can tell, introspectively or retrospectively. There is a problem, however. So far, the *subject* of public access has not been identified. On the one hand we can speak of the *public's* access via print-out or other publication to what is going on in a system, and on the other we can speak of the *print-out faculty's* computational access to the information it publishes; but surely neither of these subjects is the "I" who has access to my contents of consciousness, nor does any more suitable subject appear likely to be found in this neighborhood.[1]

The picture of a human being as analogous to a large organization, with intercommunicating departments, executives, and a public relations unit to "speak for the organization" is very attractive and useful. The basic idea is as old as Plato's *Republic*, but it seems to have a fatal flaw: it is not like anything to be such an organization. What is it like to be the Ford Administration? Nothing, obviously, even if it is like something to be a certain part of that administration. The whole is a very clever assemblage of coordinated *parts* that at its best acts with a unity not unlike the unity of a single person (Rawls, 1971), but still, it has no soul of its own, even if some of its parts do.

This apparently decisive shortcoming threatens a wide spectrum of theory-building enterprises currently receiving favorable attention in philosophy and psychology. Any philosopher of mind who (like myself) favors a "functionalist" theory of mind (see, for example, Block, this volume—Ed.) must face the fact that the very feature that has been seen to recommend functionalism over cruder brands of materialism—its abstractness and hence neutrality with regard to what could "realize" the functions deemed essential to sentient or Intentional systems—permits a functionalist theory, however realistically biological or humanoid in flavor, to be instantiated not only by robots (an acceptable or even desirable consequence in the eyes of some), but by suprahuman organizations that would seem to have minds of their own only in the flimsiest metaphorical sense.[2] Psychologists cannot escape this embarrassment merely by declining to embrace philosophers' versions of functionalism, for their own theories are vulnerable to a version of the same objection. Functionalist theories are theories of what I have called the subpersonal level. Subpersonal theories proceed by analyzing a person into an organization of subsystems (organs, routines, nerves, faculties, components—even atoms) and attempting to explain the behavior of the whole person as the outcome of the interaction of these subsystems. Thus in the present instance the shortcoming emerged because the two access notions introduced, computational access *simpliciter* and the computational access of a print-out faculty, were defined at the subpersonal level; if introduced into a psychological theory they would characterize relations not between a person and a body, or a person and a state of affairs or a person and anything at all, but rather, at best, relations between *parts* of persons (or their bodies) and other things. So far as I can see, however, every cognitivist theory currently defended or envisaged, functionalist or not, is a theory of the subpersonal level. It is not at all clear to me, indeed, how a psychological theory—as distinct from a philosophical theory—could fail to be a subpersonal theory.[3] So the functionalists' problem of capturing the person as subject of experience must arise as well for these cognitivist theories. At best a subpersonal theory will seem to give us *no grounds* for believing its instantiations would be subjects of experience, and at worst (as we have seen) a subpersonal theory will seem to permit instantiations that *obviously are not* subjects of experience. Take your favorite inchoate cognitivist theory and imagine it completed and improved along the lines of its infancy; is it not always easy to imagine the completed theory instantiated or "realized" by an entity—an engineer's contraption, for instance, or some kind of zombie—to which we have no inclination to grant an inner, conscious life?

Intuition, then, proclaims that any subpersonal theory must leave out something vital, something unobtainable moreover with subpersonal resources. Intuitions can sometimes be appeased or made to go away, however, and that is the task I set myself here. I propose to construct a full-fledged "I" out of subpersonal parts by exploiting the subpersonal notions of access already introduced.[4]

The first step is to sketch a subpersonal flow chart, a cognitivistic model that by being subpersonal "evades" the question of personal consciousness but, unlike cognitivistic psychologies with which I am familiar, prepares attachment points for subsequent explicit claims about consciousness. The flow chart will be a philosopher's amateur production, oversimplified in several dimensions, but I think it will be fairly clear how one could go about adding complications.

III

For clarity I restrict attention to six of the functional areas to which a theory of consciousness must do justice. (See Figure 1). At the output end we have the print-out component, and since this is our own Ron Nessen analogue I shall call it *PR*. *PR* takes as input *orders to perform speech acts*, or *semantic intentions*, and executes these orders. The details of the organization of the *PR* component are hotly contested by psycholinguists and others, and I do not wish to adjudicate the debates. Roughly, I suppose the breakdown to be as follows: the speech act command gets turned into an *oratio obliqua* command (to say that *p*), and this gets turned into a "deep structure" specification—in "semantic markerese" perhaps—which in turn yields a surface structure or *oratio recta* specification. We

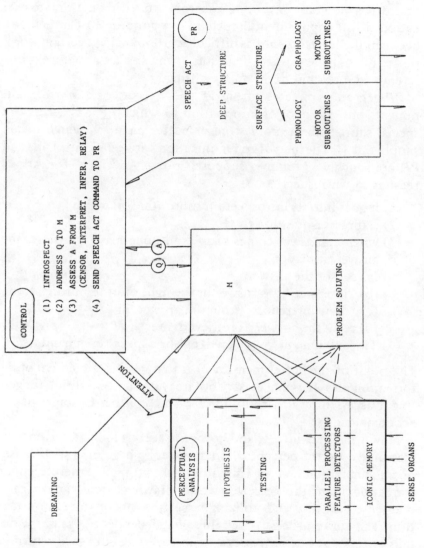

Figure 1.

can imagine this to branch into either a phonological or graphologi-
cal specification, depending on whether the initial command was to
speak or write. These specifications, finally, drive motor subroutines
that drive the vocal or writing apparatus to yield an ultimate execution of the input intention. There is a good deal of interaction
between the levels: if one has difficulty pronouncing a certain word,
this may count against its inclusion in the surface structure if one
intends to speak but not if one is writing.

PR gets all its directions from a higher executive or *Control* component, but the pool of information to which *PR* has access is a
special short-term memory store or buffer memory, which I shall
simply call *M*. The lines of communication between Control, *M*, and
PR are roughly as follows: suppose Control "decides" for various
reasons to "introspect":

(1) it goes into its introspection subroutine, in which
(2) it directs a question to *M*;
(3) when an answer comes back (and none may) it assesses the
answer: it may
    (a) censor the answer
    (b) "interpret" the answer in the light of other information
    (c) "draw inferences" from the answer, or
    (d) relay the answer as retrieved direct to *PR*
(4) The outcome of any of (a-d) can be a speech command to *PR*.

The point of the buffer memory *M* is that getting some item of information into *M* is a necessary but not sufficient condition for getting it accessed by *PR* in the form of the *content* of some speech
act command.

Now what gets into *M* and how? First let us look at perception.
I assume a tier of perceptual analysis levels beginning with sense-
organ stimulation and arriving ultimately at highly interpreted information about the perceived world, drawing often on more than
one sense modality and utilizing large amounts of stored information. The entire process is variably goal-dependent. Again, the details of this stack of processes are controversial, but I shall venture a
few relatively safe points. At the lowest levels we have what Neisser
(1967) calls "iconic memory,"[5] a very short storage of the stimuli
virtually uninterpreted. "Parallel processing" by "feature detectors"

takes us up several levels and yields crude but local-specific information about edges, corners, shapes, patches of color, and so forth. From there a process of "hypothesis generation and confirmation" takes over, a *sequential*, not parallel, process that utilizes both stored "world knowledge" (in the "expectation-driven mode") and the results of the parallel feature detectors (in the "data-driven mode") to determine the generation of hypotheses and their confirmation and disconfirmation. Perhaps the "data structures" at the highest levels of this process are Minsky's "frames" (1974), and perhaps they are not. All the processes of perceptual analysis, but especially the higher, sequential levels are governed by complicated instruction from Control. As Neisser (1967) argues convincingly, with limited cognitive resources with which to perform this sophisticated task of perceptual analysis, Control must budget wisely, allocating the available cognitive resources to the sensory modality or topic of most current importance. This allocation of cognitive resources is the essence of *attention*, Neisser argues, and I partially concur. There is a notion of attention that is very definitely a matter of allocation of cognitive resources.[6] This notion of attention, important as it is, is only very indirectly connected with consciousness, as can be seen at a glance if one considers the fact that any problem-solving or game playing computer pays attention, in this sense, first to one candidate course of action and then to another, and presumably it would not on this ground be deemed conscious. Or consider the fact that a somnambulist must no doubt allocate considerable cognitive resources to the job of navigating successfully and maintaining balance while being, in some important sense, unconscious (and unconscious *of* all this calculation) at the time. In this sense of attention, *unconscious attention* is no contradiction in terms, and in fact no hints at all have been given to suggest what *conscious* attention might be.

Now the perceptual analysis component sends information to *M from many levels*. Why? Because when one sees a complex scene and analyzes it as, say, a chair and a table in the middle of the room, one sees more than just that there are that chair and table there. One sees the shapes, colors, local details, and periphery too. I do not want to *identify* what one experiences with what one *can say*, but at least *if* one can say something about some current feature of the perceivable world, one has experienced it. This is vividly brought out by tachistoscopic experiments (Neisser, 1967). If one sees a string of four alphabetic letters flashed for a few milliseconds on a screen, one cannot usually identify them. Although the stimulus pattern persists in iconic storage after the actual external flash has ceased, this storage decays before the higher-level processors can complete their work; and once the data are lost, analysis must terminate. But one sees *something*; one can say that one has seen a flash, or a flash with some dark objects, or even four letters or symbols. Something is experienced even though perceptual analysis is not completed. In such a case, I am supposing, the results of however much analysis gets accomplished normally go to M. These results will go other places of great importance as well, no doubt, but for our purposes all that matters is what gets into M.[7]

Perception, then, sends a variety of inputs to M. Perceptual experience is not the only conscious experience we have, though, so what else must we suppose gets into M? We are normally conscious of our thinking when we set out to solve problems, so let us very artificially isolate a *problem-solving component* that sends its results to M. (At least for some sorts of problem-solving—"imagistic" problem-solving—it is tempting to suppose the processes utilize a lot of the machinery of perceptual analysis; hence the dotted lines in Figure 1.) We shall return later to this component and its interactions with M. Another unit that sends information to M is Control itself. A partial record of its goals, plans, intentions, beliefs gets installed in M for occasional publication when the situation demands it.

These are the essential units of the system for my purposes here, but just to illustrate how the model could be extended, I add the dream-production unit. It loads M as well, and, as I have argued elsewhere (Dennett, 1976), the question whether dreams are experiences is to be answered by assessing the nature of this memory-loading process (the "route taken" by the access arrow).

Before turning to the question of how such a subpersonal model could possibly say anything about consciousness, let me illustrate briefly how it is supposed to handle various phenomena. Fodor (1975) discusses an experiment by Lackner and Garrett (1973). In dichotic listening tests subjects listen through earphones to two different channels and are instructed to *attend* to just one channel. They can typically report with great accuracy what they have heard through the attended channel, but not surprisingly they can typically say little about what was going on concomitantly in the unattended channel. Thus, if the unattended channel carries a spoken sentence, the subjects can typically report they heard a voice, or even a male or female voice. Perhaps they even have a conviction about whether the voice was speaking in their native tongue, but they cannot report *what was said*. One hypothesis, based on Broadbent's (1958) filtering theory, is that a control decision is made to allocate virtually all the cognitive resources to the analysis of the attended channel, with only low-level ("preattentive") processing being done on the input from the unattended channel. Processing of the unattended channel at the level of semantic analysis, for instance, is on this hypothesis *just not done*. Lackner and Garrett's (1973) experiments disconfirm the Broadbent model in this instance, however. In the *attended* channel subjects heard ambiguous sentences, such as "He put out the lantern to signal the attack." In the unattended channel one group of subjects received disambiguating input (e.g., "He extinguished the lantern"), while another group had neutral or irrelevant input. The former group *could not report* what they heard through the unattended channel, but they favored the suggested reading of the ambiguous sentences more than the control group. The influence of the unattended channel on the interpretation of the attended signal can be explained only on the hypothesis that the unattended input is processed all the way to a semantic level, even though the subjects have no awareness of this—that is, cannot report it. On my model, this suggests that although higher-level processing of the unattended channel goes on, only low-level results are sent to M. This nicely illustrates the independence of computational access for *control* (in this case, influencing perceptual set in the attended channel) from computational access for *publication*, and gives an instance of, and an interpretation of, the well-known unreliability of introspective evidence. The *absence* of introspective evidence that a certain analysis has been performed is never reliable evidence that no such analysis has been performed. The analysis in question may simply be one of the many processes that contribute in other ways to control, perception, and action without loading M with its results. I shall discuss more subtle cases of the relationship between such processing and introspective access later.

To pave the way for this, I want to say a bit more about the interaction proposed between *PR*, Control, and *M*. Suppose *PR* gets a speech act command that for one reason or another it cannot execute. Words fail it. I propose that a failure discovery like this feeds back to Control, which will deal with the situation in a number of ways. It can alter its directions to Perceptual Analysis, producing a new perceptual set. This *may* result in a reinterpretation of the incoming stimulation, producing a *changed* input (at any level) to *M*, and then a changed speech act command to *PR*. Being unable at first to describe one's perceptual experience could lead in this way to a *change* in one's perceptual experience. (This would help explain, I suggest, the heightened capacity to discriminate—and experience— wines that comes from learning to use the exotic vocabulary of the wine-taster. What I am proposing is, of course, a very Kantian bit of machinery, designed in effect to knit intuitions and concepts together. Any psychological theory must address this problem; in some models the Kantian perspective is just more readily seen.) But if perceptual revision did not occur, Control could send to *PR* a direction to say that one finds the experience ineffable or indescribable, and this might be followed by a series of commands to say various things about what the experience was more or less like, about just how one's words are betraying one's true semantic intentions, and so forth. What I am granting is that there is no guarantee that information loaded into *M* has a publication in the native tongue that is acceptable to the system.[8]

What kind of *information* might fail to find expression in one's native tongue? Although *M* has been characterized as an information store, nothing has been said about the *form* the information must take. What sort of "data structures" are involved? Is the information encoded "propositionally" or "imagistically" or "analogically"? These important questions deserve answers, but not here. It is important here, however, to explain why I refrain from answering them, and that will require a digression.

The current debate in cognitive psychology between the propositionalists and the lovers of images[9] is multifariously instructive to philosophers, not only because it contains echoes of philosophic controversies,[10] but also because it clearly illustrates the close and systematic relationship between "pure" philosophy—especially epistemology—and empirical psychology. Psychologists, faced with the practical impossibility of answering the empirical questions of psychology by brute inspection (how does the human nervous system accomplish perception or cognition?) very reasonably ask themselves an easier preliminary question: how could *any* (physical or mechanical or biological) system accomplish perception or cognition? This question is easier because it is "less empirical"; it is an *engineering* question, a quest for a solution (any solution) rather than a discovery, but it is still dominated by a mountain of empirical facts—in particular, facts about the powers, limits, and idiosyncrasies of actual human perceivers under a wide range of conditions.

The psychological question becomes: how could any system *do all that*? It is a question one is ill-equipped to answer if one does not know what *all that* is—for instance, if one is a philosopher largely unacquainted with the psychologists' data. Yet there is a strong aprioristic element in the psychologists' investigations, because it turns out to be very difficult to compose any model at all that could conceivably *do all that*. What is wrong with most models is that they fail to satisfy some quite general constraint or constraints on all solutions. The charge often leveled against such models is thus not (or *not just*) that they fail to account for some body of data, but that they *could not conceivably* account for human perception or cognition (for instance), since they violate some proclaimed necessary condition on all solutions. This aprioristic thinking is not peculiar to psychology. Engineers can enumerate necessary conditions for being an amplifier or a motor, and biologists can set down constraints on all possible solutions to the problem of the mechanics of genetic inheritance, to give just two examples. Once one decides to do psychology this way at all, one can address oneself to the problems raised by the most particular constraints, by middling constraints, or by the most general constraints. One can ask how any neuronal network of such-and-such features can possibly accomplish human color discriminations, or one can ask how any finite organic system can possibly subserve the acquisition of a natural language, or one can ask, with Kant, how anything at all could possibly experience or know anything. Pure epistemology thus viewed is simply the limiting case of the psychologists' quest, and any constraints the philosopher finds in that most general and abstract in-

vestigation bind all psychological theories as inexorably as constraints
encountered in more parochial and fact-enriched environments.

Notice, too, that the philosophers' most abstract question is not
asked in a factual vacuum; when we ask aprioristically how experience is possible, or what knowledge is, or how anything can be a
symbol or have meaning, we appeal to, and are thus constrained
by, an enormous body of commonplace facts: the facts that anchor
what we mean by "experience," "symbol," and so forth. All the
philosopher need know in the way of facts is what can be learned
at mother's knee, but that is not nothing. The psychologist says:
the experimental results bear me out, don't they? The philosopher
says: that's what it is to understand an utterance, isn't it? If recently
many philosophers of mind, knowledge, and language have found
it useful or imperative to descend in the direction of more data, the
reason is that the issues at the less general levels are proving to be
fascinating, manipulable, and apparently useful in illuminating the
more abstract level.

This is particularly apparent in the current controversy over propositions and images as vehicles of information in cognitive systems,
a controversy of protean guise, sometimes appearing to be pure
philosophy (and hence no business of psychologists!), sometimes an
abstract engineering question for cyberneticists and the like, and
sometimes a question of hard psychological, biological, or phenomenological fact. It has grown popular to the point of becoming second
nature to talk of *information*-processing and transmission in the nervous system, but there is uncertainty and disagreement about the
a priori constraints on any such talk of information. There is often
the illusion that no problems attend the psychologists' talk of information, since information theory has presumably provided a rigorous
foundation for such talk, but it is not often that psychologists have
in mind any hard-edged information-theoretic sense of the term;
usually what is being alluded to is the information or content an
event within the system has *for the system as a (biological) whole*
(what the frog's eye tells the frog's brain, or better, as Arbib has
suggested (in conversation), what the frog's eye tells the frog.) The
content (in this sense) of a particular vehicle of information, a particular information-bearing event or state, is and must be a function
of its function in the system. This is the sense of "information"

utilized in our model (and in psychological models generally); so when I assert that, for instance, there is a transfer of information from some perceptual analysis area to M, I endow that transfer event with content, and the content it has is to be understood as a function of the function within the whole system of that event. So far, that event's function has been only circularly characterized: it has the function of conveying information about the results of analysis at that level to a functional area that is accessible to another functional area whose function is to express in a natural language just that information obtained by that level of perceptual analysis. Such a characterization is circular, but not necessarily viciously circular. The circle is a high-level holding pattern, which permits us to consider the constraints on any theory without descending to the next, more empirical level.

We can say, though, just what that next level down is. The content of a psychological state or event is a function of its function, and its function is—in the end, must be—a function of the *structure* of the state or event and the systems of which it is a part. Not just any structures can realize the functions that we determine must be realized, but the step from functional constraint to structural constraint is treacherous[11] and takes a philosopher quite far from home. When the question of "form of information" takes on this (quite proper) guise as a question of engineering, I leave it—reluctantly— to the engineers. I shall address myself shortly to the question in its "purely philosophical" or "phenomenological" guises. So, to end the digression, it would be best, for the time being, to stay in our circle and talk only of the *content* of states and events, and not the structure of the vehicles of content.

Stopping at a level of description above the stern demands of structural realizations is thus engaging in an extended exercise in more or less well-motivated handwaving,[12] but this handwaving may well be saved by ultimate realizations of these information-processing components, and if it is, it will have been not only not in vain, but an essential propaedeutic to such theorizing.

One can never be sure, however. For instance, the Control component in my model is awfully fancy. It has a superb capacity to address just the right stored information in its long-term memory, a talent for asking M just the right questions, and an ability to organize its long- and short-term goals and plans in a very versatile way. This is no homunculus that any AI researcher has the faintest idea how to realize at this time. The ever-present worry is that as we devise components — lesser homunculi — to execute various relatively menial tasks near the periphery, we shall be "making progress" only by driving into the center of our system an all-powerful executive homunculus whose duties require an almost Godlike omniscience.[13] I can make no firm claims for the soundness of my components in this model. The most I shall venture for them is that they seem to me not to reproduce the problems at deeper levels, thus merely postponing solution.

IV

With those qualifications and excuses behind me, I turn to the decisive question. Suppose an entity were all wired up in some fashion so as to realize the flow chart in Figure 1. What would it be like (if anything) to be such an entity? At first glance the answer seems to be: not like anything. The whole system has been designed to operate in the dark, as it were, with the various components accomplishing their tasks unperceived and unperceiving. In particular, we have not supposed any inner introspecting eye to be watching the perceptual analysis processes, the control decisions, the efforts of *PR* to execute its orders. And yet to us on the outside, watching such an entity, engaging it in conversation, listening to its efforts to describe the effects on it of various perceptual environments, there will be at least the illusion that it is like something to be the entity. In fact it will tell us (or at least seem to be telling us) just what it is like. But inside it is all darkness, a hoax. Or so it seems. Inside your skull it is also all darkness, and whatever processes occur in your grey matter occur unperceived and unperceiving. Can it be said that just as there is some other point of view that *you* have, there is some other point of view that *it* has?

It is hard to know how to answer that question. But the following may help. Suppose I put forward the bold hypothesis that you are a realization of this flow chart, and that it is in virtue of this fact that it seems — to us and to you — that there is something it is like to be you. Can you give good grounds for denying the hypothesis, and if so, what are they? What personal access do you have, and to what? Here I must abruptly shift the perspective of this paper and wax phenomenological for a while. I want to draw your attention to a class of phenomena. If you ever had a sudden *presentiment* that someone was looking over your shoulder, or a *premonition* that something dire was about to happen, you are acquainted with the phenomena. These events are propositional episodes, thinkings that *p*; there is normally some inclination to express them (although the inclination is easily suppressed or cancelled), and we may not even express them to ourselves in "inner speech." When they occur in us we have not the faintest idea what their etiology is (unless we have some theory about the causes of premonitions; my point is that "to introspection" they arrive from we know not where). There are other more familiar examples of coming to want to say something without knowing how or why. Witticisms "occur to us," but we do not know how we produce them (the example is Ryle's). Lashley long ago pointed out that if asked to think a thought in dactyllic hexameter we (many of us) can oblige, but we have no awareness of how we do it: the *result* arrives, and that is the extent of our direct access to the whole business. Lashley's provocative comment on his example was that "no activity of the mind is ever conscious," and the interpretation of this I am supporting is that we have access— conscious access—to the *results* of mental processes, but not to the processes themselves.

My contention is that far from being rare and anomalous occurrences, the propositional episodes, these thinkings that *p*, are our normal and continuous avenue to self-knowledge, that they exhaust our immediate awareness, and that the odd varieties, such as the presentiment that someone is looking over one's shoulder, are striking only because of their isolation from the preceding and following presentiments, only because of our inability to follow them up with related propositional episodes about the same topic.[14] Right now it occurs to me that there are pages in front of me, a presentiment whose etiology is not known directly by me, but which is, of course, perfectly obvious. It is my visual system that gives me this presentiment, along with a host of others. I *can say* all sorts of things to elaborate on and supplement my initial report. But if I am put in an abnormal perceptual environment—for instance, in a tachisto-scopic experiment—I may be less sure *why* I want to say what I do.

I sort of have a hunch that is was an English word you flashed on the screen, but did I really *see* it? I cannot say what word it was, or describe it in any detail.

Instead of cajoling you with further phenomenological persuasions, I shall enlarge upon my view by drawing an analogy to Hume (1888). Hume's revolutionary step in the analysis of causation was to suggest that we had it all backwards. Earlier attempts at an account of our belief in causation supposed that when we saw a cause and then an effect we *saw* the necessary connection between them, and *thereupon and therefore* inferred or expected the effect when we saw the cause. Hume examined the cause ("turned it on all sides") and could *find* no such necessary connection to be observed, so he suggested that it was the other way around: having been conditioned, in effect, to infer or expect the effect when seeing the cause, we *found ourselves* drawing the inference, and this gave rise to an illusion of sorts that we were *seeing* a necessary connection that explained and grounded the inference we were compelled to make. The inference itself, Hume says, is psychologically and epistemically prior, and it gives rise to the belief in a "perceived" necessary connection. I am proposing a parallel account of "introspection": we find ourselves *wanting to say* all these things about what is going on in us; this gives rise to *theories* we hold about how we come to be able to do this—for instance, the notorious but homespun theory that we "perceive" these goings on with our "inner eye," and that this *perception* grounds and explains the semantic intentions we have.

Hume might almost have arrived at this extension of his view. He claims (1888, I.iv.2) that there is a difference between our "internal impressions" and our sensations. The latter require the positing of continuously existing external bodies in order to preserve the coherence and constancy of our discontinuous impressions of sensation. (Hume's example is the fire in his study fireplace that gradually burns down, turning slowly to embers in the periods between the interrupted and different sensations he receives from the fire.) But, says Hume (p. 195), "internal impressions" do not require this postulating; "on no occasion is it necessary to suppose that they have existed and operated, when they were not perceived, in order to preserve the same dependance and connexion, of which we have had experience." This claim is virtually unavoidable for Hume—given his allegiance to a Lockean doctrine of the "transparency" of the mind to itself—but it is a fundamental error. Not only must we come to accept all manner of covert influences, unconscious problem-solving processes, and the like (recall Lashley's dictum), but *mental images themselves* are the creatures of a "posit," an inference or extrapolation exactly analogous to Hume's "posit" about external bodies. This is graphically illustrated by Shepard's (1971) experiments with "rotating mental images." The subjects in these experiments are shown pairs of line drawings like those in Figure 2, and asked whether or not the pair are different views of the same shape. In this case, as you can quickly determine, the answer is Yes. How did you do it? A typical answer is, "I rotated the image in my mind's eye." Amazingly, Shepard set out to see if he could determine the normal angular velocity of rotation of such images! How could he do this? The subjects were given buttons to press to give their answers. After tentative standard latency times were subtracted from both ends of the duration between display and answer, Shepard was left with durations that should, on his hypothesis, vary linearly (ignoring acceleration and deceleration) with the degrees of rotation required to bring the figures into superimposition. It should take

Figure 2.

roughly twice as long to rotate an image through 100 degrees as through 50 degrees. Shepard claims to have obtained significant positive results: he himself can rotate such mental images at an angular velocity of 62.6 degrees per second.

Now how can my view possibly accommodate such phenomena? Aren't we directly aware of an image rotating in phenomenal space in this instance? No. And that much, I think, you can quickly ascertain to your own satisfaction. For isn't it the case that if you attend to your experience more closely when you say you rotate the image you find it moves in discrete jumps—it flicks through a series of orientations. You cannot gradually speed up or slow down the rotation, can you? But now "look" again. Isn't it really just that these discrete steps are discrete propositional episodes: now it looks like *this*, but if I imagine it turned *that* much, it would look like *that* . . . ah yes, it would eventually look just like the other one. But the flicking, you may insist, is clearly part of a motion observed— the axis of rotation is, perhaps, vertical, not horizontal. But your reason for saying this is just that your intermediate judgments define the rotation. They are judgements that fall in an order that would be the proper order of perceptual judgments in a case of watching a real image rotate around a vertical axis. If you are inclined to argue that only an internal system that did actually proceed by some rotation in space of a representation or image could explain the sequence of judgments and their temporal relations in such cases, you might be right, but your grounds are hardly overwhelming. In fact, these discrete series of judgments bear a striking resemblance to the discrete series of small flashing lights that create the illusions of perceived motion, which have received so much attention from psychologists.[15]

We know that in these situations we all "perceive" motion—even elaborate orbital motions in three dimensions—when there is no motion. When we are confronted by a small group of these sequentially flashing lights we experience an illusion; we are led irresistibly to a nonveridical perceptual judgment that there is a single light moving in a particular way. What I am suggesting is that as the discrete series of flashes is to that nonveridical judgment, so our series of judgments in the image rotation case is to the judgment that something is really rotated in our minds (or in our brains, or anywhere).

There *may* be motion of something "behind" our judgments in the image rotation case, but if there is, it is something quite outside our present ken, and its very existence is suggested only by the most tenuous inference, however psychologically irresistible it may be.

My account of the Shepard phenomenon is that *however* the problem-solving process is accomplished, it yields *results*, both final and intermediate, that are available in *M* to be accessed by *PR*. These results, by the time they reach *PR*, are unproblematically propositional in nature: they are intentions to say that *p*. They are one product of perception or problem-solving. Another product is ducking when you see a flying object coming at you, but this is neither propositional nor imagistic so far as I can see. These products are perhaps only *indirect* products of perceptual processes; the *direct* or *immediate* product, one might wish to say, is experience itself, and the question is whether experience is propositional or imagistic or something else. My answer, counterintuitive as it may seem at first, is that if that question has any admissible interpretation at all, introspection cannot answer it. We have no direct personal access to the *structure* of contentful events within us.

V

Having given some suggestion about how the model I propose operates with a variety of phenomena, I now want to make some proposals about how the traditional categories of consciousness are to be superimposed on the model. These proposals are not supposed to be a priori truths about consciousness, or the dictates of conceptual analysis of our ordinary concepts, but rather suggestions about the best fit we can achieve between our pretheoretical intuitions (which are not entirely consistent) and a cognitive theory of the sort I have been sketching.

(1) One perceives more than one experiences. Perceptual analysis provides information about the world that is utilized in the control of behavior but is not accessible to introspection or consciousness, on any familiar understanding of these terms. In other words, there is nothing repugnant to theory in the notion of unconscious or subliminal perception or "subception," and any intuitions to the contrary should be discarded.

(2) The content of one's experience includes whatever enters (by

normal routes) the buffer memory M. What one experiences may decay before it is in fact accessed by PR, or it may be garbled in transition to PR, or it may be relatively inaccessible to PR.[16] In virtue of this possibility of error or malfunction between M and PR, *what one wants to say* is not an infallible or incorrigible determinant of what one has experienced or is currently experiencing. So the content of one's experience is given an *objective* characterization, and any intuition we have to the contrary that we are the sole and perfect arbiters of what we experience should be discarded.

(3) One experiences more at any time than one wants to say then. What fills the "periphery," adds detail to one's "percepts," inhabits "fringe consciousness," is, as phenomenologists have insisted, *there*. Where? In M. No more mysterious process of presentation or apprehension of inhabitants of phenomenal space is needed.

(4) One experiences more than one attends to—in either of two senses of attention. One experiences more than what results from higher-level allocations of cognitive resources, and one experiences, as (3) asserts, more than one is currently thinking. These are entirely different ways in which there are unattended contents of consciousness, even though there is a strong contingent link between them. Usually Control fixes things so that what one is attending to in the former sense is what one is attending to in the latter. Put otherwise, our conscious access to what we are attending to is normally excellent.

(5) One's access to one's experience is accomplished via the access relations between M and PR. As Anscombe would put it, we simply *can say* what it is we are experiencing, what it is we are up to. This is accomplished without any inner eye or introspective faculty beyond the machinery invoked in the model.

(6) Our feelings of special authority in offering introspective reports—the basis for all the misbegotten theses of introspective incorrigibility and infallibility—arises from the fact that our semantic intentions, which determine what we want to say, are the standards against which we measure our own verbal productions; hence if we say what we mean to say, if we have committed no errors or infelicities of expression, then our actual utterances cannot fail to be expressions of the content of our semantic intentions, cannot fail to do justice to the access we have to our own inner lives.[17]

VI

Having an inner life—being something it is like something to be —is on this account a matter of having a certain sort of functional organization, but the only natural entities that could be expected to have such functional organizations would be highly evolved and *socialized* creatures. The prospect of a robot artificially constructed to replicate such a functional structure is not ruled out, but when one reflects on the activities such an entity would have to engage in to be more than an instantaneous version of such a system, the claim that it would be conscious loses—at least for me—its implausibility. We might not have the imagination to engage such a thing in interpersonal relations; it might not *seem*, in its metallic skin, to have an inner life or any prospect of an inner life. Such appearances are unreliable, however, for consider the possibility of their being a truly conscious entity (whatever one supposes this involves) that was just like us except that it operated on a time scale ten thousand times slower than ours. We would have a very hard time recognizing any of its day-long emissions as speech acts, let alone witty, cheery, doleful, heartfelt speech acts, and its ponderous responses to cuts and bruises would not easily enliven our sympathies; but if so, we would *ex hypothesi* be ignoring a genuine, conscious person among us.

When we wonder if something or someone is conscious, it is tempting to view this as wondering whether or not a special light is turned on inside. This is an error, however, as we can see by asking questions about our own cases: was I conscious (or conscious of X) at time t? When we see that what settles the issues in our own case is a consideration of facts about our current capacities and past activities, and the best theory that can account for these, we are less reluctant to let the same considerations settle the issues in the case of others.

There is no *proving* that something that seems to have an inner life does in fact have one—if by "proving" we understand, as we often do, the evincing of evidence that can be seen to establish by principles already agreed upon that something is the case. In this paper I set myself the task of constructing an "I," a something it was like something to be, out of subpersonal parts of the sort encountered in cognitivistic theories. I do not now wish to claim that

I have *demonstrably* succeeded in this. Suppose we consider the two questions:

(A) Would an entity instantiating this theory sketch *seem* (to "others," to "us") to have an inner conscious life?

(B) Would such an entity *in fact* have an inner conscious life?
Question (A) is an agreeably straightforward question of engineering. Perhaps the thing whose design I have sketched would impress the keenest skeptic, and perhaps it would be lamentably (or comically) unrealistic or mute or self-defeating. Whatever flaws the design has might have philosophical or psychological significance, or might be rather trivial blunders on my part. (Is my model akin to the blueprint for a perpetual motion machine, or have I merely forgotten to provide a way out for the exhaust gases?) Most if not all objections to *details* in my model can be cast—even if not so intended—as grounds for denying (A), thus:

(C) Such an entity would not even *seem* to have an inner conscious life because

. . . it lacks any provision for such human phenomena as . . .,

. . . it ignores . . .,

. . . it would respond in situation - - - by doing . . .

I must take such objections seriously because part of my goal in this paper is to reveal, by imagined counterinstance, the implausibility of the charge that no entity describable solely by the resources of cognitivistic theory could *possibly* seem to have an inner conscious life. If that charge is nevertheless true (I cannot imagine how that could be *shown*—but perhaps I shall live and learn), then cognitivism is forlorn, and this would be a fact of great importance to philosophy and psychology.

Suppose, however, that some cognitivistic model of consciousness (not mine, no doubt, but its kin, I like to think) encouraged a positive answer to question (A). Suppose some model passed all the appearance tests we could devise. How on earth should one then address question (B)? Is there a better course than mere doctrinaire verificationism on the one hand or shoulder-shrugging agnosticism on the other? This is of course just "the problem of other minds," and I propose that progress can be made on it by reexamining *what one knows about one's own case* in the light of the most promising theories of psychology. What convinces *me* that a cognitivistic theory could capture all the dear features I discover in my inner life is not any "argument," and not just the programmatic appeal of thereby preserving something like "the unity of science," but rather a detailed attempt to describe to myself exactly those features of my life *and the nature of my acquaintance with them* that I would cite as my "grounds" for claiming that I am — and do not merely seem to be — conscious. What *I* discover are facts quite congenial to cognitivistic theorizing, and my tactic here has been to try, by persuasive redescription, to elicit the same discoveries in others. Skeptics can view the form of the argument, such as it is, as a challenge — to produce a rival description of some feature of conscious experience that is both acceptable to many (better, it should evoke enthusiastic agreement, it should ring a bell) and unassimilable by cognitivistic theorizing. I am aware of the irony of recommending something so reminiscent of the battle of descriptions that embarrassed the early introspectionists to death, but how else could anyone plausibly support the claim that one's theory was a theory of *consciousness*?

Notes

1. There are other worries as well, of course. Nonhuman, nonverbal creatures have no print-out faculties, or at best very rudimentary and unexpressive print-out faculties, yet some philosophers — notably Nagel (1974) — insist that full-blown, phenomenological consciousness is as much their blessing as ours. I think one can be skeptical of this claim without thereby becoming the Village Verificationist, but the issue deserves an unhurried treatment of its own.

2. Davis (1974) has raised a graphic version of this objection with regard to functionalist theories of pain. Let a functionalist theory of pain (whatever its details) be instantiated by a system the subassemblies of which are not such things as *C*-fibres and reticular systems but telephone lines and offices staffed by people. Perhaps it is a giant robot controlled by an army of human beings that inhabit it. When the theory's functionally characterized conditions for pain are not met we must say, if the theory is true, that the robot is in pain. That is, real pain, as real as our own, would exist in virtue of the perhaps disinterested and businesslike activities of these bureaucratic teams, executing their proper functions. It does *seem* that there must be more to pain than that. See also Shoemaker (1975) for a careful analysis and rebuttal of several kindred objections to such functional theories.

3. Ryle (1949) and Wittgenstein (1953) are the preeminent modern theorists of the personal level. In fact, in their different ways they invent the enterprise, by showing that there is work to be done, that there are questions that arise purely at the personal level, and that one misconceives the questions if one offers subpersonal hypotheses or theories as answers. Typically readers who do not understand, or accept, these difficult claims see them as evading or missing the point, and complain that neither Ryle nor Wittgenstein has any positive psychological theory to offer at all. That is true: the personal level "theory" of persons is not a psychological theory.

4. This unpromising enterprise is forced on me (as students, colleagues, and other critics have insisted over the last few years) if I am to salvage the sort of functionalist theory of the mind I have heretofore defended. Since I have no other theory of the mind to fall back on, since in fact I see no remotely plausible alternatives to tempt me, I accept this problem as mine. It is not mine alone, though, as I hope I have made clear. This is fortunate, for the problem begs for a cooperative solution; my attempt trespasses deep in psychologists' territory, and I would hope to stimulate assistance, not a boundary dispute, from that quarter.

5. Neisser now wishes to banish iconic memory from a position of importance in the thoery of perceptual processes (see his contribution to this volume, and his *Cognition and Realist* (1976); but I cannot see that he can go so far as to deny its existence. Moreover I am not convinced it is not important.

6. Cf. the discussion of "awareness$_{1,5}$" in Arbib (1972).

7. M is a special hypothesized memory location, defined functionally by its access relations to PR, and it should not be confused with any already familiar functionally or anatomically defined variety of buffer memory, short-term memory, or echoic memory posited by cognitive theories to date. It may, for all I know, *coincide* nicely with some variety of memory already proposed and studied, but eclectic as my model is, I do not intend here to be appropriating any existing notion from psychology.

8. The possibilities for interaction of this sort between PR and Control have only been crudely exhibited here, but they can be — and to some extent have been — studied systematically. Relative retrieval times, lexical biases, the reliability of "tip-of-the-tongue" judgments, similarity spaces, and the like can provide an abundance of clues to guide the model builder. Consider James's (1950, pp. 251-2) introspective account of having a forgotten name on the tip of one's tongue:

> There is a gap therein; but no mere gap. It is a gap that is intensely active. A sort of wraith of the name is in it, beckoning us in a given direction, making us at moments tingle with the sense of our closeness, and then letting us sink back without the longed for term. If wrong names are proposed to us, this singularly definite gap acts immediately so as to negate them. They do not fit into the mold. . . . The rhythm of a lost word may be there without a sound to clothe it.

This passage, for all its phenomenological glories, is strikingly suggestive of purely functional interrelationships that might realistically be postulated to hold between the components of the model (or the components of a better model, of course). Suppose a functionalistic model "inspired" by this passage were developed and supported in the usual ways; it would be part of the burden of this paper to mitigate the resistance to the claim that an instantiation of such a theory could *assert* (*knowing* what it meant, and *meaning* what it said) just what James asserts in this passage.

9. An unrepresentative but philosophically valuable sampling of this literature would include Paivio (1971), Shepard and Metzler (1971), Arbib (1972), and Pylyshyn (1973, 1975).

10. The counterpart reference to work in philosophy should include Sellars (1963), (1973), Harman (1973), Armstrong (1973), and especially two new books: Fodor (1975) and Rosenberg (1974). I disparaged images in Dennett (1969) and propositions in Dennett (1975a). The present paper rescinds all (and only) the overstatemants in those pieces.

11. Pylyshyn's papers (1973, 1975) give the clearest account of false steps from functional premises to structural conclusions. Minsky (1974) suggests that there are structures

undreamt of by the combatants in the words-versus-pictures debates that may in the end reveal that debate to be misconceived.

12. It only appears to be more specific handwaving when one talks not simply of contentful states and events but of cognitive *maps*, say, as opposed to stored *propositions*. People who like images say they are talking about images but not (of course!) about *pictures in the brain*; people who like propositions say they are talking about propositions — which are not *at all* like images — but also, of course, not *sentences in the brain*. There is plenty of doctrine about what images and propositions are *not*, but very little about what they are.

13. On the prospects and vicissitudes of homunculus theories see Dennett (1975b).

14. Cf. Ryle's (1949) illuminating account of "unstudied utterances" and Sellars's (1963, 1974) treatments of "thinkings out loud" and "proximate propensities" to think out loud. Ryle claims that our unstudied utterances "constitute our primary evidence for making self-comments" (p. 183), and I am claiming that it is our proximate propensities to make unstudied utterances that constitute this primary evidence. Ryle probably would not deny this, for he says (p. 194): "One of the things often signified by 'self-consciousness' is the notice we take of our own unstudied utterances, including our explicit avowals, whether these are spoken aloud, muttered or said in our heads. We eavesdrop on our own voiced utterances and our own silent monologues." Ryle offers no account, however, of just what one is doing when one "eavesdrops" on one's "silent monologue," nor could he give such an account without descending to the subpersonal level he wishes to avoid: *we* do not do anything in order so to eavesdrop. we *just are* aware of our own thinkings.

15. I owe this observation to Michael Hooker.

16. Ryle (1949, p. 160) says: "There is, however, a proper sense in which I can be said generally to know what has just been engaging my notice or half-notice, namely that I generally could give a memory report of it, if there was occasion to do so, This does not exclude the possibility that I might sometimes give a misreport, for even short-term reminiscence is not exempt from carelessness or bias." Ryle permits himself to call this capacity "log-keeping," and my M is apparently just Ryle's log-keeping system "paramechanized." (Another precursor of M that may have occurred to the reader is Freud's (1962, p. 10) *preconscious*: "The question, 'How does a thing become conscious?' would thus be more advantageously stated: 'How does a thing become preconscious?', and the answer would be: 'Through becoming connected with the word-presentations corresponding to it.' ") But surely Ryle's own remarks on log-keeping, if taken seriously, constitute just the sort of paramechanical hypothesis he typically condemns. Why is Ryle led to such an uncharacteristic account? Not because he is *aware* of keeping logs, and not because he finds himself or observes himself keeping logs (a Rylean would be quick to ask him embarrassing questions about how many entries he writes in his log before breakfast, and how he writes them). Ryle is led to this (happy) lapse, I suppose, because *what must be explained* (viz., our ability to report on so many different things that were just now happening) demands an explanation somehow in terms of an information — or memory — model.

17. I used to claim (Dennett, 1969) that this fact explained how we were, in a very limited and strained sense, incorrigible with regard to the contents of our awareness or consciousness. Now, thanks to the relentless persuasions of John Bender, William Talbott, Thomas Blackburn, Annette Baier, and others, I wish to claim that this fact explains not how we are in fact incorrigible, but rather why people (especially philosophers) so often think we are. The fact does provide for what Gunderson (1972) calls the investigational asymmetry of some first-person claims, but the asymmetry is not profitably to be viewed, as I used to think, as any sort of even limited incorrigibility.

References

Arbib, M. Consciousness: The secondary role of language. *Journal of Philosophy*, October 5, 1972, 69, 579-590.

Armstrong, L. *Belief, truth and knowledge*. Cambridge: Cambridge University Press, 1973.

Broadbent, D. E. *Perception and communication*. Oxford: Pergamon Press, 1958.

Davis, L. Unpublished paper delivered to the Association for Philosophy and Psychology, M.I.T., October 1974.

Dennett, D. C. *Content and consciousness*. London: Routledge & Kegan Paul, 1969, pp. 90-96.

Dennett, D. C. Brain writing and mind reading. In K. Gunderson (Ed.), *Language, mind, and knowledge*. Minneapolis, University of Minnesota Press, 1975. (a)

Dennett, D. C. Why the Law of Effect will not go away. *Journal of Theory of Social Behavior*, October 1975. (b)

Dennett, D. C. "Are dreams experiences?" *Philosophical Review*, April, 1976.

Fodor, J. *The language of thought*. New York: Crowell, 1975.

Freud, Sigmund. *The ego and the id*. New York: Norton, 1962.

Gunderson, K. *Content and consciousness* and the mind-body problem. *Journal of Philosophy*, 1972, 69, 591-603.

Harman, Gilbert. *Thought*. Princeton: Princeton University Press, 1973.

Hume, David. *A Treatise of human nature*, ed. L. A. Selby-Bigge. London: Oxford University Press, 1888.

James, William. *The principles of psychology*, vol. I. New York: Dover Publications, 1950. First published 1890.

Julesz, B. *Foundations of cyclopean vision*. Chicago: University of Chicago Press, 1971.

Lackner, J. R., & Garrett, M. "Resolving ambiguity: effects of biasing context in the unattended ear." *Cognition*, 1973, 1, 359-372.

Minsky, M. A Framework for representing knowledge. M.I.T. AI Lab Memo no. 306, 1974.

Nagel, T. What is it like to be a bat? *Philosophical Review*, 1974, 83, 435-451.

Neisser, U. *Cognitive psychology*. New York: Appleton-Century-Crofts, 1967.

Neisser, U. *Cognition and reality*. San Francisco: W. H. Freeman and Co., 1976.

Paivio, A. *Imagery and verbal processes*. New York: Holt, Rinehart and Winston, 1971.

Pylyshyn, Z. What the mind's eye tells the mind's brain. A critique of mental imagery. *Psychological Bulletin*, 1973, 1975, 86, 1-24.

Pylyshyn, Z. Representation of knowledge: non-linguistic forms. In *Theoretical issues in natural language processing*, Assoc. for Computational Linguistics Preprint, 1975.

Rawls, J. *Theory of justice*. Cambridge, Mass.: Harvard University Press, 1971.

Rosenberg, J. *Linguistic representation*. Dordrecht: Reidel, 1974.

Ryle, G. *The Concept of Mind*. London: Hutchinson, 1949.

Sellars, W. *Science, perception and reality*. London: Routledge and Kegan Paul, 1963.

Sellars, W. Meaning as functional classification. *Synthèse*, 1974.

Shepard, R. N., and Metzler, J. Mental rotation of three-dimensional objects. *Science*, 1971, 171, 701-3.

Shoemaker, S. Functionalism and qualia. *Philosophical Studies*, 1975, 27, 291-315.

Wittgenstein, L. *Philosophical investigations*. Oxford: Blackwells, 1953.

Computation and Reduction

Introduction

Nobody loses all the time; a fitful and negative glimmer illuminates the philosophy of mind. We now know that the program of behavioristic reduction of psychological theories cannot, in general, be carried through. And we know why. Let a behaviorist be someone who claims, at a minimum, that there must be a reference to behavior in any logically perspicuous specification of a psychological state. Then, whatever else may be wrong with the behaviorist program (no doubt plenty else is wrong), it is blocked by the intentionality of typical psychological terms.[1] So, for example, there is a *sense* in which there is a reference to whistling (to, as psychologists inelegantly say, Dixie-whistling behavior) in such English formulae as $\ulcorner \Psi =$ John's intention to whistle a snatch of Dixie$\urcorner$, and perhaps there would be a similar sort of reference to, say, avoidance behavior in any adequately perspicuous specification of John's pains. Perhaps, that is, John's having a pain profoundly involves his intending or desiring to avoid a painful stimulus. But, of course, that would not be good enough to make the behaviorist's case. For such "references to behavior" as are, in *this* sense, involved in logically perspicuous specifications of psychological states occur (only) in intentional contexts; which is to say that they are not, in any full-blooded sense, references to behavior at all. Briefly, whatever is required to make it true that John's intention to whistle a snatch of *Dixie* is such and such does not in general, involve the actual occurrence of any *Dixie*-whistling, and whatever is required to make it true that John's pain is such and such does not, in general, involve the actual occurrence of any avoidance behavior. Similarly, mutatis mutandis, for other psychological states and processes.

This is all familiar territory, and I mention these points only in order to set them to one side. My present interest is the following. Although it is fairly clear what kinds of problems phenomena of intentionality raise for *behavioristic* reductions of psychological predicates, very little is understood about the problems they raise for *physicalistic* reductions of the sort often contemplated by central-state identity theorists. In fact, it often happens in the standard literature on mind/body identity that this question is not so much as aired.[2] Perhaps this is due to the continuing influence of an early version of the identity theory, which was physicalist about *sensations* but behaviorist about propositional attitudes (see, for example, Place, 1956 and Smart, 1957). On that view, physicalism presupposes behavioral analyses for those psychological predicates that most evidently establish intentional contexts: verbs like "hopes," "thinks," "intends," "feels that," "believes," etc. The identity theory is thus left free to operate in the account of sensations, an area where issues of intentionality seem less pressing.

But however one construes the history, it now seems clear that behavioristic analyses of propositional attitudes will not be forthcoming, so physicalist theories will have to decide what to do about their intentionality. And it also seems clear that the problems intentionality poses for physicalism are likely to be quite different from the ones it posed for behaviorism. The reason for this is that, prima facie, what the behaviorist requires of reduction is quite different from what the physicalist requires. Behaviorism will not do unless for every true sentence in an (ideally completed) psychology there exists a canonical *paraphrase* in a proprietary vocabulary. Nonlogical expressions in this vocabulary are to be behavioral (whatever, precisely, that is supposed to mean), and all contexts in canonical paraphrases are to be extensional.

It is a good deal less clear what the physicalist wants. *Not* a paraphrase, surely, because on no plausible account does a physicalistic sentence say what the corresponding mentalistic sentence means. But, on the other hand, the physicalist presumably wants something more than an extensional sentence materially equivalent to each intentional sentence, since that is available by merest stipulation. Let 'Alfred = John's intention to whistle a snatch of *Dixie*' be a stipulated equivalence. Then, for 'John intends to whistle a s. of D.' we get, roughly, 'Here's Alfred,' which satisfies none of the traditional tests for opacity. Nor will it content the physicalist to find an extensional sentence equivalent to each intentional one such that the equivalence is nomologically necessary since, presumably, a psychophysical parallelist or epiphenomenalist could grant him that without granting him what he primarily wants. Nor, I think, should the physicalist be content with the de facto identity of the things that mental terms name with those that physical terms name since, as we shall see, there are several respects in which he might get that and not get the substantive reduction of psychology to neurology (or any more basic science). In fact, it seems difficult to me to say just what the physicalistic reductionist *does* want. In this paper, in any event, I shall consider what, in the light of the intentionality of typical psychological predicates, he is likely to get, and what it is likely to cost him.

My strategy will be the following. I shall say a few things about reduction and a few things about psychological explanation. I shall then argue that, given the notions of reduction and psychological explanation at issue, the reduction of psychology could probably be purchased only at the expense of its explanatory power. I shall suggest, too, that this situation is probably specific to psychology as opposed to other special sciences. That is, reducing psychology to (say) neurology would probably lose us something that reducing meterology to (say) mechanics would probably not lose us. This argument will turn on the special role that intentional expressions play in psychological theories. Finally, I shall discuss very briefly how we could strengthen the notion of reduction so as to guarantee that, if psychology is reducible in this stronger sense, then it *is* reducible without loss of explanatory power.

I shall not, however, argue for or against the blanket contention that psychology is reducible to neurology or physics. Indeed, it is hard to see how a sensible argument to either conclusion *could* be mounted in the present state of play. For, not only are there straightforwardly empirical questions that are pertinent and unanswered, but also what we say about the reducibility of psychology depends on what we think psychological theories should be like and what we require reduction to preserve. And we do not know much about what psychological theories should be like or about which constraints on reduction are justifiable.

Reduction

In what follows, I shall be taking "reduction" in quite a specialized sense; the sense that (if I read the literature correctly) informed much positivistic thinking about the relation between physics and the special sciences. It will be one of my points that this notion of reduction is not the only one compatible with the ontological assumptions of physicalism. But I shall start with it because it is widely known and because the considerations that are likely to make psychological theories recalcitrant to reduction in this special sense would also hold on many other construals, as far as I can tell. So as not to have to write "reduction in this special sense" whenever I wish to refer to reduction in this special sense, I shall adopt the practice of calling it simply "reduction." But the reader is encouraged to bear the qualifier in mind.

In the first place, then, "reduces to" names a relation between *theories*. When that relation holds between a pair of theories, say T_1 and T_0, T_0 is said to be a *reducer* of T_1. The reduction relation is transitive and asymmetrical, hence irreflexive. By the "unity of science" I shall mean the doctrine that all sciences except physics reduce to physics. By "physicalistic reductionism" I shall mean a certain claim that is entailed by, but does not entail, the unity of science; viz., the claim that psychology reduces to physics (presumably via neurology).

I do not know whether theories are sets of sentences, and I do not wish to prejudice that question. However, some of the conditions on reduction constrain properties of the syntax and vocabulary of expressions in the reduced and reducing sciences. So, in what follows, I shall take "theory" to mean "theory in normal form." A theory in normal form *is* a set of sentences by stipulation. I shall also sometimes write as though all the sentences that belong to a theory in normal form are universal generalizations. The interesting problems about reduction persist on this assumption, and it helps with the exposition.

Let each sentence of the set T_1 be the universal closure of a formula of the form $A_x \rightarrow B_y$ (read: it is a law that x's being A is causally sufficient for y's being B). Let each sentence of the set T_0 be the universal closure of a formula of the form $\Phi_x \rightarrow \Psi_y$. Then the crucial conditions on T_0 reducing T_1 are these.

a) (At least some) items in the vocabulary A, B . . . are not in the vocabulary Φ, Ψ. . . .

b) Let the "projected" predicates of a science be the ones that appear essentially in its laws. Then T_0 reduces T_1 only if nomologically necessary and sufficient conditions for the satisfaction of the projected predicates of T_1 can be framed in the vocabulary of T_0.

So, for example, theories in whose laws the expression 'water' (or its cognates) occurs will reduce to chemistry only if (a') chemistry contains some expression other than 'water' (say 'H_2O') such that (b') '(x) (x is water iff x is H_2O)' expresses a law.

c) Let T_2 be the set whose members are T_0 together with such laws. Then T_0 reduces T_1 only if every consequence of T_1 is a consequence of T_2.[3]

Formulae like the one quoted in (b') are said to express "bridge" laws; we can call them *bridge formulae*. For our purposes, the essence of standard reductionism is the suggestion that bridge formulae link reduced sciences to their reducers. Viewed as principles of inference, bridge formulae permit us to substitute expressions in the vocabulary of T_0 for expressions in the vocabulary of T_1 preserving nomological necessity. That is, if G is a generalization in the vocabulary of T_1, and G' is the formula derived from G by replacing every expression of T_1 by the T_0 expression that is related to it by some bridge formula, then if G is nomologically necessary, G' will be too. For essentially this reason, it is plausible to claim that any event causally explained by G is also causally explained by G'.

There are many difficulties with this notion of reduction, but I shall not pursue them here. Suffice it to mention only the following rather general points. First, on this account, reducibility involves a good deal more than the ontological claim that things that satisfy descriptions in the vocabulary of T_1 also satisfy descriptions in the vocabulary of T_0 (e.g., that every event that falls under a law of psychology satisfies a physical description). I have stressed this point elsewhere, but it may be worth repeating here in passing. Since the present account requires that bridge formulae be lawlike, it entails not only that their antecedents and consequents be expressions of the reduced and reducing science respectively, but also that they be *projectible* expressions of the reduced and reducing sciences respectively. (This is of a piece with the remark made above, that substitution under the equivalences specified by bridge formulae is supposed to preserve nomological necessity.) That this condition is stronger than the ontological requirement that whatever falls under the generalizations of T_1 should also fall under those of T_0 can be seen from the consideration that the latter could be satisfied even if bridge formulae expressed (not laws but) mere true empirical generalizations; but the requirement that nomological necessity be preserved under the substitutions that bridge formulae license would presumably *not* be satisfied in this case. (For further discussion, see Fodor, 1975.)

Second, if the present account is correct, there is an important sense in which *syntax* is preserved under reduction; on this view, the pertinent difference between a reduced generalization of T_1 and its reducing counterpart in T_0 lies just in the (nonlogical) *vocabulary* of the two formulae. To put this point the other way around, if we look only at the *form* of the sentences that constitute T_0 and T_1, disregarding such expressions as belong to the nonlogical vocabularies of the two theories, then there will not, in general, be any way of telling the sentences of T_0 and T_1 apart. Fundamentally, standard reduction just consists in substituting expressions in the nonlogical vocabulary of T_0 for expressions in the nonlogical vocabulary of T_1 under the equivalences which the bridge formulae specify.

It connects with the latter observation that the *point* of standard reduction (insofar as the point is not merely ontological) is primarily to exhibit the generalizations of T_1 as special cases of the generalizations of T_0. The idea is roughly this: events fall under the generalizations of T_1 by virtue of satisfying descriptions in the vocabulary of T_1. Reduction permits us to *re*describe these events in the vocabulary of T_0, hence to express their conformity to the generalizations of T_0. Since it is assumed that the generalizations of T_0 will normally hold in a domain that properly includes the domain of T_1 (e.g., physics is true of everything that psychology is true of, and physics is true of other things as well), progress in reduction should permit us to subsume phenomena under laws of increasing generality. But since it is said that the generality of laws is an index of the explanatory power of the theories that express them, progress in reduction turns out to be progress toward theories of increasing explanatory power. The unity of science was, perhaps, initially construed as just a way of expressing the ontological claim that everything is the kind of thing that physics is about. But we can now see that the unity of science expressed an epistemological claim as well: the claim that physical explanation subsumes explanation in the special sciences.[4]

I want to consider the application of this picture of reduction to certain kinds of theories typical of current work in cognitive psychology. In order to do so, however, I shall first have to say something about the structure of such theories.

Computation

I am interested, for present purposes, in psychological theories that propose "computational" or "information flow" accounts of mental processes. Not all psychological theories do propose such accounts; indeed, not all mental processes provide appropriate domains for theories of this kind. Roughly, and to put the cart before the horse, mental states are computationally related only when they are related in content. Psychological theories of information flow model such relations of content by (a) providing a descriptive vocabulary in which the content of a mental state can be perspicuously represented, and (b) specifying transformations over formulae in that vocabulary that predict mental states and processes of the organism; in particular, its propositional attitudes. I have elsewhere discussed such theories at considerable length (Fodor, 1975), so in this paper I shall work largely from examples.

Consider learning. I suppose that cases of learning (or, in any event, cases of learning that . . ., where what fills the blank is approximately a sentence) are typically cases of environmentally determined alterations of epistemic state. In particular, what happens when someone learns that so and so is typically that (a) what he knows or believes changes, and (b) the change is a causal consequence (inter alia) of his transactions with his environment. So, for example, you can learn that Minneapolis is in Minnesota by looking at a map of Minnesota and noticing that Minneapolis is on it, or by hearing someone say (in a language one understands) that Minneapolis is in Minnesota, or by drawing the pertinent inference from the observation that Minneapolis is in the same state as St. Paul and that St. Paul is in Minnesota, etc. In general, in such cases, certain things happen to one and, as a more or less direct consequence, what one knows or believes is altered in certain ways. I assume that "consequence" is to be construed causally here since, as far as I can see, no other way of construing it will suit the case.

But not every case of environmentally determined alteration in knowledge or belief is a case of learning. Suppose, for example, that someone were to invent a pill which, when swallowed, induces a mastery of Latin. One takes the pill and eo ipso acquires the relevant beliefs about what "eo ipso" means, how "cogitare" is conjugated, and so on. Moreover, the acquisition of these beliefs is, let us suppose, a causal consequence of taking the pill: the events of taking the pill and acquiring the beliefs fall, respectively, under the antecedent and consequent of a causal law, etc. Still, acquiring Latin by taking the pill is not *learning* Latin, any more than coming to speak the way aphasics do as a consequence of traumatic insult to Broca's area counts as learning aphasic. What is missing?

Intuitively, what is missing is this: the relation between what is acquired when one acquires Latin this way and the experiences that causally occasion the acquisition is, though nomological by hypothesis, notably arbitrary. (This contrasts with the case in which, e.g., one learns what "eo ipso" means by being told what "eo ipso" means, or by inducing its meaning from observations of occasions on which people say "eo ipso," etc.) A way to exhibit the arbitrariness is this: but for the hypothetical causal laws involved, one could imagine the situation to be reversed, so that it is insult to Broca's area that occasions the acquisition of Latin and swallowing the pill that induces aphasia. This situation seems no less gratuitous than the one we imagined initially. It is, in this sense, just an accident that the pills are connected with Latin rather than with aphasia; there is, as it were, nothing in a perspicuous description of what one learns when one learns Latin that connects it with what happens when one swallows a pill. But it is surely *not* just an accident that being told what "eo ipso" means is connected with learning what "eo ipso" means, or, for that matter, that it is English (and not Latin, Urdu, or aphasic) that children reared in English-speaking environments eventually learn to speak.[5]

Take another case. A man sees many gray elephants and, as a consequence of what he sees, comes to believe that elephants are gray. One wants to say there is a difference between this situation and one in which a man sees many gray elephants and, as a consequence of what he sees, comes to believe, say, that two is a prime number. What *kind* of difference? Well, not that the relation between seeing what he saw and coming to believe what he came to believe is causal, for we can imagine that to be true in *both* cases. Still, one wants to say, the first man learned (from his experiences) that elephants are gray, whereas the second many simply had certain experiences and came to believe that two is a prime number as a result of having had them. The relation between the second man's beliefs and his experiences is, in some important sense, arbitrary, whereas the relation between the first man's beliefs and his experiences, in the same important sense, is not. (It is, of course, connected with this that the experiences from which one can learn that so and so are often the experiences one can appeal to in justifying the belief that so and so.)

One more example, and then I shall try to say something about what the examples are examples of. A man sees many gray elephants and, as a causal consequence, comes to believe that elephants are gray. But, although each of the things he saw (the seeing of which contributed causally to the fixation of his beliefs that elephants are gray) was, in fact, a gray elephant, still what he *took* each of these things to be was, say, a very small, brown camel. Such a case is, of course, doubly grotesque; one wants to ask why a man should take elephants to be camels and why, having done so, he should come to believe that elephants are gray as a consequence of the putative camel-sightings. My point is that there need be no answer to these questions beyond adverting to the facts about the man's physical constitution and the way the world happens to impinge upon him. One can, in short, imagine a man so constructed and so situated that his experiences come to fix the right belief about the color of elephants by, as it were, the wrong route. But I think we should want to add that, prima facie, that sort of fixation of belief would not be learning.[6] For learning one needs a nonarbitrary relation (not just between the facts about the experiences and the content of the

beliefs they determine, but also) between the content of the beliefs
and what the man *takes* the facts about the experiences to be.

To a first approximation, then: in paradigmatic cases of learning
there is a relation of content between the belief that is acquired and
the events that causally determine its acquisition. But this is a poor
first approximation, because events do not, in general, have contents,
although beliefs, in general, do. A better procedure is to relativize
to descriptions and say that, in paradigmatic cases of learning, there
is a relation of content between the belief acquired, under its theoretically pertinent description, and the events that causally determine the learning, under *their* theoretically pertinent descriptions.
That is: one imagines an account of fixation of beliefs at large (hence
of learning in particular) such that descriptions in some canonical language are assigned to the beliefs and to such organism/environment
interactions as causally occasion the having of them. One further
assumes that, under this assignment, it will sometimes turn out that
there are relations of content between the former descriptions and
the latter. Presumably all cases of learning will be cases of this kind.
Indeed, one might take it to be a condition upon the adequacy of
canonical psychological descriptions that this should, in general, be
true.

But this is not good enough either. For, as we have seen, there
could be cases in which experiences that are correctly described as
experiences of gray elephants fix beliefs that are correctly described
as beliefs that elephants are gray, yet the required relations of content do not hold between the experiences and the beliefs they fix.
What is "transparently" an experience of gray elephants may be
"opaquely" an experience of brown camels: if such an experience
fixes a belief about elephant colors, the relations between the belief
and the experience is, in the relevant sense, arbitrary (see note 6).
This is a way of saying what psychologists have in mind when they
emphasize the theoretical centrality of the *proximal representation*
of the stimulus (as opposed to the distal stimulus per se) in any but
the most superficial accounts of learning. (See the discussion in
Dennett unpublished.)

We can fix this up as follows. We continue to reconstruct the
notion of learning (as distinct from undifferentiated causal fixation
of belief) in terms of content relations between experiences and

beliefs, both taken under their theoretically pertinent descriptions. But we construe theoretical pertinency as requiring an appropriate correspondence between the description the *psychological theory* assigns to the experience and the description the *subject* assigns to it. In effect, we construe theoretical pertinency of a description as requiring its psychological reality. If the subject internally represents what are in fact experiences of gray elephants as experiences of brown camels, then it is the latter description that enters into the psychological account of the relation between his experience and his beliefs. Descriptions of mental states are, in effect, read opaquely for the purposes of constructing such accounts.[7]

I have been considering the kinds of conceptual mechanisms a psychological theory will need if it is to preserve the distinction between learning that so and so and merely acquiring the belief that so and so. It appears, if the sketch I have given is even more or less correct, that at the heart of this distinction are certain constraints upon relations of content between beliefs and the experiences that fix them. It seems to follow that a psychology of learning will have to respect those constraints if it is to *be* a theory of learning; a fortiori, it will have to be able to represent the properties of mental states in virtue of which they satisfy such constraints—viz., the properties in virtue of which they have the content they do.

Now it may be thought that this sort of argument makes a great deal rest upon the preservation of a bit of ordinary language taxonomy; viz., on preserving the distinction between learning and mere causal fixation of belief. I want to emphasize, however, that that is not even slightly the sort of point I have in mind. I assume, rather, that the linguistic distinction probably corresponds to a fact *in rerum natura*; roughly, to the fact that there are generalizations that hold for learning but not for arbitrary cases of fixation of belief. I assume, moreover, that to state these generalizations we shall need to advert to the content of what is learned and to the content of the experiences that causally occasion the learning. To put the same claim the other way around, I assume that if we taxonomize mental states by their contents we shall be able to state general truths about them that we shall not be able to state otherwise; such truths, as, for example, that general beliefs tend to be fixed by experiences of their instances.[8]

I think it is, to put it mildly, very plausible that there *are* generalizations about mental states that hold in virtue of their contents, but I am not going to argue that claim here. Suffice it to emphasize its centrality not only in current approaches to the psychology of learning, but also in such adjacent fields as the psychology of perception, problem-solving, action, etc. In each case, theory construction proceeds by assigning canonical descriptions to mental states and by specifying functions from one such state to another. In each case, whether the theory represents a given mental state as falling under such a function depends on the canonical description the theory assigns to the state; the adequacy of the canonical description depends, in turn, on the accuracy with which it specifies the content of the mental state it applies to. A causal chain of mental states (e.g., the chains that run from experience to beliefs) thus gets a special sort of representation in this kind of theory: viz., a representation as a sequence of formulae related by content.

The explanatory power of such a treatment lies in its ability to predict the content of some mental states, given knowledge of the content of other, causally connected mental states. So, given a canonical representation of sensory contents, we should be able to predict the content of the percepts they give rise to. Given a canonical representation of a percept, we should be able to predict the memories it engenders; and so on, mutatis mutandis, wherever causally related mental states *are* related by content, viz., nonarbitrarily related. If, rather tendentiously, we take "coherent" to be the contradictory of "arbitrary," then the interest of computational psychological theories lies in their ability to explicate the principles according to which causally related mental states are also coherently related.

We have thus far been developing a picture of computational psychological theories as, in effect, treating causal relations among mental states as though they were derivational relations among formulae. It is, however, of prime importance to insist upon a point we encountered above: the interformulaic relations that such a theory articulates typically hold only insofar as the canonical descriptions of mental states are, as it were, construed opaquely.[9] So, for example, suppose it is true that general beliefs tend to be fixed by experiences of their instances. Then a theory of learning might tell us how

John's belief that elephants are gray is fixed by (what John takes to be) his experiences of gray elephants; e.g., given, as datum, that John took n of his experiences to be gray-elephant experiences, the theory might predict that John's belief that elephants are gray is fixed to degree m. But now 'elephant' is nonreferential in 'John believes elephants are gray' and in 'John took e to be a gray-elephant experience,' and 'gray' is nonextensional in those contexts. This is patently essential if the theory of learning is to be remotely plausible, since it seems clear that the very same experiences that fix the belief that elelphants are gray may be neutral to the belief that pachyderms reflect light of such and such a wavelength, and this may be true even though *for* elephants to be gray just *is* for pachyderms to reflect light of that wavelength. Whether a given belief is fixed by a given experience notoriously depends on how the belief and the experience are represented.

I have been arguing for the following contentions: on the one hand, information flow theories reconstruct content relations among mental states as computational relations among canonical descriptions; and on the other, because canonical descriptions specify the contents of mental states, they must be read opaquely. One way of putting the situation is this: if the general account of computational psychological theories I have sketched is right, then the possibility of constructing such theories depends on a certain approach to formulae embedded to verbs of propositional attitude in canonical psychological descriptions. Such formulae must be viewed as nonextensional but not as "fused."[10] To make this clear, I shall have to say a little about what fusion is supposed to be.

'Dog' is nonreferential in 'dogmatic.' But that is a bad way of putting it since "dog' (I mean the *word* 'dog' as opposed to the sequence of letters 'd' 'o' 'g') does not so much as *occur* in 'dogmatic.' Similarly, according to the fusion story, 'elephant' is nonreferential in 'John believes elephants are gray,' because the word 'elephant' does not so much as occur in 'John believes elephants are gray.' Rather, 'believes-elephants-are-gray' is a fused expression, analogous to a one-word predicate or an idiom, so that the logical form of 'John believes elephants are gray' is simple F_{John}, indistinguishable from the logical form of, say, 'John is purple.' It is worth remarking, for later reference, that this is a two-step story. The nonreferentiality of 'elephant' is explained by the assumption that it is not a term in 'believes elephants are gray,' and the denial of termhood is then rationalized by appeal to the notion of fusion. One can imagine alternative accounts on which 'elephant' is not construed as a term in 'believes elephants are gray' but on which verbs of propositional attitude are nevertheless *not* construed as fused with their objects. We shall return to this further on.

The present point, in any event, is this: fusion will certainly account for failures to refer; in something like the way being dead accounts for failures to be loquacious. But it is a kind of account that is not compatible with the development of psychological theories of the kind I have been describing. If "believes elephants are gray" is a fused expression, then a fortiori the canonical representation of John's mental state when he believes that elephants are gray bears no more intimate relation to the canonical representation of his mental state when he takes himself to sight a gray elephant than it does to the canonical representation of his mental state when, say, he takes himself to have sighted a brown camel.[11] Fusion is precisely a way of reading propositional attitudes as *not* exhibiting content, a fortiori as not exhibiting the relations of content.

Whereas, of course, the whole point of appealing to a notion of canonical psychological representation in the first place was to permit the development of, e.g., principles of fixation of belief that *are* sensitive to the way that mental states are related in virtue of content. So, in particular, the theory was to reconstruct the intuitive notion that there is a relation of content between experiences of elephants and beliefs about the color of elephants, and that the experiences tend to fix the beliefs in virtue of this relation. But if this whole strategy is to succeed, then it had better be that in canonical descriptions like 'believes elephants are gray' the object of 'believes' is somehow connected with the generalization *elephants are gray*, and in canonical descriptions like 'takes himself to see a gray elephant' the object of 'takes himself to see' is somehow connected with a singular statement about an elephant. Unless this condition is satisfied, we shall not be able to represent John's belief that elephants are gray *as* a general belief: a fortiori, we shall not be able to represent the fixation of that belief as falling under the principle that general beliefs tend to be fixed by experiences of their instances. Conversely, if this condition *is* satisfied, then, by that very fact, it follows that the canonical representations of situations in which *a* has such and such a propositional attitude cannot, in general, be of the form *Fa*. In short, *we can have fusion or we can have computation, but we cannot have both*.

I take it to be the moral that any operation on canonical descriptions that has the effect of fusing the expressions they deploy will thereby deprive us of the very formal mechanisms on which the (presumed) explanatory power of computational psychological theories rests. My strategy in the rest of this paper will assume this is true. I shall argue (a) that the conditions on standard reduction could be satisfied even if canonical neurological representations of mental states are fused, hence (b) that the satisfaction of the conditions upon standard reduction does *not* guarantee the subsumption of psychological explanation by neurological explanation. The form of argument is thus that fusion is a sufficient condition for loss of explanatory power and that standard reduction is compatible with fusion, hence the success of standard reduction would not, in and of itself, ensure that the kinds of explanations that computational psychological theories yield can be reconstructed in the vocabulary of the neurological theories that reduce them. One can look at such an argument as showing that there is something wrong with the standard notion of reduction (since standard reduction turns out to be compatible with loss of explanatory power). Alternatively, one can hold to the standard notion of reduction and abandon the claim that explanation in a reduced science is subsumed by explanation in the reducing science. My own inclination, for present purposes, is to take the former line and strengthen the constraints on the neurological reducers of psychological theories; I shall return to this in the last section.

Computation and Reduction

I remarked above that, in paradigm cases of classical reduction, mapping the sentences of T_1 onto sentences of T_0 is primarily a matter of replacing items in the vocabulary of the former with items in the vocabulary of the latter, such replacements being mediated by the lawful coextensions (or identities; the distinction is not germane to the present argument) that bridge laws express. But it should now be clear that this will *not* be the case in the reduction of (computational) psychological theories to, say, neurology. For, as we have seen, computational psychological theories contain canonical descriptions that make serious use of a formulae in which sentences are embedded to opaque verbs ("serious" in the sense that the generalizations the theory articulates depends critically on the form and vocabulary of such embedded sentences); whereas at least on the usual assumptions about neurology (and, a fortiori, about physics) those sciences do not employ descriptions of that kind. So the reduction of psychology to neurology (unlike, say, the reduction of meteorology to mechanics) involves alteration of the syntax of the reduced formulae, and it is easy to see from examples that the effect of such alteration will typically be the fusion of expressions that specify the objects of propositional attitudes.

Consider the reduction to neurology of a psychological theory containing the formula 'John believes elephants are gray.' Given the usual assumptions, there will be a sentence of neurological theory (say 'John is N') such that 'John believes elephants are gray iff John is N' is nomologically necessary. So let us suppose that 'John believes elephants are gray' reduces to 'John is N,' and similarly, mutatis mutandis, for 'John takes e to be a gray elephant experience,' which comes out under reduction to be, let us say, 'John is M.' Given this much, the classical constraints upon the reduction of psychology to neurology are satisfied insofar as they apply to these two sentences. And if, as we may suppose, 'John's being M brings about John's being N' instantiates a causal law, then we have a causal explanation, in the vocabulary of neurology, of the contingency of John's belief about elephant colors upon John's experiences of colored elephants. So far, so good.

Except, of course, that fusion has already occurred (taking, as the criterion of fusion, the failure of canonical—now neurological—descriptions to specify the content of the mental states they apply to). To see this, imagine that, by some or other causal quirk, not only (putative) experiences of gray elephants, but also some experiences that do not have contents (like swallowings of pills) or some experiences that have the "wrong" contents (like putative sightings of camels) happen to be causally sufficient for fixing beliefs about the color of elephants. Then, presumably, there will be an expression E that is (a) in the language of neurology, (b) such that 'John is E' is true if John swallows the pill (takes himself to sight the camel), and (c) such that 'John's being E brings about John's being N' is *also* an instance of a causal law. That is, once we go over to neurological descriptions, there need be nothing to choose between the way the theory represents the case in which John's coming to believe elephants are gray is consequent upon his sighting gray elephants and the case in which John's coming to believe elephants are gray is consequent upon his swallowing blue pills. Looked at formally, this is due to the fact that reduction permits the fusion of 'believes elephants are gray' (and/or 'takes himself to sight a gray elephant'), where the mechanism that accomplishes fusion is the substitution of some (possibly elementary) neurological expression for a psychological expression in which a verb of propositional attitude has scope over a formula that specifies the content of a propositional attitude. Looked at substantively, what has been lost is a representation of the relation of content between beliefs about elephants and elephant-experiences. If, then, there are generalizations that hold of mental states in virtue of the content relations between them (if, for example, there are generalizations that relate the content of beliefs to the content of the experiences that fix them), then the conditions on reduction may be satisfied even though such generalizations (statable by assumption in the psychological vocabulary) are not statable in the vocabulary of the reducing science. In short, insofar as there is any explanatory power to be gained by resort to a computational psychology, reduction is in danger of losing it for us.

I had better, at this point, make as clear as I can what I am *not* claiming. To begin with, I do not deny that there could be a truth of neurological theory that applies to exactly the cases in which say, a general belief is fixed by its instances. On the contrary, if the truths of psychology are to follow from the truths of neurology plus bridge laws, there had *better* be a neurological state necessary and sufficient for having any given belief, and a neurological state necessary and sufficient for having any given belief-fixing experience; and the neurological theory had better say (or, anyhow, entail) that states of the latter kind are causally sufficient for bringing about states of the former kind. The difficulty is, however, that since the contents of the beliefs and experiences presumably will not be specified by their *neurological* descriptions, it is only when we are given their *psychological* descriptions that we will be able to predict the contents of the beliefs *from* the contents of the experiences. I am saying, in effect, that beliefs and experiences reduce to neurological entities, but the contents of beliefs and experiences — the things that our beliefs and experiences relate us to — do not reduce to anything; psychological representations of content simply fuse under neurological description of mental states. So, to put it rather misleadingly, although neurology can, in principle, say anything that needs to be said about the contingency of beliefs upon experiences, it has no mechanisms whatever for talking about the contingency of the contents of beliefs upon the contents of experiences. Yet there are, it appears, such contingencies, and there are interesting things to be said about them.

It might nevertheless be held with some justification that this line of argument is unfair, if not to the spirit of standard reductionsim, then at least to the letter. For, on the reductionist view, T_0 will not reduce T_1 unless all the consequences of T_1 are consequences, not of T_0 alone, but of T_0 together with the bridge laws. Now, if there are bridge laws of the form: (x) (x has a general belief [of the appropriate content] iff N_x), and (y) (y has a belief-fixing experience [of the appropriate content] iff M_y), and if 'M brings about N' expresses a law of neurology, then neurology together with the bridge laws *does* entail whatever psychology entails about the fixation of beliefs by experiences.

Still, the present case is quite unlike what the classical reduction paradigm envisions. True, in the standard examples, we need not only T_0 but also the bridge laws to recover the entailments of T_1. But that is only for the relatively uninteresting reason that the bridge laws provide access to the (nonlogical) *vocabulary* of T_1, which is, by assumption, not included in the vocabulary of T_0. (Chemistry can entail "H_2O is wet," but only chemistry plus the bridge laws can entail "Water is wet.") Whereas the curious thing about the psychology/neurology case is that here the bridge laws provide access not just to the vocabulary of the reduced science but also to an *explanatory construct* — content — for which the reducing science offers no counterpart. Specifically, we shall need the bridge laws to unpack the fused objects of verbs of propositional attitude if, as I have argued, fusion deprives us of the appropriate theoretical mechanisms for specifying the domains in which generalizations about cognitive processes hold.

In short, we are back where we started. I have argued, *not* that the classical constraints upon reduction cannot be met in the psychology/neurology case, but rather that they fail to provide sufficient conditions for the subsumption of psychological explanations by neurological explanations. And examination of that case has shown precisely that it is possible for a pair of theories to meet the classical constraints (T_0 plus the bridge laws entails whatever T_1 does) even though intuitively (and by the fusion test) the explanations of T_1 are not subsumed by T_0. Requiring that T_0 together with the bridge laws yield the entailments of T_1 does not ensure that the explanations available in T_1 have counterparts in T_0, Q. E.D.

I have been issuing caveats. Here is another: the present argument is not that reduction *must* lose the advantages that psychological models gain; only that it *can* do so compatibly with the satisfaction of such conditions, ontological and methodological, as standard views of reduction impose. This is due to the fact that nothing in those conditions prohibits fusion as the consequence of reduction. On the contrary, in the absence of further constraints upon reduction, fusion would be its *natural* consequence, as can be seen from the following.

Reduction required, in effect, that for every psychological state of John's there exist a coextensive (or token-identical) neurological state of John's, and that every psychological sentence that attributes the former state to him should be replaced by a neurological sentence that attributes the latter state to him. But consider again the sentence, 'John believes elephants are gray.' The shortest stretch of that sentence that can be construed as expressing a state (property, etc.) of *anything* is surely 'believes elephants are gray,' since, in particular, in this sentence the occurrence of elephants is nonreferential and 'are gray' does not express a property of elephants. In short, if we are to substitute neurological-state expressions for psychological-state expressions, the natural choice is to make the substitution in the frame: ⌜John . . .⌝, i.e., to substitute simultaneously for the verb of propositional attitude and its object. And, since the classical construals of reduction do not do anything like requiring that the content of propositional attitudes can be specified by neurological representations of mental states, the consequence of substitution in this frame is likely to be, precisely, fusion.

I have a strong suspicion that this chapter would do well to stop here. For I suspect the moral just drawn is essentially the right one: reduction will probably require fusion, and fusion will entail the loss of the explanatory power that computational psychological theories are constructed to obtain. If this is true, it suggests that we will have to be very much more pluralistic about scientific explanation than classical views of the unity of science supposed. In particular, nothing in the discussion has jeopardized the ontological claim that mental states are neurological states; on the contrary, the whole argument can be run on the standard assumptions of the mind/body identity theory. But what turns out not to be true is that explanation in a reduced science is invariably subsumed by explanation in its reducer. Rather, we shall have to say something like this: Mental states have canonical psychological descriptions in virtue of which they fall under the generalizations expressed by computational principles, and they have canonical neurological descriptions in virtue of which they fall under the generalizations expressed by causal laws. Quite possibly there never will be a state of science which we can, as it were, do neurology *instead of* psychology because, quite possibly, it will never be possible to express in the vocabulary of neurology those generalizations about relations of content that computational psychological theories articulate. Pyschologists have lots of things to worry about, but technological unemployment is not likely to be one of them.

It may, however, be worth forging on. I want to sketch, very rapidly and incompletely, a way that psychology and neurology might turn out so as to make possible reduction without fusion. I am not going to defend the claim that either psychology or neurology *will* turn out that way. My primary interest is still just to make clear how much more than correlation (or contingent identity) of psychological and neurological states the substantive reduction of psychology to neurology would require.

Reduction without Fusion

What we have said so far amounts to this: we want a psychological theory that at least provides canonical descriptions of mental states, and we want canonical descriptions to reconstruct the contents of the mental states they apply to. Insofar as such a theory is formalized, its generalizations will apply to mental states in virtue of features of their canonical representations. Such a theory should therefore suffice to represent the causal sequences that constitute the mental life of an organism by sequences of transformations of canonical representations. To contemplate the substantive reduction of computational psychology is, in effect, to suppose that such theories can operate solely with neurological constructs. To put this last point slightly differently, it is to suppose that the descriptions in virtue of whose satisfaction psychological states fall under principles of computation are descriptions in the same vocabulary as those in virtue of whose satisfaction psychological states fall under neurological laws. The question is whether we can imagine a reduction of psychology to neurology that makes this true.

We have seen that the basic methodological problem is to find a way of representing the contents of mental states that avoids recourse to fusion while doing justice to the nonreferentiality of terms occurring in typical psychological contexts. There is a classical proposal here that, as far as I can see, may well point in the direction in which we ought to look: take verbs of propositional attitude to express relations between organisms and *formulae*. In particular, on this view, to believe that elephants are gray is to be related, in a certain way, to some such formula as 'elephants are gray'; to take oneself to see a gray elephant is to be related in a certain (different) way to some such formula as 'I see a gray elephant,' etc.[12]

There is a well-known difficulty with this suggestion, but I think it has been overplayed: viz., believing that elephants are gray *cannot* be being related (in whatever way) to the formula 'elephants are gray,' since, if it were, it would presumably follow that monolingual English speakers cannot have the same beliefs as, say, monolingual French speakers. And it would also presumably follow that infraverbal organisms (cats, dogs, and human infants, inter alia) can have no beliefs at all.

The most that this objection shows, however, is not that believing cannot be being related to a formula, but only that, if it is, then all organisms that can have shared beliefs must have some shared language.[13] I am convinced, for reasons I have elaborated elsewhere (Fodor, 1975), that we would be well advised to take that suggestion seriously; in fact, that it is quite impossible to make sense of the notion of a computational psychology unless some such suggestion is endorsed. The idea is, roughly, that all organisms that have a mental life at all have access to some system of internal representations; that insofar as the mental life of organisms is homogeneous (e.g., insofar as people and animals, or, for that matter, people and machines, instantiate the same psychology) there must be corresponding homogenieties between their internal representational systems; and that a major goal of information flow theories must be to characterize this system of representations and provide necessary and sufficient conditions for the having of propositional attitudes by reference to relations between organisms and the formulae of the system. On this view, for example, to believe that elephants are gray is to be in a certain relation to whatever internal formula translates the English sentence, 'Elephants are gray'; if there is a content relation between that belief and certain of the experiences that are causally responsible for fixing it, then that relation is expressed by generalizations defined over whichever internal representations are implicated in the having of the belief and experiences. In effect, there is a language of thought, and content relations among propositional attitudes are to be explicated as relations among formulae of that language.[14]

Correspondingly, the canonical representations deployed by a computational psychology are assumed to contain structural descriptions of internal formulae. Mental states fall under the generalizations articulated by psychological theories because they satisfy their canonical representations, so John's believing that elephants are gray makes true a certain psychological sentence; viz., a sentence of the form $R_{John} SD$. In that sentence, SD is the structural description of an internal representation (in particular of the internal representation which translates "elephants are gray") and R is a relation between John and that internal representation (in particular, whichever relation to an internal representation is nomologically necessary and sufficient for believing what it expresses).[15]

We are so far from having a developed cognitive psychology that it is hard to give untendentious examples. But consider the propositional attitude *remembering*, and suppose (for once *not* contrary to fact) that psychology acknowledges a relation of *storing* that holds between organisms and internal representations. Then the following might be among the sentences that psychology entails: ⌐John remembers (the fact) that elephants are gray iff John stores (the formula SD⌐, where what substitutes for 'SD' is the structural description of the internal translation of 'elephants are gray.' Note that the biconditional is extensional for the object of 'stores.' That is, it remains true whatever name of the internal formula one substitutes for 'SD.'

However, structural descriptions (unlike other kinds for names) play a special role in this sort of theory, and this connects with the fact that, strictly speaking, structural descriptions are not *names* at all. What they are, of course, is descriptions. So, suppose that 'Alfred' is a name of the internal formula SD. Then, although we preserve *truth* if we substitute 'Alfred' for a structural description of SD in psychological sentences containing the canonical representation of SD, we *do not*, in general, preserve canonicalness. A canonical representation of a mental state must specify its content. We get such a specification (ceteris paribus) insofar as the canonical representation of a mental state contains the structural description of an internal formula, but we do not get it (ceteris paribus) when it contains a noncanonical name of that formula like 'Alfred.' The general idea is that internal representations (like, for that matter, English sentences) express the content they do because they satisfy the structural descriptions they do. Structural descriptions specify those properties of a formula that determine its syntactic and semantic behavior—those properties by virtue of which a formula constitutes an expression in a language.

The assumption that canonical psychological representations typically contain structural descriptions of internal formulae allows us some of the advantages of fusion theories without their most obvious vices. In particular, if the canonical counterpart of 'John believes elephants are gray' is of the form $R_{John, SD}$, it is not surprising that the canonical counterpart of 'elephant' fails to refer to elephants when it occurs within the scope of the canonical counterpart of 'believes.' Roughly, the present account agrees with the fusion story in holding that 'elephant' is not a term in 'John believes elephants are gray.' But it provides a different rationale for the denial of termhood. Since the immediate epistemic objects of propositional attitudes are taken to be formulae, the syntactic objects of verbs of propositional attitude are taken to be structural descriptions of formulae; the word 'elephant' is not a term in 'believes elephants are gray,' but the name of that word is.

The difference between this view and the fusion story should not be minimized. Structural descriptions are unfused expressions: qua names, they purport to refer, and qua descriptions, they purport to determine their referents in virtue of the properties of their referents. Correspondingly, verbs of propositional attitude are construed relationally on the present account; in particular, they express relations between organisms and the referents of structural descriptions; i.e., relations between organisms and formulae of the internal representational system. Such relations are ontologically kosher. No fusion theory can make that statement.

Suppose, then, that canonical psychological representations turn out to contain structural descriptions of internal formulae. Is there any way of reducing this sort of psychology to neurology without committing fusion at the point of reduction? If the argument we have been pursuing is correct, that is what the issue about the possibility of substantive reduction—reduction without loss of explanatory power—boils down to in the case of cognitive psychology.

I suppose the answer goes like this: substantive reduction would at least require (1) that token computational processes turn out to be token neurological processes (storing a formula turns out to be a neurological process, etc.); (2) token internal representations turn out to be token neurological states (a token internal representation that translates 'elephants are gray' turns out to be some neurological configuration in, roughly, the way the above sentence token is a configuration of ink marks on this page); and (3) canonical names of internal formulae (viz., their structural descriptions) are specifiable in the vocabulary of neurology.

I take it that (1) and (2) are just consequences of applying the usual ontological conditions upon reduction to the special case of psychological theories that acknowledge internal representations. They do not, that is, distinguish substantive reduction from standard reduction. It is (3) that does the work. In effect, (3) requires that the canonical *neurological* description of a mental state (of a's) be of the form $R_{a, SD}$, (and not, for example, of the form $R_{a, Alfred}$). So the question that has to be faced is: what would have to be the case in order for (3) to be satisfied? Heaven knows, I am unclear about how that question should be answered, but what I *think* it comes to is this: for psychology to be substantively reducible to neurology, it must turn out that neurological entities constitute a code, and that the canonical neurological representation of such entities specifies the properties in virtue of which they constitute formulae in that code. Since the properties in virtue of which a formula belongs to a code are the ones in virtue of which it satisfies its structural description, and since the properties in virtue of which a formula satisfies its structural description are the ones in virtue of which it has the content it has, we can summarize the whole business by saying that neurology will not reduce psychology unless neurological descriptions specify the content of internal formulae. (Compare the standard view, in which what specifies the content of a mental state is its canonical neurological representation *together with the relevant bridge laws*, and in which the specification is couched in the vocabulary of the reduced rather than the reducing science.)

I have gone about as far as I can, but it is worth remarking that the notion that some neurological states do constitute a code is not exactly foreign to the speculative literature on brain and behavior. So, one might suppose, neurons are relays and canonical names of neurological states are specifications of levels of neural excitation. For this to be true, it would have to turn out that to specify the state of excitation of a set of neurons is to fix the content of a token formula, just as specifying the structural description of an English sentence fixes the content of its tokens. I do not have the foggiest idea whether anything like that *is* true, but the following, at least, is clear: if neurological representations specify those properties of states of the central nervous system in virtue of which they constitute formulae belonging to a code, then the descriptions that such states receive in sciences still more basic than neurology almost certainly do not.(Think what a particle description of a token neurological state—or, for that matter, a token English sentence—would actually look like; then try to imagine specifying, in that vocabulary, such properties as those in virtue of which a sentence token like 'elephants are gray' is content-related to a sentence token like 'there's a gray elephant.' To specify such relations, we need, e.g., notions like 'quantifier' and 'general term.' Is it plausible that such notions should be expressible in the vocabulary of particle physics? The more reason we have for thinking that neurology might substantively reduce psychology, the less reason we have for thinking that physics might substantively reduce neurology.[16]

We have come quite a long way from the suggestion that what we need to reduce psychology to neurology is just correlation (or token identity) of psychological and neurological states. And, as we anticipated at the start, it is the intentionality of psychological predicates that primarily confounds that suggestion. On the one hand, terms in formluae embedded to psychological verbs are typically nonreferential, but, on the other, it is precisely such formulae that express the contents of mental states; and, in the theoretically interesting cases, mental states are related in virtue of their content. Insofar as reduction leads to fusion, it thereby results in the failure to represent the generalizations about mental life that structure such relations. But these generalizations are, as we remarked above, involved in the very rationality of mental life. (It is constitutive of the rationality of John's beliefs about the color of elephants that they are fixed by, e.g., his elephant-sightings and not, e.g., by swallowing pills, or sighting camels, or having his cortex surgically rewired.) Small wonder that antireductionists have often held that to replace psychological explanations by neurological explanations is to lose precisely what a theory of the mind ought to be about. Given the standard notion of reduction, this objection seems to me entirely pertinent.

There is, however, an undefended premise in this whole argument, and I had better say something about it before I stop. I have argued that neurological representations will, quite possibly, fail to provide the appropriate format for such generalizations as hold in virtue of content-relations of mental states. But it might be replied that there are, in fact, no such generalizations; that the distinction between believing elephants are gray because of all those gray elephants and believing elephants are gray because of all those blue pills is not a distinction that a scientifically disciplined theory of mental states would recognize. Of course, we, pretheoretic as we are, like to draw such distinctions; and of course, insofar as they come to anything at all, there will be distinctions between causal mechanisms corresponding to (viz., coextensive with) what we take to be distinctions among relations of content. But a theory of content-relations per se would not be formulable in a first-class conceptual system. What counts, in such a system, is those descriptions under which events (including mental events) instantiate the laws of basic science. And nothing else counts.

Underlying this objection (if I understand it correctly) is the observation that no behavioral or neurological (or physical) description of an organism will uniquely determine an assignment of propositional attitudes to that organism. Any such assignment, however plausible in the light of the behavioral and neurological data, is to that extent an interpretation that we place upon the physical facts and hence not something to be mentioned in even the most exhaustive catalogue of the physical facts themselves.[17] (That assignments of propositional attitudes are interpretations of the physical facts would itself not be mentioned in such a catalogue; interpretation is not a physical category either.) But if there are not any facts about propositional attitudes, then a fortiori there is not the fact that internal formulae are nomologically implicated in the having of propositional attitudes; this is also true however plausible it turns out to be to treat neurological states as tokens in a code and however much such a treatment seems to rationalize the behavioral observations. We need internal formulae to account for propositional attitudes, and we need propositional attitudes if we are to represent such facts as that organisms act out of their beliefs and utilities. But if there are no such facts the whole pattern of explanation is otiose.

Whatever else there is to be said on this issue, however, it is essential to distinguish it from the question of the substantive reducibility of psychology. For the latter is, by hypothesis, an empirical matter, whereas the whole point about the underdetermination of mental ascriptions by physics is that, if it is true at all, it is true *however* the physics and the psychology turn out. Suppose our evidence for treating a certain neurological state as a token of a certain linguistic type were as good as our evidence for treating 'it's raining' as a token of the English type *it's raining*. That would not advance the case one jot since, on the present view, the assignment of token inscriptions to English sentences is *also* just a gloss upon the physical facts. There must be indefinitely many ways of associating objects of the physical form "it's raining" with linguistic objects *salve* the totality of physically characterizable facts about the organisms which produce such tokens.

On the other hand, there is nothing in this line of argument that stops our evidence for the linguistic analysis of token neurological states from being as good as—indeed, of the same kind as—our evidence for the linguistic analysis of English inscriptions, and, skeptical worries to one side, it is hard to believe the latter evidence is other than pretty good. There is thus room for a program of empirical research this side of skepticism: show that *if* there is good reason for treating (some) inscriptions as linguistic tokens, then there is *equally* good reason for treating (some) neurological states as linguistic tokens. It would, in short, be enormously impressive to show that neurological objects satisfy relevant necessary conditions for interpretation as a code, even if it turns out that nothing could show *which* code they (or anything else) belong to.[18] Such a demonstration would be tantamount to the substantive reduction of computational psychological theories. My point throughout has been that nothing less will do.

Notes

1. When I speak of intentionality, I shall usually have two related facts in mind. First, that psychological states (including, specifically, propositional attitudes) are typically individuated by reference to their *content*; second, that expressions that occur in linguistic contexts subordinate to verbs of propositional attitude are typically nonreferential. It is notoriously hard to say how, precisely, the first of these facts is to be construed or what, precisely, the relation between the two facts is. Some of the discussion in this paper is tangent to those issues, but I shall dodge them whenever I can. I shall not, in particular, be attempting anything so ambitious as a general theory of intentionality.

2. Quine (1960) and Dennett (1971) are perhaps the best examples of influential physicalists to whom this charge does *not* apply.

3. The sketch of classical reductionism I have just given is very inadequate from a

number of points of view. Nothing in the following discussion will exploit its inadequacies, however, and it would take considerable space to do justice to the details of the proposal.

4. I think it was a pervasive and characteristic error in positivistic thinking to infer the unity of science from the unity of the subject matter of science; viz., the epistemological thesis from the ontological one. However that may be, it is easy to find passages in the positivist literature in which the former doctrine is espoused in no uncertain terms. Thus Hempel (1949, p. 382) wrote, "The division of science into different areas rests exclusively on differences in research procedures and direction of interest; *one must not regard it as a matter of principle. On the contrary, all the branches of science are in principle of one and the same nature; they are branches of the unitary science, physics.*" (Emphasis Hempel's.) I should add that Hempel has since disavowed many of the ideas in that paper, and I do not intend to suggest that the passage I have quoted is indicative of his present views.

5. The experiences that lead to the acquisition of the rules of English are, normally, observations of utterances that formally instantiate the rules of English; there is, in that sense, a connection between the content of what is learned when one learns English and the content of the experiences that occasion the learning, and it would be a grievous error for a theory of learning to miss that connection. The equal and opposite error would be to try to parlay such connections of content into conceptual necessities, as, I think, some "ordinary language" philosophers have been inclined to do. It is not logically necessary in any useful sense of "logic" that hearing English is normally causally sufficient for speaking English; surely there are possible worlds in which it is normally causally sufficient for speaking Urdu.

6. The "prima facie" is important. For, of course, one can imagine a case in which someone knows something from which it follows (deductively or plausibly) that if small camels are brown then elephants are gray. In this case, though not only in this case, the fixation of the belief that elephants are gray by putative experiences of brown camels need not be arbitrary and might (at least to that extent) count as learning. A serious attempt to distinguish between learning and mere causal fixation of belief would, in short, need to work with a far deeper notion of "nonarbitrariness" than the examples so far might suggest. I am not, however, trying to draw such a distinction here; only to give a rough indication of the direction in which it lies. (The present case is, by the way, just a "Gettier example" transferred from "knows" to "learns", see Gettier, 1963.)

7. I do not suppose we can generally identify the internal representation that the subject assigns the stimulus with the representation he would (or could) supply if asked. Nor do I suppose this point needs, by now, to be argued.

8. I have used this example throughout as a paradigm of a generalization about relations between mental states that appears, prima facie, to be statable only by reference to their contents. I like this example because it is so pedestrian; it is hard to see how any psychology of learning could fail to have some such principle among its tenets. But I do not want to suggest that such examples are hard to come by. On the contrary, they are the cognitive psychologist's stock in trade. The contingencies that cognitive psychologists try to articulate are precisely those in which the contents of mental states are dependent or independent variables, or both.

It is worth emphasizing that the present account takes a view of the domain of cognitive psychological explanation different from the one that dominates the philosophical literature. It has become a sort of dogma that explanations that appeal to the contents of mental states can function only when the states are "rationally" related. The extreme form of this doctrine is that such explanations have literal application only to an ideally rational entity. (For versions of this story, see Dennet [1971], Quine [1960], Davidson [1970].)

Now it presumably *is* true that rationally related mental states are so related in virtue of their content. But there are plenty of cases of plausible psychological generalizations that hold for mental states that are content-related but *not* rationally related, not even on the most inflationary construal of "rational." Association by similarity (if there is such a process) is a simple and venerable example. Or consider the well-supported psycholinguistic generalization that sentences of negative import are harder to understand and to remember than corresponding affirmatives. Such a generalization would seem, on the face of it, to apply to propositional attitudes in virtue of features of their content. But there is no obvious sense in which the mental processes it envisages are usefully sigmatized as rational. On the contrary, an ideally rational creature would presumably never forget, or misunderstand, anything at all. (For further discussion, see Fodor, forthcoming.)

9. This is to put it very roughly. We shall see what it comes to in more detail as we go along.

10. The notion that the (syntactic) objects of verbs of propositional attitudes are (semantically) fused expressions (or, what comes to pretty much the same thing, that verbs of propositional attitude must be read "non-relationally") is one that a number of philosophers have flirted with, either in the context of discussions of Leibniz's Law problems about the mind/body identity theory or in the (intimately related) context of worries about the ontological commitments of psychological ascriptions. It is not clear to me that anybody actually holds the fusion theory of propositional attitudes, but for discussions in which that option is contemplated, see Quine (1960), Nagel (1965), and Dennett (1971). The term "fusion" is borrowed from Dennett.

11. For that matter, the canonical counterpart of 'John takes himself to see a gray elephant' will have no relation (other than the reference to John) to the canonical counterpart of 'John takes himself to see an elephant,' even though (one might have thought) taking oneself to see a gray elephant *is* taking oneself to see an elephant (inter alia). If, in short, the theory wants to represent these states as connected, it will have to do so by specific stipulation; e.g., by taking some such principle as 'x takes-himself-to-see-a-gray-elephant $\rightarrow$ x takes-himself-to-see-an-elephant' as a nonlogical axiom. Fused representations are, to put it mildly, semantically imperspicuous.

12. By contrast, seeing a gray elephant is not being related to a formula, it is being related to an elephant. The present proposal concerns the construal of psychological verbs whose (syntactic) object is read opaquely. I have nothing at all to say about the notoriously difficult question of how to construe such verbs when their objects are read transparently.

13. In fact, it shows less, since it would do, for these purposes, if every organism had a language and the languages were intertranslatable insofar as the mental states of organisms overlap. It is no news, of course, that issues of translation and issues of the proper treatment of propositional attitudes tend to merge.

14. I discover, very belatedly, that an account in some respects quite like this one was once proposed by Sellars (1956). Sellars's work seems remarkably prescient in light of (what I take to be) the methodological presuppositions of contemporary cognitive psychology.

15. For the benefit of those keeping score, we note that the following pieces are now in play. There are (a) internal representations. These are formulae in an internal language, and it is assumed that they are the immediate objects of propositional attitudes. In particular, nomologically necessary and sufficient conditions for the having of a propositional attitude are to be formulated in terms of (presumably computational) relations that the organism bears to internal representations.

There are also (b) structural descriptions of internal representation. These are formulae in the vocabulary of an (ideally completed) psychological theory. Structural descriptions are canonical names of internal representations (see text below). A propositional attitude has the content that it does because the internal representation that constitutes its immediate object satisfies the structural description that it does.

There are also (c) English sentences like 'Elephants are gray.' For heuristic purposes, we use such sentences to form definite (but noncanonical) descriptions of internal representations. We do this because we do not know what the structural descriptions of internal representations are like. That is: ideally completed psychological theories refer to internal representations via their structural descriptions. *We* refer to them as, e.g., the internal representation that translates 'elephants are gray.' We do so faut de mieux.

Finally, there are (d) structural descriptions of English sentences. Structural descriptions of English sentences specify the properties in virtue of which *they* have the content that they have. Roughly, structural descriptions are specifications of sentence types couched in an ambiguity-free notation. If what most psycholinguists now believe is true, the structural descriptions of English sentences must themselves function as internal representations. For, on current views, structural descriptions are normally (among) the ones that speakers intend their utterances to satisfy and that hearers recover in the course of construing the utterances of speakers. That is: in the theoretically interesting cases, the internal representation of an English sentence *is* its structural description.

16. I want to reemphasize that I am *not* denying that the (putative) neurological sentence tokens will satisfy *some physical descriptions or other*, just as the present sentence token satisfies some physical description or other. The question is whether their *physical* descriptions will turn out to be construable as *structural* descriptions which individuate the sentence types that the tokens belong to. (The corresponding question for natural language tokens is, approximately: does a formant analysis of an utterance represent its logical syntax. To which the answer is, of course, "resoundingly, no!")

17. Of course the merely notional status of propositional attitudes does not *follow* just from the observation that mental ascriptions are not entailed by physical ascriptions. what follows from that is only that behaviorism is false and physicalism is not better than contingently true. To get the result that propositional attitudes are fictions one needs to add some such premise as that their ascription would not be justified *unless* it followed from physics. I do not know how, precisely, such a premise would be formulated or how it could be defended.

It is worth mentioning, by the way, that the logical independence of mental and physical statements goes in both directions and has supported dubious arguments both ways. It used to be claimed that tables and chairs are notional on the grounds that physical object statements are not entailed by statements about percepts. Ho hum!

18. For example, internal representations must be at least as differentiated as the contents of propositional attitudes if they are to play the role that we have cast them for in individuating the contents of propositional attitudes. This is a strong condition; one that is not satisfied, e.g., by English orthographic sequences, since the latter do not constitute an ambiguity-free notation.

References

Davidson, D. Mental events. In Forster, L. & Swanson, J. (Eds.), *Experience and theory*. Amherst, Mass.: University of Massachusetts Press, 1970.

Dennett, D. Skinner skinned, a diagnosis of B. F. Skinner's Central Error. Tufts University. Unpublished.

Dennett, D. Intentional systems. *Journal of Philosophy*, 1971, 68, (4), 82-106.

Fodor, J. A. *The language of thought*. New York: Thomas Y. Crowell, 1975.

Fodor, J. A. Three cheers for propositional attitudes; a reply to Dennett's "Intentional Systems." Forthcoming.

Gettier, E. Is justified true belief knowledge? *Analysis*, 1963, 23, 121-123.

Hempel, C. G. Logical analysis of psychology. In Feigel, H. & Sellars, W. (Eds.), *Readings in philosophical analysis*. New York: Appleton-Century Crofts, 1949.

Nagel, T. Physicalism. *The Philosophical Review*, 1965, 74, 339-356.

Place, U. T. Is consciousness a brain process? *British Journal of Psychology*, 1956, 47, 44-50.

Quine, W. V. *Word and object*. Cambridge, Mass.: M.I.T. Press, 1960.

Sellars, W. Empiricism and the philosophy of mind. In Feigel, H. & Scriven, M. (Eds.), *Minnesota studies in the philosophy of science*, Vol. I. Minneapolis, Minnesota: University of Minnesota Press, 1956.

Smart, J. J. C. Sensations and brain processes. *Philosophical Review*, 1959, 68, 141-156.

Troubles with Functionalism

The functionalist approach to the philosophy of mind is increasingly popular; indeed, it may now be dominant (Armstrong, 1968; Block & Fodor, 1972; Field, 1975; Fodor, 1965, 1968a; Grice, 1975; Harman, 1973; Lewis, 1971, 1972; Locke, 1968; Lycan, 1974; Nelson, 1969, 1975; Putnam, 1966, 1967, 1970, 1975a; Pitcher, 1971; Sellars, 1968; Shoemaker, 1975; Smart, 1971; Wiggins, 1975). However, "functionalist" theories are the products of a number of rather different projects: attempts to reformulate logical behaviorism to avoid objections, attempts to exploit mind-machine analogies, attempts to apply empirical psychology to philosophy of mind, and attempts to argue for—or against—mental-neurological identity theses. Thus, though theories called 'functionalist' have a certain obvious family resemblance, it should not be surprising if there is no single doctrine about the nature of mind that all so-called functionalists share.

I shall consider those functionalist theories of mind that can be understood as *identity* theses in the tradition of claims that pain is a brain state. That is, the kinds of functionalism I shall discuss claim that there are functional states and that each mental state is identical to a functional state (or that there are functional properties and that each mental property is identical to a functional property). These functional-state identity theses are concerned with *types* of mental states or events, not (just) *tokens*—that is, pain, or the state of being in pain, rather than (just) particular datable pains—universals that can be instantiated in different people at different times, not (just) nonrecurring particulars.

I shall begin by describing functionalism and sketching the functionalist critique of behaviorism and physicalism. Then I shall argue that the troubles ascribed by functionalism to behaviorism and physicalism infect functionalism as well.

Functionalism in the sense intended here should not be confused with the distinct, though related doctrine that the method of psychology is "functional analysis"—decomposing mental processes into their component subprocesses, which are individuated with regard to the role they play in the mental life of the organism (Fodor, 1968a, 1968b; Dennett, 1975; Cummins, 1975). Functionalism in this sense is a doctrine about the nature of psychological explanation, not a doctrine about what mental states *are*. Functionalism in the sense of this chapter, on the other hand, is an ontological doctrine.

One characterization of functionalism that is probably vague enough to be accepted by most functionalists is: each type of mental state is a state consisting of a disposition to act in certain ways *and to have certain mental states*, given certain sensory inputs and certain mental states. So put, functionalism can be seen as a new incarnation of behaviorism. Behaviorism identifies mental states with dispositions to act in certain ways in certain input situations. But as critics have pointed out (Chisholm, 1957; Putnam, 1963), desire for goal G cannot be identified with, say, the disposition to do A in circumstances in which A leads to G, since, after all, the agent might not *know* A leads to G and thus might not be disposed to do A. Functionalism replaces behaviorism's "sensory inputs" with "sensory inputs and mental states"; and functionalism replaces behaviorism's "disposition to act" with "disposition to act and have certain mental states." Functionalists want to individuate mental states causally, and since mental states have mental causes and effects as well as sensory causes and behavioral effects, functionalists individuate mental states partly in terms of causal relations to other mental states. One consequence of this difference between functionalism and behaviorism is that there are organisms that according to behaviorism, have mental states but, according to functionalism, do not have mental states.

So, necessary conditions for mentality that are postulated by functionalism are in one respect stronger than those postulated by behaviorism. According to behaviorism, it is necessary and sufficient for desiring that G that a system be characterized by a certain set (perhaps infinite) of input-output relations; that is, according to behaviorism, a system desires that G just in case a certain set of conditionals of the form 'It will emit O given I' are true of it. According to functionalism, however, a system might have these input-output relations, yet not desire that G; for according to functionalism, whether a system desires that G depends on whether it has internal states which have certain causal relations to other internal states (and to inputs and outputs). Since behaviorism makes no such "internal state" requirement, there are possible systems of which behaviorism affirms and functionalism denies that they have mental states.[1] One way of stating this is that, according to functionalism, behaviorism is guilty of *liberalism* — ascribing mental properties to things that do not in fact have them.

Despite the difference just sketched between functionalism and behaviorism, functionalists and behaviorists need not be far apart in spirit. Indeed, if one defines 'behaviorism' — somewhat misleadingly — as the view that mental terms (e.g., 'pain') can be defined in nonmental terms, then functionalism in most of its forms *is* a version of behaviorism.[2] Shoemaker (1975), for example, says, "On one construal of it, functionalism in the philosophy of mind is the doctrine that mental, or psychological, terms are, in principle, eliminable in a certain way" (pp. 306-7). Functionalists have tended to treat the mental-state terms in a functional characterization of a mental state quite differently from the input and output terms. Thus in the simplest Turing-machine version of the theory (Putnam, 1967; Block & Fodor, 1972), mental states are identified with the total Turing-machine states, which are themselves *implicitly* defined by a machine table that explicitly mentions inputs and outputs, described nonmentalistically.

In Lewis's version of functionalism, mental-state terms are defined by means of a modification of Ramsey's method, in a way that eliminates essential use of mental terminology from the definitions but does not eliminate input and output terminology. That is, 'pain' is defined as synonymous with a definite description containing input and output terms but no mental terminology.[3]

Furthermore, functionalism in both its machine and nonmachine versions has typically insisted that characterizations of mental states should contain descriptions of inputs and outputs in *physical* language. Armstrong (1968), for example, says,

We may distinguish between 'physical behaviour', which refers to any merely physical action or passion of the body, and 'behavior proper' which implies relationship to the mind. . . . Now, if in our formula ["state of the person apt for bringing about a certain sort of behaviour"] 'behaviour' were to mean 'behaviour proper', then we would be giving an account of mental concepts in terms of a concept that already presupposes mentality, which would be circular. So it is clear that in our formula, 'behaviour' must mean 'physical behaviour'. (p. 84)

Therefore, functionalism can be said to "tack down" mental states only at the periphery—i.e., through physical, or at least nonmental, specification of inputs and outputs. One major thesis of this chapter is that, because of this feature, functionalism fails to avoid the sort of problem for which it rightly condemns behaviorism. Functionalism, too, is guilty of liberalism, for much the same reasons as behaviorism. Unlike behaviorism, however, functionalism can naturally be altered to avoid liberalism—but only at the cost of falling into an equally ignominious failing.

The failing I speak of is the one that functionalism shows *physicalism* to be guilty of. By 'physicalism', I mean the doctrine that pain, for example, is identical to a physical (or physiological) state.[4] As many philosophers have argued (notably Fodor, 1965, and Putnam, 1966; see also Block & Fodor, 1972), if functionalism is true, physicalism is false. The point is at its clearest with regard to Turing-machine versions of functionalism. Any given abstract Turing machine can be realized by a wide variety of physical devices; indeed, it is plausible that, given any putative correspondence between a Turing-machine state and a configurational physical (or physiological) state, there will be a possible realization of the Turing machine that will provide a counterexample to that correspondence. (See Kalke, 1969; Gendron, 1971; Mucciolo, 1974, for unconvincing arguments to the contrary; see also Kim, 1972.) Therefore, if pain is a functional state, it cannot, for example, be a brain state, because creatures without brains can realize the same Turing machine as creatures with brains.

I must emphasize that the functionalist argument against physicalism does not appeal merely to the fact that one abstract Turing machine can be realized by systems of different *material composition* (wood, metal, glass, etc.). To argue this way would be like arguing that temperature cannot be a microphysical magnitude because the same temperature can be had by objects with *different* microphysical structures (Kim, 1972). Objects with different microphysical structures, e.g., objects made of wood, metal, glass, etc., can have many interesting microphysical properties in common, such as molecular kinetic energy of the same average value. Rather, the functionalist argument against physicalism is that it is difficult to see how there *could be* a nontrivial first-order (see note 4) physical property in common to all and only the possible physical realizations of a given Turing-machine state. Try to think of a remotely plausible candidate! At the very least, the onus is on those who think such physical properties are conceivable to show us how to conceive of one.

One way of expressing this point is that, according to functionalism, physicalism is a *chauvinist* theory: it withholds mental properties from systems that in fact have them. In saying mental states are brain states, for example, physicalists unfairly exclude those poor brainless creatures who nontheless have minds.

A second major point of this paper is that the very argument which functionalism uses to condemn physicalism can be applied equally well against functionalism; indeed, any version of functionalism that avoids liberalism falls, like physicalism, into chauvinism.

I momentarily digress to note that although some philosophers have argued, as stated earlier, that if functionalism is true, physicalism is false, others (Lewis, 1971, Smart, 1971, Armstrong, 1968) have argued, contrariwise, that if functionalism is true, physicalism is *true*. The argument, briefly stated, is that we can give a functional definition of '(the state) pain' as the occupant of a certain causal role; a brain state has that causal role, so the brain state is identical to pain. But suppose that Martians are functionally equivalent to us, yet have no brain state like any of ours. To avoid contradiction (one thing identical to two different things), holders of the view that functionalism shows physicalism is true have had to retreat to narrower, e.g., species specific identities. They say human pain is one brain state and Martian pain another.[5] To say this is to give up saying what property it is *in virtue of which* Martians and humans can *both* be in pain, and to give up saying what property a (token) state has *in virtue of which* it is a pain state. (Stating the point in this manner reveals the misguided nature of proposals to identify pain with the disjunction of physical states that have realized or will realize pain in the history of the universe. Such a disjunction would hardly capture what these pain-feeling organisms have in common in virtue of which they all have pain.) We cannot allow that there is a universal, pain, that is identical to a functional state and at the same time claim that pain is one brain state in humans and another brain state in Martians. (This point is also noted in Lycan, 1974 and Wiggins, 1975.) If functionalism is true, physicalists face a dilemma. Either they must abandon the attempt to propose a theory of mental universals such as pain, anger, etc., and talk instead of human pain, Martian pain, etc. (or worse, *deny* that anything has pain or anger, etc.), or they must claim that mental states are, for example, brain states and thus embrace chauvinism.[6]

This chapter has three parts. The first argues that functionalism is guilty of liberalism, the second that one way of modifying functionalism to avoid liberalism is to tie it more closely to empirical psychology, and the third that no version of functionalism can avoid both liberalism and chauvinism.

1.1 More about What Functionalism Is

One way of providing some order to the bewildering variety of functionalist theories is to distinguish between those that are couched in terms of a Turing machine and those that are not.

A Turing-machine table lists a finite set of machine-table states, $S_1 \ldots S_n$; inputs, $I_1 \ldots I_m$; and outputs, $O_1 \ldots O_p$. The table specifies a set of conditionals of the form: if the machine is in state S_i and receives input I_j, it emits output O_k and goes into state S_l. That is, given any state and input, the table specifies an output and a next state. Any system with a set of inputs, outputs, and states related in the way specified by the table is described by the table and is a realization of the abstract automaton specified by the table.

To have the power for computing every recursive function, a Turing machine must be able to control its input in certain ways. In standard formulations, the output of a Turing machine is regarded as having two components. It prints a symbol on a tape, then moves the tape, thus bringing a new symbol into the view of the input reader. For the Turing machine to have full power, the tape must be infinite in at least one direction and movable in both directions. If the machine has no control over the tape, it is a "finite transducer," a rather limited Turing machine. Finite transducers need not be regarded as having tape at all. Those who believe that machine functionalism is true must suppose that just what power automaton we are is a substantive empirical question. If we are "full power" Turing machines, the environment must constitute part of the tape.

Machine functionalists generally consider the machine in question as a probabilistic automaton—a machine whose table specifies conditionals of the following form: if the machine is in S_a and receives I_b, it has a probability p_1 of emitting O_1; p_2 of emitting O_2 . . . p_k of emitting O_k; r_1 of going into S_1; r_2 of going into S_2 . . . r_n of going into S_n. For simplicity, I shall usually consider a deterministic version of the theory.

One very simple version of machine functionalism (Block & Fodor, 1972) states that each system having mental states is described by at least one Turing-machine table of a specifiable sort and that each type of mental state of the system is identical to one of the machine-table states. Consider, for example, the Turing machine described in the accompanying table (cf. Nelson, 1975):

	S_1	S_2
nickel input	Emit no output Go to S_2	Emit a Coke Go to S_1
dime input	Emit a Coke Stay in S_1	Emit a Coke & a nickel Go to S_1

One can get a crude picture of the simple verson of machine functionalism by considering the claim that S_1 = dime-desire, and S_2 = nickel-desire. Of course, no functionalist should claim that a Coke machine desires anything. Rather, the simple version of machine functionalism described in the table makes an analogous claim with respect to a much more complex machine table. Notice that machine functionalism specifies inputs and outputs explicitly, internal states implicitly (Putnam [1967, p. 434] says: "The S_i, to repeat, are specified only *implicitly* by the description, i.e., specified *only* by the set of transition probabilities given in the machine table"). To be described by this machine table, a device must accept nickels and dimes as inputs and dispense nickels and Cokes as outputs. But the states S_1 and S_2 can have virtually any natures, so long as those natures connect the states to each other and to the inputs and outputs specified in the machine table. All we are told about S_1 and S_2 are these relations; thus, in this sense, machine functionalism can be said to reduce mentality to input-output structures. This example should suggest the force of the functionalist argument against physicalism. Try to think of a first-order (see note 4) physical property that can be shared by all (and only) realizations for this machine table!

One can also categorize functionalists in terms of whether they regard functional identities as part of a priori psychology or empirical psychology. (Since this distinction crosscuts the machine/nonmachine distinction, I shall be able to illustrate nonmachine versions of functionalism in what follows.) The a priori functionalists (e.g., Smart, Armstrong, Lewis, Shoemaker) are the heirs of the logical behaviorists. They tend to regard functional analyses as analyses of the meanings of mental terms, whereas the empirical functionalists (e.g., Fodor, Putnam, Harman) regard functional analyses as substantive scientific hypotheses. In what follows, I shall refer to the former view as 'Functionalism' and the latter as 'Psychofunctionalism'. (I shall use 'functionalism' with a lowercase 'f' as neutral between Functionalism and Psychofunctionalism. When distinguishing between Functionalism and Psychofunctionalism, I shall always use capitals.)

Functionalism and Psychofunctionalism and the difference between them can be made clearer in terms of the notion of the Ramsey sentence of a psychological theory. Mental-state terms that appear in a psychological theory can be defined in various ways by means of the Ramsey sentence of the theory (see. p. 269). All functional-state identity theories (and functional-property identity theories) can be understood as defining a set of functional states (or functional properties) by means of the Ramsey sentence of a psychological theory—with one functional state corresponding to each mental state (or one functional property corresponding to each mental property). The functional state corresponding to pain will be called the 'Ramsey functional correlate' of pain, with respect to the psychological theory. In terms of the notion of a Ramsey functional correlate with respect to a theory, the distinction between Functionalism and Psychofunctionalism can be defined as follows: Functionalism identifies mental state S with S's Ramsey functional correlate with respect to a *common-sense* psychological theory; Psychofunctionalism identifies S with S's Ramsey functional correlate with respect to a *scientific* psychological theory.

This difference between Functionalism and Psychofunctionalism gives rise to a difference in specifying inputs and outputs. Functionalists are restricted to specification of inputs and outputs that are plausibly part of common-sense knowledge; Psychofunctionalists are under no such restriction. Although both groups insist on physical—or at least nonmental—specification of inputs and outputs, Functionalists require externally observable classifications (e.g., inputs characterized in terms of objects present in the vicinity of the organism, outputs in terms of movements of body parts). Psychofunctionalists, on the other hand, have the option to specify inputs and outputs in terms of internal parameters, e.g., signals in input and output neurons.

The notion of a Ramsey functional correlate can be defined in a variety of ways. For the purposes of this chapter, it will be useful to adopt one of them.[7] I shall define a notion of Ramsey functional correlate for a mental property *being in S*, where S is a type of mental state. Let T be a psychological theory of either common-sense or scientific psychology. Reformulate T so that it is a single conjunctive sentence, with all mental-state terms as singular terms— e.g., 'is angry' becomes 'has anger'. Suppose that T, so reformulated, can be written as

$$T(p, s_1 \cdots s_n, i_1 \cdots i_k, o_1 \cdots o_m)$$

where p designates an ideal or representative person; $s_1 \cdots s_n$ are terms for mental states, $i_1 \cdots i_k$ for inputs, and $o_1 \cdots o_m$ for outputs. T may contain generalizations such as p's being in such and such states and receiving such and such inputs causes p's emitting such and such outputs and going into such and such states.

To get the Ramsey sentence of T, replace p and $s_1 \ldots s_n$ with variables and prefix an existential quantifier for each variable. A singular term designating the Ramsey functional correlate of being in pain (with respect to T) can be formulated using a property-abstraction operator. Let an expression of the form '$\lambda x F x$' be a singular term meaning the same as an expression of the form 'the property (or attribute) of being an x such that x is F', i.e., 'F-ness'.[8] If $y, x_1 \ldots x_n$ are the variables that replaced $p, s_1 \ldots s_n$, and x_i is the variable that replaced 'pain', the Ramsey functional correlate of the property of being in pain (with respect to T) is

$$\lambda y \exists x_1 \ldots x_n \left[T\,(y, x_1 \ldots x_n, i_1 \ldots i_k, o_1 \ldots o_m) \,\&\, y \text{ is in } x_i \right]$$

Notice that this expression contains input and output terms, but no mental terms (since the mental state terms were replaced by variables). For this reason, this version of functionalism (like machine functionalism) could be said to reduce mentality to input-output structures.

An example: Let T be the theory that a person's having pain causes him to emit a loud noise. The Ramsey sentence of T is

$$\exists y\, \exists x (y\text{'s having } x \text{ causes } y \text{ to emit a loud noise})$$

and the Ramsey functional correlate of being in pain with respect to T is

$$\lambda y\, \exists x (y\text{'s having } x \text{ causes } y \text{ to emit a loud noise } \& \, y \text{ is in } x)$$

This expression (which designates pain with respect to the theory T) contains the output term 'emit a loud noise', but it contains no mental term.[9]

Thus far I have defined the Ramsey functional correlate of (the property of) being in mental state S, and I have characterized functionalism as identifying being in S (for each mental state S) with the Ramsey functional correlate of being in S (with respect to a psychological theory). But I have not yet defined the functional *state* with which functionalism identifies S. I shall introduce a state abstraction operator 'δ' analogous to the property abstraction operator 'λ', introduced above. Let an expression of the form 'δxFx' be a singular term meaning the same as an expression of the form 'the state of x's being an x such that Fx', i.e., 'the state of something's having F'. If you reexamine the expression that designates the Ramsey functional correlate of being in pain (with respect to T) and substitute 'δ' for 'λ', you have a singular term designating the Ramsey functional correlate of pain. Functionalism identifies pain with its Ramsey functional correlate (with respect to T).[10]

FUNCTIONAL EQUIVALENCE

Relations of functional equivalence for all versions of functionalism are relative to specification of inputs and outputs. For both machine and nonmachine versions of functionalism, there are functional-equivalence relations of different strengths. One could regard Turing machines x and y as functionally equivalent (relative to a given specification of inputs and outputs) just in case there is at least one machine table that lists just that set of inputs and outputs and describes both x and y. On the other hand, one could require that *every* machine table that describes x describes y and vice versa —relative to the given specifications of inputs and outputs.[11] One way of being precise though redundant—is to speak of functional equivalence relative to *both* a given specification of inputs and outputs and a given machine table.

Similar points apply to nonmachine versions of functionalism. One could regard systems x and y as functionally equivalent (relative to a given specification of inputs and outputs) just in case there is at least one psychological theory that adverts to just that set of inputs and outputs and is true of both x and y. Or one might require that all psychological theories with the set of inputs and outputs that are true of x are also true of y. Again, one way of being precise is to relativize to both inputs and outputs and to psychological theory.

In what follows, I shall sometimes speak of x and y as functionally equivalent (with respect to certain inputs and outputs) without specifying a particular psychological theory or Turing-machine table. What I shall mean is that x and y are functionally equivalent (with respect to the given inputs and outputs) with respect to at least one reasonably adequate, true psychological theory (either common-sense or empirical, depending on whether Functionalism or Psychofunctionalism is in question) or with respect to at least one reasonably adequate machine table that describes both x and y.[12] Admittedly, such notions of functional equivalence are quite vague. Unfortunately, I see no way of avoiding this vagueness. Functionalists should be consoled, however, by the fact that their chief rival, physicalism, seems beset by an analogous vagueness. As far as I know, no one has ever come up with a remotely satisfactory way of saying what a physical state or property is without quantifying over unknown, true physical theories (e.g., a physical property is a property expressed by a predicate of some true physical theory); nor has anyone been able to say what it is for x and y to be physical states of the same type without quantifying over reasonably adequate, but unknown, true physical theories.

In discussing the various versions of functionalism, I have also been rather vague about what psychology is supposed to be psychology *of*. Presumably, some animals, e.g., dogs, are capable of many of the same mental states as humans, e.g., hunger, thirst, other desires, and some beliefs. Thus, if functionalism is true, we must suppose that there is a psychological theory that applies to people and some animals that says what it is in virtue of which both the animals and the people have beliefs, desires, etc. On the other hand, there are mental states people can have that dogs presumably cannot. Further, there may be mental states that some persons can have but others cannot. Some of us can suffer *weltschmerz*, whereas others, perhaps, cannot. It is possible that there are no basic psychological differences between dogs, persons who can have *weltschmerz*, persons who cannot, etc. Perhaps the gross behavioral differences are due to different values of the same parameters in a single psychological theory that covers all the aforementioned creatures. An analogy: the same theory of nuclear physics covers both reactors and bombs, even though there is a gross difference in their behavior. This is due to different values of a single set of parameters that determine whether or not the reaction is controlled. Perhaps parameters such as information-processing capacity or memory space play the same role in psychology. But this is unlikely for scientific psychology, and it surely is not true for the common-sense psychological theories Functionalism appeals to. Thus, it seems likely that both Functionalism and Psychofunctionalism require psychological theories of different degrees of generality or level of abstraction—one for humans who can have *weltschmerz*, one for all humans, one for dogs and humans, etc. If so, different mental states may be identical to functional states at different abstractness levels. The same point applies to functional-equivalence relations. Two creatures may be functionally equivalent relative to one level of abstractness of psychological theory, but not with respect to another.

The Ramsey functional-correlate characterization of functionalism captures relativities to both abstractness level and input-output specification. According to both Functionalism and Psychofunctionalism, each functional state is identical to its Ramsey functional correlate with respect to a psychological theory. The intended level of abstractness is automatically captured in the level of detail present in the theory. The input and output specifications are just those mentioned. For example, suppose the Ramsey functional correlate of pain with respect to the theory is $\delta y \exists x$ (y's being pricked by a pin causes y to be in x & y's being in x causes y to scream & y is in x). The input and output specifications are 'pin pricks' and 'screaming', and the level of abstractness is determined by those two causal relations being the only ones mentioned.

Until Section 3.1, I shall ignore considerations concerning level of abstractness. When I say that two systems are "functionally equivalent," I shall assume that my "reasonable adequacy" condition ensures an appropriate level of concreteness.

(The reader can skip to page 277 without loss of continuity.)

I mentioned two respects in which Functionalism and Psychofunctionalism differ. First, Functionalism identifies pain with its Ramsey functional correlate with respect to a common-sense psychological theory, and Psychofunctionalism identifies pain with its Ramsey functional correlate with respect to a scientific psychological theory. Second, Functionalism requires common-sense specification of inputs and outputs, and Psychofunctionalism has the option of using empirical-theory construction in specifying inputs and outputs so as to draw the line between the inside and outside of the organism in a theoretically principled way.

I shall say a bit more about the Psychofunctionalism/Functionalism distinction. According to the preceding characterization, Psychofunctionalism and Functionalism are theory relative. That is, we are told not what pain *is*, but, rather, what pain is *with respect to this or that theory*. But Psychofunctionalism can be defined as the doctrine that mental states are constituted by causal relations among whatever psychological events, states, processes, and other entities—as well as inputs and outputs—actually obtain in us in whatever ways those entities are actually causally related to one another. Therefore, if current theories of psychological processes are correct in adverting to storage mechanisms, list searchers, item comparators, and so forth, Psychofunctionalism will identify mental states with causal structures that involve storage, comparing, and searching processes as well as inputs, outputs, and other mental states.

Psychofunctional equivalence can be similarly characterized without overt relativizing to theory. Let us distinguish between weak and strong equivalence (Fodor, 1968a). Assume we have agreed on some descriptions of inputs and outputs. I shall say that organisms x and y are weakly or behaviorally equivalent if and only if they have the same output for any input or sequence of inputs. If x and y are weakly equivalent, each is a weak simulation of the other. I shall say x and y are *strongly* equivalent relative to some branch of science if and only if (1) x and y are weakly equivalent, and (2) that branch of science has in its domain processes that mediate inputs and outputs, and x's and y's inputs and outputs are mediated by the same processes. If x and y are strongly equivalent, they are strong simulations of each other.

We can now give a characterization of a Psychofunctional equivalence relation that is not overtly theory relative. This Psychofunctional-equivalence relation is strong equivalence with respect to psychology. (Note that 'psychology' here denotes a branch of science, not a particular theory in that branch.)

This Psychofunctional equivalence relation differs in a number of respects from those described earlier. For example, for the sort of equivalence relation described earlier, equivalent systems need not have any common output if they share a given sequence of inputs. In machine terms, the equivalence relations described earlier require only that equivalent systems have a common machine table (of a certain type); the current equivalence relation requires, in addition, that equivalent systems be in the same state of the machine table. This difference can be eliminated by more complex formulations.

Ignoring differences between Functionalism and Psychofunctionalism in their characterizations of inputs and outputs, we can give a very crude account of the Functionalism/Psychofunctionalism distinction as follows: Functionalism identifies mental states with causal structures involving conscious mental states, inputs, and outputs; Psychofunctionalism identifies mental states with the same causal structures, elaborated to include causal relations to *unconscious* mental entities as well. That is, the causal relations adverted to by Functionalism are a subset of those adverted to by Psychofunctionalism. Thus, weak or behavioral equivalence, Functional equivalence, and Psychofunctional equivalence form a hierarchy. All Psychofunctionally equivalent systems are Functionally equivalent, and all Functionally equivalent systems are weakly or behaviorally equivalent.

Although the characteristics of Psychofunctionalism and Psychofunctional equivalence just given are not overtly theory relative, they have the same vagueness problems as the characterizations given earlier. I pointed out that the Ramsey functional correlate characterizations suffer from vagueness about level of abstractness of psychological theory—e.g., are the psychological theories to cover only humans who are capable of *weltschmerz*, all humans, all mammals, or what? The characterization of Psychofunctionalism just given allows a similar question: what is to count as a psychological entity or process? If the answer is an entity in the domain of some true psychological theory, we have introduced relativity to theory. Similar points apply to the identification of psychofunctional equivalence, with strong equivalence with respect to psychology.

Appeal to unknown, true psychological theories introduces another kind of vagueness problem. We can allocate current theories among branches of science by appealing to concepts or vocabulary currently distinctive to those branches. But we cannot timelessly distinguish among branches of science by appealing to their distinctive concepts or vocabulary, because we have no idea what concepts and vocabulary the future will bring. If we did know, we would more or less have future theories now. Worse still, branches of science have a habit of coalescing and splitting, so we cannot know whether the science of the future will countenance anything at all like psychology as a branch of science.

One consequence of this vagueness is that no definite answer can be given to the question, Does Psychofunctionalism as I have described it characterize mental states partly in terms of their relations to *neurological* entities? I think the best anyone can say is: at the moment, it seems not. Psychology and neurophysiology seem to be separate branches of science. Of course, it is clear that one must appeal to neurophysiology to explain some psychological phenomena, e.g., how being hit on the head causes loss of language ability. However, it seems as if this should be thought of as "descending" to a lower level in the way evolutionary biology appeals to physics (e.g., cosmic rays hitting genes) to partially explain mutation.

If correct, the characterization that I have given of functionalism as being theory relative should be a source of difficulty for the functionalist who is also a realist. Since psychological theories can differ considerably—even if we restrict our attention to true theories— the functionalist would identify pain with one state with respect to one theory and another state with respect to another theory. But how can pain be identical to nonidentical states? Notice that this problem is not avoided by construing functionalism as a theory of type-identity conditions on mental states—e.g., (x) (x is a pain $\equiv$ x is a token of functional state S)—rather than as an identity theory—e.g., pain = S. For mental state token a can be type identical to b with respect to one theory and to c with respect to another, even though b is not type identical to c on either theory. It makes no more sense to suppose that a is type identical to two nontype identical states than to suppose pain is identical to two nonidentical states.

I see only two avenues of escape that have even a modicum of plausibility. One would be to argue that true psychological theories simply do not differ in ways that create embarrassment for realist functionalists. Certain views about the varieties of true psychological theories may be conjoined with those about identity conditions for states in order to argue that the Ramsey functional correlates of pain with respect to the true psychological theories are not different from one another. The second approach is to argue that there is only one true psychological theory (or set of equivalent theories) that provides the *correct* Ramsey functional correlate of pain. According to Lewis (1971, 1972) and Shoemaker (1975), the theory that contains all the truths of meaning analysis of psychological terms has this property. I argue against their claim in Section 1.6.

One final preliminary point: I have given the misleading impression that functionalism identifies *all* mental states with functional states. Such a version of functionalism is obviously far too strong. Let X be a newly created cell-for-cell duplicate of you (which, of course, is functionally equivalent to you). Perhaps you remember being bar-mitzvahed. But X does not remember being bar-mitzvahed, since X never was bar-mitzvahed. Indeed, something can be functionally equivalent to you but fail to know what you know, or {verb}, what you {verb}, for a wide variety of "success" verbs. Worse still, if Putnam (1975b) is right in saying that "meanings are not in the head," systems functionally equivalent to you may, for similar reasons, fail to have many of your other propositional attitudes. Suppose you believe water is wet. According to plausible arguments advanced by Putnam and Kripke, a condition for the possibility of your believing water is wet is a certain kind of causal connection between you and water. Your "twin" on Twin Earth, who is connected in a similar way to XYZ rather than H_2O, would not believe water is wet.

If functionalism is to be defended, it must be construed as applying only to a subclass of mental states, those "narrow" mental states such that truth conditions for their application are in some sense "within the person." But even assuming that a notion of narrowness of psychological state can be satisfactorily formulated, the interest of functionalism may be diminished by this restriction. I mention this problem only to set it aside.

I shall take functionalism to be a doctrine about all "narrow" mental states.

1.2 Homunculi-Headed Robots

In this section I shall describe a class of devices that embarrass all versions of functionalism in that they indicate functionalism is guilty of liberalism—classifying systems that lack mentality as having mentality.

Consider the simple version of machine functionalism already described. It says that each system having mental states is described by at least one Turing-machine table of a certain kind, and each mental state of the system is identical to one of the machine-table states specified by the machine table. I shall consider inputs and outputs to be specified by descriptions of neural impulses in sense organs and motor-output neurons. This assumption should not be regarded as restricting what will be said to Psychofunctionalism rather than Functionalism. As already mentioned, every version of functionalism assumes *some* specificiation of inputs and outputs. A Functionalist specification would do as well for the purposes of what follows.

Imagine a body externally like a human body, say yours, but internally quite different. The neurons from sensory organs are connected to a bank of lights in a hollow cavity in the head. A set of buttons connects to the motor-output neurons. Inside the cavity resides a group of little men. Each has a very simple task: to implement a "square" of a reasonably adequate machine table that describes you. On one wall is a bulletin board on which is posted a state card, i.e., a card that bears a symbol designating one of the states specified in the machine table. Here is what the little men do: Suppose the posted card has a 'G' on it. This alerts the little men who implement G squares — 'G-men' they call themselves. Suppose the light representing input I_{17} goes on. One of the G-men has the following as his sole task: when the card reads 'G' and the I_{17} light goes on, he presses output button O_{191} and changes the state card to 'M'. This G-man is called upon to exercise his task only rarely. In spite of the low level of intelligence required of each little man, the system as a whole manages to simulate you because the functional organization they have been trained to realize is yours. A Turing machine can be represented as a finite set of quadruples (or quintuples, if the output is divided into two parts) — current state, current input; next state, next output. Each little man has the task corresponding to a single quadruple. Through the efforts of the little men, the system realizes the same (reasonably adequate) machine table as you do and is thus functionally equivalent to you.

I shall describe a version of the homunculi-headed simulation, which is more clearly nomologically possible. How many homunculi are required? Perhaps a billion are enough; after all, there are only about a billion neurons in the brain.

Suppose we convert the government of China to functionalism, and we convince its officials that it would enormously enhance their international prestige to realize a human mind for an hour. We provide each of the billion people in China (I chose China because it has a billion inhabitants.) with a specially designed two-way radio that connects them in the appropriate way to other persons and to the artificial body mentioned in the previous example. We replace the little men with a radio transmitter and receiver connected to the input and output neurons. Instead of a bulletin board, we arrange to have letters displayed on a series of satellites placed so that they can be seen from anywhere in China. Surely such a system is not physically impossible. It could be functionally equivalent to you for a short time, say an hour.

"But," you may object, "how could something be functionally equivalent to me for *an hour*? Doesn't my functional organization determine, say, how I would react to doing nothing for a week but reading *Reader's Digest*?" Remember that a machine table specifies a set of conditionals of the form: if the machine is in S_i and receives input I_j, it emits output O_k and goes into S_l. Any system that has a set of inputs, outputs, and states related in the way described realizes that machine table, even if it exists for only an instant. For the hour the Chinese system is "on," it *does* have a set of inputs, outputs, and states of which such conditionals are true. Whatever the initial state, the system will respond in whatever way the machine table directs. This is how *any* computer realizes the machine table it realizes.

Of course, there are signals the system would respond to that you would not respond to, e.g., massive radio interference or a flood of the Yangtze River. Such events might cause a malfunction, scotching the simulation, just as a bomb in a computer can make it fail to realize the machine table it was built to realize. But just as the computer *without* the bomb *can* realize the machine table, the system consisting of the people and artifical body can realize the machine table so long as there are no catastrophic interferences, e.g., floods, etc.

"But," someone may object, "there is a difference between a bomb in a computer and a bomb in the Chinese system, for in the case of the latter (unlike the former), inputs as specified in the machine table can be the cause of the malfunction. Unusual neural activity in the sense organs of residents of Chungking Province caused by a bomb or by a flood of the Yangtze can cause the system to go haywire."

Reply: the person who says what system he or she is talking about gets to say what counts as inputs and outputs. I count as inputs and outputs only neural activity in the artificial body connected by radio to the people of China. Neural signals in the people of Chungking count no more as inputs to this system than input tape jammed by a saboteur between the relay contacts in the innards of a computer count as an input to the computer.

Of course, the object consisting of the people of China + the artificial body has *other* Turing machine descriptions under which neural signals in the inhabitants of Chungking *would* count as inputs. Such a new system (i.e., the object under such a new Turing-machine description) would not be functionally equivalent to you. Likewise, any commerical computer can be redescribed in a way that allows tape jammed into its innards to count as inputs. In describing an object as a Turing machine, one draws a line between the inside and the outside. (If we count only neural impulses as inputs and outputs, we draw that line inside the body; if we count only peripheral stimulations as inputs and only bodily movements as outputs, we draw that line at the skin.) In describing the Chinese system as a Turing machine, I have drawn the line in such a way that it satisfies a certain type of functional description—one that you *also* satisfy, and one that, according to functionalism, justifies attributions of mentality. Functionalism does not claim that every mental system has a machine table of a sort that justifies attributions of mentality with respect to *every* specification of inputs and outputs, but rather, only with respect to *some* specification.

Objection: The Chinese system would work too slowly. The kind of events and processes with which we normally have contact would pass by far too quickly for the system to detect them. Thus, we would be unable to converse with it, play bridge with it, etc.[13]

Reply: It is hard to see why the system's time scale should matter. What reason is there to believe that *your* mental operations could not be very much slowed down, yet remain mental operations? Is it really contradictory or nonsensical to suppose we could meet a race of intelligent beings with whom we could communicate only by devices such as time-lapse photography. When we observe these creatures, they seem almost inanimate. But when we view the time-lapse movies, we see them conversing with one another. Indeed, we find they are saying that the only way they can make any sense of us is by viewing movies greatly slowed down. To take time scale as all important seems crudely behavioristic. Further, even if the time-scale objection is right, I can elude it by retreating to the point that a homunculus-head that works in normal time is *metaphysically* possible, even if not nomologically possible. Metaphysical possibility is all my argument requires (see Section 1.3).[14]

What makes the homunculi-headed system (count the two systems as variants of a single system) just described a prima facie counter-example to (machine) functionalism is that there is prima facie doubt whether it has any mental states at all—especially whether it has what philosophers have variously called "qualitative states," "raw feels," or "immediate phenomenological qualities." (You ask: What is it that philosophers have called qualitative states? I answer, only half in jest: As Louis Armstrong said when asked what jazz is, "If you got to ask, you ain't never gonna get to know.") In Nagel's terms (1974), there is a prima facie doubt whether there is anything which it is like to be the homunculi-headed system.

The force of the prima facie counterexample can be made clearer as follows: Machine functionalism says that each mental state is identical to a machine-table state. For example, a particular qualitative state, Q, is identical to a machine-table state, S_q. But if there is nothing it is like to be the homunculi-headed system, it cannot be in Q even when it is in S_q. Thus, if there is prima facie doubt about the homunculi-headed system's mentality, there is prima facie doubt that $Q = S_q$, i.e., doubt that the kind of functionalism under consideration is true.[15] Call this argument the Absent Qualia Argument.

So there is prima facie doubt that machine functionalism is true. So what? After all, prima facie doubt is only prima facie. Indeed, appeals to intuition of this sort are notoriously fallible. I shall not rest on this appeal to intuition. Rather, I shall argue that the intuition that the homunculi-headed simulation described above lacks mentality (or at least qualia) has at least in part a rational basis, and that this rational basis provides a good reason for doubting that Functionalism (and to a lesser degree Psychofunctionalism) is true. I shall consider this line of argument in Section 1.6. Before I do that, however, I must tie up a number of loose ends; I shall sketch homunculi-headed, prima-facie counterexamples for other versions of functionalsm and defend, from a few obvious objections, what I have said so far.

(The remainder of this section, and section 1.3 and 1.4, can be omitted without loss of continuity.)

The homunclui-headed system is a prima facie counterexample to one version of functionalism. In the remainder of this section, I shall briefly sketch a few other versions of functionalism and argue that this or similar examples also provide counterexamples to those versions of functionalism. Every version of functionalism I know of seems subject to this type of difficulty. Indeed, this problem seems so close to the core of functionalism that I would be tempted to regard a doctrine not subject to it as ipso facto not a version of functionalism.

The version of functionalism just discussed (mental states are machine-table states) is subject to many obvious difficulties. If state M = state P, then someone has M if and only if he or she has P. But mental and machine-table states fail to satisfy this basic condition, as Fodor and I pointed out (Block & Fodor, 1972).

For example, people are often in more than one psychological state at a time, e.g., believing that P and desiring that G. But a Turing machine can be in only one machine-table state at a time. Lycan (1974) argues against Fodor's and my objection. He says the problem is dissolvable by appeal to the distinction between particular, physical Turing machines and the abstract Turing machine specified by a given description. One abstract machine can be realized by many physical machines, and one physical machine can be the realization of many abstract machines. Lycan says we can identify the *n* mental states a person happens to be in at one time with machine-table states of *n* abstract automata that the person simultaneously realizes. But this will not do, for a Functionalist should be able to explain how a number of simultaneous mental states jointly produce an output, e.g., when a belief that action A will yield goal G, plus a desire for G jointly cause A. How could this causal relation be captured if the belief and the desire are identified with states of different abstract automata that the person simultaneously realizes?

The "one-state-at-a-time" problem can be avoided by a natural reformulation of the machine-table state identity theory. Each machine-table state is identified not with a single mental state, but with a conjunction of mental states, e.g., believing that P and hoping that H and desiring that G. . . . Call each of the mental states in such a conjunction the "elements" of the machine-table state. Then, each mental state is identical to the disjunction of the machine-table states of which it is an element. This version of Functionalism is ultimately unsatisfactory, basically because it has no resources for appropriately handling the content relations among mental states, e.g., the relation between the belief that P and the belief that (P or Q).

Fodor and I (1972) raised a number of such criticisms. We concluded that Turing-machine functionalism could probably avoid such difficulties, but only at the cost of weakening the theory considerably. Turing-machine functionalism seemed forced to abandon the idea that mental states could be identified with machine-table states or even states definable in terms of just machine-table states, such as the disjunction of states already suggested. It seemed, rather, that mental states would have have to be identified instead with *computational* states of a Turing machine—that is, states definable in terms of table states *and* states of the tape of a Turing machine.

However, the move from machine-table state functionalism to computational-state functionalism is of no use in avoiding the Absent Qualia Argument. Whatever Turing machine it is whose computational states are supposed to be identical to your mental states will have a homunculi-headed realization of the sort described earlier, i.e., a realization whose mental states are subject to prima facie doubt. Therefore, if a qualitative state, Q, is supposed to be identical to a computational state, C_q, there will be prima facie doubt about whether the homunclui-headed system is in Q even if it is in C_q, and hence prima facie doubt that $Q = C_q$.

Now let us turn briefly to a version of functionalism that is not framed in terms of the notion of a Turing machine. Like machine functionalists, nonmachine functionalists emphasize that characterizations of mental states can be given in entirely nonmental—

indeed, they often say physical—terminology. The Ramsey functional-correlate expression designating pain (p. 270) contains input and output terms but not mental terms. Thus, nonmachine versions, like machine versions, can be described as "tacking down" mental states only at the periphery. That is, according to both versions of functionalism, something can be functionally equivalent to you if it has a set of states, of whatever nature, that are causally related to one another and to inputs and outputs in the appropriate way.

Without a more precise specification of nonmachine functionalism (e.g., a specification of an actual psychological theory of either the Functionalist or Psychofunctionalist varieties), it would be hard to *prove* that nonmachine versions of functionalism are subject to the kind of prima facie counterexample described earlier. But this does seem fairly obviously the case. In this regard, the major difference between machine and nonmachine versions of functionalism is that we cannot assume that the homunculi-headed counterexample for nonmachine functionalism is "discretized" in the way a Turing machine is. In our new homunculi-headed device, we may have to allow for a continuous range of values of input and output parameters, whereas Turing machines have a finite set of inputs and outputs. Further, Turing-machine descriptions assume a fixed time interval, t, such that inputs occur and instructions are executed every t seconds (t = 10 nanoseconds in an IBM 370). Turing machines click, whereas our homunculi-headed device may creep. However, it is not at all obvious that this makes any difference. The input signals in the mechanical body can be changed from on-off lights to continuously varying lights; continuously variable potentiometers can be substituted for the output buttons. We may suppose that each of the little men in the body carries a little book that maps out your functional organization. The little men designate states of themselves and/or their props to correspond to each of your mental states. For example, your being in pain might correspond to a certain little man writing 'pain' on a blackboard. The intensity of the pain might be indicated by the (continuously variable) color of the chalk. Having studied his book, the little man knows what inputs and other mental states cause your pains. He keeps an eye open for the states of his colleagues and the input lights that correspond to those conditions. Little men responsible for simulating states that are contin-

gent on pain keep their eye on the blackboard, taking the appropriate configurations of 'pain' written on the board + input lights
and actions of other men as signals to do what they have designated
to correspond to states caused by pain. If you, a big man, have an
infinite number of possible mental states, the same can be assumed
of the little men. Thus, it should be possible for the simulation to
have an infinite number of possible "mental" states.

One difference between this simulation and the one described
earlier is that these little men need more intelligence to do their
jobs. But that is all to the good as far as the Absent Qualia Argument is concerned. The more intelligence exercised by the little
men in simulating you, the less inclined we are to ascribe to the
simulation the mental properties they are simulating.

1.3 What Kind of Possibility Does
the Absent Qualia Argument Appeal to?

According to functionalism, each mental state, e.g., Q, is identical
to a functional state, e.g., S_q. The Absent Qualia Argument argues
that there is a possible system that has S_q but whose possession of Q
is subject to prima facie doubt, and thus there is prima facie doubt
that Q = S_q. What notion of possibility does the Absent Qualia Argument appeal to? And what is the basis for the assumption that if
Q = S_q, it is not possible for something to have S_q without Q?

Let us take the notion of possibility to be nomological possibility.
And let us restrict our attention to identity statements of the form
$\ulcorner a = \beta \urcorner$, where a and β are rigid designators. It is hard to conceive of
a mildly plausible criterion of identity for properties (or for types
of states) that allows both that F = G *and* that it is nomologically
possible for something to have or be in F but not in G. As Kripke
(1972) has shown, true identities are necessarily true. Thus, if F = G,
there is no possible world and hence no nomologically possible world
in which F ≠ G; hence, there is no nomologically possible world in
which something is in (or has) F but is not in (or lacks) G.

I conclude that on the nomological reading of 'possible', the Absent Qualia Argument is valid. Further, if the Chinese system described earlier is nomologically possible, and if there is prima facie
doubt about its qualia, the argument is sound. However, even if
such a homunculi-headed simulation is not nomologically possible,

it is surely metaphysically possible. Therefore, assuming there is prima facie doubt about the qualia of the homunculi-headed simulations, understanding 'possible' as 'metaphysically possible' ensures the soundness of the Absent Qualia Argument, while retaining validity. Kripke has shown that true identities are metaphysically necessary. Thus, if $Q = S_q$, then (assuming 'Q' and 'S_q' are rigid designators) it is necessary that $Q = S_q$. And it is necessary that something has Q just in case it has S_q. Since there is a possible object (a homunculi-headed simulation) that has S_q but whose possession of Q is subject to prima facie doubt, there is prima facie doubt about whether $Q = S_q$.

Kripke's arguments against materialism (based on his principle that identities are necessary) are subject to a number of difficulties. If the Absent Qualia Argument is forced to rely on Kripke's principle (i.e., if homunculi-headed simulations are not nomologically possible), is the Absent Qualia Argument subject to the same difficulties as Kripke's argument against materialism? In the remainder of this section I shall argue that none of the serious difficulties that beset Kripke's arguments against materialism besets the Absent Qualia Argument.

Kripke argues (against an opponent who says pain is stimulation of c-fibers) that we can conceive of a possible world in which c-fiber stimulation occurs in the absence of pain and that we can also conceive of a possible world in which pain occurs in the absence of c-fiber stimulation. So far, so good: but how do we judge the truth of claims to conceive of such possible worlds? (Notice that I am using 'conceive' such that if anyone can conceive of a possible world in which such and such obtains, then there is such a possible world. 'Imagine' has no such implication.) Kripke provides us with a way of ruling out false conceivability claims. Suppose someone, call him 'Epistemagine', claims he can conceive of a world which contains heat but no corresponding molecular agitation. Kripke argues that what Epistemagine is really imagining is being in the epistemic situation we would have been in had we discovered that heat phenomena (e.g., our sensation of heat) were caused by something other than molecular agitation, say, y-radiation. Thus, what Epistemagine is really conceiving is a possible world in which the sensation that heat causes in the actual world is caused by something else, y-radiation.

If heat exists in the world at all, it is molecular agitation. This ploy is Kripke's major tool for ruling out false conceivability claims. Does this tool serve to rule out Kripke's own claim to conceive of a world with pain but no c-fiber stimulation? No, Kripke says, because a possible world in which I am in the epistemic situation I am in when I am in pain in the real world is a possible world in which I *have pain*. Pain and its epistemic counterpart (the experience of pain) are not different, whereas heat and the sensation of heat *are* different. But Kripke's reply is inadequate because *c-fiber stimulation* and *its* epistemic counterpart *are* different. (Pointed out independently by Boyd & Putnam, in conversation: see Boyd, forthcoming.) Kripke's ability to imagine pain without c-fiber stimulation can be ascribed not to the real conceivability of a possible world with pain but no c-fiber stimulation, but rather to the imaginability of the epistemic situation we would have been in had we discovered that pain is not correlated with c-fiber stimulation. In other words, the world Kripke imagines may be one where his pain is c-fiber stimulation, but he fails to be aware of it, e.g., because his cerebroscope does not work or because c-fibers are invisible, or they look like d-fibers under certain conditions, or for some such reason.

The matter does not end here, however, for Kripke can reply to the Boyd-Putnam point that there is a disanalogy between (a) the epistemic situation when one's cerebroscope does not work or c-fibers look like d-fibers, etc., and (b) the epistemic situation when y-radiation causes the sensation that in the real world is caused by molecular agitation — namely, in case a but not b one is imagining an epistemic situation in which one is being *misled*. Does this difference make a difference? How are we to decide? Kripke might also reply to the Boyd-Putnam point that he can conceive of a possible world in which he has a pain and a *working* cerebroscope shows no c-fiber stimulation; or to put the same point somewhat differently, he can conceive of a pain with no corresponding c-fiber stimulation, without imagining any epistemic situation at all. There is something attractive about this line of thought, but to accept it is to abandon Kripke's tool for ruling out false conceivability claims; and without this or some other such tool, there seems no remotely objective way to settle claims that a certain sort of world is or is not possible.

The dispute just sketched seems to me to end in a stalemate. But

I do not inherit Kripke's difficulties. Rather than simply asserting that there is a possible world which contains a present functional state and an absent quale, I have given *reason to think* there is such a world. I have told a story suggesting that something can be functionally equivalent to you, yet there be prima facie doubt about its qualia. In other words, I did not ask you to imagine two things (a present functional state and an absent quale); I asked you to imagine one thing (a homunculi-headed system), then I claimed that what you had *already* imagined was such that there is prima facie doubt about its qualia.

Another difference between Kripke's attack on materialism and the Absent Qualia Argument is that Kripke's attack is meant to apply to token materialism as well as type materialism, whereas the Absent Qualia Argument is addressed only to type functionalism. That is, a variant of Kripke's argument is supposed to apply against the claim that there is even a single datable individual pain that is a c-fiber stimulation. On the other hand, it is perfectly compatible with the Absent Qualia Argument that *all* token qualitative states are token functional states. Kripke argues against token materialism, but I do not argue against token functionalism. (Of course, if the Absent Qualia Argument is correct, it is prima facie doubtful that any of the token functional states in homunculi-headed robots are token qualitative states.)

Kripke's argument against token materialism proceeds from the claim that he can conceive of a possible world that contains *this very* c-fiber stimulation but not pain. If this very pain, denote it rigidly by 'Philbert,' were identical to this very c-fiber stimulation, call it 'Sam,' there would be no such possible world. "But," it might be objected, "the world you have conceived of may be a world in which Philbert exists (and is identical to Sam) but has no qualitative content" (Feldman, 1973). In reply to the (foreseen) objection, Kripke, in effect, invokes the claim that Philbert (and every other pain) necessarily has qualitative content, that is

$$(e) \ (e \text{ is a pain} \supset \Box \ (e \text{ has qualitative content}))$$

(Note that Kripke does not need this claim in the argument against *type* materialism. There he requires instead: $\Box$ (e) (e is a pain $\equiv$ e has a certain qualitative content). This claim allows Kripke to mount an even simpler attack on token materialism, based on the indiscernability of identicals: viz, each pain has a property (necessarily having qualitative content) which each c-fiber stimulation lacks. Hence, no pain is a c-fiber stimulation. But how are we to ascertain that Kripke is right when he says that each c-fiber stimulation lacks the property of necessarily having qualitative content? By ascertaining whether we can conceive of a possible world that contains a given c-fiber stimulation, but not pain? This task would involve us in just the morass depicted on p. 287 above. Indeed, how are we to ascertain that Kripke is right in saying that each *pain has* qualitative content in all possible worlds? Once again, the argument seems to turn on an appeal to intuitions that we have no moderately objective means of evaluating.

Again, I do not inherit Kripke's difficulties. Nothing in the Absent Qualia Argument dictates anything controversial about the essential qualitativeness of any particular qualitative or functional state.

1.4 What If I Turned Out to Have Little Men in My Head?

Before I go any further, I shall briefly discuss a difficulty for my claim that there is prima facie doubt about the qualia of homunculi-headed realizations of human functional organization. It might be objected, "What if *you* turned out to be one?" Let us suppose that, to my surprise, X-rays reveal that inside my head are thousands of tiny, trained fleas, each of which has been taught (perhaps by a joint subcommittee of the American Philosophical Association and the American Psychological Association empowered to investigate absent qualia) to implement a square in the appropriate machine table.

Now there is a crucial issue relevant to this difficulty which philosophers are far from agreeing on (and about which I confess I cannot make up my mind): Do I know on the basis of my "privileged access" that I do not have utterly absent qualia, no matter what turns out to be inside my head? Do I know there is something it is like to be me, even if I am a flea head? Fortunately, my vacillation on this issue is of no consequence, for either answer is compatible with the Absent Qualia Argument's assumption that there is doubt about the qualia of homunculi-headed folks.

Suppose the answer is no. It is not the case that I know there is something it is like to be me even if I am a flea-head. Then I should admit that my qualia would be in (prima facie) doubt if (God forbid) I turned out to have fleas in my head. Likewise for the qualia of all the other homunculi-headed folk. So far, so good.

Suppose, on the other hand, that my privileged access does give me knowledge that I have qualia. No matter what turns out to be inside my head, my states have qualitative content. There is something it is like to be me. Then if I turn out to have fleas in my head, at least one homunculi-head turns out to have qualia. But this would not challenge my claim that the qualia of homunculi-infested simulations is in doubt. Since I do, in fact, have qualia, supposing I have fleas inside my head is supposing someone with fleas inside his head has qualia. But this supposition that a homunculi-head has qualia is just the sort of supposition my position doubts. Using such an example to argue against my position is like twitting a man who doubts there is a God by asking what he would say if he turned out to *be* God. Both arguments against the doubter beg the question against the doubter by hypothesizing a situation which the doubter admits is logically possible, but doubts is *actual*. A doubt that there is a God entails a doubt that I am God. Similarly, (given that I do have qualia) a doubt that flea heads have qualia entails a doubt that I am a flea head.

1.5 Putnam's Proposal

One way functionalists can try to deal with the problem posed by the homunculi-headed counterexamples is by the ad hoc device of stipulating them away. For example, a functionalist might stipulate that two systems cannot be functionally equivalent if one contains parts with functional organizations characteristic of sentient beings and the other does not. In his article hypothesizing that pain is a functional state, Putnam stipulated that "no organism capable of feeling pain possesses a decomposition into parts which separately possess Descriptions" (as the sort of Turing machine which can be in the functional state Putnam identifies with pain). The purpose of this condition is "to rule out such 'organisms' (if they count as such) as swarms of bees as single pain feelers" (Putnam, 1967, pp. 434-439).

One way of filling out Putnam's requirement would be: a pain feeling organism cannot possess a decomposition into parts *all* of which have a functional organization characteristic of sentient beings. But this would not rule out my homunculi-headed example, since it has nonsentient parts, such as the mechanical body and sense organs. It will not do to go to the opposite extreme and require that *no* proper parts be sentient. Otherwise pregnant women and people with sentient parasites will fail to count as pain-feeling organisms. What seems to be important to examples like the homunculi-headed simulation I have described is that the sentient beings *play a crucial role* in giving the thing its functional organization. This suggests a version of Putnam's proposal which requires that a pain-feeling organism has a certain functional organization and that it has no parts which (1) themselves possess that sort of functional organization and also (2) play a crucial role in giving the whole system its functional organization.

Although this proposal involves the vague notion "crucial role," it is precise enough for us to see it will not do. Suppose there is a part of the universe that contains matter quite different from ours, matter that is infinitely divisible. In this part of the universe, there are intelligent creatures of many sizes, even humanlike creatures much smaller than our elementary particles. In an intergalctic expedition, these people discover the existence of our type of matter. For reasons known only to them, they decide to devote the next few hundred years to creating out of their matter substances with the chemical and physical characteristics (except at the subelementary particle level) of our elements. They build hordes of space ships of different varieties about the sizes of our electrons, protons, and other elementary particles, and fly the ships in such a way as to mimic the behavior of these elementary particles. The ships also contain generators to produce the type of radiation elementary particles give off. Each ship has a staff of experts on the nature of our elementary particles. They do this to produce huge (by our standards) masses of substances with the chemical and physical characteristics of oxygen, carbon, etc. Shortly after they accomplish this, you go off on an expedition to that part of the universe, and discover the "oxygen," "carbon," etc. Unaware of its real nature, you set up a colony, using these "elements" to grow plants for food, pro-

vide "air" to breathe, etc. Since one's molecules are constantly being exchanged with the environment, you and other colonizers come
(in a period of a few years) to be composed mainly of the "matter"
made of the tiny people in space ships. Would you be any less capable of feeling pain, thinking, etc. just because the matter of which
you are composed contains (and depends on for its characteristics)
beings who themselves have a functional organization characteristic
of sentient creatures? I think not. The basic electrochemical mechanisms by which the synapse operates are now fairly well understood.
As far as is known, changes that do not affect these electrochemical
mechanisms do not affect the operation of the brain, and do not
affect mentality. The electrochemical mechanisms in your synapses
would be unaffected by the change in your matter.[16]

It is interesting to compare the elementary-particle-people example with the homunculi-headed examples the chapter started with.
A natural first guess about the source of our intuition that the initially described homunculi-headed simulations lack mentality is that
they have *too much* internal mental structure. The little men may
be sometimes bored, sometimes excited. We may even imagine that
they deliberate about the best way to realize the given functional
organization and make changes intended to give them more leisure
time. But the example of the elementary-particle people just described suggests this first guess is wrong. What seems important is
how the mentality of the parts contributes to the functioning of
the whole.

There is one very noticeable difference between the elementary-
particle-people example and the earlier homunculus examples. In
the former, the change in you as you become homunculus-infested
is not one that makes any difference to your psychological processing (i.e., information processing) or neurological processing but only
to your microphysics. No techniques proper to human psychology
or neurophysiology would reveal any difference in you. However,
the homunculi-headed simulations described in the beginning of the
chapter are not things to which neurophysiological theories true of
us apply, and *if they are construed as Functional* (rather than Psychofunctional) simulations, they need not be things to which psychological (information-processing) theories true of us apply. This
difference suggests that our intuitions are in part controlled by the

not unreasonable view that our mental states depend on our having the psychology and/or neurophysiology we have. So something that differs markedly from us in both regards (recall that it is a Functional rather than Psychofunctional simulation) should not be assumed to have mentality just on the ground that it is Functionally equivalent to us.[17]

1.6 Is the Prima Facie Doubt Merely Prima Facie?

The Absent Qualia Argument rested on an appeal to the intuition that the homunculi-headed simulations lacked mentality, or at least qualia. I said that this intuition gave rise to prima facie doubt that functionalism is true. But intuitions unsupported by principled argument are hardly to be considered bedrock. Indeed, intuitions incompatible with well-supported theory (e.g., the pre-Copernican intuition that the earth does not move) thankfully soon disappear. Even fields like linguistics whose data consist mainly in intuitions often reject such intuitions as that the following sentences are ungrammatical (on theoretical grounds):

The horse raced past the barn fell.
The boy the girl the cat bit scratched died.

These sentences are in fact grammatical, though hard to process.[18]

Appeal to intuitions when judging possession of mentality, however, is *especially* suspicious. *No* physical mechanism seems very intuitively plausible as a seat of qualia, least of all a *brain*. Is a hunk of quivering gray stuff more intuitively appropriate as a seat of qualia than a covey of little men? If so, perhaps there is a prima facie doubt about the qualia of brain-headed systems too.

However, there is a very important difference between brain-headed and homunculi-headed systems. Since we know that *we are brain-headed systems*, and that *we* have qualia, we know that brain-headed systems can have qualia. So even though we have no theory of qualia which explains how this is *possible*, we have overwhelming reason to disregard whatever prima facie doubt there is about the qualia of brain-headed systems. Of course, this makes the Absent Qualia Argument partly *empirical*—it depends on knowledge of what makes us tick. But since this is knowledge we in fact possess, dependence on this knowledge should not be regarded as a defect.

There is another difference between us meat-heads and the homunculi-heads: they are systems designed to mimic us, but we are not designed to mimic anything (here I rely on another empirical fact). This fact forestalls any attempt to argue on the basis of an inference to the best explanation for the qualia of homunculi-heads. The best explanation of the homunculi-heads' screams and winces is not their pains, but that they were designed to mimic our screams and winces.

Some people seem to feel that the complex and subtle behavior of the homunculi-heads (behavior just as complex and subtle—even as "sensitive" to features of the environment, human and nonhuman, as your behavior) is itself sufficient reason to disregard the prima facie doubt that homunculi-heads have qualia. But this is just crude behaviorism.

I shall try to convince the reader of this by describing a machine that would act like a mental system in a situation in which only verbal inputs and outputs are involved (a machine that would pass the "Turing Test").

Call a string of sentences whose members, spoken one after another, can be uttered in an hour or less, a speakable string of sentences. A speakable string can contain one very long sentence, or two shorter ones. Consider the set of all speakable strings of sentences. Since English has a finite number of words (indeed, a finite number of sound sequences forming possible words short enough to appear in a speakable string), this set has a very large but finite number of members. Consider the subset of the set of all speakable strings of sentences, each of whose member strings can be understood as a conversation in which at least one party is "making sense." Call it the set of smart speakable strings. For example, if we allot each party to a conversation one sentence per "turn," each even-numbered sentence of each string in S would be a sensible contribution to the ongoing discussion. We need not be too restrictive about what is to count as making sense. For example, if sentence 1 is "Let's see you talk nonsense," then sentence 2 could be nonsensical. The set of smart speakable strings is a finite set which could in principle be listed by a very large team working for a long time with a very large grant. Imagine that the smart speakable strings are recorded on tape and deployed by a very simple machine, as follows. An interrogator utters sentence A. The machine searches the set of smart speakable strings, picks out those strings that begin with A, and picks one string at random (or it might pick the first string it finds beginning with A, using a random search). It then produces the second sentence in that string, call it 'B'. The interrogator utters another sentence, call it 'C'. The machine picks a string at random that starts with A, followed by B, followed by C, and utters its fourth sentence, and so on.

Now, if the team has been thorough and imaginative in listing the smart speakable strings, this machine would simulate human conversational abilities. Indeed, if the team did a brilliantly creative job, the machine's conversational abilities might be superhuman (though if it is to "keep up" with current events, the job would have to be redone often). But this machine clearly has no mental states at all. It is just a huge list-searcher plus a tape recorder.

Thus far in this section, I have admitted that the intuition that the homunculi-head lacks qualia is far from decisive, since intuition balks at assigning qualia to any physical mechanism. But I went on to argue that although there is good reason to disregard any intuition that brain-headed systems lack qualia, there is no reason to disregard our intuition that homunculi-headed simulations lack qualia. I now want to argue that the intuition that homunculi-headed simulations lack qualia can be backed up by argument. The rest of this section will be devoted to Functionalism and Functional simulations. The next section will be devoted to parallel considerations with respect to Psychofunctionalism.

Think of the original homunculi-headed example as being designed to be Functionally equivalent to you. Since it need not be Psychofunctionally equivalent to you (see the next section), it need not be something to which any scientific psychological theory true of you applies. Obviously, it would not be something to which neurological theories true of you apply. Now as I pointed out in the last few paragraphs of the last section, it is a highly plausible assumption that mental states are in the domain of psychology and/or neurophysiology, or at least that mentality depends crucially on psychological and/or neurophysiological processes and structures. But since the homunculi-headed Functional simulation of you is markedly unlike you neurophysiologically (insofar as it makes sense to speak of something with no neurons at all being neurophysiologically un-like anything) and since it need not be anything like you psycho-logically (that is, its information processing need not be remotely like yours), it is reasonable to doubt that it has mentality, even if it is Functionally equivalent to you. Further, the comparison made in the last section with the person infected with homunculi at the elementary-particle level suggests that this argument is at least part of the source of the intuition that the homunculi-headed functional simulation does not have mentality.[19]

This is not an overwhelmingly powerful argument, but it does seem sufficient to throw the onus of argument on Functionalists. If there is no minimally decent argument *for* Functionalism, it seems the argument against Functionalism supported by the homunculi-headed examples should be regarded as showing Functionalism is false.

In spite of the widespread belief in forms of Functionalism, I know of only one kind of argument for it in the literature. It is claimed that Functional identities can be shown to be true on the basis of analyses of the meanings of mental terminology. According to this argument, Functional identities are to be justified in the way one might try to justify the claim that the state of being a bachelor is identical to the state of being an unmarried man. A similar argument appeals to commonsense platitudes about mental states instead of truths of meaning. Lewis says that Functional characterizations of mental states are in the province of "common sense psychology — folk science, rather than professional science" (Lewis, 1972, p. 250. See also Shoemaker, 1975, and Armstrong, 1968. Armstrong equivo-cates on the analyticity issue. See Armstrong, 1968, pp. 84-85, and p. 90.). And he goes on to insist that Functional characterizations should "include only platitudes which are common knowledge among us — everyone knows them, everyone knows that everyone else knows them, and so on" (Lewis, 1972, p. 256). I shall talk mainly about the "platitude" version of the argument. The analy-ticity version is vulnerable to essentially the same considerations, as well as Quinean doubts about analyticity.

Because of the required platitudinous nature of Functional defi-nitions, Functionalism runs into serious difficulties with cases such as paralytics and disembodied brains hooked up to life-support systems. Suppose, for example, that C is a cluster of inputs and mental states which, according to Functionalism, issues in some characteristic behavior, B. We might take C to consist in part in: pain, the desire to be rid of the pain, the belief that an object in front of one is causing the pain, and the belief that the pain can easily be avoided by reverse locomotion. Let B be reverse locomotion. But a paralytic could typically have C without B. It might be objected, "If C typically issues in B, then one of the elements of C would have to be the belief that *B is possible*, but a paralytic would not have this belief." Reply: Imagine a paralytic who does not know he/she is paralyzed and who has the kind of hippocampal lesion that keeps him/her from learning, or imagine a paralytic whose paralysis is *intermittent*. Surely someone in intense pain who believes the only way to avoid intense pain is by reverse locomotion and who believes he or she *might* be capable of reverse locomotion will (other things equal) attempt to locomote in reverse. This is as platitudinous as any of the platitudes in the Functionalist collection. But in the case of an intermittent paralytic, attempts to locomote in reverse might *typically fail*, and, thus, he/she might typically fail to emit B when in C. Indeed, one can imagine that a disease strikes worldwide, resulting in intermittent paralysis of this sort in all of us, so that *none* of us typically emits B in C.

It would seem that such a turn of events would require Functionalists to suppose that some of the mental states which make up C no longer occur. But this seems very implausible.

This objection is further strengthened by attention to brain-in-bottle examples. Perhaps the day will come when our brains will be periodically removed for cleaning. Imagine that this is done initially by treating neurons attaching the brain to the body with a chemical that allows them to stretch like rubber bands, so that no connections are disrupted. As technology advances, in order to avoid the inconvenience of one's body being immobilized while one's brain is serviced, brains are removed, the connections between brain and body being maintained by radio, while one goes about one's business. After a few days, the customer returns and has the brain reinserted. Sometimes, however, people's bodies are destroyed by accidents while their brains are being cleaned. If hooked up to input sense organs (but not output organs) these brains would exhibit *none* of the usual platitudinous connections between behavior and clusters of inputs and mental states. If, as seems plausible, these brains could have almost all the same (narrow) mental states as we have, Functionalism is wrong.

It is instructive to compare the way Psychofunctionalism attempts to handle cases like paralysis and brains in bottles. According to Psychofunctionalism, what is to count as a system's inputs and outputs is an empirical question. Counting neural impulses as inputs and outputs would avoid the problems just sketched, since the brains in bottles and paralytics could have the right neural impulses even without bodily movements. Objection: there could be paralysis that affects the nervous system, and thus affects the neural impulses, so the problem which arises for Functionalism arises for Psychofunctionalism as well. Reply: nervous system diseases can actually *change mentality*, e.g., they can render victims incapable of having pain. So it might actually be true that a widespread nervous system disease that caused intermittent paralysis rendered people incapable of certain mental states.

According to plausible versions of Psychofunctionalism, the job of deciding what neural processes should count as inputs and outputs is in part a matter deciding *what malfunctions count as changes in mentality and what malfunctions count as changes in peripheral input and output connections*. Psychofunctionalism has a resource that Functionalism does not have, since Psychofunctionalism allows us to *adjust the line we draw between the inside and the outside of the organism so as to avoid problems of the sort discussed*. All versions of Functionalism go wrong in attempting to draw this line on the basis of only commonsense knowledge; "analyticity" versions of Functionalism go especially wrong in attempting to draw the line a priori.

Objection: Sydney Shoemaker suggests (in correspondence) that problems having to do with paralytics, and brains in vats of the sort I mentioned, can be handled using his notion of a "paradigmatically embodied person" (see Shoemaker, 1976). Paradigmatic embodiment involves having functioning sensory apparatus and considerable voluntary control of bodily movements. Shoemaker's suggestion is that we start with a functional characterization of a paradigmatically embodied person, saying, inter alia, what it is for a physical state to realize a given mental state in a paradigmatically embodied person. Then, the functional characterization could be extended to nonparadigmatically embodied persons by saying that a physical structure that is not a part of a paradigmatically embodied person will count as realizing mental states, if, without changing its internal structure and the sorts of relationships that hold between its states, it could be incorporated into a larger physical system that would be the body of a paradigmatically embodied person in which the states in question played the functional roles definitive of mental states of a paradigmatically embodied person. Shoemaker suggests that a brain in a vat can be viewed from this perspective, as a limiting case of an amputee—amputation of everthing but the brain. For the brain can (in principle) be incorporated into a system so as to form a paradigmatically embodied person without changing the internal structure and state relations of the brain.

Reply: Shoemaker's suggestion is very promising, but it saves functionalism only by retreating from Functionalism to Psychofunctionalism. Obviously, nothing in prescientific commonsense wisdom about mentality tells us what can or cannot be paradigmatically embodied *without changing its internal structure and state relations*. Imagine an entire human nervous system, including peripheral nerve endings in a vat. Think of a gram of the peripheral tissues removed. Then another gram removed, then another, and so on. At what point (and given what kinds of removal) do we have something which can no longer be paradigmatically embodied "without changing its internal structure and state relations"? This is not merely a conceptual question. Indeed, the scientific issues involved in answering this question may well be very similar to the scientific issues involved in the Psychofunctionalist question about the difference between defects in or damage to input-output devices, as opposed to defects in or damage to central mechanisms. That is, the scientific task of drawing the Psychofunctionalist line between the inside and the outside of an organism seems pretty much the same as Shoemaker's task of drawing the line between what can and what cannot be paradigmatically embodied without changing its internal structure and state relations.

I shall briefly raise two additional problems for Functionalism. The first might be called the Problem of Differentiation: there are mental states that are different, but that do not differ with respect to platitudes. Consider different tastes or smells that have typical causes and effects, but whose typical causes and effects are not known or are not known to very many people. For example, tannin in wine produces a particular taste immediately recognizable to wine drinkers. As far as I know, there is no standard name or description (except "tannic") associated with this taste. The causal antecedents and consequents of this taste are not widely known, there are no platitudes about its typical causes and effects. On experiencing this taste and being asked, "What is this taste?" even cooperative people do not typically reply "tannic" since they typically do not know the word. Moreover, there are sensations that not only have no standard names but whose causes and effects are not yet well understood by anyone. Let A and B be two such (different) sensations. Neither platitudes nor truths of meaning can distinguish between A and B. Since the Functional description of a mental state is determined by the platitudes true of that state, and since A and B do not differ with respect to platitudes, Functionalists would be committed to identifying A and B with the same Functional state, and thus they would be committed to the claim that A = B, which is ex hypothesi false.

A second difficulty for Functionalism is that platitudes are often wrong. I suppose it is a platitude that the particular olfactory sensation which we associate with skunks is *typically* caused by skunks. But surely it could turn out that this sensation is more often than not caused by another animal or a fungus. Indeed, maybe this is already known to experts and has not yet penetrated to the general public. So the platitude-based Functional description of this smell will fail to pick it out.

Let us call this problem the Problem of Truth. Lewis suggests, by way of dealing with this problem, that we specify the causal relations among mental states, inputs and outputs, not by means of the conjunction of all the platitudes, but rather by "a cluster of them—a disjunction of conjunctions of *most* of them (that way it will not matter if a few are wrong.)" This move may exacerbate the problem of Differentiation, however, since there may be pairs of different mental states that are alike with respect to *most* platitudes.

2.1 Arguments for Psychofunctionalism,
and What Is Wrong with Them

I said there is good reason to take seriously our intuition that the homunculi-headed Functional simulations have no mentality. The good reason was that mentality is in the domain of psychology and/or physiology, and the homunclui-headed Functional simulations need not have either psychological (information-processing) or physiological mechanisms anything like ours. But this line will not apply to a homunculi-headed *Psycho*functional simulation. Indeed, there is an excellent reason to disregard any intuition that a homunculi-headed Psychofunctional simulation lacks mentality. Since a Psychofunctional simulation of you would be Psychofunctionally equivalent to you, a reasonably adequate psychological theory true of you would be true of it. Indeed, without changing the homunculi-headed example in any essential way, we could require that *every* reasonably adequate psychological theory true of you be true of it. What better reason could there be to attribute to it whatever mental states are in the domain of psychology? In the face of such a good reason for attributing mental states to it, prima facie doubts about whether it has those aspects of mentality which are in the domain of psychology should be rejected.

I believe this argument shows that a homunculi-headed simulation could have nonqualitative mental states. However, in the next section I shall describe a Psychofunctional simulation in more detail, arguing that there is nonetheless prima facie doubt that it has *qualitative* mental states (i.e., states, that, like pain, involve qualia). Moreover, the argument on which this doubt rests is also an argument that qualia are not in the domain of psychology at all. So at least with respect to qualitative states, the onus of argument is still on Psychofunctionalists. I shall now argue that none of the arguments that have been offered for Psychofunctionalism are any good.

Here is one argument for Psychofunctionalism that is implicit in the literature. It is the business of branches of science to tell us the nature of things in the branches' domains. Mental states are in the domain of psychology, and, hence, it is the business of psychology to tell us what mental states are. Psychological theory can be expected to characterize mental states in terms of the causal relations among mental states, and other mental entities, and among mental entities, inputs, and outputs. But these very causal relations are the ones which constitute the Psychofunctional states that Psychofunctionalism identifies with mental states. So Psychofunctionalism is just the result of applying a plausible conception of science to mentality; Psychofunctionalism is just the doctrine that mental states are the "psychological states" it is the business of psychology to characterize.

That something is seriously amiss with this form of argument can be seen by noting that it would be fallacious if applied to other branches of science.

Consider the analogue of Psychofunctionalism for physics. It says that protonhood, for example, is the property of having certain lawlike relations to certain other physical properties. With respect to current physical theory, protonhood would be identified with a property expressible in terms of the Ramsey sentence of current physical theory (in the manner described on p. 269 above). Now there is an obvious problem with this claim about what it is to be a proton. Namely, this physico-functionalist approach would identify being an anti-proton *with the very same property*. According to current physical theory, protons and anti-protons are "dual" entities: one cannot distinguish the variable which replaced 'protonhood' from the variable that replaced 'anti-protonhood' (in any nontrivial way) in the Ramsey sentence of current physical theory. Yet protons and anti-protons are different types of particles; it is a law of physics that particles annihilate their anti-particles; thus, protons annihilate anti-protons, even though protons get along fine with other protons.[20]

Suppose someone were to argue that 'protonhood = its Ramsey functional correlate with respect to current physical theory' is our best hypothesis as to the nature of protonhood, on the gound that this identification amounts to an application of the doctrine that it is the business of branches of science to tell us the nature of things in their domains. The person would be arguing fallaciously. So why should we suppose that this form of argument is any less fallacious when applied to psychology?

In the preceding few paragraphs I may have given the impression that the analogue of Psychofunctionalism in physics can be used to

cast doubt on Psychofunctionalism itself. But there are two important disanalogies between Psychofunctionalism and its physics analogue. First, according to Psychofunctionalism, there is a theoretically principled distinction between, on one hand, the inputs and
outputs described explicitly in the Ramsey sentence, and, on the
other hand, the internal states and other psychological entities
whose names are replaced by variables. But there is no analogous
distinction with respect to other branches of science. An observa-
tional/theoretical distinction would be analogous if it could be made
out, but difficulties in drawing such a distinction are notorious.

Second, and more important, Psychofunctionalism simply need
not be regarded as a special case of any general doctrine about the
nature of the entities scientific theories are about. Psychofunctionalists can reasonably hold that only *mental* entities—or perhaps only
states, events, and their ilk, as opposed to substances like protons
—are "constituted" by their causal relations. Of course, if Psychofunctionalists take such a view, they protect Psychofunctionalism
from the proton problem at the cost of abandoning the argument
that Psychofunctionalism is just the result of applying a plausible
conception of science to mentality.

Another argument for Psychofunctionalism (or, less plausibly,
for Functionalism) which can be abstracted from the literature is
an "inference to the best explanation" argument: "What *else* could
mental states be if not Psychofunctional states?" For example, Putnam (1967) hypothesizes that (Psycho)functionalism is true and
then argues persuasively that (Psycho)functionaism is a *better* hypothesis than behaviorism or materialism.

But this is a very dubious use of "inference to the best explanation." For what guarantee do we have that *there is* an answer to
the question "What are mental states?" of the sort behaviorists,
materialists, and functionalists have wanted? Moreover, inference
to the best explanation cannot be applied when none of the available explanations are any good. In sum, in order for inference to
the best explanation to be applicable, two conditions have to be
satisfied: we must have reason to believe an explanation is possible,
and at least one of the available explanations must be minimally
adequate. Imagine someone arguing for one of the proposed solutions to Newcomb's Problem on the ground that despite its fatal

flaw it is the best of the proposed solutions. That would be a joke. But is the argument for functionalism any better? Behaviorism, materialism, and functionalism are not theories of mentality in the way Mendel's theory is a theory of heredity. Behaviorism, materialism, and functionalism (and dualism as well) are attempts to solve a problem: the mind-body problem. Of course, this is a problem which can hardly be guaranteed to have a solution. Further, each of the proposed solutions to the mind-body problem has serious difficulties, difficulties I for one am inclined to regard as fatal.

Why is functionalism so widely accepted, given the dearth of good arguments for it, implicit or explicit? In my view, what has happened is that functionalist doctrines were offered initially as hypotheses. But with the passage of time, plausible-sounding hypotheses with useful features can come to be treated as established facts, even if no good arguments have ever been offered for them.

2.2 Are Qualia Psychofunctional States?

I began this chapter by describing a homunculi-headed device and claiming there is prima facie doubt about whether it has any mental states at all, especially whether it has qualitative mental states like pains, itches, and sensations of red. The special doubt about qualia can perhaps be explicated by thinking about *inverted* qualia rather than *absent* qualia. It makes sense, or seems to make sense, to suppose that objects we both call green look to me the way objects we both call red look to you. It seems that we could be functionally equivalent even though the sensations fire hydrants evoke in you is qualitatively the same as the sensation grass evokes in me. Imagine an inverting lense which when placed in the eye of a subject results in exclamations like "Red things now look the way green things used to look, and vice versa." Imagine futher, a pair of identical twins one of whom has the lenses inserted at birth. The twins grow up normally, and at age 21 are functionally equivalent. This situation offers at least some evidence that each's spectrum is inverted relative to the other's. (See Shoemaker, 1975, footnote 17, for a convincing description of intrapersonal spectrum inversion.) However, it is very hard to see how to make sense of the analogue of spectrum inversion with respect to nonqualitative states. Imagine a pair of persons one of whom believes that p is true and that q

($\neq$ p) is false, while the other believes that q is true and that p is false. Could these persons be functionally equivalent? It is hard to see how they could.[21] Indeed, it is hard to see how two persons could have only this difference in beliefs and yet there be no possible circumstance in which this belief difference would reveal itself in different behavior. Qualia seem (though perhaps not to adherents of Davidsonian Anomalous Monism) to be supervenient on functional organization in a way that beliefs are not.

In part because of this feature of qualia, I called the argument against functionalism the 'Absent Qualia Argument.' But there is another reason for firmly distinguishing between qualitative and nonqualitative mental states in talking about functionalist theories: Psychofunctionalism avoids Functionalism's problems with nonqualitative states, e.g., propositional attitudes like beliefs and desires. But Psychofunctionalism may be no more able to handle qualitative states than is Functionalism. The reason is that qualia may well not be in the domain of psychology.

To see this, let us try to imagine what a homunculi-headed realization of human psychology would be like. Current psychological theorizing seems directed toward the description of information-flow relations among psychological mechanisms. The aim seems to be to decompose such mechanisms into psychologically primitive mechanisms, "black boxes" whose internal structure is in the domain of physiology rather than in the domain of physiology. (See Fodor, 1968b, Dennett, 1975, and Cummins, 1975; interesting objections are raised in Nagel, 1968.) For example, a near-primitive mechanism might be one that matches two items in a representational system and determines if they are tokens of the same type. Or the primitive mechanisms might be like those in a digital computer, e.g., they might be (a) *add 1 to a given register*, and (b) *subtract 1 from a given register, or if the register contains 0, go to the nth (indicated) instruction*. (These operations can be combined to accomplish any digital computer operation; see Minsky, 1967, p. 206.) Consider a computer whose machine language code contains only two instructions corresponding to (a) and (b). If you ask how it multiplies or solves differential equations or makes up payrolls, you can be answered by being shown a program couched in terms of the two machine-language instructions. But if you ask how it adds 1 to a given register, the appropriate answer is given by a wiring diagram, not a program. The machine is hard-wired to add 1. When the instruction corresponding to (a) appears in a certain register, the contents of another register "automatically" change in a certain way. The computational structure of a computer is determined by a set of primitive operations and the ways nonprimitive operations are built up from them. Thus it does not matter to the computational structure of the computer whether the primitive mechanisms are realized by tube circuits, transistor circuits, or relays. Likewise, it does not matter to the psychology of a mental system whether its primitive mechanisms are realized by one or another neurological mechanism. Call a system a "realization of human psychology" if every psychological theory true of us is true of it. Consider a realization of human psychology whose primitive psychological operations are accomplished by little men, in the manner of the homunculi-headed simulations discussed. So, perhaps one little man produces items from a list, one by one, another compares these items with other representations to determine whether they match, etc.

Now there is good reason for supposing this system has some mental states. Propositional attitudes are an example. Perhaps psychological theory will identify remembering that P with having "stored" a sentencelike object which expresses the proposition that P (Fodor, 1975). Then if one of the little men has put a certain sentencelike object in "storage," we may have reason for regarding the system as remembering that P. But unless having qualia is just a matter of having certain information processing (at best a controversial proposal—see later discussion), there is no such theoretical reason for regarding the system as having qualia. In short, there is perhaps as much doubt about the qualia of this homunculi-headed system as there was about the qualia of the homunculi-headed Functional simulation discussed early in the chapter.

But the system we are discussing is ex hypothesi something of which any true psychological theory is true. *So any doubt that it has qualia is a doubt that qualia are in the domain of psychology.*

It may be objected: "The kind of psychology you have in mind is *cognitive* psychology, i.e., psychology of thought processes; and it is no wonder that qualia are not in the domain of *cognitive* psychology!" But I *do not* have cognitive psychology in mind, and if it sounds that way, this is easily explained: nothing we know about the psychological processes underlying our conscious mental life has anything to do with qualia. What passes for the "psychology" of sensation or pain, for example, is (a) physiology, (b) psychophysics (i.e., study of the mathematical functions relating stimulus variables and sensation variables, e.g., the intensity of sound as a function of the amplitude of the sound waves), or (c) a grabbag of descriptive studies (see Melzack, 1972, Ch. 2). Of these, only psychophysics could be construed as being about qualia per se. And it is obvious that psychophysics touches only the *functional* aspect of sensation, not its qualitative character. Psychophysical experiments done on you would have the same results if done on any system Psychofunctionally equivalent to you, even if it had inverted or absent qualia. If experimental results would be unchanged whether or not the experimental subjects have inverted or absent qualia, they can hardly be expected to cast light on the nature of qualia.

Indeed, on the basis of the kind of conceptual apparatus now available in psychology, I do not see how psychology in anything like its present incarnation *could* explain qualia. We cannot now conceive how psychology could explain qualia, though we *can* conceive how psychology could explain believing, desiring, hoping, etc. (see Fodor, 1975). That something is currently inconceivable is not a good reason to think it is impossible. Concepts could be developed tomorrow that would make what is now inconceivable conceivable. But all we have to go on is what we know, and on the basis of what we have to go on, it looks like qualia are not in the domain of psychology.

Objection: if the Psychofunctional simulation just described has the same beliefs I have, then among its beliefs will be the belief that it now has a headache (since I now am aware of having a headache). Is its belief mistaken?

Reply: if it has beliefs, yes. The objection evidently assumes some version of the Incorrigibility Thesis (if x believes he has a pain, it follows that he does have a pain). I believe the Incorrigibility Thesis to be false. But even if it is true, it is a double-edged sword. For one can just as well use it to argue that Psychofunctionalism's difficulties with qualia infect its account of belief too. For if the homunculi-headed simulation is in a state Psychofunctionally equivalent to believing it is in pain, yet has no qualia, and hence no pain, then if the Incorrigibility Thesis is true, it does not believe it is in pain either. But if it is in a state Psychofunctionally equivalent to belief without believing, belief is not a Psychofunctional state.

Objection: at one time it was inconceivable that temperature could be a property of matter, if matter was composed only of particles bouncing about; but it would not have been rational to conclude temperature was not in the domain of physics. Reply: first, what the objection says was inconceivable was probably never inconceivable. When the scientific community could conceive of matter as bouncing particles, it could probably also conceive of heat as something to do with the motion of the particles. Bacon's theory that heat was motion was introduced at the inception of theorizing about heat—a century before Galileo's primitive precursor of a thermometer, and even before distinctions among the temperature of x, the perceived temperature of x, and x's rate of heat conduction were at all clear (Kuhn, 1961). Second, there is quite a difference between saying something is not in the domain of physics and saying something is not in the domain of psychology. Suggesting that temperature phenomena are not in the domain of physics is suggesting that they are not explainable at all.

It is no objection to the suggestion that qualia are not psychological entities that qualia are the very paradigm of something in the domain of psychology. As has often been pointed out, it is in part an empirical question what is in the domain of any particular branch of science. The liquidity of water turns out not to be explainable in chemistry, but rather by subatomic physics. Branches of science have at any given time a set of phenomena they seek to explain. But it can be discovered that some phenomenon which seemed central to a branch of science is actually in the purview of a different branch.

Suppose psychologists discover a *correlation* between qualitative states and certain cognitive processes. Would that be any reason to think the qualitative states are identical to the cognitive states they are correlated with? Certainly not. First, what reason would there be to think this correlation would hold in the homunculi-headed systems that Psychofunctionally simulate us? Second, although a case can be made that certain sorts of general correlations between Fs and Gs provide reason to think F is G, this is only the case when the predicates are predicates of different theories, one of which is reducible to the other. For example, there is a correlation between thermal and electrical conductivity (asserted by the Wiedemann-Franz Law), but it would be silly to suggest that this shows thermal conductivity is electrical conductivity (see Block, 1971, Ch. 3).

I know of only one serious attempt to fit "consciousness" into information-flow psychology: the program in Dennett, 1978. But Dennett fits consciousness into information-flow psychology only by claiming that the contents of consciousness are exhausted by judgments. His view is that to the extent that qualia are not judgments (or beliefs), they are spurious theoretical entities that we postulate to explain why we find ourselves wanting to say all sorts of things about what is going on in our minds.

Dennett's doctrine has the relation to qualia that the U.S. Air Force had to so many Vietnamese villages: he destroys qualia in order to save them. Is it not more reasonable to tentatively hypothesize that qualia are determined by the physiological or physico-chemical nature of our information processing, rather than by the information flow per se?

The Absent Qualia Argument exploits the possibility that the Functional or Psychofunctional state Functionalists or Psychofunctionalists would want to identify with pain can occur without any quale occurring. It also seems to be conceivable that the latter occur without the former. Indeed, there are facts that lend plausibility to this view. After frontal lobotomies, patients typically report that they still have pains, though the pains no longer bother them (Melzack, 1973, p. 95). These patients show all the "sensory" signs of pain (e.g., recognizing pin pricks as sharp), but they often have little or no desire to avoid "painful" stimuli.

One view suggested by these observations is that each pain is actually a *composite* state whose components are a quale and a Functional or Psychofunctional state.[22] Or what amounts to much the same idea, each pain is a quale playing a certain Functional or Psychofunctional role. If this view is right, it helps to explain how people can have believed such different theories of the nature of pain and other sensations: they have emphasized one component at the expense of the other. Proponents of behaviorism and functionalism have had one component in mind; proponents of private ostensive definition have had the other in mind. Both approaches err in trying to give one account of something that has two components of quite different natures.

3.1 Chauvinism vs. Liberalism

It is natural to understand the psychological theories Psychofunctionalism adverts to as theories of *human* psychology. On Psychofunctionalism, so understood, it is logically impossible for a system to have beliefs, desires, etc., except insofar as psychological theories true of us are true of it. Psychofunctionalism (so understood) stipulates that Psychofunctional equivalence to us is necessary for mentality.

The alternative characterization of Psychofunctionalism mentioned on p. 274 *explicitly* made Psychofunctional equivalence to us necessary for mentality. That characterization was: mental states are states that consist in being causally related to whatever psychological events, states, and processes, and other entities [as well as inputs and outputs] actually obtain *in us* in whatever way those entities are causally related to one another. But even if Psychofunctional equivalence to us is a condition on our *recognition of mentality*, what reason is there to think it is a condition on mentality itself? Could there not be a wide variety of possible psychological processes that can underlie mentality, of which we instantiate only one type? Suppose we meet Martians and find that they are roughly Functionally (but not Psychofunctionally) equivalent to us. When we get to know Martians, we find them about as different from us as humans we know. We develop extensive cultural and commercial intercourse with them. We study each other's science and philosophy journals, go to each other's movies, read each other's novels, etc. Then Martian and Earthian psychologists compare notes, only to find that in underlying psychology, Martians and Earthians are very different. They soon agree that the difference can be described as follows. Think of humans and Martians as if they were products of conscious design. In any such design project, there will be various options. Some capacities can be built in (innate), others learned. The brain can be designed to accomplish tasks using as much memory capacity as necessary in order to minimize use of computation capacity; or, on the other hand, the designer could choose to conserve memory space and rely mainly on computation capacity. Inferences can be accomplished by systems which use a few axioms and many rules of inference, or, on the other hand, few rules and many axioms. Now imagine that what Martian and Earthian psychologists find when they compare notes is that Martians and Earthians differ as if they were the end products of maximally different design choices (compatible with rough Functional equivalence in adults). Should we reject our assumption that Martians can enjoy our films, believe their own apparent scientific results, etc? Should they "reject" their "assumption" that we "enjoy" their novels, "learn" from their textbooks, etc.? Perhaps I have not provided enough information to answer this question. After all, there may be many ways of filling in the description of the Martian-human differences in which it would be reasonable to suppose there simply is no fact of the matter, or even to suppose that the Martians do not deserve mental ascriptions. But surely there are many ways of filling in the description of the Martian-Earthian difference I sketched on which it would be perfectly clear that even if Martians behave differently from us on subtle psychological experiments, they nonetheless think, desire, enjoy, etc. To suppose otherwise would be crude human chauvinism. (Remember theories are chauvinist insofar as they falsely *deny* that systems have mental properties and liberal insofar as they falsely *attribute* mental properties.)

So it seems as if in preferring Psychofunctionalism to Functionalism, we erred in the direction of human chauvinism. For if mental states are Psychofunctional states, and if Martians do not have these Psychofunctional states, then they do not have mental states either. In arguing that the original homunculi-headed simulations (taken as Functional simulations) had no mentality, I appealed, in effect, to the following principle: if the sole reason to think system x has mentality is that x was built to be Functionally equivalent to us, then differences between x and us in underlying information processing and/or neurophysiology are prima facie reasons to doubt whether x has mental states. But this principle does not dictate that a system can have mentality only insofar as it is Psychofunctionally equivalent to us. Psychofunctional equivalence to us is a sufficient condition for at least some aspects of mentality (those in the domain of psychology), but it is not obvious that it is a necessary condition of any aspects of mentality.

An obvious suggestion of a way out of this difficulty is to identify mental states with Psychofunctional states, taking the domain of psychology to include *all creatures with mentality*, including Martians. The suggestion is that we define "Psychofunctionalism" in terms of "universal" or "cross-system" psychology, rather than the human psychology I assumed earlier. Universal psychology, however, is a suspect discipline. For how are we to decide what systems should be included in the *domain* of universal psychology? What systems are the generalizations of universal psychology based on? One possible way of deciding what systems have mentality, and are thus in the domain of universal psychology, would be to use some *other* developed theory of mentality, e.g., behaviorism or Functionalism. But such a procedure would be at least as ill-justified as the other theory used. Further, if Psychofunctionalism must presuppose some other theory of mind, we might just as well accept the other theory of mind instead.

Perhaps universal psychology will avoid this "domain" problem in the same way other branches of science avoid it or seek to avoid it. Other branches of science start with tentative domains based on intuitive and prescientific versions of the concepts the sciences are supposed to explicate. They then attempt to develop natural kinds in a way which allows the formulations of lawlike generalizations which apply to all or most of the entities in the prescientific domains. In the case of many branches of science—including biological and social sciences such as genetics and linguistics—the prescientific domain turned out to be suitable for the articulation of lawlike generalizations.

Now it may be that we shall be able to develop universal psychology in much the same way we develop Earthian psychology. We decide on an intuitive and prescientific basis what creatures to include in its domain, and work to develop natural kinds of psychological theory which apply to all or at least most of them. Perhaps the study of a wide range of organisms found on different worlds will one day lead to theories that determine truth conditions for the attribution of mental states like belief, desire, etc., applicable to systems which are pretheoretically quite different from us. Indeed, such cross-world psychology will no doubt require a whole new range of mentalistic concepts. Perhaps there will be families of concepts corresponding to belief, desire, etc., that is, a family of belieflike concepts, desirelike concepts, etc. If so, the cross-world psychology we develop shall, no doubt, be somewhat dependent on which new organisms we discover first. Even if cross-world psychology is in fact possible, however, there will certainly be many possible organisms whose mental status is indeterminate.

On the other hand, it may be that universal psychology is *not* possible. Perhaps life in the universe is such that we shall simply have no basis for reasonable decisions about what systems are in the domain of psychology and what systems are not.[23]

If cross-world psychology *is* possible, the problem I have been raising vanishes. Cross-world Psychofunctionalism avoids the liberalism of Functionalism and the chauvinism of human-Psychofunctionalism. But the question of whether cross-world psychology is possible is surely one which we have no way of answering now. What if cross-world psychology is not possible? Are we forced to choose between the liberalism of Functionalism and the chauvinism of Psychofunctionalism? There is reason to think that cross-world psychology ought to be partially possible and that the extent to which it is possible may resolve the problem of the Martians mentioned above. What makes us want to attribute mentality to the Martians is that they are (a) Functionally equivalent to us, and (b) they have a psychology as rich as ours, e.g., they do not operate by means of mechanisms like the tree-searcher described above (p. 294). Now if this fact that the Martian psychology is as rich as ours can be made precise, it should allow us to state a psychological generalization true of both us and the Martians. But then this psychological generalization, added to the generalizations that ground the Functional description that applies to both the Martians and us, should allow us to formulate a "reasonably adequate" psychological theory suitable for framing a Psychofunctional equivalence relation stronger than Functional equivalence, but weaker than the Psychofunctional equivalence relation based on human psychology. This Psychofunctional equivalence relation will license the application of mental terminology to Martians.[24]

If no more cross-world psychology than this is possible, the attribution of mental states to newly discovered organisms will be largely the product of the kind of linguistic legislation required for practical purposes when a familiar concept must be extended to cover cases of a sort such that there is no matter of fact about whether it applies or not, e.g., in the way terms like 'stomach ulcer' or 'sprained ankle' might be applied in intergalactic medicine.

To summarize my conclusions so far: First, given the reasonable assumption that mental states are in the domain of psychology and/or physiology, the homunculi-head example shows that Functionalism is false. Second, none of the arguments in the literature for either Functionalism or Psychofunctionalism are persuasive. Third: the claim that beliefs and desires are Psychofunctional states is impervious to arguments based on homunculi-heads; but since there is a doubt that qualia are in the domain of psychology, there is a doubt that qualitative states are Psychofunctional states. Finally, I considered chauvinism/liberalism problems for Psychofunctionalism and concluded that some version of Psychofunctionalism may yet steer between the Scylla of liberalism and the Charybdis of chauvinism. So, even if there is no good reason for thinking Psychofunctionalism true, still I have provided only weak reason for thinking it false. In the next section, I bring up a difficulty for Psychofunctionalism (and Functionalism) which may not be easily evaded.

3.2 The Problem of the Inputs and the Outputs

I have been supposing all along (as Psychofunctionalists often do—see Putnam, 1967) that inputs and outputs can be specified by neural impulse descriptions. But this is a chauvinist claim, since it precludes organisms without neurons (e.g., machines) from having functional descriptions. How can one avoid chauvinism with respect to specification of inputs and outputs? One way would be to characterize the inputs and outputs *only as* inputs and outputs. So the functional description of a person might list outputs by number: $output_1$, $output_2$, . . . Then a system could be functionally equivalent to you if it had a set of states, inputs, and outputs causally related to one another in the way yours are, no matter what the states, inputs, and outputs were like. Indeed, though this approach violates the demand of some functionalists that inputs and outputs be physically specified, other functionalists—those who insist only that input and output descriptions be *nonmental*—may have had something like this in mind. This version of functionalism does not "tack down" functional descriptions at the periphery with relatively specific descriptions of inputs and outputs; rather, this version of functionalism treats inputs and outputs just as all versions of functionalism treat internal states. That is, this version specifies states, inputs, and outputs only by requiring that they *be* states, inputs, and outputs.

The trouble with this version of functionalism is that it is wildly liberal. Economic systems have inputs and outputs, e.g., influx and outflux of credits and debits. And economic systems also have a rich variety of internal states, e.g., having a rate of increase of GNP equal to double the Prime Rate. It does not seem impossible that a wealthy sheik could gain control of the economy of a small country, e.g., Bolivia, and manipulate its financial system to make it functionally equivalent to a person, e.g., himself. If this seems implausible, remember that the economic states, inputs, and outputs designated by the sheik to correspond to his mental states, inputs, and outputs need not be "natural" economic magnitudes. Our hypothetical sheik could pick *any* economic magnitudes at all—e.g., the fifth time derivative of the balance of payments. His only constraint is that the magnitudes he picks be economic, that their having such and such values be inputs, outputs, and states, and that he be able to set up a financial structure which realizes the intended causal structure. The mapping from psychological magnitudes to economic magnitudes could be as bizarre as the sheik requires.

This version of functionalism is far too liberal and must therefore be rejected. If there are any fixed points when discussing the mind-body problem, one of them is that the economy of Bolivia could not have mental states, no matter how it is distorted by powerful hobbyists. Obviously, we must be more specific in our descriptions of inputs and outputs. The question is: is there a description of inputs and outputs specific enough to avoid liberalism, yet general enough to avoid chauvinism? I doubt that there is.

Every proposal for a description of inputs and outputs I have seen or thought of is guilty of either liberalism or chauvinism. Though this paper has focused on liberalism, chauvinism is the more pervasive problem. Consider standard Functional and Psychofunctional descriptions. Functionalists tend to specify inputs and outputs in the manner of behaviorists: outputs in terms of movements of arms and legs, sound emitted and the like; inputs in terms of light and sound falling on the eyes and ears. As I argued earlier, this conception is chauvinist, since it denies mentality to brains in vats and to paralytics. But the chauvinism inherent in Functional descriptions runs deeper. Such descriptions are blatantly *species-specific.* Humans have arms and legs, but snakes do not—and whether or not snakes have mentality, one can easily imagine snakelike creatures that do. Indeed, one can imagine creatures with all manner of input-output devices, e.g., creatures that communicate and manipulate by emitting strong magnetic fields. Of course, one could formulate Functional descriptions for each such species, and somewhere in disjunctive heaven there is a disjunctive description which will handle all species that ever actually exist in the universe (the description may be infinitely long). But even an appeal to such suspicious entities as infinite disjunctions will not bail out Functionalism, since even the amended view will not tell us what there is in common to pain-feeling organisms in virtue of which they all have pain. And it will not allow the ascription of pain to some hypothetical (but nonexistent) pain-feeling creatures. Further, these are just the grounds on which functionalists typically ascerbically reject the disjunctive theories sometimes advanced by desperate physicalists. If functionalists suddenly smile on wildly disjunctive states to save themselves from chauvinism, they will have no way of defending themselves from physicalism.

Standard Psychofunctional descriptions of inputs and outputs are also species-specific (e.g., in terms of neural activity) and hence chauvinist as well.

The chauvinism of standard input-output descriptions is not hard to explain. The variety of possible intelligent life is enormous. Given any fairly specific descriptions of inputs and outputs, any high-school-age science-fiction buff will be able to describe a sapient sentient being whose inputs and outputs fail to satisfy that description.

I shall argue that *any physical description* of inputs and outputs (recall that many functionalists have insisted on physical descriptions) yields a version of functionalism that is hopelessly chauvinist.

Imagine yourself so badly burned in a fire that your optimal way of communicating with the outside world is via modulations of your EEG pattern in Morse Code. You find that thinking an exciting thought produces a pattern that your audience agrees to interpret as a dot, and a dull thought produces a "dash." Indeed, this fantasy is not so far from reality. According to a recent newspaper article (*Boston Globe*, March 21, 1976), "at UCLA scientists are working on the use of EEG to control machines. . . . A subject puts electrodes on his scalp, and thinks an object through a maze." The "reverse" process is also presumably possible: others communicating with you in Morse Code by producing bursts of electrical activity that affect your brain (e.g., causing a long or short afterimage). Alternatively, if the cerebroscopes that philosophers often fancy become a reality, your thoughts will be readable directly from your brain. Again, the reverse process also seems possible. In these cases, *the brain itself becomes one's input and output device*. But this possibility has embarrasing consequences for functionalism. You will recall, that as functionalists have emphasized in criticizing physicalism, a single mental state can be realized by an indefinite variety of physical states, that have no necessary and sufficient physical characterization. But if this functionalist point against physicalism is right, since the device which physically realizes mental states can serve as a mental system's input and output devices, *the same point applies to mental systems' input and output devices*. That is, on any sense of 'physical' in which the functionalist criticism of physicalism is correct, *there will be no physical characterizations that apply to all mental systems' inputs and outputs. Hence, any attempt to formulate a functional description with physical characterizations of inputs and outputs will exclude some systems with mentality, and thus will be chauvinist.*

If the functionalist argument against physicalism is right, any functional description that specifies inputs and outputs physically will be chauvinist. Moreover, mental or "action" terminology (e.g., 'punching the offending person') may not be used either, since to use such specifications of inputs or outputs would be to give up the functionalist program of characterizing mentality in nonmental terms. On the other hand, you recall, characterizing inputs and outputs simply *as* inputs and outputs is inevitably liberal. I, for one, do not see how functionalism can describe inputs and outputs without falling afoul of either liberalism or chauvinism, or abandoning the original project of characterizing mentality in nonmental terms. I do not claim that this is a conclusive argument against functionalism. Rather, like the functionalist argument against physicalism, it is perhaps best construed as a burden of proof argument. The functionalist says to the physicalist: "It is hard to see how there could be a single physical characterization of the internal state of every possible organism functionally equivalent to a human." I say to the functionalist: "It is very hard to see how there could be a single characterization of inputs and outputs that applies to all and only mental systems." In both cases, it seems enough has been said to make it the responsibility of those who think there could be such characterizations to sketch how they could be possible.[25]

Notes

1. The converse is also true.

2. It would be misleading to define 'behaviorism' in this way because although functionalists, like behaviorists, typically want to be able to eliminate mental *terms*, unlike behaviorists, they accomplish this by means which typically presuppose the existence of mental *states*. For example, Lewis's functional definitions of mental state terms contain no mental state terms, but they *quantify over* mental states.

3. Lewis's functional definitions are constructed as follows: We formulate an account consisting mainly of all the common-sense platitudes about causal relations among mental states, inputs, and outputs. Then we reformulate the account so that all the mental-state terms are singular terms (e.g., 'is angry' becomes 'has anger'). We write the account as a single sentence, $\ulcorner T(t_1 \ldots t_n) \urcorner$, where $t_1 \ldots t_n$ are mental state terms. We replace $t_1 \ldots t_n$ by variables $x_1 \ldots x_n$, and form the modified Ramsey sentence (what Lewis sometimes calls the unique realization sentence), $\ulcorner \exists_1 \langle x_1 \ldots x_n \rangle T(x_1 \ldots x_n) \urcorner$. This says there is exactly one n-tuple of entities that realizes the original common-sense account. We can define the n-tuple of mental state terms by means of the modified Ramsey sentence: $\ulcorner \langle t_1 \ldots t_n \rangle = \iota \langle x_1 \ldots x_n \rangle T(x_1 \ldots x_n) \urcorner$. Any single mental-state term can be defined in an obvious way. For example,

$$t_1 = \iota y_1 \exists y_2 \ldots y_n \forall x_1 \ldots x_n \ (T[x_1 \ldots x_n] \equiv [y_1 = x_1 \& \ldots y_n = x_n])$$

Lewis (1971 and 1972) does not, strictly speaking, espouse a version of the doctrine I am calling 'functionalism'. He claims not that pain is a functional state, but that pain can be *functionally characterized*, i.e., picked out by a certain sort of definite description (as indicated in the preceding paragraph). However, I occasionally consider Lewis a functional-state identity theorist, because his view is easily transformed into a clear and useful version of a functional-state identity thesis (see p. 269). Further, given that Lewis claims his functional characterizations are analytic, he seems committed to a functional-*property* identity thesis. In my view, this amounts to much the same thing as a functional-state identity thesis.

4. State type, not state token. Throughout the chapter, I shall mean by 'physicalism' the doctrine that says each distinct type of mental state is identical to a distinct type of physical state; for example, pain (the universal) is a physical state. Token physicalism, on the other hand, is the (weaker) doctrine that each particular datable pain is a state of some physical type or other. Functionalism shows that type physicalism is false, but it does not show that token physicalism is false.

By 'physicalism', I mean *first order* physicalism, the doctrine that, e.g., the property of being in pain is a first-order (in the Russell-Whitehead sense) physical property. (A first-order property is one whose definition does not require quantification over properties; a second-order property is one whose definition requires quantification over first-order properties.) The claim that being in pain is a second-order physical property is actually a (physicalist) form of functionalism. See Putnam, 1970.

'Physical property' could be defined for the purposes of this chapter as a property expressed by a predicate of some true physical theory or, more broadly, by a predicate of some true theory of physiology, biology, chemistry, or physics. Of course, such a definition is unsatisfactory without characterizations of these branches of science. See Hempel, 1970 for further discussion of this problem.

5. Kim, 1972, p. 190; Lewis, 1969. Lewis makes it clear that he thinks *both* functionalist and materialist identities can be true. It is worth noting that if P is the functional state nonphysicalist functionalists want to identify with pain, those who assert both functionalist and materialist identities would have to claim *human P* is one brain state and *Martian P* is another. In fairness to Lewis, the version of functionalism espoused in Lewis 1971 and 1972 is exempt from the kind of criticism I make here. In these articles, he claims only that the meaning of 'pain' can be captured by a certain definite description of the form: 'the occupant of causal role R'. Clearly, the occupant of causal role R can be one thing in the case of humans and another thing in the case of Martians. In the new footnotes to "An Argument for the Identity Theory" (1971), Lewis says that in his view, 'pain' is a contingent name, a name with different denotations in different possible worlds, but 'the attribute of having pain' is a noncontingent name, denoting the same thing in each possible world. Those who share Lewis's doctrine that 'pain' is a contingent name need not thereby reject the arguments of this chapter. I would be satisfied to put all the points I make in terms of functionalism as a property or attribute identity theory viz., the claim that each mental attribute is identical to a functional attribute.

6. Functionalists who are also physicalists have formulated broadly physicalistic versions of functionalism. As functionalists often point out (Putnam, 1967), it is logically possible for a given abstract functional description to be satisfied by a nonphysical object, e.g., a soul. One can formulate a physicalistic version of functionalism simply by explicitly ruling out this possibility. One such physicalistic version of functionalism is suggested by Putnam (1970), Field (1975 and forthcoming) and Lewis (in conversation): having pain is identified with a second-order physical property, a property that consists of having certain first-order physical properties if certain other first-order physical properties obtain (see note 3 for an explication of 'order'). This doctrine combines functionalism (which can be formulated as the doctrine that having pain is the property of having certain properties if certain other properties obtain) with token physicalism (see note 3). Of course, the Putnam-Lewis-Field doctrine is *not* a version of type physicalism; indeed, the P-L-F doctrine is incompatible with type physicalism.

7. My approach differs in a number of ways from Lewis's method. The main difference is that Lewis claims that 'pain' can be analytically defined as the state with such and such a causal role. According to the version of functionalism that I shall present, a state

S is defined as the state with such and such a causal role, and the functionalist claim becomes: pain = S. In Lewis's version, pain is a *functionally characterized* state, not a functional state; pain can be a functionally characterized *brain* state. That is, the definite description that defines 'pain' can pick out a neurophysiological state. In my version, S is itself a functional state. Since Lewis is committted to the analyticity of the claim that pain = the state with such and such a causal role, he is also committed to the claim that being in pain = being in the state with such and such a causal role. But since the property of being in the state with such and such a causal role is a functional property — not merely a functionally characterized property (see Lewis, 1971, pp. 164-165) — Lewis is committed to a functional-property thesis of the sort I am discussing.

8. Correctly stated: where ψ is a predicate ϕa, let $\ulcorner \lambda a \psi \urcorner$ be a singular term for the property expressed by ϕa. I am grateful to George Boolos for this formulation and for the advice not to use it.

9. The example may be somewhat misleading in that it leaves out causal relations among mental states. It is easy to construct an example which lacks this flaw using the Coke machine described earlier. Let us think of the Coke machine as having two desire-like states, nickel-shmesire and dime-shmesire. The following four sentences describe the causal relations among the Coke machine's mental states, inputs, and outputs:

1. M's having dime-shmesire + 5¢ input causes M's having nickel-shmesire + (no Coke, 0¢) output.
2. M's having dime-shmesire + 10¢ input causes M's having dime-shmesire + (Coke, 0¢) output.
3. M's having nickel-shmesire + 5¢ input causes M's having dime-shmesire + (Coke, 0¢) output.
4. M's having nickel-shmesire + 10¢ input causes M's having dime-shmesire + (Coke, 5¢) output.

'5¢ input' means that a nickel is put into the machine; '(Coke, 5¢) output' means a Coke and a nickel are emitted by the machine; '+' should be read as 'together with'' T = 1&2&3&4. The Ramsey sentence of T is formed by replacing 'M', 'nickel-shmesire' and 'dime-shmesire' with variables and by existentially quantifying. The property of having dime-shmesire is identified with its Ramsey functional correlate, viz.,

$$\lambda z \exists x \exists y \ [(z\text{'s having } x + 5 ¢ \text{ input causes } z\text{'s having } y + (\text{no Coke, } 0¢) \text{ output})$$
$$\& \ (z\text{'s having } x + 10 ¢ \text{ input causes } z\text{'s having } x + (\text{Coke, } 0¢) \text{ output})$$
$$\& \ (z\text{'s having } y + 5 ¢ \text{ input causes } z\text{'s having } x + (\text{Coke, } 0¢) \text{ output})$$
$$\& \ (z\text{'s having } y + 10 ¢ \text{ input causes } z\text{'s having } x + (\text{Coke, } 5¢) \text{ output})$$
$$\& \ z \text{ is in } x]$$

10. The comparison between a functional state identity theory of the sort I have just described and a functional characterization view of the sort that Lewis advances can be clarified if we think of a state type as a certain sort of property, viz., the property each token of that state type has in virtue of being a token of that type. For example, the state pain would be identified with the property of *being a pain*, i.e., the property each pain has in virtue of which it is a pain. (Notice the difference between being a pain and being in pain; the latter is a property of organisms, the former is a property of pains.) On this assumption, if a psychological theory can be written as

$$T(s_1 \ . \ . \ . \ s_n)$$

(I omit input and output terms, for brevity), where $s_1 \ . \ . \ . \ s_n$ designate mental states, then, oversimplifying somewhat (see Lewis, 1972, footnote 7), Lewis would functionally define 'pain' as follows:

$$pain = \iota x_1 \exists x_2 \ldots \exists x_n T(x_1 \ldots x_n)$$

where x_1 is the variable that replaces 'pain'. That is, pain would be defined as the state that has a certain causal role. The functional state identity theory approach, on the other hand, would replace Lewis's iota with lambda:

$$pain = \lambda x_1 \exists x_2 \ldots \exists x_n T(x_1 \ldots x_n)$$

That is, pain would be identified with the property of having a certain causal role.

11. This distinction (one machine table in common/all machine tables in common) is arguably a distinction without a difference, given certain plausible conditions on what is to count as a realization of a machine table. That is, it is arguable that any pair of machines that share one machine table share all machine tables (with respect to a given set of inputs and outputs).

12. If, as suggested in note 11, there is no difference, then any machine table that describes the two machines (with respect to a given set of inputs and outputs) will be reasonably adequate.

13. This point has been raised with me by persons too numerous to mention.

14. One potential difficulty for Functionalism is provided by the possibility that one person may have two radically different Functional descriptions of the sort that justify attribution of mentality. In such a case, Functionalists might have to ascribe two radically different systems of belief, desire, etc., to the same person, or suppose that there is no fact of the matter about what the person's propositional attitudes are. Undoubtedly, Functionalists differ greatly on what they make of this possibility, and the differences reflect positions on such issues as indeterminacy of translation.

15. Shoemaker, 1975, argues (in reply to Block & Fodor, 1972) that absent qualia are logically impossible, that is, that it is logically impossible that two systems be in the same functional state yet one's state have and the other's state lack qualitative content. If Shoe- is right, it is wrong to doubt whether the homunculi-headed system has qualia. I attempt to show Shoemaker's argument to be fallacious in Block, forthcoming.

16. Since there is a difference between the role of the little people in producing your functional organization in the situation just described and the role of the homunculi in the homunculi-headed simulations this chapter began with, presumably Putnam's condition could be reformulated to rule out the latter without ruling out the former. But this would be a most ad hoc maneuver. Further, there are other counterexamples which suggest that a successful reformulation is likely to remain elusive.

Careful observation of persons who have had the nerve bundle connecting the two halves of the brain (the *corpus callosum*) severed to prevent the spread of epilepsy, suggest that each half of the brain has the functional organization of a sentient being. The same is suggested by the observation that persons who have had one hemisphere removed or anesthetized remain sentient beings. It was once thought that the right hemisphere had no linguistic capacity, but it is now known that the adult right hemisphere has the vocabulary of a 14-year-old and the syntax of a 5-year-old (*Psychology Today*, 12/75, p. 121). Now the functional organization of each hemisphere is different from the other and from that of a whole human. For one thing, in addition to inputs from the sense organs and outputs to motor neurons, each hemisphere has many input and output connections to the other hemisphere. Nonetheless, each hemisphere may have the functional organization of a sentient being. Perhaps Martians have many more input and output organs than we do. Then each half brain could be functionally like a whole Martian brain. If each of our hemispheres has the functional organization of a sentient being, then a Putnamian proposal would rule us out (except for those of us who have had hemispherectomies) as pain-feeling organisms.

Further, it could turn out that other parts of the body have a functional organization similar to that of some sentient being. For example, perhaps individual neurons have the same functional organization as some species of insect.

(The argument of the last two paragraphs depends on a version of functionalism that construes inputs and outputs as neural impulses. Otherwise, individual neurons could not have the same functional organization as insects. It would be harder to think of such examples if, for instance, inputs were taken to be irradiation of sense organs or the presence of perceivable objects in the "range" of the sense organs.)

17. A further indication that our intuitions are in part governed by the neurophysiological and psychological differences between us and the original homunculi-headed simulation (construed as a Functional simulation) is that intuition seems to founder on an intermediate case: a device that simulates you by having a billion little men each of whom simulates one of your neurons. It would be like you in psychological mechanisms, but not in neurological mechanisms, except at a very abstract level of description.

There are a number of differences between the original homunculi-heads and the elementary-particle-people example. The little elementary-particle people were not described as knowing your functional organization or trying to simulate it, but in the original example, the little men have *as their aim* simulating your functional organization. Perhaps when we know a certain functional organization is intentionally produced, we are thereby inclined to regard the thing's being functionally equivalent to a human as a misleading fact. One could test this by changing the elementary-particle-people example so that the little people have the aim of simulating your functional organization by simulating elementary particles; this change seems to me to make little intuitive difference.

There are obvious differences between the two types of examples. It is *you* in the elementary case and the change is *gradual*; these elements seem obviously misleading. But they can be eliminated without changing the force of the example much. Imagine, for example, that your spouse's parents went on the expedition and that your spouse has been made of the elementary-particle-people since birth.

18. Compare the first sentence with 'The fish eaten in Boston stank.' The reason it is hard to process is that 'raced' is naturally read as active rather than passive. See Fodor, Bever, & Garrett, 1974, p. 360. For a discussion of why the second sentence is grammatical, see Fodor & Garrett, 1967; Bever, 1970; and Fodor, Bever, & Garrett, 1974.

19. This argument backs up the suggestion of the end of the previous section that the "extra" mentality of the little men per se is not the major source of discomfort with the supposition that the homunculi-headed simulation has mentality. The argument of the last paragraph does not advert at all to the mentality of the homunculi. The argument depends only on the claim that the homunculi-headed Functional simulation need not be either psychologically or neurophysiologically like a human. This point is further strengthened by noticing that it is provable that each homunculus is replaceable by an extremely simple object—a McCullough-Pitts "and" neuron, a device with two inputs and one output that fires just in case the two inputs receive a signal. (The theorem assumes the automaton is a finite automaton and the inputs enter one signal at a time—see Minsky, 1967, p. 45.) So the argument would apply even if the homunculi were replaced by mindless "and" neurons.

20. One could avoid this difficulty by allowing *names* in one's physical theory. For example, one could identify protons as the particles with such and such properties contained in the nuclei of all atoms of the Empire State Building. No such move will save this argument for Psychofunctionalism, however. First, it is contrary to the idea of func-

tionalism, since functionalism purports to identify mental states with abstract causal structures; one of the advantages of functionalism is that it avoids appeal to ostension in definition of mental states. Second, tying Psychofunctionalism to particular named entities will inevitably result in chauvinism. See Section 3.1.

21. Sylvain Bromberger has pointed out that the spectrum inversion cases carry with them "belief inversion" for qualitative beliefs. That is, someone whose spectrum is inverted will have abnormal beliefs about the qualia usually associated with 'red' and 'green'. My point is not really undermined by this sort of example, since it is the qualitative aspect of the beliefs in question which makes the example work. My point can be restricted to beliefs that have no such qualitative aspect.

22. The quale might be identified with a physico-chemical state. This view would comport with a suggestion Hilary Putnam made in the late '60s in his philosophy of mind seminar. See also Ch. 5 of Gunderson, 1971.

23. To take a very artificial example, suppose we have no way of knowing whether inhabitants of civilizations we discover are the builders of the civilizations or simulations the builders made before departing en masse.

24. I am indebted to Hartry Field for clarification on this point.

25. I am indebted to Sylvain Bromberger, Hartry Field, Jerry Fodor, David Hills, Paul Horwich, Bill Lycan, Georges Rey, and David Rosenthal for their detailed comments on one or another earlier draft of this paper. Parts of the earlier versions were read at Tufts University, Princeton University, University of North Carolina at Greensboro, and SUNY at Binghamton.

References

Armstrong, D. *A materialist theory of mind*. London: Routledge & Kegan Paul, 1968.

Bever, T. The cognitive basis for linguistic structures. In J. R. Hayes (Ed.), *Cognition and the development of language*. New York: Wiley, 1970.

Block, N. *Physicalism and theoretical identity*. Unpublished doctoral thesis, Harvard University, 1971.

Block, N. Are absent qualia impossible? forthcoming.

Block, N. & Fodor, J. What psychological states are not. *Philosophical Review*, 1972, 81, 159-81.

Boyd, R. Materialism without reductionism. In N. J. Block (Ed.), *Readings in philosophy of psychology*. New York: Crowell, forthcoming, 1978.

Chisholm, Roderick. *Perceiving*. Ithaca: Cornell University Press, 1957.

Cummins, R. Functional analysis. *Journal of Philosophy*, 1975, 72, 741-64.

Davidson, D. Mental events. In L. Swanson & J. W. Foster (Eds.), *Experience and theory*. Amherst, University of Massachusetts Press, 1970.

Dennett, D. *Content and consciousness*. London: Routledge & Kegan Paul, 1969.

Dennett, D. Why the law of effect won't go away. *Journal for the Theory of Social Behavior*, 1975, 5, 169-87.

Dennet, D. A cognitive theory of consciousness. This volume, Ch. 10.

Dennett, D. Why a computer can't feel pain. In *Synthese*, forthcoming. This article as well as the two preceding articles are to be reprinted in a collection of Dennett's papers: *Metapsychology: Essays in the philosophy of mind and psychology*, Montgomery, Vt.: Bradford, 1978.

Feldman, F. Kripke's argument against materialism. *Philosophical Studies*, 1973; 416-19.

Field, H. *Mental representation*. Erkentniss, forthcoming.

Field, H. Conventionalism and instrumentalism in semantics. *Nous*, 1975, 9, 375-405.

Fodor, J. Explanations in psychology. In M. Black (Ed.), *Philosophy in America*, London: Routledge & Kegan Paul, 1965.

Fodor, J. *Psychological explanation*. New York: Random House, 1968a.

Fodor, J. The appeal to tacit knowledge in psychological explanation. *Journal of Philosophy*, 1968b, 65, 627-40.

Fodor, J. Special sciences. *Synthese*, 1974, 28, 97-115.

Fodor, J. *The language of thought*. New York: Crowell, 1975.

Fodor, J., Bever, T. & Garrett, M. *The psychology of language*. New York: McGraw-Hill, 1974.

Fodor, J. & Garrett, M. Some syntactic determinants of sentential complexity. *Perception and Psychophysics*, 1967, 2, 289-96.

Gendron, B. On the relation of neurological and psychological theories: A critique of the hardware thesis. In R. C. Buck and R. S. Cohen (Eds.), *Boston studies in the philosophy of Science VIII*. Dordrecht: Reidel, 1971.

Grice, H. P. Method in philosophical psychology (from the banal to the bizarre). *Proceedings and Addresses of the American Philosophical Association*, 1975.

Gunderson, K. *Mentality and machines*. Garden City: Doubleday Anchor, 1971.

Harman, G. *Thought*. Princeton: Princeton University Press, 1973.

Hempel, C. Reduction: Ontological and linguistic facets. In S. Morgenbesser, P. Suppes & M. White (Eds.), *Essays in honor of Ernest Nagel*. New York: St. Martin's Press, 1970.

Kalke, W. What is wrong with Fodor and Putnam's functionalism? *Nous*, 1969, 3, 83-93.

Kim, J. Phenomenal properties, psychophysical laws, and the identity theory. *The Monist*, 1972, 56(2), 177-92.

Kripke, S. Naming and necessity. In D. Davidson & G. Harman (Eds.), *Semantics and natural language*. Dordrecht: Reidel, 1972.

Kuhn, T. The Function of measurement in modern physical science. *Isis*, 1961, 52(8), 161-93.

Lewis, D. An argument for the identity theory. *Journal of Philosophy*, 1966, 63, 1. Reprinted (with new footnotes) in D. Rosenthal (Ed.), *Materialism and the mind-body problem*. Englewood Cliffs: Prentice Hall, 1971. Page references are to the reprinted version.

Lewis, D. Review of *Art, mind and religion*. *Journal of Philosophy*, 1969, 66, 23-35.

Lewis, D. How to define theoretical terms. *Journal of Philosophy*, 1970, 67, 427-44.

Lewis, D. Psychophysical and theoretical identifications. *Australasian Journal of Philosophy*, 1972, 50(3), 249-58.

Locke, D. *Myself and others*. Oxford: Oxford University Press, 1968.

Lycan, W. Mental States and Putnam's Functionalist Hypothesis. *Australasian Journal of Philosophy*, 1974, 52, 48-62.

Melzack, R. *The puzzle of pain*. New York: Basic Books, 1973.

Minsky, M. *Computation*. Englewood Cliffs: Prentice-Hall, 1967.

Mucciolo, L. F. The identity thesis and neuropsychology. *Nous*, 1974, 8, 327-42.

Nagel, T. The boundaries of inner space. *Journal of Philosophy*, 1969, 66, 452-58.

Nagel, T. Armstrong on the mind. *Philosophical Review*, 1970, 79, 394-403.

Nagel, T. Review of Dennett's *Content and consciousness*. *Journal of Philosophy*, 1972, 50, 220-34.

Nagel, T. What is it like to be a bat? *Philosophical Review*, 1974, 83, 435-50.

Nelson, R. J. Behaviorism is false. *Journal of Philosophy*, 1969, 66, 417-52.

Nelson, R. J. Behaviorism, finite automata & stimulus response theory. *Theory and Decision*, 1975, 6, 249-67.

Oppenheim, P. and Putnam, H. Unity of science as a working hypothesis. In H. Feigl, M. Scriven & G. Maxwell (Eds.), *Minnesota studies in the philosophy of science II*. Minneapolis: University of Minnesota Press, 1958.

Pitcher, G. *A theory of perception*. Princeton: Princeton University Press, 1971.

Putnam, H. Brains and behavior. 1963. Reprinted as are all Putnam's articles referred to here (except "On properties") in *Mind, language and reality; philosophical papers*, Vol. 2). London: Cambridge University Press, 1975.

Putnam, H. The mental life of some machines. 1966.

Putnam, H. The nature of mental states. (This was originally published under the title *Psychological Predicates*.) 1967.

Putnam, H. On properties. In *Mathematics, matter and method; philosophical papers*, Vol. 1. London: Cambridge University Press, 1970.

Putnam, H. Philosophy and our mental life. 1975a.

Putnam, H. The meaning of 'meaning'. 1975b.

Rorty, R. Functionalism, machines and incorrigibility. *Journal of Philosophy*, 1972, 69, 203-20.

Scriven M. *Primary philosophy*. New York: McGraw-Hill, 1966.

Sellars, W. Empiricism and the philosophy of mind. In H. Feigl & M. Scriven (Eds.), *Minnesota studies in the philosophy of science I*. Minneapolis: University of Minnesota Press, 1956.

Sellars, W. *Science and metaphysics*. (Ch. 6). London: Routledge & Kegan Paul, 1968.

Shoemaker, S. Functionalism and qualia. *Philosophical studies*, 1975, 27, 271-315.

Shoemaker, S. Embodiment and behavior. In A. Rorty (Ed.), *The identities of persons*. Berkeley: University of California Press, 1976.

Shallice, T. Dual functions of consciousness. *Psychological Review*, 1972, 79, 383-93.

Smart, J. J. C. Reports of immediate experience. *Synthese*, 1971, 22, 346-59.

Wiggins, D. Identity, designation, essentialism, and physicalism. *Philosophia*, 1975, 5, 1-30.

Tryouts toward the Production of Thought

This paper explores what we might mean by terms like "sense," "perceive," "know," "consciousness," "self," "short-term memory," "analog," "schema" and "cognitive model," by trying to find what they refer to in actual computer programs. The different types of systems for perception are briefly surveyed, to indicate structures that they must have in common. Then more wholistic cognitive systems are described.

One system (Uhr, 1975a, b, 1976a) called a SEER[1] attempts to handle simultaneously all the cognitive processes—including perception, remembering, deductive problem-solving, language processing, acting, and learning—that are usually studied separately by psychologists and computer scientists. SEERs are first attempts to develop well-integrated wholistic cognitive systems that are designed to do a variety of things, albeit drably (much as most human beings go about their everyday tasks of thinking), rather than one particular difficult thing well (like chess or proving theorems). They are therefore required to decide what type of thing to do, and when, and to choose, organize, integrate, and orchestrate the sets of cognitive transforms needed to carry out the chosen actions, cutting across the separate cognitive systems.

RATIONALE

Our problem is the development of a science of information-processing entities, a science coordinate with physics—the science of matter/energy. Psychology and the building of "artificial intel-

Note: The author's research described in this paper was partially supported by the National Science Foundation and the University of Wisconsin Graduate School.

ligences" will someday be viewed as the natural and artifactual applications of our science, just as geology and engineering are today viewed as the natural and artifactual applications of physics. Therefore I shall treat the "modeling of intelligent thinking entities" and "artificial intelligence" (or "simulation") as one and the same science. That we act as though we have two separate sciences is just another indication of how primitive our present science is. Think what geology or engineering would be like without any science of physics.

Our problem is not to simulate all the details of human thought, or to direct all the power of the computer's speed and size to specific peculiarly well-suited intellectual tasks, but to increase our understanding of the processes whereby a system comes to perceive, know, understand, manipulate, and interact fruitfully with its larger world. We then can particularize our general model into specific models, for example, of ants or humans. (But remember, this process is not as simple as it sounds. Even physics progresses fruitfully; applications often must be handled by cookbooks, not by theoretical analysis. So it is with our science.)

I think most workers in the field would reject this view, if only because it suggests that our problems are huge and that we have hardly begun to solve them. But we shall never solve our problems by evading them. We must take the proper path, and we may turn out to be luckier than we think. Perhaps we shall find the path to be short or discover that we have already come a longer way.

Some Prototypical Approaches to Perception

Some forty years ago, in a society of physicists and physiologists, I proposed for discussion the question, why geometrically similar figures were optically similar. I remember quite well the attitude taken with regard to this question, which was accounted not only superfluous, but even ludicrous. Nevertheless, I am now as strongly convinced as I was then that this question involves the whole problem of form-vision. That a problem cannot be solved which is not recognized as such is clear. In this non-recognition, however, is manifested, in my opinion, that one-sided mathematico-physical direction of thought, which alone accounts for the opposition (Mach, 1906, p. 109).[2]

"Perception" refers to the gathering of relevant information: information that is usually (but not always) about objects, and objects that are important enough to have been ennobled with names. As William James suggests, "the consciousness of particular material things present to sense is nowadays called perception" (1950, Vol. 2, p. 76). Thus pattern recognition is probably the central purpose of perception. Often the object must be further described, especially to record its unusual qualities and its missing or aberrant parts. Often a whole scene—that is, the interrelations among several objects—must be described.

Let us briefly survey the approaches that have been taken to perception. The perception systems devised thus far have often had their greatest success in recognizing or describing particular types of objects—e.g. letters, or chromosomes, or polyhedra. (See Duda and Hart, 1973, and Uhr, 1973a, 1974 for recent surveys.) These systems have a common basic structure that may help illuminate what we mean by the terms "sense," "perceive," "sense-data," and "know." The various systems are described below.

(A) A *TEMPLATE* system (Figure 1a) stores a complete and detailed representation of each possible scene that might be input to it (e.g., Hannan, 1962). It matches each new input scene with stored "templates" until it finds an exact match, and then outputs the string of symbols (which might be a name like "B" or "TABLE" or "DACHSHUND" or "DOG" or "JOE") associated with the matching template.

(B) An *IMAGE* system (Figure 1b) stores a set of "typical" representations of possible scenes. These might be prototype templates, or they might be "probability contour maps" or other ways of describing "typical" or "prototypical" or "average" scenes (e.g., Baran & Estrin, 1960, Highleyman, 1962). The system computes the "similarity" between a new input scene and each of the stored "images." ("Similarity" is an obscure and complex concept and many measures have been used. One measure correlates the values stored in each cell of the probability contour map, stored for each possible image, with the values at corresponding cells in the input.) The system outputs the name associated with the image judged most similar to the input scene.

(C) Serial *DISCRIMINATION* nets (Figure 2b) apply a series of tests to the input (e.g., Unger, 1959; Naylor, 1971). Each test

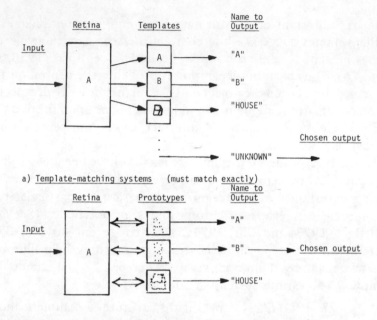

a) <u>Template-matching systems</u>   (must match <u>exactly</u>)

b) <u>Systems that measure "similarity" to stored prototype "images"</u>

Figure 1. Perceivers that use templates and prototypes

determines which test to apply next, until the name to output is finally implied. This is the technique typically used for programs for "concept formation" (e.g., Hunt, 1962; Kochen, 1961; Towster, 1970). But it has had little success in pattern recognition, because it depends upon perfect tests that never make mistakes, whereas real-world patterns are so variable that their properties cannot be so easily captured. This weakness can be remedied by having a whole set of transforms make a probabilistic choice, or using a powerful algorithm, at each node. But that turns such a system into a structural perceiver, as discussed below.

(D)   *FEATURE DETECTION* systems look for features and merge the possible name or names associated with each successfully found feature into a list of possibilities (Figure 2a) (e.g., Doyle, 1960; Munson, 1968). The most highly implied possibility is chosen and output. The system can use one, a few,

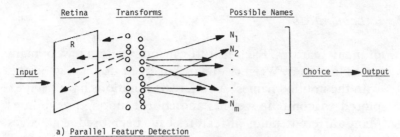

a) Parallel Feature Detection

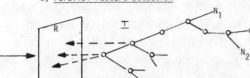

b) Serial Discrimination Net

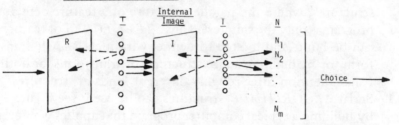

c) 2 Layer

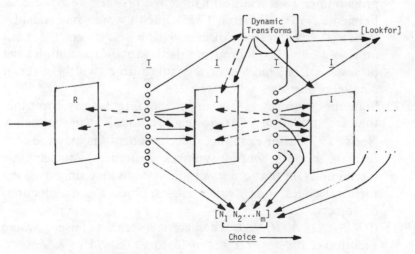

d) A Parallel-Serial Structural

System where Names as well as internal images can be implied at any layer, along with things to lookfor and dynamically implied transforms to apply, in glancing about.

Figure 2. Some structures of perception systems

or many features. Each feature can imply one, a few, or many possible names. Weights might, but need not, be associated with the implied names. A variety of functions have been explored to combine weights and choose among possibilities. Many different kinds of features have been used; e.g., edges, cavities, curves, angles, contours, loops, enclosures, area, center of gravity, dispersion. Different systems use different combinations of these features, chosen carefully to handle the types of patterns (e.g., printed letters, chromosomes, X-rays, aerial photos) the system must recognize.

(E)   A feature can also be a whole set, a whole configuration, of features. And features can be embedded in a variety of larger structures, where the parallel structure of a feature-detector program is only the simplest. Thus *STRUCTURES* of features can be built, and looked for, either within each single transform, or by building larger structures of transforms, or both. I shall mention three roughly different kinds of structures.

(E.1)   Serial *ALGORITHMIC* structures can be used (see Figure 3) by building a typical computer program that applies whatever functions, and makes whatever interspersed decisions, the programmer feels will best handle the problem (e.g., Brice & Fennema, 1970; Winston, 1975). Such a system has, roughly, the serial structure of a discrimination net, except that each node is a complex subroutine that embodies a complex set of tests. Often, hidden in this subroutine, will be a set of parallel processes.

(E.2)   Sometimes processes are organized into large subroutines that are applied in *STAGES* (e.g., Reddy, Erman, Fennell & Neely, 1973). For example, speech recognizers may look for formats, phones, words, syntactic structures, and semantic interactions, in that order. Vision systems may similarly look for local edges, long strokes, angles, objects, and collections of objects.

(E.3)   *CONFIGURATIONAL* characterizers can be used, where each looks for a whole set of features (e.g., Uhr & Vossler, 1963; Zobrist, 1971). And these can be structured into larger configurations, whether layered, hierarchical, heterarchical, or any other architecture (e.g., Uhr, 1972, 1973b, 1976b;

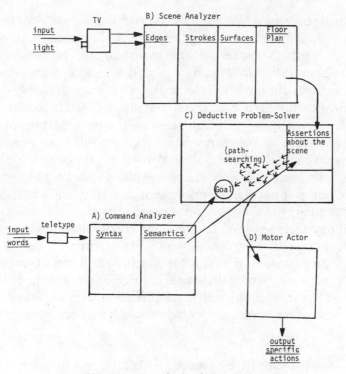

Figure 3. A typical robot system

Williams, 1975; Riseman & Hanson, 1974). Whereas the feature-detector builds one list of possibilities from which an overall choice is made, a configurational system builds many lists, both intermediate and final (see Figures 2c, 2d, and 4 for a few examples), and makes choices from each of these lists. And a wide variety of different inner- and outer-directed processes thus become possible, increasing the likelihood of power and success, and also the problems in finding good systems.

Simple templates are obviously impossible with real-world patterns that vary in unknown nonlinear ways. Far too many templates would be needed for all the variants, and the system would never be able to handle a slightly different new variant without being given a template for it. Image systems do not seem to work very well, but that may be because we do not have a very good grasp of how to compute "similarity" between complex patterns. I suspect that the right way is to break the pattern down into strokes and other features. But that turns the image system into a feature-detecting system.

The systems that use more complex structures probably do the best job. But the particular set of transforms used is probably the most important factor in the success of the system. It is not at all clear what types of structure are most powerful. Most researchers today seem to prefer deterministic algorithms, although I think that probabilistic configurations are more like the brain's network of neurons and give much more promise of flexibility and adaptability. Unfortunately, there are as yet no experimental comparisons to settle the issue. Inner-directed "glancing about" becomes increasingly important with complex scenes. Serial algorithms can be carefully pre-programmed to do this for specific small sets of known-in-advance patterns. But parallel-serial configurations should do better over a wide variety of unanticipated patterns, although very likely at the cost of occasional errors that could have been avoided if anticipated.

Wholistic Cognitive Systems: Piecemeal and Integrated

Where the sign and what it suggests are both concretes which have been coupled together on previous occasions, the inference is common to both brutes and men, being really nothing more than association by contiguity. . . . Our "perceptions," or recognitions of what objects are before us, are inferences of this kind. . . .

In reasoning we pick out essential qualities.

Let us make this ability to deal with NOVEL data the technical differentia of reasoning. . . . Reasoning may then be very well defined as the substitution of parts and their implications for consequences or wholes (James, 1950, Vol. 2, pp. 326-30).

This idea [central to Buddhist logic] is that our knowledge has two heterogeneous sources, Sensibility and Understanding. Sensibility is a direct reflex of reality. The understanding creates concepts which are but indirect reflexes of reality. Pure sensibility is only the very first moment of a fresh sensation, the moment x. In the measure in which this freshness fades away, the intellect begins to "understand." Understanding is judgment. Judgment is x = A where x is sensibility and A is understanding. Inference, or syllogism, is an extended judgment, $x = A + A^1$. The x is now the subject of the minor premise. It continues to represent sensibility. The $A + A^1$ connection is the connection of the Reason with the Consequence. This reason . . . is divided in only two varieties, the reason of Identity and the reason of Causation (Stcherbatsky, 1962, p. 545).

I shall briefly describe some of the things that today's wholistic systems can do, with emphasis on the integrated SEER systems I have been developing.

TOWARD MODELING ORDINARY EVERYDAY INTELLIGENCE

Most of us human beings spend most of our time doing very ordinary things, things that, I suggest, are of the essence of intelligence. We constantly make complex decisions that take into account an enormous variety of relevant information. These decisions are designed to maximize our satisfactions, achieve a variety of goals, and avoid many anticipated and unanticipitaed dangers and pitfalls. But they are about ordinary and obvious things, and on the surface they may appear too mundane to glorify with the term "intelligence."

These include such things as deciding when, where, and what to eat; deciding how to get the food to our mouths (e.g., go to a restaurant, phone a friend, scream "ma-ma," or make it ourselves). We similarly decide what to do during a vacation, or during the evening; what to talk about with a friend; how to respond to a comment. Even ordinary perception uses a mixture of remembered and deduced information, as when we plan how to carve a turkey, or deal with a traffic cop.

These activities sound far simpler than proving a theorem, or playing a middling game of chess, or extracting cube roots. But they are far more difficult to program, and we are only beginning to get a grasp on the problem. We must get the computer to assess relevance, to take only small relevant subsets of large bodies of information into account, to decide in a flexible manner what type of process to effect next (given a continuing contextual interaction from the rich variety of pertinent information that the system attempts to gather as it surveys its external environment and its internal memory stores).

"ARTIFICIAL INTELLIGENCE" ROBOTS

Several robots have been programmed—notably at MIT (Winston, 1972), Stanford (Feldman, et al., 1971), and SRI (Nilsson, 1969)—to (a) input, parse, and "understand" a command teletyped in simple English, (b) sense and describe a room containing several cubes, wedges, platforms, and pyramids, as viewed by a television camera, (c) deduce how to carry out the command on the perceived objects, and (d) actually compose and effect the necessary motor actions. Each of these four major processes is handled by a separate (very large) program, with a minimum of information passed from one program to another.

Commands that have been successfully understood and carried out include the following (see Fikes & Nilsson, 1971):

ROBOT GATHER BOXES (the robot must deduce the sequence: MOVETO BOXA; PUSH BOXA BOXB; MOVETO BOXC; PUSH BOXC BOXB)

ROBOT TOUCH PYRAMID (the pyramid rests on a platform. If a wedge is pushed so its high edge is next to the platform, the robot can roll up the wedge and onto the platform, turn, and roll to the pyramid. Therefore the robot must deduce the sequence: MOVETO WEDGE; PUSH WEDGE PLATFORM: MOVETO LOC(I) (up the wedge and onto the platform); TURN 90° RIGHT: MOVETO PYRAMID.)

A scene analysis program converts the television image into local edges, long straight edges, angles, contours, objects, and, finally, a floor plan of the recognized objects in the room. Some of this information is extracted and converted into a set of logical assertions that are passed on to the problem-solver, as grist for its deductive mill. The typed command is analyzed by a separate language "understanding" program, and used to describe the needed solution and start the problem-solver on its task of finding a solution-path.

Thus an extremely complex set of programs applies a pre-programmed set of stages to the various aspects of the problem. Information is first obtained from the perceived scene and the understood command and then passed to the problem-solver. Everything that the problem-solver might need to know must be anticipated in advance. The problem-solver does not call on the perceptual system to look for new objects that might serve in a conjectured solution.

The sequence of actions to effect a solution is worked out in advance, and then effected without any perceptual feedback.

WHOLISTIC INTEGRATED "SEER" SYSTEMS

According to the analysis of the psyche rendered by the Sāṅkhya, and taken for granted in the disciplines of Yoga, man is "active" (kartar) through the five "organs of action" and "receptive" (bhoktar) through the five "organs of perception." These two sets of five are the vehicles, respectively, of his spontaneity and receptivity. They are known as the "faculties working outward" (Bahyendriya) and function as so many gates and doors, while "intellect" (manas), "egoity" (ahankara), and "judgment" (buddhi) stand as the doorkeepers. The latter three, taken together, constitute the so-called "inner organ" (antahkarana); they are the powers that open and close the gates—inspecting, controlling, and registering whatever is carried through.

The body is described as a town or kingly palace in which the king dwells inactive (according to the Oriental style) amidst the activities of his staff. For the human mind, with its contents and wisdom, is conditioned, in every specific case, by the peculiar balance of the gunas [activities] within the character and disposition of the given individual. His ideas, beliefs, and insights, and even the things that he sees around him, are, finally, but the functions or reflexes of his particular manner of not-knowing-better (Zimmer, 1956, p. 317).

In my own work I have been trying to develop simpler, more general and better integrated, wholistic systems. One of these—the SEER system—is described later; capital letters refer to processes or lists used. (See Uhr, 1975 a, b, 1976 a, b for fuller descriptions.)

Briefly, the SEER system looks for hierarchical Structures of Configurations (see Figure 4). It successively transforms a scene input to its "retina,"extracting, abstracting, coalescing, compounding, until all implied possibilities are finally merged back into a single "CENTRAL" cell upon which more central cognitive transforms (called "IDEAS") continue to act. The perceptual subsystem has the overall architecture of a many-layered cone that gives a parallel-serial hierarchical structure to its set of transforms. Transforms are implied from within, by desired expectations, actions, and objects, as well as from without, by the external scene and relevant information extracted from it so far. These dynamically implied transforms are all merged into the GLANCE list, which is applied along with fixed transforms.

The fixed transforms reside at all locations at all levels of depth

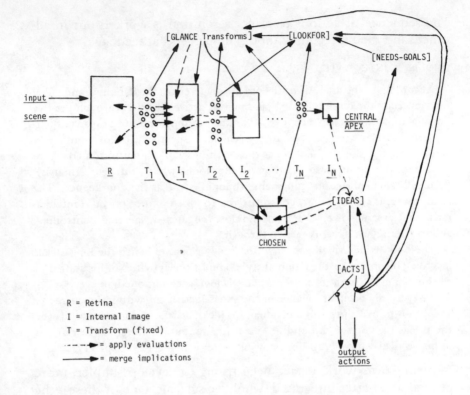

The single general type of transform means that any process can call on, and imply information into, any other process.

Variant systems merge all choices into the CENTRAL APEX, others into the separate CHOSEN list. The IDEAS are applied to either, or both, as appropriate.

Figure 4. A wholistic integrated "SEER" system

of the cone (depth comes in layers, but this is only for convenience, and to model living systems—it need not). Each successful transform merges its implied images and names into the corresponding cell at the next layer, finally achieving the grand merge into the CENTRAL apex. Implied transforms to apply and things to look for are merged into the appropriate lists. Choices among possibilities are made in the CENTRAL apex; but choices can also be made in any of the other cells, since among the things that a transform can

imply is the decision to choose, in a specified cell, among a specified class of possibilities.

Thus there are many nodes where things are looked for and processes are applied (we might consider calling these nodes of "awareness") and many cells at which decisions are made. (When would
we want to consider these nodes and cells as loci for "consciousness"
or "conscious choice?")

I am ignoring a number of other important features, and much
detail, describing only what seems relevant to the issues examined
in this chapter.

The cognitive transforms that look at the CENTRAL list are of
two general types: (a) links and pointers into a network of information stored in memory (that is, for remembering), and (b) deductions, computations, and other stored information and/or processes of the sort we normally call deductive problem-solving.

The single most highly weighted transform in the IDEAS list is
applied to the CENTRAL apex. If it succeeds (that is, enough of
the tests it specifies are passed so that its threshold for success is
reached), its implied associations and deductions are merged into
CENTRAL, implied transforms to apply are merged into IDEAS
and also into the list of GLANCE transforms to apply to the external scene, and implied acts are merged into an ACTS list. Thus perception, remembering, and deduction all intermingle, helping and
calling upon one another. When an ACT is chosen (see Uhr, 1975a, b
for details of how this is effected in a system that handles a static
scene, and 1975d in an extended system that begins to interact with
scenes of objects that move about and change over time), the system generates a specific sequence of actions needed to effect that
act, binding each action with specific objects that have been perceived. This in turn calls for more perception and/or cognition, by
implying further things to LOOKFOR, which in turn imply further
GLANCE transforms to apply.

A number of variant systems have been coded, to explore the
possible interactions among the various processes. One of these uses
a list of HYPOTHESES to give more coherence and direction to
the act. Now needs, goals, and expectations imply "hypotheses"
that, if acted upon, might lead to their satisfaction. The system
chooses the most highly implied hypothesis, which in turn implies

acts upon types of objects, which the system looks for, or thinks about in order to arrive at alternative courses of action. The hypothesis also lists expected intermediate and final consequences, intermediate and final consequences, including feedback and need-satisfactions. These now serve to keep the act moving in the desired direction toward the goal, and to set the system to look for confirming or disconfirming evidence to use in assessing the hypothesis.

Perceptual transforms must also handle language. Real-world organisms have no special input channel, like the robots' teletype, for referential information. And that is inevitable, unless we establish artificially simplified relations between the knower and its environment. For signs, symbols, words, commands, suggestions, descriptions, and any kind of language are part of the single environment, and must be input through sensory channels, like eyes and ears, in mixed scenes of words, objects, and other things. Thus, for example, local edges will compound and grow into longer edges; then into several joined edges, or contours; then into larger wholes like a table top, window, tree, or (the letter) D; then into larger wholes like table, house, forest, (the word) DOG. Then DOG might imply such things as "animal" and "bark," and also some perceptual characterizers that will be applied to the successive images of the scene to try to find the object-dog that has been suggested by this recognized word-dog. If "LOOK FOR THE DOG" or "POINT TO THE DOG" is recognized as a larger structure over DOG and the other similarly recognized related words, then the perceptual characterizers needed to recognize and find a dog will be implied with very strong weights.

It would be hard—I suspect impossible—to draw a line in the SEER system where perception ends and remembering and ideation begin. For such a system compounds and associates to higher-level wholes and more abstract classes, qualities, and other concepts. Nor can we reasonably separate language processing from perceptual processing. It therefore seems crucial to use a single general type of transform to handle all aspects of the system's processes. Consequently, the same general transform type is used for memory associations, deductive processes, and also perceptual and linguistic processes.

The system must further decide what type of act to effect—whether to *name* a recognized object, *describe* the input scene, *answer* a question, *solve* a posed problem, *find* and *touch* a particular object, or *find*, *touch*, and *move* one object to another. These it does in very primitive and simple-minded ways. But the important point is that it must be able to choose among a variety of acts, in response to a variety of cognitive problems. It must itself decide which is the appropriate *type* of thing to do. It must also decide *when to decide* this, since there is no fixed sequence of steps to its processes. It must be able to use a mixture of its different types of processes in order to amass the relevant information, decide that it has done so, and therefore choose and effect the appropriate consequent actions.

Finally, these processes are not simply a function of the perceived scene of objects and commands. Rather, the system also has internal needs and goals which imply acts that might serve them and objects that might be needed for these acts, either as tools (e.g., a stick to reach), or as objects (e.g., the banana to eat). These needs and goals also imply classes of things, and particular things, to LOOKFOR, and characterizing transforms to GLANCE at the scene to effect that perceptual process. The transforms implied by needs and goals merge with transforms implied by transforms that have been implied so far, e.g., by partially recognized things. Thus the presses of needs, goals, and expectations from within and from prior percepts serve to direct processing, along with the presses of input from the outer world.

What Seems Necessary to Intelligent Systems?

In answering this question let us look first at perceptual systems, in which several basic structures are present in almost all programs, and then at the wholistic cognitive systems.

ASPECTS OF PERCEPTION

The raw image of the scene must be input to the system, to be stored as a digital iconlike representation in a first "retinal" input buffer. Then characterizing transforms must be applied. In the simplest whole-template systems, the first transform that succeeds will imply the chosen name. In simple parallel systems, characterizing feature-detectors will immediately imply possible names to assign to the input. In the simplest serial systems each transform will imply which transform to apply next. In more sophisticated parallel-serial systems each transform will imply several possible kinds of things, including internal images, new transforms to apply, possible names to choose, and triggers to choose.

In all cases we find a structure consisting of (a) the retinal input image, and (b) the chosen names (or set of names, or description). This structure suggests that we call the retinal input the "sensed image" and the final choice of name or description the "percept."

Almost any system that perceives with any degree of power also transforms the raw sensed input into successively more abstract internal images and makes one or more choices among alternative possibilities. We might want to equate the whole set of internal images (probably including the retinal image) with "sense-data." And the places where choices are made might be considered as very low-level and primitive loci of "awareness." Those loci where names or other elements of the descriptions are chosen might be considered loci where perception is achieved.

In a system that successively transforms the image by smoothing, filling gaps, enhancing edges, and building larger wholes, we have an example of the active constructive processes that tend toward object constancy. If the system further describes a recognized image by outputting elements of an internally stored description of an object-class, as well as a description of the characteristics actually perceived in this particular sensed instance, we begin to get the flavor of the higher-level kinds of construction found in human perception, where major distortions or missing parts are regularized or filled in during perception and thus not noticed by the perceiver.

"KNOWING," BELIEVING," AND "KNOWING THAT"

In a wholistic system the output of the perceiver is not a name or description printed by a teletype, but a piece of internal information used by other cognitive processes within the system to access or deduce related information. We might consider saying that the larger system "knows" what the perceiving subsystem tells it; or, if weights or probabilities are associated with the parts of the output of perception, that it "believes" with a certain degree of certainty.

There is some inclination to say that the perceiving subsystem itself "knows" what it perceives, to the extent that the term "know" carries connotations of an "ego" or "locus of consciousness" identical with the knower. One might for this reason want to equate "knowing" with the larger system into which the perceptual subsystem outputs. Thus in the SEER systems we might say that the IDEAS list of transforms, which looks at the CENTRAL list of chosen names and descriptive information, "knows."

Would we be inclined to say that the system "knows" if it rarely, or even never, outputs the correct answer to a question or the correct name for a pattern? Or would we ask for a high percentage of correct responses over a whole sequence of problems? Or would we insist that all responses be correct (but we would not do that with humans)?

These criteria would force us to say that any simple program that accesses any kind of data base "knows" the accessed information. For example, the system might access the addresses of anybody who filed an income tax return, doing it in the most stupid and "unknowing" ways, e.g., by matching the name in question with every name in memory until a match was found.

We might insist that the thing known be in some sense worth knowing, and that the knowing of it be a major achievement, and that the process of coming to know it be done in the "right way." These are extremely stringent requirements. And to traditional psychologists they will appear impossible to satisfy; for how can we look inside a living mind/brain to see whether it does things "in the right way?" But in fact this set of requirements is too easily satisfied, e.g., by programs for arithmetic. Such programs do indeed add, multiply, or extract roots in the right way, according to any of the procedures that we humans use (because we learned them in school). Arithmetic is worth knowing; the answers are indeed computed and generated, not stored; and a sequence of 10-digit multiplications is a major achievement.

These considerations seem to force us to accept a definition of (primitive) knowing that, like our definition of perceiving, will include many clearly unintelligent, uninteresting systems. And it forces us to consider higher-level aspects of the system, ones that we might want to insist must be present for more complex, powerful, and interesting kinds of knowing.

Interesting issues arise in trying to distinguish between "believing" and "knowing" in terms of the certainty of such systems choices. Suppose we stipulate that a system knows only if its choices are 100 percent certain, or certain beyond some unacceptable margin of error. Then we are forced to say that probabilistic systems believe rather than know—unless we find in or give to such systems routines that convert beliefs into certainty, in which case the system would, I think, be self-delusional in an important sense.

A second more straightforward alternative is to identify the knower with a special subsystem. This amounts to saying that the system does not know its answer, or know that its answer is right, unless the system contains some subject (ego) separate from the subsystem that actually achieved that answer, that accepts the answer as in its judgment right, certifying and outputting it. The difficulty with this second alternative is that the question-answerer or arithmetic unit has many more guarantees of the correctness of its answer than does the "ego" (which might merely be a program that prints out payroll checks) that later looks at the answer to check that it is right. For what could the ego do? It might itself check the answer—recomputing possibly in some different way; thus it would then be, or use, just another arithmetic unit. Or it might simply know that its arithmetic unit is correct in the way that a computer knows each of its processors is correct; then we might better call this "knowing" blind absolute trust.

This is not to say that "knowing that" or a "self that knows" are not valid constructs. I think in fact they are necessary, and we already begin to see them exemplified in primitive form in systems that are required to make higher-level choices and flexibly decide what kinds of processes to effect. Such systems are always deciding, in effect, that "more must be known or done about this or that." The places where such decisions are made—especially if they are few, or singular—begin to have some of the features of a "knowing self" or ego which "knows that things are the case."

But it is interestingly paradoxical that this supposedly "higher" type of ego that "knows that" is not identical with the processor that knows or achieves the knowledge. Such an ego inevitably makes fallible judgments, judgments it is in a poorer position to make than the "lower-level" routines (very likely under its control) that actually did the dirty work of knowing. The ego is, therefore, something of an "illusion," to borrow an idea from Indian philosophy. (Or is it the judgment ("buddhi") that lies beneath the western ego of the persona?)

When might we also say that a system "knows that it knows?" Possibly the use of an expectation to guide its perceptual search for feedback about an hypothesis upon which it has acted is the germ.

ONE "ENDURING EGO" AND "CENTRAL CONSCIOUSNESS?"

These terms suggest a kind of ego and consciousness that are not easily exemplified in information-processing systems. An easy way to introduce their germ is to put the system under the control of an executive who decides at the highest level what to do next, like the executive in a separated problem-solving system who uses its set of heuristics to decide what step to take next in searching for a solution-path. The executive thus has the same structure as any other node where lists of things are compared and choices are made, and it is hard to see why it should be singled out as "the central consciousness." Dennett (this volume) points out how difficult it is to examine one's consciousness and suggests, "we have access— conscious access—to the *results* of mental processes, but not to the processes themselves" (p. 217). I am inclined to call this consciousness of which we are aware "central consciousness," as opposed to the far larger network of unconscious consciousnesses that permeates the mind/brain with points of judgments and choices.

Thus this central consciousness is hard to pinpoint and may be relatively unimportant in the network as a whole. Most thinking may well go on in unconscious consciousnesses. But there are many simple examples of conscious consciousness, as when we try to remember a phone number, do mental arithmetic, memorize a person's name, recall a name, or recall and reconstruct the layout of furniture in a familiar room. In such cases we are conscious of a structured set of information and we make a conscious effort to process this information. Even though most of the attendant processes still go on unconsciously—so that we are not conscious of the details, much less the neuronal events, that lead to the recognition or the recalling of a name—a central consciousness seems to be present, and seems more than just the slot where the answer appears. It seems reasonable to think of all choice nodes as loci of local consciousness. But some of these are more central than others, and if we construct our system with a single executive we get an obvious candidate for central consciousness.

The mind is at every stage a theatre of simultaneous possibilities. Consciousness consists in the comparison of these with each other, the selection of some, and the suppression of the rest by the reinforcing and inhibiting agency of attention. The highest and most elaborated mental products are filtered from the data chosen by the faculty next beneath, out of the mass offered by the faculty below that, which mass was sifted from a still larger amount of yet simpler material, and so on (James, 1950, Vol. 2, p. 288).

But I do not think this central consciousness will have much of the flavor of human consciousness without a good bit more—something that would give the system some subjective feeling (which could indeed have illusory aspects) that it is conscious, making a conscious effort, is consciously aware, is directing and choosing its processes consciously.

We tend to equate all these various aspects of consciousness with a central unified process, and one pretty much in control, as executive. But James's shifting unpredictable stream of consciousness is a better model. In this model the external press of the environment and the internal presses of more or less enduring needs, goals, plans, and expectations impinge upon and control all decisions. Although a system with a single executive may resemble the social structures we have found easiest to implement in business and political organizations, it is not necessarily the most efficient or productive. The succession of choices among many loci of consciousness may weave a unifying thread and thus replace the single executive. Nature may well evolve systems with several executives, or systems with no executives, in which different subsystems simply interact. In the parallel-serial probabilistic systems that nature seems to use, the fact that at some points choices are made may make it appear that the system has an executive. But there may well be only choice nodes, including the for each moment relatively final choices.

LOCI FOR "UNCONSCIOUS CONSCIOUSNESSES"

An obvious place to look for consciousness is at the point of heuristic serial choice and application of the transforms that have been merged into the IDEAS list to the CENTRAL store of implied and chosen things. At an even lower level, any locus of choice might be considered a local node of consciousness. Fairly global organization is given to a system when the chosen ACT controls what is to be done (whether to perceive, remember, or problem-solve; which problem to work on). Still more global organization is provided when a list of HYPOTHESES is used to handle not only information-processing but also the expectations that guide that processing— motor acts, perceptual consequences, and deductive processes, and also expectations of consequent feedback.

Thus we have several possible loci of possible conscious awareness: (1) at each transform's application; (2) at each and any locus of choice; (3) at the CENTRAL list, as looked at by the IDEAS list; (4) at the ACT that is being executed and therefore directs processing; and (5) at the HYPOTHESIS that controls all processes, binding them together by local expectations and using overall expectations to look forward to feedback. (6) Conscious awareness can also be attributed to a learning-controled system that has higher-level hypotheses to the effect "if this is learned, [I] will better be able to cope."

These loci are, of course, extremely conjectural (I think it is quite premature to take achieved systems seriously as in any way "conscious"). But they do posit precise and completely open lists and processes; and so it seems instructive to look at them in the larger context of the total program, see what roles they play, and begin to ask, in a precise way, what still needs doing, and how else consciousness could be modeled.

EGO, AND THE CONTINUITY OF SELF

But to ask that the observer should imagine himself as standing upon the sun instead of the earth [to see earth revolve around sun] is a mere trifle in comparison with the demand that he should consider the Ego to be nothing at all, and to resolve it into a transitory connexion of changing elements. (Note: Cp. the standpoint of Hume and Lichtenberg. For thousands of years past Buddhism has been approaching this conception from the practical side. Cp. Paul Carus, *the Gospel of Buddha*) (Mach, 1906, p. 356).

Ego, like central consciousness, might also be illusory. Quite possibly a hypothesis controls and guides actions and expectations for a while (maybe seconds, maybe hours or days), and then, or even interspersed, other hypotheses take over. But all these hypotheses will be related, like a loose family, in that they were learned to serve the same set of needs and goals in relation to a common set of experiences with a common environment. And they are all chosen because implied by the same set of transforms. Might that not be enough to give the rather vague feeling of continuity that leads us all to the (illusory?) conclusion that we have a continuing ego? "The ego must be given up. . . . Ego-consciousness can be of many different degrees and composed of a multitude of chance memories" (Mach, 1906, pp. 24-25).

In some sense there seems to be an observer of the above process, a "self-awareness" that has at least some "free will" and some impact on what the whole system does—e.g., whether it plays chess, bakes cakes, or sings—and seems to be observing, even savoring, the whole process. But all we have in our programs is the locus where the choice of hypotheses is made, and the related loci where prior choices that implied those hypotheses were made. Is there then a need for some highest-level processor that can search about to put that kind of information together, much as a special routine may well be needed to compose an "appropriate" description from the mass of potentially interesting descriptive information that perception implies? Such a processor would give the system the illusion of coherence and self-control; but what productive functions would it serve?

FEELINGS AND PROTEIN

If consciousness belongs to all protoplasm, by what mechanical constitution is this to be accounted for? . . . This question cannot be evaded or pooh-poohed. Protoplasm certainly does feel; and unless we are to accept a weak dualism, the property must be shown to arise from some peculiarity of the mechanical system. . . . It can never be explained, unless we admit that physical events are but degraded or undeveloped forms of psychical events (Peirce, 1971, vol. 6, pp. 172-73).

Primitive feelings, like hunger, pain, and redness, may well be the most troublesome problem of all. How can a program feel the sharp pinches of pain, or model the difference between a color-blind person, who always correctly understands that certain shades of for-him grey are actually red, and the person who feels the sensual power of the redness? We might argue that such primitive feelings are not necessary for intelligence; but it seems likely that their close relation with perception and with need-motivation will indeed make them necessary. In any case they exist, and it would seem strange to have a model of the mind/brain that could not encompass them.

To explain pain we might posit some complex overloading of information, some pervasive very high weight of implication from multiple sensory sources, both external and internal. Pain signals would thus be qualitatively stronger than and would override all other processes, and would seem overwhelmingly salient. Similarly, "redness" might be a rich welter of strong associations to a variety of sensory experiences. This suggests some complex of information, rather like that posited for consciousness and self. But I think the suggestion is even less satisfactory in the present context.

Alternately, we might say with Peirce that "protoplasm certainly does feel" (1931, vol. 6, p. 173), that these primitive feelings are simply qualities of protein. But what might that mean or entail? We could not have just protein sensors, for they would then have to send information to the nonprotein central computer, which would not be able to "feel." And a protein-based general-purpose computer would not have, at the level of its actual information-transforming processes, anything different from an electronic, mechanical, or optical computer, unless we made it a continuous analog computer.

SUMMARY

I think some perceptual processes are illuminated by today's programs. We can, if we wish, equate them with various parts of a recognizer. But it seems more useful to posit ever higher and more global levels of perceiving and knowing, rather than to insist that one function resides exactly here and another exactly there.

It may be premature to attribute awareness, feelings, consciousness, and self to any existing, or any conceivable, program. Until recently I had been inclined against such attributions at this early stage of our model building. But some suggestions for the various loci where choices are made seem intriguing. The most intriguing suggestion seems to me that these complex constructs may lie not at any single locus, but are subjective constructs from the complex set of processes that play back and forth over many nodes of awareness. This suggestion seems the most consonant with what psychology and neuroscience tell us about living mind/brains, and with intuition and introspection.

An alternate suggestion is that a single highest-level executive reflects and controls decisions. But even if such an executive did make all the decisions, what would give it an awareness and self-awareness of that, or a feeling of its own existence as a sentient ego?

"Iconic," "Short-Term," and "Long-Term" Memories

The first "retinal" input buffer seems a good candidate for iconic memory. It results from a transduction that minimally distorts the energy emitted from the scene to be perceived. It is as much a "picture" as a digital computer (or a living eye of discrete rods and cones) can receive and store. But it is important to note that, although the image is an icon of the actual scene, it has already been transformed into a discrete set of symbols. For that is all that a digital computer is capable of handling. Thus the "icon," along with any other possibly "analog" representations, is handled with a discretized approximation. Whether it is treated as an analog will now depend upon the procedures that transform and interpret it.

The internal buffers into which successful transforms merge their implications (including transformed and abstracted images) are all candidates for short-term memory (STM). All are a function of recently fired transforms. All must fade away relatively rapidly (unless reinforced because they continue to be salient) to make room for new information. Thus all the internal buffers at every layer of the perceptual cone—including the central apex and the lists of ideas to apply, things to look for, dynamic transforms to apply, and acts to effect—are short-term memories.

It may seem reasonable to think of perceptual memories as unconscious and to regard the central apex and ideas lists as what we ordinarily mean by short-term memory. But this would imply that we are subjectively aware of these stores and therefore give them special status. It would be more appropriate to call these stores STM that are also loci of attention. In any case it seems quite unreasonable to assume that there is only one STM involved in temporarily storing directions to a party, memorizing a date, or trying to remember a poem.

The perceptual transforms are an especially permanent part of long-term memory, rather than, as usually pictured, something rather different. They may differ from other parts of long-term memory by being more iconic or analogical (as is a feature-detector for an edge or a stroke, or a configurational characterizer of a set of parts composing a complex shape, such as a B, chair, or face). But they must be handled in the brain by the same substrate—a set of neurons. The use of a single general type of transform in SEER systems shows how we can at least begin to handle perceptual transforms in our programmed models.

Passive vs. Active; Outer- vs. Inner-Directed Perception

The typical pattern recognition system is frequently criticized as too passive, too determined by the sensed input. Minsky (1975) has proposed an inner directed use of "frames" (which, he notes, are quite similar to Bartlett's (1932) "schemata"). Vernon (1952) and Neisser (1976) have pointed out that human perception is usually active; we glance about, walk about, and conduct experiments, in a continuing attempt to achieve perceptual understanding.

But I think this criticism is unfair, since even in the earliest programs, pattern recognizers used inner-directed processes and schemata. Thus MacKay's (1956) early suggestion of "analysis through synthesis," taken up by Eden and Halle (1961) among others, essentially said: "dynamically build a structure that comprehends the input." Indeed, I think one of the best expressions of this suggestion is found in Sāṅkhya psychology of about the third century B.C.:

> The foremost point of the thinking principle, when meeting objects through the senses, assumes their form. Because of this the process of perception is one of perpetual self-transformation. The mind-stuff is compared, therefore, to melted copper, which when poured into a crucible assumes its form precisely (Zimmer, 1956, p. 288).

The inner-directed application of the "frame" (or "schema" or "map") was used in much the way that Minsky suggests by Grimsdale, Sumner, Tunis, and Kilburn (1959) ("turn the scene into a graph; then look for stored graphs in that representation"). It was also used by Marill, et al. (1963) in a more extreme way, since their system's search for features was entirely inner-directed and under control of the internal description of the object.

A further step is taken when new things to look for and transforms to apply are implied by what has been found and implied so far, as in Uhr's "flexible" systems (1973a, ch. 8). Now the system can begin to glance about, to entertain and follow up hypotheses. The SEER systems have needs, acts, cognitive associations and deductions that imply things into these dynamic lists of things to look for and transforms to apply, and thus achieve a rich contextual interaction of internally and externally implied processes. This, I suggest, is what is needed—a mixture of inner- and outer-directed processes, dynamically changing over time as a function of what has been perceived, thought of, and tried out so far.

Thus cognitive processes play an intimate role in perception. And once we put implied actions into the loop—so that, for example, the system moves itself physically to the right of an object in order to see it better, or rub it, rather than simply applying new visual characterizers to the right—perception will exhibit the motor aspects that Neisser emphasizes. The problem, then, becomes one of selecting the sources (outer or/and inner) of information that imply the transforms to apply and the set of processes (including motor actions) involved in the continuing perceptual loop.

Perception and Complexity

Do today's programs for perception really "perceive" the letter "B" or the "CHAIR" or the "DACHSHUND" that they *correctly* name? They certainly do something interesting, and rather difficult, something that we did not know how to do until we started coding such computer programs. And they share this capacity only with the higher animals. I do not think it is terribly important whether we call this capacity "perception" or "recognition" or "identification" or "classification." (I must mention that I do not think definitions serve much purpose except to point and orient.)

It seems very hard to distinguish between programs that do and do not perceive. Does a template program perceive? Even when it has only five or two templates or even one template? Does a card reader perceive? (Remember, the brush that finds the hole in the card is just a template.) Does the riverbed perceive the flowing water or the river? I think that on the usual definition of perception—on the gathering of information about external environment—we must attribute perception to all these things. We might try to grade perception, e.g., "trivial," "real," "realer," etc. Or we might try to construct a set of dimensions that underlies perception.

We can profitably examine the complexity of the precept. We can consider the number of alternate possible names that might be assigned to an input, or the number of combinations of names when the input is a scene that might contain several objects. Another dimension of complexity is the number of possible variants of each object—e.g., all the different bananas, or faces, or expressions on your mother's face. This within-object variability might be quite simple (e.g., when the object is rigid and a linear transformation suffices) or terribly complex (e.g., when the object can be distorted as though made of stretching rubber, or of crumbling and stretching rubber, or of a growing and learning system of muscles).

The interactions between within-object variability and across-object variability are crucial and complicate things further. A jug vs. a knife may be a rather easy distinction to make, even though there is an enormous variety of each. But consider distinguishing higher mammal A vs. higher mammal B from pictures of their faces with many different expressions. If the mammals are from a different race or species from the perceiver, the distinction becomes even more difficult, since relevant features are not as easily learned. And what if the mammals are sisters or identical twins? We can extend dimensionality here to include such things as depth, time, color, texture. On the one hand this may increase the complexity of the problem (the moving object must be tracked, the several color components combined). On the other hand it may simplify, since more information is input (the several moments, or colors).

If we increase the repertoire of possibles we further complicate: 10 numbers; 26 letters, thousands of faces; many thousands of words and objects. Such numbers necessitate, I think, a structure for our perceivers that successively builds larger and larger wholes, thereby reducing a single unmanageable task to an interlocking set of smaller tasks.

Thus we get into issues of the size and difficulty of the problems handled and the internal structure of our system. Here we enter into the scientific enterprise of building and evaluating a theory, for our system can best be taken as a theory of the set of scenes of objects that might be set in its view. So we must apply the familiar canons of hypothetico-deductive method: parsimony, generality, power, fruitfulness, elegance. (This raises another unsolved problem: for we do not yet know how to assess these terribly complex programs for their generality, elegance, or power, and we rarely try to evaluate the size, much less complexity, of the problems they attempt to handle, or the degree of success they attain.)

"General-Purpose" Computers, Analogs, and Discrete Approximations

Today's "general-purpose digital computers" are just enormously large and fast embodiments of the "universal Turing machine," which is a very general logistic system *plus* the specification of the actual procedures (the "machine") needed to effect transformations in that system. Church (1936), Kleene (1952), and Turing (1936) independently developed the lambda-calculus, recursive functions and Turing computable functions. These were quickly proved to be equivalent (see Kleene, 1952, Arbib, 1969). They are generally regarded as defining the broadest concept of effective calculation that can be used in developing a firm foundation for mathematics (and for thinking in general in the view of Turing and many scientists involved in getting computers to "think"—see, for example, Minsky, 1967, pp. 108-11).

And, despite a great deal of effort since, nobody has been able to define any broader concept of calculation except in terms of continuous, analog systems (which can be approximated with discrete digital representations).

Any of today's computers can, when given the proper program, carry out any set of describable processes that could be carried out by *any other* computer, whether hardware or software (although if the computer is too small, or slow, or inappropriately designed for the particular program, it may need more time than could ever be made available to it). But everything input to a computer must be expressed in sets of discrete symbols (e.g., a language, but also a graph, or an array like a television raster). And any internal representation, whether we call it "picture," "icon," "image," "schema," "map," "model," "semantic net," or something else with an analog flavor, is always represented as a discrete approximation.

Using the computer, then, entails the assumption that the mind/brain can be described by structures of discrete symbols. This seems a reasonable working assumption. And the variety of complex functions computers can effect is the largest possible set of functions. Therefore they give the psychologist the broadest possible range of potential theories and the greatest possible expressive power as a vehicle for describing his or her theories. And running the program actually tests its consequences.

But it is by no means certain that the computer is adequate for the formidable task of intelligent thinking or, even more troubling, for more homely processes like feeling pain or seeing red. If we feel that these can be handled only by new hardware, as Gunderson (1971) seems to suggest for such "program-resistive" processes, then we are asking for something very different and difficult. We are asking for a broadening of the definition of a computer, since the meaning of "general-purpose" is precisely that any conceivable hardware-embodied computer can be described in a program so that it can be simulated exactly by any general-purpose computer.

If we feel that "analog" computers are needed, we must specify the analog. Today's "analog computers" typically use a set of simple circuits to integrate and differentiate. But to recognize objects or represent images we would need very different kinds of analogs, in tandem with the procedures that manipulate and transform them, and extract and compute information from them. Most research on perception, question-answering, and memory representation consists precisely in the search for and exploration of different, usually at least partially analog, possibilities. We usually find it convenient, and plausible, to use the digital computer to make discrete approximations. So whenever we talk about "analog" processes on today's computers we mean processes that are actually being realized digitally. If we insist that true continuity exists in the real physical world, and that it is vital for intelligence, we are again insisting upon the inadequacy of today's computers. Today (because we are still tooling up) we can still approximate; but tomorrow we may have to join Peirce and use analog configurations of protoplasm to capture the conscious feelings of continuous life.

DIGITAL VS. ANALOG; STORED VS. COMPUTED; DESCRIPTIONS VS. MODELS

We see, then, that it makes little or no difference in what sort of mind-stuff, in what quality of imagery, our thinking goes on. The only images *intrinsically* important are the halting-places, the substantive conclusions, provisional or final, of the thought. Throughout all the rest of the stream, the feelings of relation are everything, and the terms related almost naught. These feelings of relation, these psychic overtones, halos, suffusions, or fringes about the terms, may be the same in very different systems of imagery (James, 1892, p. 169).

Input to the computer inevitably gives a discrete approximation of the sensed scene. Perceptual transforms, at least at the earlier layers, almost certainly must be analogical, e.g., edge, stroke, and feature-detectors. Transforms can imply abstracted analogs and/or symbols, or strings of symbols including words in a natural language. When such symbol strings are arranged linearly, as in sentences, it is probably best to think of them as nonanalogical, nonpictorial, non-image-like descriptions or propositions. But if symbols are arranged in list-structures or in graphs and are connected by relational symbols (like "above" or "near-left" or "60°") that are interpreted by procedures that compute these relations, I think it is best to say that these relations, and their resulting structure, and these procedures, and their resulting transformations, give an analogical aspect to the representation. But we cannot exclude even linear strings, because any arbitrary graph or n-dimensional array can be expressed in a linear string, using symbols like parentheses and commas to embed and indicate structure.

The analog flavor emerges, I think, when the representation has some model-like aspects; in the sense that not everything is spelled out and stored explicitly, but an enormous, even a potentially infinite, amount of information can be derived in a reasonably efficient way. For example, a model of the robot's room and its position in that room allows us to compute its location relative to any object, or any point, in that room. But it will be impossibly cumbersome to deduce these relative positions from a small set of logical propositions about the objects in the room.

Nor is a picture or icon an analog, in the sense of allowing for a dense set of useful derivations. The raw picture can be used only as a rigid template, to be matched exactly. A picture of a particular rectangle is a very bad analog concept of "rectangle," for it would be of no help with any other rectangle. Rather, we need an abstract structural description that allows all rectangles to be handled. This will—as in the analytic geometry representation—almost certainly be a mixture of symbols and relations that give an (analogical) structure from which an enormous set of possibilities can conveniently and powerfully be derived.

It seems reasonable to think of terms like "image," "schema," "map," and "model" as vague overlapping suggestions of the analog aspects of the representation. But the actual analog qualities reside not in whether a memory contains symbols or pictures, but in the structure of the representation, the richness and power of the procedures that can manipulate and transform it, and the resulting potential richness of the information that can be derived. Thus is makes eminent sense for Peirce to hold the most extreme conception of mind as a continuous analog and simultaneously develop the deepest of "semeiotic" theories of this mind as a discrete symbolic "existential graph": "the mind is a sign, developing according to the laws of inference" (1931, vol. 5, p. 188).

WHAT DOES REALITY BECOME WHEN COMPUTERS BEGIN TO THINK?

Bodies do not produce sensations, but complexes of elements (complexes of sensations) make up bodies. If, to the physicist, bodies appear real, abiding existences, whilst "elements" are regarded merely as their evanescent, transitory appearance, the physicist forgets, in the assumption of such a view, that all bodies are but thought-symbols for complexes of elements (complexes of sensations) (Mach, 1906, p. 29).

A computer program to model a world that contains an intelligent organism would have to specify the things in that world, including the organisms that perceive them, and the rules of interaction between things and organisms. As with all computer programs, these specifications must be made in strings of symbols that define spaces, networks, graphs, or other structures.

If we can describe and model an intelligent organism with a computer program, the rest of the model, of its microcosm world, should be easier to construct—since it consists of merely a few additional intelligent organisms, plus other, much simpler, structures. Such a project will probably never succeed: either because no computer will be large enough to contain a sufficiently large piece of the world to present an interesting environment to the intelligent organism that forms a part of it or because the computer must be a continuous analog.

But it is instructive to examine this situation, from the point of view of the simulated organism's attempts to examine how it perceives, what it knows, and what is the reality out there. We know the reality because we have programmed it all, and can examine it all with detachment. Assume that we someday achieve intelligent programs that satisfy all our criteria for "thinking" and "intelligence," and that assert such things as "I know" and "that object is real." Then we shall have an existence proof of a perceived and constructed reality whose "ultimate stuff" *we* know to be merely a description, a construct of symbols. Our programs believe in this "reality" just as we believe in our reality, and we give them just as much credit for intelligence as we give each other. Such a constructed reality would then be the *only bona fide* reality whose structure we *knew*.

Once again we move toward Peirce:

> The universe is a vast representamen, a great symbol of God's purpose, working out its conclusions in living realities. Now every symbol must have, organically attached to it, its Indices of Reactions and its Icons of Qualities; and such part as these reactions and these qualities play in an argument that, they of course, play in the universe—that Universe being precisely an argument. In the little bit that you or I can make out of this huge demonstration, our perceptual judgments are the premises *for us* and these perceptual judgments have icons as their predicates, in which *icons* Qualities are immediately presented. But what is first for us is not first in nature (1931, vol. 5, pp. 75-76).

Summary and Some Troublesome Comments

This paper explores aspects of perception and cognition of special interest to philosophers and to psychologists by examining the relevant structures and processes of actually programmed models.

The many programs for perception are briefly described and categorized, to elicit several common structures that help give precise meaning to the concepts of "sensation," "percept," and "sense-data."

Wholistic cognitive systems are examined by a brief look at today's robots and a more detailed description of the author's attempt to develop better-integrated, contextually interactive, probabilistic SEER systems that perform a variety of intellectual tasks in a flexible way that intermingles the separate cognitive processes.

Perception is examined from an empirical point of view, by studying programs that give increasing power and generality over various dimensions of complexity. Cognitive systems are then examined for the light that their necessary structures and processes throw on such basic concepts as "perceiving," "thinking," "knowing," "understanding," "ego," and "self." It is suggested that systems are needed whose behavior is a function of both the external environment's presses and internal needs, goals, and ideas.

Possible loci of "iconic," "short-term," and "long-term" memories are posited. It is suggested that the interrelated issues of "analog" vs. "symbolic" representations, "computed" vs. "stored" information, and "models" vs. "descriptions" boil down to a question of the degree to which relevant but unanticipated information can conveniently be derived from the internal representation.

Mathematical logicians have been successful in defining a very broad class of "effective procedures" that Turing machines (and that means today's "general-purpose" computers) can embody: such machines will effect any procedure, no matter how complex, that is described by a "program" input to them. This development shows that computers are the most general vehicle for information-processing man has been able to devise. Therefore, writing a computer program is the most general, powerful, and convenient way to model the mind/brain.

But it is not easy to judge how difficult is this time-honored task or how far we have come. Nor do we have any firm results or guidelines relating to the type of program needed—whether it be given predigested knowledge or learn; describe discursively or model analogically; have the flavor of deductive problem-solving or inductive perception; be parallel, serial, or parallel-serial; be deterministic or probabilistic. These are issues of efficiency, power, and generality, to be settled by the hypothetico-deductive method, as we test, evaluate, and rebuild our models—something we have not yet learned to do.

I have tried to argue that certain structures and processes are necessary for thinking. But are they sufficient? Or are some of the essential characters (like the feelings of redness, pain, and love), or even the protagonist (like the conscious self), still missing? We may not even know enough to send out a casting notice.

I have suggested that a unified consciousness, the ego, and (somehow in a more troubling way) feelings might be semi-illusions built up from the complex structure of experience. But how can a system know its external and internal reality? One insight comes from the ancient Indian philosophies of Sāṅkhya, the Yoga-sūtras of Patanjali (see Zimmer, 1956) and Buddhist logic (see Stcherbatsky, 1962). Perception, thinking, ego, and personality reflect the superficial surface agitations of everyday life. Beneath these lies the still, aware self, at one with all being, all consciousness.

Could we attain this deeper level of awareness in our programs? Does this suggest some new kinds of organization with a reflective meta-level that does not in any way control or direct, but rather assesses dispassionately if it is allowed to? Does it suggest that we must program in, must start with, a pervasive universal consciousness? Or is Peirce correct in saying that "matter is effete mind, inveterate habits becoming physical laws" (1931, vol. 6, p. 30)? Computers, whatever their material embodiment, are part of the universal mind-stuff. So we should be able to get them to embody conscious minds that are aware with feelings and thoughts, possibly simply by freeing them to be continuous, analog, probabilistic, and imprecise (protoplasm?). Indeed they already offer us examples of a perceiver that knows and apprehends external objects.

Notes

1. For *SEE* and to *ER*r is human; *SE*mantic learn*ER*; *S*ensed *E*nvironment *E*ncoder, *R*ecognizer and *R*esponder; and, above all, for short.

2. The liberal quotes from James, Mach, and Peirce in this paper are attempts to show that today's programmed models, the problems they attack, and the issues they raise are the children of (a) a central tradition of western psychology that was sidetracked by attempts to push oversimple associationism too far (e.g., the Mills, Pavlov); (b) weird and wondrous flights into introspection turned fantasy (e.g., Wundt, Freud); and (c) a know-nothing behaviorist reaction (e.g., Watson, Skinner) that misapplies the scientific method,

pragmatism, and physicalism and has shamed psychology into ignoring its most central questions. This is an oversimplification (I am not a historian of philosophy or psychology). But I want to emphasize how congenial are the thoughts of a tradition that has its beginnings in Indian as well as Greek philosophy, and how liberating.

Computer programs allow us to return to a precise and sensible examination of complex internal processes. How refreshing, and contemporary, is talk of the stream of consciousness as the processes of judgment and choice, of reality as consisting in constructions over relations, of existential graphs as (the medium for) thought.

References

Arbib, M. A. *Theories of abstract automata.* Englewood-Cliffs, N.J.: Prentice-Hall, 1969.

Baran, P., & Estrin, G. An adaptive character reader. *IRE WESCON Convention Record*, 1960, 4 (pt. 4), 29-36.

Bartlett, F. C. *Remembering: A study in experimental and social psychology.* Cambridge: Cambridge University Press, 1932.

Brice, C. R., & Fennema, C. L. Scene analysis using regions. *Artificial Intelligence*, 1970, 1, 205-226.

Church, A. An unsolvable problem of elementary number theory. *American Journal of Mathematics*, 1936, 58, 345-363.

Dennett, D. C. Toward a cognitive theory of consciousness (this volume).

Doyle, W. Recognition of sloppy, hand-printed characters. *Proceedings of the IFIP WJCC*, 1960, 17, 133-142.

Duda, R. O., & Hart, P. E. *Pattern classification and scene analysis.* New York: Wiley, 1973.

Eden, M., & Halle, M. The characterization of cursive writing. In Colin Cherry (Ed.), *4th London Symposium on Information Theory.* Washington: Butterworth, 1961, 287-299.

Feldman, J. A., et al. The Stanford hand-eye project. *Proceedings of the 2nd International Joint Conference on Artificial Intelligence*, 1971, 521-526.

Fikes, R. E., & Nilsson, N. J. STRIPS: a new approach to the application of theorem proving to problem solving. *Proceedings of the 2nd International Joint Conference on Artificial Intelligence*, 1971, 608-620.

Grimsdale, R. L., Sumner, F. H., Tunis, C. J., & Kilburn, T. A system for the automatic recognition of patterns. *Proceedings of the Institute of Electrical Engineers*, 1959, 106 (pt. B), 210-221.

Gunderson, K. *Mentality and machines.* New York: Anchor, 1971.

Hannan, W. J. The RCA Multi-font reading machine. In G. L. Fischer, Jr., et al. (Eds.), *Optical character recognition.* Washington: Spartan, 1962.

Highleyman, W. H. Linear decision functions with application to pattern recognition. *Proceedings of the IRE*, 1962, 50, 1501-1514.

Hunt, E. B. *Concept formation: An information processing approach.* New York: Wiley, 1962.

James, W. *Psychology (briefer course).* New York: Holt, 1892.

James, W. *The principles of psychology.* New York: Dover, 1950 (2 vols.) (orig. 1890).

Kleene, S. C. *Introduction to metamathematics.* Princeton: Van Nostrand, 1952.

Kochen, M. An experimental program for the selection of disjunctive hypotheses. *Proceedings of the Western Joint Computer Conference*, 1961, 19, 571-578.

Mach, E. *The analysis of sensations.* New York: Dover, 1959 (orig. 1906).

MacKay, D. M. The epistemological problem for automata. In C. E. Shannon and J. McCarthy (Eds.), *Automata studies.* Princeton: Princeton University Press, 1956.

Marill, T., et al. Cyclops-I: A second-generation recognition system. *AFIPS FJCC Conference Proceedings*, 1963, 24, 27-34.

Minsky, M. *Computation: Finite and infinite machines*. Englewood-Cliffs, N.J.: Prentice-Hall, 1967.

Minsky, M. A framework for representing knowledge. In P. H. Winston (Ed.), *The psychology of computer vision*. New York: McGraw-Hill, 1975.

Munson, J. H. Experiments in the recognition of hand-printed text. *Proceedings of the Spring Joint Computer Conference*, 1968, 33, 279-290.

Naylor, W. C. Machine imitation. Unpublished Ph.D. thesis, University of Wisconsin, 1971.

Neisser, U. *Cognition and reality*. San Francisco: W. H. Freeman and Co., 1976.

Neisser, U. Perceiving, anticipating, and imagining (this volume).

Nilsson, N. J. A mobile automaton: An application of A. I. techniques. *Proceedings of the 1st International Joint Conference on Artifical Intelligence*, 1969, 509-520.

Peirce, C. S. *Collected papers*. Cambridge, Mass.: Harvard University Press, 1931-1958 (8 vols.) (orig. 1859-1908).

Reddy, D. R., Erman, L. D., Fennell, R. D., & Neely, R. B. The hearsay speech understanding system. *Proceedings of the 3rd International Conference on Artificial Intelligence*, 1973, 185-193.

Riseman, E. M., & Hanson, A. R. Design of a semantically directed vision processor. *Technical Report 74C-1*, Computer Science Department, University of Massachusetts, January 1974.

Stcherbatsky, T. *Buddhist logic*. New York: Dover, 1962.

Towster, E. Studies in concept formation. Unpublished Ph.D. thesis, University of Wisconsin, 1970.

Turing, A. M. On computable numbers, with an application to the Entscheidungsproblem. *Proceedings of the London Mathematical Society* (ser. 2), 1936, 42, 230-265.

Uhr, L. Layered "recognition cone" networks that preprocess, classify and describe. *IEEE Transactions Computers*, 1972, 21, 758-768.

Uhr, L. *Pattern recognition, learning and thought*. Englewood-Cliffs, N.J.: Prentice-Hall, 1973(a).

Uhr, L. Describing, using "recognition cones." *Proceedings of the 1st International Joint Conference on Pattern Recognition*, 1973(b).

Uhr, L. Form perception and scene description: Toward a theoretical and experimental science of complex structures. *Computer Science Department Technical Report 231*, 1974.

Uhr, L. Toward integrated cognitive systems, which *must* make fuzzy decisions about fuzzy problems. In L. Zadeh et al. (Eds.), *Fuzzy sets*. New York: Academic Press, 1975(a).

Uhr, L. A wholistic cognitive system (SEER-2) for integrated perception, action and thought. *Proceedings of the 3rd MSACC Conference*, 1975(b).

Uhr, L. A wholistic integrated cognitive system (SEER-T2) that interacts with its environment over time. *Proceedings of the 4th MSACC Conference*, 1976(a).

Uhr, L. "Recognition cones" that perceive and describe scenes that move and change over time. *Proceedings of the 3rd International Joint Conference on Pattern Recognition*, 1976(b).

Uhr, L., & Vossler, C. A pattern recognition program that generates, evaluates and adjusts its own operators. *Proceedings of the Western Joint Computers Conference*, 1961, 19, 555-570. (Reprinted, with additional results, in E. Feigenbaum and J. Feldman (Eds.), *Computers and thought*. New York: McGraw-Hill, 1963.)

Unger, S. H. Pattern detection and recognition. *Proceedings of the IRE*, 1959, 47, 1737-1752.

Vernon, M. D. *A further study of visual. perception.* Cambridge: Cambridge University Press, 1952.

Williams, H. A net-structure for learning and describing patterns in terms of subpatterns. *Proceedings of the 3rd MSACC Conference*, 1975, 3, 99-108.

Winston, P. H. The MIT robot. In B. Melzer and D. Michie (Eds.), *Machine intelligence 7.* Edinburgh: Edinburgh University Press, 1972.

Winston, P. H. (Ed.), *The psychology of computer vision.* New York: McGraw-Hill, 1975.

Zimmer, H. *Philosophies of India.* New York: Meridian, 1956.

Zobrist, A. L. The organization of extracted features for pattern recognition. *Pattern Recognition*, 1971, 3, 23-30.

Rigid Designators and Mind-Brain Identity

A kind of mind-brain identity theory that is immune to recent objections by Kripke (1971 and 1972)[1] is outlined and defended in this paper. For reasons, the details of which will be given later, I have characterized the view as a *nonmaterialist physicalism*. It is nonmaterialist in that it does not attempt to eliminate or in any way deemphasize the importance of the "truly mental." On the contrary, it accords central roles to *consciousness*, "private experience," subjectivity, "raw feels," "what it's like to be something,"[2] thoughts, pains, feelings, emotions, etc., as we live through them in all of their qualitative richness. The theory also claims, however, that all of these genuinely mental entities are also genuinely physical, from which it follows that some genuinely physical entities are genuinely mental. This should occasion no shock, for it is a consequence of any authentic mental-physical identity thesis. Of course, some call themselves identity theorists and, at the same time, deny the existence of the genuinely mental (in my sense); but the result of this is always some kind of physical-physical identity thesis rather than a genuine mental-physical identity claim. One of the main reasons that Kripke's arguments do not hold against this theory is that it incorporates a significant revision of our basic beliefs about the nature of "the physical." The revision, however, is by no means ad hoc. It is virtually forced upon us, quite independently of Kripke's argument—indeed, quite apart from the mind-brain issue—by contemporary physics, physiology, neurophychology, and psychophysiology. It will turn out that Kripke's arguments *do* reveal, in a novel and cogent manner, the inadequacies of materialism. At the same time they provide valuable considerations that can be used to bolster the case for nonmaterialist physicalism.

Note: This research was supported in part by the National Science Foundation and the Minnesota Center for Philosophy of Science of the University of Minnesota.

All of this will become more clear later, I hope, when more detail is given. But, even at this point, perhaps I should attempt a crude and somewhat inaccurate characterization of "the physical." *The physical* is, very roughly, the subject matter of physics. By 'subject matter' I mean *not* the *theories*, *laws*, *principles*, etc., of physics, but rather what the theories and laws are about. *The physical* thus includes tables, stars, human bodies and brains, and whatever the constituents of these may be. The crucial contention is that contemporary science gives us good reason to suppose that these constituents are quite different from what common sense *and* traditional materialism believe them to be. While "the dematerialization of matter" has perhaps been overplayed in some quarters, its advocates do make an important point (see, e.g., Hanson, 1962 and Feigl, 1962); and this point is crucial for the mind-body problem. A nonmaterialist physicalism is one that rejects those erroneous prescientific beliefs about physical entities that I shall argue are endemic to common sense and are carried over, to a great extent, into traditional *and* contemporary materialism. The elimination of these beliefs clears the way for a mind-brain identity theory that avoids the antimentalist reductionism of materialism, behaviorism, and similar views. (No contempt of common sense is involved here at all. Science, at best, is modified and improved common sense. Often the improvement is minimal; but, if it is genuine, surely it ought to be preferred to the unimproved version.)

Before considering Kripke's argument against mind-brain identity, I should remark that I am assuming that his ("quasi-technical") system of "rigid designation," "reference-fixing," etc., is a viable system. This is not to assume that it provides, necessarily, an account that is in perfect accord with our customary modes of conceptualization, inference, ascription of necessity, etc. Kripke, I think, intends and believes that it does, but many disagree. This explains, no doubt, why they feel that some of his conclusions are wrong or at best highly counterintuitive or based on eccentric terminology. Be this as it may, I believe that his terminology is clear and consistent and that his system provides, if not an "analysis," at least a tenable alternative "reconstruction" of conceptualization, reasoning, etc., both in everyday and in scientific contexts. (I am *not* so sure about his *essentialism*. However, for the sake of argument —

that is, for the purpose of defending the identity thesis against his objections—I shall accept his essentialism insofar as I am able to understand it.)

Let me now introduce the elements of Kripke's system that are needed for the argument in question. A *rigid designator* is a symbol the referent of which remains the same in our discourse about all possible worlds *provided two conditions obtain*. The first is the rather trivial one that the language must remain the same. Obviously if we change the meaning or the conventional (*or* stipulated) use of a term, its referent will not necessarily remain constant. The second condition is that the referent exist in the possible world in question, and this condition will, of course, fail to obtain in many possible worlds. Another way of stating the matter is to say that the referent of a rigid designator either remains constant or becomes null as our discourse ranges over different possible worlds. Proper names are, for Kripke, paradigm examples of rigid designators. As long as the term 'Richard Nixon' has its standard and established role in our language, it refers to the same entity, namely Nixon, no matter what possible world we may be talking about, *unless*, of course, we happen to be talking about a possible world in which Nixon does not exist. (Instead of using the "possible worlds" terminology, we could say that a rigid designator has the same referent in every occurrence no matter whether the statement in which it occurs is about an actual or a counterfactual state of affairs.) The most common instances of nonrigid or "accidental" designators are descriptive phrases. To use an example of Kripke, the phrase 'the inventor of bifocals' refers to Benjamin Franklin; but obviously the phrase is not a rigid designator. There are many possible worlds in which bifocals were invented by someone else—or we can easily imagine counterfactual situations such that bifocals were invented, say, by Thomas Paine. In discourse about the latter situation the referent of the phrase 'the inventor of bifocals' would be Thomas Paine instead of Benjamin Franklin.

We come now to a crucial juncture in Kripke's system. In attempting to make it as clear as possible, I shall use an example of different from and somewhat simpler than those employed by Kripke. Suppose we are convinced that one and only one man invented the incandescent electric light bulb but that we do not know who he was.

Nevertheless, suppose that we stipulate that the term 'Oscar' is to be used to *rigidly designate* this so far unidentified inventor. What does this mean? It means that 'Oscar' always refers to the man who invented, as a contingent matter of fact in this the actual world, the incandescent bulb. And this referential relation holds whether or not our discourse is about the actual world or about other possible worlds—whether it is about actual or counterfactual states of affairs. There are, of course, many possible worlds in which Oscar did not invent the bulb, worlds in which someone else invented it or in which it was not invented at all. This is just to say that there are possible worlds in which the bulb was not invented by the man who actually did invent it (in this, the actual world—to be redundant). Nevertheless, in our discourse about these worlds 'Oscar' still refers to the same man—the man who invented the bulb in this, the actual world.

It is evident that 'Oscar' is *not* being used as an abbreviation of the descriptive phrase 'the inventor of the incandescent electric light bulb.' The referent of the descriptive phrase changes, being dependent on which possible world (or set of possible worlds) our discourse is about, whereas we have made the referent of 'Oscar' constant (or null) by stipulation.[3] The stipulation alone, however, is *not sufficient* to *fix the reference* of 'Oscar.' The crucial point, alluded to above, may now be put as follows: There is, on the one hand, the *stipulation* that the referent of 'Oscar' is always to be the the man who invented, in this, the actual world, the incandescent electric light bulb. On the other hand, there is *the (contingent) fact* that one specific man did invent it. This stipulation *plus* this contingent fact *fixes* or *picks out* this specific man as the referent of 'Oscar.'[4] This emphasis on the crucial role of contingent facts in *fixing the reference* of terms in the language is perhaps the most striking aspect of Kripke's system.

Whether Kripke would endorse the following explication of this mode of reference-fixing, I do not know. I have found it helpful in organizing my thinking about the matter. Instead of issuing stipulations in a metalanguage about the referent of 'Oscar,' we can use instead a *reference-fixing postulate* stated in the object language (analogous to Carnapian "meaning postulates." See, e.g., Carnap, 1952, and Maxwell, 1961). The postulate would be something like:

If one and only one person invented the incandescent electric light bulb, then that person was Oscar.

or:

$(\exists x)\ [Ixb \cdot (y)\ (Iyb \supset x = y)] \supset [Iob \cdot (y)\ (Iyb \supset o = y)]$
where '*Ixb*' stands for '*x* invented the incandescent electric light bulb' and '*o*' stands for 'Oscar.'

The "postulate" fixes the *reference* of 'Oscar' (or '*o*'), but, in contrast to a Carnapian "meaning postulate," it is not intended to fix a *connotation* or a *sense* of the term(s) in question.

This procedure can be generalized in an interesting manner. Let 'T' stand for any conjuction of sentences that expresses the content of a given scientific theory, and let 'R_T' stand for the *Ramsey sentence* of the theory. ('R_T' is formed from 'T' by replacing each theoretical term of the theory with an existentially quantified variable of appropriate logical type.) Carnap (1957) proposed that the expression '$R_T \supset T$' be taken as a meaning postualte, fixing the meanings of the theoretical terms of the theory (assuming—correctly, I believe—that 'R_T' expresses the contingent or the factual content of the theory). It is considerably better, I believe, to take '$R_T \supset T$' as a *reference-fixing postulate* for the theoretical terms. Prima facie, the difference may seem subtle and minimal, but I am convinced that it has important implications for our understanding of the structure of scientific theories, and indeed, of the nature of most of our knowledge. Explanation of the details of these matters, however, belongs to another project.

Before proceeding to the mind-brain identity thesis, it will be helpful to continue examination of the "Oscar" example in order to understand better Kripke's views about identity in general. Suppose that, after fixing the referent of 'Oscar' as we did above, we make the (contingent) discovery that Thomas A. Edison invented the incandescent electric light bulb. It follows, obviously, that Oscar and Edison are identical—that "they" are one and the same person. It also follows, given the Kripkean system, that Edison and Oscar are *necessarily* identical. This follows simply because both 'Oscar' and 'Thomas A. Edison' are rigid designators. This means that 'Oscar' *always* refers to the same man and that, of course, the referent of 'Thomas A. Edison' *always* remains constant, whether our discourse is about the actual world (or about actual situations) or about any other possible world or any counterfactual situation. It follows that, if Edison and Oscar are identical in any possible world (including the actual world, of course), then "they" are identical in all possible worlds (in all actual and counterfactual situations). Therefore, "They" are *necessarily* identical, since something holds *necessarily* if and only if it holds in all possible worlds—in all actual and counterfactual situations.

It may seem highly counterintuitive to claim that it is *necessarily true* that Oscar is Thomas A. Edison. Knowledge that Oscar is Thomas A. Edison *seems* to be genuine contingent knowledge. Kripke provides an explanation of the existence of such "illusions of contingency." Although knowledge that Oscar is Edison is knowledge of a necessary truth, *we come to know* it by means of what he calls a "contingent associated discovery." In this case, the contingent associated discovery is the discovery that Edison invented the incandescent bulb (and nobody else did). This discovery plus our stipulation that 'Oscar' rigidly designates the inventor of the bulb entails that Oscar and Edison are necessarily identical.

It is helpful, I believe, to expand somewhat this explanation. Let us say that the reference-fixing stipulation (plus the contingent fact that one and only one person invented the bulb) *fixed the referent* of 'Oscar' *ontologically*. At that point, however, we did not know (so the example supposes) *who* the referent *was* or, let us put it, the referent was not *epistemically determined*. When we discover, subsequently, that Edison invented the bulb, we discover what (who) the referent of 'Oscar' is; i.e., the discovery that Edison invented the bulb *epistemically determines* the referent of 'Oscar.' (More accurately, the discovery plus the ontological reference-fixing postulate produces the epistemic determination.) The status of the statement, 'Oscar is identical with Thomas A. Edison,' may now be explained as follows. Although the statement is *necessarily* true, it *conveys*, but *does not assert*, the *contingent* information that 'Oscar' (rigidly) designates Thomas A. Edison, which is tantamount to conveying the contingent information that Edison invented the bulb (given our reference-fixing postulate to the effect that Oscar invented the bulb). What, then, does the statement, 'Oscar is identical with Thomas A. Edison,' *assert*? Given the apparatus we are employing, we must say, I believe, that it asserts that the man in question, call him 'Oscar' or 'Edison,' or 'the man who invented the bulb'—*that this man is identical with himself.* Small wonder that it is necessarily true!

This result, if I am correct and it *is* a result, of the Kripkean system might seem to signal a serious defect or at best to trivialize Kripke's treatment of identity. Trivial or not, I do not believe that it indicates a defect. On the contrary, it emphasizes the crucial point that *every identity is an identity of something with itself* (in the sense of 'identity' that is the concern of this paper—the sense that is relevant for mind-brain identity). As Kripke notes, identity is that relation that holds *always and only* between an entity and itself. So all identities are self-identities; and, since all self-identities hold necessarily, it follows that all identities are necessary identities.

This is a good point at which to give a somewhat truncated but forceful sketch of Kripke's argument against the mind-brain identity thesis. The sketch follows:

(1) There seems to be *no way* for a brain state (or brain event) to be *necessarily* identical with a mental state (or a mental event). So, (1') if mind-brain identities exist, they are contingent identities. But (as we have seen above) (2) there *are no* contingent identities. Therefore, there are no mind-brain identities.

Obviously the argument is valid; if we are to reject the conclusion, we must reject at least one premise. Many—probably most—mind-brain identity theorists accept the first premise. Indeed, they emphasize and insist that mental-physical identities are contingent identities. They then proceed, either explicitly or tacitly, to reject premise (2). Needless to say, I accept (2) and shall argue that (1) and therefore (1') are false.

Kripke emphasizes that this is just what the identity theorist *must* do if he is to retain any hope of rejecting the argument's conclusion. He then argues at some length that the first premise seems quite invulnerable. I shall argue that the first premise is false.

Kripke notes and indeed emphasizes that his apparatus provides what might seem to offer an escape route for the identity theorist, and we have already touched upon the matter earlier. If we could show that the apparent truth of premise (1) is due entirely to an *illusion of contingency*, we would have produced conclusive grounds for rejecting the premise. In order to do this we would need to indicate how there could be a *contingent associated fact* that is responsible for this "illusion of contingency." Kripke argues that the existence of such a fact seems out of the question. Before examining these arguments, it will be helpful to continue our discussion of identity and necessity.

It was contended above that 'Oscar is Edison' *conveyed*, although it did *not assert*, the contingent information that 'Oscar' designates Edison, which, in conjunction with the reference-fixing postulate for 'Oscar,' entails that Edison invented the bulb. Coming from the opposite direction, it was our contingent discovery that Edison invented the bulb that informed us that 'Oscar' designates (rigidly) Edison, i.e., this discovery *epistemically determined* the referent of 'Oscar.' And this, in turn, gives us the a posteriori (!) knowledge of the necessary truth that Edison and Oscar are one and the same man. The aura of mystery or paradox about a posteriori necessity disappears when we recognize that we have rigged our language so that the reference of 'Oscar' depends on a contingent fact and, moreover, that it remains epistemically undermined until we discover what that contingent fact is. The necessity of Oscar's being Edison should present no mystery. It derives entirely from the nature or the function of the language used plus the necessary truth that everything is identical with itself. We do not *fully* understand the complete function of the term 'Oscar' until we discover the contingent fact which, by virtue of our own stipulation, fixes its reference. This is how we come to know, a posteriori, that 'Oscar is Edison' expresses a truth and, indeed, a necessary one.

Frege is faulted, correctly, by Kripke for suggesting that identity should be construed as a relation holding between linguistic symbols rather than as a relation holding between objects (or between an object and itself). However, I believe that there is a valid insight behind Frege's mistake. Identity statements often *convey*, even though they do not *assert*, information about the referents of some of the symbols used. This information, in turn, when conjoined with (either tacit or explicit) knowledge about our conventional linguistic usage yields whatever contingent, nonlinguistic information that the identity statement provides. The valid insight, then, is that the unasserted but conveyed *contingent* information about the symbols used *plus* explicit or tacit knowledge about the *conventional* linguistic functions of the symbols conveys the extralinguistic, contingent information that identity statements provide.

Strictly speaking, what I have just claimed holds for those identity statements in which the identity sign is flanked on both sides by names or other rigid designators (e.g., 'Oscar = Edison' or 'Water = H_2O'). If statements such as 'Scott is the author of *Waverly*' are to be classified as identity statements, as I suppose they usually are, then the following holds. On Russell's analysis, the illustrative statement not only conveys but also asserts the contingent fact that Scott wrote *Waverly* (and nobody else did), i.e., that one and only one man wrote *Waverly* and that Scott wrote *Waverly*. On Strawson's analysis, it is not asserted but rather presupposed that one and only one man wrote *Waverly*. I prefer Russell's analysis, but it does not matter for the moment. The point that concerns us is that the existence of contingent identity *statements* (such as these) by no means entails that there are contingent *identities*. The *statement* in the example tells us that Scott wrote *Waverly* and that nobody else did. However, long ago Russell made it clear that there is no relation of identity that somehow holds between the author of *Waverly* and Scott. The relevant identity relation is the one that holds between Scott and himself, and this of course holds necessarily. As I see it, this is what is behind Russell's contention that the author of *Waverly* is "not a constituent of the proposition that Scott is the author of *Waverly*." Thus his position clearly seems to be that the identity sign must always be flanked on both sides by names (or other rigid designators) or by variables whose only permissible values are rigid designators. If this is observed, then we can always *salvae veritate* and otherwise properly attach the necessity operator to every sentence and every function of the form '$x = y$,' viz. '$\Box (x = y)$.' For example, 'Scott is the author of *Waverly*' becomes:

$$(\exists x) \, [Wxw \cdot (y) \, (Wyw \equiv \Box \, y = s)]$$

The necessity of the *identity relation* is made explicit although the so-called *identity statement* is contingent.

Let us now consider, with Kripke, the allegedly contingent identities that have been unearthed by scientific inquiry. According to him, long before the important discoveries of Clausius, Rumford, and others, the users of our language had fixed, rigidly, the referent of 'heat' as being *that which causes heat sensations*.[5] (This was accomplished, no doubt, by tacitly accepted linguistic conventions rather than by explicit stipulations. It should also be noted parenthetically here that many will object to Kripke's taking "common nouns" to be rigid designators in this manner, especially since, as he sees it, this amounts to treating them analogously to proper names, i.e., to giving them referents but no *connotation* or *sense*. I am inclined to agree with Kripke about this but hope that it is not necessary to argue the matter here; for the main point at present is to consider the mind-brain problem within the context of Kripke's framework.) Eventually it was discovered that heat sensations are caused by molecular motion (or by a certain level of mean molecular kinetic energy—this is all somewhat inaccurate, of course, but it does not matter here). This is the "contingent associated discovery" that provides us, a posteriori, with knowledge of the necessary identity of heat and molecular motion. As counterintuitive as this may seem, I believe that it is impeccable, given the Kripkean framework. Moreover, this is precisely analogous to the necessary identity of Oscar and Edison. (Let us grant Kripke, for the moment, at least, that 'molecular motion' *is* a rigid designator.) Since 'heat' and 'molecular motion' are both rigid designators, it follows that, if heat is identical with molecular motion in any world, it is identical with molecular motion in all possible worlds; therefore the identity is necessary. (This does not mean, of course, that molecular motion causes "heat sensation" in all possible worlds—any more than the necessary identity of Oscar and Edison implies that Edison [alias Oscar] invented the incandescent bulb in all possible worlds.)

Returning now to the mind-brain identity thesis, consider a claim that, say, a certain *determinate* kind of pain, call it 'pain$_{39}$' is identical with a certain *determinate* kind of brain state b_{76}.[6] Rather than speaking of *states*, it is much better, I believe, to (attempt to) identify mental *events* with physical *events*. So let us change the matter a little and take 'pain$_{39}$' to refer to the *occurrence* of a certain determinate kind of pain and let 'b_{76}' refer to a certain determinate kind of brain event. (This is actually more in line with Kripke's main example. In it, the physical entity is *C*-fiber stimulation, which is a process or an event.) Let us suppose further that 'b_{76}' is the genuine rigid designator for the relevant physical event that

Kripke suggests we use just in case 'C-fiber stimulation' is not a rigid designator.

Now, since 'pain$_{39}$' and 'b_{76}' are both rigid designators, it follows that, if pain$_{39}$ and b_{76} are identical, they are necessarily identical. So, if the identity does hold, there must be some contingent associated fact involved in fixing the reference either of 'pain$_{39}$' or of 'b_{76},' a fact, moreover, that would explain the all but overwhelming "illusion of contingency" about the claim of identity. Kripke argues convincingly and, in my opinion, conclusively that no such fact can exist for a designator such as 'pain$_{39}$.' He says that the referent of 'pain' is picked out by a *necessary* (or "essential") property of pain, by, indeed, the property of *being pain*. This precludes the existence of a contingent reference-fixing fact for 'pain' (and for 'pain$_{39}$'); for the reference of 'pain' (and 'pain$_{39}$') is fixed *ontologically without* any reference fixing fact. It is fixed *solely* by virtue of conventional linguistic practice. In contrast, fixing the reference of 'Oscar' and 'heat' involved contingent facts *in addition* to the linguistic factors. Finally, and equally importantly, language alone not only fixes ontologically the reference of 'pain,' it also *epistemically determines* what its referent *is*; in this case no contingent associated fact is involved.

So the referent of 'pain' is picked out by a necessary truth about pain, namely, the truth that pain is necessarily pain. It is *not possible* that pain (or pain$_{39}$) could have been something that was not pain. This necessary truth may seem quite trivial, and in a sense it is. Note, however, that is is not a necessary truth about the inventor of the incandescent bulb that he invented the incandescent bulb. Under the appropriate arrangement of Russell's "scope operator," we can even say truthfully that it is not necessarily true that the inventor of the bulb was the inventor of the bulb; i.e., the man who *did* invent it *might* not have (cf. Kripke, p. 279). Someone other than Edison might have done it. (Or more than one person might have invented it, or it might not have been invented at all.) Or, to say it in still another manner; the man who in this, the actual, world invented the bulb did not invent it in every possible world. Or, returning to the essentialist framework, being the inventor of the bulb is not an *essential* property of the inventor of the bulb. (Or course, however, being the inventor of the bulb *is* an essential property of *being* the inventor of the bulb [as is the property of being an inventor, etc.] .) Consider another example. Neither being red nor being crimson is an essential property of my sweater, which *is*, as a matter of contingent fact, crimson. But being red is of course an essential property of being crimson. Being red, therefore, is an essential property of an "accidental" property of my sweater. So we see that there are not only "illusions of contingency" but, as in the case of the inventor being the inventor, "illusions of necessity" as well. Something which, prima facie, seems necessary may turn out on closer examination to be contingent.

These considerations will stand us in good stead shortly, but another point needs to be made before we proceed. We saw above that our conventional linguistic practice vis a vis the word 'pain' precludes the existence of a contingent reference-fixing fact for the word 'pain' (pain and our mode of awareness of it being what they are). This, however, by no means precludes the existence of *another rigid designator* whose referent is also pain (or pain39) by virtue, moreover, of a contingent associated fact. Consider a contrived but simple example. Let us suppose that it occurs to our friend Jones that once or twice a week lately he has been quite irritable in the mornings, yelling at his kids, being cross with his wife, etc. He becomes convinced that this is due to some unidentified physiological or psychological factor in himself. He wonders what it could be and begins to speculate about it. To facilitate his thinking, he selects the term 'factor a' as a rigid designator, fixing its reference with the description, 'the cause of my recent undesirable behavior towards my family.' Jones has also noticed that he has been having a unique kind of headache recently to which, in line with his characteristic pedantic practices, he ostensively gives the name 'pain39.' One day it occurs to Jones that he has blindly failed to notice that the undesirable behavior occurs when and only when he is afflicted with pain39. He decides that *factor a* is probably one and the same as pain39. If this is true, then 'pain39 = factor a' expresses a necessary truth, since 'pain39' and 'factor a' are both rigid designators. There is an *illusion of contingency* here, however, because of the *contingent associated discovery* that pain39 is the cause of the undesirable behavior. This contingent fact picks out pain39 as the referent of 'factor a,' and when this fact becomes *known*, the reference of 'factor a' becomes epistemically determined.

I hope that it is unnecessary to emphasize that I am *not* laying the groundwork for any kind of behaviorist or "functionalist"*analysis* of mental events. I agree with Kripke (p. 336) that such *analyses* of mental entities in terms of their causal roles are self-evidently absurd. This example just reminds us that mental events do, however, *have* causal (or "functional") properties in addition to their "essential" (and other intrinsic) properties. Just as (one of) the causal properties of molecular motion picked it out as being the referent of 'heat,' there is nothing to prevent a causal property of a mental event from picking *it* out as the referent of a rigid designator—a designator, moreover, other than its original, *ostensively fixed* one. This distinction between the fixing of the reference of a term by means of a contingent (causal) fact, on the one hand, and an *analysis* that aims to give the *meaning*, *sense*, or *connotation* of a term, on the other, is obviously a crucial distinction for the Kripkean framework (as I believe it must be for *any* viable framework).

Returning once again to Kripke's arguments, I have agreed very strongly with him that the referent of the *word* 'pain' (and the referent of the word 'pain$_{39}$') is picked out by a necessary fact about (or an "essential" property of) the referent; i.e., the word 'pain$_{39}$' rigidly designates the event *pain$_{39}$* by virtue of the necessity of pain$_{39}$'s *being* pain$_{39}$. This precludes the possibility of fixing the reference of the term 'pain$_{39}$' by means of any contingent fact. But we have seen above that this by no means precludes the existence of another, different word, say 'factor a' that rigidly designates the *event* pain$_{39}$ and *that*, moreover, *rigidly designates it by virtue of a contingent fact*. It seems to me that such a possibility is overlooked by Kripke. However this may be, I claim that *terms referring to certain kinds of brain events*, properly construed,—terms such as b_{76}'—*do rigidly refer to mental events* (events such as pain$_{39}$). *Such reference is accomplished*, moreover, *by means of the (contingent) neurophysiological causal roles of the relevant events*. These "accidental" causal properties of the events *fix their reference ontologically*. However, due to our lack of neurological, psycho-physiological, and neuropsychological knowedge about the details of these causal properties, the reference has *not* been, so far, *epistemically determined*. Nevertheless, the identity theorist speculates that it is mental events that are the real actors in *some* of these neurophysiological causal roles. More specifically, he speculates that there is a certain brain event, call it 'b_{76},' which plays, contingently, a certain neurophysiological causal role. Moreover, the referent of 'b_{76}' can, in principle, be fixed by means of this (contingent) role; i.e., the relevant neurophysiological details, if only we knew them, could pick out the referent of 'b_{76}' ontologically. Next, he continues, the relevant (contingent) psychophysiological or neuropsychological details, if only we knew them, could epistemically determine that it is pain$_{39}$ that plays the neurophysiological role in question.

Kripke stresses the disanalogies between claiming that heat (or an instance of heat) is identical with molecular motion, on the one hand, and claiming that a brain event is identical with a pain, on the other. He concludes that, although heat and molecular motion are necessarily identical, these disanalogies preclude the possibility of a brain event and a pain's being necessarily identical and therefore preclude their being identical at all. He is correct about the existence of the disanalogies but wrong, I believe, in inferring that they preclude the necessity of mind-brain identities. He summarizes his argument on this matter (p. 340) as follows:

Thus pain, unlike heat, is not only rigidly designated by 'pain' but the reference of the designator is determined by an essential property of the referent. Thus it is not possible to say that although pain is necessarily identical with a certain physical state, a certain phenomenon can be picked out in the same way we pick out pain without being correlated with that physical state. If any phenomenon is picked out in exactly the same way we pick out pain, then that phenomenon is pain.

This is certainly correct. However, it does not preclude mind-brain identities. For what we *can* say is that, although pain$_{39}$ is necessarily identical with a certain brain event (call it 'b_{76}'), a (different!) brain event could, in some possible worlds, be picked out in the same way that we (in the actual world) pick out b_{76} without being identical with or even correlated with pain. This is true because the referent of 'b_{76}' is fixed as being the event that plays such and such a neurophysiological causal role *in this world*. In some other possible worlds *that role* will be played by entities other than b_{76}. The identity theorist maintains, of course, that the role in question is played by pain$_{39}$ *in this world*, although it could be played by another event (which might not even be a mental event) in some other possible world. This is what is responsible for *the illusion of contingency* concerning the necessary identity of pain39 and b_{76}.

It seems that Kripke assumes, tacitly at least, that designators such as 'pain39' correspond to the designator 'heat' and thus that those such as 'b_{76}' correspond to 'molecular motion.' I contend that the relevant analogies are rather between 'heat' and 'b_{76}' on the one hand and 'molecular motion' and 'pain39' on the other. For the reference of 'heat' and the reference of 'b_{76}' are fixed by contingent facts (by "accidental properties" of the referents). And it is the contingent associated discoveries that molecular motion causes heat sensations and that pain39 plays such and such a neuro-physiological causal role that account for, respectively, the illusions of contingency about the necessary identity of heat and molecular motion and the necessary identity of pain39 and the brain event b_{76}.

Now it may seem that Kripke has protected his flank on this score, for he does contend (p. 336) that *"being a brain state* is evidently an essential property of *B* (the brain state)."* In other words, he would claim that every brain state of necessity *had* to be a brain state (and surely he would make the analogous claim about brain events). He goes on to say, "even being a brain state of a specific type is an essential property of [the brain state] *B*." If the same *is* true of brain *events* (whether Kripke so contends or not), then my counterargument *would* be unsound; for this would entail that the reference of 'b_{76}' is fixed by means of a necessary truth (i.e., that an "essential property" of b_{76} fixes it as the referent of 'b_{76}'). This would preclude fixing the reference of 'b_{76}' by means of one of the "accidental properties" of the referent, and therefore there could not exist any contingent associated fact to account for the apparent contingency of the correlation between b_{76} and pain39. Following Kripke (p. 336), the difficulty may also be put: "If $A = B$, then the identity of A with B is necessary, and any essential property of one must be an essential property of the other." Now suppose that being a brain event *is* an essential property of b_{76}. Since being a brain event is *not* an essential property of pain39, it would follow that b_{76} and pain39 do not share all of their essential properties and thus cannot be identical.

It is time now for one of the central and, perhaps, one of the most counterintuitive contentions of this paper: *being a brain event* is not, in general, an essential property of brain events. (Although, of course, *being a brain event* is an essential property of *being* a brain event.) Again, this is a matter of *scope* (in Russell's sense of "scope"). Just as Russell pointed out long ago how it is that we can say that a given inventor might not have been an inventor (e.g., Edison might have spent his life writing mystery novels, never inventing even a mouse trap), we are now in a position to understand how *a given brain event might not have been a brain event.* For, I claim, *to be a brain event* is to play a neurophysiological causal role of an appropriate, broadly specifiable ("determin*able*") kind; and to be a brain event of a specific ("determin*ate*") kind is to play a specific, determinate kind of neurophysiological causal role (e.g., of the kind we are supposing b_{76} to play), and if we assume (in agreement with Hume) that *to say of a given event (or kind of event) that it plays a certain kind of causal role is to say something contingent*, then we see immediately that *to say of a given event (or kind of event) that it is a brain event is to say something contingent.* This follows, of course, because to say of an event that it is a brain event is merely to say that it plays a certain kind of causal role. And to say that this very brain event might not have been a brain event is merely to say that although this event, as a matter of contingent fact, plays a certain causal role, it is possible that it might not have played such a role; in some possible worlds it plays a very different role. As to the case at hand, although pain$_{39}$ (alias b_{76}) plays a certain specific neurophysiological causal role and is thereby (contingently) a brain event (of a certain kind), it *might not* have played such a role. It might not even have played any kind of neurological role, and thus it might not have been a brain event. Exactly the same holds for b_{76}—which is, in effect, to say the same thing again, for b_{76} and pain$_{39}$ are necessarily identical; 'b_{76}' and 'pain$_{39}$' refer to one and the same event. Moreover and *obviously* by now, *being a brain event* is *not* an essential property of *the brain event b_{76}*; but *being a pain is* an essential property of *the brain event b_{76}.* And, of course, being a brain event is *not* an essential property of the *brain* (!) *event*, pain$_{39}$; but being a pain *is* an essential property of the brain event,[7] pain$_{39}$. Pain$_{39}$ and b_{76} *do* share all of "their" properties, including all of "their" essential properties; they are one and the same event. To paraphrase Russell, there is no more difficulty about a pain being both a sensation and a brain event than there is about a man being both a rational animal and a barber.

The apparent difficulties involved in claiming that to be a brain event is to play a certain kind of neurophysiological causal role and that pain and other mental events play such neurophysiological roles will be considered presently. First I should like to assume, just for the moment, that these difficulties are not insuperable. This will permit me to answer a reformulation of Kripke's argument (p. 340) which, he says, may be "more vivid [and be made] without such specific reference to the technical apparatus [that has been developed]." I shall summarize this version of his argument very briefly, but I believe that none of its essentials will be omitted. Let us imagine God creating the world. What shall we say about the act of creation of molecular motion? Is it not true that this very act was the creation of heat? When molecules became sufficiently agitated, Kripke says, there were fires, things were hot, temperatures were high, etc. And this held before and independently of the creation of any sentient beings. What, then, gives us the *illusion* that, after creating molecular motion, God still had substantive work to do in order to make it identical with heat? Kripke answers that what *was* a substantive task for the Deity was to make molecular motion produce heat sensations. To do this, He had to create sentient beings such that this *contingent causal connection*[8] between molecular motion and their heat sensations holds. Only after God has done this, Kripke continues, "will there be beings who can learn that the sentence 'Heat is the motion of molecules' expresses an *a posteriori* [but necessary] truth in precisely the same way we do."

What about the creation of brain events and mental events? Kripke holds that our strong feeling that the creation of a certain kind of brain event, e.g., b_{76}, and the creation of a certain kind of mental event, e.g., $pain_{39}$, are two separate acts of creation is *not* an illusion. When God brought about the existence of C-fiber stimulation, he says, He still had further substantive creative work to do in order for pain to come into existence (and in order for it to be correlated with C-fiber stimulation).

I shall not, at this point, summarize his argument for this latter contention, for I believe that, again, he takes the term 'molecular motion' from the "heat" example to be analogous to the term 'C-

fiber stimulation.' As I explained earlier, I hold that the relevant analogy holds between 'molecular motion' and the term 'pain.' He does make an important point about C-fiber stimulation, but I shall return to it later.

What I want to do next is to argue directly that, when God made the relevant kind of brain event, say b_{76}, this very act of creation was the creation of (the mental event—the sensation) $pain_{39}$. After God created b_{76}, there did *not* remain for Him the substantive task of creating $pain_{39}$ (nor the task of then correlating it with b_{76}). The creation of b_{76} *was* the creation of $pain_{39}$, for "they" are one and the same event. What *was* a substantive task for the Deity was to give $pain_{39}$ (alias b_{76}) the kind of (contingent) neurophysiological causal role that it has. He *could* have decided to give it a different neurophysiological role or even not to give it *any neurophysiological* role at all (just as He *could* have decided not to give molecular motion the causal role of producing "heat sensations"). Our implicit recognition that the Deity had to make this contingent decision about the causal role of b_{76} is responsible for our *mistaken* feeling that the creation of b_{76} was a different act from the act of creation of $pain_{39}$ and thus for the *illusion of contingency* about the *actual necessity* of the identity of (the mental event) $pain_{39}$ and (the brain event) b_{76}.

The following, I believe, has now been established: *If* to be a brain event is to play a kind of neurophysiological causal role and if sensations (and other mental events) can play such roles, *then* it is possible that some brain events just *are* (identical with) mental events; and, moreover, it has been established that any such identity that holds between a mental event and a brain event *holds necessarily*. I must now try to provide some support for the claim that to be a brain event is to play a kind of neurophysiological causal role and the claim that it is possible that mental events play (some of) these roles. Let me begin this task by returning to Kripke's contention about C-fiber stimulation, which was mentioned above.

The relevant passage (from pp. 340-341) follows:

What about the case of the stimulation of C-fibers? To create this phenomenon, it would seem that God need only to create beings with C-fibers capable of the appropriate type of physical stimulation; whether the beings are conscious or not is irrelevant here. It would seem though, that to make the C-fiber stimulation correspond to pain, or be felt as pain, God must do something in addition to the mere creation of the C-fiber stimulation; He must let the creatures feel the C-fiber stimulation as *pain*, and not as a tickle, or as warmth, or as nothing, as apparently would also have been within His powers. If these things in fact are within His powers, the relation between the pain God creates and the stimulation of C-fibers cannot be identity. For if so, the stimulation could exist without the pain; and since 'pain' and 'C-fiber stimulation' are rigid, this fact implies that the relation between the two phenomena is not that of identity. God had to do some work, in addition to making the man himself, to make a certain man be the inventor of bifocals; the man could well exist without inventing any such thing. The same cannot be said for pain; if the phenomenon exists at all, no further work should be required to make it into pain.

Now we must ask ourselves: What kind of phenomenon *is* C-fiber stimulation?[9] Obviously, 'C-fiber stimulation' cannot refer merely to an external stimulus, i.e., to a stimulus *external to the C-fibers*. It *would* be self-evidently absurd to hold that an external stimulus could be identical with pain. On the other hand, such an external stimulus is presumably almost always a crucial factor in the *production* of pain. But pain itself surely must correspond more closely with activity *within* the C-fibers than with any external stimulus. It follows, I believe, that, if the term 'C-fiber stimulation' is to be retained in this discussion, it must be taken to refer to an appropriate kind of *internal C-fiber activity* rather than to an *external* stimulus which, in reality, produces (as a *response*) this appropriate kind of activity. Otherwise the dice would be unfairly loaded against any identity thesis—a result that Kripke almost certainly would want to avoid. The question now becomes: Is it possible that some of the events that occur in C-fiber regions of the brain are such that it is feasible to identify them with mental events? Or more bluntly: Is it possible that some of the events that comprise C-fiber activity are mental events? The identity theorist must, or course, answer in the affirmative.

Does it follow from such an answer that the identity theorist thereby denies Kripke's contentions quoted above? This question is by no means as unequivocal as it may seem. For much the same reasons, neither is the question as to whether or not the mind-brain identity thesis is a contingent claim. To consider these questions we shall need to develop a small amount of "quasi technical" apparatus of our own. We need the notion of *causal structure* and the notion of a *causal network*. The accompanying greatly oversimplified sketch will serve both to explain these notions and to help answer the questions at issue. In the diagram, the circles represent events, and the arrows connecting them represent causal connections. A lower-case letter indicates that an event is a brain event. If the letter is from the beginning portion of the alphabet, the brain event is (also) a mental event; letters toward the end of the alphabet indicate brain events (or other neurological events) that are not mental events. Capital letters indicate "input" and "output" events —input into the neurological network and output from the network. For example, the event, A, might be light striking the eyes and B sound waves entering the ears, while X and Y might be lifting an arm and uttering a word, respectively. Dots and arrows with no circles at their heads or no circles at their tails indicate that large portions of (indeed, most of) the network is not shown in the diagram.

The entire diagram represents a *causal network*, and every item shown is an essential part of the particular network that is illustrated. In other words, a causal network consists of a number of (causally connected) events and of the causal connections among them. The *causal structure* of the network consists entirely of the causal connections and the positions or loci of the events in the network. For example, if in the diagram event B were replaced by another event or even by an event of another *kind*, the result would be a *different*

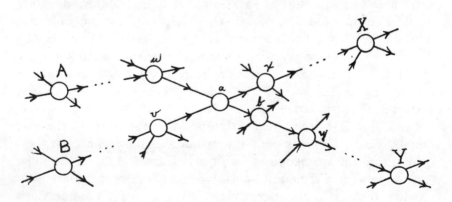

Figure 1

causal *network*, but the causal *structure* would remain *exactly the same*. The same holds for event a, event y, or any and all other events.

Let us now suppose that the events represented in the central part of the diagram occur in the *C*-fiber regions of the brain and that the event labeled 'a' is pain$_{39}$ (alias b_{76}). Pain$_{39}$ is, thus, a part of the activity taking place in this region of the *C*-fibers. Its immediate causal ancestors u and v are also a part of this activity, although, unlike a (alias pain$_{39}$, alias b_{76}), they are not mental events. Among pain$_{39}$'s causal descendants are b, a brain event that is also a mental event (anger$_{64}$, perhaps), and y, a brain event and perhaps a *C*-fiber event that is *not* a mental event.

At this point, I should emphasize that the view being advocated is much easier to present and defend when an *event ontology*, as opposed to a *substance* or *thing ontology*, is presupposed. This is to presuppose that the universe consists entirely of *events* and the causal relations that hold among them. For example, what we commonsensically take to be a *thing* (or a *substance* or a *portion of matter*) consists entirely, according to the event ontology, of a family of events intimately related to each other in certain ways.[10] But, it might be asked by way of objection, what *are* events? Are they not what *happen* to *things* or what *things* (or groups of *things*) *do*? How then is it possible to eliminate *things* in favor of *events*? We may reply, first, that, even in the commonsense framework, there are some events that do not involve *things* or *pieces of matter* in a necessary or obvious way. Let us call such events "pure events." If I could be assured of not being taken too seriously, I would say that a pure event is (something like) the instancing of a property or the exemplification of a property, in a suitably broad sense of 'property'. This is not to be taken as a definition (we are taking events to be primitives) but, rather, a crude, informal characterization. Now, for example, the presence of ambient light, heat, etc., as well as fluctuations of them are *events* that do not, in any obvious manner, involve *substances* or *portions of matter*. Certainly they are conceptually independent of substances. The existence in their own right of such *pure events* is not impugned by the fact that physics tells us that they are *caused* by other events; and whether these other events involve "substances" or are themselves pure events does not matter either as far as the autonomous existence of the pure events

is concerned. The same considerations hold for the presence of gravitational and other kinds of fields and for fluctuations therein. Other
examples of *pure events* are: a twinge of pain, a feeling of nausea,
and a surge of pleasure or joy. In fact, I should say that all mental
events are, rather obviously, pure events. *Assuming an event ontology*, then, *amounts to assuming that the universe consists entirely of*
pure events. What we commonsensically believe to be *things*, or
"substances" or hunks of matter are, according to the event ontolo-
gist, families of (pure) events, families of families of pure events,
etc., related to each other in certain, intimate ways.

Now, I have been convinced by Russell and by reflecting on implications of contemporary physics that such an event ontology is
correct or, at the very worst, that it is no more incorrect than a *thing*
or *substance* ontology; and, as remarked earlier, it is more convenient for the view that I am proposing in this paper. However, the
view does not *have* to presuppose an event ontology; so I hope that
those who find such an ontology unpalatable will bear with me a
little longer. On the other hand, it must be emphasized that *the
view does have to assume that some physical events are pure events
and that all mental events are pure events*. Unless this is explicitly
recognized, the position is very difficult to understand and, I believe, impossible to accept. For example, if C-fiber activity is thought
of as consisting of threadlike pieces of matter (the "C-fibers") waving around and perhaps stroking each other, then any attempt to
identify such activity with pain (as felt in all of its excruciating im-
mediacy) does become patently absurd. However, if we recognize
that C-fiber activity is a complex causal network in which at least
some of the events are pure events and that neurophysiology, physics, chemistry, etc., provide us *only* with knowledge of the *causal
structure* of the network, the way is left entirely open for the neuro-
psychologist to theorize that some of the events in the network *just
are pains* (in all of their qualitative, experiential, mentalistic richness).

Let us now return to Kripke's claim that, in order to create C-fiber
stimulation (C-fiber activity, in our terms), "it would seem that
God need only to create beings with C-fibers capable of the appropriate type of *physical* . . . [activity]; whether the beings are conscious or not is irrelevant" [my italics]. Interpreted in one way, this

claim is true; but under this interpretation, it in no way counts against the identity thesis. Interpreted in another way, the claim is inconsistent with the identity thesis; however, under this second interpretation, I contend, it becomes false. Under the first interpretation, 'C-fiber activity' refers to a *causal structure*; more specifically, it refers to a certain kind of causal structure of a complex of events in the C-fiber regions of the brain. Now, quite obviously, it is (logically) possible for one and the same causal structure to be exemplified by many different complexes of events (by many different causal networks). So in order for God to create C-fiber activity *in this sense*, all He has to do is create a complex of events that has the appropriate causal structure. *The nature of the events in the complex* is *irrelevant*; some or all of them may be tickles, feelings of warmth, or, even, pain; or, on the other hand, every one of them could be entirely nonmental. In this sense of 'C-fiber activity', Kripke is entirely correct in his claim that whether or not conscious beings are involved is irrelevant. However, the identity thesis, properly formulated, does *not* attempt to identify mental activity with C-fiber activity *in this sense*; i.e., it does *not* identify pain with the *causal structure of the complex of events—just as Kripke does not identify heat with the causal structure of heat-sensation production.* What is identified with (a specific kind of) pain is a (specific kind of) event, or complex of events, in the causal *network*—a (kind of) event, moreover, that has the position it has in the network *in this, the actual, world*. (Analogously, what is identified with heat is a [specific kind of] event, or complex of events, that causes the heat sensations in this, the actual world.) If the term 'C-fiber activity' is used to refer to such events (or complexes of events)—events that have the appropriate position in the causal network in this, the actual world—then, according to the identity thesis, 'C-fiber activity' *in this* (second) *sense* refers to pain and *does so rigidly*. If Kripke's claim is interpretated according to this sense of 'C-fiber activity,' then it must be denied; for, in this sense, 'C-fiber activity' rigidly designates pain, and the existence of sentient beings is necessarily involved with the existence of pain and, therefore, necessarily involved with the existence of C-fiber activity *in this sense* (just as the existence of mobile molecules is necessarily involved with the existence of heat).

It is not part of my purpose to speculate about what sense of 'C-fiber activity' (or 'C-fiber stimulation') Kripke has in mind. But surely he would agree that the identity theorist can legitimately use the term in the second sense that I have discussed and that, if he is to be refuted, the refutation must be accomplished under the aegis of such a use. Let us now ask whether or not it can be plausibly contended that in order to create C-fiber activity, *in the second sense of 'C-fiber activity'*, all God has to do is create beings with C-fibers capable of the appropriate kind of *physical* activity and whether or not the beings are sentient is irrelevant. I have argued, of course, that such a contention is false, but I think that it is instructive to inquire as to why it may seem so prima facie plausible. This, too, has already been answered—at least implicitly, I believe. As noted, we may tend to think of the *physical* activity of C-fibers as being nothing but (inert) threadlike pieces of matter waving about and perhaps rubbing against each other; and, it certainly would be absurd to claim that such goings-on are identical with occurrences of pains (in the genuinely mentalistic sense of 'pain' that we and Kripke are using throughout). So that Kripke's claim about the irrelevance of consciousness vis-à-vis the appropriate kind of *physical* activity is plausible, it seems to me, *only* if *the physical* is conceived in such a rather naive and, I claim, such a scientifically inaccurate manner. That such a conception is scientifically inaccurate follows from considerations that are quite independent of the mind-brain identity thesis. I have contended this at length elsewhere (e.g., 1970, 1972, 1976), following Russell (1948, 1956), Schlick (1974), and others. In other words, C-fiber activity, *in the sense required*, does not consist of "impure" events like threads of matter waving about; rather, C-fiber activity (or the component of it with which we are concerned) is a complex of *pure events* such that physical science has something to say about their causal structure but absolutely nothing about their "intrinsic nature" (more on this presently).

But we must not be too hasty in faulting Kripke for operating with the naive, inadequate notion of the physical (if, indeed, he does so). For, I believe, traditional (Hobbesian) materialists *as well as many contemporary ones* attempt to identify "the mental" with "the physical" *in* something very much like *this defective sense of* '*physical*'. (Eliminative [or "replacemant"] materialism does not do so. However, we shall soon see that it is not a genuine mind-brain identity theory and, therefore, is not within the scope of our present concerns—although both Kripke and I seem to find it difficult to resist the temptation to reject it as being "self-evidently absurd.") As I have already indicated, if the identity thesis is interpreted materialistically, then Kripke's objections are not only cogent, but, in my opinion, virtually conclusive.

Returning to the main point, let us examine again the term 'C-fiber activity'—or, better and less subject to ambiguity, the rigid designator that I, in response to Kripke's suggestion, have been using in its stead, 'b_{76}'. Once more we must emphasize that the referent of this rigid designator is *epistemically undetermined* as far as neurophysiology and other "purely physical" sciences are concerned. Physical science leaves us completely ignorant as to *what* the referent of 'C-fiber activity' (or better, 'b_{76}') *is*; it provides us *only* with knowledge about the locus of the referent in the causal network. Or, stated without the quasi-technical, rigid-designator terminology, physical science leaves us entirely ignorant as to *what* C-fiber activity *is* and provides us *only* with knowledge about its causal structure (including, of course, its causal connections to the rest of the neurophysiological causal network).

We see now that when God created the *C*-fiber event, $pain_{39}$ (alias a, alias b_{76}), the existence of an essentially involved conscious being was *not* irrelevant; it was *necessarily* required. The creation of *this* particular bit of *C*-fiber activity *just was* the creation of $pain_{39}$ (alias a, alias b_{76}). Nothing *else* had to be done in order to make it be *felt* as pain; its "essence" *is* being *felt as pain*. And, of course, it would *not* be in God's powers to make $pain_{39}$ (alias a and b_{76}) be felt as a tickle, or as warmth, or as nothing, rather than felt as pain. Feeling a certain determinate kind of pain is one and the same event as $pain_{39}$. (To *be* pain is to be *felt* as pain.) On the other hand, in addition to creating $pain_{39}$ (alias b_{76}, alias a), God did do *something* else; He made the contingent decision to give $pain_{39}$ the causal role that is indicated in the diagram. He *could* have decided to give it an entirely different neurophysiological causal role or even to give it no neurophysiological role at all; for example, He might have decided to cast the world in a Cartesian mold. Analogously, God could have decided to give molecular motion (alias heat) a different causal role from the one that it has; He might, for example, have decided *not* to have it cause heat sensations. And, just as He could have decided to have events of a different kind, say low-frequency radio waves, be the principal and proximal cause of heat sensations, he also could have decided to have an event of a quite different kind play the neurophysiological causal role that, as a matter of contingent fact, is played by pain$_{39}$. In particular, he could have decided to have this role played by a nonmental event.

The points illustrated by these examples follow from the more general principle: *it is* (logically) *possible for different causal networks to have the same causal structure*; or, in other words, one and the same causal structure may be realized in a number of different ways, i.e., may be exemplified by a number of different causal networks. Thus God could have created a causal network such that it differed from the one in the diagram only in that the positions occupied by a and b were occupied by different events—perhaps by events that were nonmental. This creation would have been a different causal network, but it would have been the same causal structure. Or, giving the Diety a rest, *in some possible worlds, mental events are* (some of the) *elements of C-fiber activity*, and, *in other possible worlds, none of the elements of C-fiber activity are mental events*. More generally, *in some possible worlds, mental events are brain events*, and, *in other possible worlds, no mental events are brain events*. This is true, I claim, because to be a brain event is to occupy a position in an appropriate portion of the neurophysiological causal network, and it is a contingent matter as to what kind of events occupy any such position. *With this understanding*, we may take the *identity thesis* to be *the thesis that all mental events are brain events*. *Such a thesis is contingent*, as we have just seen. But *this*, of course, *does not by any means entail that there are contingent identities*. A fortiori, it is entirely consistent with what, indeed, *must* be the case: *all the identities* that hold between mental events and brain events *hold necessarily*. How all of this comes to be the case has already been explained repeatedly, perhaps ad nauseum, and with several variations above. Nevertheless, since it *is* the heart of the matter, I shall make one more try.

We have just formulated the identity thesis as the claim that all mental events are brain events. This may be reformulated to become: Any mental event is identical with some brain event. We may write this as

$$(x) [Mx \supset (\exists y) (By \cdot \square \, x = y)]$$

(where 'Mx' stands for 'x is a mental event,' 'By' for 'y is a brain event,' and '$\square \, x = y$' for 'x and y are necessarily identical'). Now *the statement as a whole is contingent*. But if the statement is true, then the following holds: Consider any value of 'x' that satisfies 'Mx,' say 'pain$_{39}$,' where pain$_{39}$ *is* a mental event. Then there must be (exactly) one value of 'y' say 'b_{76},' such that the expression '$\square$ pain$_{39} = b_{76}$' expresses a true proposition, i.e., such that it is necessarily true that pain$_{39}$ is identical with b_{76}. This, along with what has gone on before, removes, I hope, any obstacles in the way of accepting the claim that the identity thesis is a contingent thesis, although all identities that hold between mental events and brain events hold necessarily. Recall once more that *there are contingent identity statements*, but *there are no contingent identities*. The identity thesis is a *statement* (or is expressed by a statement). *It* is not an identity, but, rather, it asserts the existence of identities of a certain kind. The *statement* is contingent, but the *identities*, if they hold at all, hold necessarily.

It is true that many, perhaps most, identity theorists speak of contingent identities. But surely this is because they are misled by illusions of contingency. These "illusions" arise because the more interesting and important identity *statements* are either contingent or involve "associated contingent facts" in the ways that are now familiar to us.

Unfortunately, the strongest objection to the identity thesis is, in my opinion, yet to come. Just how it is related to Kripke's objections remains to be seen. Given what physiology and physics tell us about C-fibers and their activity, is it reasonable or even coherent to suppose that mental events comprise (a portion of) such activity? A prime—perhaps *the* prime—ingredient of this activity seems to be neuronal activity, which, let us assume, consists of chemical and (the associated) electrical activity. Chemical and electrical events, in turn, involve the transfer and transportation of electrons, ions, etc. How can one claim that (some of) the goings-on of these tiny charged particles of matter are identical with pains, joys, sorrows, thoughts that two plus two equals four, etc.? Surely, it may seem, such a claim is absurd! I once heard Benson Mates remark that it makes no more sense to identify a mental event with a brain event than it does to identify a quadratic equation with a billy goat. It is not difficult to empathize with his sentiments. Let us state the objection in a more general manner: (1) We know from common sense, from physics, from neurophysiology, etc., what brain events are like. (2) We know ("by acquaintance"—and perhaps better than we know anything else) what mental events are like. (3) This knowledge reveals that brain events differ radically from mental events; more specifically, it reveals that mental events have properties that brain events lack and that brain events have properties that mental events lack. Therefore, the objection concludes, no mental events are brain events.[11]

This, in my opinion, is *the* argument against the identity thesis, and the most important specific objections to the thesis, including Kripke's, depend upon it in one way or another. The details of the dependence need not concern us. What should be done, rather, is to acknowledge the obvious: premise (or, rather, intermediate conclusion) number (3) above must be denied if the identity thesis is to be maintained; if the thesis is to be plausible, it must be plausible to contend that some brain events share *all* of their properties, both "essential" and "accidental" ones, with mental events. More precisely:

$$(x) \left\{ Mx \supset (\exists y) \left[By \cdot (\Phi) (\Phi x \equiv \Phi y) \right] \right\}$$

where 'Mx' stands for 'x is a mental event,' 'By' for 'y is a brain event,' and '(Φ)' is to be read as 'for any property, Φ.'

The typical materialist move is to deny premise (2) above. Materialists tend to hold that knowledge of mental events, if it exists at all, is at best second or third rate knowledge. The belief that we are directly acquainted with the (ingredients of) mental events that comprise our very being is, according to them, at least partly and perhaps totally mistaken. Some go on to maintain that knowledge claims about our mental events (about "private experience," etc.) are so defective that they should, in principle, be abandoned entirely—that, as our knowledge from physics, physiology, etc. increases, we shall see that talk about (allegedly) mental events, private experience, etc., is on a par with talk about witches, demons, or perhaps phlogiston and epicycles. When that happy day arrives, they tell us, we shall talk only about brain events, molecules and electrons, and other "scientifically respectable" entities. This position has been called the *replacement* or the *disappearance* version of the identity thesis (see, e.g., Feyerabend, 1963, and Rorty, 1965). Quite obviously, however, it is not an identity thesis at all; it purports to eliminate mental entities altogether rather than to identify them with brain events. This is not the place to give detailed arguments against such a view. I *will* say more about it later, but now I just want to remark that this position is certainly rejected by Kripke. It is fair to say, I believe, that both he and I find it "self-evidently absurd."

Some materialists who reject premise (2) take a different tack. According to them, knowledge claims (purporting to be) about mental entities are so confused or otherwise defective that they should be "translated" into "topic-neutral" statements. The following example is given by J. J. C. Smart (1959):

When a person says 'I see a yellowish-orange after-image' he is saying something like this: 'There is something going on which is like what is going on when I have my eyes open, am awake, and there is an orange illuminated in good light in front of me, that is, when I really see an orange.'

The idea seems to be that the troublesome, mentalistically tainted term 'yellowish-orange after-image' is replaced by the descriptive phrase 'something going on which is like . . .' The descriptive phrase, we are told, is *topic-neutral* in that it makes no commitment as to *what* its referent *is*; it merely indicates, the materialist tells us, that it (the referent) has certain relations[12] to epistemically and metaphysically respectable entities such as oranges, normal illumination, etc. The materialist might then go on to point out that, since this cleaned-up way of referring to what *were* allegedly mental entities leaves their *intrinsic nature*[13] entirely open and unspecified, it makes perfectly good sense to advance the contingent hypothesis that they are brain states (or brain events).

It is easy to anticipate, I believe, Kripke's reaction to this move, although I am reluctant to put words into his mouth: neither can the "topic-neutral" descriptive phrase be a *translation* of the term 'yellowish-orange after-image', nor can it be used to fix its reference. For being a yellowish-orange after-image is surely an essential property of yellowish-orange after-images; and, even more importantly, being an item in direct experience, being or involving a (visual) sensation, and (therefore) being a mental entity are all essential properties of yellowish-orange after-images. As was explained at some length earlier, this precludes fixing the reference of 'yellowish-orange after-image' entirely by means of relationships between after-images and nonmental items.

We have also seen, it is true, that this does not prevent us from *referring* to entities like after-images by means of descriptions (including "topic-neutral" ones) or even by means of "topic-neutral" rigid designators. In fact, we could just stipulate that the rigid designator 'b_{77}' refers to a type of brain event that is very similar to the brain event produced "when I have my eyes open, am awake, and there is an orange illuminated in good light . . . etc." We could then propose the contingent hypothesis that a yellowish-orange after-image is what is so produced, which, if true, would entitle us to assert a posteriori the necessary truth that b_{77} is a yellowish-orange after-image.

This move, in fact, *should* be made by the *identity theorist*, I maintain. It is not, however, open to the *materialist*, for to make it is to abandon materialism. Far from eliminating the "truly mental," this tactic yields the result that some brain events just *are*, intrinsically, nothing but "truly mental" events. These considerations show, I believe, that this variety of materialism must retreat to the following position:

We do not *translate* mentalistic discourse into topical-neutral discourse, the materialist must hold; rather we *replace* the former with the latter, and, moreover, the replacement does not result in the loss of any cognitive content that is important, significant, scientifically respectable, etc.

Thus the so-called *topic-neutral translation* thesis turns out to be a variety of—or rather an implementation of—the "disappearance" or "replacement" thesis. These views have been considered here as examples of unsuccessful attempts by materialists to answer the main objection to the identity thesis. They turn out *not* to be genuine mind-brain identity theses, and they "solve" the mind-brain problem by sweeping the genuinely mental under the rug.

This failure of materialism results from the fact that it must attack the objection at its strongest point, premise (2). I say this *not* because I believe that knowledge about our mental events is certain, infallible, or complete (I do not so believe), but rather because it provides us with the best (perhaps the only) knowledge that we have of the *intrinsic* properties of individual events (as opposed to *causal* and other *structural* properties). Moreover, if the objection is to retain anything at all of its great intuitive potency, premises (1) and (2) as well as intermediate conclusion (3) must be taken to refer to knowledge about *intrinsic* properties.

There is a widespread tendency to identify[14] the mind-body identity thesis with materialism. To do so, however, is to miss the point *entirely* of any genuine mind-brain identity claim. Materialism, as it is typically proposed and defended, seeks to eliminate the *genuinely mental* realm, to deny that genuinely mental events exist. But, if there *are* no mental events, then the thesis that all mental events are brain events is either nonsensical or vacuously true. A *genuine mind*-brain identity thesis must hold that there are both mental events and brain events, that all mental events are brain events, and that therefore *some brain events are mental events*—in the most full-blown "mentalistic" sense of 'mental.' Such a view I have called *nonmaterialist physicalism*[15] (see, e.g., Maxwell, 1976).

As should be apparent by now, I propose to defend the identity thesis against the prime objection by denying premise (1). More specifically: although physics, neurophysiology, etc., *do* provide us with the best knowledge we have of the *structure* of the neurophysiological causal networks that comprise the brain, they provide us with *no knowledge* (or precious little) about the *intrinsic* properties of individual brain events.[16] *Thus the possibility is entirely open that some of these brain events* just are *our twinges of pain, our feelings of joy and sorrow, our thoughts that two plus two equals four, etc.* Such a brain event would, of course, "share"[17] all of its properties with the mental event which it *is*—all "essential" properties and all "accidental" properties, all intrinsic properties and all causal properties, etc., etc. By now, I hope, this is no more mysterious than the fact that the 51-year-old brother of Billy Carter "shares" all of his properties, be they accidental, essential, intrinsic, relational, etc., with the present (February 1977) president of the United States.

Well, perhaps it *is somewhat* more mysterious, for reasons to be discussed in a moment. But first it should be emphasized that the materialist has the matter entirely backwards and reversed: there is no need whatever to replace mentalistic terms with "topic-neutral" ones. For, I hold, premise (2) is correct: we *do* know (*by acquaintance*) the intrinsic nature of our mental events, i.e., we know *what* the "topic" of discourse about mental events *is*. On the other hand, we do not have this kind of knowledge about anything in the non-mental realm, i.e., we reject premise (1) insofar as it pertains to the intrinsic nature of the entities involved. Therefore, with one kind of exception, we *must* refer to physical events in a *topic-neutral* manner, unless we are willing to introduce a certain amount of confusion and unnecessary puzzlement.[18] We can refer to such physical events only with descriptions or with terms whose reference has been fixed by means of descriptions or by other *topic-neutral*, non-ostensive means.[19] This is not, of course, a "disappearance" or "replacement" view of the physical. It is just that our references to physical events by means of *topic-neutral designators* is an explicit signal of our ignorance of their intrinsic nature — our ignorance as to *what* such physical entities *are*. It is a reminder that our knowledge of them is limited to their causal and other structural properties. The kind of exception to all this mentioned above is comprised by those physical events that are mental events.

I have been trying to remove, layer by layer, the obstacles that stand in the way of maintaining a mind-brain identity thesis — emphasizing along the way the untenability of accomplishing this by means of antimentalist stratagems such as materialism. So far the task has been relatively easy, if somewhat tedious and repetitive due to the fact that layers tend to overlap each other. We approach now what is perhaps the last and certainly the thickest and most formidable layer. This difficulty arises from our rejection, or, rather from our *qualified* acceptance, of premise (1). We agreed that (physical[20]) science provides us with the best information that we have about the structure of the physical realm, including the structure of the brain. But, we insist, science is in the main completely silent about the intrinsic, qualitative properties exemplified by physical events.[21] The difficulty is two-fold: (a) Science does seem, sometimes, to deal explicitly with intrinsic properties. For example, we certainly seem to be dealing directly with intrinsic properties when we say that electrons are negatively charged—indeed, that each electron has a charge of 4.8 x 10 $^{-10}$ e.s.u. It would appear that having a negative electrical charge of 4.8 x 10 $^{-10}$ e.s.u. is an intrinsic property of an electron; moreover, *being an electron* seems to be an intrinsic property. (b) The structures exemplified in our (private) experience, i.e., the structures we know by "acquaintance," are prima facie quite different from any known *or* hypothesized brain structures—from any structures exemplified in brain events. If these differences are actual rather than merely apparent, then the identity thesis is refuted: *unless each mental event "shares" all of its properties, both intrinsic and structural with some brain event, identity cannot hold*.

The first difficulty is not serious. *To be an electron* is to play a certain kind of *causal* (and/or otherwise *structural*) role: or more precisely, the reference of the term 'electron' is fixed (ontologically) by specifying the positions that electrons occupy in causal-structural networks. Similarly the reference of 'having a negative charge of 4.8 x 10 $^{-10}$ e.s.u.' is (ontologically) fixed by the causal-structural role played by such charges. However, the reference of such terms is not (to this date) *epistemically determined*. The terms do refer to intrinsic properties, but we do not know *what* the referents *are*, e.g., we do not know what a negative electrical charge *is* — just as we did not know what heat *was* until we discovered that molecular motion caused heat sensation. (Actually, just as we do not know what an electron *is*, we *still* don't know what heat [alias molecular motion] *is*. We just know more about its causal roles than we used to.) Our earlier statement that physical science provides us with knowledge of structural properties but not with knowledge of intrinsic properties was an oversimplification: science *does* assert the *existence* of instances of a variety of intrinsic properties; moreover, it provides information about the various causal-structural roles that such instances play. However, it *does* leave us completely ignorant as to *what* these intrinsic properties *are*. This crucial matter calls for repeated emphasis: physics, chemistry, physiology, etc., leave us entirely ignorant about the intrinsic nature of physical entities in general and of brain events in particular; the physical sciences, properly construed, do refer to intrinsic properties, but they do so via *topic-neutral* designators—designators that leave us entirely in the dark as to *what* their referents *are*; their referents remain epistemically *un*determined. This disposes of the first difficulty, (a). For it leaves entirely open the possibility that some brain events just *are* events such as the occurrence of a twinge of pain, the occurrence of a red expanse in the visual field, thinking that two plus two equals four, and exemplification of other intrinsic properties that characterize our experience (our "mental processes"). This consequence that (at least) *a portion of the physical realm may be intrinsically mental* must be entertained in complete literalness by anyone who wishes to entertain seriously a genuine mind-brain identity thesis.

What the statement of the second difficulty, (b), amounts to is a somewhat more precise statement of the "grain objection" referred to in a footnote on p. 392 above. The objection asks, for example, how is it that the occurrence of a smooth, continuous expanse of red in our visual experience can be identical with a brain process that must, it would seem, involve particulate, discontinuous affairs such as transfers of or interactions among large numbers of electrons, ions, or the like? Surely being smooth or continuous is a *structural* property, and being particulate or discontinuous is also a structural property, one moreover that is incompatible with being smooth and continuous. This strongly suggests, the objection continues, that at least some mental events exemplify structural properties that are not exemplified by any brain event, or, at any rate, not in any brain event that is an otherwise feasible candidate for being identical with the mental event. It follows that the mental event and the brain event do not share all of their (structural) properties, and thus, the objector concludes, they cannot be identical.

The difficulty is genuine and crucial. Unless there is good reason to hope that it can be overcome, there is no good reason to hope that mind-brain identity is possible. This difficulty is not, however, the one that has been the main concern of this paper, which has been the difficulty posed by Kripke. Nevertheless our answer to Kripke's challenge has emphasized the indirectness, the abstractness, and the incompleteness of our knowledge of the physical realm, and reflection upon this makes the "grain objection" appear—to me, at least —somewhat less formidable. It is true that we have not, in principle, set any limits on the scope of our knowledge about the structure of the physical realm; but the indirect, highly theoretical nature of such knowledge strongly suggests that it *is* quite incomplete and imperfect. There are also strong independent grounds for the same conclusion. Surely very few historians, philosophers, and practitioners of the physical sciences believe that our knowledge of the structure of the manifold of physical events is nearing perfection or completeness. For example, what many consider to be the unsatisfactory status of the foundations of quantum theory may well be due to crucial gaps in our knowledge of structure at the micro-level; and perhaps it is not too fanciful to suspect that the failure to integrate quantum theory and general relativity is due in part to a lack of knowledge of structures of causal networks that are somewhere between the very small ones and the very large ones. Perhaps it is precisely this "middle-sized" realm that provides the relevant context for investigation of mind-brain identities. In sum, as our knowledge grows about the various manifolds of events that constitute the physical realm, perhaps we shall discover that some of the structures that are exemplified by them *are* entirely isomorphic and quite possibly identical with instances of the structures with which we are acquainted in our "private" experience.

Even within the bounds of present physical theory, we might consider a fanciful but logically coherent possibility. Fields—electrical, magnetic, or gravitational—and fluctuations in fields are, *as far as their structures are concerned*, viable candidates for identification with (some kinds of) mental states or mental events. There are, no doubt, strong objections against supposing that, say a fluctuation in an electrical field could be a mental event (such as a twinge of pain). However, such objections could not be based on a difference in structure or "grain"; as far as I can see, such a fluctuation could be entirely isomorphic in all respects with a twinge of pain. The identity theorist must hope that continued developments in physics, neurophysiology, etc., will make manifest the existence of physical entities that have such appropriate structures and that are also otherwise more feasible candidates for being identified with mental entities.

Fortunately some neurophysiologists and neuropsychologists are devoting detailed attention to these problems. For example, the holographic theories of Pribram and others represent attempts to incorporate the structural features of mental functions (e.g., memory) and the structural features of brain processes into *one* (self-identical!) model (Pribam, Baron, & Nuwer, 1974). More accurately, they attempt to describe models in which the structural properties that characterize brain processes are ("also") structural properties of mental functions, and conversely. In other words, they are searching for a model such that, in any given case, there is only *one* process (or function), and it is both a brain process and a mental process.

Whether or not the holographic approach will survive long-range investigation is not a matter about which I would care to forecast, even if I felt competent about its details. It does seem clear that this general *kind* of approach is a necessary condition for significant future development and progress in dealing with mind-body problems. A model such as the holographic one should, obviously, warm the heart of an identity theorist. If it turned out to be "successful" —if it stood up to experimental testing, successfully predicted startling new experimental outcomes, etc.—this would provide a considerable degree of confirmation (by no means conclusive, of course) of the identity thesis.

Let us suppose the holographic model turned out to be unsuccessful. Would this refute or "falsify" the identity thesis? Would it even count very strongly against it (strongly disconfirm it)? Both questions must be answered, I believe, in the negative. This seems to me an instance of a kind of methodological situation that frequently obtains in scientific inquiry, a situation such that positive experimental results would strongly confirm the hypothesis being tested but such that negative results, far from refuting the hypothesis (*pace* Popper), would disconfirm it only very slightly. (For discussion of a notorious example, the experimental "detection" of the neutrino, see Maxwell, 1974.) It is true that, if there followed *repeated* failures of *other* various identity theoretic models in addition to failure of the holographic model, then the identity thesis would begin to be appreciably, perhaps strongly, disconfirmed, especially if all of this were accompanied by impressive successes of dualistic models. I mention this matter to illustrate the complexity of the relationships between experimental evidence and contingent scientific (*cum* philosophical) problems *such as the mind-body problem*! I have discussed this in some detail in Maxwell 1976; and I argue there that it leads to the conclusion that, in several of the traditional problem areas, the mind-body problem being a prime example, there is no sharp line or very helpful distinction between scientific inquiry and philosophical inquiry. In other words, philosophical investigation is *not* exhausted without remainder by logical, conceptual, and linguistic considerations however important, difficult, and interesting these may be. For this very general reason coupled with more specific ones such as the "grain" problem just discussed, I do not believe that philosophers are going to contribute a great deal more to the "solutions" of mind-brain issues until they attain something close to specialists' competence in neurophysiology, neuropsychology, etc. I am willing to go one step further and predict that the next important breakthrough, if it comes at all, will come from the neurosciences. On the other hand, the neuroscientists will probably not contribute much either unless they understand and appreciate the logical, conceptual and, *yes* (!), the contingent components of the "mind-body problem" that have concerned philosophers over the centuries. The work of Kripke that we have been considering provides valuable, fresh perspectives on these crucial components.

Notes

1. In subsequent references to Kripke, page numbers refer to his 1972 essay.

2. Cf. Thomas Nagel, 1974.

3. In natural languages, of course, such results are accomplished by (implicit) rules of language or conventional language practice, etc., rather than by explicit stipulations.

4. Kripke maintains — correctly, it seems to me — that the reference of proper names, especially those of persons, is hardly ever fixed in the simple way that it is in our case of Oscar. The example is therefore, as far as proper names are concerned, somewhat artificial; I have used it because of its relative transparence and simplicity and, moreover, because reference-fixing relevant for cases of the so-called contingent identities discovered by scientific investigation (e.g., common salt is sodium chloride) *does* parallel, very closely for Kripke, that for the *Oscar* example.

5. As far as actual linguistic practice is concerned, this seems quite wrong to me. But it does not matter; let us suppose that we did and do use a language in which 'heat' does rigidly designate whatever it is that causes "heat sensations."

6. Kripke directs his arguments mainly against "type-type" mental-physical identities and says that advocates of "token-token" identities are perhaps partially immune to his criticism. The reason for the immunity is not clear to me. However, I shall also consider, in the main, type-type identities. Absolving them of Kripke's charges will also absolve token-token identities, since these are entailed by the type-type ones.

7. Although, as indicated earlier, being a brain event *is* an essential property of *being* a brain event; and being a brain event *is* an essential property of *being* a brain event of a specific kind. Also, being a pain is *never* an essential property of *being* a specific kind of

brain event. Again, all of this is true simply because it *is necessarily* true that all neuro-physiological roles are neurophysiological roles, but it is not necessarily true that pain plays any neurophysiological role at all.

8. This is *my* way of putting this point.

9. Kripke says (p. 337), "I know virtually nothing about *C*-fibers except that the stimulation of them is said to be correlated with pain." My ignorance about *C*-fibers is, I am sure, at least as great as Kripke's. Unfortunately, however, we have to consider some questions about their nature if we are to deal adequately with the possibility of identifying their stimulation with pain.

10. As Russell, 1956, has put the matter:

The world is composed of events, not of things with changing states, or rather, everything that we have a right to say about the world can be said on the assumption that there are only events and not things. Things, as opposed to events, are an unnecessary hypothesis. This part of what I have to say is not exactly new, since it was said by Heraclitus. His view, however, annoyed Plato and has therefore ever since been considered not quite gentlemanly. In these democratic days this consideration need not frighten us. Two kinds of supposed entities are dissolved if we adopt the view of Heraclitus: on the one hand, persons, and on the other hand, material objects. Grammar suggests that you and I are more or less permanent entities with changing states, but the permanent entities are unnecessary, and the changing states suffice for saying all that we know on the matter. Exactly the same sort of thing applies to physical objects. If you go into a shop and buy a loaf of bread, you think that you have bought a "thing" which you can bring home with you. What you have in fact bought is a series of occurrences linked together by certain causal laws.

11. The "grain" objection, attributed to Wilfrid Sellars (1965) and elaborated by Paul E. Meehl (1966), is a special case of this objection.

12. In this example the relation is asserted to be just "bare" similarity. I shall ignore any difficulties that may plague such a relation (see, s.g., Shaffer, 1961).

13. My terms or, rather, Russell's (used toward another end, of course).

14. You should pardon the expression!

15. *Physicalism* because to be a physical event is to have a locus in the spatio-temporal causal network.

16. The claim is a general one, holding out only for the brain but for all physical systems. See, e.g., Russell, 1948, and Maxwell, 1970.

17. The word 'share' is put in "shudder quotes" because what we are talking about, of course, is a thing "sharing" all of its properties with itself. This seems to be a somewhat atypical way of talking. The same is true of saying that if "two [!] things" are identical, "they" "share" all of "their" properties, etc. All of this results, does it not, because reflexive relations, especially identities, are somewhat atypical?

18. In most of our practical, everyday discourse, such confusion does not, of course, arise. In such contexts, there is no more need to reform our customary beliefs and modes of reference than there would be to replace, in most of its uses, the word 'salt'' with the words 'sodium chloride' on the grounds that common table salt, sodium chloride, is just one out of thousands of kinds of salts, most of which are inedible and poisonous.

19. In a full-scale program, such reference-fixing can be accomplished systematically by using either Ramsey sentences or model-theoretic techniques. See above, p. 369, and Maxwell, 1970.

20. Psychology and some social sciences, properly conducted, do deal explicitly with intrinsic as well as structural properties.

21. This paper cannot provide a systematic account of the distinction between intrin-

sic and structural properties. I *have* made preliminary efforts in this direction in Maxwell, 1970. I believe that the examples used here, however, coupled with our common-sense grasp of the distinction, will be sufficient for the purposes of this paper.

References

Carnap, R. Meaning postulates, *Philosophical Studies*, 1952, 3, 65-73.

Carnap, R. Beobachtungsprache und theoretische sprache. *Dialectica*, 1957, 12, 236-248.

Feigl, H. Matter still largely material. *Philosophy of Science*, 1962, 29, 39-46.

Feyerabend, P. K. Materialism and the mind-body problem. *Review of Metaphysics*, 1963, 17, 46-64.

Hanson, N. R. The dematerialization of matter. *Philosophy of Science*, 1962, 29, 27-38.

Kripke, S. Naming and necessity. In D. Davidson & G. Harman (Eds.), *Semantics of natural language*. Boston and Dordrecht: Reidel, 1972.

Kripke, S. Identity and necessity. In M. Munitz (Ed.), *Identity and individuation*. New York: New York University Press, 1971.

Maxwell, G. Meaning postulates in scientific theories. In H. Feigl & G. Maxwell (Eds.), *Current issues in the philosophy of science*. New York: Holt, Rinehart, & Winston, 1961.

Maxwell, G. Structural realism and the meaning of theoretical terms. In M. Radner & S. Winokur (Eds.), *Analyses of theories and methods of physics and psychology: Minnesota studies in the philosophy of science* (Vol. 4). Minneapolis: University of Minnesota Press, 1970.

Maxwell, G. Russell on perception: A study in philosophical method. In D. Pears (Ed.), *Bertrand Russell: A collection of critical essays*. New York: Doubleday (Anchor Paperbacks), 1972.

Maxwell, G. Corroboration with demarcation. In P. A. Schlipp (Ed.), *The philosophy of Karl Popper*. LaSalle, Ill.: Open Court, 1974.

Maxwell, G. Scientific results and the mind-brain issue: Some afterthoughts. In G. Globus, G. Maxwell, & I. Savodnik (Eds.), *Consciousness and the brain: A scientific and philosophical inquiry*. New York: Plenum Press, 1976.

Meehl, P. E. The compleat autocerebroscopists: A thought experiment on Professor Feigl's mind-body identity thesis. In P. K. Feyerabend & G. Maxwell (Eds.), *Mind, matter, and method: Essays in philosophy and science in honor of Herbert Feigl*. Minneapolis: University of Minnesota Press, 1966.

Nagel, T. What is it like to be a bat? *Philosophical Review*, 1974, 83, 435-450.

Pribram, K. H., Baron, R., & Nuwer, M. The holographic hypothesis of memory in brain function and perception. In R. C. Atkinson, D. H. Krantz, R. C. Luce, & P. Suppes, (Eds.), *Contemporary developments in mathematical psychology*. San Francisco: W. H. Freeman, 1974.

Rorty, R. Mind-body identity, privacy, and categories. *Review of Metaphysics*, 1965, 19, 24-54.

Russell, B. *Human knowledge: Its scope and limits*. New York: Simon & Schuster, 1948.

Russell, B. *Portraits from memory*. New York: Simon & Schuster, 1956.

Schlick, M. *General theory of knowledge* (Albert E. Blumberg, trans.). Vienna and New York: Springer-Verlag, 1974.

Sellars, W. S. The identity approach to the mind-body problem. *Review of Metaphysics*, 1965, 18, 430-451.

Shaffer, J. Could mental states be brain processes? *Journal of Philosophy*, 1961, 58, 812-822.

Smart, J. J. C. Sensations and brain processes. *Philosophical Review*, 1959, 68, 141-156.

An Evolutionary Naturalist Realist
Doctrine of Perception
and Secondary Qualities

In this paper I outline an approach to perception that is characteristic of the position I call evolutionary naturalist realism (ENR hereafter), and sketch the way in which it supports a particular doctrine of secondary qualities. These doctrines I first set down in a thesis (Hooker, 1970). Elaborated, they form part of a book in preparation on the naturalist conception of *Homo Sapiens Sapiens*.

§ 1. Meta-Philosophy and Theory of Perception

I have developed both the metaphilosophy and the philosophy of a consistent, thoroughgoing evolutionary and naturalist approach to *Homo Sapiens Sapiens*, especially to that activity of the species called science, elsewhere (Hooker, 1974, 1975a, b and c), and the reader must turn there for detail and defense. Suffice it here to note that two consequences of the approach are that philosophical doctrines have the same epistemological and normative status as do scientific theories, and that the primary aim of ENR philosophy is to construct the most adequate, coherent, 'global' conception of the universe possible.

From the ENR standpoint a philosophical doctrine of perception is a *theory* of the perceptual process which answers the following questions:

Q_1: What is the process by which we acquire perceptual information concerning the external world?

Q_2: What is the relationship between the character and content of the conscious perceptual experience and the perceptual process?

Q_3: What is it about the perceptual process that justifies our calling the end-product perceptual *knowledge*, and knowledge *of the external world*?

Q_4: What is the correct account of those epistemic failures of perception: illusion and hallucination?

Historically, doctrines of perception have indeed had the orientation presupposed in these four questions and have usually dealt with the questions in the order stated. They have also changed with changing factual knowledge.

Contemporary students of philosophy can be forgiven for supposing that discussion of perception over the last two centuries has been dominated by arguments concerning the nature and existence of sense data (sensations, elementary perceptions, etc.), and that, despite such lavish attention, the issues involved are still somewhat obscure. In fact, the motives for introducing sensory items between the world and perceptual knowledge of the world seem to have been mixed. Roughly speaking, such sensory items have been required to play one or more of the following four roles. R_1: they are the representatives to consciousness of the entities in the external world; R_2: they are the component parts of conscious (phenomenal) content; R_3: they are the sources of knowledge concerning the external world; R_4: their possession is the ground of the justification of our knowledge concerning the world. Not all these roles have had equal weight in philosopher's minds when they wrote of such sensory items; very likely some were not even consciously considered as such. Still, the motives for each role are plain enough: each worthy philosophical doctrine of perception is supposed to address itself to questions Q_1-Q_4, and the introduction of sense data in their various guises was designed to answer these questions.

This is to approach perception with epistemology foremost. But those who have done so have typically chosen their ontology to suit their epistemological ends. Behind the epistemic approach lie some tacit and undefended assumptions that show great power in determining the character of the resulting doctrine. Five of these are:

A_1: The mind is epistemically transparent to itself.

A_2: Conscious awareness is propositional awareness, i.e., epistemic states are propositionally defined states.

A_3: The acquisition of perceptual knowledge demands an act of conscious apprehension, i.e., a particular conceptual content must come 'before' consciousness and be examined.

A$_4$: Sensory items, i.e., conceptually distinguishable contents, are individuals of the ontology, i.e., are objects.

A$_5$: Perception is veridical if and only if what is before the mind is an exact replica of what is in the world.

The first of these assumptions one associates especially with Descartes—is has run through philosophy of mind ever since, a deadly thread. From it, together with Cartesian scruples about the certainty of true knowledge, the second, third, and fourth assumptions follow naturally (the fourth aided by Lockean representational theory). And from these assumptions (coupled to a confusion of "sense data are the direct objects of knowledge" with "empirical knowledge is of objects; what is represented to consciousness in perception are the conditions of objects"), we obtain the last assumption.

ENR rejects all five of these assumptions. The arguments that lead to them, when there are any, are a tissue of falsehoods and non-sequiturs. This, because scientific evidence runs against them and arguments for them logically require metaphilosophical premises that ENR rejects. (Both these claims are reviewed in my book, mentioned in the introduction to this chapter; cf. Hooker, 1975a.) I shall not take time here to rehearse the well-known objections to the main alternatives to a direct realist doctrine of perception, i.e., to phenomenalism and representative realism (see e.g., Armstrong, 1966, 1968; Sellars, 1963; Smart, 1963), nor to their common model of the structure of mind, the inner scanner model (there is not the slightest neurophysiological evidence for this functional structure to the brain).[1]

What picture shall we adopt of the senses? The senses are aids to survival. They are our evolutionary heritage in the field of information-gathering about the environment. Physiologically, the human brain developed about the primitive visual perception center. Actual survival value, however, has ranked at least as high for other senses (e.g., smell, touch) in the case of some species as it has for vision in *Homo Sapiens*. Evolutionary development produces an ever-changing array of "sense"; from the point of view of adaptation there is no reason to believe that the senses are at all limited in their possible forms, except by the very general character of the environment and the organism (cf. also Grossman, 1974; Thomas, 1975). By contrast with this casual pragmatism, one might easily gain the impression from the way philosophers often write about the specifically human senses that they were divinely given, ineluctable servants of the passing play of consciousness, theater directors for an inner *son et lumiere* (etc., etc.) an alternative to which could not be imagined.

How then shall we conceive of the senses? First as *systems*, second as *information-processing* systems, and third as *environmentally oriented*. The senses are environmentally oriented, information-processing systems, i.e., *perceptual* systems. Roughly, our perceptual systems receive a pattern of physical stimuli, select and abstract from it (i.e., transform it), and feed it to the entire central nervous system for action.[2] At some point in this process conceptualization and consciousness set in.

According to my view of concepts as information-processing structures (Hooker, 1975d), conceptualization sets in early, e.g., at the retina; some of it will be genetically programmed ('hard') and some learned ('soft'); any boundaries between 'hard' and 'soft' drawn on linguistic grounds will be arbitrary, for language as such is not central to brain function (Hooker, 1975d).

The naturalist must still face the question of the relation of consciousness to perception.

Contemporary materialists have not fared well trying to answer the question. So strongly embedded is the inner-eye model of consciousness that most materialists seem to have assumed themselves to be on the horns of a dilemma: either admit consciousness and with it all the epistemic and scientific difficulties of the inner-eye model (especially for the materialist account) or eschew consciousness as a distinctive element of perceptual life at all. Most materialists seem to have chosen the second horn of the dilemma and eschewed any reference to distinctive conscious states. There is a second assumption, also arising out of the general history of philosophy, that aids in driving the materialist to avoid or denude consciousness; it is the belief that if one admits a distinctive conscious experience, a rich phenomenal life, one is bound ultimately to reject a materialist account of mind. It seems to be assumed that one can do justice to the distinctiveness of conscious experience, if at all, only by introducing special qualities of a special mind which turn out to have a quite ethereal nature to them.

For my part, I am sufficiently convinced that the phenomenon of consciousness is important enough that one ought to face it head on and not attempt to eliminate it. However, I also do not accept either of the assumptions just discussed. Following the earlier discussion, the view I am inclined to accept is that consciousness is only one limited aspect or phase of neurological functioning. This view is supported both by neurophysiological research and by comparative species studies; the former having begun to unravel the extent and importance of the undergirding subconscious neurological functions of the central nervous system (CNS) and the latter by displaying a cohering pattern of neurophysiological development that is associated with a gradual and late development of consciousness.[3]

The evolutionary approach to the central nervous system and hence to consciousness quite generally suggests three theses that run counter to most philosophical presumptions, namely, that (1) language, (2) consciousness, (3) personal unity are peripheral to nervous function. These theses are based upon the late evolutionary appearance of all three characteristics and the presumption that the older, more common functions of the nervous system continue to characterize its basic structure and function in later developments. One wants to give an evolutionary/neurophysiological explanation of language ability as a specialization of information-processing ability generally, of consciousness as a specialized phase of nervous function, of personal unity as an abstracted reflection at some 'higher' functional level of the relative integration of the subsystems of the nervous system. Although the levels of ignorance, ambiguity, and controversy are all high in this area, it currently seems to me that all the scientific evidence, e.g., that from aphasia, subconscious function, schizophrenia, brain-bisection etc., supports these theses.[4]

Therefore, I shall assume a unified mind-brain and 'fuse' the corresponding descriptive sentences (cf. Dennett, 1969). In my view there are no *objects* of conscious-awareness, there are only certain indissoluble experiences which we describe as 'My-being-consciously-aware-of-(that)-_____'. The experience is indissoluble in that one cannot remove the hyphens in this phrase to identify an object of awareness and a distinct subject that is aware. There *is*, in most experiences, a legitimate object of awareness, namely the situation of which the organism is directly *perceptually* aware (cf. below § 2), but that awareness is of the world, it is not of the experience of the world. Conscious-awareness is an *experience had*, it is not an awareness *of* any objects, nor is it, in the special sense I have reserved for the terms here, an awareness *that* anything (but more about the conceptual content of the experience shortly).[5]

Not surprisingly, the ENR approach to perception does not sit well with the epistemological approach. A central tenet, then, of my view of perception is that perceptual experience is the end-product of a process. Consider again what is the raw physical information reaching the perceiver's senses. It is not a set of beautifully polished *data*, a set of visual pictures of the world for example. It is, rather, the kinds of information a television camera or tape recorder receives: a more or less systematic pattern of fluctuations of physical magnitudes.[6] The perceptual process reflects a radical process of *selection* and *abstraction*. Moreover, the knowledge that is gained in perception, and the resulting content of the conscious perceptual experience, is a function not only of the state of the perceived world but also of the perceiver's processing capabilities, memory state, current situation, interests, and so forth. This point is a commonplace of everyday experience (cf. the chicken sexer who sorts without a conscious description and the inexperienced person who cannot; the altered perception of familiar situation often had upon waking in gloomy light, etc.) and has been strikingly demonstrated in laboratory and anthropological fieldwork (cf. Gregory, 1966; Snyder & Sendon, 1952; note 2 references).

Now, this view of perceptual data places the notion of *data* in its proper context. *It is only of the end-products of this perceptual process, i.e., the beliefs that are formed, that we can sensibly say that they are data.* A datum is something from which an inference can be made. It is not until incoming information has been abstracted, conceptualized etc., and trained into something resembling propositional beliefs that anything properly called data emerges. For only then can inferences (from this data) be made. But the original perceiving is then already complete, so clearly it is not itself a process of inferring to the world from some kind of perceptual data. The world is directly perceived, that is, we acquire noninferential knowledge of it through the senses, and *after that* inferences may be made. Perception results in the acquisition of knowledge and beliefs concerning the world; such knowledge and beliefs may form the basis for further inferences about the world, that is, they can act as data. To repeat: the objects of perception are not data, data are to be found, if anywhere, in the *results* of perception. Sense data theories of perception, then, locate data in the wrong place in the perceptual process.

From the point of view of the ENR approach, we might well re-construe sense data as theoretical entities and identify them with some features of the nervous process; but this would be more or less arbitrary. Certainly it is extremely unlikely that all four roles for sense data mentioned earlier could be fulfilled at all, let alone by the same entities, and the resulting divisions will probably not be theoretically interesting.

The foregoing discussion should have made it clear in just what way I believe a scientifically adequate theory of perception and mind requires the rejection of all five assumptions of the epistemological approach. The importance of the role of the subconscious/unconscious in mental functioning and our ignorance of it is evidence enough that A_1 is false. Language is peripheral to nervous function, and the transformations occurring in the nervous system can be expected to be richer and nongrammatical in form. So A_2 is false. Consciousness being a phase of nervous function in a nervous system dominated by unconscious processes, perception does not require a conscious act at all, nor is there plausibly a subject/object structure to conscious processes. So A_3 is false. The nervous system processes information in a manner dependent jointly upon environment and organism. Thus sense data, if we choose to introduce them as theoretical entities, will be structural features of nervous-system states, not objects of any sort, and not in any sort of subject/object relation to consciousness. Perception depends on structure-preserving mappings, not identities; it depends on the extraction of information to make *identifications* rather than achieving identities. So A_4 and A_5 are false.

This last remark deserves a little elaboration because of the role A_4 and A_5 have played in the philosophic treatment of illusion and hallucination (cf. e.g., Robinson, 1975 and § 3). Perception is the organism's key to action. What is extracted in perception, how it is encoded, and what the mind itself supplies is a function of the priorities and information the organism has accrued. There is a large accumulation of evidence that the ways we perceive the world are indeed constructed in this fashion (cf. references to the psychological literature herein). The features of the world that are mapped and the way they are mapped into the existing informational state of the organism are idiosyncratically selected according to the organism's ends, in the light of its capacities; thus we expect no identities, only transformations and embeddings appropriate to making appropriate identifications for action. And this position provides a proper framework for understanding illusion and hallucination (see § 3 below).

Now is the time to discuss the nature of the relations and content of perception.

§ 2. Perceptual Relations and Perceptual Content

Perception is directly of the external world (perception is first for survival). When the causal relationships involved are of the appropriate sort and the perceptual processing is also appropriate, I shall say that the perceiver acquires *directly* knowledge concerning the properties and state of the object concerned. Thus for a person A to be directly perceptually aware of X (where X may be an object, scene, and so on), that is, for A to directly perceive X, is for A to stand in an appropriate causal relationship to X such that there is caused (by X) to arise in A appropriate knowledge and/or belief states concerning X's state or properties. If either knowledge of X is gained in this process or all beliefs acquired in this process concerning X are true, the perception is veridical; otherwise it is partially or completely illusory.[7]

No hyphen appears in "perceptually aware" to contrast it with "consciously-aware" introduced earlier. Perceptual awareness is subject/object in structure, conscious-awareness is not. To be directly perceptually aware of something is for two kinds of "appropriate" qualifiers to be fulfilled: (1) the causal process must be an appropriate one, i.e., that specified by the best scientific theory of veridical perception,[8] (2) the knowledge and beliefs must be appropriate, i.e., they must be those that are the immediate culmination of the perceptual process, again as specified by our best scientific theory of the process (when we have it), rather than later deductions made from these, from memories, and so on. The 'directness' or immediateness of direct perception consists, then, in the scientific specification of causal relevance. It should not be thought of as some peculiarly clear 'eyeball-to-eyeball confrontation' with the world— as if indirect perception means *indistinct* perception. Nor is there anything else involved in the direct perception of the world than the *overall* relationship specified above. Moreover, my definition of direct perception does not involve reference to conscious experience. This is deliberate, because we need to allow for subliminal and other forms of unself-conscious perception. That is, it is not that direct perception cannot involve conscious experience—it does quite often —but only that it need not do so.[9]

To do justice to traditional concerns and our experience it is necessary to include an explanation of the relation of the content of conscious perceptual experience to the whole perceptual process. Here I can offer no more than a sketch.

Conscious perceptual experience certainly has a content. It is doubtful if this content is really adequately captured in any propositional formula. (Consider, e.g., the experience of looking at a new aesthetic work marking a creative breakthrough.) But the appropriate propositional formulas capture what is linguistically expressible and usually dominate attention. (Cf. "I see a black cat" and the experience of seeing the relevant situation.)[10]

Whence comes this complex description, why is this the way we choose to describe our experience?

At least part of the answer lies in the fact that, fundamentally, our entire perceptual/conceptual situation is goal-centered and directed toward external objects and situations, our language and sense organs have evolved in this setting. Our belief formation goes much deeper than our conscious-awareness and it seems reasonable to suppose that that deeper structure is the wellspring of speech responses as well as of conscious experience. Thus it is not too surprising that we describe our perceptual activity in terms of external situations. Such descriptions simultaneously reflect our dominant interests, inform others of our current beliefs and intended activity, and inform them in the only relevant and intersubjective terms we have, namely those dealing with the particular external situations that are the subject of our beliefs and focus of our activity. (Correlatively, we do not possess a very detailed phenomenal language for describing our private experience. It should be noted, though, that there are occasions when we are so intent on directing attention to the qualities of our perceptual experience that we introduce a specifically phenomenological vocabulary. Such situations are typically aesthetic, as witness the vocabularies for discussing wines, music, paintings, and so on. Our ability to develop such a vocabulary when forced to shows that we should not attach more importance to the form of our normal perceptual descriptions than it can carry.)

At the present stage of development of neurophysiology nothing very precise can be said concerning the relation of the conscious phases of information processing to the whole process. Very roughly, some hypothesis of the following sort seems required: The perceptual-processing states in general, and the belieflike states formed in the perceptual process in particular, determine, or are a major factor in the determination of, the conscious phase of perception. If something like this were true neurophysiologically, it would give us a plausible basis for claiming what I shall now assert as part of my doctrine: *our experience in perception is the conscious-awareness (phase) of our perceptual awareness states*. The contents of our experience in perception are precisely those states that are caused to arise when objects are directly perceived. *The specific conceptual contents of our perceptual experiences then derive from the fact that such experiences are, centrally, conscious-awarenesses of belieflike states*, the descriptions with which we characterize our experience being precisely the statements of the corresponding beliefs concerned.

Thus if I now offer as a description of my perceptual experiences, "I see that the sun is eclipsed," or "I see the eclipsed sun," the knowledge state "The sun is eclipsed" is precisely the state caused to arise in me in my becoming directly perceptually aware of the eclipsed sun. In thus describing our perceptual experience, we are in fact identifying the central states, the conscious-awareness of which is the having of that experience.[11] And on my account of consciousness (§ 1), these conscious states are not themselves objects of an inner perception, we are simply consciously-aware of them.

This general line is surely at least plausible. Consciousness is some phase of the sequence of global nervous states induced in the perceptual process, and central among these latter are surely the knowledge and belief states formed. In any event I am prepared to stake my doctrine of perception on there turning out to be a correlative, adequate, neurophysiological description of nervous-system functioning.[12]

This account of our perceptual experiences explains how they can be just that, experiences, and yet also be correct or incorrect (correspond or fail to correspond with the world). The experience, qua experience, cannot be right or wrong, but the perceptual knowledge and beliefs that determine the content of the experience can be either right or wrong, can correspond or fail to correspond with the world. And this fact, together with the fact that the perceptual processing that plays a large role in determining the knowledge and beliefs acquired (and hence the experience had) involves our assumptions and expectations concerning the perceptual situation, explains how direct perceptual awareness, though yielding noninferential knowledge, nonetheless has a judgmental component or aspect to it.[13]

How, then, are perceptual claims justified? Given my metaphilosophy, the answer which I shall adopt should be clear: they are not justified, at least not in the certainty-granting sense usually demanded by philosophers. Perceptual claims are justified, ultimately, only relative to other perceptual claims. Let me elaborate. I hold that (1) there is a basic range of perceptual claims that we all habitually, and reasonably, do fall back upon as the ultimate justification of claims to empirical knowledge; and that (2) these claims are made within a characteristic range of perceptual situations where we habitually make correct perceptual judgments (for example, they might include simple visual situations such as seeing a table in normal circumstances); (3) these situations are precisely those under which, according to the realist doctrine of perception and our scientific knowledge of the processes involved, we are habitually directly aware of our environment, that is, we habitually acquire, through the senses, noninferential knowledge of that environment. To be thus supported is, I claim, a fundamental part of the true nature of empirical knowledge.

Finally, it is not hard to see how one can utilize the resources of this position to respond to two well-known arguments that prove troublesome for sense-data theories, the arguments from intransitivity and indeterminateness of perceptual judgments. The arguments can be found e.g., in Armstrong (1961). The first argument is to the effect that a sequence of perceptual stimuli may be indiscriminable when taken pairwise successively but discriminable when n-place-separated comparisons are made, n ⩾ 2; but according to the sense-data theory the sense data will have to be pairwise successively identical and identity is transitive. The second argument is to the effect that many perceptual experiences are indeterminate in various respects (e.g., how many stripes on the tiger?), yet the corresponding sense datum, being an image or replica of the object perceived, must be everywhere determinate. Once the sense-data model is dropped in favor of an information-processing model, these phenomena cease to pose difficulties; encodings may be such that pairwise successive stimuli are encoded as identical but not n-separated successors and of course efficient encoding, given the organism's priorities, may often call for indeterminate encoding (that it is a tiger is usually more important than the number of stripes shown). The point is that whatever conceptualizations, i.e., processings, are most appropriate to the organism's priorities and capacities can be employed and these may cut across any replicating or imaging boundaries. Identification, not identity, is the issue. Which brings me directly to the phenomena of illusion and hallucination.

§ 3. The Nature of Illusion

The external world is directly perceived when the appropriate causal relations exist between the world perceived and the perceiver. The external world is *adequately* perceived when the appropriate perceptual skills are brought to bear in the processing of incoming physical information. Such perceptual processing may be either well adjusted or maladjusted, that is, appropriate or inappropriate to the perceptual situation.

There is good reason to believe that there is still some flexibility in the processing techniques we actually employ. The evidence is contained in the psychological references cited earlier. Simple examples occur when, upon wakening or entering ill-lit and unfamiliar surroundings, we first "see" one scene (respective examples being a nearby pencil as distant and tree-sized, a blowing scarf as a running cat) and then correct our perceiving as more information flows in. We adapt our processings, within evolutionary constraints, to suit our needs and situations.

This last remark gives the clue to the nature of illusion. There are times when we encounter situations for which our processing techniques are inadequate, and yet we do not correct those techniques for one reason or another (the situations are sufficiently difficult to correct for, or rare, or unimportant, or uninteresting, and so on). Under these conditions we experience *perceptual illusion*. We prefer, or are compelled, to explain away these illusions rather than to remove them by correcting for them in the perceptual processing.

Thus, for example, we have learned to correct for shape change as a function of orientation (at least for sufficiently small, sufficiently close, objects). There are no illusions in these cases except, significantly enough, when we are *unfamiliar* with the *type* of object involved. But we have not learned to correct for shape change as a function of refractive index, so that objects immersed in fluids are usually seen as undergoing a shape change.[14]

The existence of illusions and hallucinations has always been an important problem for direct realist doctrines of perception. Their occurrence makes it clear that if we sometimes do perceive the external world directly, we do not always do so when undergoing perceptual experience (hallucinations), and we do not always perceive it accurately when we do perceive it directly (illusions). From this it seems to follow that what we are directly aware of in perception, under *all* circumstances, is never the external world but something else—a sense datum, for example. So it seems that direct realism must be abandoned. The argument may be stated as follows:[15]

P_1: Sensory illusions and hallucinations are logically possible (in fact they occur).

P_2: Veridical perception is indistinguishable, qua perceptual experience, from sensory illusion and hallucination.

P_3: In sensory illusion and hallucination I am always perceiving something.

P$_4$:   Because in sensory illusion and hallucination what I perceive is not identical with anything existing, what I perceive in these cases is never the external world.

P$_5$:   Therefore, what I perceive in veridical perception is never
the external world.

This argument is a more precise version of what is usually offered
in argument. The first thing to note about it is that it is *invalid*. It
would be formally valid if, but only if, the indistinguishability of P$_2$
implied indistinguishability in *all* respects. But as it stands, P$_2$ asserts *perceptual* indistinguishability only, and the indistinguishability of two perceptual experiences does not imply the identity in kind
of the objects (if any) of those experiences. Only the pernicious belief that our perceptual experiences must be fully identical with the
objects of those perceptions allows this gap to be bridged. To be a formally valid argument, either the phrase "qua perceptual experience"
would have to be deleted from P$_2$ (but who, then, would accept P$_2$?)
or an additional premise would have to be added, a premise roughly
to the effect that in all perceptual experience there is always an
object that is identically that described by reports of perceptual experience. But this latter is among the claims rejected in this paper.

What the direct realist claims is that veridical and illusory perception *are* distinct from hallucinatory experience precisely because in
the former cases we are directly perceiving the external world and
in the latter case we are not. And the doctrine claims that illusory
perception *is* distinguishable from veridical perception precisely in
terms of the adequacy of the perceptual processing applied, the accuracy of the beliefs formed, and so on. This vital flaw in the argument has tended to go unnoticed, however, because philosophers of
perception have tended to make the identity assumption.

I reject P$_3$ for the case of hallucinations (and after-images). I claim
that in hallucinatory experience we may be aware, *consciously-
aware*, of many things, but we do not perceive, are not *perceptually
aware* of anything. To have an hallucinatory experience of X is to
be in the same internal states as one would be in were X to exist
and one were veridically perceiving X, except that these states on
this occasion have purely (or predominantly) *internal* causes.

Moreover, the account of perception I have offered also leads directly to the rejection of P$_4$. P$_4$ is acceptable only if it is also ac-

cepted that if the external world is perceived at all, the content of perception is identical with what is perceived. It is clear that in my account of illusion I reject this assumption, the world may be inadequately perceived as well as adequately perceived, but in both cases it is the world that is perceived. Here is a second point at which the argument rests on this pernicious identity assumption. Once this assumption has been rejected, the existence of illusions ceases to become a problem. Illusions are accounted for as inadequate perceptual adjustments on our part. It is not that identity fails in these cases (it never did hold anywhere) but that we prefer to explain these situations away rather than attempt to correct for them.[16]

In order to reveal this ubiquitous argument in all its presumptuous regalia, let me attempt an even more explicit formal statement:

P_1: Sensory illusions and hallucinations are logically possible (indeed they occur).

P_2: Veridical perception is indistinguishable to the mind from illusory and hallucinatory perception, qua perceptual experience.

A_1: The mind is epistemically self-transparent.

A_3: Perception logically requires a consciously examined content.

A_4: Perceptual contents are objects, i.e., individuals of the ontology.

C_1: What is before the mind in veridical perception are objects of the same role, type, and status as are those objects before the mind in illusory and hallucinatory perception.

A_5: Perception is veridical if an only if what is before the mind is identical with what is in the external world.

P_3: The contents of illusory and hallucinatory perceptions differ from the actual external situation presented to the perceiving subject.

C_2: The objects before the mind in illusion and hallucination are not objects in the external world.

C_3: What is before the mind in veridical perception are not objects in the external world.

P_4: The objects of perception either belong to the external world or belong internally to the mind.

C_4: What is before the mind in veridical perception are objects in the mind.

Although I accept P_1, P_2, P_3, and, let us say, P_4 (this is what makes the argument plausible, when the other premises are suppressed), I reject A_1, A_3, A_4, A_5, and the conclusions C_1, C_2, C_3.

Now we are in a position to use my doctrine in an attempt at a new-old resolution of the problem of the secondary qualities.

§ 4. The Problem Stated

Contemporary science (especially biochemistry and neruophysiology) make a naturalistic materialism an increasingly plausible doctrine.[17] The position has always been attractive because it is one expression of the drive for unity in science. Central to this conception of unity is the adoption of some form of realist doctrine of perception and a naturalistic materialistic account of mind.

It is in this general context that I am attempting to offer an account of secondary qualities. Certainly they are intimately bound up with doctrines of mind on the one side and doctrines of perception on the other. For the primary/secondary quality distinction is just the distinction between those properties of the immediate objects of perception that belong to objects in themselves (these are the primary properties) and those properties that belong only to our perceptions of those objects (these are the secondary properties). But this means that on the one side the nature and status of the primary/secondary distinction hinges on the doctrine of perception adopted and on the other side, since perceiving is a mental activity and perceptual states are mental states, the nature and status of secondary qualities themselves depends crucially on the doctrine of mind adopted. The problem thus raised for secondary qualities is well known: in contrast to the primary properties, secondary properties play no explicit role in any of the naturalistic sciences, hence form no part of the characterization of the naturalistic ontology, either of the external world or of the mind-brain, yet they play a central role in the description of conscious experience and the perceptual characterization of the world. (See e.g., Natsoulos' review of the psychological literature, in Nicholas, 1976.)

Since the secondary qualities will at the very least have to be smoothly integrated with those of the natural sciences, ENR has essentially only three choices of doctrine: secondary qualities can be construed as (1) additional objective properties (a) of all physical objects, (b) of specific mind-brain processes, or (2) as reductively identical with complexes of primary properties (a) of physical situations generally, (b) of specific mind-brain processes, or (3) as non-existent qua individual properties. Position (1a) commits its proponents to claiming the causal incompleteness of the scientific account of the causal perceptual process and introduces highly causally idiosyncratic, yet fundamental, natural properties. Position (1b) is entirely implausible on the prevailing evidence. Position (2b) strongly suggests an inner-screen representative realist account of the perceptual process. None of these positions sits well with ENR. Given the general, if tacit, assumption that (3) is to be rejected on phenomenological grounds (we experience the secondary qualities as individual properties), it is not surprising that materialists have tended to prefer (2a). Moreover, (2a) fits nicely with the prevalent assumption that purely functional, qualitatively denuded conscious states are necessary for a defensible materialism (see § 1).

But (2a) has a well-known difficulty associated with it: it is simply not the case, in general, that there are complexes of primary properties, or finite disjunctions of these, which correspond one-one with occurrences of secondary qualities (see, for example, Campbell in Rollins, 1969). And where the correspondence does obtain, there is reason to believe it merely a result of relative crudity of physiological response and/or evolutionary accident, rather than (2a) being in the right direction. Moreover, I believe the functionalist variety of topic-neutral reductionism advanced by materialistic defenders of (2a) fails of itself.[18]

This, then, poses the problem for ENR; for its solution it seems necessary to choose one of the alternatives (1)-(3), but none of them appear acceptable. I am going to state and defend a version of alternative (3). So far as I am aware no one has taken this alternative seriously since Broad laughingly dismissed Pritchard's statement of it at the turn of the century. Perhaps it will turn out that this was for good reason. Nevertheless, I attempted a preliminary defense in my doctoral dissertation (Hooker, 1970), and I attempt a more elaborate defense in my forthcoming book (see introduction). What follows is a sketch of that defense.

§ 5. A Solution Stated (1): Sensory Awareness and the Relations between the Primary and Secondary Qualities

Perception is fundamentally an information flow from environment to organism, where the information is sorted, processed, and used. Conscious perception is conscious experience of this information flow as it affects our internal states and processes. Now every information flow requires a medium, for information is just the structuring of some medium. The incoming physical patterns need to be represented by the organism in its media, so encoding principles are also required.

Consider normal visual perceptions. The physical, external medium of information flow is the electromagnetic field, and the encoding principles are physical laws referring to the behavior of both those fields and physical objects. The physical information is the fluctuation pattern of this field. Within the human body, the physical medium is the electrochemical substances making up the optical nervous system, and the encoding principles are laws referring to the structure and responses to electrical stimulation of the biochemical substances in the eye, optic nerve, and brain. The physical information is now the pattern of electrochemical changes.

There are, then, two internal components involved in any perceptual process, the encoding medium and the encoded information. We may be consciously-aware of both, though perceptually aware of neither. We experience this twin conscious-awareness as a perceptual field, i.e., as *primary structure embedded in a secondary medium*. If the media of all senses are distinct, we obtain the sensory commonness of the primary properties and the sensory specificity of the secondary properties.

When, for example, we are directly perceptually aware of our environment through vision, the medium of the information flow is the electromagnetic field, but we are not aware of the field. Internally, the medium of information flow is the electrochemical "field," and the encoding principles are determined by the physical structure of our retina, postretinal ganglia, etc. In being aware of objects in our environment we are not perceptually aware of, do not perceive the internal medium either. The encoding principles of our visual receptors, together with the nature of our visual neural subsystem, determines the resulting internal perceptual states, thus determining also the special character of our conscious experience of these states. Our experience of (i.e., conscious-awareness of) our visual mode of *perceptual* awareness is unique to that sense. We experience the visual field as the embedding of primary (i.e., primary-qualitied) information (e.g., location, size, motion) in a secondary-qualitied medium (the medium of colors). The information is embedded (encoded) as color differences. I am self-consciously-aware of it as perception "through" colored shapes. The unique character of it as a *color* medium derives from the unique characteristics of the internal states that such direct perceptual awareness produces in me.

In short: the distinctive character of our experience of each of our five senses is due to our conscious-awareness of the characteristic inner perceptual states of each sense. The distinctive general character of the perceptual states of any given sense is in turn determined by the distinctive *mode* of perceptual awareness of that sense, that is, by the distinctive encoding principles and/or encoding media associated with that sense. We experience our sensory states as perceptual fields, i.e., as the embedding of primary-qualitied information in a secondary-qualitied medium.

To repeat: we do not perceive (are not perceptually aware of) perceptual fields. It is important to distinguish sharply between what it is that we are directly perceptually aware of and our experience of, i.e., conscious-awareness of, the direct perceptual awareness. *The perceptual states of which we are consciously-aware are not what is perceived.* Only the external world is perceived. And our conscious perceptual experience arises, not from *perceiving* (= being perceptually aware of) our perceptual awareness states, but from being *consciously-aware* of (experiencing) the perceptual awareness states arising as part of the perceiving of the external world.

In sum, to experience a secondary quality of sense S at time T is to be consciously-aware of, or experience, the T time-slice of the perceptual awareness states arising in consequence of our mode S of perception of the world.

Thus it should be clear that color experience, for example, is *no mere accompaniment* or perception but is an integral part of it. Color experience is the form of all conscious visual perception.[19] Similar remarks apply to the other senses and their unique characteristics.

This account explains how it is possible, for example, for (conscious) visual perception to involve both colors and shapes (as colored shapes) and yet the aspects remain quite distinct in status, the former being subjective and the latter objective. We distinguish sharply between the information encoded and the mode and medium of its encoding. The information is the origin of the objective component of visual experience, the mode and medium provide the origin of the subjective component of the experience. (Being aware of colors is bound up intimately with being aware of the character of the encoding medium.) Both components are consciously experienced together as the *embedding* of one in the other: we perceive colored shapes.

The account also explains why secondary qualities, but not primary qualities, are sense-specific, and how exactly they depend upon perception and alter as the conditions of perception alter. My account also explains why some secondary qualities are more closely associated with corresponding primary quality complexes than are others (the sensory receptor is cruder, thus producing a simple medium state/external state correspondence). And my account explains, finally, why primary, but not secondary, qualities play significant causal roles in the world and how black can be a secondary quality, though no perception of objects may be involved.[20]

§ 6. A Solution Stated (II): The Apparent Objectivity of Colors Explained

Our visual experience is, for the most part, that of perceiving colored bodies. Yet colors are not objective physical properties of bodies. How is this conflict to be resolved? Briefly, my reply is that our beliefs in this regard (namely, that colors are "on" the surfaces of bodies), are mistaken and our "seeing" illusory. That much of the reply is dictated by the theory of the nature and origin of the secondary qualities put forward above. The remaining question is: How did this situation come about? I shall argue that on any evolutionary (developmental) view of human perception, the situation as I have described it is a likely end-product.

We use visual perception to identify the shapes, sizes, positions, and motions of objects, and to gain some information concerning their physical states (on fire, angry-with-X, etc.). The external primary information is encoded as differences in the state of the visual medium, and to this extent the epistemic intrusion of colors is unavoidable for us.

Least interestingly (for survival) we discover the colors of bodies in this way also, for colors are associated with few interesting causal processes. Their main function is to help as identifiers of objects ("The *yellow* brick in the corner . . . ," etc.). But though perceptual data concerning colors are the least important perceptual information, it is, on my account, intimately bound up with other perceptual data on whose acquisition our survival depends. It is reasonable to assume, therefore, that when the processing of visual sensory information that human beings employ was being developed, a processing was selected that accorded colors the same ontological status as the objects being perceived. Within the visual field, color differences often coincide with boundaries and are fundamental to visually guided function. Under life circumstances in which we place an enormous epistemic reliance on vision, and in which no great difficulties arise from such a choice or processing, the pressure to adopt it must surely have been overwhelming.

Perceptual processing techniques develop during the early years of each individual human being. But human beings are born with a neural organization already geared to certain kinds of processing as a result of countless years of evolutionary selection. Now the developmental theories of Piaget and his general school[21] emphasize ontogenesis. On Piaget's view, the newborn infant's perceptual world is a vast blur of sensory stimulation, out of which order is finally created as the cortex hits on the most effective methods of selection, abstraction, etc. In this process of highly successful interpretive development, it is entirely natural and plausible—in the face of the experienced inseparability of colors and geometric information, and an increasing degree of epistemic reliance on vision—to accord colors the same positive status accorded geometric properties. For the processing strategy that treats colors as objective properties of enduring external bodies is in fact largely successful.

On the other hand, there is now evidence that colors begin to be objectified in infancy.[22] This evidence suggests that ontogeny recapitulates phylogeny: that the human race as a whole (and perhaps prehuman species as well) have passed countless years of past experience on to us as hereditary structures.

Whether the phylogenetic or the ontogenetic viewpoint is correct, or to what extent each is correct, is of lesser importance here since the explanation of how colors came to be accorded objective status is the same for both viewpoints.[23]

There is no doubt that our primitive way of looking at the world has served us fairly well. It is true that colors are puzzlingly causally inert, unlike their geometric counterparts which play causally active roles in the world. It is also true that they show a variability and illusion-proneness not possessed by shapes and sizes. But, since physical conditions do not in general change much for man (that is, since physical conditions that produce stimulating new perceptual situations are in general absent), we have not had any serious reason to modify our primitive interpretive stance. But once we begin to investigate the situation carefully, the disparity between geometric and color components of visual perception becomes increasingly obvious. However, our general lack of difficulties under normal conditions reinforces our primitive adjustment.

In this connection the situation in regard to the other secondary qualities is illuminating. As a rough generalization the secondary qualities of a sense S tend to be attributed to external bodies as objective properties of those bodies just in proportion as the sense S involves, or is closely connected with, the tactile sense. Thus the tactile secondary qualities ("the rough surface" etc.) themselves are virtually always attributed to the surfaces of bodies.[24] Apart from the visual and tactile qualities that are attributed directly to external bodies, there are sounds, tastes, and smells. We do not universally say of any of these three that they are presented to us as intrinsic properties of external bodies. Such attribution becomes progressively less strained in the order: sounds, smells, and tastes. Tastes we most readily attribute to an external body, sounds least readily. In all three cases we more often than not speak about the associated object (if there is one) as the *cause*, or *source* (origin), of the sound, taste, or smell.

All of this is nicely consistent with the evolutionary view that the fundamental objectively understood properties are the non-sense-specific primary properties, with the secondary qualities, which are sense specific, given an interpretation whose degree or character of objectivity depends upon their closeness of association with the primary properties. It is also illuminating to realize that the strength of our tendency to give to a particular group of secondary qualities such an interpretation depends upon the epistemic centrality or otherwise of the sense concerned. For this reason, it can be misleading to commence the analysis of the secondary qualities with colors and the tactile secondary qualities.

In the perception of colors and of tactile secondary qualities, then, we are under *systematic illusion* when we perceive them as "on" the surfaces of bodies. For illusion is nothing but inadequate and incorrect perceptual adjustment on our part.

§ 7. A Solution State (III): Defense against Criticism

The claim that there are no colored bodies (in the strict sense) and the concomitant claim that visual perception is systematically illusory may come as a shock to common intuition. But common intuition has more than once in recent times been shown to be mistaken. It has, indeed, been shown to be precisely what one would expect: the end-product of countless years of collective experience and countless episodes of individual experience, *at the scientifically unaided level*. It is thus natural to expect that, though our intuitive perceptual-conceptual adjustment will be the best suited to our experience, it will contain many errors of adjustment which only careful scientific investigation can reveal and which were, at a more primitive level, pragmatically justified as the simplest, most efficient way to organize experience. Such is the nature of what evidently are intuition's many errors concerning space and time, as revealed by modern physics. And such, I claim, is its error in the case of colors. As I have argued, our present way of seeing the world is, though incorrect, pragmatically the least confusing and simplest way of organizing our visual experience. That intuition is shocked to discover this fact is of no great importance. So long as an adequate scientific account of the perceptual situation is available and a reasonable account of the origin of perceptual error is at hand, the claims of intuition must be ignored.

By the same token, arguments against my doctrine of colors based on conceptual claims drawn from our everyday natural language can also be ignored. The conceptual system we possess evolves simultaneously with, and parallel to, our perceptual organization. Thus the conceptual framework may also be expected to contain conceptual reflections of those perceptual errors we develop in the course of maturing. Both are but differing aspects of the same organizational development. Therefore very often the conditions under which perceptual experience can be treated as illusory are also conditions under which conceptual organization can be treated as erroneous.[25]

No bodies in the external world literally possess secondary qualities. But "This is red," e.g., has not lost its truth value; it is true just in case the object referred to is perceived as red by the utterer of the statement.[26] It is clear that I shall have to regard talk about color properties, *qua genuine individual properties of bodies*, as, strictly, inappropriate. There are no colors, no real individual properties referred to by color terms; there are only *color experiences*. These are not experiences *of colors*, where distinct properties, colors, hold some relation to a conscious mind, but simply kinds of experience. The hypen in "color-experiences" signifies all this.

What I must maintain, therefore, is roughly the following: "This is red for S," S a perceiver, has a significant analysis in terms of the power of what is referred to by "This" to give rise to impressions-of-red in S, but "impressions-of-red" has itself no significant ontologically perspicuous analysis in which "red" occurs predicated of a logical subject. The connotation of "This is red" is determined ostensively. "S's having-an-impression-of-red" is true just when S is in some particular state; whether this state is physical or nonphysical is not thereby decided.

The same approach is to be taken to all of the secondary qualities. Thus although "This is C for S," where C is some secondary-quality term, has a significant analysis in terms of the power of what is referred to by "This" to give rise to *impressions-of-C* in S, "impressions-of-C" has no significant analysis—it is ostensively defined. "S's having-an-impression-of-C" is true just when S is in some particular state, whether mental or physical is not thereby decided.

The principal objection to my account lies in the belief that for secondary qualities in general, and for colors in particular because of their apparent 'equality' with primary properties, there ought to be separately identifiable properties of *something* of which we can say "They are the secondary qualities."

This objection assumes the following principle, (P): No account of our experience is to be regarded as satisfactory that does not provide an ontologically realized 'archetype' for every phenomenally distinct aspect of our experience; that is, no account of experience is satisfactory that does not provide a distinguishable entity corresponding to a very distinguishable feature of our experience.[27]

Thus, in the case of colors, the argument would run: since colors are experienced as individual properties of objects, for every reductive identification of "S is having-an-impression-of-red" there should be a specific, separable identification of "red" *within* it. The intuitive idea is roughly as follows. In visual perception we can distinguish geometric properties of objects, states of objects, and (apparently) colors of objects. Now, by P, each one of these distinct aspects is to be assigned a basis in the ontology. Thus the geometrical properties are actual geometric properties of external objects and the states are actual states of external objects. Therefore, to complete the picture, the colors must be actual properties of something: external object, mental entity, or whatever.

The general principle P seems to have been implicitly adopted, in effect, by almost every philosophy of perception. In the case of colors, these archetypes are placed either in the external world (Objectivisms) or in the mind (Representative Realism or Phenomenalism). The very demand of *identity* between veridical perceptual experience and what is perceived (assumption A_5), adopted by most philosophies of perception, is tantamount to adopting P and the assumptions A_3, A_4, tantamount to the claim that there ought to be a special perceived object with the relevant secondary quality as property, make it plausible.

But why should this principle be adopted? In isolation it has nothing that I can see to recommend it. Moreover, I reject the assumptions, A_3-A_5, which have led so may philosophers (including materialists) to find P plausible.[28]

Consider the following, very crude, analogy: a liquid undergoes wave motion whose amplitude varies with time. The total wave motion is to be associated with a visual experience. Now the wave motion can be reduced to the collective motions of the fluid particles and, analogously, the total visual experience can be reduced to an overall physical and/or mental process (involving, if necessary, the entire body and mind). In the reduction of the wave, the *phase* of the wave and the *amplitude* of the wave cannot be individually reduced to distinct structural properties; they are both complex functions of *the same thing*, the totality of particle motions; nevertheless, phase and amplitude are two conceptually distinguishable aspects of wave motion appearing in certain theoretical descriptions of it. Another illuminating example is provided by the aerodynamic descriptions of birds' wings. At the whole-systems level engineers distinguish the functions of lift and propulsion and in modern aircraft these are indeed provided by distinct design features (wing and engine). But birds' wings typically combine these two functions in the one wing movement, and descriptions presupposing their separation fail. Rather, to obtain an adequate theoretical description one must go to a more theoretically basic level of description, to direct applications of fluid or gaseous dynamics.

In the same way, though there must be *some basis* in inner states for secondary-quality experiences, this in itself provides no grounds for claiming that secondary qualities are reductively identical with properties of this basis (whatever it be), much less for claiming that secondary qualities are properties of some special class of inner states. It is perfectly possible, I claim, that an entire visual experience should be no more than an internal process and yet that there should exist no way in which to isolate every conceptually or experientially distinguishable component of the experience as a distinct and similar property of the process occurring.

True, the inner states will need to possess structures of the right kind to explain the perceptual processing that occurs; and they will need a dynamical structure correlative to the processing to explain the transmission of information from the world to the perceiver. However, that we distinguish geometrical properties, states of objects, and secondary qualities in perception gives us no warrant to believe that, in addition to the dynamical process, there must be distinct features of the process corresponding to these three categories and related analogously as they are related. Indeed, this belief betrays a profound misconception of the nature of the perceptual process; it assumes that perceptual realization of concepts is like building a literal internal copy of an external scene. Where perceiving is viewed correctly, as an information-processing activity, a perceptually instantiated concept means simply that an incoming pattern is processed in a certain manner; only abstracted structural information need be preserved, under any mapping that preserves the relevant structural relations. Only clinging to the assumptions $A_1 \to A_5$ (especially $A_3 \to A_5$) could make the misconceived view plausible.

This disposes of the main objection to the doctrine based upon assuming principle P. But considerations of a semantical sort may rekindle faith in the employment of P against my position. I shall consider two such objections. The first, and more naive, of the two simply asks what account I can give of the fact that predicates designating primary and secondary properties appear on a grammatical par in perceptual reports, yet I do not accord these properties the same ontological status. But an insistence that grammatical or syntactic structure always transfer to ontological commitment is just P again. I can see no compelling reason why the deep logical structures of sentences should reflect in their (model-theoretic) semantics the same features as the corresponding surface grammatical structures, indeed so much is implied in the recognition of deep structure underlying surface structure. Moreover, I hold the view that in many (possibly all) cases what ultimately dictates choice of deep structure, hence semantics and ontological commitment, is theory, theory of the subject matter involved. And in the present case there is theoretical motivation for a distinction in treatment between primary and secondary predicates, namely just the distinction between conscious-awareness, which is not subject/object in nature (if it were, there would have to be 'objects', i.e., some basis, corresponding to our awareness of colors), and perceptual awareness, which does have a subject-relation-object structure. Rather, we use secondary-quality descriptions to identify (both internal experiences and their causing situations), not to cite identities (between experience, as-object, and world).

There is, however, some specific semantic backing for the doctrine P, which gives rise to a second and sharper line of criticism. Consider the following sentences:

> p: X has an impression of color.
> q: X has an impression of red.
> r: X has an impression of bright red.

We have r entails q and q entails p. Generally, sentences containing secondary-quality terms enter into a complex of logical relations because the secondary-quality terms they contain stand in certain determinate-determinable relations. It seems inescapable therefore that secondary-quality terms must appear as distinct semantic components of such sentences if any semantical account of these logical relations is to be given. Conversely, anyone who insists, as I do, on treating such sentences as semantical wholes can apparently offer no satisfactory[29] account of these logical relations (indeed, can apparently have little or nothing to say about the determinable-determinate hierarchy at all, in or out of sentences).

I can see no other way to make sense of the semantical role of the determinable-determinate structure but to grant the initial demand. Any move from this concession to the conclusion that there are individual secondary qualities qualifying some members of the ontology is, however, too fast and too unsubtle.

What I have stated is that hyphenated expression of the form 'X has-an-impression-of-ϕ have not *ontologically significant* analysis; more precisely, the ontologically perspicuous form of these sentences is 'X is in a state of kind K'. I shall now argue for two theses: (1) this latter ontologically perspicuous form regenerates the only relevant determinable-determinate hierarchy, and (2) this ontological analysis is compatible with a grammatical/semantical analysis of the earlier form that recognizes the distinctive semantical role of secondary-quality terms. These theses together constitute a rebuttal of the objection while granting its initial claim.

Of what kind are the states associated with having-impressions-of-ϕ? Recall that they have in common at least a certain structuring of the neurological medium. But such structurings themselves must instance a determinable-determinate hierarchy, since there will be more and less general structural properties and descriptions. (Consider, for example, "Medium varying sinusoidally" and "Medium varying sinusoidally with period T and wavelength L".)

Of course we are not consciously-aware of the character of the sensory states; rather, we seem to be aware only of the quality or kind of experience that they cause in their conscious phases. Not surprisingly, the quality differences and similarities recapitulate part of the state differences and similarities, without being the same thing. It is useful, therefore, to replace the sentence p with "X is having a visual experience," q with "X is visually experiencing somewhere in the typically long wavelength-caused range" and q with "X is visually experiencing somewhere in the range typically caused by long-wavelengths with a high intensity." The point of these replacements is to emphasize that our secondary-quality talk is a way of identifying experiences that ultimately have their basis elsewhere than literal colors, namely in the neurological character of our sensory states. And this explains why their semantical structure is relevant; for their logical relations recapitulate sensory-state relations without being ontologically binding, because the recapitulation is accomplished through identifications, not identities (see § 3). Claims couched in secondary-quality language such as p, q, r identify sensory states K, K_q, K_r, but the logical form of the corresponding claims "X is in State K" is F(X)," which is the ontologically appropriate form.

Given that principles of deep structure analysis are theoretically motivated, it emerges that P gains whatever appeal it has from the silent assumption of one or more of $A_1 \rightarrow A_5$ (cf. the argument from illusion, § 3). With the rejection of these assumptions, P loses its attractiveness and with the rejection of P the intuitive core of the objection against my account is also done away with.[30]

My view of secondary qualities also brings with it a number of advantages in the form of plausible solutions to standard issues — issues which have often provided difficulties for other materialist positions. Thus for example, I am able to explain how a percipient's color experiences may be reversed without producing any difference in his/her behavior, survival value, and so on: the same external stimuli simply cause different (reversed) internal perceptual states *but with the same information encoded*. Moreover, I am freed from having to take a firm stand on the issue of whether perceptual experiences are distinct from the corresponding belief states that arise (contrast Armstrong 1961), though my own view is that such perceptual experiences are distinct from and richer than the corresponding linguistically defined belief states. I am able to explain, in principle, the phenomenon of intersensory connectedness among secondary qualities (trumpet blast↔red, for example) by postulating media similarity and/or causal connectivity of the corresponding perceptual states. I am able to account for the causal inactivity (or irrelevance) of most secondary qualities (causal irrelevance of corresponding perceptual states) and also to provide plausible explanations of the few exceptions (correlation of causally active external factor and arising of appropriate perceptual state). Finally, I am able to account for the sense of exclusion we feel among secondary qualities of the same sort (nothing can be red and green all over, etc.) in terms of mutual exclusion among the corresponding perceptual states.

Space limitations preclude any expansion upon these advantages here or critical discussion of alternative doctrines of perception. I am content to re-emphasize the importance of a systematic and unifying conception of ourselves.

Notes

1. See references, note 3 below. I have not been arguing that no account of perceptual awareness involving mental states or entities (ideas, sense data) is acceptable. I have been arguing only that no account of perceptual awareness in which mental states or entities were *the immediate objects of perception* was acceptable—and that is a very different matter. There is no objection so far—and none to come—to saying that mental states or entities are involved in perceptual awareness, so long as they are not what is immediately perceived.

2. Such approaches to perceptual systems are now increasingly common and coherent; see, for example, Gibson (1967, 1968), Gregory (1966), Haber (1969), Kabrinsky (1966), Rock & Harris (1967), and especially Neisser (1967) vis-à-vis Neisser (1976) and the references in note 3 below.

3. If readers wish they can think of these phases of CNS states as the physical correlates of the nonphysical conscious states; the important thing is to get the relation between consciousness and other central nervous functions into the right perspective: consciousness is a minor phase of these other functions; it is not the central area in which all mental activities take place. (Let doubting readers recall the importance of the emotional subconscious since Freud, the phenomena of subconscious solution to problems not solvable while conscious ("sleep on it"), hypnotic effects, sleep learning, etc.). Moreover it is a phase of functions; it is not an arena—central or not—in which objects are presented and parade themselves. So far as I am aware, there is not the slightest evidence that consciousness, conscious states or whatever are sharply separated from other CNS processes, or that there is a special object-subject ('arena-audience') structure to conscious awareness. To the contrary, all the evidence seems to support the view adopted here of consciousness as an integrated phase of general CNS functioning. One of the several contributions of a generalized information-processing conceptual scheme for describing nervous functions is to break the grip on us of our ordinary English descriptions of mental functioning which are (naturally) biased heavily toward conscious functioning and which tacitly

build in the arena-object model. Another advantage is the sophistication possible in the discussion of analogue and digital communication.

On this general approach to the central nervous system and consciousness see, for example, Arbib (1972), Ashby (1952), Harnad et al. (1976), Jerison (1973), McCulloch (1965), Mackay (1956), Pribram (1971), Simon (1969), and Sommerhoff (1974).

4. Cf. e.g., references in note 3 and discussion in my book referred to in the introduction. Of course these considerations do not logically prevent one from separating out conscious activity as distinctively mental in some way that conflicts with materialism, or even of separating out a 'complete mind' (subconscious plus conscious components) as distinctively mental; but they suggest to me that a more plausible line to take is that consciousness is a phase of neurological activity, integrated into all other bodily processes in the fashion that modern analytical science and the utilities of survival suggest. Moreover, I believe that this view can be made satisfyingly compatible with the admission of a rich phenomenal life.

5. I want to point out, by way of achieving parity, an important way in which materialists who have even superficially plausible doctrines of perception make use of just this account of experience: when accounting for hallucinatory perception. For whatever a sense-data theorist might say about the reality of the dagger MacBeth saw, no materialist can admit that such a dagger occurs anywhere, inside or outside the head. In these cases, therefore, the perceptual experience cannot be construed along subject-relation-object lines. (A materialist, committed to the inner-scanner model might try to say that MacBeth inner-scanned a neurological screen which he saw, in disguise as it were, as a dagger; but there is the additional difficulty of developing an adequate notion of disguise here on top of the implausibility of the inner-scanner model.) Often this use of the no subject-object structure doctrine contrasts with a general preference for the inner-scanner model. Why the model is not entirely dropped can only be guessed at, as I have done.

6. That is, "physical information" is here intended in the sense treated by information theory. Incidentally, the fact that there is a retinal *image* formed in visual perception does not undermine my claims here, because our perception of that image is itself an end-product of a perceptual process whose starting point is physical information. The retinal 'image' is itself only a pattern of electromagnetic radiation, (and/or a pattern of chemical states in the retina —depending on the extension of the term). There are no corresponding images for the other senses, and none required.

7. The cumbersome formulation in terms of both knowledge and true beliefs is to show that my account of perception does not presuppose a completed epistemological doctrine; rather, the epistemology follows on the account of perception. I am not fundamentally concerned with developing a detailed epistemology in this study, and I do not analyze the relations between knowledge and belief.

8. It is not appropriate, e.g., for person B to perceive X and then report to A, or to allow A's sensory organs to be stimulated but to interrupt the neural development and cause A to have beliefs by some other means (e.g., probes), even though A may in these ways arrive at true beliefs concerning X, and other similar interruptions of the causal chain are ruled out.

9. I reject the argument that we can be aware only of the last link in the causal chain. Cf. Armstrong (1961, chapter 11), and Hirst (1959, pp. 282-82). Also, note that the proper 'units' of perceptual judgments are really whole situations ("There are no crows in the sky," "She's angry because he smiled"), not 'simple' properties of single objects. These latter judgments are sophisticated end-products of the development of perceptual judgment. Only the implicit atomism of the sense-data epistemology in ontology could lead us to think otherwise.

10. The mere fact that the experiences are describable using a sentence with grammatical subject/object structure does not in the least imply that the mental states involved must have a structural analysis in subject/object terms. The descriptions are not *of-the-visual-field* but *of-the-content-of* the visual field. The latter may well have this structure when pressed into propositional form; the visual field need not also be thereby construed as itself a complex object of the same sort.

11. I believe that in offering these descriptions we are offering only a *definite description* of the mental states involved by describing the conditions under which the particular (veridical) perceptual experience can be had, for I believe that such states can only be ostensively *defined*. Note that it would have been incorrect to drop the adjective "belieflike" in favor of just "belief," for it is often the case that we are both perfectly well aware that a particular situation is illusory or hallucinatory and yet continue to be under illusion or hallucinated. On the pure belief acquisition model of perception we should then be entertaining contradictory beliefs, a belief that the world was in a particular condition (e.g., that a particular stick immersed in water is bent), and a contrary belief that the former belief is false (e.g., that the stick is in fact straight). Of course, one could simply grasp the nettle and claim that the beliefs we form in perception are simply not under our voluntary control, so it is not surprising that we sometimes find ourselves forced to hold contradictory beliefs. Perhaps so, but we surely do not feel the sense of tension in these cases that we do in other circumstances when it is pointed out to us that our beliefs are contradictory. In these cases we know very well which statements are true and the persistent recurrence of the perceptual experience becomes merely a nuisance.

Armstrong (1961) comes closer to the actual phenomenological situation when he speaks of perceptual experience as constituting a *prima facie pressure* to believe, or to assent to claims that are being pressed upon us. That is, did we not have countervailing reasons to believe that the perceptual experience was illusory or hallucinatory, our perceptual experience would culminate in our believing that the world was the way it appears to be, and sometimes even when we do have these reasons the pressure to accept appearance as reality is nearly overwhelming.

We have plenty of leeway for a distinction between belieflike states and actual belief states in the neurophysiological model because of its present lack of detail; belieflike states are information states in the postconceptual stage of the processing which are (presumably) very like belief states, except that they have not yet been linked into the battery of systematic evaluative considerations that lead to the final decision to assent to, or dissent from, them. Tentatively I envisage them as states structurally similar to belief states, arising directly in the information processing of perception, and presented, as it were, to the nervous system at large as candidate belief (and knowledge) states for acceptance or rejection. In the normal course of events, these candidate states pass the various filtering procedures that are the neurophysiological operations corresponding to comparison with past examples, stored generalizations, etc., and become, or cause, full-fledged belief states. It is presentation of the belieflike states in combination with their habitual acceptance as belief states in normal conditions that constitutes the pressure to believe of which Armstrong writes. Only under special conditions will this normal process be prevented from occurring.

My theory thus explains how it is that our perceptual experience can contain elements known to be inaccurate, and yet we do not find this logically discomforting.

Of course, when all the details of neurophysiology are assembled it may well turn out that the correct explanation of this situation is rather more complex, and just possibily considerably different in structure, then the simple hypothesis I have offered. But it seems plausible at this time that something along the lines I have suggested captures the appropriate phase of the correct structure of the perceptual process. In any event, as I said, I am prepared to stake my doctrines on there being the appropriate neurophysiological structures to back them.

12. In particular, other cortical states may also contribute to the quality of our conscious-awareness besides knowledge and belief states, for example, states of the sensory systems involved, memory states, and so forth; but these are not of immediate interest here. Precisely which states are involved, and how, is a problem for science to answer.

13. This feature of perceptual experience is discussed, for example, by Hirst (1959, pp. 238ff.).

14. This is probably because such situations occur but rarely in the experience of the young child when processing is most flexible, and are not important to him or her when they do so. If we lived beneath the sea like fish, I venture to suggest that shape constancy under changing fluid conditions would be something which we would all master very quickly. There would then be no more illusions of that type.

15. It is presented clearly, for example, by Armstrong (1961, chapter 1) and by Ayer (1961). It is argued very persuasively by Price (1964).

16. It can be seen, therefore, that there are two points at which I reject the move from "I seem to see an X" to "I see a seeming X," where that move might seem plausible (namely, under illusory or hallucinatory conditions). I reject it for the case of hallucinatory perception and deny that there is any *object* of the perceptual experience at all. I reject it for the case of illusory perception and claim that the object of perception is the usual external physical object or situation, but perceived inadequately. The move has no plausibility by itself at all in the case of veridical perception. The reply shows, for example, how I would reply to similar moves of Price (1964). A final remark: of course in some sense of the word every doctrine of perception that expects to offer an account of transformation of information from the world to human heads must posit structural transforms of the external world in the head, of some sort or other, and these might be called representatives of the world in the mind (= head). On this basis my own doctrine has been labeled Representative Realism by some. But, used in this way, the label is so general as to be useless: it applies to every plausible doctrine of perception whatever, and entirely fails to do justice to the historical doctrine so named whose epistemology, ontology, and psychology are so radically opposed to my own.

17. I call the materialism naturalistic because all the natural sciences are included as possibly equifundamental for our understanding of the nature of the physical world. Such materialism, although richer than its original mechanical version, is also less sharply demarcated from some of the older opposing positions.

18. This claim cannot be argued here, but see, e.g., the arguments cited by Smart (1963, p. 81) and Armstrong (1968, pp. 257-60), Bradley (1964), and Sellars (1963).

19. This is not a Kantianlike remark to the effect that a colored medium is logically necessary for visual perception. To the contrary, that the visual medium is a color medium is dependent upon the facts of our constitution, namely, that our visual perception has the encoding principles and medium that it does as a matter of fact have. Things might well have been otherwise. It is hoped that we shall someday be able to give an explanation of why there are just the colors there are, in terms of the character of the encoding medium and encoding principles, and perhaps we shall be able to change the qualitative medium of visual perception in consequence of that understanding.

20. For consistency and completeness we may also suppose that conscious-awareness itself has an evolutionary explanation. Roughly, the explanation is that the higher inte-

gration levels characteristic of conscious mind-brains are more efficient feedback control devices than a larger number of lower-level unconscious subsystems (especially when abstract symbolic manipulation is involved — see references to literature in § 1).

21. See Piaget (1929, 1951, 1954, 1971), as well as Berlyne (1957) and Gessell (1940, 1949).

22. See, for example, Bower (1966), Gibson & Walk (1960), and Rock & Harris (1967).

23. A point to be stressed is that the choice of a particular processing is *not* to be regarded as a choice of inference rules, or as a projection of inner features out in the world. Thus to so process visual information that colors are accorded an objective status is not to project anything (colors, for example) out into the world. The word "projection" suggests a quite misleading picture of the entire process. It suggests that we first perceive the colors internally and then project them out into the world, rather like a movie projector. This is an erroneous picture of conscious perception. There is no inner perception and no consequent projection. There is simply a *way* of perceiving, i.e., a manner of processing information and the conscious experience of that way of perceiving. But what is directly perceived in this way of perceiving is the enduring external world.

24. In light of my comments, it can be seen, however, that we actually have to do here with a *double* attribution. There is the attribution of physical properties to the surface: roughly, having a surface geometry such that variations in depth are larger than δ and occur over areas larger than ϵ. And there is the reference to the tactile (secondary) quality experience which touching that surface causes us to have. So few are the tactile illusions encountered in everyday life, however, that these two aspects tend not to be distinguished.

25. One must take the *fact* of the current conceptual scheme seriously, to be sure. But this attitude may find expression in an explanation of how the scheme came to embody the errors which it does embody. Natural language as a mature individual possesses it is the end result of the trial and error process of adjustment, collectively of the human race over the centuries and individually of that person's personal and social experiences. As with our perceptual organization and the rest of our more conscious beliefs in general, it is not guaranteed free of error or inadequacy, or the possibility of revision.

26. This simple statement is often complicated by an implicit pragmatic content, referring beyond the immediate sensory situation, which such statements often carry. That is, the utterer is usually making a claim about a body's *standing* color, not its transitory color (cf. Campbell in Rollins, 1969). But this is an inessential complication here.

27. The real situation is probably more closely reflected in the conjecture that we are driven to demand such an *individual* basis for colors because of their *appearance* of objectivity. But only something like the above principle, which does in any case have a grip of its own upon philosopher's minds, is strong enough to support the demand.

28. Let me call attention to the ambivalent attitude of contemporary materialist philosophies to principle P. On the one hand, these philosophies conform to the principle by attempting to reduce all distinguishable experienced qualities to distinguishable properties of the external world. But on the other hand, they are forced to deny (implicitly) the principle (just as I would do), when it comes to hallucinations, for materialists deny that there is, strictly, any object of the hallucinatory perceptual experience. Rather, they simply assert that the total hallucinatory experience is reducible to an internal process alone. Thus it is somewhat perverse for materialists to press the above objections against my position, though they often do so. Contemporary materialists place great emphasis on the ability to say what any given hallucination was *like — phenomenologically like*. The typical formula is "it (the hallucination) was like the veridical perception of . . ." This ability tends to create the (spurious) feeling that the *nature* of hallucinations has thereby

been adequately accounted for. But if there is any gap at all, there is as much or more of a gap in the account of materialists as there is in my account, and no amount of talk about *phenomenological similarities* can wipe out the (concealed) problem of accounting for the *ontological dissimilarities* that exist. For we have in hallucinatory experience a *perceptual* experience and yet we are perceptually aware of nothing; this is as much of a problem for materialists (who hold a direct realist account of perception), as it is for anyone else. In fact it is more of a problem for those who hold to P, for P is violated in the case of hallucinatory perceptual experience but not, apparently, in the case of veridical perceptual experience. What must be done, at minimum, is to show that though P may be violated in hallucinatory experience it must remain valid everywhere else. This has never been done — or even attempted — to my knowledge. Nor, in view of my reasons for rejecting P, can I see how it could be successfully attempted. (Note also that the specification of phenomenological content by the use of the quoted formula above is a device which I and anyone else can also use.)

29. I have in mind as unsatisfactory an unexplained postulation of all of the requisite logical relations among claims of the form p, q, r treated as wholes.

30. There are other ways to defend P, of course; among these the most powerful known to me is that of Sellars. For an articulation, examination, and rejection of his argument, see Hooker (1977).

References

Arbib, M. *The metaphorical brain*. New York: Wiley-Interscience, 1972.

Armstrong, D. M. *Perception and the physical world*. London: Routledge & Kegan Paul, 1961.

Armstrong, D. M. *A materialist theory of the mind*. New York: Humanities Press, 1968.

Ashby, W. R. *Design for a brain*. London: Chapman and Hall, 1952.

Ayer, A. J. *The problem of knowledge*. Baltimore, Md.: Penguin Books, 1961.

Berlyne, D. E. Recent developments in Piaget's work. *British Journal of Educational Psychology*, 1957, 27, 1-12.

Bower, T. G. R. The visual world of infants. *Scientific American*, 215 (December, 1966), 80-92.

Bradley, M. C. J. J. C. Smart's 'Philosophy and Scientific Realism'. *Australian Journal of Philosophy*, 1964, 42, No. 2.

Dennett, D. *Content and consciousness*. London: Routledge & Kegan Paul, 1969.

Gessell, A., et al. *The first five years of life*. New York: Harper, 1940.

Gessell, A., et al. *Vision: Its development in infant and child*. New York: Harper, 1949.

Gibson, E. J., & Walk, R. D. The visual cliff. *Scientific American*, 203 (April, 1969), 2-9.

Gibson, J. J. New reasons for realism. *Synthese*, 1967, 17, 162-72.

Gibson, J. J. *The senses considered as perceptual systems*. London: George Allen & Unwin, 1968.

Gregory, R. L. *Eye and brain*. New York: McGraw-Hill (World Univeristy Library), 1966.

Grossman, N. Empiricism and the possibility of encountering intelligent beings with different sense-structure. *Journal of Philosophy*, 1974, 61, 815-21.

Haber, R. N. *Information-processing approaches to visual perception*. New York: Holt, Rinehart and Winston, 1969.

Harnad, S. R., Steklis, H. D., & Lancaster, J. (Eds.), *Origins and evolution of language and speech*. New York: New York Academy of Sciences, 1976.

Hirst, R. J. *Problems of perception*. New York: Humanities Press, 1959.

Hooker, C. A. Systematic philosophy and the secondary qualities. Ph.D. dissertation, York University, Canada, 1970.

Hooker, C. A. Systematic Realism. *Synthese*, 1974, 26, 409-97.

Hooker, C. A. Systematic philosophy and meta-philosophy of science: Empiricism, Popperianism and realism. *Synthese*, 1975, 32, 177-231. (a)

Hooker, C. A. On global theories. *Philosophy of Science*, 1975, 42, 153-79. (b)

Hooker, C. A. Toward an adequate conception of scientific rationality. To appear. Invited paper for an international workshop on the Philosophy and Methodology of Science, Kronberg, July 1975 (c)

Hooker, C. A. The philosophical ramifications of the information-processing approach to the brain-mind. *Philosophy and Phenomenological Research*, 1975, 36, 1-15. (d)

Hooker, C. A. Sellars and the elimination of sensa. *Philosophical Studies*, 1977, 32, 335-48.

Jerison, H. J. *Evolution of the brain and intelligence.* New York: Academic Press, 1973.

Kabrinsky, L. *An information processing theory of vision.* Urbana: Ill.: University of Illinois Press, 1966.

Mackay, D. M. An information-flow model of human behaviour. *British Journal of Psychology*, 1956, 46, 30-43.

McCulloch, W. S. *Embodiments of mind.* Cambridge, Mass.: M.I.T. Press, 1965.

Nicholas, J. *Images, perception and knowledge.* Dordrecht, Holland: Reidel, 1976.

Neisser, U. *Cognitive psychology.* New York: Appleton-Century-Crofts, 1967.

Neisser, U. *Cognition and reality.* New York: W. H. Freeman, 1976.

Piaget, J. *The child's conception of the world.* New York: Harcourt, Brace Jovanovich, 1929.

Piaget, J. *Language and thought in the child.* New York: Humanities Press, 1951.

Piaget, J. *The construction of reality in the child.* New York: Basic Books, 1954.

Piaget, J. *Insights and illusions of philosophy.* New York: Meridian Books. 1971.

Pribram, K. *Languages of the brain.* Englewood Cliffs, N.J.: Prentice-Hall, 1971.

Pribram, K., & Baron, R. The holographic hypothesis of memory structure in brain function and perception. To appear in R. C. Atkinson, D. S. Krants, R. C. Luce, and F. Suppes (Eds.), *Contemporary developments in mathematical psychology.*

Price, H. H. Appearing and appearance. *American Philosophical Quarterly*, 1964, 1, 3-19.

Robinson, H. J. *Renascent rationalism.* Toronto: Macmillan, 1975.

Rock, I. & Harris, C. S. Vision and touch. *Scientific American* 1967, 216, 96-104.

Rollins, C. N. *Contemporary philosophy in Australia.* London: George Allen & Unwin, 1969.

Sellars, W. *Science, perception and reality.* London: Routledge & Kegan Paul, 1963.

Simon, H. A. *The sciences of the artificial.* Cambridge, Mass.: M.I.T. Press, 1969.

Smart, J. J. C. *Philosophy and scientific realism.* London: Routledge & Kegan Paul, 1963.

Snyder, F. W., & Sendon, N. H. *Vision and spatial inversion.* Wichita, Kansas: University of Wichita Press, 1952.

Sommerhoff, G. *The logic of the living brain.* New York: Wiley, 1974.

Thomas, W. J. Communication Without Sensory Overlap. *Journal of Philosophy*, 1975, 62, 256-57.

On the Status of "Direct" Psychophysical Measurement

Whether the water in a pot feels cold, cool, warm, or hot depends both on how long the pot has been on the fire and how long the testing hand has been in from the cold. In the recognition of such primitive facts one can discern the beginnings of both physics and psychophysics.

The fundamental invariances of physics began to emerge in pure, mathematically expressible form only when it became possible (a) to refine the scale of descriptive labels that could be applied to an object under study (e.g., from four such crude labels as "cold," "cool," "warm," and "hot" to a hundred or more distinguishable

Note: I first set forth the basic ideas underlying this essay over a decade ago in an unpublished but rather widely circulated note dated November 15, 1966 and titled "What does the psychophysicist measure?" Principally, these ideas were (a) that psychophysical judgments are essentially relative judgments, (b) that magnitude estimation and cross-modality matching determine no more than the ordinal structure of internal magnitudes, and (c) that what the psychophysicist measures on a "ratio scale" is a parameter that characterizes each sensory continuum — not the magnitude of any one sensation within such a continuum. Except for minor editing, the addition of some more recent references, and a number of deletions, the present paper is essentially identical to the draft of a more extensive development of these ideas that I prepared, under the present title, before leaving Harvard in June of 1968. It represents my most ambitious attempt to come to terms with the psychophysical claims of my late Harvard colleague, Professor S. S. Stevens. Regrettably, following my shift in geographical location and field of research, I had not until now found the occasion to return to the task of revising this manuscript for publication. In the meantime other writers have further explored some of these ideas. I believe the most elegant (and generous) published statements along these lines to be those of David H. Krantz (1972a, b). As I note in the relevant section, some of the formalizations presented in the present paper owe much to suggestions made to me by David V. Cross (personal communication, 1968). I want also to acknowledge the support provided by the National Science Foundation (Grants GS-1302 and BMS 75-02806) during the preparation and revision of this essay.

levels in the height of a column of mercury), and (b) to ensure that the descriptive label obtained from such a refined scale would relate more to the state of the object itself and less to the extraneous state of the measurer or his measuring instrument.

Once physics had attained this degree of quantitative precision and independence of the imperfectly correlated reactions of the human observer, the question arose as to whether these purely "psychological" responses — now that they had been conceptually distinguished from their purely physical correlates — might not be found to possess a certain kind of order of their own. If so, one could begin to contemplate a science of *psycho*physics; that is, a science that would have as its goal the quantitative specification of any relations that hold between such a psychological order, on the one hand, and the independently established physical order, on the other. I have attempted in this chapter to clarify the extent to which we have approached this goal.

The Problem of the Construction of Psychophysical Scales

In the development of purely physical science, mathematically formulated laws of predictive precision and generality were of course made possible only through the extensive refinement of physical scales of measurement such, for example, as the scale of temperature. It was therefore natural, in attempting the subsequent development of a psychophysical science, to strive for a similar refinement of psychological scales of measurement. For, as long as the responses of the human observer were limited to just a few ill-defined qualitative labels, the relations between these responses and the physical variables could not approach the kind of precision and generality characteristic of the laws relating purely physical variables.

CONSTRUCTION OF SCALES FOR
THE MEASUREMENT OF PHYSICAL MAGNITUDES

In the case of physics, the perfection of scales of measurement was critically dependent upon the development of theory. The earliest temperature-sensitive devices, such as the "thermoscope" or "weather glass" of 1600, provided only a somewhat more purified and objective way of gauging "warmth." The still largely intuitive notion of temperature had not yet acquired sufficient theoretical articulation to support more than an ordinal structure. That is, although it could consistently be determined whether one object was warmer or cooler than another (even when the difference was quite small), there was little basis for asserting anything further about the quantitative magnitude of such a difference in temperature. Indeed, even when the thermoscope was transformed into the first crude thermometer by the addition of a graduated scale some time around 1610 (Middleton, 1966), the scale was necessarily quite arbitrary and so did not really provide an adequate basis for assigning numerical values to temperatures in any unique way.

It was the considerably later developments of thermodynamics and the kinetic theory of heat that furnished the structure necessary for the transformation of the original, intuitive notion of warmth into the present, fully articulated concept of temperature. It was only by recourse to abstract thermodynamic arguments concerning "ideal heat engines" (see, e.g., Becker, 1967, pp. 18-20) that in 1848 William Thomson (Lord Kelvin) was able to present a satisfactory rationale for the specification of temperatures by numerical values that were uniquely determined except for multiplication by a positive constant (the arbitrary unit of measurement that determines whether we are talking, say, about degrees Kelvin or degrees Rankine).

On the resulting "thermodynamic scale" the difference between two temperatures can be defined in terms of the mechanical work extractable by a Carnot engine working between the two temperatures. Thus it became for the first time fully meaningful to say that the difference in temperature between two cool objects, A and B, is equal to the difference in temperature between two warm objects, C and D. In terms of the classificatory scheme of scale types set forth by Stevens (1946, 1951), the merely "ordinal scale" of warmth had at this point become an "interval scale" of temperature. Further, with the conceptualization of the absolute zero point of temperature, which can only be approached but never attained (and which, according to the kinetic theory, corresponds to the cessation of all relative molecular motion), it became meaningful to talk about ratios as well as differences. Of two objects, A and B, not only could one say that the temperature of B is greater than the temperature of A, one could further state that it is twice as great, three times as great, or whatever the case might be. At this point, the scale of temperature finally emerged as what would be classified in Stevens's scheme as a full-fledged "ratio scale."

Apparently, then, the interval and ratio properties of the thermodynamic scale of temperature can be fully justified only by reference to physical theory. It is of course a convenient (and not entirely adventitious) outcome that the equally spaced graduations on the laboratory thermometer correspond to nearly (though, significantly, not precisely) equal differences on the thermodynamic scale. But even the hydrogen thermometer, which most closely approximates the theoretically ideal thermodynamic scale, is subject to correction owing to the departure of hydrogen from a perfect gas (with the consequence that the desired "thermometric" property is approximated only as the product of pressure times volume is extrapolated to zero pressure). Again, the real reason for specifying temperature on this scale (and for imposing slight corrections on the equally spaced graduation of the thermometer) is the resulting simplification in the mathematical structure of physical theory as a whole. For this theory is concerned not just with temperature, but also with a host of other variables and concepts that are related to temperature and to each other in a vast, interdigitated complex.

In the last analysis, of course, the justification for the whole theoretical edifice must be sought in the account that it provides for concrete empirical observations. Nevertheless, it appears that the variables (such as temperature) that are measured by means of physical scales as now refined are themselves essentially of the nature of theoretical constructs. For, to the extent that we identify the temperature of a macroscopic body with the kinetic energy of its microscopic constituents, the temperature itself recedes from the realm of concrete, directly experienceable entities.

CONSTRUCTION OF SCALES FOR
THE MEASUREMENT OF PSYCHOLOGICAL MAGNITUDES

I have argued that refined scales for the measurement of purely physical quantities originally evolved out of attempts to eliminate the influence of the variable internal states of the observer upon his evaluations of the state of an external object. This suggests the possibility of using a reverse strategy to develop comparably refined scales for the measurement of what might be called purely psychological magnitudes; namely, those very states of the observing subject that, in the process of perfecting physical measurement, had finally been cast entirely aside.[1]

Within the original use of such crude, descriptive labels as "hot" and "cold," that is, one can discern the precursors of two quite distinct concepts: (a) that of a purely physical magnitude (temperature) that is conceived as residing entirely within the external object, and (b) that of a purely psychological magnitude (perceived warmth) that is conceived as residing entirely within the observing subject. Indeed, either magnitude can exist quite independently of the other. The physical temperatures of objects can be registered automatically without the occurrence of any sensation of warmth, and (during direct electrical excitation of the cortex, spontaneous hallucinations, or dreams) a sensation of warmth can occur in the total absence of a corresponding physical stimulus.

It might seem that I have ignored a fundamental asymmetry between the two types of magnitudes. For even if physical temperature is a theoretical construct, inaccessible to direct observation, the corresponding sensation of warmth is surely directly experienced by the subject who reports its occurrence. However, with the adoption of the behavioristic orientation toward sensations required for the intersubjective development of a public science, statements about sensations assume fundamentally the same status as statements about the theoretical variables of physics. If the concept of a sensation of warmth is introduced into behavioral theory, it is for the same reason that the concept of a temperature is introduced into physical theory—not because it is demanded by any single observation, but because it simplifies the theory as a whole. Just as a temperature is identified, theoretically, with a certain unobserved state of molecular agitation in the external object, a sensation of warmth would presumably be identified, theoretically, with some unobserved pattern or level of neuronal activity in the brain.

Now physical measurement owes its great power not only to its independence of the variable state of the observer but also to its high degree of quantitative precision. To what extent can this same kind of precision be achieved in the measurement of purely psychological variables—variables such as visual brightness, auditory loudness, or tactual warmth? Such sensations do seem to have certain definite subjective magnitudes. But to what extent can we specify explicit procedures of measurement that will enable us to pin such magnitudes down on anything approaching the refined structure of a numerical scale?

The history of physical measurement indicates that, if this is to be accomplished, its accomplishment will hinge critically upon the available theoretical structure. A subject can of course say more about his thermal sensations than merely whether each is "cold," "cool," "warm," or "hot." He can, for example, report the judgment that one such sensation seems about twice as strong (i.e., hot) as another. But we cannot safely conclude that the one sensation is, in fact, twice the other just because the subject makes such a verbal report—any more than we could conclude that the temperature is twice the other just because the mercury rises to twice the height. The direct, quantitative indication of either the subject or the thermometer might even be true, but, in the one case as much as in the other, a more than trivial theory is needed to substantiate the claim.

ROLE OF PSYCHOPHYSICAL
RELATIONS IN THE CONSTRUCTION OF SCALES

A physical magnitude such as temperature evidently derives much of its significance from its relations with other physical variables. Similarly, if procedures could be devised for making quantitative determinations of psychological magnitudes, the most significant advance in our understanding would come not from the mere measurement of this or that sensation per se. Rather, it would come from the relations that might thus be found to hold between such psychological magnitudes and other measurable variables. The enterprise becomes psycho*physical* (rather than purely psychological) to the extent that some of the most important of these relations are with physical variables.

So far, psychophysical investigations have endeavored principally to determine the functional form of one particular type of relation; namely, the relation between the psychological strength of a sensation (such as perceived loudness, brightness, or warmth) and the physical intensity of the eliciting proximal stimulus (measured, say, in terms of energy—whether acoustic, electromagnetic, or kinetic). Before such a determination can be made, however, it would seem necessary to meet two conditions.

First, other physical variables that might also influence the psychological magnitude under study must be carefully controlled. One such variable (emphasized at the outset) is the intensity of stimulation to which the receptive organ has previously been adapted. However, although such control may not always be easy in practice, it does not appear to depend upon the resolution of any major theoretical issues and so will not be further considered here.

The second condition is quite another matter. It is that the psychological magnitude in question must be measurable on a scale with more than a merely ordinal structure. We must be able to find out more about a sensation than merely whether it exceeds or falls short of some other sensation. Otherwise, the findings could as well be accounted for by *any* monotonic function of physical intensity. And yet, just how the necessary further structure can be secured remains an issue of continuing dispute.

Actually, as the example of the temperature scale suggests, it is simplistic to suppose that one first erects a fully structured scale and *then* proceeds to relate the variable measured on this scale to other variables. Rather, what seems to have happened in physics is a bi-directional, mutually constraining interaction between these two processes. It was, in fact, the attempt to perfect and simplify the relations with other variables that prescribed what form the internal structure of the temperature scale itself would finally have to take. Perhaps, then, the development of psychophysics can progress only by means of a similar kind of cooperative alternation between the tightening of the structure of a scale and the simplifying of its relations with other variables.

DISCRIMINABILITY AS A BASIS FOR PSYCHOPHYSICAL SCALING

In view of the difficulties that have appeared to confront any attempt to measure psychological magnitudes directly, some psychophysicists, notably Fechner and Thurstone, have turned to discriminability as a method for inferring psychological magnitudes, so to speak, indirectly. In practice, all such approaches evidently depend upon the variability of subjects' responses and, indeed, depend upon some specific assumption about the relation between that variability and psychological magnitude.

Although he did not conceive of it in precisely these terms, Fechner (1860), who is generally credited with the founding of psychophysics, assumed in effect that this variability is constant and independent of magnitude on the underlying psychological scale. Thus he was led to identify the difference in the psychological magnitudes of two intensities on the same sensory continuum with what amounts to the number of intervening differences in intensity that could be discriminated some specified fraction of the time (i.e., the number of intervening "just noticeable differences" or "*jnds*").

In order to secure a ratio scale, then, Fechner had only to assume that a zero (or subthreshold) physical intensity leads to a zero psychological magnitude. For, on the resulting scale, one can numerically specify both the *difference* between two sensations (the number of *jnds* from the one to the other) and the *ratio* between those sensations (the number of *jnds* from zero to the one divided by the number of *jnds* from zero to the other).

In his much later approach to psychophysics, Thurstone (1927) was more explicit about its dependence upon the variability of the subject's responses. In particular, he expressly postulated that the same external stimulus leads to an internal psychological magnitude, the "discriminal process," that varies from occasion to occasion. Moreover, in a manner that strongly foreshadowed the modern theory of signal detection (Green & Swets, 1966), he went on to specify a decision rule, according to which the subject's overt response to a particular stimulus was determined by whether the psychological magnitude to which it gave rise on a given occasion exceeded or fell short of some internal criterion magnitude.

However, although he thus provided an explicit mechanism to account for Fechner's *jnd*, Thurstone himself preferred to take a somewhat different aspect of the subject's variability as fundamental for the construction of psychological scales. Specifically, instead of assuming that the distribution of the discriminable process has a fixed variance on the underlying psychological scale, he assumed that this distribution has a fixed functional form—namely, the form of the normal (or Gaussian) error function. Under this assumption, the normal distributions of discriminal processes arising from different stimuli could have different variances; in that case, equally often noticed differences would not necessarily correspond to equal differences in psychological magnitude.

Scaling methods in considerable variety have evolved out of Fechner's and Thurstone's original attempts to base psychophysics on discriminability. Essentially these methods are designed to find a spacing of stimuli on the "psychological scale" such that the overt responses of subjects can best be accounted for by some model of the Thurstonian type in which the hypothetical distributions of psychological magnitudes all have either (a) the same variance, as suggested by Fechner, (b) the normal functional form, as proposed by Thurstone, or perhaps (c) merely the same, unspecified functional form (Klemmer & Shrimpton, 1963; Kruskal & Shepard, 1974, p. 154; Levine, 1970, 1972; Shepard, 1965), or even (d) just an optimum degree of smoothness or "continuity" (Carroll, 1963; Shepard & Carroll, 1966).

Since these methods lead to interval or ratio scales (i.e., to scales that are determined essentially to within a linear or even a similarity transformation), they possess enough structure to support some determination of the "psychophysical function." Fechner, as I noted, claimed to have what amounts to a ratio scale of psychological magnitude. All he then needed was the empirical fact, already established by Weber, that the size of a *jnd* in units of phsyical intensity is approximately proportional to intensity. From this empirical invariance (since known as "Weber's Law"), Fechner deduced that the psychological magnitude of a sensation, as he defined it, must be a logarithmic function of physical intensity.

Fechner's proposed solution to the psychophysical problem appears rather weak, however, when we compare his scale of psychological magnitude with physical scales, such as that for temperature. For the structure of the thermodynamic scale of temperature was, so to speak, conferred on that temperature scale—not just by one relation, but by a richly interconnected web of mutually reinforcing theoretical and empirical relations. By contrast, the structure of Fechner's scale was dictated by the attempt to secure just one relation; viz., the relation that a just noticeable difference subtend the same separation in psychological magnitude regardless of its position on the scale.

This weakness is not, however, inherent in the general choice of discriminability as a basis for psychophysics. Within the broader, Thurstonian framework there is at least the possibility of establishing mutually reinforcing relations among diverse kinds of experimental tasks. It could for example happen that one scale of psychological magnitude would be found to provide a simple and unified account of (a) the distribution of stimuli classified as "same" or "different" or as "greater than" or "less than" any given stimulus (Woodworth, 1938; Torgerson, 1958), (b) the pattern of errors made in tasks of absolute identification or paired-associate learning (Garner, 1952; Luce & Galanter, 1963; Shepard, 1958b), (c) the shape of the "gradient" of stimulus generalization (Guttman & Kalish, 1956; Shepard, 1965) or of discriminative reaction time (Curtis, Paulos, & Rule, 1973; Falmagne, 1971; Shepard, Kilpatric, & Cunningham, 1975, pp. 127 ff.; Welford, 1960), (d) the way in which accuracy of comparative judgment decays with the delay of the second stimulus (Shepard, 1958a; Wickelgren, 1969), and even (e) phenomena of stimulus-response compatibility (Shepard, 1961) and of classification learning (Shepard & Chang, 1963; Shepard, et al., 1975, pp. 134-135). Then, surely, one could begin to have some confidence in such a psychological scale. (See in particular the more recent work of Falmagne, 1971.)

The extent to which such a synthesis can eventually be achieved for these various sorts of discrimination data appears to be a largely empirical question. In any case the logical status of such a discriminability scale now seems reasonably clear. So the remainder of this paper will be devoted to the examination of the entirely different proposal that, quite apart from the possibility of inferring psychological magnitudes indirectly on the basis of discriminability, we can —and perhaps should—obtain the desired estimates more directly by simply asking the subject himself for a straightforward, quantitative judgment of these magnitudes.

DIRECT JUDGMENT AS A BASIS FOR PSYCHOPHYSICAL SCALING

The late S. S. Stevens, who was undoubtedly the foremost proponent of psychophysics in recent years, launched a sustained attack against the whole attempt to base psychophysics on discriminability. He pointed out that, in physics, the analogue of discriminability would be error variability—the converse of resolving power. But (except when we approach the irreducible limitations of quantum physics) resolving power is clearly more dependent upon the particular measuring instrument used than it is upon the underlying physical quantity to be measured. Thus the recommendation that we adjust our scale of psychological magnitude solely in order that error variability will be constant across the scale would be like calibrating a scale of electric current just so that the inaccuracy in the deflection of the pointer will be constant across the scale of the galvanometer. But in this latter case (as in the case of temperature), it is relations other than those having to do with such variability that furnish the most fundamental basis for an operational definition of the underlying physical quantity. Possibly this is true as much for the definition of the strength of a sensation as for the definition of the strength of an electric current. Certainly it can be seen as a curious aspect of scaling procedures based on discriminability that they essentially depend upon the presence of what we usually seek to minimize—namely, variability or error.

At a turning point in his long endeavor to develop a method for estimating psychological magnitudes without depending on variability, Stevens (1956) proposed to have subjects simply report direct, quantitative estimates of the strengths of their sensations. In the instructions to the subject, he explicitly specified that the numbers given should be proportional to the strengths of the corresponding sensations. Suppose, for example, that the first stimulus had been called "40." Then the instructions evidently required that, if the psychological magnitude of the second stimulus seemed twice as great as that of the first, it should be called "80"; if half as great, "20"; and so on.

Now the responses obtained from subjects in this method of "direct magnitude estimation" have manifested an undeniable degree of consistency and order for a wide class of sensory continua; namely, the class of what Stevens (1957) has called "prothetic" continua. Principally this class includes the "intensive" and "extensive" dimensions of stimuli along which variation is perceived as the purely *quantitative* addition or subtraction of the same homogeneous quality, as in loudness, brightness, or length. This class is thus contrasted with the class of "metathetic" continua along which variation is perceived, rather, as the *qualitative* substitution of one kind of experience for another, as in auditory pitch or, perhaps, visual hue.

If we confine our attention specifically to "prothetic" continua, then, we find that the (geometric) mean of the numbers produced by the subjects for each stimulus closely approximates a power function of the physical intensity of the stimulus. Moreover, although the numerical value of the exponent in the best-fitting power function does vary somewhat from subject to subject, when the values are averaged over even a small group of subjects, the resulting average value turns out to be a rather stable characteristic of the particular sensory continuum. Such average values range from between 0.3 to 0.6, for the continuum of intensity of a light (depending on the visual size of the source), all the way up to 4.5, for the continuum of intensity of an electric shock (Stevens, 1966a).

On the basis of these results, Stevens (1961) proclaimed that the logarithmic function that Fechner had derived for the central psychophysical relation should be rejected in favor of a power function (a conclusion, incidently, that he notes had been first advanced and then withdrawn, without the benefit of sufficient evidence, some 100 years earlier by Fechner's contemporary, Plateau).

Even with the large body of evidence that Stevens and his followers have amassed, however, the claims that the power function rather than the logarithmic function is in fact the true psychophysical law and that one can, and should, now measure sensations by direct magnitude estimation have continued to come under assault (e.g., Graham, 1958; Helson, 1964; Luce, 1972; Savage, 1970; Torgerson, 1960; Treisman, 1963, 1964). For the most part, these attacks seem to be aimed at the implications that Stevens claims to draw from this evidence, more than at the empirical evidence itself.

With respect to the empirical evidence, it is generally conceded that systematic departures from the overall power function are found near threshold, near other "anchoring" background or reference stimuli, or when the stimuli to be judged are themselves drawn from a set of intensities that is unevenly spaced, bunched, or truncated on the "true" underlying psychological scale. But such departures seem susceptible to correction in principle—for example, by the rational introduction of an appropriate, empirically estimable threshold constant, by the avoidance of undesired "anchors," and by "iterative" experiments designed to converge on an optimum distribution or spacing of stimulus intensities (e.g., see Pollack, 1965). What follows here, in any case, will take the validity of the basic empirical generalizations for granted and will focus instead on the implications of these generalizations for the measurement of psychological magnitudes and for the development of psychophysical theory.

SOME APPARENT LIMITATIONS OF DIRECT MAGNITUDE ESTIMATION

The first problem that we confront here is basically like the problem that the mere affixing of a numbered scale to a thermoscope provided no sound basis for saying whether one temperature was twice or three times another. Indeed it later became apparent that the numbers inscribed on these early scales very definitely were *not* proportional to the corresponding absolute temperatures required by physcial theory. Without a theory, then, how can we assume that the numbers proffered by a subject—any more than the numbers indicated on the arbitrary scale of the thermoscope—are proportional to any underlying quantity?

We cannot answer this question merely by insisting that the subject is expressly instructed to give a number that *is* proportional to the underlying psychological magnitude. For, in the absence of any independent access to that psychological magnitude, how could we be certain that the subject is following our instruction? How, indeed, could we ever have taught the subject to make such reports correctly in the first place? Surely it would be a risky business to assume, just because an instruction was issued, that it was followed. (What if we were to instruct the subject to repeat back a 24-digit number, or to report the direction of a weak magnetic field?)

The difficulty inherent in this "direct" approach can be brought out in even clearer, mathematical terms as follows: According to Stevens (1957) the fundamental psychophysical relation is of the general form

$$\Psi = f_1(S), \tag{1}$$

where S is the physically measured intensity of a stimulus, Ψ is the resulting psychological magnitude, and f_1 is the "psychophysical" function that transforms one into the other. Clearly, though, this formulation is incomplete. It takes us only from the external, measurable stimulus, S, into the internal, unobservable sensation, Ψ.

In order to complete the formulation and to give it any empirical content, we must get back out to the externally recordable response, R, by means of a second, reverse "psychophysical" transformation

$$R = f_2(\Psi). \tag{2}$$

But, as has previously been noted (e.g., by Treisman, 1964), since the intervening variable, Ψ, is not itself observable, the responses of the subject can at most determine the form of the single, overall "physical-physical" relation

$$R = f_3(S) = f_2\{f_1(S)\}, \tag{3}$$

in which Ψ does not explicitly appear.

Apparently, unless we arbitrarily fix one of the two component functions of f_3 (viz., either f_1 or f_2), both of the two component functions must remain wholly unknown. Hence the conclusion that Stevens has drawn from the results of magnitude estimation—namely, that the function f_1 is a power function—evidently depends upon the implicit assumption that the instructions have sufficed to ensure that f_2 is itself a power function (hopefully with an exponent of unity). But the grounds for assuming that the instructions would have precisely this effect seem never to have been adequately explained.

In fact the situation is even worse than this. For what the subject really gives us in a magnitude estimation is, after all, only a discrete, learned response (i.e., a word). It is not anything that itself even possesses a definite quantitative magnitude. So, as a number of psychophysicists have noted, whether it is legitimate to speak of "ratios" or "differences" between these verbal responses or, indeed, to compute their geometric means is not something that can safely be taken for granted (Garner, 1954; Graham, 1958, p. 68; Luce & Galanter, 1963, p. 274; McGill, 1960, p. 67; Oyamo, 1968); it needs to be justified.[2]

But those who have considered how a child might learn to use such phrases as "twice as great," "three times as great," etc., have tended to argue that the relations among the public or objective quantities, S, rather than the relations among the private or subjective magnitudes, Ψ, generally furnish the criteria for correct use (Skinner, 1945, 1957; Treisman, 1964; Warren, 1958; Wittgenstein,

1953). Thus, in a situation of comparing sticks of different lengths, the child may learn that the phrase "twice as long" is appropriate when two of the equal, shorter sticks laid end-to-end reach just as far as the single, longer stick.

It may even be that what he really learns is to infer these objective relations among the physical quantities S from the subjective relations among his immediately given psychological magnitudes Ψ. But no matter what these latter, purely subjective relations may be, his commerce with the public, physical world is likely, in the words of Thouless (1931), to favor a "regression," in his overt responses, to the "real objects." Whatever the relevant psychological distances, someone who is attempting to jump from stone to stone across a stream had better regulate each response so that it will carry him over the appropriate *physical* distance. It is not perhaps too surprising, then, that the empirically determined exponent in the power law for visual extent is found to be close to unity (Stevens & Guirao, 1963; Teghtsoonian, 1965).

Just how subjects learn to make judgments on intensive, as opposed to extensive, continua is not entirely clear. It is however a suggestive fact (Stevens, 1960, p. 64) that exponents close to ½ rather than close to 1 have been obtained for intensities presented to the "distance" receptors of vision (0.5 for the brightness of a point source), audition (0.6 for the loudness of a binaural tone), and olfaction (0.55 for the strength of the odor of coffee). Possibly the judgment of an intensive magnitude is in part based on the appreciation of an extensive magnitude. Certainly, if a source that is twice as far away is called half as bright, loud, or strong, then the inverse square law might help to explain the clustering of these fitted exponents about the value 0.5 (Treisman, 1964; Warren, 1958; Warren, Sersen, & Pores, 1958).

On the other hand, one must agree with Stevens (1964) that it seems unlikely that each individual subject has had the opportunity to learn to apply numbers in this way to each separate continuum, *de novo* —particularly in the case of the more novel continua that have been studied, such as strength of electric shock or apparent viscosity (Stevens & Guirao, 1964). Possibly, then, much of this "learning" has been accomplished, not in the individual subject, but in the preceding biological evolution of higher organisms in general (cf. Shepard, 1964, pp. 63-65; 1975, pp. 96, 115). In this connection there is reason to suppose that output transformations are more readily learnable if the function f_2 in Equation (2) is of a suitably standard or "simple" form (Carroll, 1963). If so, natural selection would tend to favor the development of input transformations in which the resulting subjective magnitude represents an appropriate "phenomenal regression," if not always to a "real object," at least to the physical magnitude relevant to the widest range of adaptive responses.

Regardless of how subjects come to be able to assign numbers consistently to stimuli differing along a sensory continuum, the fact remains that what this assignment directly reveals is not the form of the transformation of S into Ψ, but rather the form of the complete transformation of S into R. Here we come back, then, to the essential dependence of measurement on theory. For surely we cannot safely turn about and take the numerical face value of the overt response R as a direct measure of the intervening, covert psychological magnitude Ψ, unless we have an acceptable theory as to why the output function f_2 in (2) should be precisely the one of simple proportionality, $R = k\Psi$.

For this purpose, moreover, such a theory should presumably be more fully articulated and confirmed than either the rather vague evolutionary argument offered above or the remotely connected argument of simplicity seemingly invoked in the discussion of this matter by Stevens (1964). Given that the overall relation $R = f_3(S)$ is empirically found to be a power function, it may in some sense be simpler (as Stevens implied) to assume that the two component functions, f_1 and f_2, are themselves both power functions than to assume that the input function is logarithmic (as proposed by Fechner) while the output function is the counteracting exponential. Later, however, Stevens adopted the attractive and plausible hypothesis that magnitude estimation is really just a special case of "cross-modality matching;" and, within that more general framework, the argument based on simplicity changes so as to lose much of its force.

SOME APPARENT LIMITATIONS OF CROSS-MODALITY MATCHING

Partly in order to answer some of the persistent objections to his interpretation of the numerical responses obtained under direct magnitude estimation, Stevens (1959) introduced and subsequently placed increasing stress on results of experiments in what he called "cross-modality matching." In these experiments the subject is presented, one by one, with stimuli that differ along some sensory continuum just as in magnitude estimation; but, instead of giving a number for each stimulus, the subject adjusts another, variable stimulus along a second sensory continuum until it seems to "match" each presented stimulus. Thus he may adjust a tone of variable intensity until its apparent loudness seems psychologically equivalent to each apparent brightness in a series of lights varying only in intensity.

As in the method of direct magnitude estimation, the subject may be explicitly instructed to maintain proportionality of psychological magnitudes. So, if the second light seems just twice as bright as the first, say, the second tone should be adjusted to sound just twice as loud as the first, and so on. Indeed, Stevens came to hold that magnitude estimation can itself best be regarded as a kind of cross-modality matching (Stevens, 1966b, p. 388). The same can also be claimed for the reverse procedure of "magnitude production," in which a number is given to the subject who then tries to match it by producing an appropriate physical intensity (whether indirectly, by adjusting the attenuator on a tone generator, or directly, by simply singing the desired tone).

The only special features of these latter two varieties of cross-modality matching is that, for one of the two "modalities," a physically given continuum of intensity (or extensity) is replaced by the conventionally established continuum of numbers. In all of these cases, according to Stevens, what the subject really does is to search for the psychological magnitude on one continuum that appears to "match" the psychological magnitude on another continuum. The results tend to substantiate his claim that it makes little difference whether both of the continua are physical or whether one is the learned or conventional "continuum" of numbers.

Indeed the overall consistency of the results that have emerged from these various types of experiments is quite impressive. Specifically, for each pair of continua studied, the intensities chosen on the one continuum have been found to be closely fitted by a power function of the corresponding given intensities on the other continuum. Moreover, the exponent of this fitted power function is uniformly in close agreement with the value predicted simply by taking the appropriate ratio of the exponents obtained by magnitude estimation for each of the two continua separately (e.g., Stevens, 1959, 1966a). The exponent estimated for each of the sensory continua apparently does represent a real, psychophysical property of that continuum.

However, the basic objection evidently remains that we are still only relating physical magnitudes. Although it is now clearly legitimate to speak of ratios or differences between these physical magnitudes, it is not clear that we have moved any closer to the measurement of the intervening, purely psychological magnitude Ψ.

The model for magnitude estimation, which was formally stated in the earlier Equations (1) and (2), is now replaced by the model for cross-modality matching, which I propose to express in the form

$$\Psi = f(S),$$
$$\Psi' = f'(S'), \tag{4}$$
$$\text{``Match'' when } \Psi = \Psi'.$$

Here the prime indicates a second sensory continuum (or, in application to magnitude estimation, the "continuum" of conventional number words). The derived relation between empirical variables, which earlier took the stimulus-response form of Equation (3), now takes the stimulus-stimulus form

$$S = f^{-1}\{f'(S')\},$$
$$S' = f'^{-1}\{f(S)\}. \tag{5}$$

Although this revised model seems more general and is more consonant with Stevens's later view that all psychophysical judgments are based upon matching, a comparison of Equations (3) and (5) reveals that, as far as their empirical implications are concerned, the two models are formally equivalent. In either case we simply end up with a functional relation of the general $X = g(Y)$; and, regardless of whether X is conceived as a response or as a stimulus, X and Y are both observables, so the functional relation g between them is equally susceptible to empirical determination.

More significantly, however, the two models are also alike in that neither provides any empirical basis for deciding among alternative

factorings of the overall function g into its two theoretical components (f_1 and f_2 in the magnitude estimation model, or f and f' in
the "matching" model). The basic empirical finding, viz., that the
physcial intensities that are matched between any two continua are
closely describable by a power function, is undisputed. But, contrary
to the impression given by Stevens, this finding does not by itself
entail that the inner, psychological magnitudes, on the basis of which
the subject is assumed to be achieving these matches, are themselves
power functions of the external intensities.

As several commentators have noted (e.g., Ekman, 1964; Luce &
Galanter, 1963, p. 280; MacKay, 1963; Treisman, 1963), the very
same finding could as well be explained by assuming (with Fechner)
that the directly-to-be-matched psychological magnitudes all arise,
not through a power transformation of the form $\Psi = aS^\beta$, but
through a logarithmic transformation of the form $\Psi = a + \beta \log S$.
For suppose (with Stevens) that intensities S and S' on two different
continua (the unprimed and the primed continuum) result in the
desired psychological match, $\Psi = \Psi'$, whenever

$$aS^\beta = a'S'^{\beta'}$$

(where β and β' are fixed parameters, each associated with its own
continuum). But this equations is exactly equivalent, mathematically, to the equation

$$\log a + \beta \log S = \log a' + \beta' \log S',$$

which defines a match according to the logarithmic model.[3]

Stevens himself uniformly applied a logarithmic transformation
to the physical intensities, S and S', before plotting the resulting
"matching functions." This is, of course, a perfectly natural and
convenient thing to do—particularly since engineers commonly express physical intensities in terms of a logarithmic transformation
of energy (i.e., in decibels). However, there are two more reasons
for applying such a transformation here. First, the power relation
between S and S' is made, in this way, to appear as the graphically
simpler linear relation between $\log S$ and $\log S'$. And, second, the
variability of the judgments will, in accordance with Weber's law,
appear of more uniform size in the resulting log-log plot. (One might
even argue that, since the unit of discriminability is approximately
constant only on the logarithmic scale, considerations of simplicity

of the overall psychophysical picture—including data on both direct judgment and discriminability—favors the logarithmic over the power model.)

In any case, when magnitude estimation is recast into the general framework of cross-modality matching, it is no longer necessary to invoke an exponential output transformation to counteract a logarithmic input transformation. For now, in place of one input transformation (1) and a separate output transformation (2), we have two symmetrically related input transformations (4). Clearly all such input transformations could be either logarithmic or power functions, and, in view of the above discussion, the previously mentioned argument against the logarithmic alternative on grounds of overall simplicity no longer commands much conviction.

Hypothetical magnitudes Ψ_i that can be reached only through inherently indeterminate functions such as those contained in Equations (3) and (5) have the unsatisfactory status of "nomological danglers" (Feigl, 1958, pp. 382, 428) and ordinarily would suggest a hasty recourse to Ockham's razor. In the present case, however, to bypass the intervening variable Ψ would be to forfeit the major part of our predictive power. For only by factoring the overall, empirically determined relations (3) or (5) into their two theoretical components does it become possible to predict the overall relation to be found between new combinations of previously studied continua. It is on such grounds that Stevens might argue—as have Hull (1943, pp. 111, 122) and others, including myself (Shepard, 1958b) —for the retention of an intrinsically unobservable variable intervening between the observable stimuli and responses.

Regardless of the ontological status accorded such intervening magnitudes in general, though, they appear to play a curiously indeterminate role in the two models for direct psychophysical judgment considered here. We are left with the following rather awkward state of affairs: In order to provide a simple account for the whole range of cross-modality data, it appears desirable to assume that, corresponding to the external, physical magnitudes, there are internal, psychological magnitudes with definite, quantitative values. But, unless we arbitrarily assume some particular form for the input (or output) functions, nothing can be learned about these values beyond their merely ordinal relations. In such a case it does not seem wholly justifiable to speak of the "measurement" of a psychological magnitude such as the loudness of a tone or the brightness of light.

FAILURE TO REPRESENT THE RELATIVITY OF PERCEPTION

All of the above objections have taken for granted the traditional psychophysical presupposition that a single stimulus intensity S gives rise, quite by itself, to a quantitatively unique magnitude Ψ —i.e., without reference to any other comparison stimulus. That is, both of the two models considered were models for "absolute" psychophysical judgment. In addition to the objections already raised, I want now to raise the different objection that this traditional presupposition may itself be wrong. For, if an isolated stimulus gives rise to a unique magnitude Ψ, the subject himself seems strangely incapable of making any use of it. The uncertainty and variability of absolute judgments are notorious.

Typically a subject cannot reliably distinguish more than about six or seven *absolute* levels along any one unidimensional continuum (Miller, 1956). This is in striking contrast to a subject's refined sensitivity to *relative* differences between stimuli that differ only slightly, which underlies the hundred or more discriminable steps of Fechner's *jnd* scale. Even in the case of widely separated intensities, a subject may be able to report with considerable reliability and confidence that, with respect to one intensity, the other is greater by half again, by three and one half times, by nearly twenty times, or whatever the case may be.

This superiority of relative judgments is understandable in physiological terms. As we noted at the outset, the absolute level of neural activity depends upon both the intensity of the stimulus and the physiological state of the receptive system. Hence the absolute level of neuronal activity can provide only a very crude and variable indication of the absolute intensity of the external stimulus, and it would not be adaptive for an organism to rely on it for anything more. But, although the absolute rates for two fixed stimuli may thus vary over a wide range, some relationship *between* those rates (such as their difference or ratio) may remain relatively constant (Cornsweet, 1970, pp. 245 ff.). Thus it could well be adaptive for an organism to rely, instead of on the absolute rates of firing, on something like *relative* rates as valid indicators of what is going on in the external world. In the case of physical measuring instruments, of course, it is elementary that determinations of relative energy are both easier and more accurate than determinations of absolute energy.

It is not surprising, then, that the preferred operations of the psychophysicist typically require the comparison of two or more stimuli. In the method of magnitude estimation, for example, little significance is customarily attached to the number that the subject produces in response to the first stimulus in the series. Although this number may be to some extent influenced by the intensity of the first stimulus, it is typically regarded as a more or less arbitrary "modulus," and the subject will, in fact, accept a quite arbitrary number for this "modulus." It is only with the presentation of the second stimulus that the quantitative value of the subject's responses become of real interest. For at that point he is for the first time constrained by the instruction that, relative to the modulus, the numbers given to succeeding stimuli should be proportional to the magnitudes of the sensations to which they give rise.

A subject can of course tell us something about the intensity of an individual stimulus, if only to assign it to one of a small number of levels (such as "cold," "cool," "warm," and "hot"). However, it is debatable whether a stimulus is ever presented in total isolation, so the judgment may always be at least in part relative. Thus, in judging the brightness of a single spot of light, the subject may compare the spot with the spatially adjacent and temporally coincident surround or with the temporally adjacent and spatially coincident adapting field. We can of course attempt to eliminate all bases for a relative judgment. In the case of brightness, we could reduce the spatial adjacency by substituting a completely uniform field ("*ganzfeld*") for the circumscribed spot, and we could reduce the temporal adjacency by bringing the illumination up to its final physical intensity only gradually. Significantly, however, we then come face to face with the problems of shifting adaptation and, more importantly, with the curious instability, indeterminacy, and even intermittent cessation of visual experience that is characteristic under prolonged *ganzfeld* conditions (Cohen, 1957; Hochberg, Triebel, & Seaman, 1951).

Conditions that would truly force an absolute judgment may be realizable only in *gedanken* experiments. Imagine a line segment that, although it does have a definite physical length (e.g., on the retina), is somehow presented in such a way as to prevent comparison of its visual extent with any reference extent (such as its distance, its width, another visual object, or even the apparent extent of the visual field as a whole). Although the line could presumably still appear to be extended under such hypothetical conditions, it is doubtful whether its extent could be appreciated as a uniquely defined psychological magnitude Ψ. Not only do subjects have difficulty in assessing truly absolute retinal extent within the same eye (Rock, 1975, p. 37), they are often unable even to determine which eye has been stimulated (Pattie, 1935; Pickersgill, 1961). Again, natural selection has favored nervous systems that are primarily tuned to what is "out there" in the external world; and, as in the case of physical measurements, what is out there is most easily and accurately determined by making comparisons.

Those instances in which there does appear to be some basis for genuinely absolute judgment seem to involve the "metathetic" continua such as those of auditory pitch or, possibly, visual hue rather than the intensive or extensive "prothetic" continua considered here. Moreover, even on metathetic continua, relative judgment may typically play a more prominent role than absolute judgment. In the case of pitch, although anyone with a "musical ear" can identify one tone as a third above, or a fifth below another, say, only a very small fraction of the population is able to identify the pitch of a single note absolutely (Siegel, 1972; Ward, 1963). The familiar ability of normal subjects to identify a spectral hue (as red, orange, yellow, green, blue, or violet) might be considered a commonly occurring visual analogue of auditory absolute pitch. But Land's compelling demonstrations show that the experience of a particular color, although it may have a subjectively unique quality, generally depends upon a comparison across a color boundary (Land, 1964, 1966; McCann, 1972). And, again, when the possibility of such comparison is removed under *ganzfeld* conditions, the experienced color tends to desaturate and even to disappear entirely (Hochberg et al., 1951).

Whether or not all perception is relative, it does appear that the perceived magnitude of a stimulus on a prothetic continuum, at least, is generally largely, if not totally, relative to some comparison magnitude on that same continuum. But, if so, any model that deals with but a single stimulus at a time on each continuum may already impose the wrong sort of structure.

Reinterpretation via a "Relation Theory" of Psychophysical Judgment

It was the recognition of the importance of the relativity of perception that led me, over ten years ago, to investigate the consequences of this relativity for the fundamental indeterminacy of "direct" psychophysical scaling demonstrated in the preceding sections of this paper. Toward this end I proposed, in place of either of the two models for absolute psychophysical judgment given in Equations (1-3) or (4-5), a rather different model, which Krantz, in his well-formulated development of it, has named the "relation theory" (Krantz, 1972a).[4] The following sections are devoted to the examination of this alternative theory, its justification, and its consequences for the problem of "direct" psychophysical measurement.

RECONSIDERATION OF THE
FUNDAMENTAL MATCHING OPERATIONS OF PSYCHOPHYSICS

Stevens's suggestion that all psychophysical judgment amounts to the matching or equating of external, physically specifiable things with respect to their inner, psychological effects has considerable appeal. As Stevens pointed out, this suggestion uniformly places the subject in the conceptually simple role of a sort of "null instrument." Or, in the spirit of the cybernetic analysis of control through feedback (cf. MacKay, 1963; Powers, 1973), to produce a response (whether by squeezing a hand dynamometer in "magnitude production" or by finding an appropriate number in "magnitude estimation") is really to instate a certain stimulus; namely, the one that results in a match of the corresponding internal magnitude Ψ' to the appropriate comparison magnitude Ψ. Thus, when the subject in a magnitude estimation experiment gives a particular number, say "45," to a particular intensity of tone, he is merely telling us which number matches the given tone with respect to the two corresponding internal magnitudes, Ψ (for the tone) and Ψ' (for the number).

However, according to the preceding argument for the relativity of perception, even if every psychophysical judgment amounts to the establishment of a match between two things, the two things that are thus said to be psychologically equivalent may not be two individual stimuli but, at least, two *pairs* of stimuli.

In some situations this structure may be imposed quite explicitly, as when the subject is given a pair (S_i, S_j) and is asked to adjust a variable stimulus S_x in a second pair (S_k, S_x) until the two pairs become in some way psychologically equivalent. If the physical intensity of S_j is just twice the physical intensity of S_i, this might happen when, for example, the physical intensity of S_x is adjusted to just twice the physical intensity of S_k. The same sort of operation can of course be performed, too, when there are only three stimuli—as when the pairs to be compared are, in effect, (S_i, S_j) and (S_j, S_x).

In other situations, such as cross-modality matching, the composition of the pairs may not be explicitly specified. Suppose a subject is required to adjust the loudness of a variable tone S'_x until it matches the brightness of a fixed spot of light S_i (where the prime indicates that the variable stimulus is on a different continuum). The subject may not be able to do this directly, but only derivatively —by comparison of the pairs (S_0, S_i) and (S'_0, S'_x), where S_0 and S'_0 are corresponding implicit reference stimuli for the two continua (perhaps the initial or background levels of visual and auditory stimulation respectively).

The response to the first stimulus in a magnitude estimation task could be generated in a similar manner, provided that numbers are treated like stimuli on any purely sensory continuum. The variable and often seemingly arbitrary character of this first response could still be explained in terms of the subject's uncertainty about the unspecified reference levels S_0 and (for the number continuum) S'_0. (Then too, this uncertainty might be subject to amplification owing to the generally great distance of the presented stimulus S_i from the chosen reference stimulus S_0.) So, again, it is only with the presentation of the second, explicitly constraining stimulus that we can expect an orderly pattern to emerge in the subject's responses.

Now it might seem that, with the presentation of the third and subsequent stimuli, our analysis must rapidly increase in complexity. It might even appear that we should have to specify whether each successive stimulus is related just to the immediately preceding stimulus or to some weighted combination of those presented most recently—a specification that could easily involve us in unresolved issues concerning temporal information processing, mechanisms of short- and long-term memory, attention, and the like. Fortunately, according to the relation theory, an understanding of the logical basis of psychophysical scale construction can be gained without making such further specifications. For it follows from that theory that all of the information is internally consistent ("transitive") in such a way that, except for distortions introduced by memory itself, a subject's judgment should be the same regardless of which preceding stimuli are taken as a basis for the judgment.[5]

EQUIVALENCE CLASSES OF PAIRS OF STIMULI

Instead of starting, as in classical psychophysics, with a mapping of S into Ψ, we begin, in the relation theory, with a mapping of the Cartesian product set $S \times S$ into Ψ. That is, the results of the fundamental matching operations define equivalence classes of all pairs (S_i, S_j) that are judged to be psychologically equivalent and that, for this reason, are assigned to the same subjective magnitude Ψ. The psychophysical data also enable us to establish an ordering of these equivalence classes. For, if two pairs (S_i, S_j) and (S_h, S_k) are clearly *not* equivalent, the subject can tell us, not only that they are not equivalent, but also in what direction they depart from equivalance. He can say whether the contrast presented by the pair (S_i, S_j) is greater or less than the contrast presented by the pair (S_h, S_k). Since such judgments are generally consistent (i.e., transitive) for all except marginally equivalent pairs, they define an ordering on the set of psychological magnitudes, Ψ.

In order to go further, we need to specify something about the structure of these equivalence classes or, in other words, about the nature of the function $\Psi(S_i, S_j)$, mapping each pair, S_i and S_j, into an element of the ordered set Ψ. For this purpose we must, for any given continuum, adopt a particular measure of the physical magnitude of any stimulus on that continuum. What we want is some measure of the *amount* of the stimulus, so that the physical measure is properly additive if we combine stimuli. For intensive continua, the most reasonable measure seems to be the traditional one of physical energy.

The psychophysical data of Stevens and his students then show that, to a first approximation, *it is equal ratios of physical magnitude that are psychologically equivalent*. This amounts to saying that, if we increase the physical magnitudes of any two stimuli by the same constant factor k, the psychological relation between them remains invariant; in functional notation,

$$\Psi(S_i, S_j) = \Psi(kS_i, kS_j), \tag{6}$$

provided, of course, that S_i, S_j, and k are all greater than zero.

This is, moreover, a rule with considerable adaptive utility. As Plateau noted in 1872, an object with surfaces of characteristic reflectances could then be recognized as the same object under widely different levels of illumination (Herrnstein & Boring, 1966, pp. 75-79). Likewise, figures composed of lines of different lengths could be recognized as the same figure when viewed from different distances (cf. Rock & Ebenholtz, 1959); speech sounds could be recognized whether loud or soft; music would sound much the same whether a record is played at 33 or 45 rpm; and, perhaps similarly, speech could be understood whether uttered by a young child or an adult male.

The implications of Equation (6) are perhaps easier to see if we display the iso-Ψ contours, graphically, in the $S_i \times S_j$ space, as shown in Figure 1. What (6) requires is that these contours all be straight lines radiating from the origin. (The origin itself as well as narrow regions all along both zero-intensity axes should, as indicated by the broken lines, be excluded by proper ancillary conditions on this equation.)

Each of these linear contours is defined by the similarity relation $S_j = c \cdot S_i$ or, in other words, by the requirement that the ratio S_j/S_i is a constant, c. Now (6) also requires that $\Psi(S_i, S_i) = \Psi(S_j, S_j)$ for all i and j. Clearly then, the function Ψ must have the form

$$\Psi(S_i, S_j) = f\left(\frac{S_j}{S_i}\right), \tag{7}$$

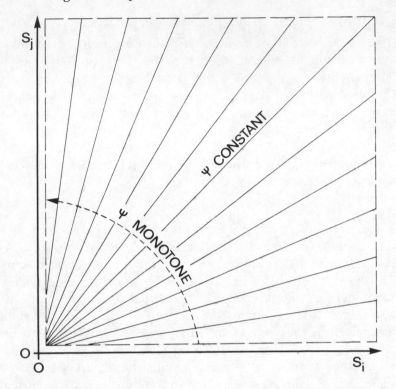

Figure 1. Loci of points corresponding to pairs of physical magnitudes, S_i and S_j, on the same sensory continuum that produce psychological contrasts of the same magnitude Ψ.

where f is any function. Whereas in the classical formulation Ψ is the subjective magnitude corresponding to the intensity of a single stimulus, in the present formulation Ψ is the subjective magnitude corresponding to the ratio of two stimuli.

In addition, we noted that we can establish an ordering on these subjective magnitudes. Within any one continuum, this ordering is determined by the requirement that

$$\Psi(S_h, S_k) > \Psi(S_i, S_j) \tag{8}$$
$$\text{whenever } S_k/S_h > S_j/S_i.$$

From this further condition it then immediately follows that the function f in (7) is monotone increasing, as indicated in Figure 1.

Now. if we are given any two intensities S_1 and S_2 on the same continuum, we can construct a sequence, $S_1, S_2, S_3, S_4, \ldots$, such that the psychological magnitude Ψ is the same for all adjacent pairs; i.e., so that for any j

$$\Psi(S_i, S_{i+1}) = \Psi(S_{i+1}, S_{i+2}) = \text{const.} \tag{9}$$

But, according to (8), this psychological equivalence entails a physical relation in which the ratios between successive intensities are all the same; i.e., in which

$$\frac{S_2}{S_1} = \frac{S_3}{S_2} = \frac{S_4}{S_3} = \cdots \frac{S_i}{S_{i-1}} = \text{const.}$$

And from this it follows that the intensity S must be expressable in terms of the two originally given intensities, S_1 and S_2, as follows:

$$S_i = \left(\frac{S_2}{S_1}\right)^{i-1} \cdot S_1 \tag{10}$$

In short, the assumption (6) leads directly to the conclusion that, if the psychological relations between successive stimuli are to be constant, the stimuli must form a geometric series: viz.,

$$S_1, cS_1, c^2 S_1, c^3 S_1, \ldots ,$$

where c is the ratio between the two initially given intensities.[6]

RELATIONS AMONG DIFFERENT CONTINUA

The results obtained so far have shown how we might construct a sequence of stimuli such that the psychological effect is the same for any pair of stimuli separated by the same number of steps along the sequence. In this sense, of course, we might be said to have provided a basis for a scaling of the physical stimuli with respect to their psychological effects. We have not, however, provided any basis for a scaling of those psychological effects themselves; and surely, it would not be correct to say that we are now in a position to measure any internal, psychological magnitudes. Stevens's work suggests that if a basis for such a scaling or such measurements is to be found, it is probably to be found in the psychological relations among different sensory continua. Let us turn, therefore, to a consideration of "cross-modality" matching which, as we shall see, does place one further constraint on our model for relative psychophysics.

Suppose, then, that we have two sensory continua, the primed and the unprimed (corresponding, for example, to continua of auditory and visual intensity). If our psychological matching operations can be extended from one continuum to the other, they will define a mapping of the Cartesian product sets $S \times S$ and $S' \times S'$ into either the same ordered set, Ψ, or equivalently, into two ordered sets, Ψ and Ψ', with a uniquely defined one-to-one correspondence between them. In order to be consistent with the formulation of the matching model, we shall adopt the latter interpretation.

It then follows that, if we are given any pair (S_1, S_2) on the unprimed continuum, we can not only construct a sequence S_1, S_2, S_3, . . . on that same continuum satisfying (9), we can also construct a sequence S'_1, S'_2, S'_3, ... on the primed continuum such that

$$\Psi'(S'_i, S'_{i+1}) = \Psi(S_i, S_{i+1}) = \text{const.} \tag{11}$$

The first stimulus, S'_1, on the primed continuum may be arbitrarily supplied by the experimenter or it may be left to the subject to choose either arbitrarily or, possibly, by resorting to comparisons with some implicit reference stimuli, S_0 and S'_0, to achieve at least a rough match between the pairs (S_0, S_1) and (S'_0, S'_1). (We do not suppose that a pair such as (S_1, S'_1) produces a unique psychological magnitude directly when the two intensities are on different continua.) In any case, once S'_1 has been fixed, the remainder of the sequence of stimuli needed to satisfy the matching condition (11) on the primed continuum will be rigidly determined. Indeed, just as in the case of the unprimed continuum, this sequence will form a geometric series:

$$S'_i = \left(\frac{S'_2}{S'_1}\right)^{i-1} \cdot S'_1. \tag{12}$$

The two geometric sequences and the correspondence between them are illustrated graphically in Figure 2. If the first two stimuli on the unprimed continuum had been at the intensities of S_2 and S_4 (instead of at the intensities of S_1 and S_2), while S'_1 was still retained as the first stimulus on the primed continuum, then the second corresponding stimulus on the primed continuum would have been S'_3 and the new correspondence would be as shown by the dashed lines.

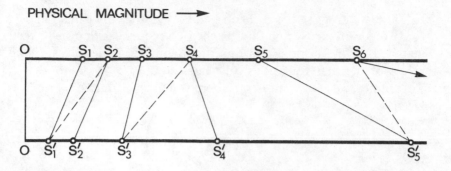

Figure 2. Psychological correspondences between physical magnitudes on two different continua, such as those for brightness and loudness.

So far, we have two geometric series of stimuli: one (12) on the primed continuum and one (10) on the unprimed continuum. From the assumptions, two things follow. First, within either series, stimuli separated by the same number of steps constitute psychologically equivalent pairs. And, second, between the two series, pairs separated by one step in one series are psychologically equivalent to pairs separated by one step in the other series, as required by (11). However, for $n > 1$, it does not yet follow that pairs separated by n steps in one series (although equivalent with each other) are also equivalent with pairs separated by n steps in the other series. This further correspondence between the two series apparently requires the explicit introduction of an additional assumption.

My former colleague David Cross, who first made me aware of the importance of this additional assumption, proposed that it be called the assumption of "transitivity" of equivalence relations. It takes the form

$$\text{if } \Psi'(S'_i, S'_j) = \Psi(S_i, S_j)$$
$$\text{and } \Psi'(S'_j, S'_k) = \Psi(S_j, S_k), \tag{13}$$
$$\text{then } \Psi'(S'_i, S'_k) = \Psi(S_i, S_k).$$

This assumption seems to be well supported by the empirical results obtained by Stevens and others from experiments on cross-modality matching. As we shall see, it implies that the function f in (7) cannot have an arbitrarily different form for each continuum.

What, then, must the relation be between the functions f and f' for two continua? Notice that, in the two sequences that have been matched on the primed and unprimed continua, regardless of the values of the first four physical magnitudes $S_1, S_2, S'_1,$ and S'_2, (always finite, positive numbers), there will exist a unique number p given by

$$p = \log\left(\frac{S'_2}{S'_1}\right)\bigg/\log\left(\frac{S_2}{S_1}\right).$$

Hence, the relation between the ratios of the first two intensities on the two continua can always be expressed in the form

$$\frac{S'_2}{S'_1} = \left(\frac{S_2}{S_1}\right)^p \tag{14}$$

If, now, we substitute (14) into (12), we obtain

$$S'_i = \left(\frac{S_2}{S_1}\right)^{p(i-1)} \cdot S'_1.$$

But according to (10),

$$\left(\frac{S_2}{S_1}\right)^{(i-1)} = \frac{S_i}{S_1},$$

which can be substituted into the preceding equation to obtain

$$S'_i = \left(\frac{S_i}{S_1}\right)^p \cdot S'_1$$

or, after rearranging terms,

$$\frac{S_i{}^p}{S'_i} = \frac{S_1{}^p}{S'_1}.$$

This, of course, must hold for any j as well as for any i, so it follows more generally that

$$\frac{S_i{}^p}{S'_i} = \frac{S_j{}^p}{S'_j} = \frac{S_1{}^p}{S'_1}.$$

A final rearrangement of terms in the left and middle ratios then yields

$$\frac{S'_j}{S'_i} = \left(\frac{S_j}{S_i}\right)^p \tag{15}$$

for any i and j.

Moreover, the exponent p depends only upon the two continua themselves, and not at all upon the particular stimuli S_1, S_2, and S'_1 arbitrarily chosen to construct the two matching sequences on these continua. Thus, in Figure 2, the alternative correspondence between stimuli indicated by the broken lines still leads to the very same exponent p. Apparently, then, the inherent differences in the way two prothetic continua operate psychologically can be fully accommodated simply by expressing the relation between the two continua in terms of a power transformation with a uniquely defined exponent or power p as indicated in (15).

Indeed, the relations among all such continua can be most parsimoniously explained simply by associating with each of the individual sensory continua, say, S, S', S'', etc., a characteristic power, p, p', p'', etc., such that the exponent characterizing the relation between any two of these continua is given simply by the appropriate ratio of the two powers associated with the continua compared. A consequence is that, while the exponent relating any two continua is determined completely (i.e., up to the identity transformation), the exponents associated with the individual continua themselves are determined only up to multiplication by an arbitrary constant. Hence in (15) the exponents associated with the primed and unprimed ratios could as well have been q and qp (with any arbitrary q), instead of simply 1 and p.

In practice, of course, this arbitrary factor q can be fixed for all continua by adopting the convention that the exponent characterizing some particular or preferred continuum (such as the continuum of visual length or that of the number responses in direct magnitude estimation) shall be unity. The empirical results of the cross-continuum matching experiments, together with this convention, then suffice to determine the exponents for all other continua uniquely (to within experimental error).

Apparently, then, the fundamental relation of relative psychophysics can be written in the final, more explicit form

$$\Psi(S_i, S_j) = g \left\{ \left(\frac{S_j}{S_i} \right)^p \right\},\tag{16}$$

where, again, g is any monotone increasing function. Now, however, in order to ensure satisfaction of the "transitivity" condition (13), the function g, whatever its form, must be regarded as having the *same* form for all continua. The difference between the psychophysical functions, f and f', for any two different continua is thus entirely absorbed into the power function indicated by the exponent p.

THE IRREDUCIBLE INDETERMINACY OF THE PSYCHOPHYSICAL FUNCTION

It is clear that, if we are given any sequence of physical magnitudes $S_a, S_b, S_c, \ldots$ on one continuum, and any one intensity S'_a on a second continuum, we can construct a sequence $S'_a, S'_b, S'_c, \ldots$ on the second continuum such that, for any i and j

$$g \left\{ \left(\frac{S_j}{S_i} \right)^p \right\} = g \left\{ \left(\frac{S'_j}{S'_i} \right)^{p'} \right\},\tag{17}$$

where p and p' are the powers associated with the two continua in question. Clearly, too, the form of the monotone increasing function g is totally irrelevant to the outcome. (Application of g^{-1} to both sides has no empirical consequences.)

In order to account for the principal results that Stevens and his followers have found for cross-modality matching (including magnitude estimation and magnitude production), then, we need not assume that there is, corresponding to a given intensity S_i, any uniquely defined subject magnitude $\Psi(S_i)$. Instead we need merely assume that for any pair of intensities S_i and S_j there is some subjective magnitude

$$g \left\{ \left(\frac{S_j}{S_i} \right)^p \right\},$$

where g is some fixed, monotone increasing function whose form is not otherwise constrained by the psychophysical data.

We could, of course, assume that

$$g(x) = ax^\beta \tag{18}$$

(where, as an even more special case, we could take $a = \beta = 1$). Then we would have

$$\Psi(S_i, S_j) = a\left(\frac{S_j}{S_i}\right)^{\beta p}, \tag{19}$$

and none of the previous conclusions would be altered by this specialization. If, then, we take $S_i = S_0$, this amounts to the power law adopted by Stevens.

On the other hand, we could as well assume that

$$g(x) = a + \beta \log x, \tag{20}$$

in which case we would find that

$$\Psi(S_i, S_j) = a + \beta p (\log S_j - \log S_i). \tag{21}$$

Again nothing would be changed, although in this case we see that, with respect to the new physical variable $\log S$, Ψ can be regarded as a difference rather than as a ratio of physical magnitudes.

ALTERNATIVE DERIVATION USING FUNCTIONAL EQUATIONS

By taking advantage of known solutions to certain functional equations, the above-demonstrated irreducible indeterminacy of the psychophysical function can be established by an alternative, more elegant derivation, subsequently proposed to me by David Cross. Strictly, in addition to the Invariance Assumption (6), stated separately for the primed as well as the unprimed continuum, and the Transitivity Assumption (13), we need to make an implicit Comparability Assumption explicit, as follows: For any S_i and S_j in the unprimed continuum and any S_i' in the primed, there exists a S_j' in the primed continuum such that

$$\Psi(S_i, S_j) = \Psi'(S_i', S_j'). \tag{22}$$

As we already noted in deriving Equation (7) from (6), the most general solutions to the functional equations in the Invariance Assumption are

$$\Psi(S_i, S_j) = f\left(\frac{S_j}{S_i}\right) \quad \text{and} \quad \Psi'(S_i', S_j') = g\left(\frac{S_j'}{S_i'}\right),$$

where f and g are arbitrary functions.

However, by the Comparability Assumption (22),

$$f\left(\frac{S_j}{S_i}\right) = g\left(\frac{S_j'}{S_i'}\right).$$

By applying g^{-1} to both sides, we obtain

$$\frac{S_j'}{S_i'} = h\left(\frac{S_j}{S_i}\right), \text{ where } h = g^{-1}f.$$

Then, by the Transitivity Assumption (13),

$$\frac{S_k'}{S_j'} = h\left(\frac{S_k}{S_j}\right) \quad \text{and} \quad \frac{S_k'}{S_i'} = h\left(\frac{S_k}{S_i}\right).$$

But

$$\frac{S_k'}{S_i'} = \frac{S_k'}{S_j'} \cdot \frac{S_j'}{S_i'} = h\left(\frac{S_k}{S_j}\right) \cdot h\left(\frac{S_j}{S_i}\right).$$

Thus

$$h\left(\frac{S_k}{S_i}\right) = h\left(\frac{S_k}{S_j}\right) \cdot h\left(\frac{S_j}{S_i}\right). \tag{23}$$

For some $a > 0$ and $b > 0$,

$$S_j = aS_i, S_k = bS_i, \text{ and hence } S_k = abS_i.$$

Substituting into (23), we have

$$h(a \cdot b) = h(a) \cdot h(b).$$

This classical functional equation of Cauchy has, as its most general continuous solution, the power form

$$h(t) = t^p$$

Hence, for any i and j, if

$$f\left(\frac{S_j}{S_i}\right) = g\left(\frac{S'_j}{S'_i}\right),$$

the forms of f and g, instead of being arbitrary, are constrained by the composition

$$g^{-1}f\left(\frac{S_j}{S_i}\right) = \left(\frac{S_j}{S_i}\right)^p. \tag{24}$$

Cross noted that two classes of functions that satisfy the functional composition (24) are the class of logarithmic functions

$$f(x) = k \ln x, \qquad g(y) = c \ln y,$$

and the class of power functions

$$f(x) = x^a, \qquad g(y) = y^\beta.$$

On further consideration, however, it appeared to me that there is a more general class of functions (which subsumes the above two classes) that also satisfies the same functional composition (24); viz.,

$$f(x) = h(x^a) \quad \text{and} \quad g(y) = h(y^{a/p}),$$

where h is *any* monotone increasing function. For if

$$g(x) = f_1[f_2(x)],$$

then

$$g^{-1}(x) = f_2^{-1}[f_1^{-1}(x)],$$

so

$$g^{-1}\left[f\left(\frac{x'}{x}\right)\right] = h^{-1}\left[h\left\{\left(\frac{x'}{x}\right)^a\right\}\right]^{p/a} = \left[\left(\frac{x'}{x}\right)^a\right]^{p/a} = \left(\frac{x'}{x}\right)^p.$$

Again, therefore, I conclude that the functions f and g can be of any monotone increasing form, although (owing to transitivity) they must always be of the *same* form for all continua. As before, whether these functions are taken, for all continua, to be power functions, log functions, or functions of some other form must be decided on the basis of considerations other than the results of magnitude estimation or cross-modality matching.

Discussion and Conclusions

The relation theory has led to the conclusion that the operations of magnitude estimation and cross-modality matching are not sufficient to determine anything beyond the ordinal relations among the psychological magnitudes, Ψ_i. I want to conclude by explicitly setting down what I take to be the implications of this result for perennial questions concerning (a) what it is that the psychophysicist measures, (b) what the status is of the so-called psychophysical law, and (c) what type of scale it is that is constructed in psychophysical scaling. But first some clarification is in order concerning what appears to be a possible dependence of the relation theory upon implicit absolute psychophysical judgments, and concerning the extent to which the present conclusions are dependent upon the relation theory.

RELATIVE VERSUS ABSOLUTE
PERCEPTION, AND THE ROLE OF MEMORY

In the preceding analysis, relative psychophysical judgment has been described as if the resulting psychological magnitude, say $\Psi(S_i, S_j)$, is something that arises from the comparison of two stimuli, S_i and S_j, that are both available simultaneously. Actually the stimuli within any one continuum are usually presented successively. In most cases, then, it is not entirely correct to say that the two stimuli S_i and S_j are compared directly. At best, each presented stimulus in these cases can be compared only with some sort of memory trace of any preceding stimulus.

This, however, raises a perplexing conceptual problem for the notion that a well-defined psychological magnitude, such as Ψ, arises only upon the presentation of at least two stimuli from any one continuum. For surely, if $\Psi(S_i, S_j)$ assumes a well-defined value even though S_i was removed before the presentation of S_j, then the trace of S_i alone must have had a well-defined value. In other words, how could the ratio S_j/S_i, upon which $\Psi(S_i, S_j)$ depends, be available to the subject unless definite, quantitative information about S_i was somehow preserved within the subject? But, if such quantitative information about individual stimuli is thus represented within the subject, in what sense can it properly be claimed that a definite psychological magnitude Ψ comes into being only upon comparison with a second stimulus?

Indeed the same problem remains even when the two stimuli are presented simultaneously. Even if they are not separated in time, they are nevertheless separated in some other way (e.g., in space). But the two external stimuli are not themselves brought together within the subject's nervous system; what is brought together can only be some internal representation of these two stimuli. Again, if the result of this comparison depends upon the ratio of the two physical magnitudes, then the quantitative information necessary to determine this ratio must be contained in the two internal representations—even before they are brought together.

What, then, is the explanation for the fact that relative judgments are more stable and precise than absolute judgments? Even though there must indeed be some quantitative representation of each stimulus separately, I have already argued that these separate representations will necessarily be highly dependent upon such external variables as distance and condition of illumination that are not inherent in the perceived object itself. Moreover, these separate representations are likely to vary widely with the internal state of the organism. It seems reasonable to suppose that changes in internal state (like variations in external conditions) tend to affect the neurophysiological encoding of magnitudes in a similar way. Rate of neural firing, for example, might be affected additively or multiplicatively. If so, it would be only when two such separate representations are brought together and a difference or ratio formed that a quantitative representation would be obtained that has a suitably invariant relation to the external stimulus.

Such a supposition would explain the well-know fact that even relative comparisons become less stable and precise as the two stimuli are separated in time, space, or along some other dimensions (e.g., wavelength for colors to be matched in brightness, or frequency for tones to be matched in loudness). For, as two stimuli are separated in any way, it becomes more probable that the local internal states prevailing in the relevant nervous centers will differ significantly and thus fail to be canceled out in the subsequent computation of the ratio or difference. This is particularly clear in the case of a separation in time and seems, therefore, to provide a plausible account of the well-established decay in recognition memory with time (cf. Shepard, 1958a; Wickelgren, 1969).

Under favorable conditions, in which the separation is not too great, on the other hand, the computed ratio or difference will be relatively independent of the perturbing physiological parameters since these will affect both components entering into the computation alike. It would not be surprising, then, if natural selection had favored an organization of the brain such that these purified ratios or differences are readily connectable to voluntary responses (including verbal reports), whereas the contaminated raw components of these ratios or differences are kept relatively inaccessible in order to decrease the probability of an inappropriate response to the external world.

Nevertheless, since there must be some sort of quantitative, internal representation or magnitude for each individual stimulus even before any comparison takes place, we cannot dismiss the possibility that subjects may sometimes be able to report truly absolute psychophysical judgments. The only points that I wish to emphasize about such absolute judgments are the following two: First, according to the arguments made just above (and earlier in this paper), such judgments are likely to be less reliable than relative judgments. And second, even under conditions in which such judgments are sufficiently reliable, the analyses presented here—particularly following Equations (3) and (5)—and elsewhere by other commentators indicate that the constraints provided by absolute judgments are no greater than those provided by relative judgments. Our basic conclusion as to the quantitative indeterminacy of the psychological magnitudes Ψ_i does not depend, then, upon the adoption of the relation theory. What, then, must our answers be to the long-debated questions concerning psychophysical "measurements," "laws," and "scales"?

WHAT DOES THE PSYCHOPHYSICIST MEASURE?

Usually when one speaks of measuring something, one has in mind the assignment of a number on a numerical (i.e., interval or ratio) scale. Having measured some objects in this sense, one can legitimately report such facts as that one object is twice as long as another, or is equal in weight to the sum of two others, and so on. Naturally, then, when someone speaks of measuring a sensation, it suggests that the sensation has likewise been fixed on a numerical scale, and that one can thereby determine whether one sensation is twice another, is equal to the sum of two others, and so on.

According to the analysis presented above, however, the operations of magnitude estimation and cross-modality matching upon which Stevens proposed to base psychophysical measurement do not determine any more than an ordinal structure on the psychological magnitudes Ψ_i. So, although the subject himself can tell us that one such inner magnitude is greater than another, the psychophysical operations that we have considered are powerless to tell us anything further about *how much* greater the one is than the other. My conclusion—like those of Krantz (1972a, b), Luce (1972), and Savage (1970)—is that these operations do not in themselves permit us to measure inner sensations in any quantitative sense.

What the psychophysical operations of magnitude estimation and cross-modality matching *do* enable one to measure on a ratio scale is the exponent p that characterizes a given (prothetic) sensory continuum for a given subject or population of subjects. In short, what the psychophysicist measures is an important constant governing how a subject transduces any stimulus from a particular sensory continuum, such as the continuum of lights varying in intensity, tones varying in amplitude, or lines varying in length. He does not measure the magnitude of any one inner subjective sensation produced by one stimulus or pair of stimuli as opposed to another along any such continuum.

WHAT IS THE STATUS OF THE PSYCHOPHYSICAL LAW?

Although it is possible to determine, for each prothetic continuum, the exponent p that characterizes that particular continuum uniquely (up to multiplication of all such exponents by an arbitrary constant), the psychophysical *relations* between physical magnitudes and the postulated inner psychological magnitudes Ψ_i for all such continua are seen to contain the same indeterminate function g. Stevens's claims that the psychophysical law is a power law appear to be implicitly based on the argument that g should be taken, on grounds of simplicity, to be a power function—indeed the identity function. But such an argument seems to me to lack the richness of supportive interconnections with the rest of the sciences of sensation, perception, cognition, and neurophysiology to inspire conviction.

Indeed, a consideration of the neurophysiology of sensory perception suggests that the notion that a physical stimulus gives rise to some *one* unique inner magnitude Ψ_i is rather simplistic. Such a notion seems to be based on the tacit assumption that there is some *one* stage, during the propagation of the sensory signal through the nervous system, at which a coded representation is displayed before some "homunculus" or "ghost in the machine." Instead I find it more satisfactory to suppose that this propagation proceeds through a whole series of transformations. The results of different ones of these transformations may well correspond to different forms of the function *g*.

Such a view is consonant, also, with evolutionary considerations. For, if it is adaptive for an organism to be able to learn new responses without also having to master, each time, some new and nonlinear function *de novo*, then it will also be useful for the organism to have, for each important physical variable, a choice of representations corresponding to different, generally useful transformations (linear, logarithmic, etc.). Much as in the "pandemonium" model of Selfridge (1958), then, the process of learning would be one in which the response becomes attached to the most appropriate (i.e., simply related) of these available alternative representations. Even if an elucidation of the psychophysical problem along these lines has no other virtue, it at least accounts for the troublesome fact that diverse psychophysical procedures often lead to equally diverse results!

WHAT TYPE OF SCALE IS
CONSTRUCTED IN PSYCHOPHYSICAL SCALING?

In Stevens's celebrated classification scheme, scales are assigned to a type on the basis of the group of transformations under which the empirically significant properties of the scale remain invariant (Stevens, 1946, 1951). The most commonly considered types are the *ordinal scale*, in which only order is significant, so any monotone transformation is permissible; the *interval scale*, in which the equivalence or nonequivalence of differences (i.e., intervals) is significant, so the monotone transformation must also be linear; and the *ratio scale*, in which the equivalence or nonequivalence of ratios (as well as differences) is significant, so the linear transformation must be restricted to a similarity (i.e., to multiplication by a constant). When they can be constructed, ratio scales are preferable to interval scales, which in turn are preferable to merely ordinal scales. The reason is that the former types provide greater quantitative leverage. Indeed, since determination on a merely ordinal scale really provides only qualitative rather than quantitative information, it seems to be stretching the usual meaning of the word "measurement" to apply it to the ordinal case at all.

Whereas Stevens claimed that his psychophysical operations permitted measurement on a ratio scale, this appears to be the case only for the measurement of the parameter p governing each prothetic continuum—not for the measurement of the magnitude of a sensation within any continuum. There is, however, another possible way of construing Stevens's contention concerning scale type. Although we cannot obtain a quantitative determination of the psychological magnitudes themselves, we nevertheless can use the empirically determined equivalences among these magnitudes to construct a spacing or "scale" that does have some quantitatively unique properties *with respect to a particular, designated physical variable*. Thus, if we take energy as our fundamental measure of physical magnitude on a certain prothetic continuum, the psychological equivalences that are determined by cross-modality matching lead to a geometric spacing on that physical variable. Now this spacing is unique (on that variable) up to a power transformation; a geometric series remains geometric after, and only after, all terms are multiplied by a constant and/or raised to a power. Since more general, monotonic transformations destroy this property, the result is stronger than a merely ordinal scale.

It does not, however, correspond to either an interval or a ratio scale in Stevens's sense. Rather, it appears to amount to a different type of scale based upon the equivalence of ratios *without* the prior equivalence of differences. It is somewhat curious, then, that with regard to this new type of scale, later recognized by Stevens and dubbed the "logarithmic interval type,"[7] Stevens stated that "it has thus far proved empirically useless" (1957, p. 176). On the one hand, he was clearly aware that, in order to convert such a logarithmic interval scale into a full ratio scale, we must be able either (a) to equate differences or else (b) to determine the numerical values —rather than just equivalences—of ratios. But, on the other hand, he seems not to have made clear how his psychophysical operations provide a satisfactory basis for doing either of these things.

Whatever the type of such a scale, it is not strictly a scale that permits the quantitative measurement of psychological magnitudes. If there are unique psychological magnitudes, these could, as we saw, be related to this scale by any monotonic function. Furthermore, any measurement performed on such a scale would be "derived" rather than "fundamental" measurement (Suppes & Zinnes, 1963), since it depends upon the existence of a previously established physical scale; viz., the ratio scale of energy. Such a measurement is arbitrary in the sense that a change to a different physical variable (say number of decibels, which is logarithmically related to energy) can induce a nonadmissable transformation in the derived scale (the geometric series can become arithmetic).

CONCLUDING REMARKS

The reinterpretation of the results of direct psychophysical judgment in terms of the relation theory seems to offer several advantages. It takes account of the well-established superiority of relative over absolute judgments. It is consonant with evolutionary arguments for the selective advantage of a perceptual system that responds principally to ratios of intensities and extensities. It suggests a general neurophysiological basis for a variety of phenomena of comparative judgment and memory. And, as Krantz (1972) has noted, it leads to empirically testable consequences beyond those directly suggested by the traditional theories of absolute psychophysical judgment. The reinterpretation made possible by the relation theory does not, however, provide a way of circumventing the fundamental indeterminacy of the implications of magnitude estimation and cross-modality matching concerning the subjective magnitudes of sensations.

I conclude that, if we are to pin down any of what may well be several monotonically related types of internal representations of the magnitude of a stimulus quantitatively, we are going to have to move outside the circumscribed system of relationships provided by these "direct" psychophysical operations. Possibly depending on the type of internal representation, we may find the necessary additional relationships in the neurophysiological results of single-cell recording (Kiang, 1965; Luce & Green, 1972; Mountcastle, Poggio, & Werner, 1963; Perkel & Bullock, 1968; Rushton, 1961); in the behavioral results of experiments on stimulus generalization (Shepard, 1965), discrimination, and disjunctive reaction time (Curtis, et al., 1973; Falmagne, 1971; Shepard, et al., 1975); or in the cognitive results of experiments on the mental combining of perceived magnitudes (Anderson, 1970; Birnbaum & Veit, 1974; Falmagne, 1976; Levelt, Riemersma, & Bunt, 1972; Luce & Tukey, 1964; Sternberg, 1966). According to the theoretical analysis I have presented, the empirical findings of Stevens imply that the internal representations of sensory magnitude that are compared with each other in any given task are all related to physical magnitude by the same function, g. This result must, I believe, have some empirical significance. It encourages me, in any case, to believe that the search for further relationships at the neurophysiological, behavioral, and cognitive levels will not go unrewarded.

Notes

1. The development of chronometric measurement in the physical and then psychological sciences shows a parallel history. Bessel's 1820 discovery that astronomers differed systemmatically in determining the time of transit of a star led to two successive developments (Boring, 1950, p. 136): First, physical devices were perfected in order to reduce and then eliminate dependence on the "personal equation" of the human observer and, second, experimental psychologists, starting with Donders in 1868 and continuing to the present day (Sternberg, 1969) have turned such improved chronometric techniques back onto the problem of studying the temporal course of information processing within the human subject.

2. *Gedanken* experiments on psychophysical scaling with animals as subjects can be valuable in this connection. Such experiments confront us with the issue of how the experimenter is to train the subject to make responses that will somehow reveal the magnitudes of the subject's sensory experiences without at the same time biasing the subject toward some particular psychophysical relationship.

3. In the logarithmic model just as much as in the power model the parameter β must be regarded as an empirically determinable property of each continuum and not merely as an arbitrary scale factor. Thus, as Treisman has noted, the supposition by Stevens (1964) that the predictability of the interrelations among the exponents discovered in cross-modality matching would be sacrificed in the case of the logarithmic model appears unfounded. (Also see Luce & Galanter, 1963, p. 280.)

4. In revising the present section, I have adopted Krantz's now relatively entrenched term "relation theory" instead of speaking, as I did in my original 1968 draft, of "interpretation via a model for relative psychophysical judgment." Otherwise, I have retained my original exposition and derivations rather than attempting a reformulation along the

somewhat different, though in parts more elegant, formulation offered by Krantz (1972a). Krantz's Equations (18) and (12) correspond, respectively, to my invariance and transitivity Equations (6) and (13) and, from these, he arrives at essentially the same conclusions as I did. Also see Krantz (1972b, 1974) for his further work along related lines.

5. After this section was originally written, Ross and DiLollo (1968, 1971) independently reported new psychophysical results and analyses (including some theoretical developments related to those described here) that, however, complicate the unidimensionally consistent picture presented above. In the case of magnitude estimation of heaviness of lifted weights in particular, Ross and DiLollo found that the dimension that is effectively being judged tends to shift back and forth between the nonlinearly related attributes of weight and density depending upon the context of recently presented weights. As they noted, other continua might also be susceptible to such shifts in the basis for judgment (as, in the case of size judgments, between linear extent and area). In such cases, the above claim that all the judged ratios should be consistent with each other might need some modification.

6. In the original 1968 version of this paper, I had also explored the possibility that, in some tasks, subjects might equate differences rather than ratios of physical magnitudes. In preparing the present version, I have eliminated that discussion because I believe that the treatment of this possibility by Krantz, Luce, Suppes, and Tversky (1971) is much more satisfactory. The judgment of sense distance as opposed to sense ratios underlies widely used methods of *multi*dimensional scaling. It is noteworthy that, whereas I conclude here that merely ordinal information about ratios does not permit the recovery of a ratio scale of magnitude, in the context of nonmetric multidimensional scaling, I have shown that merely ordinal information about distances does permit the recovery of a ratio scale of distance (Shepard, 1962, 1966).

7. After independently noting the possibility of this type of scale, I proposed to Stevens (personal communication, 1956) that, for overall consistency in his classificatory scheme, the designation "ratio scale" should properly be reserved for scales of this new type (in which equivalences are defined for ratios only) while scales that he had been designating in this way should more properly be called "interval-ratio scales" (since, in them, equivalences are defined for both differences and ratios). However, when he subsequently extended his classificatory scheme to encompass scales of this new variety (Stevens, 1957), he preferred to introduce, for them, the new term "logarithmic interval scales," in order to avoid a departure from the earlier usage of the term "ratio scale."

References

Anderson, N. H. Functional measurement and psychophysical judgment. *Psychological Review*, 1970, 77, 153-170.

Becker, R. *Theory of heat*. New York: Springer-Verlag, 1967.

Birnbaum, M. H., & Veit, C. T. Scale convergence as a criterion for rescaling: Information integration with difference, ratio, and averaging tasks. *Perception & Psychophysics*, 1974, 15, 7-15.

Boring, E. G. *A history of experimental psychology*. New York: Appleton-Century-Crofts, 1950.

Carroll, J. D. *Functional learning: The learning of continuous functional mappings relating stimulus and response continua* (ETS RB 63-26). Princeton, N.J.: Educational Testing Service, 1963.

Cohen, W. Spatial and textural characteristics of the Ganzfeld. *American Journal of Psychology*, 1957, 70, 403-410.

Cornsweet, T. N. *Visual perception*. New York: Academic Press, 1970.

Curtis, D. W., Paulos, M. A., & Rule, S. J. Relation between disjunctive reaction time and stimulus difference. *Journal of Experimental Psychology*, 1973, 99, 167-173.

Ekman, G. Is the power law a special case of Fechner's law? *Perceptual and Motor Skills*, 1964, 19, 730.

Falmagne, J.-C. The generalized Fechner problem and discrimination. *Journal of Mathematical Psychology*, 1971, 8, 22-43.

Falmagne, J.-C. Random conjoint measurement and loudness summation. *Psychological Review*, 1976, 83, 65-79.

Fechner, G. T. *Elemente der Psychophysik*. Leipzig: Breitkopf und Hartel, 1860. (Translation of Volume I reprinted as *Elements of psychophysics*, New York: Holt, Rinehart & Winston, 1966.)

Feigl, H. The "mental" and the "physical." In H. Feigl & M. Scriven (Eds.), *Minnesota studies in the philosophy of science* (Vol. II). Minneapolis: University of Minnesota Press, 1958.

Garner, W. R. An equidiscriminability scale for loudness judgments. *Journal of Experimental Psychology*, 1952, 43, 232-238.

Garner, W. R. Context effects and the validity of loudness scales. *Journal of Experimental Psychology*, 1954, 48, 218-224.

Graham, C. H. Sensation and perception in an objective psychology. *Psychological Review*, 1958, 65, 65-76.

Green, D. M., & Swets, J. A. *Signal detection theory and psychophysics*. New York: Wiley, 1966.

Guttman, N., & Kalish, H. I. Discriminability and stimulus generalization. *Journal of Experimental Psychology*, 1956, 51, 79-88.

Helson, H *Adaptation level theory*. New York: Harper & Row, 1964.

Herrnstein, R. J., & Boring, E. G. (Eds.). *A source book in the history of psychology*. Cambridge, Mass.: Harvard University Press, 1966.

Hochberg, J. E., Treibel, W., & Seaman, G. Color adaptation under conditions of homogeneous visual stimulation (Ganzfeld). *Journal of Experimental Psychology*, 1951, 41, 153-159.

Hull, C. L. *Principles of behavior*. New York: Appleton-Century-Crofts, 1943.

Kiang, N. Y.-S. *Discharge patterns of single fibers in the cat's auditory nerve*. Cambridge: Mass.: M.I.T. Press, 1965.

Klemmer, E. T., & Shrimpton, N. Preference scaling via a modification of Shepard's proximity analysis method. *Human Factors*, 1963, 5, 163-168.

Krantz, D. H. A theory of magnitude estimation and cross-modality matching. *Journal of Mathematical Psychology*, 1972, 9, 168-199. (a)

Krantz, D. H. Measurement structures and psychological laws. *Science*, 1972, 175, 1427-1435. (b)

Krantz, D. H. Measurement theory and qualitative laws in psychophysics. In D. H. Krantz, R. C. Atkinson, R. D. Luce, & P. Suppes (Eds.), *Contemporary developments in mathematical psychology*. San Francisco: Freeman, 1974.

Krantz, D. H., Luce, R. D., Suppes, P., & Tversky, A. *Foundations of measurement* (Vol. 1). New York: Academic Press, 1971.

Kruskal, J. B., & Shepard, R. N. A nonmetric variety of linear factor analysis. *Psychometrika*, 1974, 39, 123-157.

Land, E. H. The Retinex. *American Scientist*, 1964, 52, 247-264.

Land, E. H. Color vision: From retina to Retinex. William James Lectures, presented at Harvard University, November 1966.

Levelt, W. J. M., Riemersma, J. B., & Bunt, A. A. Binaural additivity of loudness. *British Journal of Mathematical and Statistical Psychology*, 1972, 25, 51-68.

Levine, M. V. Transformations that render curves parallel. *Journal of Mathematical Psychology*, 1970, 7, 410-443.

Levine, M. V. Transforming curves into curves with the same shape. *Journal of Mathematical Psychology*, 1972, 9, 1-16.

Luce, R. D. *Individual choice behavior: A theoretical analysis*. New York: Wiley, 1959.

Luce, R. D. What sort of measurement is psychophysical measurement? *American Psychologist*, 1972, 27, 96-106.

Luce, R. D., & Galanter, E. Psychophysical scaling. In R. D. Luce, R. R. Bush, and E. Galanter (Eds.), *Handbook of mathematical psychology* (Vol. I). New York: Wiley, 1963.

Luce, R. D., & Green, D. M. A neural timing theory for response times and the psychophysics of intensity. *Psychological Review*, 1972, 79, 14-57.

Luce, R. D. & Tukey, J. Simultaneous conjoint measurement: A new type of fundamental measurement. *Journal of Mathematical Psychology*, 1964, 1, 1-27.

MacKay, D. M. Psychophysics of perceived intensity: A theoretical basis for Fechner's and Stevens' laws. *Science*, 1963, 139, 1213-1216.

McCann, J. J. Rod-cone interactions: Different color sensations from identical stimuli. *Science*, 1972, 176, 1255-1257.

McGill, W. The slope of the loudness function: A puzzle. In H. Gulliksen & S. Messick (Eds.), *Psychological scaling: Theory and applications*. New York: Wiley, 1960.

Middleton, W. E. K. *A history of the thermometer and its uses in meteorology*. Baltimore: Md.: Johns Hopkins Press, 1966.

Miller, G. A. The magical number seven, plus or minus two: Some limits on our capacity for processing information. *Psychological Review*, 1956, 63, 81-97.

Mountcastle, V. B., Poggio, G. F., & Werner, G. The relation of thalamic cell response to peripheral stimuli varied over an intensive continuum. *Journal of Neurophysiology*, 1963, 26, 807-834.

Oyamo, T. A behavioristic analysis of Stevens' magnitude estimation method. *Perception & Psychophysics*, 1968, 3, 317-320.

Pattie, F. A. A report of attempts to produce uniocular color blindness by hypnotic suggestion. *British Journal of Medical Psychology*, 1935, 15, 230-241.

Perkel, D. H. & Bullock, T. H. Neural coding. *Bulletin, Neurosciences Research Program*, 1968, 6, 221-348.

Pickersgill, M. J. On knowing with which eye one is seeing. *Quarterly Journal of Experimental Psychology*, 1961, 13, 168-172.

Pollack, I. Iterative techniques for unbiased rating scales. *Quarterly Journal of Experimental Psychology*, 1965, 17, 139-148.

Powers, W. T. *Behavior: The control of perception*. Chicago: Aldine, 1973.

Rock, I. *An introduction to perception*. New York: Macmillan, 1975.

Rock, I., & Ebenholtz, S. The relational determination of perceived size. *Psychological Review*, 1959, 66, 387-401.

Ross, J., & DiLollo, V. A vector model for psychophysical judgment. *Journal of Experimental Psychology Monograph Supplement*, 1968, 77, (3, Part 2).

Ross, J., & DiLollo, V. Judgment and response in magnitude estimation. *Psychological Review*, 1971, 78, 515-527

Rushton, W. A. H. Peripheral coding in the nervous system. In W. A. Rosenblith (Ed.), *Sensory communication*. Cambridge, Mass.: M.I.T. Press, 1961.

Savage, C. W. *The measurement of sensation*. Berkeley: University of California Press, 1970.

Selfridge, O. G. Pandemonium, a paradigm for learning. In *Proceedings of symposium on the mechanization of thought processes*. National Physical Laboratory, Teddington, England. London: H. M. Stationery Office, 1958.

Shepard, R. N. Stimulus and response generalization: Deduction of the generalization gradient from a trace model. *Psychological Review*, 1958, 65, 242-256. (a)

Shepard, R. N. Stimulus and response generalization: Tests of a model relating generalization to distance in psychological space. *Journal of Experimental Psychology*, 1958, 55, 509-523. (b)

Shepard, R. N. Role of generalization in stimulus-response compatibility. *Perceptual and Motor Skills*, 1961, 13, 59-62.

Shepard, R. N. The analysis of proximities: Multidimensional scaling with an unknown distance function. I & II. *Psychometrika*, 1962, 27, 125-140, 219-246.

Shepard, R. N. Computers and thought: A review of the book edited by Feigenbaum and Feldman. *Behavioral Science*, 1964, 9, 57-65.

Shepard, R. N. Approximation to uniform gradients of generalization by monotone transformations of scale. In D. I. Mostofsky (Ed.), *Stimulus generalization*. Stanford, Calif.: Stanford University Press, 1965.

Shepard, R. N. Metric structures in ordinal data. *Journal of Mathematical Psychology*, 1966, 3, 287-315.

Shepard, R. N. Form, formation, and transformation of internal representations. In R. Solso (Ed.), *Information processing and cognition: The Loyola Symposium*. Hillsdale, N.J.: Lawrence Erlbaum Associates, 1975.

Shepard, R. N., & Carroll, J. D. Parametric representation of nonlinear data structures. In P. R. Krishnaiah (Ed.), *Multivariate analysis*. New York: Academic Press, 1966.

Shepard, R. N., & Chang, J.-J. Stimulus generalization in the learning of classifications. *Journal of Experimental Psychology*, 1963, 65, 94-102.

Shepard, R. N., Kilpatric, D. W., & Cunningham, J. P. The internal representation of numbers. *Cognitive Psychology*, 1975, 7, 82-138.

Siegel, J. A. The nature of absolute pitch. In I. Gordon (Ed.), *Studies in the psychology of music* (Vol. 8). Iowa City: University of Iowa Press, 1972.

Skinner, B. F. The operational analysis of psychological terms. *Psychological Review*, 1945, 52, 270-277.

Skinner, B. F. *Verbal behavior*. New York: Appleton-Century-Crofts, 1957.

Sternberg, S. Four theories of the effect of distance on apparent size. Paper read at the Psychonomic Society meeting, St. Louis, October, 1966.

Sternberg, S. The discovery of processing stages: Extensions of Donders' method. *Acta Psychologica*, 1969, 30, 276-315.

Stevens, J. C. & Stevens, S. S. Warmth and cold—dynamics of sensory intensity. *Journal of Experimental Psychology*, 1960, 60, 183-192.

Stevens, S. S. On the theory of scales of measurement. *Science*, 1946, 103, 677-680.

Stevens, S. S. Mathematics, measurement, and psychophysics. In S. S. Stevens (Ed.), *Handbook of experimental psychology*. New York: Wiley, 1951.

Stevens, S. S. The direct estimation of sensory magnitudes—Loudness. *American Journal of Psychology*, 1956, 69, 1-25.

Stevens, S. S. On the psychophysical law. *Psychological Review*, 1957, 64, 153-181.

Stevens, S. S. Cross-modality validation of subjective scales for loudness, vibration, and electric shock. *Journal of Experimental Psychology*, 1959, 57, 201-209.

Stevens, S. S. Ratio scales, partition scales, and confusion scales. In H. Gulliksen & S. Messick (Eds.), *Psychological scaling: Theory and applications.* New York: Wiley, 1960.

Stevens, S. S. To honor Fechner and repeal his law. *Science*, 1961, 133, 80-86.

Stevens, S. S. Concerning the psychophysical power law. *Quarterly Journal of Experimental Psychology*, 1964, 16, 383-385.

Stevens, S. S. Matching functions between loudness and ten other continua. *Perception & Psychophysics*, 1966, 1, 5-8. (a)

Stevens, S. S. On the operation known as judgment. *American Scientist*, 1966, 54, 385-401. (b)

Stevens, S. S., & Guirao, M. Subjective scaling of length and area and the matching of length to loudness and brightness. *Journal of Experimental Psychology*, 1963, 66, 177-186.

Stevens, S. S., & Guirao, M. The scaling of apparent viscosity. *Science*, 1964, 144, 1157-1158.

Suppes, P., & Zinnes, J. L. Basic measurement theory. In R. D. Luce, R. R. Bush, and E. Galanter (Eds.), *Handbook of mathematical psychology* (Vol. I). New York: Wiley, 1963.

Teghtsoonian, M. The judgment of size. *American Journal of Psychology*, 1965, 78, 392-402.

Thouless, R. H. Phenomenal regression to the "real" object. I & II. *British Journal of Psychology*, 1931, 21, 339-359; 22, 1-30.

Thurstone, L. L. A law of comparative judgment. *Psychological Review*, 1927, 34, 273-286.

Torgerson, W. S. *Theory and methods of scaling.* New York: Wiley, 1958.

Torgerson, W. S. Quantitative judgment scales. In H. Gulliksen & S. Messick (Eds.), *Psychological scaling: Theory and applications.* New York: Wiley, 1960.

Treisman, M. Laws of sensory magnitude. *Nature*, 1963, 198, 914-915.

Treisman, M. Sensory scaling and the psychophysical law. *Quarterly Journal of Experimental Psychology*, 1964, 16, 11-22.

Ward, W. D. Absolute pitch. *Sound*, 1963, Part I, 2, 14-41; Part II, 3, 33-41.

Warren, R. W. A basis for judgment of sensory intensity. *American Journal of Psychology*, 1958, 71, 675-687.

Warren, R. M., Sersen, E. A., & Pores, E. B. A basis for loudness judgments. *American Journal of Psychology*, 1958, 71, 700-709.

Welford, A. T. The measurement of sensory-motor performance: Survey and reappraisal of twelve years' progress. *Ergonomics*, 1960, 3, 189-230.

Wickelgren, W. A. Associative strength theory of recognition memory for pitch. *Journal of Mathematical Psychology*, 1969, 6, 13-61.

Wittgenstein, L. *Philosophical investigations* (G. E. M. Anscombe, trans.). New York: Macmillan, 1953.

Woodworth, R. S. *Experimental psychology.* New York: Henry Holt, 1938.

INDEXES

Author Index

493

Subject Index